BRITISH AND COMMONWEALTH
# MERCHANT SHIP LOSSES
TO AXIS SUBMARINES
1939–1945

ALAN J. TENNENT

SUTTON PUBLISHING

First published in 2001 by
Sutton Publishing Limited · Phoenix Mill
Thrupp · Stroud · Gloucestershire · GL5 2BU

Reprinted in 2002

British Library Cataloguing in Publication Data
A catalogue record for this book is available from the British Library.

ISBN 0-7509-2760-7

Typeset in 10/12pt Bembo.
Typesetting and origination by
Sutton Publishing Limited.
Printed and bound in England by
J.H. Haynes & Co. Ltd, Sparkford.

*This book is dedicated to the men of the Merchant Service who gave their lives during the 1939–1945 war*

# CONTENTS

# ACKNOWLEDGEMENTS AND SOURCES

In compiling this reference book I should like to thank the staff of the following organisations for their kind help and assistance:

The Guildhall Library, Lloyd's Collection, London
Lloyd's Register of Shipping, London
Ministry of Defence, Naval Historical Branch, London
Norsk Sjofartsmuseum, Oslo
Royal Navy Submarine Museum, Gosport
The Corporation of Trinity House, London
The Public Record Office, Kew
The Norrish Central Library (Naval Section), Portsmouth

The following documents were researched at the Public Record Office:

  AIR 15/136 – U–Boat Assessment Forms
  ADM 1 – Reports on attacks/sinkings of U–boats
  ADM 53 – Logbooks of HM ships
  ADM 199 – Reports on attacks/sinkings of U–boats
  ADM 199/2032/2056 – U–boat incidents
  ADM 199/2057/2062 – Monthly anti–submarine reports
  ADM 199/2061/2062 – Awards to U–boat commanders
  ADM 199/2130/2148 – Survivors' reports
  ADM 199 and ADM 237 – Various convoy reports

# INTRODUCTION

From the first day of the Second World War, the most ferocious sea battles were fought to keep the lifelines of the oceans of the world open to merchant shipping for the movement of war materials and food from our Empire and the Americas to the factories of the United Kingdom. The battles that raged in the Atlantic Ocean were to become known as the Battle of the Atlantic and were fought over hundreds and thousands of square miles, from the frozen wastes of the North Cape, Arctic Ocean and Barents Sea to the warmer climates of the Southern Oceans, the eastern seaboard of the United States to the Caribbean, and the Gulf of Mexico to the shores of the United Kingdom. The battle with the enemy submarines raged for month after month over this vast expanse of ocean between the hunter and the hunted.

The first vessel to fall victim to the U-boat aggression, shortly after the declaration of war, was the liner *ATHENIA*, sunk by U-30. The liner was on passage from Liverpool to Montreal; among the passengers were Jewish refugees escaping persecution in Nazi Germany and American tourists returning home. The great naval bases for the German Kriegsmarine fleet of submarines were the North Sea ports of Kiel and Wilhelmshaven. On the occupation of France in 1940 the Germans built bombproof U-boat pens on the French Atlantic coast at Bordeaux, Brest, La Pallice, Lorient and St Nazaire, thereby extending the operating range of the U-boats. Similar bases were also constructed in occupied Norway.

The Kriegsmarine had a number of different types of U-boats constructed in their naval yards at Bremen, Hamburg, Kiel and Wilhelmshaven. The most numerous of those built was the Type VIIC, a seagoing combat craft – surface/submerged displacement 769/871 tons, overall length 67.10m, draught 4.74m and beam 6.18m; main armament five torpedo tubes with fourteen torpedoes, with a complement of 44/48 crew. Over 570 of these U-boats were built, and on the cessation of the war most had been destroyed by the action of the British and Allied naval forces and aircraft of RAF Coastal Command, Commonwealth and other Allied forces.

The convoy system was first introduced in the First World War to protect merchant ships plying the Atlantic. The first convoy of the Second World War sailed from Gibraltar for Cape Town on 2 September 1939. The main convoy routes were across the Atlantic to North America. These were designated OB – Liverpool outward to North America; ON (former OB fast convoy, 10 knots) UK to North America; ONS slow convoys UK – North America; HX – Halifax (NS)/New York – UK; SC – Sydney (CB) – UK. These convoys sailed approximately every three/four days with as many as twenty to forty ships or more in each convoy. Owing to the limited range of British and Allied anti-submarine ships and aircraft to protect friendly shipping, large areas of the ocean were free for enemy submarines to attack unmolested. For month after month these convoys were attacked ruthlessly by the U-boats with heavy loss of life and tonnage. During December 1941 Germany declared war on the United States of America and Hitler ordered his wolf packs to attack in the plentiful hunting grounds off the east coast of America, the Caribbean and the US Gulf of Mexico; this was known as 'Operation Paukenschlag' (Drumbeat). On their arrival the U-boat commanders were able to see the lights of US coastal cities and towns, and they plundered the heavy shipping lanes of every type of merchant vessel, including neutral tonnage. No mercy was shown.

The heavy oil tankers moving oil from the Gulf and Caribbean ports to the United States and the United Kingdom fell easy prey to the enemy, for at this stage no convoy systems were in operation by the Americans. This was to become known to the U-boat commanders as the 'Second Happy Time', the first being the autumn of 1940, or the U-boats' Paradise, from January through to July 1942. Upon the entry of the USA into the Battle of the Atlantic a large construction programme was undertaken to build warships at US shipyards and long-range aircraft like the Liberator, Flying Fortress and the Catalina to combat the enemy. The vast numbers of new ships, the availability of the long-range aircraft and the newly acquired bases at the Azores, Greenland and Iceland, meant that the 'black hole' in the Atlantic was closed and for the first time the convoys were given sea and air protection throughout the voyage to the United Kingdom. The loss to merchant shipping was greatly reduced, the losses to the Kriegsmarine increased daily.

In order to keep their wolf packs at sea for a longer operational period, the Kriegsmarine ordered a number of large U-boats known as Milch-Cows to be built for the purpose of supplying the U-boats at sea with fuel, torpedoes and stores. This type was known as XIV with a surface displacement at full load of 1688 tons, a maximum surface speed of 15 knots and a cruising range of 12,350 miles. All fourteen of these U-tankers were destroyed; most were caught on the surface while refuelling other boats, the majority of which were destroyed by strike aircraft flown from the newly built escort carriers as the result of British and Allied intelligence gained from Enigma decrypts. An Enigma machine was captured by the destroyer HMS *BULLDOG* on the sinking of U-110 (Lemp) in the North Atlantic during May 1941. The machine and its code books was one of several taken to the top secret home of the government Code and Cypher School at Bletchley Park where the codes of the Kriegsmarine, Luftwaffe and Wehrmacht were eventually broken. This was one of the best-kept secrets of the war, and for long after the end of the war the enemy never knew that their codes had been broken.

Some of the hardest convoy battles were fought during winter 1942 and spring 1943. Convoy ONS 5 sailed from Liverpool on 21 April 1943, and proceeded westward through the North Channel on 22 April bound for the USA and the West Indian ports. It comprised 42 merchant ships flying the flags of many nations with an escort of 12 warships. In appalling weather conditions, mountainous seas, poor visibility, fog and snowstorms the convoy was attacked on 4 May by a wolf pack of between 28 and 40 U-boats. In the ensuing battle thirteen merchantmen were lost and the U-boats suffered a heavy defeat with the loss of seven boats. Dönitz then realised that the battle was lost and the rule of the U-boat was in rapid decline.

The loss of life in the Battle of the Atlantic and other theatres of the war at sea was enormous. The British Merchant Service lost over 31,000 men and about 1,600 merchant ships; over 8,000,000 gross tonnage. The German U-boat arm sustained heavy losses with over 32,000 men lost, as well as over 720 U-boats. A war memorial to the Merchant Navy at Trinity Gardens, Tower Hill, London, lists the names of merchant seamen who gave their lives in the course of the war. At Möltenort, Germany, a memorial was erected to German submariners who gave their lives.

## Author's note

Entries are listed alphabetically by shipping line, with individual vessels listed in chronological order by date of loss. At the end of each section are listed merchant vessels of allied governments in exile, requisitions, or ships taken as prizes, that were commandeered and operated nominally under the command of the British government's Ministry of War Transport (MOWT), but in practice operated by private shipping companies.

# THE SHIPS

## ABERDEEN COAL & SHIPPING COMPANY – ABERDEEN

*FERRYHILL* • GRT 1086 • Built 1919
21.1.40: Struck a mine laid on 11.12.1939 by German submarine U-61 (Oesten), and sank in
the North Sea 1½ miles N from St Mary's Lighthouse near Blyth, in position 55.05N 01.27W
while sailing independently on a voyage from Blyth to Aberdeen, with a cargo of 1200 tons
of coal. The Master, Capt Williamson John Taylor Stephen, and 8 crew were lost. 2 crew
were rescued by HM minesweeper *YOUNG JACOB* 99/14 (FY.975) (Skipper T. Williamson)
and landed at North Shields.

## ADELLEN SHIPPING CO. LTD – LONDON

*ADELLEN* (tanker) • GRT 7984 • Built 1930
22.2.42: Torpedoed and sunk by German submarine U-155 (Piening), part of 'Operation
Paukenschlag' (Drumbeat) first wave of five U-boats, in the Atlantic S of Cape Farewell,
Greenland, in position 49.20N 38.15W while on government service on a voyage from
Newport, Mon. to Trinidad, BWI, in ballast, part of convoy ONS 67 comprising 37 ships.
The Master, Capt John Brown, 9 crew and 2 gunners were rescued by HMCS corvette
*ALGOMA* 925/40 (K.127) (Lt J. Harding), transferred to rescue ship *TOWARD* 1571/23
(Capt Arthur James Knell DSC MBE) and landed at Halifax, Nova Scotia 1.3.1942. 29 crew
and 7 gunners were lost.

## ADMIRALTY, THE – LONDON

*CAIRNDALE* (Royal Fleet Auxiliary tanker) laid down as *ERATO* • GRT 8129 • Built 1939
30.5.41: Torpedoed and sunk by Italian submarine *GUGLIELMO MARCONI* (Pollina), in the
Atlantic 170 miles WSW of Cape Trafalgar, Spain, in position 35.19N 08.33W while sailing
independently on a voyage from Gibraltar 26.5.41 to Curacao, NWI, in ballast. The Master,
Capt Reginald John Harland, and survivors were rescued by HM rescue tug *ST DAY* 860/18
(W. 55) and landed at Gibraltar. 4 crew were lost.

*DARKDALE* ex-*EMPIRE OIL* (RFA tanker) • GRT 8145 • Built 1940
22.10.41: Torpedoed and sunk by German submarine U-68 (Merten), in the South Atlantic
while anchored in Jamestown harbour, St Helena, as a storage ship, in position 16.00S
05.37W, while on a voyage from Durban to St Helena with a cargo of 3000 tons of fuel oil,
850 tons of aviation gasoline, 500 tons of diesel oil and lubricating oil. The Master, Capt
Thomas H. Card, and 7 crew were rescued by harbour craft. 37 crew and 4 gunners were
lost. The sinking of the *DARKDALE* was the first British ship sunk by a U-boat south of the
Equator.

**SLAVOL** (RFA tanker) • GRT 2623 • Built 1917

26.3.42: Torpedoed and sunk by German submarine U-205 (Bürgel), in the Mediterranean off Sidi Barrani, Egypt, in approximate position 31.36N 26.04E while in convoy on a voyage from Alexandria to Tobruk, Cyrenaica, with a cargo of fuel oil. The Master, Capt George Sydney Perry and 19 crew were rescued by RHN destroyer *VASILISSA OLGA* 1350/39 (known as *QUEEN OLGA*) and landed at Alexandria. 36 crew were lost. One of the escorts HM destroyer *JAGUAR* 1690/38 (F.34) (Lt P.F. Cole) was sunk the same day by U-652 (Fraatz). U-205, commanded by Oberleutnant zur See Friedrich Bürgel, was damaged on 17.2.43 in the Mediterranean 40 miles NW of Derna, Cyrenaica, in position 32.56N 22.01E while attacking convoy TX 1, damaged by a Bristol Blenheim 'W', pilot Capt C.R. Brinton of No. 15 Squadron South African Air Force, based at Landing Ground 29, Amiriya, Egypt, and HM destroyer *PALADIN* 1540/41 (G.69) (Lt E.A.S. Bailey). U-205 was taken in tow by HM corvette *GLOXINIA* 925/40 (K.22) (Lt A.F. Harkness OBE DSC) with an attempt to salvage but sank off Ras el Hilal, in position 32.57N 22.10E about 100 miles W of Tobruk. The U-boat commander and 41 crew were taken prisoner by HMS *PALADIN* and HM destroyer leader *JERVIS* 1695/39 (F.00) (Capt A.F. Pugsley). 8 crew were lost. U-652 commanded by Oberleutnant zur See George-Werner Fraatz was badly damaged on 2.6.42 in the Gulf of Sollum off Sollum, in position 31.55N 25.13E by a Bristol Blenheim bomber of No. 203 Squadron Royal Air Force, based at Landing Ground 39, Burgh al Arab S, Egypt, and a Fairey Swordfish torpedo-bomber 'L' V407, pilot Sub-Lt G.H. Bates of No. 815 Squadron, Fleet Air Arm. U-652 was later sunk by a torpedo fired by U-81. The U-boat commander and crew of 45 were rescued by U-81, commanded by Kapitänleutnant Friedrich Guggenberger, who was awarded the Knight's Cross (10.12.41), with Oak Leaves (8.1.43), and landed at Salamis, Greece on 3.6.42. The qualification for the Knight's Cross was sinking 100,000 tons of shipping, and the Oak Leaves sinking 200,000 tons. This honour could also be awarded for the successful carrying out of specially difficult or dangerous operations.

**MONTENOL** (RFA tanker) • GRT 2646 • Built 1917

21.5.42: Torpedoed and damaged by German submarine U-159 (Witte), in the Atlantic about 140 miles ESE of Santa Maria, Azores, in position 36.41N 22.45W while on a voyage from Greenock to Freetown, Sierra Leone, in ballast, part of convoy OS 28 comprising 37 ships. Later sunk by gunfire by HM corvette *WOODRUFF* 925/41 (K.53) (Lt-Cdr F.H. Gray). The Master, Capt Edward Emile August Le Sage, 52 crew and 8 gunners were rescued by HM sloop *WELLINGTON* 990/34 (L.65) (Lt-Cdr W.F.R. Segrave) and landed at Freetown. 3 crew were lost. Kapitänleutnant Helmut Witte was awarded the Knight's Cross (22.10.42).

**DINSDALE** ex-*EMPIRE NORSEMAN* (RFA tanker) • GRT 8254 • Built 1942

31.5.42: Torpedoed and sunk by Italian submarine *COMDTE. ALFREDO CAPPELLINI* (Revedin), in the South Atlantic 120 miles SSW of St Paul Rocks, Brazil, in position 00.45S 29.50W while sailing independently on a voyage from Trinidad to Port Elizabeth, with a cargo of aviation spirit. The Master, Capt Thomas H. Card, and 43 crew were rescued by Spanish ship *MONTE ORDUNA* 5529/22 and landed at Las Palmas, Canary Islands, and brought to Cadiz by Spanish ship *CIUDAD DE VALENCIA* 2497/31. 13 crew were lost. *COMDTE. ALFREDO CAPPELLINI* was captured by the Germans at Sabang, Sumatra, and renamed UIT-24; later ceded to the Japanese and renamed I-503; scrapped at Kobe in 1946.

***BRAMBLELEAF*** ex-*RUMOL* (RFA tanker) • GRT 5912 • Built 1917
10.6.42: Torpedoed and damaged by German submarine U–559 (Heidtmann), in the Mediterranean off Ras Alem, Egypt, in position 31.12N 28.10E while on a voyage from Alexandria to Tobruk, with a cargo of fuel oil, diesel oil and motor spirit, part of convoy AT 49 comprising 4 ships. Beached near Port Said later became an oil hulk at Alexandria. The Master, Capt Herbert Allister Shackblock, 54 crew and 3 gunners were rescued by RHN destroyer *VASILISSA OLGA* 1350/39 and landed at Alexandria. 2 crew were lost. U–559, commanded by Kapitänleutnant Hans Otto Heidtmann (Knight's Cross 12.4.43), was lost on 30.10.42, sunk in the Mediterranean 60 miles NE of Port Said, in position 32.30N 33.00E by HM destroyers *PAKENHAM* 1550/41 (G.17) (Capt Eric B.K. Stevens), *PETARD* 1540/41 (G.56) (Lt-Cdr P.C. Egan), *HERO* 1340/36 (H.99) (Lt-Cdr W.S. Scott), *DULVERTON* 1050/41 (L.63) (Cdr W.N. Petch) and *HURWORTH* 1050/41 (L.28) (Lt D.A. Shaw), and Vickers Wellesley bomber 'N' from No. 47 Squadron RAF based at Shandur, Egypt. The U-boat commander and 36 crew were taken prisoner by HMS *PETARD* and landed at Port Said 31.10.42. 8 crew were lost. The Knight's Cross was awarded to Kapitänleutnant Hans Otto Heidtmann while he was a prisoner-of-war.

***ALDERSDALE*** (RFA tanker) • GRT 8402 • Built 1937
5.7.42: Attacked and damaged by German Ju-88s aircraft of 111/KG 30 Bomber Group based at Banak, North Cape, in the Barents Sea N of the Kola Peninsula, in position 75.00N 45.00E while on a voyage from Reykjavik, Iceland, to Archangel, USSR, with a cargo of aviation spirit, dispersed from the ill-fated convoy PQ 17 comprising 36 ships. The damaged tanker was taken in tow by HM minesweeper *SALAMANDER* 815/36 (N.86) (Lt W.R. Mottram), abandoned on 7.7.42 then torpedoed and sunk by German submarine U–457 (Brandenburg), part of the 'Eistenfel' (Ice Devil) patrol group of six U-boats. The Master, Capt Archibald Hobson, and crew of 53 were rescued by HM minesweeper *SALAMANDER* 815/36 (N.86) and landed at Archangel 11.7.42.

***GREY RANGER*** (RFA tanker) • GRT 3313 • Built 1941
22.9.42: Torpedoed and sunk by German submarine U–435 (Strelow), in the North Atlantic NE of Iceland, in position 71.23N 11.03W while on a voyage from Archangel 13.9.42 to the UK via Loch Ewe, in ballast, part of convoy QP 14 comprising 20 ships. The Master, Capt Howard Douglas Gausden DSO, and 32 crew were rescued by rescue ship *RATHLIN* 1600/36 (Capt August Banning DSO) and landed at Gourock 26.9.42. 6 crew were lost. Two of the convoy's escorts were lost: HM minesweeper *LEDA* 815/37 (N.93) (Cdr A.H. Wynne-Edwards) was sunk on 20.9.42 by German submarine U–435 (Strelow) in the Greenland Sea NW of Bear Island, in position 76.30N 05.00E, and HM destroyer leader *SOMALI* 1870/37 (F.33) (Lt-Cdr C.C. Maud DSC) was damaged on 20.9.42 by German submarine U–703 (Bielfeld) in the Greenland Sea NW of Jan Mayen Island, in position 75.40N 02.00W, taken in tow by HM destroyer *ASHANTI* 1870/37 (F.51) (Cdr R.D. Onslow DSO) and lost after 420 miles towage during a gale on 24.9.42.

**ALEXANDER, DAVID & SONS – GLASGOW**
**Grove Line (Glasgow) Ltd**

***OLIVEGROVE*** • GRT 4060 • Built 1929
7.9.39: Torpedoed and sunk by German submarine U–33 (v. Dresky), in the Atlantic 420 miles WSW of Land's End, in position 49.05N 15.58W while sailing independently on a

voyage from Puerto Padre, Cuba, to London, with a cargo of 4500 tons of sugar. The Master, Capt James Barnetson, and crew of 32 were rescued by US liner *WASHINGTON* 24289/33 and landed at Southampton 9.9.39.

*ALDERGROVE* ex-*ELBA* ex-*GLENPARK* • GRT 1974 • Built 1918
23.8.41: Torpedoed and sunk by German submarine U-201 (Schnee), in the Atlantic NW of Lisbon, in position 40.43N 11.39W while on a voyage from Cardiff to Lisbon, with 1 naval rating and a cargo of 2650 tons of patent fuel, part of convoy OG 71 comprising 21 ships. The Master, Capt Hugh William McLean, crew of 32 and 5 gunners were rescued by HM corvette *CAMPANULA* 925/40 (K.18) (Lt-Cdr R.V.E. Case DSC) and landed at Gibraltar 24.8.41. The naval rating was lost.

## MINISTRY OF WAR TRANSPORT (MOWT)

*MICHAEL JEBSEN* • GRT 2323 • Built 1927
14.8.42: Torpedoed and sunk by German submarine U-598 (Holtorf), in the Atlantic 30 miles SW of Bahamas, in position 21.45N 76.10W while on a voyage from Barbados, BWI, to the UK via Trinidad 8.8.42, with a cargo of 2750 tons of sugar, part of convoy TAW 12 comprising 47 ships. The Master, Capt R. Nielsen, 35 crew and 4 gunners were rescued by a USN patrol boat and landed at Guantanamo Bay, Cuba. 6 crew and 1 gunner were lost. U-598 commanded by Kapitänleutnant Gottfried Holtorf was sunk on 23.7.43 in the South Atlantic 130 miles ENE of Cape San Roque, Brazil, in position 04.05S 33.23W by two Consolidated B-24 Liberator bombers, pilots Lt George E. Waugh and Lt-Cdr Renfro Turner of the US Navy Bombing Squadron VB-107 based at Natal, Brazil. The U-boat commander and 42 crew were lost. 2 crew were taken prisoner by US Navy tug *SENECA* 1235/43 (ATF.91).

## ALLAN, BLACK & COMPANY – SUNDERLAND
**Albyn Line Ltd**

*THISTLEGARTH* • GRT 4747 • Built 1929
15.10.40: Torpedoed and sunk by German submarine U-103 (Schütze), in the Atlantic 45 miles WNW of Rockall, in position 58.43N 15.00W while on a voyage from Scapa Flow, Orkney Islands 13.10.40, to Father Point, New Brunswick, for orders, in ballast, part of convoy OB 228 comprising 47 ships. The Master, Capt Donald Plummer MM, 28 crew and 1 gunner were lost. 9 crew were rescued by HM corvette *HEARTSEASE* 925/40 (K.15) ex-HMS *PANSY* (Lt-Cdr E.J.R. North).

*THISTLEGLEN* • GRT 4750 • Built 1929
10.9.41: Torpedoed and sunk by German submarine U-85 (Greger), part of the 'Markgraf' patrol group of fourteen U-boats, in the North Atlantic NE of Cape Farewell, in position 62.14N 39.29W while on a voyage from New York to Glasgow via Sydney CB 30.8.41, with a cargo of 2400 tons of pig iron and 5200 tons of steel, part of convoy SC 42 comprising 65 ships. The Master, Capt Gordon Frederick Dodson, 39 crew and 6 gunners were rescued by British ship *LORIENT* 4737/21 and landed at Belfast. 3 crew were lost.

## MOWT

***EMPIRE CLOUD*** • GRT 5969 • Built 1941
19.8.42: Torpedoed and damaged by German submarine U-564 (Suhren), in the Atlantic NE of Trinidad, in position 11.58N 62.38W while on a voyage from Durban to New York and Philadelphia via Trinidad 18.8.42, in ballast, part of convoy *TAW* 13 comprising 13 ships. Later sank in tow of Dutch tug *ROODE ZEE* 468/38 on 21.8.41 in position 10.54N 62.10W. The Master, Capt Charles Cottew Brown, 42 crew and 8 gunners were rescued by ships in the convoy and landed at Key West, Florida, and Mobile, Alabama. 3 crew were lost. Korvettenkapitän Reinhard Suhren was awarded the Knight's Cross (3.11.40) with Oak Leaves (31.12.41) and the Swords (1.9.42). U-564, commanded by Oberleutnant zur See Hans Fiedler, was sunk on 14.6.43 in the Atlantic 120 miles WNW of Cape Ortegal, Spain, in position 44.17N 10.25W by an Armstrong Whitworth Whitley bomber 'G' BD220, pilot Sgt Arthur J. Benson (Australian) of 10 OTU, Bomber Command, based at St Eval. The aircraft sustained damage and ditched in the sea, to be rescued 3 days later by a French fishing boat. The pilot was awarded the DFM while in Stalag Luft 3. The U-boat commander and 27 crew were lost. 18 crew were rescued by German submarine U-185, commanded by Kapitänleutnant August Maus (Knight's Cross 21.9.43), was later transferred to German destroyers Z24 1870/40 and Z25 1870/40.

## AMBROSE DAVIES & MATTHEWS LIMITED – LONDON
## Brynymor SS Co. Ltd

***GER-Y-BRYN*** • GRT 5108 • Built 1941
5.3.43: Torpedoed and sunk by German submarine U-130 (Keller), in the Atlantic NW of Cape Finisterre, in position 43.50N 14.45W while on a voyage from Lagos, Nigeria to Hull via Gibraltar, with 8181 tons of West African produce, part of convoy XK 2 comprising 20 ships. The Master, Capt Theodore John Butler Beard, crew of 37 and 9 gunners were rescued by HM corvette *COREOPSIS* 925/40 (K.32) (Lt B.C. Hamilton), transferred to HM trawler *LOCH OSKAIG* 543/37 (FY.175) (Lt G.F.S. Clampitt) and landed at Londonderry. Oberleutnant zur See Siegfried Keller and crew of 52 were lost while shadowing convoy UGS 6 comprising 45 ships on 12.3.43 when U-130, part of the 'Unverzagt' (Intrepid) patrol group of six U-boats was sunk in the Atlantic 550 miles SW of the Azores, in position 37.10N 40.21W by US destroyer *CHAMPLIN* 1620/42 (DD-601) (Cdr Charles L. Melson).

***AELYBRYN*** • GRT 4986 • Built 1938
11.3.43: Torpedoed and sunk by German submarine U-160 (Lassen), part of the 'Seehund' (Seal) patrol group of five U-boats, in the Indian Ocean ENE of Durban, in position 29.08S 34.05E while sailing independently on a voyage from Calcutta and Cochin to the UK via Durban, with 7935 tons general cargo. The Master, Capt Harold William Brockwell, 27 crew and 4 gunners were rescued by Portuguese ship *LOURENCO MARQUES* 6281/05 and landed at Cape Town. 9 crew were lost. Kapitänleutnant George Lassen was awarded the Knight's Cross (10.8.42) with Oak Leaves (7.3.43). U-160, under the command of Oberleutnant zur See Gerd von Pommer-Esche, and crew of 56 were lost on 14.7.43, sunk in the Atlantic 250 miles SSW of San Miguel, Azores, in position 33.54N 27.13W by a Grumman F4F Wildcat fighter-bomber, pilot Lt H. Brinkley Bass and a Grumman TBF Avenger torpedo bomber, pilot Lt John H. Ballentine of US Navy Composite Squadron VC-29 from US escort carrier

*SANTEE* 11400/42 (CVE-29) (Capt H.F. Fick), part of the Task Group 21.11. The *AELYBRYN* was torpedoed and damaged on 10.5.41 by German submarine U-556 (Wohlfarth), in the North Atlantic SE of Cape Farewell, in position 59.23N 35.25W, part of convoy OB 318 comprising 38 ships. Towed to Reykjavik by HM corvette *HOLLYHOCK* 925/40 (K.64) (Lt-Cdr T.E. Davies OBE). The Master, Capt Harold William Brockwell, and 44 crew were rescued by HM trawler *DANEMAN* 516/37 (FY.123) (Lt A.H. Ballard).

## MOWT

**DIONE II** ex-*DIONE* • GRT 2669 • Built 1936
4.2.41: Damaged by Fw 200 Condor aircraft of I/KG 40 Bomber Group on 3.2.41 and sunk by gunfire by German submarine U-93 (Korth), in the Atlantic NW of Aran Island, Co. Galway, in position 55.50N 10.30W while on a voyage from Wabana, Conception Bay, Newfoundland to Cardiff via Sydney, Cape Breton, with a cargo of 2650 tons iron ore, a straggler from convoy SC 20 comprising 38 ships. The Master, Capt Robert Squirrell, 26 crew and 1 gunner were lost. 5 crew were rescued by British ship *FLOWERGATE* 5166/21 and landed at Glasgow. Kapitänleutnant Klaus Korth was awarded the Knight's Cross (29.5.41). Oberleutnant zur See Horst Elfe was lost on 15.1.42 when U-93, part of the 'Seydlitz' patrol group of six U-boats, was sunk in the Atlantic 300 miles W of Cape St Vincent, Portugal, in position 36.40N 15.52W by HM destroyer *HESPERUS* 1340/39 (H.57) ex-HMS *HEARTY* ex-Brazilian *JURUENA* (Cdr Donald G. MacIntyre), escorting convoy SL 97 comprising 20 ships. The U-boat commander and 35 crew were taken prisoner by HMS *HESPERUS* and landed at Gibraltar, and 4 crew by HM destroyer leader *LAFOREY* 1935/41 (F.99) (Capt R.M.J. Hutton). 6 crew were lost.

## ANCHOR LINE (HENDERSON BROS) LTD – GLASGOW

*SCOTSTOUN* ex-*CALEDONIA* • GRT 17046 • Built 1925
13.6.40: Torpedoed and sunk by German submarine U-25 (Beduhn), part of the 'Prien' (named after a U-boat commander) patrol group of seven U-boats, in the Atlantic about 80 miles W of Barra Island, Outer Hebrides, in position 57.00N 09.57W. *SCOTSTOUN* was on government service employed as an Armed Merchant Cruiser (F.) part of the 10th Cruiser Squadron. Capt S.G. Smyth, 340 officers and ratings were saved. 6 ratings were lost. Kapitänleutnant Heinz Beduhn and crew of 48 were lost on 3.8.40 when U-25 struck a mine in British field No. 7 and sank in the North Sea N of Terschelling, West Frisian Islands, in position 54.00N 05.00E.

*TRANSYLVANIA* • GRT 16923 • Built 1925
10.8.40: Torpedoed and sunk by German submarine U-56 (Harms), in the Atlantic 40 miles NW of Malin Head, Co. Donegal, in position 55.50N 08.03W. She was on government service employed as an Armed Merchant Cruiser (F.65), part of the 10th Cruiser Squadron (Capt F.N. Miles). About 300 officers and ratings were rescued. 48 officers and ratings were lost. U-56 commanded by Oberleutnant zur See Joachim Sauerbier was sunk at Kiel, Germany, on 28.4.45 by RAF and USAAF aircraft.

*TAHSINIA* • GRT 7267 • Built 1942
1.10.43: Torpedoed and sunk by gunfire by German submarine U-532 (Junker), part of the 'Monsun' (Monsoon) patrol group of nine U-boats, in the Indian Ocean NE of the Maldive

Islands, in position 06.51N 74.38E while sailing independently on a voyage from Calcutta and Colombo 28.9.43 to Aden and the UK, with 7038 tons of general cargo, including tea, manganese ore and pig iron. The Master, Capt Charles Edward Stewart, 39 crew and 8 gunners were rescued: the Master and 24 survivors were rescued 10 miles W of Alleppey Lighthouse after 7 days in an open boat by British India ship *NEVASA* 9071/13 and landed at Bombay 11.10.43, and 23 survivors landed on Mahdu Atoll, Maldive Islands 6.10.43, and were brought to Colombo by an Indian dhow.

## MOWT

***EMPIRE KUMARI*** ex-*STURMFELS* • GRT 6288 • Built 1920
26.8.42: Torpedoed and damaged by German submarine U-375 (Koenenkamp), in the Mediterranean NE of Port Said, Egypt, in position 31.58N 34.21E while on a voyage from Haifa, Palestine 26.8.42, to Port Said, Egypt, with a part cargo of 450 tons of bagged potash, part of convoy LW 38 (codenamed Theta). Taken in tow by HM corvette *GLOXINIA* 925/40 (K.22) (Lt A.F. Harkness OBE DSC), then at a later stage by HM tug *BRIGAND* 840/37 (W.83) and the Haifa harbour tug *ROACH* 259/35 to Haifa harbour; arrived 27.8.42 but sank at anchor during the evening of 27/28.8.42. The Master, Capt Robert Cunningham Streets, 84 crew and 4 gunners were rescued by HMS *GLOXINIA* and landed at Haifa. 3 crew were lost. The German *STURMFELS* was scuttled on 25.8.41 at Bandar Shapur, Persia, salvaged by the Royal Navy and taken as a prize.

***EMPIRE KOHINOOR*** ex-*CABOTO* ex-*WAR CELT* • GRT 5225 • Built 1919
2.7.43: Torpedoed and sunk by German submarine U-618 (Baberg), in the Atlantic 250 miles SW of Freetown, in position 06.20N 16.30W while sailing independently on a voyage from Alexandria to Cape Town 18.6.43 and the UK via Freetown, with 6000 tons of general cargo. The Master, Capt R. Black, 72 crew and 8 gunners were rescued. The 1st boat was rescued by HM destroyer *WOLVERINE* 1220/19 (D.78) (Cdr J.P. Meney) and landed at Takoradi, the 2nd was rescued by British ship *GASCONY* 4716/25 and the 3rd boat landed at Lumley Beach, Sierra Leone 7.7.43. 6 crew were lost. Oberleutnant zur See Erich Faust and crew of 50 were lost when U-618 was damaged on 14.8.44 in the Bay of Biscay by a Leigh Light-equipped Liberator aircraft 'G', pilot F/L Gilbert Potier DFC of No. 53 Squadron RAF, based at St Eval, Cornwall, part of 15 Group and later sunk 60 miles W of Belle Ile, in position 47.22N 04.39W by HM frigates *DUCKWORTH* 1300/43 (K.351) (Cdr R.G. Mills) and *ESSINGTON* 1300/43 (K.353) (Lt-Cdr W. Lambert) of the 3rd Support Group. The Italian *CABOTO* was scuttled on 25.8.41 at Bandar Shapur, Persia, salvaged and taken as a prize.

## ANGLO-AMERICAN OIL CO. LTD – LONDON

***KENNEBEC*** ex-*WAR MOGUL* (tanker) • GRT 5548 • Built 1919
8.9.39: Torpedoed and damaged by German submarine U-34 (Rollman), in the Atlantic about 70 miles W by S of the Scilly Isles, in position 49.18N 08.13W while sailing independently on a voyage from Aruba to Avonmouth, with a cargo of 7000 tons of fuel oil. Later sunk by gunfire by HM destroyer *VERITY* 1120/19 (D.63) (Lt-Cdr A.R.M. Black). The Master, Capt Edward John Instone, and crew were rescued by HMS *VERITY* and landed at Milford Haven 10.9.39.

**CHEYENNE** (tanker) • GRT 8825 • Built 1930
15.9.39: Torpedoed and sunk by gunfire by German submarine U-53 (Heinicke), in the Atlantic SW of Ireland, in position 50.20N 13.30W while sailing independently on a voyage from Aruba to Swansea, with a cargo of 12600 tons of benzine. The Master, Capt Hugh Kerr, and 36 crew were rescued by Norwegian ship *IDA BAKKE* 5455/38 and landed at Baltimore, Co. Cork. 6 crew were lost.

**SARANAC** (tanker) • GRT 12070 • Built 1918
25.6.40: Torpedoed and sunk by gunfire by German submarine U-51 (Knorr), part of the 'Prien' patrol group of seven U-boats, in the Atlantic about 270 miles WSW of Land's End, in position 48.24N 15.05W while on a voyage from Fawley to Aruba, in ballast, part of convoy OA 172 comprising 56 ships. The Master, Capt Vernon Horace Alcock, and 30 crew were rescued by HM destroyer *HURRICANE* 1340/39 (H.06) ex-Brazilian *JAPARUA* (Lt-Cdr H.C. Simms) and landed at Plymouth, and 9 crew by British trawler *CALIPH* 226/06 were landed at Berehaven, Co. Cork. 4 crew were lost.

**APPALACHEE** (tanker) • GRT 8826 • Built 1930
1.12.40: Torpedoed and sunk by German submarine U-101 (Mengersen), in the Atlantic 340 miles W of Bloody Foreland, Co. Donegal, in position 54.30N 20.00W while on a voyage from Baytown, Texas, to Avonmouth via Bermuda, with a cargo of 11706 tons of aviation spirit, part of convoy HX 90 comprising 35 ships. The Master, Capt Warwick Armstrong, and 31 crew were rescued by British ship *LOCH RANZA* 4958/34 transferred to HM corvette *HELIOTROPE* 925/40 (K.03) (Lt-Cdr J. Jackson) and landed at Londonderry. 7 crew were lost.

**CARDILLAC** (tanker) • GRT 12062 • Built 1917
1.3.41: Torpedoed and sunk by German submarine U-552 (Topp), in the Atlantic NE of Rockall, in position 59.44N 11.16W while on a voyage from Aruba to Avonmouth via Halifax NS 13.2.41, with 3 passengers and a cargo of 17000 tons of aviation spirit, part of convoy HX 109 comprising 36 ships. The Master, Capt John Fraser Jefferson, 32 crew, 2 gunners and 2 passengers were lost. 4 crew and 1 passenger were rescued by HM destroyer leader *MALCOLM* 1804/19 (D.19) (Cdr C.D. Howard Johnston) and landed at Stornoway 3.3.41.

## MOWT

**EMPIRE MICA** (tanker) • GRT 8032 • Built 1941
29.6.42: Torpedoed and sunk by German submarine U-67 (Muller-Stöckheim), in the Gulf of Mexico SW of Cape St George, Florida, in position 29.25N 85.17W while sailing independently on a voyage from Houston, Texas, and New Orleans, Louisiana, to the UK via Key West, with a cargo of 12000 tons of vapourising oil. The Master, Capt Hugh Gordon Bradford Bentley, 7 crew and 6 gunners were rescued by a US coastguard cutter and landed at Panama City. 33 crew were lost.

**EMPIRE OIL** (tanker) • GRT 8029 • Built 1941
10.9.42: Torpedoed and damaged by German submarine U-659 (Stock), part of the 'Vorwärts' (Forward) patrol group of ten U-boats, later sunk by *coup de grâce* by German

submarine U-584 (Deecke), part of the same patrol, in the Atlantic SW of Iceland in position 51.23N 28.13W while on a voyage from Swansea to New York via Milford Haven 3.9.42, in ballast, part of convoy ON 127 comprising 34 ships. The Master, Capt Edward Marshall, 28 crew and 6 gunners were rescued, the Master, 12 crew and 6 gunners were rescued by HMCS destroyer ST CROIX 1190/19 (I.81) (Lt-Cdr A.N. Dobson) ex-USN four-stack McCOOK landed at St John's, Newfoundland 15.9.42 and 29 crew and 5 gunners by HMCS destroyer OTTAWA 1375/31 (H.60) (Lt-Cdr Clark A. Rutherford) ex-HMS CRUSADER. 13 crew and 5 gunners from the EMPIRE OIL were lost when HMCS OTTAWA was sunk on 14.10.42 by U-91 (Walkerling) in position 47.55N 43.27W. The captain, 4 officers and 114 ratings were lost. 76 officers and ratings were rescued by HM corvettes CELANDINE 925/40 (K.75) (Lt P.V. Collins) and HMCS ARVIDA 925/40 (K.113) (Lt A.I. Mackay). Kapitänleutnant Joachim Deecke and crew of 52 were lost on 31.10.43 when U-584 was sunk in the Atlantic 745 miles NW by N of Flores, Azores, in position 49.14N 31.55W by three Avengers, pilots Lt Letson S. Balliett, Lt Wilma S. Fowler and Lt Alexander C. McAuslan from US Navy Composite Squadron VC-9 from US escort carrier CARD 9800/42 (CVE-11) (Cdr Arnold J. Isbell), part of Task Group 21.14.

## ANGLO-SAXON PETROLEUM CO. LTD – LONDON

*TELENA* (tanker) • GRT 7406 • Built 1927
29.5.40: Damaged and set on fire by gunfire from German submarine U-37 (Oehrn), in the Atlantic SW of Cape Finisterre, in position 42.25N 09.08W while sailing independently on a voyage from Tripoli, Syria to Pauillac, with a cargo of 9368 tons of crude oil. The Master, Capt Harold Fitch Gosling, and 17 crew were lost. 36 crew were rescued by Spanish trawlers *BUENA ESPERANZA* and *JOSE IGNACIO de C* 300/16 and landed at Mari and El Grove near Vigo. The *TELENA*, abandoned, was seized by the Spanish authorities, towed to Vigo and arrived at Bilbao 17.8.40 for repairs. Later she was sold to Compania Espanola de Petroles of Madrid and renamed *GERONA*. Scrapped at Barcelona 5.1975.

*THIARA* (tanker) • GRT 10364 • Built 1939
27.7.40: Torpedoed and sunk by German submarine U-34 (Rollman), in the Atlantic 170 miles SW of Rockall, in position 56.37N 17.56W while on a voyage from Falmouth and Milford Haven to Curacao, NWI, with 4 passengers, in ballast, part of convoy OB 188 comprising 37 ships. The Master, Capt Robert William Thompson, 31 crew and passengers were rescued by HM destroyer *WINCHELSEA* 1300/17 (F.40) (Lt-Cdr W.A.F. Hawkins) and landed at Liverpool. 25 crew were lost.

*PECTEN* (tanker) • GRT 7725 • Built 1927
25.8.40: Torpedoed and sunk by German submarine U-57 (Topp), in the Atlantic 75 miles N of Tory Island, in position 56.22N 07.55W while on Admiralty service on voyage from Trinidad to the Clyde, with a cargo of 9546 tons of Admiralty fuel oil, a straggler from convoy HX 65 comprising 51 ships. The Master, Capt Herbert Edward Dale, and 15 crew were lost. 8 crew were rescued by British ship *TORR HEAD* 5021/37, transferred to HM trawler *ROBINA* 306/14 and landed at Belfast; 36 crew were rescued by Norwegian ship *CETUS* 2014/20 and landed at Stornoway. U-57 commanded by Oberleutnant zur See Erich Topp was rammed and sunk on 3.9.40 in the North Sea E of Brunsbuttel, in position 53.53N

09.09E by Norwegian steamer *RONA* 1376/94. 6 crew were lost. U-57 was later salvaged, decommissioned and scuttled at Kiel on 2.5.45.

**TORINIA** (tanker) • GRT 10364 • Built 1939
21.9.40: Torpedoed and damaged by German submarine U-100 (Schepke), later sunk by HM destroyer *SKATE* 900/17 (H.39) (Lt F.B. Baker DSC) in the Atlantic 340 miles W of Bloody Foreland, Co. Donegal, in position 55.00N 19.00W while on Admiralty service on a voyage from Curacao to the Clyde, with a cargo of 13815 tons of Admiralty fuel oil, part of convoy HX 72 comprising 47 ships. The Master, Capt Henry Jackson, and crew of 54 were rescued by HMS *SKATE* and landed at Londonderry 23.9.40.

**CAPRELLA** (tanker) • GRT 8230 • Built 1931
20.10.40: Torpedoed and sunk by German submarine U-100 (Schepke), in the Atlantic about 130 miles SW of Rockall, in position 56.28N 17.53W while on a voyage from Curacao to the Mersey, with a cargo of 11300 tons of fuel oil, part of convoy HX 79 comprising 49 ships. The Master, Capt Percy Prior, and 51 crew were rescued by HM trawler *LADY ELSA* 518/37 (FY.124) (Lt J.G. Rankin) and landed at Belfast. 1 crew was lost.

**SITALA** (tanker) • GRT 6218 • Built 1937
20.10.40: Torpedoed and sunk by German submarine U-100 (Schepke), in the Atlantic 130 miles SW of Rockall, in position 56.28N 17.53W while on a voyage from Curacao to Manchester, with a cargo of 8444 tons of crude oil, part of convoy HX 79 comprising 49 ships. The Master, Capt John Lewis Morgans, and 42 crew were rescued by HM trawler *LADY ELSA* 518/37 (FY.124) (Lt J.G. Rankin) and landed at Belfast. 1 crew was lost.

**CONCH** (tanker) • GRT 8376 • Built 1931
2.12.40: Torpedoed and damaged by German submarines U-47 (Prien) and U-95 (Schreiber), and finally sunk on 3.12.40 by German submarine U-99 (Kretschmer), in the Atlantic 370 miles W of Bloody Foreland, Co. Donegal, in position 54.21N 19.30W while on Admiralty service on a voyage from Trinidad to the Clyde via Bermuda, with a cargo of 11214 tons of Admiralty fuel oil, part of convoy HX 90 comprising 35 ships. The Master, Capt Charles George Graham, and crew of 52 were rescued by HMCS destroyer *ST LAURENT* 1375/31 (H.83) ex-HMS *CYGNET* (Lt R.P. Welland) and landed at Greenock.

**CLEA** (tanker) • GRT 8074 • Built 1938
13.2.41: Torpedoed and sunk by German submarine U-96 (Lehmann-Willenbrock), in the Atlantic SE of Iceland, in position 60.25N 17.11W while on Admiralty service on a voyage from Curacao to Loch Ewe and Scapa Flow, with a cargo of Admiralty fuel oil, a straggler from convoy HX 106 comprising 41 ships. The Master, Capt Leonard Walter George Boyt, and crew of 58 were lost.

**CHAMA** (tanker) • GRT 8077 • Built 1938
23.3.41: Torpedoed and sunk by German submarine U-97 (Heilmann), in the Atlantic WSW of Fastnet, in position 49.35N 19.13W while on a voyage from Ardrossan to New York, in ballast, a straggler from convoy OG 56 comprising 35 ships. The Master, Capt Hubert Stanley Sivell, crew of 54 and 4 gunners were lost.

**CONUS** (tanker) • GRT 8132 • Built 1931
4.4.41: Torpedoed and sunk by German submarine U-97 (Heilmann), in the Atlantic SE of Cape Farewell, in position 56.14N 31.19W while on Admiralty service on a voyage from Swansea and Milford Haven to Curacao, in ballast, part of convoy OB 304 comprising 36 ships. The Master, Capt Charles Asquith, and crew of 58 were lost.

**AURIS** (tanker) • GRT 8030 • Built 1935
28.6.41: Torpedoed and sunk by Italian submarine *LEONARDO DA VINCI* (Calda), in the Atlantic E of Madeira, in position 34.27N 11.57W while sailing independently on Admiralty service on a voyage from Trinidad to Gibraltar, with a cargo of 11493 tons of Admiralty fuel oil. The Master, Capt Norman Redvers Reed, 26 crew and 5 gunners were rescued by HM destroyer *FARNDALE* 1050/40 (L.70) (Cdr S.H. Carlill) and landed at Gibraltar. 32 crew were lost.

**HORN SHELL** (tanker) • GRT 8272 • Built 1931
26.7.41: Torpedoed and sunk by Italian submarine *BARBARIGO* (Murzi), in the Atlantic W of Madeira, in position 33.23N 22.18W while sailing independently on government service on a voyage from Gibraltar to Curacao, in ballast. The Master, Capt Archibald MacDougall, and 11 crew were rescued by Brazilian ship *CUYABA* 6489/06 and landed at Pernambuco (Recife); 12 crew rescued by Portuguese ship *AFRICA OCIDENTAL* 1268/39 were landed at the Cape Verde Islands. 17 crew were lost.

**BULYSSES** (tanker) • GRT 7519 • Built 1927
11.9.41: Torpedoed and sunk by German submarine U-82 (Rollmann), in the North Atlantic S of Cape Farewell, in position 62.40N 38.50W while on a voyage from New York to Stanlow via Sydney CB 30.8.41, with a cargo of 9300 tons of gas oil, part of convoy SC 42 comprising 65 ships. The Master, Capt Bartram Lamb, 53 crew and 6 gunners were rescued by Finnish ship *WISLA* 3106/28 and landed at Liverpool. 1 crew was lost.

**CARDITA** (tanker) • GRT 8237 • Built 1931
31.12.41: Torpedoed and sunk by German submarine U-87 Berger), in the Atlantic 110 miles 307° from St Kilda, in position 59.42N 11.58W while on a voyage from Curacao to Shellhaven, with a cargo of 11500 tons of motor spirit and white spirit, a straggler from convoy HX 166 comprising 35 ships. The Master, Capt John Osmond Evans, 16 crew and 6 gunners were rescued by HM destroyer *ONSLOW* 1540/41 (G.17) (Capt H.T. Armstrong DSC) and 10 crew by HM destroyer *SABRE* 905/18 (H.18) (Lt Peter W. Gretton OBE DSC) and landed at Reykjavik. 27 crew were lost.

**DIALA** (tanker) • GRT 8106 • Built 1938
15.1.42: Torpedoed and damaged by German submarine U-553 (Thurmann), in the Atlantic 300 miles ESE of Cape Race, Newfoundland, in position 44.50N 46.50W while sailing independently on a voyage from Stanlow to Los Angeles via Panama, in ballast, dispersed on 11.1.42 from convoy ON 52 comprising 42 ships. Abandoned and presumed sunk on 19.3.42 in position 47.00N 37.00W. The Master, Capt Herbert John Adler Peters, 6 crew and 1 gunner were rescued by British ship *TELEFORA DE LARRINAGA* 5780/20 and landed at New York. 48 crew and 9 gunners were lost.

**CIRCE SHELL** (tanker) • GRT 8207 • Built 1931
21.2.42: Torpedoed and sunk by German submarine U–161 (Achilles), in the Atlantic 20 miles WNW of Port of Spain, Trinidad, in position 11.03N 62.03W while sailing independently on government service on a voyage from Glasgow to Trinidad, in ballast, dispersed from convoy ON 60 comprising 45 ships. The Master, Capt John Thomas Sinclair, 51 crew and 5 gunners were rescued by the Admiralty tug *BUSY* 300/41 ex-USN *BYT 1* and landed at Port of Spain, Trinidad 23.2.42. 1 crew was lost.

**ANADARA** (tanker) • GRT 8009 • Built 1935
24.2.42: Torpedoed and damaged by gunfire by German submarine U–558 (Krech), attacked later in the day by U–587 (Borcherdt) and finally sunk by U–558, in the Atlantic E of Halifax, Nova Scotia, in position 43.45N 42.15W while on a voyage from Heysham 9.2.42 to Curacao via Halifax NS, in ballast, a straggler from convoy ONS 67 comprising 37 ships. The Master, Capt William Thomas Walmsley, crew of 53 and 8 gunners were lost.

**DARINA** (tanker) • GRT 8113 • Built 1939
20.5.42: Torpedoed and sunk by German submarine U–158 (Rostin), in the Atlantic 500 miles ESE of Bermuda, in position 29.17N 54.25W while on a voyage from Stanlow 6.5.42 to Texas City, Texas, in ballast, dispersed on 17.5.42 from convoy ON 93 comprising 25 ships. The Master, Capt John Murray Cuthill, 44 crew and 5 gunners were rescued, the Master's boat and 17 survivors were rescued by British tanker *BRITISH ARDOUR* 7124/28 and landed at Charleston, South Carolina 27.5.42; the Chief Officer's boat was rescued afer 6½ days 150 miles SSE of Bermuda by US ship *EXANTHIA* 6533/42 and landed at Norfolk, Virginia, and the 3rd Officer's boat was rescued after 6 days by Norwegian ship *DAGRUN* 4562/28 and landed at Cape Town 23.6.42. 5 crew and 1 gunner were lost.

**HAVRE** (tanker) • GRT 2073 • Built 1905
10.6.42: Torpedoed and sunk by German submarine U–431 (Dommes), in the Mediterranean about 50 miles W of Alexandria, while on a voyage from Alexandria 9.6.42 to Tobruk, with a cargo of 2125 tons of cased benzine, part of convoy AT 49 comprising 4 ships. The Master, Capt George Christopher Pearson, 17 crew and 2 gunners were lost. 27 crew, 2 gunners and 1 signalman were rescued by HM whaler *PARKTOWN* 250/25 and landed at Mersa Matruh, Egypt.

**DONOVANIA** (tanker) • GRT 8149 • Built 1941
21.7.42: Torpedoed and sunk by German submarine U–160 (Lassen), in the Atlantic, off Grand Matelot Point, Trinidad, in position 10.56N 61.10W while sailing independently on a voyage from Lagos 13.7.42 to Trinidad, in ballast. The Master, Capt Douglas Bartholomew Edgar, 42 crew and 2 gunners were rescued by HM motor torpedo boats and US destroyer *LIVERMORE* 1620/40 (DD.429) and landed at Port of Spain, Trinidad. 3 crew and 2 gunners were lost.

**TRICULA** (tanker) • GRT 6221 • Built 1936
3.8.42: Torpedoed and sunk by German submarine U–108 (Scholtz), in the Atlantic 250 miles NE of Trinidad, in position 11.35N 56.51W while sailing independently on a voyage from Curacao and Trinidad 1.8.42 to Cape Town, with 2 passengers and a cargo of 8000 tons

of fuel oil. The Master, Capt Oswald Eustace Sparrow, 42 crew, 5 gunners and 1 passenger were lost. 8 crew, 1 gunner and 1 passenger were rescued by Argentinian ship *RIO SAN JUAN* 2328/36 and landed at Fernando, Cuba. Kapitänleutnant Klaus Scholtz was awarded the Knight's Cross (26.12.41) with Oak Leaves (10.9.42). U-108, commanded by Oberleutnant zur See Matthias Brünig, was scuttled at Settin 24.4.45.

**DONAX** (tanker) • GRT 8036 • Built 1938
22.10.42: Torpedoed and damaged by German submarine U-443 (v. Puttkamer), part of the 'Puma' patrol group of ten U-boats, in the Atlantic SW of Fastnet, in position 49.51N 27.58W while on a voyage from Avonmouth to New York via Milford Haven 15.10.42 and Belfast 17.10.42, in ballast, part of convoy ON 139 comprising 38 ships. Later sank on 29.10.42 in position 48.04N 24.41W while under tow by HM rescue tug *NIMBLE* 890/41 (W.123) and HM tug *MARAUDER* 840/38 (W.98) (Lt F. Jennings). The Master, Capt John Murray Cuthill, crew of 54 and 8 gunners were rescued: 38 crew by HMCS corvette *DRUMHELLER* 925/41 (K.167) (Lt G.H. Griffiths) and landed at St John's, Newfoundland, 10 crew by HM destroyer *CAMPBELTOWN* 1090/19 (I.42) (Lt-Cdr S.H.B. Beattie) ex-USN four-stack *BUCHANAN* and landed at Greenock, and 15 crew by HM rescue tug *NIMBLE* and landed at Greenock.

**BULLMOUTH** (tanker) • GRT 7519 • Built 1927
30.10.42: Torpedoed and sunk by German submarines U-409 (Massmann) and U-659 (Stock), part of the 'Streitaxt' (Battleaxe) patrol group of eight U-boats, in the Atlantic about 100 miles NNW of Madeira, in position 33.20N 18.25W while on a voyage from Freetown 16.10.42 to the Tyne, in ballast, part of convoy SL 125 comprising 40 ships. The Master, Capt John Wilfred Brougham, 44 crew and 5 gunners were lost. The Chief Officer and 5 crew landed on the island of Bugio near Madeira.

**OTINA** (tanker) • GRT 6217 • Built 1938
20.12.42: Torpedoed and sunk by German submarine U-621 (Kruschka), part of the 'Raufbold' (Brawler) patrol group of twelve U-boats, in the Atlantic W of Ireland, in position 47.40N 33.06W while on a voyage from Belfast to New York, in ballast, a straggler from convoy ON 153 comprising 43 ships. The Master, Capt George Lowery Forrest, crew of 52 and 7 gunners were lost.

**EULIMA** (tanker) • GRT 6207 • Built 1937
23.2.43: Torpedoed and sunk by German submarine U-186 (Hesemann), part of the 'Knappen' (Shieldbearer) patrol group of four U-boats, in the Atlantic about 310 miles S of Cape Race, in position 46.48N 36.18W while on a voyage from Liverpool 11.2.43 to New York, in ballast, a straggler from convoy ON 166 comprising 48 ships. The Master, Capt Frederick William Wickera, 52 crew and 9 gunners were lost. The 3rd Officer J. Campkin was taken prisoner, landed at Lorient 5.3.43 and taken to Milag Nord prisoner-of-war camp near Bremen. Kapitänleutnant Siegfried Hesemann and crew of 52 were lost when U-186, part of the 'Elbe 2' (German river) patrol group of thirteen U-boats, was sunk while shadowing convoy SC 129 comprising 26 ships on 12.5.43 in the Atlantic 170 miles N by W of Flores, Azores, in position 41.54N 31.49W by HM destroyer *HESPERUS* 1340/39 (H.57) ex-HMS *HEARTY* (Cdr Donald G. MacIntyre), part of Escort Group B2.

**CORBIS** (tanker) • GRT 8132 • Built 1931
18.4.43: Torpedoed and sunk by German submarine U-180 (Musenberg), in the Indian Ocean 500 miles ESE of Port Elizabeth, South Africa, in position 35.20S 35.37E while sailing independently on a voyage from Abadan 21.3.43 and Bandar Abbas 25.3.43 to Cape Town, with a cargo of 11310 tons of diesel oil and 50 tons of aviation spirit. The Master, Capt Stanley Wilfred Appleton, 47 crew and 2 gunners were lost. 4 crew and 6 gunners were rescued after drifting for 13 days in an open boat by a SAAF crash launch and landed at East London. Oberleutnant zur See Rolf Riesen and crew of 55 were lost when U-180 struck a British mine on 22.8.44 in the Bay of Biscay NW of Bordeaux, in position 45.00N 02.00W.

**DORYSSA** (tanker) • GRT 8078 • Built 1938
25.4.43: Torpedoed and sunk by Italian submarine *LEONARDO DA VINCI* (Gazzana), in the Indian Ocean 200 miles S of Mossel Bay, South Africa, in position 37.03S 24.03E while sailing independently on a voyage from Cape Town 24.4.43 to Abadan, Persia, in ballast. The Master, Capt Walter Fraser, 49 crew, 1 gunner and 2 passengers were lost. 5 crew and 4 gunners were rescued by HM whaler *SOUTHERN BREEZE* 314/36 (T.28) (Lt C.A. Johnson) and landed at Cape Town. *LEONARDO DA VINCI* commanded by Lt-Cdr Gianfranco Gazzana-Priaroggia, Knight's Cross, was sunk on 23.5.43 in the Atlantic 20 miles W by S of Cape Finisterre, in position 42.16N 15.40W by HM destroyer *ACTIVE* 1350/29 (H.14) (Lt-Cdr P.G. Merriman) and HM frigate *NESS* 1370/42 (K.219) (Cdr T.G.R. Crick DSC).

**MAJA** (tanker) • GRT 8181 • Built 1931
15.1.45: Torpedoed and sunk by German submarine U-1055 (Meyer), in the Irish Sea SE of Drogheda, in position 53.40N 05.14W while sailing independently on a voyage from Swansea to Belfast and Reykjavik, with a cargo of 10680 tons of gas oil and motor spirit. The Master, Capt William Cecil Robinson, 37 crew and 2 gunners were rescued by Belgian trawler *HENDRIK CONSCIENCE* 90/31 and landed at Holyhead. 17 crew and 8 gunners were lost. Oberleutnant zur See Rudolf Meyer and crew of 48 were lost by an unknown cause in the Atlantic WSW of Brest, in position approximately 52.00N 11.00W after 23.4.45.

**MOWT**

**PRESIDENT SERGENT** (tanker) • GRT 5344 • Built 1923
18.11.42: Torpedoed and sunk by German submarine U-624 (v. Soden), part of the 'Kreuzotter' (Viper) patrol group of nine U-boats, in the Atlantic SSE of Cape Farewell, in position 54.07N 38.26W while on government service on a voyage from Liverpool 7.11.42 to Trinidad via New York, in ballast, part of convoy ONS 144 comprising 28 ships. The Master, Capt Patrick Gerald Gordon Dove, Commodore J.K. Brook CBE DSO RNR RD, 6 naval staff, 24 crew and 7 gunners were rescued by the rescue ship *PERTH* 2208/15 (Capt Keith Williamson OBE) and landed at Halifax, Nova Scotia 25.11.42. 20 crew were lost. One of the convoy's escorts RNoN corvette *MONTBRETIA* 925/25 (K.208) was sunk on 18.11.42 by German submarine U-262 (Franke) in the Atlantic, SSE of Cape Farewell, in position 53.37N 38.15W. Capt Patrick G.G. Dove was the Master of the coastal tanker *AFRICA SHELL* 706/39 which was captured with her crew of 28 and sunk on 15.11.39 by German pocket battleship *ADMIRAL GRAF SPEE* 10000/34 (Kapitän zur See Hans Langsdorff), in the Indian Ocean 10½ miles SW by S of Cape Zavora Lighthouse, in position 24.40S 25.00E while on a voyage from Quelimane to Lourenco Marques, Portuguese East Africa, in ballast.

**EMPIRE SPENSER** (tanker) • GRT 8194 • Built 1942
8.12.42: Torpedoed and sunk by German submarine U-524 (v. Steinaecker), part of the 'Panzer' (Armour) patrol group of seven U-boats, in the Atlantic SE of Cape Farewell, in position 57.04N 36.01W while on her maiden voyage from Curacao to Stanlow via New York 27.11.42, with a cargo of 10000 tons of motor spirit, part of convoy HX 217 comprising 26 ships. The Master, Capt John Barlow Hodge, 47 crew and 9 gunners were rescued by rescue ship PERTH 2208/15 (Capt Keith Williamson OBE) and landed at Greenock 13.12.42. 1 crew was lost. Kapitänleutnant Walter Freiherr von Steinaecker and crew of 51 were lost on 22.3.43 when U-524, part of the 'Wohlgemut' (Optimistic) patrol group of five U-boats was sunk in the Atlantic 70 miles N of Palma, Canary Islands, in position 30.15N 18.13W by Liberator T/2, pilot Lt William L. Sandford, of the 1st Squadron, 480th Antisubmarine Group USAAF, based at Craw Field, Port Lyautey, French Morocco. Kapitänleutnant Nikolaus von Jacobs and crew of 44 were lost on 8.12.42 in the Atlantic 300 miles SE of Cape Discord, Greenland, in position 57.25N 35.19W when U-611, part of the 'Draufgänger' (Daredevil) patrol group of eleven U-boats, was sunk while shadowing convoy HX 217 by Liberator 'H' AM929 pilot, S/Ldr Terry M. Bullock DFC of No. 120 Squadron RAF, based at Reykjavik.

## ANNING BROTHERS – CARDIFF
### Exmouth SS Co.

**STARCROSS** • GRT 4662 • Built 1936
20.5.41: Torpedoed and sunk by Italian submarine OTARIA (Vocaturo), in the Atlantic about 400 miles W of Valentia Island, Co. Kerry, in position 51.45N 20.45W while on a voyage from Lagos and Freetown to Hull, with a cargo of 7458 tons of West African produce, part of convoy SL 73 comprising 36 ships. The Master, Capt Henry Burgess, crew of 35 and 4 gunners were rescued by HMCS destroyer ST FRANCIS 1190/19 (I.93) (Lt Clark A. Rutherford) ex-USN four-stack BANCROFT and landed at Greenock.

## MOWT

**EMPIRE GUIDON** • GRT 7041 • Built 1942
31.10.42: Torpedoed and sunk by German submarine U-504 (Poske), part of the 'Eisbär' (Polarbear) patrol group of five U-boats, in the Indian Ocean 180 miles ESE of Durban, in position 30.48S 34.11E while sailing independently on a voyage from New York 30.10.42 and Durban to Alexandria, with 3 passengers and a cargo of 7032 tons of military stores, general and coal. The Master, Capt Henry Burgess, 43 crew and 8 gunners were rescued by British ship CLAN ALPINE 5442/18 and landed at Port Elizabeth. 1 crew, 1 gunner and passengers were lost.

## ASIATIC STEAM NAVIGATION CO. LTD – LONDON

**KOHINUR** • GRT 5168 • Built 1922
15.11.40: Torpedoed and sunk by German submarine U-65 (v. Stockhausen), in the Atlantic 250 miles N of the Equator, in position 04.24N 13.46W while on government service sailing independently on a voyage from Port Talbot to Alexandria and Port Said, with a cargo of government stores, dispersed on 31.10.40 from convoy OB 235 comprising 32 ships. The Master, Capt Leslie Hugh Bonnand, 45 crew and 2 gunners were lost. 36 crew were rescued by British ship CITY OF PITTSBURG 7377/22. 1 crew was taken prisoner.

**BAHADUR** • GRT 5424 • Built 1929
7.4.42: Torpedoed and sunk by Japanese submarine I-6 (Inaba), in the Arabian Sea NW of Bombay, in position 19.44N 68.28E while sailing independently on a voyage from Bombay 6.4.42 to Basrah, Iraq, with a cargo of 5100 tons of government stores including ammunition. The Master, Capt Henry H. Gibson, and 24 crew were rescued, landed at Bombay, and the remaining crew of 61 were rescued by US ship VOLUNTEER 7717/18. Lt Nozo Fumon and crew were lost on 14.7.44 when I-6 was sunk in the Pacific 110 miles N by W of Guam Island, in position 15.81N 144.26E by US destroyer escort WILLIAM C. MILLER 1140/43 (DE–259) (Lt-Cdr D.F. Francis USNR).

**NURMAHAL** • GRT 5419 • Built 1923
9.11.42: Torpedoed and damaged by German submarine U-154 (Schuch), in the Atlantic 300 miles E of Martinique, in position 14.45N 55.45W and finally sank on 11.11.42 while sailing independently on a voyage from Safaga Island, Egypt, to Charleston and New York via Table Bay 15.10.42, in ballast. The Master, Capt W.R. Gordon, and an unknown number of crew were saved. 14 crew were lost.

**SHAHJEHAN** • GRT 5454 • Built 1942
6.7.43: Torpedoed and damaged by German submarine U-453 (v. Schlippenbach), in the Mediterranean NE of Benghazi, Cyrenaica, in position 33.01N 21.32E, taken in tow but sank in position 32.55N 21.10E the next day while on government service on a voyage from Alexandria 3.7.43 to Sicily, with 230 troops and 2000 tons of military stores, including trucks and invasion barges, part of convoy MWS 36 comprising 30 ships. The Master, Capt Bertram E. Brewin, crew of 77, 20 gunners, 229 military, naval and RAF personnel were rescued by HM rescue tug ST MONANCE 860/19 (W.63) (Skipper J. Inglish) and HM river gunboat APHIS 625/15 (T.57) (Lt-Cdr F.Y. Bethell) and landed at Benghazi. 1 service personnel was lost. Kapitänleutnant Egon Reiner von Schlippenbach was awarded the Knight's Cross (19.11.43).

**SHAHZADA** • GRT 5454 • Built 1942
9.7.44: Torpedoed and sunk by German submarine U-196 (Kentrat), in the Arabian Sea SW of Bombay, in position 15.30N 65.30E while sailing independently on a voyage from Mormugao, WC India, to Aden and Suez, with a cargo of 5000 tons of groundnuts. The Master, Capt Allan Scott Hamilton, 36 crew and 9 gunners were lost. 15 crew and 1 gunner were rescued by Norwegian ship MAGNA 1788/29 and landed at Aden 21.7.44, 15 crew by British ship CHAUGON 3619/11 and landed at Bombay 17.7.44 and 21 crew landed at Goa 18.7.44. Korvettenkapitän Eitel-Friedrich Kentrat was awarded the Knight's Cross (31.12.41). U-196 commanded by Oberleutnant zur See Johannes Werner Striegler and crew of 64 were lost on 30.11.44 in the Sunda Strait by an unknown cause.

**NAIRUNG** • GRT 5414 • Built 1942
18.8.44: Torpedoed and sunk by German submarine U-862 (Timm), in the Mozambique Channel NE of Mozambique, Portuguese East Africa, in position 14.00S 45.00E while sailing independently on a voyage from Durban 13.8.44 and Dar es Salaam, Tanganyika, to Bombay, with general cargo. The Master, Capt John Murray, and 15 crew were lost. The number of survivors was 76.

## ASSOCIATED HUMBER LINES – HULL
**Hull & Netherlands SS Co. Ltd**

*MELROSE ABBEY* • GRT 2473 • Built 1936
27.12.42: Torpedoed and sunk by German submarine U–356 (Ruppelt), part of the 'Spitz' (Sharp) patrol group of ten U-boats, in the Atlantic NNE of the Azores, in position 47.30N 24.30W while on a voyage from Tyne 13.12.42 and Loch Ewe 18.12.42 to Boston, Mass and Trinidad, with a cargo of 3403 tons of coal and 70 tons bags of mail, part of convoy ONS 154 comprising 45 ships. The Master, Capt Frederick J. Ormrod, 22 crew and 4 gunners were rescued by rescue ship *TOWARD* 1571/23 (Capt Arthur James Knell MBE DSC), transferred to HMCS corvette *SHEDIAC* 925/41 (K.110) (Lt J.E. Clayton) and landed at Ponta Delgada, Azores. 6 crew and 1 gunner were lost.

## ATHEL LINE, LIMITED – LONDON
**United Molasses Ltd**

*ATHELLAIRD* (tanker) • GRT 8999 • Built 1930
2.7.40: Torpedoed and sunk by German submarine U–29 (Schuhart), in the Atlantic 350 miles NW of Finisterre, in position 47.24N 16.49W while on a voyage from Liverpool 29.6.40 to Cuba, in ballast, part of convoy OB 176 comprising 28 ships. The Master, Capt Hugh Roberts, and crew of 41 were rescued by HM sloop *SANDWICH* 1045/28 (L.12) (Cdr H.J. Yeatman) and landed at Greenock.

*ATHELCREST* (tanker) • GRT 6825 • Built 1940
25.8.40: Torpedoed and damaged by German submarine U–48 (Rösing), in the Atlantic 90 miles E by N of Flannan Isles, in position 58.24N 11.25W while on a voyage from Aruba NWI to London, with a cargo of diesel oil, part of convoy HX 65 comprising 51 ships. The wreck was sunk by gunfire by HM corvette *GODETIA* 925/41 (K.226) (Lt A.H. Pierce OBE). The Master, Capt Llewellyn Vincent F. Evans, and 5 crew were rescued by HMS *GODETIA* and landed at Methil. 30 crew were lost. Kapitän zur See Hans Rudolf Rösing was awarded the Knight's Cross (29.8.40) and was later appointed Senior Officer, Submarines (West), the deployment of U-boats from bases at Bordeaux, Brest, La Pallice, Lorient and St Nazaire in the Bay of Biscay.

*ATHELBEACH* (tanker) • GRT 6568 • Built 1931
7.3.41: Torpedoed and sunk by gunfire by German submarine U–70 (Matz), in the North Atlantic SE of Iceland, in position 60.30N 13.30W while on a voyage from Greenock to New York, in ballast, part of convoy OB 293 comprising 37 ships. The Master, Capt Malcolm McIntyre, and 6 crew were lost. 37 crew were rescued by HM corvette *CAMELLIA* 925/40 (K.31) (Lt Cdr A.E. Willmot) and landed at Greenock. U-70 commanded by Kapitänleutnant Joachim Matz was sunk the same day in the Atlantic 150 miles N of Rockall, in position 60.15N 14.00W by HM corvettes *ARBUTUS* 925/40 (K.86) (Lt-Cdr H. Lloyd–Williams) and *CAMELLIA* 925/40 (K.31). The U-boat commander and 26 crew were taken prisoner by HMS *ARBUTUS*. 20 crew were lost.

*ATHELCROWN* (tanker) • GRT 11999 • Built 1929
22.1.42: Torpedoed and sunk by German submarine U–82 (Rollmann), in the Atlantic SE of Cape Race, Newfoundland, in position 45.06N 40.56W while sailing independently on a

voyage from Cardiff 8.1.42 and Belfast Lough to Aruba NWI, in ballast, dispersed from convoy ON 56 comprising 36 ships. The Master, Capt Isaac Burkill, 26 crew and 6 gunners were rescued by British ship *ARGOS HILL* 7178/22 landed at Halifax, Nova Scotia, 4 crew were rescued from the wreck of the Shell tanker *DIALA* 8106/38 which was found abandoned in position 47.28N 49.19W and remained on board 8 days before rescue by Swedish ship *SATURNUS* 9965/40 landed on the Faröes Isles and 8 crew by HM ship. 5 crew were lost. Kapitänleutnant Siegfried Rollmann and crew of 44 were lost on 6.2.42 when U-82 was sunk in the Atlantic 380 miles N of San Miguel, Azores, in position 44.10N 23.52W while shadowing convoy OS 18 comprising 46 ships by HM sloop *ROCHESTER* 1105/31 (L.50) (Cdr C.B. Allen) and HM corvette *TAMARISK* 925/41 (K.216) (Lt N.C. Dawson).

***ATHELQUEEN*** (tanker) • GRT 8780 • Built 1928
15.3.42: Torpedoed and sunk by Italian submarine *ENRICO TAZZOLI* (Fecia di Cossato), part of the 'Da Vinci' patrol group of five Italian submarines, in the Atlantic NE of Eleuthera Island, Bahamas, in position 26.50N 75.40W while sailing independently on a voyage from Hull to Port Everglades, Florida, in ballast, dispersed from convoy OS 20 comprising 55 ships. The Master, Capt Robert John Roberts, 39 crew and 6 gunners landed at Nassau, Bahamas. 3 crew were lost.

***ATHELEMPRESS*** (tanker) • GRT 8941 • Built 1930
30.4.42: Torpedoed and sunk by gunfire by German submarine U-162 (Wattenberg), in the Atlantic 180 miles E of Barbados, in position 13.21N 56.16W while sailing independently on Admiralty service on a voyage from Southampton and Milford Haven 11.4.42 to Trinidad, in ballast, dispersed from convoy OS 25 comprising 41 ships. The Master, Capt Walter Jackson, and 18 crew landed at Gros Inlet Bay, St Lucia. The Chief Officer and 27 crew were rescued by Norwegian tanker *ATLANTIC* 7342/25 and landed at Trinidad. 2 crew and 1 gunner were lost.

***ATHELKNIGHT*** (tanker) • GRT 8940 • Built 1930
27.5.42: Torpedoed and sunk by gunfire by German submarine U-172 (Emmermann), in the Atlantic SE of Bermuda, in position 27.50N 46.00W while sailing independently on a voyage from Barry to Curacao, NWI, in ballast, dispersed from convoy OS 28 comprising 37 ships. The Master, Capt Hugh Roberts, 39 crew and 3 gunners were rescued, the Master and 24 survivors after 28 days by British ship *EMPIRE AUSTIN* 7057/42 and landed at Cape Town; the 2nd Officer and 17 survivors landed on St Bartholomew Island, Leeward Islands, 23.6.42 after sailing in an open boat for about 1200 miles. 4 crew and 5 gunners were lost.

***ATHELTEMPLAR*** (tanker) • GRT 8992 • Built 1930
14.9.42: Torpedoed and damaged by German submarine U-457 (Brandenberg), in the Greenland Sea SW of Bear Island, in position 76.10N 18.00E while on Admiralty service on a voyage from the Tyne to Archangel via Loch Ewe and Hvalfiordur, Iceland, with a cargo of 9400 tons of Admiralty fuel oil, part of convoy PQ 18 comprising 43 ships. Abandoned and later sunk by gunfire by HM minesweeper *HARRIER* 815/34 (HN.71) (Cdr A.D.H. Jay DSO). The Master, Capt Carl Ray, 42 crew and 18 gunners were rescued by the rescue ship *COPELAND* 1526/23 (Capt W.J. Hartley DSC) and HM destroyer *OFFA* 1540/41 (G.29) (Lt-Cdr R.A. Ewing), transferred to HM minesweepers *HARRIER* and *SHARPSHOOTER* 835/36 (N.68) (Lt-Cdr W.L. O'Mara) then to HM cruiser *SCYLLA* 5450/40 (98) (Capt J.A.P. MacIntyre CBE) and landed at

Scapa Flow, Orkneys. 16 crew later died from their injuries. Capt W.J. Hartley was awarded the Lloyd's War Medal for bravery at sea. Korvettenkapitän Karl Brandenberg and 44 crew were lost on 16.9.42 when U-457 was sunk in the Barents Sea 500 miles NW of North Cape, in position 75.05N 43.15E by HM destroyer *IMPULSIVE* 1370/37 (D.11) (Lt-Cdr E.G. Roper DSC).

*ATHELSULTAN* (tanker) • GRT 8882 • Built 1929
23.9.42: Torpedoed and sunk by German submarine U-617 (Brandi), part of the 'Pfeil' (Arrow) patrol group of seven U-boats, in the Atlantic SE of Cape Farewell, in position 58.42N 33.38W while on a voyage from Port Everglades, Florida, to Liverpool via Halifax NS 12.9.42, with a cargo of 13250 tons of molasses and alcohol, part of convoy SC 100 comprising 20 ships. The Master, Capt James Dominic Donovan, and 2 crew were rescued by HMCS corvette *WEYBURN* 925/41 (K.173) (Lt Thomas M.W. Golby) and 7 crew by HM corvette *NASTURTIUM* 925/40 (K.207) (Lt C.D. Smith DSC) ex-French *LA PAIMPOLAISE* and landed at Londonderry. Commodore N.H. Gale DSO RNR RD, 37 crew, 7 gunners and 6 naval staff were lost. Capt J.D. Donovan was awarded the Lloyd's War Medal for bravery at sea. Kapitänleutnant Albrecht Brandi was awarded the Knight's Cross (21.1.43) with Oak Leaves (11.4.43), the Swords (9.5.44) and the Diamonds (23.11.44).

*ATHELPRINCESS* (tanker) • GRT 8882 • Built 1929
23.2.43: Torpedoed and sunk by German submarine U-522 (Schneider), part of 'Delphin' (Dolphin) patrol group of sixteen U-boats, in the Atlantic W of Madeira, in position 32.02N 24.38W while on government service on a voyage from Liverpool to Curacao, in ballast, a straggler from convoy UC 1 comprising 33 ships. The Master, Capt Egerton Gabriel B. Martin OBE, 42 crew and 7 gunners were rescued by HM sloop *WESTON* 1060/32 (L.72) ex-HMS *WESTON-SUPER-MARE* (Cdr L.F. Durnford-Slater) transferred to US destroyer *HILARY P. JONES* 1620/39 (DD.427) and landed at San Juan, Puerto Rico. 1 crew was lost. Kapitänleutnant Herbert Schneider (Knight's Cross 16.1.43) and crew of 50 were lost when U-552 was sunk the same day in the Atlantic 380 miles WNW of Palma, Canary Islands, in position 31.27N 26.22W by HM escort sloop *TOTLAND* 1546/31 (Y.88) (Lt-Cdr L.E. Woodhouse) ex-US coastguard cutter *CAYUGA*, part of the Escort Group 44 (Cdr L.F. Durnford–Slater).

*ATHELMONARCH* (tanker) • GRT 8995 • Built 1928
15.6.43: Torpedoed and sunk by German submarine U-97 (Trox), in the Mediterranean NW of Jaffa, Palestine, in position 32.20N 34.39E while on Admiralty service on a voyage, escorted by RHN destroyer *AETOS* 1050/11, from Beirut, Lebanon, to Alexandria, with a cargo of 13600 tons of Admiralty fuel oil. The Master, Capt Robert John Roberts, 35 crew and 11 gunners were rescued by RHN *AETOS* and landed at Beirut. 4 crew were lost. U-97 commanded by Kapitänleutnant Hans-Georg Trox was sunk on 16.6.43 in the Mediterranean 40 miles W of Haifa, in position 33.00N 34.00E by Lockheed Hudson bomber 'T' FH311, pilot F/Sgt David T. Barnard RAAF of No. 459 Squadron RAAF, based at Gambut, Cyrenaica. The U-boat commander and 26 crew were lost. 21 crew were taken prisoner by HM ship. The pilot was awarded the DFM.

*ATHELVIKING* ex-*JAVA* (tanker) • GRT 8779 • Built 1926
14.1.45: Torpedoed and sunk by German submarine U-1232 (Dobratz), in the Atlantic S of Halifax, Nova Scotia, in position 44.20N 63.24W while on a voyage from Port Everglades,

Florida, to the UK via Boston, Mass with a cargo of 11630 tons of molasses and 14 landing craft on deck, part of convoy BX 141 comprising 18 ships. The Master, Capt Egerton Gabriel B. Martin OBE, and 3 crew were lost. 39 crew and 8 gunners were rescued by HMCS motor launch No. 102 57/40 (Lt J.K. Macdonald) and landed at Halifax NS. Kapitänleutnant Kurt Dobratz was awarded the Knight's Cross (23.1.45). U-1232, commanded by Oberleutnant zur See Götz Roth, was scuttled on 2.5.45 at Wesermünde.

*ATHELDUKE* (tanker) • GRT 8966 • Built 1929
16.4.45: Torpedoed and sunk by German submarine U-1274 (Fitting), in the North Sea E of Newcastle, in position 55.39N 01.31W while on a voyage from Port Everglades, Florida, to Salt End via Loch Ewe, with a cargo of 12600 tons of molasses, part of coastal convoy FS 1784. The Master, Capt Joseph Errett, 41 crew and 4 gunners were rescued by British ship *KING NEPTUNE* 5224/28. 1 crew was lost. Oberleutnantz zur See Hans–Herman Fitting and crew of 43 were lost on the same day when U-1274 was sunk in the North Sea 6 miles E of Sunderland, in position 55.36N 01.24W by HM destroyer escort *VICEROY* 1325/17 (F.38) (Lt-Cdr J.M.J. Sinclair).

## ATKINSON & PRICKETT LIMITED – HULL
## MOWT

*MARGIT* • GRT 1735 • Built 1924
8.2.44: Torpedoed and sunk by German submarine U-985 (Kessler), part of the 'Igel 1' (Hedeghog) patrol group of fifteen U-boats, in the North Atlantic SE of Iceland, in position 61.30N 10.30W while on a voyage from the Tyne to Reykjavik, with a cargo of coal, part of convoy RA 56 comprising 37 ships. The Master, Capt Holger Johansen, and crew of 23 were lost. U-985 commanded by Kapitänleutnant Heinz Wolff was decommissioned at Kristiansand, Norway, on 15.11.44 after damage by a German mine off Lister 23.10.44.

## ATLANTIC TRANSPORTATION CO. LTD – MONTREAL

*J.B. WHITE* ex-*JADDEN* (Canadian flag) • GRT 7375 • Built 1919
16.3.41: Torpedoed and damaged by German submarine U-99 (Kretschmer), later sunk by a *coup de grâce* by U-99, in the North Atlantic WSW of the Faroes, in position 60.57N 12.27W while on a voyage from Mobile, Alabama, to Manchester and Ellesmere Port via Halifax NS 1.3.41, with a cargo of 2500 tons of steel and 4500 tons of newsprint, part of convoy HX 112. comprising 41 ships. The Master, Capt J.W.R. Woodward and 37 crew were rescued by HM destroyer *WALKER* 1100/17 (D.27) (Lt-Cdr A.A. Tait) and landed at Liverpool. 2 crew were lost.

## BALTIC TRADING CO. LTD – LONDON

*SHIRAK* tanker) • GRT 6023 • Built 1926
19.10.40: Torpedoed and damaged by German submarine U-47 (Prien), later torpedoed and sunk by German submarine U-48 (Bleichrodt), in the Atlantic 90 miles SW of Rockall, in position 57.00N 16.53W while on a voyage from Aruba to London via Halifax NS 8.10.40, with a cargo of 7771 tons of refined petroleum products, part of convoy HX 79 comprising

49 ships. The Master, Capt Lawrence Robert Morrison, and crew of 36 were rescued by HM trawler *BLACKFLY* 482/37 ex-HMS *BARNETT* (Lt A.P. Hughes) and landed at Belfast.

**SHIRVAN** (tanker) • GRT 6017 • Built 1925
10.11.44: Torpedoed and sunk by German submarine U-300 (Hein), in the North Atlantic off Skagi, Iceland, in position 64.08N 22.50W while on a voyage from Bowling via Loch Ewe to Hvalfiordur, Iceland, with a cargo of 8050 tons of gas oil, a straggler from convoy UR 142 comprising 4 ships. The Master, Capt Edward F. Pattenden, 13 crew and 2 gunners were lost. 24 crew and 7 gunners were rescued by HM rescue tug *REWARD* 1118/44 (W.164) and RNoN trawler *HONNINGSVAAG* ex-*MALANGEN* 487/40 (4.277) and landed at Reykjavik.

## BARR CROMBIE & COMPANY – GLASGOW
## MOWT

**EMPIRE WAVE** • GRT 7463 • Built 1941 – Catapult Armed Merchantman (CAM–ship)
2.10.41: Torpedoed and sunk by German submarine U-562 (Hamm), part of the 'Brandenburg' (district of Berlin) patrol group of eleven U-boats, in the Atlantic 500 miles E of Cape Farewell, in position 59.08N 32.56W while on a voyage from Sunderland to Halifax NS, in ballast, part of convoy ONS 19 comprising 49 ships. The Master, Capt Clement Porter Maclay, 19 crew and 9 RAF personnel were lost. 23 crew, 6 gunners and 2 RAF personnel were rescued by Icelandic trawler *SURPRISE* 313/19 landed at Patrick's Fjord, Iceland.

## BERMUDA & WEST INDIES STEAMSHIP CO. – HAMILTON, BERMUDA

**NERISSA** • GRT 5583 • Built 1926
1.5.41: Torpedoed and sunk by German submarine U-552 (Topp), in the Atlantic SE of Rockall, in position 57.57N 10.08W while on a voyage from Halifax NS and St John's, Newfoundland, to Liverpool, with 175 passengers and a general cargo of 3049 tons including aluminium, motor trucks and shells, a straggler from convoy HX 121 comprising 48 ships. The Master, Capt Gilbert Radcliffe Watson, 82 crew and 124 passengers were lost. 23 crew, 6 gunners, 3 stowaways and 51 passengers were rescued by HM destroyer *VETERAN* 1120/19 (D.72) (Cdr W.T. Couchman OBE) transferred to HM corvette *KINGCUP* 925/40 (K.33) (Lt R.A.D. Cambridge) and landed at Londonderry.

**CASTLE HARBOUR** ex-*MID OCEAN* • GRT 730 • Built 1929
16.10.42: Torpedoed and sunk by German submarine U-160 (Lassen), in the Atlantic 50 miles ENE of Trinidad, in position 11.00N 61.10W while on a voyage from Trinidad 16.10.42 to Pernambuco, Brazil, in ballast, part of convoy T 19 comprising 16 ships. The Master, Capt Francis Theaker, and 13 crew were rescued by USN submarine chaser No. 53 landed at Trinidad. 9 crew were lost. The *CASTLE HARBOUR* sank in 20 seconds.

## BIBBY LINE – LIVERPOOL

**YORKSHIRE** • GRT 10183 • Built 1920
17.10.39: Torpedoed and sunk by German submarines U-37 (Hartmann) and U-46 (Sohler), in the Atlantic 160 miles WNW of Cape Finisterre, in position 44.52N 14.31W while on a

voyage from Rangoon, Burma, to Liverpool, with 151 passengers and general cargo, part of the unescorted convoy HG 3 comprising 25 ships. The Master, Capt Victor Charles Patrick Smalley, 24 crew and 33 passengers were lost. 160 crew and 118 passengers were rescued by US ship *INDEPENDENCE HALL* 5050/20 and landed at Bordeaux, France.

**SHROPSHIRE** • GRT 10550 • Built 1926
13.5.41: Torpedoed and sunk by German submarine U-98 (Gysae), part of the 'West' patrol group of eight U-boats, in the Atlantic 400 miles SE of Cape Farewell, in position 56.43N 38.57W while escorting convoy SC.30 comprising 28 ships. 278 officers and ratings were rescued by HM ship. She was lost while on government service employed as an Armed Merchant Cruiser HMS *SALOPIAN* (F.94) (Capt Sir John N. Allegre Bt DSO DSC).

## MOWT

**PRESIDENT DOUMER** • GRT 11898 • Built 1934
30.10.42: Torpedoed and sunk by German submarine U-604 (Höltring), part of the 'Streitax' (Battleaxe) patrol group of eight U-boats, in the Atlantic NE of Madeira, in position 35.08N 16.44W while on government service on a voyage from Freetown 16.10.40 to the UK, with troops and general cargo, part of convoy SL 125 comprising 40 ships. The Master, Capt Jean Paul Mantelet, 173 crew, 23 gunners and 63 troops were lost. 78 crew and 7 gunners were rescued by Norwegian ship *ALASKA* 5681/18, transferred to HM corvette *COWSLIP* 925/41 (K.196) (Sub-Lt K.J. Pearson) and landed at Gibraltar.

## BILLMEIR J.A. & CO. LTD – LONDON
### Stanhope Steamship Co. Ltd

**STANBROOK** ex-*POLYFLOISVIOS* ex-*STANBROOK* ex-*LANCER* • GRT 1383 • Built 1909
19.11.39: Torpedoed and sunk by German submarine U-57 (Korth), in the North Sea WNW of the North Hinder Lightship while sailing independently on a voyage from Antwerp to Blyth, in ballast. The Master, Capt Alexander Dickson, and crew of 19 were lost.

**STANHOLME** ex-*GOLETA* • GRT 2473 • Built 1927
25.12.39: Struck a mine, laid on 5.12.39 by German submarine U-28 (Kuhnke) and sank in the Bristol Channel off Foreland Point, in position 51.20N 03.39W while sailing independently on a voyage from Cardiff to London, with a cargo of 4500 tons of coal. The Master, Capt David Llewellyn Hook, and 11 crew were rescued by Norwegian ship *LIV* 3068/96 and landed at Cardiff. 12 crew were lost.

**STANCLIFFE** ex-*HUNCLIFFE* ex-*DORNOCH* • GRT 4511 • Built 1936
12.4.40: Torpedoed and sunk by German submarine U-37 (Hartmann), in the North Sea 45 miles NE of Muckle Flugga, Shetlands, while sailing independently on a voyage from Narvik to Immingham, with a cargo of 7200 tons of iron ore. The Master, Capt Henry Herbert Sudbury, and 20 crew were lost. 16 crew landed at Haroldswick, Unst Island, Shetland.

**STANHALL** ex-*KEPWICKHALL* • GRT 4831 • Built 1932
30.5.40: Torpedoed and sunk by German submarine U-101 (Frauenheim), in the Atlantic 35 miles NNW of Ushant, in position 48.59N 10.17W while sailing independently on a voyage

from Townsville, Queensland, to Liverpool, with a cargo of 7630 tons of raw sugar and 350 tons of onions. The Master, Capt William Ewart Herbert, and 35 crew were rescued by British ship *TEMPLE MOAT* 4427/28 and landed at Weymouth. 1 crew was lost.

**STANCOR** ex-*ALBURN* ex-*ALGARDI* ex-*CHERRYBROOK* • GRT 790 • Built 1904
5.6.40: Sunk by gunfire by German submarine U-48 (Rösing), in the Atlantic 80 miles NW of Butt of Lewis, in position 58.48N 08.45W while sailing independently on a voyage from Reykjavik to Fleetwood, with a cargo of 300 tons of fish. The Master, Capt William Bibbings, 16 crew and 2 gunners survived: the Master and 8 survivors were rescued by British trawler *KINALDIE* 197/14 landed at Stornoway 7.6.40 and 10 survivors landed at Crowlista near Uig, Isle of Lewis.

**STANGRANT** ex-*CLAN GRANT* ex-*CAMBRIAN MARCHIONESS* ex-*PORT MACQUARIE*
GRT 5817 • Built 1912
13.10.40: Torpedoed and sunk by German submarine U-37 (Oehrn), in the Atlantic NE of Rockall, in position 58.27N 12.36W while on a voyage from Hampton Roads, Virginia, to Belfast via Halifax NS, with a cargo of 7715 tons of steel, a straggler from convoy HX 77 comprising 40 ships. The Master, Capt Evan David Rowlands, 28 crew and 1 gunner were rescued by a Short Sunderland flying boat of No. 10 Squadron RAAF and landed at Oban. 8 crew were lost. Korvettenkapitän Viktor Oehrn was awarded the Knight's Cross (21.10.40).

**WELCOMBE** • GRT 5122 • Built 1930
4.4.41: Torpedoed and sunk by German submarine U-98 (Gysae), in the Atlantic S of Iceland, in position 59.09N 22.00W while on a voyage from Baltimore, Maryland, to Loch Ewe via Halifax NS, with a cargo of 7900 tons of grain, part of convoy SC 26 comprising 24 ships. The Master, Capt Richard Edgar Johnson, and 19 crew were lost. 19 crew and 2 gunners were rescued by HM destroyer *HAVELOCK* 1340/39 (H.88) (Cdr C.H. Thomas DSC) ex-Brazilian *JUTANY* and landed at Liverpool.

**STANGARTH** • GRT 5966 • Built 1942
12.3.42: Torpedoed and sunk by German submarine U-504 (Poske), in the Atlantic NE of San Juan. Puerto Rico, in position 22.00N 65.00W, while sailing independently on her maiden voyage from New York to Cape Town and India, with general cargo. The Master, Capt William Ewart Herbert, crew of 39 and 6 gunners were lost.

**STANBANK** • GRT 5966 • Built 1942
5.5.42: Torpedoed and sunk by German submarine U-103 (Winter), in the Atlantic NE of Bermuda, in position 34.55N 76.47W while sailing independently on a voyage from New York to Cape Town and Alexandria, with a cargo of 6488 tons of military stores. The Master, Capt George Albert Niddrie, 34 crew and 4 gunners were rescued after 10 days in open boats by British ship *RHEXENOR* 7957/22 landed at Bermuda. 7 crew and 2 gunners were lost. Korvettenkapitän Werner Winter was awarded the Knight's Cross (5.6.42).

**STANMORE** • GRT 4970 • Built 1940
2.10.43: Torpedoed and damaged by German submarine U-223 (Wächter), in the Mediterranean near Cape Ivi, Algeria, in position 36.41N 01.10E while on government service on a voyage from Middlesbrough to Sicily, with a cargo of 2500 tons of government stores including explosives, part of convoy KMS 27 comprising 8 ships. Taken in tow by HM

trawler *FILLA* 545/42 (T.212) (Lt J.B. Hornby), later towed by HM rescue tug *CHARON* 700/41 (W.109) and HM tug *SALVONIA* 571/39 (W.43) (Lt G.M.H. Robinson) and beached at Cape Tenes, Algeria 3.10.43; it later broke in two. The Master, Capt Howard Cecil Lewis Phillips, crew of 41 and 17 gunners were rescued by HM trawler *FILLA* 545/42 (T.212) and landed at Algiers. U-223 commanded by Oberleutnant zur See Peter Gerlach was sunk on 30.3.44 in the Mediterranean 60 miles NE of Palermo, Sicily, in position 38.48N 14.10E by HM destroyer leader *LAFOREY* 1935/41 (F.99) (Capt H.T. Armstrong), HM destroyers *TUMULT* 1710/42 (R.11) (Lt-Cdr L. Lanyon), *HAMBLEDON* 907/39 (L.37) (Lt J.G. Toone) and *BLENCATHRA* 1050/40 (L.24) (Lt E.G. Warren). The U-boat commander and 22 crew were lost. 27 crew were taken prisoner by HMS *BLENCATHRA*, *HAMBLETON* and *TUMULT*. U-223 torpedoed and sank HM destroyer leader *LAFOREY* 1935/41 (F.99) prior to being sunk. 69 officers and ratings survived and 152 officers and ratings were lost. HMS *LAFOREY* was the last Royal Naval ship to be sunk in the Mediterranean by a U-boat.

## MOWT

**EMPIRE LAKE** • GRT 2852 • Built 1941
15.7.43: Torpedoed and sunk by German submarine U-181 (Lüth), in the Indian Ocean about 240 miles E of Madagascar, in position 20.56S 51.47E while sailing independently on a voyage from Durban to Aden, with a cargo of coal. The Master, Capt Richard John Sproul, 24 crew and 6 gunners were lost. 5 crew and 2 gunners landed at Farafangana, Madagascar.

## BLANE & EVANS – CARDIFF
**Blane Steamship Co. Ltd**

**ULVA** ex-*POZNAN* ex-*CARRONPARK* • GRT 1401 • Built 1912
3.9.40: Torpedoed and sunk by German submarine U-60 (Schnee), in the Atlantic 180 miles WNW of Inishtrahull, in position 55.45N 11.45W while sailing independently on a voyage from Newport, Mon. to Gibraltar, with a cargo of coal. The Master, Capt Henry Barnfather, and 16 crew landed at Castlebay, Isle of Barra, Hebrides. 3 crew were lost. U-60 commanded by Käpitanleutnant Herbert Giesewetter was scuttled at Wilhelmshaven on 1.5.45.

## BLUE STAR LINE – LONDON

**SULTAN STAR** • GRT 12306 • Built 1929
14.2.40: Torpedoed and sunk by German submarine U-48 (Schultze), in the Atlantic SW of the Scilly Isles, in position 48.54N 10.03W while sailing independently on a voyage from Buenos Aires to Liverpool, with a cargo of 7803 tons of refrigerated meat and general cargo. The Master, Capt William Henry Bevan, and crew of 72 were rescued by HM destroyers *WHITSHED* 1120/19 (D.77) (Cdr E.R. Condor) and *VESPER* 1090/17 (D.55) (Lt-Cdr W.F.E Hussey DSC) and landed at Plymouth.

**WELLINGTON STAR** • GRT 12382 • Built 1939
16.6.40: Torpedoed and sunk by gunfire by German submarine U-101 (Frauenheim), in the Atlantic about 300 miles W of Cape Finisterre, in position 42.39N 17.01W while sailing independently on a voyage from Sydney NSW and Melbourne to Falmouth via Panama, with

refrigerated and general cargo. The Master, Capt Trevor Williams, and 17 crew landed at Figueira near Oporto and 52 crew were rescued by French ship *PIERRE L D* 5795/35 and landed at Casablanca, Morocco.

### AVELONA STAR ex-*AVELONA* • GRT 12858 • Built 1926

30.6.40: Torpedoed and damaged by German submarine U-43 (Ambrosius), in the Atlantic 220 miles NW of Cape Finisterre, in position 46.46N 12.17W and later sank on 1.7.40 in position 46.59N 11.39W while on a voyage from Buenos Aires to London via Freetown 15.6.40, with 5630 tons of frozen meat and 1000 tons of oranges, part of convoy SL 36 comprising 41 ships. The Master, Capt George Ernest Hopper, and crew of 83 were rescued by British ship *BEIGNON* 5218/39. The *BEIGNON* was later sunk on 1.7.40 by German submarine U-30 (Lemp); 80 crew from *AVELONA STAR* and 30 from *BEIGNON* were rescued by escorting destroyers HMS *VESPER* 1090/17 (D.55) (Lt-Cdr W.E.F. Hussey DSC) and *WINDSOR* 1140/18 (D.42) (Lt-Cdr P.P.H.R. Pelly) and landed at Plymouth. 4 crew from *AVELONA STAR* were lost.

### ARANDORA STAR ex-*ARANDORA* • GRT 14694 • Built 1927

2.7.40: Torpedoed and damaged by German submarine U-47 (Prien), in the Atlantic about 125 miles E by N of Malin Head, Co. Donegal, in position 55.20N 10.33W and later sank in position 56.30N 10.38W while sailing independently on government service on a voyage from Liverpool to St John's, Newfoundland, with 479 German internees, 734 Italian internees, 86 German prisoners-of-war and 200 military guards. The Master, Capt Edgar Wallace Moulton, 55 crew, 91 military guards, 713 German and Italian internees and prisoners were lost. 118 crew, 109 military guards and 586 internees and prisoners were rescued by HMCS destroyer *ST LAURENT* 1375/31 (H.83) ex-HMS *CYGNET* (Lt-Cdr A.H. Hope) and landed at Greenock. Capt E.W. Moulton was awarded the Lloyd's War Medal for bravery at sea.

### AUCKLAND STAR • GRT 12382 • Built 1939

28.7.40: Torpedoed and sunk by German submarine U-99 (Kretschmer), in the Atlantic 80 miles WNW of Valentia Island, Co. Kerry, in position 52.17N 12.32W while sailing independently on a voyage from Townsville 25.5.40 to Liverpool via Panama, with 10700 tons of general cargo including hides, lead, steel, refrigerated and wheat. The Master, Capt David Rattray MacFarlane, and 54 crew landed at Dingle, Co. Kerry, and 19 crew landed at Slyne Head near Clifden, Co. Galway.

### NAPIER STAR ex-*RALEIGHSTAR* ex-*NAPIER STAR* • GRT 10116 • Built 1927

18.12.40: Torpedoed and sunk by German submarine U-100 (Schepke), in the Atlantic 321 miles 285° from Rockall, in position 58.58N 23.13W while on government service sailing independently on a voyage from Liverpool to New Zealand via Panama, with 16 passengers and 8200 tons general cargo. The Master, Capt William Walsh, 67 crew and 11 passengers were lost. 14 crew, 1 gunner and 5 passengers were rescued by Swedish motor ship *VAALAREN* 3406/36 and landed at Liverpool 23.12.40. U-100, commanded by Korvettenkapitän Joachim Schepke (Knight's Cross 24.9.40, with Oak Leaves 20.12.40), was sunk while attacking convoy HX 112 comprising 41 ships on 17.3.41 in the North Atlantic 240 miles NW of the Butt of Lewis, in position 61.00N 12.00W by HM destroyers *WALKER*

1300/17 (G.22) (Cdr Donald G.F.W. MacIntyre) and *VANOC* 1300/17 (F.27) (Lt-Cdr J.G.W. Deneys), part of the 5th Escort Group. The U-boat commander and 37 crew were lost. 6 crew were taken prisoner by HMS *VANOC* and landed at Liverpool.

**ALMEDA STAR** ex-*ALMEDA* • GRT 14935 • Built 1926
17.1.41: Torpedoed by German submarine U-96 (Lehmann-Willenbrock), in the Atlantic about 35 miles NE of Rockall, in position 58.16N 13.40W and sank in position 58.40N 13.38W while sailing independently on a voyage from Liverpool to Buenos Aires, with 194 passengers and general cargo. The Master, Capt Harry Cecil Howard, Commodore of the Blue Star Line, crew of 136, 29 gunners and passengers were lost.

**RODNEY STAR** ex-*RODNEYSTAR* • GRT 10583 • Built 1926
16.5.41: Torpedoed and sunk by gunfire by German submarine U-105 (Schewe), in the Atlantic 420 miles WSW of Freetown, in position 05.08N 19.15W while sailing independently on a voyage from Fray Bentos, Uruguay to Glasgow via Santos and Freetown, with 7000 tons of general and refrigerated cargo. The Master, Capt Samuel John Clement Phillips, and 19 crew were rescued after six days by HM destroyer *BOREAS* 1360/30 (H.77) (Lt-Cdr D.H. Maitland-Makgill Crichton) and 47 crew by British ship *BATNA* 4399/28 and landed at Takoradi, Gold Coast 23.5.41.

**TACOMA STAR** ex-*WANGARATTA* laid down as *WAR THESEUS* • GRT 7924 • Built 1919
1.2.42: Torpedoed and sunk by German submarine U-109 (Bleichrodt), part of 'Operation Paukenschlag' (Drumbeat), the first wave of five U-boats, in the Atlantic 500 miles E of Hampton Roads, Virginia, in position 37.33N 69.21W while sailing independently on a voyage from Buenos Aires and Hampton Roads, Virginia to Liverpool, with 5107 tons of refrigerated and general cargo. The Master, Capt Robert George Whitehead, and crew of 86 were lost.

**SCOTTISH STAR** ex-*MILLAIS* • GRT 7224 • Built 1916
20.2.42: Torpedoed and sunk by Italian submarine *LUIGI TORELLI* (de Giacomo), part of the 'Da Vinci' patrol group of five Italian submarines, in the Atlantic E of Barbados, in position 13.24N 49.36W while sailing independently on a voyage from London to Buenos Aires, with 2000 tons general cargo including whisky, dispersed from convoy ONS 63 comprising 31 ships. The Master, Capt Edgar Newton Rhodes, and 51 crew were rescued by HM light cruiser *DIOMEDE* 4765/19 (I.92) (Capt D. Orr Ewing) and landed at Port of Spain, Trinidad, and the Chief Officer and 16 crew landed at Barbados 27.2.42. 4 crew were lost. The *LUIGI TORELLI* was taken by the Germans at Singapore when Italy surrendered and renamed UIT-25 (Meier) later transferred to Japan and renamed I-504 at Kawasaki 14.8.45, VJ Day.

**AVILA STAR** ex-*AVILA* • GRT 14443 • Built 1926
6.7.42: Torpedoed and sunk by German submarine U-201 (Schnee), in the Atlantic NE of the Azores, in position 38.04N 22.48W while sailing independently on a voyage from Buenos Aires to Liverpool via Freetown 28.6.42, with 30 passengers and a cargo of 5659 tons of frozen meat. The Master, Capt John Fisher, 66 crew and 17 passengers were lost. 93 crew, 6 gunners and 13 passengers were rescued by Portuguese destroyer *LIMA* 1238/33 (D.333) and Portuguese sloop *PEDRO NUNES* 1090/35 (A.528) and landed at Ponta Delgada, Azores.

**VIKING STAR** ex-*VIKINGSTAR* ex-*LUSIADA* • GRT 6445 • Built 1919
25.8.42: Torpedoed and sunk by German submarine U-130 (Kals), in the Atlantic 160 miles SSW of Freetown, in position 06.00N 14.00W while sailing independently on a voyage from Buenos Aires and Montevideo 9.8.42 to the UK via Freetown, with 4519 tons of refrigerated cargo and 200 tons of fertilisers. The Master, Capt James Edward Mills, and 6 crew were lost. 31 crew and 5 gunners landed after 6 days near Bonthe, Sierra Leone, and 18 crew on a raft landed after 18 days on the coast of Sierra Leone.

**TUSCAN STAR** • GRT 11449 • Built 1929
6.9.42: Torpedoed and sunk by German submarine U-109 (Bleichrodt), in the Atlantic SW of Cape Palmas, in position 01.34N 11.39W while sailing independently on a voyage from Buenos Aires and Santos to Liverpool via Freetown 27.8.42, with 25 passengers and 7840 tons of meat and 5000 tons general cargo. The Master, Capt Edgar Newton Rhodes, 35 crew, 4 gunners and 22 passengers were rescued by Orient liner *OTRANTO* 20026/25 and landed at Freetown 10.9.42. 40 crew, 8 gunners and 3 passengers were lost. The 2nd Wireless Operator was taken prisoner, landed at Lorient 6.10.42 and taken to Milag Nord.

**ANDALUCIA STAR** ex-*ANDALUCIA* • GRT 14943 • Built 1926
7.10.42: Torpedoed and sunk by German submarine U-107 (Gelhaus), in the Atlantic 180 miles SW of Freetown, in position 06.38N 15.46W while sailing independently on a voyage from Buenos Aires 25.9.42 to Liverpool via Freetown, with 80 passengers and 5 Distressed British Seamen (DBS), a cargo of 5374 tons of frozen meat and 32 tons of eggs. The Master, Capt James Bennett Hall, 157 crew, 9 gunners, 79 passengers and DBS were rescued by HM corvette *PETUNIA* 925/40 (K.79) (Lt-Cdr J.M. Rayner) and landed at Freetown 9.10.42. 3 crew and 1 passenger were lost.

**EMPIRE STAR** • GRT 11093 • Built 1935
23.10.42: Torpedoed and sunk by German submarine U-615 (Kapitzky), part of the 'Wotan' (God of the Vikings) patrol group of ten U-boats, in the Atlantic N of the Azores, in position 48.14N 26.22W while sailing independently on a voyage from Liverpool 20.10.42 to East London, with 19 passengers and 1055 tons general and government stores. The Master, Capt Selwyn Norman Capon CBE, 29 crew, 6 gunners and 6 passengers were lost. 45 crew, 3 gunners and 13 passengers were rescued by HM sloop *BLACK SWAN* 1250/39 (L.57) (Cdr T.A.C. Pakenham) and landed at Liverpool. U-615, commanded by Kapitänleutnant Ralph Kapitzky, was damaged on 7.8.43 by a Martin PBM Mariner flying boat, pilot Lt John M. Erskine of US Navy Composite Squadron VP-204, a Mariner, pilot Lt Anthony R. Matuski of US Navy Composite Squadron VP-205, a Lockheed B34/PV Harpoon bomber, pilot Lt Theodore M. Holmes of US Navy Antisubmarine Squadron VB-130 and a Douglas B-18 bomber from US Army Bombing Squadron No. 10 based at Chaguaramas naval base, Trinidad. U-615 scuttled herself on the approach of US destroyer *WALKER* 1620/43 (DD-517) (Lt-Cdr Townsend) in the Caribbean Sea 175 miles W by N of Grenada, in position 12.38N 64.15W. The U-boat commander and 3 crew were lost. 43 crew were taken prisoner by USS *WALKER* and landed at Port of Spain, Trinidad.

**PACIFIC STAR** ex-*STANFLEET* ex-*CLAN ROBERTSON* ex-*OTAKI* laid down as *WAR JUPITER* • GRT 7951 • Built 1919
27.10.42: Torpedoed and damaged by German submarine U-509 (Witte), part of the 'Streitaxt' (Battleaxe) patrol group of eight U-boats, in the Atlantic NW of the Canary

Islands, in position 29.15N 20.57W. On 28.10.42 she was abandoned by her crew in position 21.29N 19.28W and later sank while on a voyage from Rosario to Liverpool via Freetown 16.10.42, with 5037 tons of frozen meat and general cargo, part of convoy SL 125 comprising 40 ships. The Master, Capt Griffith Lawrence Evans, 59 crew and 11 gunners landed at Santa Cruz de la Palma, Canary Islands, and were brought to Gibraltar by Spanish tanker *CAMPILO* 3971/41; 25 crew landed at Tenerife and were brought to Santa Cruz de la Palma by Spanish ship *CIUDAD DE VALENCIA* 2497/31. The Master was awarded the OBE.

**CALIFORNIA STAR** • GRT 8300 • Built 1938
4.3.43: Torpedoed and sunk by German submarine U-515 (Henke), part of the 'Unverzagt' (Intrepid) patrol group of six U-boats, in the Atlantic NW of the Azores, in position 42.32N 37.20W while sailing independently on a voyage from Wellington and Cristobal, Panama, to Liverpool, with 7 passengers and 6434 tons of general and refrigerated cargo. The Master, Capt Sydney Foulkes, 18 crew and 3 passengers landed at Flores, Azores. 40 crew, 8 gunners and 4 passengers were lost.

**CANADIAN STAR** • GRT 8293 • Built 1938
18.3.43: Torpedoed and sunk by German submarine U-221 (Trojer), part of the 'Dränger' (Harrier) patrol group of ten U-boats, in the Atlantic SE of Cape Farewell, in position 53.24N 28.34W while on a voyage from Sydney NSW to Liverpool via New York 8.3.43, with 24 passengers and 7806 tons of refrigerated cargo, part of convoy HX 229 comprising 40 ships. The Master, Capt Robert David Miller, 22 crew, 2 gunners and 9 passengers were lost. 33 crew, 6 gunners and 15 passengers were rescued by HM corvettes *ANEMONE* 925/40 (K.48) (Lt-Cdr P.G.A. King) and *PENNYWORT* 925/41 (K.11) (Lt O.G. Stuart) and landed at Gourock. Capt R.D. Miller was posthumously awarded the Lloyd's War Medal for bravery at sea. Kapitänleutnant Hans Trojer (Knight's Cross 24.3.43) and crew of 49 were lost on 27.9.43 in the Atlantic 425 miles NW by N of Cape Villano, Spain, in position 47.00N 18.00W when U-221 was sunk by Handley Page Halifax bomber 'B' HR982, pilot F/O Eric L. Hartley of No. 58 Squadron RAF, based at Holmsley South, Hampshire, part of 19 Group. The aircraft was hit by gunfire from U-221 and ditched in the sea; the six aircrew were adrift for 11 days before being rescued in position 45.20N 15.53W by HM destroyer *MAHRATTA* 1920/42 (G.23) ex-HMS *MARKSMAN* (Lt-Cdr E.A.F. Drought). 2 aircrew were lost. The pilot was awarded the DFC.

**CELTIC STAR** ex-*CELTICSTAR* ex-*CAMANA* • GRT 5574 • Built 1917
30.3.43: Torpedoed and sunk by Italian submarine *GIUSEPPE FINZI* (Rossetto), in the Atlantic SW of Freetown, in position 04.16N 17.44W while sailing independently on a voyage from Manchester and Greenock to Montevideo and Buenos Aires via Freetown, with 2 passengers and 4410 general cargo and mails. The Master, Capt James Hunter Andrew Mackie, 52 crew, 9 gunners and 2 passengers were rescued by HM whaler *WASTWATER* 560/39 (FY.239) ex-HMS *GRASMERE* (Lt W.L.J. Storey) and landed at Freetown 2.4.43. 2 crew were lost and 1 crew was taken prisoner. *GIUSEPPE FINZI* was taken by the Germans when Italy surrendered on 9.9.43, renamed UIT-21 (Steinfeldt) and scuttled at Bordeaux, France, on 25.8.44.

**MELBOURNE STAR** • GRT 12806 • Built 1936
2.4.43: Torpedoed and sunk by German submarine U-129 (Witt), in the Atlantic some 500 miles ESE of Bermuda, in position 28.05N 57.30W while sailing independently on a voyage

from Liverpool 22.3.43 and Greenock 24.3.43 to Cristobal, Melbourne and Sydney NSW, with 31 passengers and 8285 tons of government stores and general cargo, including ammunition and torpedoes. The Master, Capt James Bennett Hall, 82 crew, 11 gunners and passengers were lost. 4 crew drifted in an open boat for 39 days and were rescued by a US Navy Consolidated PBY Catalina flying boat and landed at Bermuda. The ship blew up 90 seconds after being torpedoed. The four survivors were later each awarded the British Empire Medal (BEM) for their courage and fortitude. Kapitänleutnant Hans Witte was awarded the Knight's Cross (17.12.42).

## MOWT

**EMPIRE LAKELAND** • GRT 7015 • Built 1942
8.3.43: Torpedoed and sunk by German submarine U-190 (Wintermeyer), part of the 'Ostmark' (East German mark) patrol group of eleven U-boats, in the Atlantic NW of Rockall, in position 58.00N 15.00W while on a voyage from New York 23.2.43 to Glasgow, with 7805 tons of refrigerated and general cargo, a straggler from convoy SC 121 comprising 57 ships. The Master, Capt Frederick John Gudgin, crew of 55 and 8 gunners were lost. U-190 commanded by Oberleutnant zur See Hans–Edwin Reith surrendered off Bay Bulls, Newfoundland, to HMCS corvette *THORLOCK* 925/44 (K.394) (Lt J.F. Francois) and HMCS frigate *VICTORIAVILLE* 1370/44 (K.684) (Lt-Cdr L.A. Hickey MBE) on 16.5.45 on the cessation of hostilities. On Trafalgar Day 21.10.47 U-190 was towed out and sunk by HMCS destroyer *NOOTKA* 1927/44 (R.96) (Cdr H.S. Rayner DSC) and HMCS minesweeper *NEW LISKEARD* 850/44 (J.397) (Lt-Cdr B.P. Young MBE) and aircraft from Nos 826 and 883 Squadrons RCAF, in 'Operation Scuttled' off Halifax, Nova Scotia, in position approximately 44.28N 63.10W where U-190 sank HMCS minesweeping sloop *ESQUIMALT* 590/41 (Lt R.C. Macmillan DSC and bar) on 16.4.45 with the loss of 44 crew.

**EMPIRE JAVELIN** laid down as *CAPE LOBOS* • GRT 7177 • Built 1944
28.12.44: Torpedoed and sunk by German submarine U-772 (Rademacher), in the English Channel 40 miles S of St Catherine's Point, Isle of Wight, in position 50.04N 01.00W while on passage from Southampton to Le Havre, with 1448 US troops, part of the coastal convoy TBC 21. The Master, Capt John McLean, 121 crew, 28 gunners and US troops were rescued by Free French frigate *L'ESCARMOUCHE* 1370/43 (K.267) ex-HMS *FROME* and landed at Le Havre. 7 crew were lost. *EMPIRE JAVELIN* was employed by the Admiralty as a Landing Ship Infantry. Kapitänleutnant Ewald Rademacher and crew of 47 were lost when U-772 was sunk on 30.12.44 in the English Channel 30 miles S of Portland Bill, in position 50.05N 02.31W by Leigh Light-equipped Vickers Wellington bomber XIV 'L' NB855, pilot S/Ldr C.J.W. Taylor DFC of No. 407 Squadron RCAF, based at Chivenor, Devon, part of 19 Group.

## BOLTON, F. & CO. LTD – LONDON
### Bolton Steamship Co. Ltd

**RAMSAY** • GRT 4855 • Built 1930
10.6.42: Torpedoed and sunk by German submarine U-94 (Ites), part of the 'Hecht' (Pike) patrol group of six U-boats, in the Atlantic SE of Cape Farewell, in position 51.53N 34.59W while on a voyage from the Tyne to New York, in ballast, part of convoy ONS 100 comprising 38 ships. The Master, Capt Brinley Frederick Roberts Thomas, 6 crew and 1 gunner were

rescued by HM corvette *VERVAIN* 925/41 (K.190) ex-HMS *BROOM* (Lt H.P. Crail) and landed at St John's, Newfoundland. 35 crew and 5 gunners were lost. The 'Hecht' patrol group was the first to attempt to carry out a planned 'wolf pack' (Die Rudeltactic) operation in the Atlantic. Oberleutnant zur See Otto Ites was awarded the Knight's Cross (28.3.42).

**REYNOLDS** • GRT 5113 • Built 1927
31.10.42: Torpedoed and sunk by German submarine U-504 (Poske), part of the 'Eisbär' (Polarbear) patrol group of five U-boats, in the Indian Ocean 210 miles E of Durban, in position 30.02S 35.02E while sailing independently on a voyage from New York to Karachi via Durban, with a cargo of military stores. The Master, Capt Roderick David McLeod, crew of 39 and 7 gunners were lost. Korvettenkäpitan Fritz Poske was awarded the Knight's Cross (6.11.42). Kapitänleutnant Wilhelm Luis and crew of 52 were lost on 30.7.43 when U-504 was sunk in the Atlantic 165 miles NW of Cape Ortegal, in position 45.33N 10.47W by HM sloops *KITE* 1350/42 (U.87) (Cdr Frederic John Walker CB DSO DSC), *WOODPECKER* 1300/42 (U.08) (Lt-Cdr R.E.S Hugonin), *WREN* 1300/42 (U.28) (Lt-Cdr R.N. Aubrey) and *WILD GOOSE* 1300/42 (U.45) (Lt-Cdr D.E.G. Wemyss), part of the 2nd Support Group.

**BOOKER BROS, McCONNELL & CO. LTD – LIVERPOOL**
**Arakaka SS Co. Ltd**

**ARAKAKA** • GRT 2379 • Built 1933
22.6.41: Torpedoed and sunk by German submarine U-77 (Schonder), part of the 'West' patrol group of fifteen U-boats, in the Atlantic E of St John's, Newfoundland, in position 47.00N 40.00W while employed on government service as a weather ship. The Master, Capt William Walker, crew of 32 and 12 Admiralty personnel were lost.

**AMAKURA** • GRT 1987 • Built 1924
25.8.42: Torpedoed and sunk by German submarine U-558 (Krech), in the Atlantic E of Port Morant, Jamaica, in position 17.46N 75.52W while on a voyage from Liverpool to Demerara, British Guiana via Key West 18.8.42 and Trinidad, with 2260 tons general cargo, a straggler from convoy TAW 15 comprising 29 ships. The Master, Capt Thomas Orford, 25 crew and 5 gunners landed at Point Morant Lighthouse, Jamaica. 13 crew were lost.

**BOOTH LINE – LIVERPOOL**

**CRISPIN** • GRT 5051 • Built 1934
3.2.41: Torpedoed and damaged by German submarine U-107 (Hessler), in the Atlantic NNW of Rockall, in position 56.38N 20.05W; she sank the following day in position 56.52N 20.22W, dispersed from convoy OB 280 comprising 27 ships. *CRISPIN* was lost while employed on Admiralty service as an Ocean Boarding Ship. Cdr B. Moloney DSO DSC RNR, 120 officers and ratings were rescued by HM destroyer *HARVESTER* 1340/39 (H.19) ex-HMS *HANDY* ex-Brazilian *JURUA* (Lt C.M. Thornton DSC) and landed at Liverpool.

**ANSELM** • GRT 5954 • Built 1935
5.7.41: Torpedoed and sunk by German submarine U-96 (Lehmann-Willenbrock), in the Atlantic 300 miles N of the Azores, in position 44.25N 28.35W while sailing

independently on government service on a voyage from Gourock to Freetown, with about 1210 RAF and military personnel. The Master, Capt Andrew Elliott, 93 crew, 3 gunners and about 970 RAF and military personnel were rescued by HM survey vessel *CHALLENGER* 1140/31 (J.98) (Cdr W.C. Jenk OBE) and 240 survivors by HM corvette *STARWORT* 925/41 (K.20) (Lt-Cdr N.W. Duck), transferred to HM armed merchant cruiser *CATHAY* 15104/39 (F.05) (Capt C.McC. Merewether) and landed at Freetown. 4 crew and 250 service personnel were lost.

## Ministry of Shipping

*POLYCARP* • GRT 3577 • Built 1918
2.6.40: Torpedoed and sunk by German submarine U-101 (Frauenheim), in the Atlantic 41 miles S of Land's End, in position 49.19N 05.35W while sailing independently on a voyage from Para, Brazil to Heysham and Liverpool, with 1530 tons general cargo including cork, rubber and hides. The Master, Capt Alexander Allan, and crew of 42 were rescued by French ship *ESPIGUETTE* 1109/20 and landed at Newlyn.

## MOWT

*EMPIRE ENDURANCE* ex-*ALSTER* • GRT 8570 • Built 1928
20.4.41: Torpedoed and sunk by German submarine U-73 (Rosenbaum), in the Atlantic SW of Rockall, in position 53.05N 23.14W while sailing independently on government service on a voyage from Swansea to Alexandria via Cape Town, with 5 passengers, general cargo, military stores and two motor launches ML1003 40/41 and ML1037 40/41. The Master, Capt William Willis R.D. Torkington, 63 crew and 1 passenger were lost. 5 crew were rescued after 20 days by Royal Mail liner *HIGHLAND BRIGADE* 14131/29 and landed at Liverpool, and 20 crew and 4 passengers were rescued on 21.4.41 in position 52.50N 22.50W by HMCS corvette *TRILLIUM* 925/40 (K.172) (Lt P.C. Evan) and landed at Greenock 25.4.41. U-73 sank HM aircraft carrier *EAGLE* 22790/18 (94) (Capt E.G.N. Rushrooke DSC) on 11.8.42 in the Mediterranean 65 miles S of Majorca in position 38.05N 03.02E. 690 officers and ratings were rescued by HM destroyer leader *LAFOREY* 1935/41 (F.99) (Capt R.M.J. Hutton), HM destroyers *LOOKOUT* 1920/40 (F.32) (Cdr C.P.F. Brown DSC), and *MALCOLM* 1530/19 (D.19) (Cdr A.B. Russell) and Admiralty tug *JAUNTY* 700/41 (W.30). 260 crew were lost. Kapitänleutnant Helmut Rosenbaum was awarded the Knight's Cross (12.8.42). The German *ALSTER* was captured off Vestfjord, Norway, on 10.4.40 by HM destroyer *ICARUS* 1370/36 (D.03) (Lt-Cdr W.N. Petch) and escorted by HM submarine *ULLSWATER* 545/40 (P.31) (Sub-Lt D.R. Stavert).

*FORT LA MAUNE* • GRT 7130 • Built 1942
25.1.44: Torpedoed and sunk by German submarine U-188 (Lüdden), part of the 'Monsun' (Monsoon) patrol group of nine U-boats, in the Arabian Sea ENE of Socotra Island, in position 13.04N 56.30E while sailing independently on a voyage from New York, Suez and Aden to Cochin, Vizagapatam and Calcutta, with 8130 tons general cargo and military stores. The Master, Capt James William Binns OBE, crew of 48 and 7 gunners landed on the Arabian coast and were brought by HM corvette *NIGELLA* 925/40 (K.19) (Lt C.L.L. Davies) to Aden 6.2.44.

## BOWATER'S NEWFOUNDLAND PULP & PAPER MILLS LTD – ST JOHN'S, NEWFOUNDLAND

*HUMBER ARM* • GRT 5758 • Built 1925
8.7.40: Torpedoed and sunk by German submarine U-99 (Kretschmer), in the Atlantic 60 miles S of Fastnet, in position 50.36N 09.24W while on a voyage from Corner Brook, Newfoundland to Ellesmere Port via Halifax NS 25.6.40, with 1 passenger and a cargo of 1000 tons of steel, 5450 tons of newsprint, 300 tons of lumber and 450 tons of pulp, part of convoy HX 53 comprising 44 ships. The Master, Capt Jack Rowland Morbey, crew of 41 and passenger were rescued by HM destroyers *SCIMITAR* 905/18 (H.21) (Lt R.D. Franks OBE) and *VANQUISHER* 1090/17 (D.54) (Lt F.D. Cole) and landed at Milford Haven.

*KITTY'S BROOK* ex-*SIRIO* ex-*SANTA CATHARINA* ex-*SAN JORGE* ex-*SAPELE* ex-*ABONEMA* • GRT 4031 • Built 1907
10.5.42: Torpedoed and sunk by German submarine U-588 (Vogel), in the Atlantic about 35 miles SE of Cape Sable, Nova Scotia, in position 42.56N 63.59W while sailing independently on a voyage from New York 7.5.42 to Argentia, Newfoundland, with a cargo of US Army stores. The Master, Capt Jack Rowland Morbey, and 24 crew landed at Lockeport, Nova Scotia. 9 crew were lost.

*WATERTON* • GRT 2115 • Built 1928
11.10.42: Torpedoed and sunk by German submarine U-106 (Rasch), in the Gulf of St Lawrence N of Cape Breton Island, in position 47.07N 59.54W while on a voyage from Corner Brook, Newfoundland 10.10.42 to Cleveland, Ohio, with a cargo of 2000 tons of wood sulphate and newsprint, part of convoy BS 31 comprising 2 ships. The Master, Capt William Lutjens, crew of 24 and 2 gunners were rescued by HMCS anti-submarine yacht *VISON* ex-*AVALON* 422/31 (Lt W.E. Nicholson) and landed at Sydney, Cape Breton. Kapitänleutnant Herman Rasch was awarded the Knight's Cross (29.12.42). U-106, commanded by Oberleutnant zur See Wolfdietrich Damerow, was sunk on 2.8.43 in the Atlantic 240 miles NW of Cape Ortegal, in position 46.35N 11.55W by Sunderland flying boat 'N' JM708, pilot F/O Reader D. Hanbury of No. 228 Squadron RAF, and Sunderland 'M' DV968, pilot F/Lt Irwin A.F. Clarke No. 461 Squadron RAAF, both based at Pembroke Dock, part of 19 Group. The U-boat commander and 35 crew were rescued by German torpedo boats T 22 600/40, T 24 600/40 and T 25 600/40. 25 crew were lost.

*LIVINGSTON* • GRT 2115 • Built 1928
3.9.44: Torpedoed and sunk by German submarine U-541 (Petersen), in the Atlantic NE of Louisburg, Nova Scotia, in position 46.15N 58.05W while on a voyage from Boston and Halifax to St John's, Newfoundland, with 2867 tons general cargo, part of convoy ON 251 comprising 140 ships. The Master, Capt Reuben Thomas Robinson, 12 crew and 1 gunner were rescued by HMCS corvette *BARRIE* 925/40 (K.138) (Lt W.D. Stokvis) and landed at St John's, Newfoundland. 13 crew and 1 gunner were lost. U-541, commanded by Kapitänleutnant Kurt Petersen, surrendered at Gibraltar on 14.5.45, and sailed to Lisahally. It was towed from Lisahally, Lough Foyle, on 5.1.46 by HM frigate *COSBY* 1300/43 (K.559) ex-HMS *REEVES* (Lt-Cdr L.A. Pepperwell), the tow parted the same day at 23.55 hrs and U-541 was sunk by gunfire by HM destroyer *ONSLAUGHT* 1540/41 (G.04) ex-HMS

*PATHFINDER* (Lt-Cdr C.G. Cowley) in the Atlantic NW of Moville, in position 55.38N 07.35W, part of 'Operation Deadlight', the disposal by the Royal Navy of 116 U-boats.

## BOWRING, C.T. & COMPANY – LONDON

**REGENT TIGER** (tanker) • GRT 10177 • Built 1938
8.9.39: Torpedoed and sunk by German submarine U-29 (Schuhart), in the Atlantic 220 miles W of Ireland, in position 49.57N 15.34W while sailing independently on a voyage from Trinidad to Avonmouth, with a cargo of 10600 tons of motor spirit and 3400 tons of diesel oil. The Master, Capt William Roberts, and crew were rescued by Belgian ship *JEAN JADOT* 5859/29 and landed at Ramsgate.

**EL OSO** (tanker) • GRT 7267 • Built 1921
6.1.40: Struck a mine, laid on the same day by the German submarine U-30 (Lemp) and sank in the Irish Sea 6 miles 280° from Liverpool Bar Lightship while on a voyage from Lobitos, Angola, to Ellesmere Port via Halifax NS, with a cargo of 9238 tons of crude oil and 511 tons of casinghead gasoline, dispersed from convoy HX 14 comprising 40 ships. The Master, Capt Frank Herbert Simpson, and 31 crew were rescued by HM destroyer *WALKER* 1120/17 (D.27) (Lt-Cdr A.A. Tait) and landed at Liverpool. 11.1.40. 3 crew were lost.

**URLA** • GRT 5198 • Built 1924
28.1.41: Torpedoed and sunk by Italian submarine *LUIGI TORELLI* (Longobardo), in the Atlantic 180 miles WNW of Inishtrahull, Co. Donegal, in position 54.54N 19.00W while on a voyage from Boston, Mass. and Halifax NS to Manchester, with a cargo of 3805 tons of steel and 3000 tons of lumber, a straggler from convoy HX 102 comprising 30 ships. The Master, Capt Edward Christopher Marsden, crew of 39 and 2 gunners were rescued by the British ship *SIRIS* 5242/19 and landed at Oban.

**CAPULET** (tanker) • GRT 8190 • Built 1930
28.4.41: Torpedoed and damaged by German submarine U-552 (Topp), in the North Atlantic S of Iceland, in position 60.16N 16.10W and later sunk by gunfire by the German submarine U-201 (Schnee), S of Iceland, in position 60.00N 16.00W while on Admiralty service on a voyage from Curacao to Scapa Flow, Orkneys, with 3 passengers and a cargo of 11200 tons of fuel oil, part of convoy HX 121 comprising 48 ships. The Master, Capt Edward Henry Richardson DSC, and 17 survivors were rescued by HM destroyer leader *DOUGLAS* 1800/18 (D.9) (Cdr W.E. Banks DSC) and landed at Londonderry, and 17 survivors by rescue ship *ZAAFAREN* 1559/21 (Capt Charles Kavanagh McGowan DSC) and landed at Greenock 1.5.41. 8 crew and 1 passenger were lost.

**CORDELIA** (tanker) • GRT 8190 • Built 1930
3.2.43: Torpedoed and sunk by German submarine U-632 (Karpf), part of the 'Landsknecht' (Mercenary) patrol group of twenty U-boats, in the Atlantic S of Iceland, in position 56.37N 22.58W while on Admiralty service on a voyage from Curacao to the Clyde via New York 22.1.43, with a cargo of 12000 tons of Admiralty fuel oil, a straggler from convoy HX 224 comprising 57 ships. The Master, Capt Edward Marshall, 37 crew and 8 gunners were lost. The sole survivor was rescued by U-632 and carelessly gave

information about convoy SC 118 which was reported to BdU (U-boat Commander-in-Chief). SC 118 was subsequently attacked with the loss of 9 ships (including rescue ship *TOWARD*). The survivor landed at Brest 14.2.43 and was taken to Milag Nord. Kapitänleutnant Hans Karpf and crew of 47 were lost while shadowing convoy HX 231 comprising 61 ships on 6.4.43 when U-632. part of the 'Löwenherz' (Lionhearted) patrol group of fourteen U-boats, was sunk in the Atlantic 390 miles SW of Reykjavik, in position 58.02N 28.42W by Liberator 'R' FL930, pilot F/Lt Cyril W. Burcher, of No. 86 Squadron RAF, based at Aldergrove, Co. Antrim, part of 15 Group. Oberleutnant zur See Leonard Aufhammer and crew of 47 were lost on 3.2.43 when U-265 was sunk in the Atlantic 540 miles W of Malin Head, in position 56.35N 49W while shadowing convoy HX 224 by Fortress II 'N' FL456, pilot P/O K. Ramsden of No. 220 Squadron RAF, based at Ballykelly, Co. Londonderry, part of 15 Group.

*REGENT LION* (tanker) • GRT 9551 • Built 1937
17.2.45: Torpedoed and damaged by German submarine U-300 (Hein), in the Atlantic about 8 miles E of Tangiers, in position 35.56N 05.45W while on a voyage from New York to Suez, with a cargo of 12440 tons of aviation gasolene, part of convoy UGS 72 comprising 53 ships. Taken in tow by the Admiralty dockyard tug *ROLLICKER* 620/08 (W.21) and HM trawler *ARCTIC RANGER* 493/37 (FY.186) (Lt J. Howson) on 19.2.45, later grounded on Pearl Rock near Gibraltar and declared a total loss. The Master, Capt Colin Thomas Pitt, 40 crew and 4 gunners were rescued by HM trawler *ARCTIC RANGER* and US destroyer *ROBINSON* 1620/43 (DD.562) and landed at Gibraltar. 7 crew were lost. U-300 commanded by Oberleutnant zur See Fritz Hein was sunk on 22.2.45 in the Atlantic 45 miles SE of Cape St Vincent, Portugal, in position 36.29N 08.20W by HM minesweepers *RECRUIT* 850/43 (J.298) (Cdr E.A. Dorn) and *PINCHER* 850/43 (J.294) (Lt-Cdr T. Fraser) and HM armed yacht *EVADNE* 581/31 (FY.009) (Lt-Cdr N.H. Richards). The U-boat commander and 7 crew were lost. 41 crew were taken prisoner by HMS *PINCHER* and HMS *RECRUIT*.

## BRIGHT NAVIGATION CO. LTD – LONDON

*MUNERIC* • GRT 5229 • Built 1919
10.9.41: Torpedoed and sunk by German submarine U-432 (Schultze), part of the 'Markgraf' patrol group of fourteen U-boats, in the North Atlantic S of Cape Farewell, in position 61.38N 40.40W while on a voyage from Rio de Janeiro to Middlesbrough via Sydney CB 30.8.41 with a cargo of 7000 tons of iron ore, part of convoy SC 42 comprising 65 ships. The Master, Capt Frank Baker, crew of 55, 5 gunners and 2 stowaways were lost.

## BRISTOL STEAM NAVIGATION CO. LTD – BRISTOL

*CATO* • GRT 710 • Built 1914
11.3.40: Struck a mine laid on 3.3.40 by German submarine U-29 (Schuhart), and sank in the Bristol Channel 2½ miles SE of Nash Point, in position 51.24N 03.33W while on a voyage from Dublin to Bristol, with 400 tons of general cargo. The Master, Capt Richard Martin, 10 crew and 2 gunners were lost. 2 crew were rescued by HM minesweeper *AKITA* 314/39 (FY.610) (Capt W.A. Walker DSC).

## BRITISH & CONTINENTAL SS CO. LTD – LIVERPOOL

*TRINGA* • GRT 1930 • Built 1925
11.5.40: Torpedoed and sunk by German submarine U-9 (Lüth), in the English Channel N of Dunkirk, in position 51.21N 02.25E while on a voyage from Antwerp to Glasgow, with a cargo of 1000 tons of potash and 1200 tons of iron ore. The Master, Capt Hugh Conway, 15 crew and the Belgian pilot were lost. 6 crew were rescued by HM destroyer *MALCOLM* 1530/19 (D.19) (Capt T.E. Halsey) and landed at Ramsgate 13.5.40. U-9 commanded by Oberleutnant zur See Heinrich Klapdor was sunk by Russian aircraft at Constanza, Roumania, on 20.8.44.

*DAFILA* • GRT 1940 • Built 1927
18.3.43: Torpedoed and sunk by German submarine U-593 (Kelbling), in the Mediterranean Sea near Derna, Cyrenaica, in position 32.59N 22.21E while on government service on a voyage from Tripoli to Alexandria, with a cargo of empty drums. The Master, Capt George Mugford, 9 crew and 5 gunners were rescued by the SAN whaler *SOUTHERN MAID* 344/36 (T.27) and landed at Derna. 19 crew and 3 gunners were lost.

## BRITISH & CONTINENTAL COAL & INVESTMENT CO. LTD – CARDIFF
**Ministry of Shipping**

*AURILLAC* • GRT 7733 • Built 1921
15.4.41: Torpedoed and sunk by gunfire by Italian submarine *ENRICO TAZZOLI* (di Cossato), in the Atlantic W of Madeira, in position 37.09N 18.42W while sailing independently on a voyage from Takoradi, Gold Coast, to Workington via Madeira, with a cargo of 5500 tons of manganese ore and 70 tons of willow. The Master, Capt Alec Charles Radley, and 20 survivors landed on the island of Porto Santo and were brought to Funchal; the Chief Officer and 18 survivors were rescued on 25.4.41 by Portuguese ship *GORGULHO* 428/31 and landed at Madeira 27.4.41. 1 crew was lost.

## BRITISH INDIA STEAM NAVIGATION CO. LTD – LONDON

*NALGORA* • GRT 6579 • Built 1922
2.1.41: Torpedoed and sunk by gunfire by German submarine U-65 (v. Stockhausen), in the Atlantic 350 miles N of the Cape Verde Islands, in position 22.24N 21.11W while sailing independently on a voyage from Leith and Rosyth to Aden and Alexandria, with passengers and a cargo of boom defence gear, dispersed on 22.10.40 from convoy OB 261 comprising 41 ships. The Master, Capt Aubrey Devereux Davies, 101 crew and 3 passengers were rescued after 8 days adrift in open boats. The British ship *NOLISEMENT* 5084/28 rescued 52 survivors who were landed at Freetown and British ship *UMGENI* 8180/38 rescued 34 survivors in position 21.35N 20.59W who were landed at Glasgow 13.1.41, and 19 crew in a lifeboat were landed at San Antonio, Cape Verde Islands. Korvettenkapitän Hans-Gerrit von Stockhausen was awarded the Knight's Cross (14.1.41). U-65, commanded by Kapitänleutnant Joachim Hoppe, and crew of 49 were lost on 28.4.41 while shadowing convoy HX 121. She was sunk in the North Atlantic 260 miles NW of Barra Head, Hebrides, in position 60.04N 15.45W by HM destroyer leader *DOUGLAS* 1530/18 (D.90) (Cdr W.E. Banks).

**GAIRSOPPA** ex-*WAR ROEBUCK* • GRT 5237 • Built 1919
17.2.41: Torpedoed and sunk by German submarine U-101 (Mengersen), in the Atlantic 50 miles W of Fastnet, in position 50.00N 14.00W while on a voyage from Calcutta to London via Freetown 30.1.41, with a cargo of 2600 tons of pig iron, 1765 tons of tea, 2369 tons of general cargo and £600,000 of silver ingots, a straggler from convoy SL 64 comprising 28 ships. The Master, Capt Gerald Hyland, crew of 81 and 2 gunners were lost.

**NARDANA** ex-*WAR SYBIL* • GRT 7951 • Built 1919
8.3.41: Torpedoed and sunk by German submarine U-124 (Schulz), in the Atlantic 600 miles NE of the Cape Verde Islands, in position 20.51N 20.32W while on a voyage from Bombay and Cape Town to London via Freetown 1.3.41, with 5662 tons general cargo including linseed, palm kernels, pig iron and seeds, part of convoy SL 67 comprising 56 ships. The Master, Capt Cyril Edward White, 104 crew and 2 gunners were rescued by HM destroyers *FAULKNOR* 1457/34 (H.62) (Capt A.F. de Salis) and *FORESTER* 1350/34 (H.74) (Lt-Cdr E.B. Tancock DSC) and landed at Gibraltar 16.3.41. 19 crew were lost.

**CHILKA** • GRT 4360 • Built 1922
11.3.42: Damaged by gunfire and set on fire by Japanese submarine I-2 (Inada), in the Indian Ocean near Padang, Sumatra, in position 00.23S 95.41E while sailing independently on government service on a voyage from Calcutta to Padang, Sumatra, to evacuate civilians and service personnel. She later sank 60 miles S of Padang, in position 00.30S 95.50E. The Master, Capt Walter Bird, and 6 crew were rescued on 4.5.42 35 miles NE of Madras after 54 days adrift by Greek ship *PIPINA* 2650/04 and landed at Cuddalore, EC India. 112 crew landed on the Mentawei Islands and were taken prisoner by the Japanese. 7 crew were lost. Capt W. Bird was awarded the Lloyd's War Medal for bravery at sea. I-2 commanded by Lt Kazuo Yamaguchi was sunk on 7.4.44 in the Pacific N of New Ireland, Admiralty Islands, in position 02.17S 149.14E by US destroyer *SAUFLEY* 2050/42 (DD-465) (Lt-Cdr D.E. Cochrane).

**FULTALA** • GRT 5051 • Built 1940
8.4.42: Torpedoed and sunk by Japanese submarine I-3 (Tonozuka), in the Indian Ocean 300 miles W of Ceylon, in position 06.52N 76.54E while sailing independently on a voyage from Calcutta 1.4.42 to Karachi, with 8000 tons of coal. The Master, Capt W.A. Welsh, 73 crew and 2 gunners were rescued. The Master's boat and the 2nd Officer's boat were rescued by unknown ships. Three officers, 16 crew and 1 gunner were rescued by British ship *LYEEMOON* 2885/08 and landed at Cochin 12.4.42. I-3 commanded by Lt I. Togami was sunk on 9.12.42 in the Pacific off Cape Esperance, Guadalcanal, Solomon Islands, in position 09.13S 159.40E by US motor torpedo boat PT-59 35/42.

**MUNDRA** • GRT 7275 • Built 1920
6.7.42: Torpedoed and sunk by gunfire by Japanese submarine I-18 (Otani), in the Indian Ocean off Santa Lucia Bay, Natal, in position 28.45S 32.20E while sailing independently from Calcutta and Madras to the UK via Cape Town, with 75 passengers and 15 survivors from the Swedish ship *EKNAREN* 5243/22, Dutch ships *GOVIKEN* 4854/17 and *DE WEERT* 1805/12 and 8100 tons of general cargo. The Master, Capt Fred Robinson, 36 crew and 19 passengers landed at Durban, 45 survivors were rescued by South African whaler *SIR LIEGE* 158/08 and 8 survivors were rescued by Union Castle ship *DUNDRUM CASTLE* 5259/19 and landed at Durban. 101

crew, passengers and survivors were lost. Cdr Tomiichi Muraoka and crew were lost on 2.1.43 when I-18 was sunk in the Pacific SW of Rendova Island, Solomon Islands, in position 08.49S 157.09E by the US submarine *GRAYBACK* 1475/41 (SS-208) (Lt-Cdr E.C. Stephan).

**GARMULA** laid down as *WAR REYNARD* • GRT 5254 • Built 1920
23.7.42: Torpedoed and sunk by German submarine U-752 (Schroeter), part of the 'Hai' (Shark) patrol group of six U-boats, in the Atlantic 200 miles SW of Freetown, in position 05.32N 14.45W while sailing independently on a voyage from Melbourne to the UK via Cape Town 8.7.42 and Freetown, with a cargo of 6009 tons of grain. The Master, Capt Robert C. Brown, 61 crew and 5 gunners were rescued by HM trawler *PICT* 462/36 (FY.132) (Lt-Cdr W.N.H. Faichney) and landed at Freetown. 20 crew and 1 gunner were lost. U-752 commanded by Kapitänleutnant Karl-Ernst Schroeter, part of the 'Mosel' (German river) patrol group of twenty U-boats was damaged while shadowing convoy HX 239 comprising 42 ships on 3.5.43 by Swordfish 'G', pilot Sub-Lt Harry Horrocks of No. 819 Squadron, Fleet Air Arm and Grumman F4F-4 Martlet fighter bomber 'B', pilot Sub-Lt W.G. Bowles of No. 892 Squadron FAA from HM escort carrier *ARCHER* 9000/39 (D.78) (Capt J.I. Robertson) and was scuttled in the Atlantic 750 miles W of Ireland, in position 51.40N 29.49W when approached by HM destroyers *KEPPEL* 1750/20 (D.84) (Cdr J.E. Broome) and *ESCAPADE* 1375/34 (H.17) (Lt-Cdr E.N.V. Currey DSC), part of the Escort Group B3 (Cdr A.A. Tait). The U-boat commander and 28 crew were lost. 13 crew were taken prisoner by HMS *ESCAPADE* and 4 crew were rescued by U-91 (Hungershausen) and landed at Brest 7.6.43. U-752 was the first U-boat to be sunk by rocket-firing aircraft from a British escort carrier.

**HATARANA** ex-*WAR SAILOR* • GRT 7522 • Built 1917
18.8.42: Torpedoed and damaged by German submarine U-214 (Reeder), part of the 'Blücher' patrol group of seven U-boats, later sunk by gunfire by HM corvette *PENTSTEMON* 925/41 (K.61) (Lt-Cdr J. Bryon), in the Atlantic ENE of the Azores, in position 41.07N 20.32W while on a voyage from Calcutta, Karachi and Cape Town to Glasgow via Freetown 4.8.42, with 8300 tons of general cargo, part of convoy SL 118 consisting of 34 ships. The Master, Capt Percival Arthur Clifton James, crew of 97 and 10 gunners were rescued. 20 survivors were rescued by HMS *PENTSTEMON* and landed at Londonderry, and 88 survivors by British ship *CORABELLA* 5682/37. Oberleutnant zur See Gerhard Conrad and crew of 47 were lost on 26.7.44 when U-214 was sunk in the English Channel 16 miles SSE of Start Point, in position 49.55N 03.31W by HM frigate *COOKE* 1085/43 (K.471) ex-USS *DEMPSEY* (DE-260) (Lt-Cdr L.C. Hill).

**HARESFIELD** ex-*WAR ASTER* • GRT 5299 • Built 1919
9.9.42: Torpedoed and sunk by Japanese submarine I-29 (Izu), in the Arabian Sea E of Socotra Island, in position 13.05N 54.35E while sailing independently on a voyage from Suez and Aden 7.9.42 to Colombo and Calcutta, in ballast. The Master, Capt Thomas Eric Cooper Earle, and 65 crew landed at Karachi, the 3rd and 4th engineers and 17 crew landed at Muscat, and were brought by British ship *HUNAN* 2827/32 to Karachi 26.9.42.

**HATIMURA** ex-*WAR OPAL* • GRT 6666 • Built 1919
4.11.42: Torpedoed and damaged by German submarine U-132 (Vogelsang), later sunk by German submarine U-442 (Hesse), part of the 'Veilchen' (Violet) patrol group of thirteen

U-boats, in the Atlantic 500 miles SE of Cape Farewell, in position 55.38N 39.52W while on a voyage from New York 24.10.42 to Holyhead and Manchester, with 8950 tons of general cargo including TNT and incendiaries, part of convoy SC 107 comprising 42 ships. The Master, Capt Willie Furneaux Putt, 76 crew and 9 gunners were rescued by US tugs *PECASSUS* and *UNCAS* 147/41, transferred to rescue ship *STOCKPORT* 1683/11 (Capt Thomas Ernest Fea OBE) and landed at Reykjavik 8.11.42. 3 crew and 1 gunner were lost. Kapitänleutnant Ernst Vogelsang and crew of 46 were lost on the same day when U-132 was destroyed by the explosion of the *HATIMURA*.

**TILAWA** • GRT 10006 • Built 1924
23.11.42: Torpedoed by Japanese submarine I-29 (Izu), in the Indian Ocean NW of the Maldive Islands, in position 07.36N 61.08E, and later sank, in position 07.45N 61.10E while sailing independently on a voyage from Bombay to Mombasa and Durban, with passengers and 6400 tons of general cargo. The Master, Capt Fred Robinson, 193 crew, 4 gunners and 480 passengers were rescued by HM cruiser *BIRMINGHAM* 9100/36 (19) (Capt H.B. Crane) and landed at Bombay 27.11.42. 4 survivors were rescued by HM armed merchant cruiser *CARTHAGE* 14253/31 (F.99) (Capt W.H.V. Woods MVO DSC) and landed at Bombay. The survivors were rescued from 10 lifeboats and 43 life-rafts. 28 crew and 252 passengers were lost.

**CRANFIELD** ex-*WAR VERBENA* • GRT 5322 • Built 1919
23.11.42: Torpedoed and sunk by Japanese submarine I-166 (Tanaka), in the Arabian Sea S of Cape Comorin, India, in position 08.26N 76.42E while sailing independently on a voyage from Calcutta and Madras to Suez. The Master, Capt George A. Paterson, 63 crew and 3 gunners were landed on the coast of Travancore, EC India. 9 crew were lost. Lt Cdr Shoichi Nichiuchi and crew were lost on 17.7.43 when I-166 was sunk in the Strait of Malacca off Penang, in position 05.10N 100.00E, by HM submarine *TELEMACHUS* 1090/43 (P.321) (Cdr King).

**NIRPURA** • GRT 5961 • Built 1921
3.3.43: Torpedoed and sunk by German submarine U-160 (Lassen), part of the 'Seehund' (Seal) patrol group of five U-boats, in the Indian Ocean off Port St Johns, South Africa, in position 32.03S 30.33E while on a voyage from Durban to Karachi, with 39 South African Defence troops and a consignment of 800 mules, part of convoy DN 21 comprising 11 ships. The Master, Capt Thomas George Hodgkinson, and 87 men were rescued by SAAF crash launch R 8 and landed at Durban. 38 men were lost.

**UMARIA** • GRT 6852 • Built 1941
29.3.43: Torpedoed and damaged by German submarine U-662 (Müller), later sunk by gunfire on 30.3.43 by HM frigate *WEAR* 1370/42 (K.230) (Lt G.D. Edwards) in the Atlantic SW of Cape Clear, in position 46.44N 16.38W while on a voyage from Bombay to Manchester via Cape Town and Freetown 12.3.43, with 1 passenger and 7376 tons of general cargo including 2500 tons of manganese ore, 1000 tons of rubber, 1000 tons of tea and copra, part of convoy SL 126 comprising 36 ships. The Master, Capt Aubrey Devereux Davies OBE, crew of 91, 10 gunners and passenger were rescued by HM frigate *WEAR* and landed at Liverpool.

**GOGRA** ex-*GORISSA* • GRT 5181 • Built 1919
2.4.43: Torpedoed and sunk by German submarine U-124 (Mohr), in the Atlantic 320 miles W of Oporto, in position 41.02N 15.39W while on a voyage from Glasgow 26.3.43 to Cape Town, Karachi and Bombay, with a cargo of 7000 tons of military stores including ammunition, part of convoy OS 45 comprising 42 ships. The Master, Capt John Drummond, 75 crew and 6 gunners were lost. 5 crew and 3 gunners were rescued by British ship *DANBY* 4258/37. Kapitänleutnant Johann Mohr (Knight's Cross awarded 27.3.42; with Oak Leaves 13.1.43), and crew of 52 were lost when U-124 was sunk on the same day in the Atlantic 320 miles W of Oporto, in position 41.02N 15.39W by HM sloop *BLACK SWAN* 1250/39 (L.57) (Cdr L.B.A. Majendie) and HM corvette *STONECROP* 925/41 (K.142) (Lt-Cdr J. Patrick Smythe), part of the 37th Escort Group, escorting convoy OS 45 comprising 42 ships.

**WAROONGA** ex-*HORORATA* • GRT 9365 • Built 1914
5.4.43: Torpedoed and damaged by German submarine U-635 (Eckelmann), part of the 'Löwenherz' (Lionhearted) patrol group of fourteen U-boats, later sunk by HM corvette *LOOSESTRIFE* 928/41 (K.105) (Lt A.A. Campbell) in the Atlantic 500 miles SE of Cape Farewell, in position 57.10N 35.30W while on a voyage from Sydney NSW to Liverpool via Panama and New York 25.3.43, with 8 passengers, 3 DBS and 8500 tons of general cargo, including 1500 tons of lead, 2000 tons of canned meat, 5000 tons of butter and mail, part of convoy HX 231 comprising 61 ships. The Master, Capt Charles Campbell Taylor, 97 crew, 7 gunners, 6 passengers and 2 DBS were rescued by HM corvette *LOOSESTRIFE* and the US liberty ship *JOEL ROGER POINSETT* 7196/43 and landed at Londonderry 9.4.43. 12 crew, 1 gunner, 5 passengers and 1 DBS were lost. Oberleutnant zur See Heinz Eckelmann and crew of 47 were lost on 6.4.43 when U-635 was sunk in the Atlantic 440 miles SW of Reykjanes, Iceland, in position 58.25N 19.22W by Liberator 'N', pilot F/O Gordon L. Hatherly of No. 120 Squadron RAF, based at Reykjavik, Iceland.

**NAGINA** • GRT 6551 • Built 1921
30.4.43: Torpedoed and sunk by German submarine U-515 (Henke), in the Atlantic 90 miles S of Freetown, in position 07.19N 13.50W while on a voyage from Calcutta, Cochin and Takoradi, Gold Coast 26.4.42, to the UK via Freetown, with 8000 tons of general cargo including 2750 tons of pig iron, jute, oil seeds, mica and tea, part of convoy TS 37 comprising 19 ships. The Master, Capt Walter Bird, 100 crew and 10 gunners were rescued by HM trawler *BIRDLIP* 750/41 (T.218) (Lt E.N. Groom) and landed at Freetown. 2 crew were lost.

**GHARINDA** laid down as *WAR MAVIS* • GRT 5306 • Built 1919
5.5.43: Torpedoed and sunk by German submarine U-266 (v. Jessen), part of the 'Amsel 2' (Blackbird) patrol group of five U-boats, in the Atlantic S of Cape Farewell, in position 53.10N 44.40W while on a voyage from Glasgow 21.4.43 to Portland, Maine and New York, in ballast, part of convoy ONS 5 comprising 42 ships. The Master, Capt Rodney Rosbrook Stone, crew of 81 and 10 gunners were rescued by HM frigate TAY 1370/42 (K.232) (Cdr Peter W. Gretton OBE DSO DSC) and landed at St John's, Newfoundland. Kapitänleutnant Ralf von Jessen and crew of 46 were lost on 14.5.43 while U-266 was shadowing convoy SC 129 comprising 26 ships. She was sunk in the Atlantic 360 miles SW of Land's End, in position 47.28N 10.20W by Halifax 'M' HR746, pilot W/Cdr Wilfred E. Oulton of No. 58 Squadron RAF, based at St Eval, part of 15 Group.

*DUMRA* • GRT 2304 • Built 1922
5.6.43: Torpedoed and sunk by German submarine U-198 (Hartmann), in the Indian Ocean 190 miles NE of Durban, in position 28.10S 33.25E while sailing independently on government service on a voyage from Tulear, Madagascar, to Durban, with a cargo of lorries. The Master, Capt Wilfred Charles Cripps, 24 crew and 1 gunner were lost. 65 crew and 1 gunner landed at Santa Lucia Bay, Natal. The Chief Engineer was taken prisoner, landed at Bordeaux 24.9.43 and taken to Milag Nord.

*DUMANA* • GRT 8428 • Built 1923
24.12.43: Torpedoed and sunk by German submarine U-515 (Henke), in the Atlantic W of Sassandra, Ivory Coast, in position 04.27N 06.58W while on government service on a voyage escorted by HM trawlers *ARRAN* 545/40 (T.06) (Lt W.G.N. Aplin) and *SOUTHERN PRIDE* 582/36 (K.249) (Lt G.B. Angus DSC), from Freetown to Takoradi 23.12.43, with 22 RAF personnel and a cargo of 300 tons of RAF stores. The Master, Capt Archibald Richard George Drummond, 107 crew, 7 gunners and 15 RAF personnel were rescued by the escorts and landed at Takoradi 25.12.43. 30 crew, 2 gunners and 7 RAF personnel were lost. U-515, commanded by Kapitänleutnant Werner Henke (Knight's Cross 17.12.42; with Oak Leaves (4.7.43), was sunk on 9.4.44 in the Atlantic 160 miles NW by N of Madeira, in position 34.35N 19.18W by an Avenger, pilot Lt Douglas W. Brooks of the US Navy Composite Squadron VC-58 from US escort carrier *GUADALCANAL* 7800/43 (CVE-60) (Cdr Daniel V. Gallery), US destroyer escorts *PILLSBURY* 1200/43 (DE-133) (Lt Cdr George W. Casselmann), *POPE* 1200/43 (DE-134) (Cdr Edwin H. Headland), *FLAHERTY* 1200/43 (DE-135) (Lt Cdr Means Johnson) and *CHATELAIN* 1200/43 (DE-149) (Cdr James L. Foley), part of Task Group 21.12. The U-boat commander and 42 crew were taken prisoner and landed at Norfolk, Virginia 26.4.44. 16 crew were lost.

*SURADA* • GRT 5427 • Built 1920
26.1.44: Torpedoed and sunk by German submarine U-188 (Lüdden), part of the 'Monsun' (Monsoon) patrol group of nine U-boats, in the Arabian Sea 40 miles ENE of Socotra Island, in position 13.00N 55.15E while sailing independently on a voyage from Calcutta and Colombo to Aden and Suez, with 7 passengers and 5000 tons of general cargo. The Master, Capt Ellis Henderson Brady, crew of 86, 9 gunners and passengers were rescued by British ship *DARRO* 9732/43 and landed at Aden 29.1.44. U-188, commanded by Kapitänleutnant Siegfried Lüdden, Knight's Cross (awarded 11.2.44) was scuttled at Bordeaux on 25.8.44.

**MOWT**

*MOHAMED ALI EL KEBIR* ex-*TENO* • GRT 7527 • Built 1922
7.8.40: Torpedoed and sunk by German submarine U-38 (Liebe), in the Atlantic 230 miles W of Bloody Foreland, Co. Donegal, in position 55.22N 13.18W while sailing independently on government service on a voyage from Avonmouth to Gibraltar, with about 697 troops, 66 naval personnel including marines, government stores and mail. The Master, Capt John Pratt Thomson, 153 crew, 1 gunner and 732 troops including naval personnel were rescued by HM destroyer *GRIFFIN* 1335/35 (H.31) (Lt W.A. Juniper) and landed at Greenock. 10 crew, 4 naval personnel and about 95 troops were lost.

**CALABRIA** ex-*WERRA* • GRT 9515 • Built 1922
8.12.40: Torpedoed and sunk by German submarine U-103 (Schütze), in the Atlantic 295 miles 262° from Slyne Head, Co. Galway, in position 52.43N 18.07W while on a voyage from Calcutta to Belfast and Liverpool via Freetown, with 230 Indian seamen and 8921 tons of general cargo, including 4000 tons of iron, 3050 tons of tea and 1870 tons of oilcake, a straggler from convoy SL 56 comprising 40 ships. The Master, Capt David Lonie, crew of 128, 1 gunner and the Indian seamen (crews for other ships) were lost. 21 crew were rescued by HM destroyer *SIKH* 1870/37 (F.82) (Cdr G.H. Stokes) and landed at Londonderry. The name *EMPIRE INVENTOR* was allocated but not adopted. The Italian *CALABRIA* was taken on 10.6.40 as a prize at Calcutta.

**JOHANNE JUSTESEN** ex-*FIONA* • GRT 4681 • Built 1909
15.2.42: Torpedoed and sunk by Japanese submarine I-165 (Harada), in the Arabian Sea 40 miles W of Cochin, in position 09.04N 75.58E while sailing independently on a voyage from Akyab, Burma, to Cochin, in ballast. The Master, Capt Wilhelm Rasmussen and 57 crew were landed at Alleppy, WC India. 1 crew was lost.

**MANON** ex-*SURSUM CORDA* ex-*GILGAI* ex-*WILDENFELS* • GRT 5597 • Built 1901
7.10.42: Torpedoed and sunk by Japanese submarine I-162 (Shimose), in the Bay of Bengal 400 miles ESE of Masulipatam, EC India, in position 15.00N 80.30E while sailing independently on a voyage from Calcutta and Vizagapatnam to Colombo, with a cargo of 7100 tons of coal. The Master, Capt Harry Douglas Clark, 70 crew and 3 gunners were saved. The first ship's boat landed at Iskapalli and the second and third boats landed at Bangara Pallaur, EC India. 8 crew were lost. The Italian *MANON* was taken by British troops when Kismayu, Italian Somaliland, was captured on 14.2.41.

**KHEDIVE ISMAIL** ex-*ACONCAGUA* • GRT 7513 • Built 1922
12.2.44: Torpedoed and sunk by Japanese submarine I-27 (Fukumura), in the Indian Ocean S of the Maldive Islands near Addu Atoll, in position 00.57N 72.16E while on government service on a voyage from Mombassa to Colombo, with troops and medical staff, part of convoy KR 8 comprising 5 troop ships. The Master, Capt Roderick William Macauly Whiteman DSC, 119 crew, 12 gunners, 5 medical staff and 1134 troops were lost. 51 crew and 56 troops were rescued by HM destroyers *PALADIN* 1540/41 (G.69) (Lt E.A.S. Bailey DSC), transferred to HMS *PETARD* 1540/41 ex-HMS *PERSISTENT* (G.56) (Lt-Cdr Rupert C. Egan) and landed at Addu Atoll, Maldive Islands, then embarked on HM cruiser *HAWKINS* 9860/17 (I.86) (Capt J.W. Josselyn DSC) and landed at Colombo 17.2.44. Lt Toshiaki Fukumura and crew were lost on the same day when I-27 was sunk in the Indian Ocean in the One and a Half Degree Channel, Maldive Islands, in position 01.25N 72.22E by HM destroyers *PETARD* and *PALADIN*. The *KHEDIVE ISMAIL* sank in less than 40 seconds.

## BRITISH MEXICAN PETROLEUM COMPANY – LONDON

**VICTOR ROSS** (tanker) • GRT 12247 • Built 1933
2.12.40: Torpedoed and sunk by German submarine U-43 (Lüth), in the Atlantic 355 miles 210° from Bloody Foreland, Co. Donegal, in position 56.04N 18.30W while on a voyage from Liverpool to New York, in ballast, dispersed on 1.12.40 from convoy OB 251 comprising 33 ships. The Master, Capt Ernest Butler Case, crew of 41 and 1 gunner were lost.

*INVERARDER* ex-*WAR HAGARA* (tanker) • GRT 5578 • Built 1919
24.2.42: Torpedoed and sunk by German submarine U-558 (Krech), in the Atlantic SE of St John's, Newfoundland, in position 44.34N 42.37W while on government service on a voyage from Londonderry to Trinidad via Halifax NS, in ballast, part of convoy ONS 67 comprising 35 ships. The Master, Capt Albert George Robins, 33 crew and 8 gunners were rescued by British ship *EMPIRE FLAME* 7069/41, transferred to rescue ship *TOWARD* 1571/23 (Capt Arthur James Knell MBE DSC) and landed at Halifax NS 1.3.42.

*NARRAGANSETT* (tanker) • GRT 10389 • Built 1936
25.3.42: Torpedoed and sunk by German submarine U-105 (Schuch), part of 'Operation Paukenschlag' (Drumbeat), the fourth wave of eleven U-boats, in the Atlantic about 400 miles E of Hampton Roads, Virginia, in position 34.46N 67.40W while sailing independently on a voyage from Port Arthur, Texas, to the UK via Halifax NS, with a cargo of 14000 tons of clean petroleum product. The Master, Capt Michael Blackburn Roberts, crew of 42 and 6 gunners were lost.

## BRITISH TANKER CO. LTD – LONDON

*BRITISH INFLUENCE* (tanker) • GRT 8431 • Built 1939
14.9.39: Torpedoed and sunk by gunfire by the German submarine U-29 (Schuhart), in the Atlantic 180 miles SW of Cape Clear, in position 49.43N 12.49W while sailing independently on a voyage from Abadan, Persia, to Hull, with a cargo of 12000 tons of diesel oil and fuel oil. The Master, Capt Ingersoll Hall McMichael and crew of 41 were rescued by Norwegian ship *IDA BAKKE* 5455/38, transferred 15.9.39 off Old Head of Kinsale to Courtmacsherry lifeboat, Co. Cork, and landed at Kinsale Harbour.

*BRITISH ENDEAVOUR* (tanker) • GRT 4580 • Built 1927
22.2.40: Torpedoed and sunk by German submarine U-50 (Bauer), in the Atlantic 100 miles W of Vigo, in position 42.11N 11.35W while on a voyage from Glasgow to Abadan, in ballast, part of convoy OGF 19 comprising 28 ships. The Master, Capt Thomas Weatherhead, and 32 crew were rescued by British ship *BODNANT* 5342/19 and landed at Funchal, Madeira 26.2.40. 5 crew were lost. Kapitänleutnant Max-Hermann Bauer and crew of 43 were lost on 6.4.40 when U-50 was sunk by a mine in the British Barrage Field No. 7 in the North Sea N of Terschelling Island, in position 61.59N 00.14W.

*BRITISH FAME* (tanker) • GRT 8406 • Built 1936
12.8.40: Torpedoed and sunk by Italian submarine *ALESSANDRO MALASPINA* (Leoni), in the Atlantic S of the Azores, in position 37.44N 22.56W while sailing independently from Avonmouth to Abadan via Cape Town, in ballast, dispersed from convoy OB 193 comprising 48 ships. The Master, Capt William George Knight, 43 crew and 1 gunner were rescued by Portuguese destroyer *DAO* 1400/34 and landed at Lisbon. 3 crew were lost and 1 crew was taken prisoner. This was the first merchant ship sunk by an Italian submarine during the Second World War.

*BRITISH GENERAL* (tanker) • GRT 6989 • Built 1922
6.10.40: Torpedoed and damaged by German submarine U-37 (Oehrn), in the Atlantic 550 miles W of Valentia Island, in position 51.42N 24.03W, again torpedoed by U-37 on 7.10.40

and sank in position 51.42N 24.50W while sailing independently on a voyage from the Tyne 27.9.40 and Methil 30.9.40 to Abadan, in ballast, dispersed from convoy OA 222 comprising 30 ships. The Master, Capt Frank Oswald Armstrong, and crew of 46 were lost.

**BRITISH PREMIER** (tanker) • GRT 5872 • Built 1922
24.12.40: Torpedoed and sunk by German submarine U-65 (v. Stockhausen), in the Atlantic 200 miles SW of Freetown, in position 06.20N 13.20W while on a voyage from Abadan to Swansea via Freetown 22.12.40, with a cargo of 8000 tons of crude oil, part of convoy SL 60 comprising 31 ships. The Master, Capt Francis Dalziel, 30 crew and 1 gunner were lost. 9 crew were rescued on 3.1.41 by HM cruiser *HAWKINS* 9750/17 (I.86) (Capt F.H. Pegram DSO) and others on 3.2.41 off the west coast of Africa after 41 days in an open boat (25 days without food) by HM destroyer leader *FAULKNOR* 1457/34 (H.62) (Capt A.F. de Salis) and landed at Freetown.

**BRITISH GUNNER** (tanker) • GRT 6894 • Built 1922
24.2.41: Torpedoed and sunk by German submarine U-97 (Heilmann), in the North Atlantic 273 miles NW of Cape Wrath, in position 61.09N 12.04W while on a voyage from Swansea to Aruba, in ballast, part of convoy OB 289 comprising 25 ships. The Master, Capt James William Kemp, 38 crew and 2 gunners were rescued by HM corvette *PETUNIA* 925/40 (K.79) (Lt-Cdr G.V. Legassisk) and landed at Stornoway, Hebrides. 3 crew were lost.

**BRITISH RELIANCE** (tanker) • GRT 7000 • Built 1928
2.4.41: Torpedoed and sunk by German submarine U-46 (Endrass), in the Atlantic SW of Iceland, in position 58.21N 28.30W while on a voyage from Aruba to the Clyde via Halifax NS, with 2 passengers and cargo of 9967 tons of gas oil, part of convoy SC 26 comprising 24 ships. The Master, Capt Alexander Henney, crew of 47 and passengers were rescued by British ship *TENNESSEE* 2342/21, landed at Reykjavik and brought to Gourock by British ship *ROYAL ULSTERMAN* 3244/30.

**BRITISH VISCOUNT** (tanker) • GRT 6895 • Built 1921
3.4.41: Torpedoed and sunk by German submarine U-73 (Rosenbaum), in the North Atlantic SSW of Iceland, in position 58.15N 27.30W while on government service on a voyage from Curacao to Scapa Flow via Sydney CB, with a cargo of 9500 tons of Admiralty fuel oil, part of convoy SC 26 comprising 24 ships. The Master, Capt William Coghill Baikie, and 27 crew were lost. 18 crew and 2 gunners were rescued by HM destroyer *HAVELOCK* 1340/39 (H.88) ex-Brazilian *JUTAHY* (Cdr E.H. Thomas DSC) and landed at Liverpool.

**BRITISH SECURITY** (tanker) • GRT 8470 • Built 1937
20.5.41: Torpedoed and set on fire by German submarine U-556, in the Atlantic S of Cape Farewell, in position 57.28N 41.07W, and later sank on 23.5.41 in position 57.14N 39.23N while on a voyage from Curacao to Bowling via Halifax NS, with a cargo of 11200 tons of benzine and kerosene, part of convoy HX 126 comprising 29 ships. The Master, Capt Arnold James Akers, crew of 48 and 4 gunners were lost.

**BRITISH GRENADIER** (tanker) • GRT 6857 • Built 1922
22.5.41: Torpedoed and sunk by German submarine U-103 (Schütze), in the Atlantic SW of Freetown, in position 06.20N 12.50W while sailing independently on government service on

a voyage from Freetown to Aruba, in ballast. The Master, Capt Henry George Jeary, 22 crew and 2 gunners were rescued by Portuguese steamer *GANDA* 3333/07 and 24 crew by Spanish tanker *JOSE CALVO SOTELO* 8452/41 and landed at Freetown.

**BRITISH MARINER** (tanker) • GRT 6996 • Built 1922
20.10.41: Torpedoed and damaged by German submarine U–126 (Bauer), in the Atlantic W of Freetown, in position 07.43N 14.20W while on government service on a voyage from Freetown to Curacao, in ballast. Towed by Dutch tug *DONAU* 239/10 and HM harbour tug *HUDSON* 294/39 (W.02) to Freetown, considered a constructive total loss (CTL) and used as an oil hulk in Freetown harbour. The Master, Capt Henry Beattie, 44 crew and 3 gunners were rescued by HMS *HUDSON* and landed at Freetown. 3 crew were lost.

**BRITISH RESOURCE** (tanker) • GRT 7209 • Built 1931
14.3.42: Torpedoed and sunk by German submarine U–124 (Mohr), in the Atlantic N of Bermuda, in position 36.04N 65.38W while sailing independently on a voyage from Curacao 4.3.42 to the UK, with a cargo of 10000 tons of benzine and white spirit. The Master, Capt James Kennedy, 41 crew and 3 gunners were lost. 1 crew and 3 gunners were rescued by HM corvette *CLARKIA* 925/40 (K.88) (Lt-Cdr F.J.G. Jones) and landed at Hamilton, Bermuda.

**BRITISH PRUDENCE** (tanker) • GRT 8620 • Built 1939
23.3.42: Torpedoed and sunk by German submarine U–754 (Oestermann), part of 'Operation Paukenschlag' (Drumbeat), the fourth wave of eleven U-boats, in the Atlantic NE of Halifax NS, in position 45.28N 56.13W while on government service on a voyage from Trinidad to the Clyde via Halifax NS 21.3.42, with a cargo of 12000 tons of fuel oil, part of convoy HX 181 comprising 25 ships. The Master, Capt George Albert Dickson, 41 crew and 5 gunners were rescued by HM destroyer *WITHERINGTON* 1325/19 (D.76) (Lt R. Horncastle) and landed at Halifax NS 24.3.42. 3 crew were lost.

**BRITISH SPLENDOUR** (tanker) • GRT 7138 • Built 1931
7.4.42: Torpedoed and sunk by German submarine U–552 (Topp), part of 'Operation Paukenschlag' (Drumbeat), the fourth wave of eleven U-boats, in the Atlantic E of Cape Hatteras, North Carolina, in position 35.07N 75.19W while on a voyage, escorted by HM trawlers *ST ZENO* 608/40 (FY.280) (Lt J.K. Craig) and *HERTFORDSHIRE* 458/39 (FY.176) (Cdr J.A. Shater), from Galveston, Texas, to the UK via Halifax NS, with a cargo of 10000 tons of benzine. The Master, Capt John Hall, 35 crew and 5 gunners were rescued by HM trawler *ST ZENO* and landed at Norfolk, Virginia. 11 crew and 1 gunner were lost.

**BRITISH WORKMAN** (tanker) • GRT 6994 • Built 1922
3.5.42: Torpedoed and sunk by German submarine U–455 (Giessler), part of the 'Pfadfinder' (Pathfinder) patrol group of eight U-boats, in the Atlantic SSE of Cape Race, in position 44.07N 51.53W while on a voyage from Greenock 23.4.42 to Galveston, in ballast, dispersed from convoy ON 89 comprising 49 ships. The Master, Capt Arthur W. Wilson, 39 crew and 7 gunners were rescued by HMCS destroyer *ASSINIBOINE* 1390/31 (D.18) (Lt John H. Stubbs) ex-HMS *KEMPENFELT* and HMCS corvette *ALBERNI* 925/40 (K.103) (Lt-Cdr G.O. Baugh) and landed at St John's, Newfoundland. 6 crew were lost.

**BRITISH COLONY** (tanker) • GRT 6917 • Built 1927
14.5.42: Torpedoed and sunk by German submarine U-162 (Wattenberg), in the Atlantic 90 miles NE of Bridgetown, Barbados, in position 13.12N 58.10W while sailing independently on government service on a voyage from Trinidad 12.5.42 to Gibraltar, with a cargo of 9800 tons of Admiralty fuel oil. The Master, Capt R. Wood-Thorburn, 39 crew and 3 gunners were landed 13 miles N of Bridgetown, Barbados. 4 crew were lost. U-162, commanded by Freggattenkapitän Jürgen Wattenberg, was sunk on 3.9.42 in the Atlantic 50 miles NE of Tobago, in position 12.21N 59.29W by HM destroyers *VIMY* 1300/17 (G.04) (Lt-Cdr H.G.D. de Chair), *PATHFINDER* 1540/41 (G.10) (Cdr E.A. Gibbs) and *QUENTIN* 1705/41 (G.78) (Lt-Cdr A.H.P. Noble). The U-boat commander and 48 crew were taken prisoner and landed at Port of Spain. 2 crew were lost.

**BRITISH YEOMAN** (tanker) • GRT 6990 • Built 1923
15.7.42: Torpedoed and sunk by gunfire by German submarine U-201 (Schnee), part of the 'Hai' (Shark) patrol group of six U-boats, in the Atlantic SW of the Canary Islands, in position 26.42N 24.20W while sailing independently on government service on a voyage from Curacao 1.7.42 to Gibraltar, with a cargo of 9700 tons of Admiralty fuel oil. The Master, Capt Edward Paul Spencer Attewill, 35 crew and 7 gunners were lost. 10 crew were rescued by Spanish tanker *CASTILLO ALMENARA* 6170/23 and landed at St Vincent, Cape Verde Islands. Kapitänleutnant Adalbert Schnee was awarded the Knight's Cross (30.8.41) with Oak Leaves (15.7.42). U-201, commanded by Oberleutnant zur See Gunther Rosenberg, and crew of 48 were lost on 17.2.43 when U-201, part of the 'Haudegen' (Broadsword) patrol group of twenty-one U-boats was sunk while shadowing convoy ON 165 comprising 32 ships in the Atlantic 500 miles NE of Cape Race, Newfoundland, in position 50.50N 40.50W by HM destroyer *VISCOUNT* 1120/17 (D.92) (Lt-Cdr J.V. Waterhouse).

**BRITISH CONSUL** (tanker) • GRT 6940 • Built 1924
19.8.42: Torpedoed and sunk by German submarine U-564 (Suhren), in the Atlantic 85 miles NW of Boca Grande, Trinidad, in position 11.58N 62.38W while on government service on a voyage from Trinidad 18.8.42 to Key West, Florida, for orders, in ballast, part of convoy TAW(S) comprising 11 ships. The Master, Capt James Kennedy, 34 crew, 4 gunners and 1 DBS were rescued by HM corvette *CLARKIA* 925/40 (K.88) (Lt-Cdr F.J.G. Jones) and landed at Guantanamo Bay, Cuba. 2 crew were lost. The convoy TAW(S) comprised damaged ships escorted by two tugs en route to Key West, Florida, to US ports for repairs.

**BRITISH VIGILANCE** (tanker) • GRT 8093 • Built 1942
3.1.43: Torpedoed and damaged by German submarine U-514 (Auffermann), in the Atlantic 900 miles NE of Barbados, in position 20.58N 44.40W while on a voyage from Curacao and Trinidad to Gibraltar, with a cargo of 11000 tons of clean petroleum products, part of convoy TM 1 comprising 9 tankers. The Master, Capt Evan Owen Evans, 21 crew and 5 gunners were rescued by HM corvette *SAXIFRAGE* 925/41 (K.04) (Lt N.L. Knight) and landed at Gibraltar. 25 crew and 2 gunners were lost. The wreck was sunk by German submarine U-105 (Nissen) on 24.1.43. Kapitänleutnant Hans-Jurgen Auffermann and 53 crew were lost when U-514 was sunk while shadowing convoy SL 130 comprising 37 ships on 8.7.43 in the Atlantic 50 miles W of Cape Ortegal, in position 43.37N 09.59W by Liberator 'R' BZ721, pilot S/Ldr Terry M. Bulloch DSO DFC of No. 224 Squadron RAF, based at St Eval, part of

19 Group. Kapitänleutnant Jurgen Nissen and crew of 53 were lost on 2.6.43 when U–105 was sunk in the Atlantic 25 miles SSW of Dakar, in position 14,15N 17.35W by a Potez flying boat 'Antares' of No. 141 Free French Squadron, based at Dakar.

**BRITISH DOMINION** (tanker) • GRT 6983 • Built 1928
11.1.43: Torpedoed and damaged by German submarine U–522 (Schneider), part of the 'Delphin' (Dolphin) patrol group of sixteen U-boats, in the Atlantic NW of the Canary Islands, in position 30.30N 19.55W, abandoned and later sunk by German submarine U–620 (Stein) by a *coup de grâce* while on a voyage from Curacao and Trinidad to Gibraltar, with a cargo of 9000 tons of aviation spirit, part of convoy TM 1 comprising 9 tankers. The Master, Capt Joseph Douglas Miller, 10 crew and 5 gunners were rescued by HM corvette *GODETIA* 925/41 (K.226) ex-HMS *DART* (Lt A.H. Pierce OBE) and landed at Gibraltar. 33 crew and 4 gunners were lost. Kapitänleutnant Heinz Stein and crew of 45 were lost on 14.2.43 when U–620, part of the 'Delphin' patrol group, was sunk while shadowing convoy KMS 9 comprising 46 ships in the Atlantic 115 miles W by N of Lisbon, in position 39.27N 11.34W by Catalina FP223 'J', pilot F/Lt Harry R. Sheardown RCAF, of No. 202 Squadron RAF, based at Gibraltar.

**BRITISH ARDOUR** (tanker) • GRT 7124 • Built 1928
5.4.43: Torpedoed and damaged by German submarine U–706 (v. Zitzewitz), part of the 'Löwenherz' (Lionhearted) patrol group of fourteen U-boats, later sunk by HM destroyer *VIDETTE* 1090/18 (D.48) (Lt-Cdr R. Hart) and HM corvette *SUNFLOWER* 925/40 (K.41) (Lt-Cdr J. Plomer), in the Atlantic W of Ireland, in position 58.08N 34.04W while on government service on a voyage from New York 25.3.43 to Greenock, with a cargo of 10000 tons of Admiralty fuel oil, part of convoy HX 231 comprising 61 ships. The Master, Capt Thomas Copeman, crew of 53 and 8 gunners were rescued by HMS *SUNFLOWER* and landed at Londonderry 9.4.43.

**BRITISH VENTURE** (tanker) • GRT 4696 • Built 1930
24.6.43: Torpedoed and sunk by Japanese submarine I–27 (Fukumura), in the Gulf of Oman, SE of Jask, Persia, in position 25.13N 58.02E while sailing independently on a voyage from Abadan 21.6.43 to Bombay, with a cargo of 7000 tons of kerosene and gasoil. The Master, Capt Darley Campbell Barton, 36 crew and 5 gunners were lost. 18 crew and 1 gunner were rescued by British ship *VARELA* 4651/14 and landed at Hormuz, Persia. The *BRITISH VENTURE* was ablaze within two minutes of being torpedoed.

**BRITISH CHIVALRY** (tanker) • GRT 7118 • Built 1929
22.2.44: Torpedoed and sunk by Japanese submarine I–37 (Nakagawa), in the Indian Ocean SW of Addu Atoll, Maldive Islands, in position 00.50S 68.00E while sailing independently on a voyage from Melbourne to Abadan, in ballast. The Master, Capt W. Hill, was taken prisoner. The crew in two ship's boats and four rafts were machine gunned in the water by the submarine. 29 crew and 9 gunners were rescued after being adrift for 37 days by British ship *DELANE* 6054/38, in position 04.55S 65.00E on 29.3.44 and landed at Durban. 15 crew and 5 gunners were lost.

**BRITISH FREEDOM** (tanker) • GRT 6985 • Built 1928
14.1.45: Torpedoed and sunk by German submarine U–1232 (Dobratz), in the Atlantic E of Halifax NS, in position 44.28N 63.28W while on Admiralty service on a voyage from New

York to the UK, with a cargo of 9723 tons of US Navy special fuel oil, part of convoy BX 141 comprising 18 ships. The Master, Capt Frank Llewellyn Morris, 46 crew and 9 gunners were rescued by HMCS trawler *GASPE* 460/38 (Lt A.J. Burke) and landed at Halifax NS. 1 crew was lost.

## MOWT

### EMPIRE GEM (tanker) • GRT 8139 • Built 1942

24.1.42: Torpedoed and sunk by German submarine U-66 (Zapp), part of 'Operation Paukenschlag' (Drumbeat), the first wave of five U-boats, in the Atlantic E of Cape Hatteras, North Carolina, in position 35.06N 74.58W while sailing independently on a voyage from Port Arthur, Texas, to the UK via Halifax NS, with a cargo of 10692 tons of motor spirit and 920 tons of machinery. The Master, Capt Francis Reginald Broad, and the wireless operator were rescued by a US Coastguard cutter and landed at Hatteras Inlet, North Carolina 25.1.42. 43 crew and 6 gunners were lost. Korvettenkapitän Robert Richard Zapp was awarded the Knight's Cross (23.4.42).

### MELPOMENE (tanker) • GRT 7011 • Built 1923

6.3.42: Torpedoed and sunk by Italian submarine *GIUSEPPE FINZI* (Giudice), part of the 'Da Vinci' patrol group of five Italian submarines, in the Atlantic 330 miles NE of Puerto Rico, in position 23.25N 62.39W while sailing independently on a voyage from Falmouth and Belfast Lough 12.2.42 to Baton Rouge, Louisiana, in ballast, dispersed from convoy OS 19 comprising 39 ships. The Master, Capt Alexander Henney, crew of 41 and 7 gunners were rescued by US ship *IDAHO* 6418/19 and landed at San Juan, Puerto Rico.

### EMPIRE CORPORAL ex-BRITISH CORPORAL (tanker) • GRT 6972 • Built 1922

14.8.42: Torpedoed and sunk by German submarine U-598 (Holtorf), in the Atlantic NW of Barlovento Point, Cuba, in position 21.45N 76.10W while on a voyage from Curacao 9.8.42 to Key West, Florida, for orders, with a cargo of 4532 tons of motor spirit and 4745 tons of white spirit, part of convoy TAW 12 comprising 47 ships. The Master, Capt George Eric Hodgson, 39 crew and 9 gunners were rescued by US motor torpedo boat PT 498 38/42, transferred to US destroyer *FLETCHER* 2051/42 (DD.445) (Cdr W.M. Cole) and landed at Guantanamo Bay, Cuba. 5 crew and 1 gunner were lost.

### OLTENIA II ex-OLTENIA (tanker) • GRT 6394 • Built 1928

8.1.43: Torpedoed and sunk by German submarine U-436 (Seibicke), part of the 'Delphin' (Dolphin) patrol group of sixteen U-boats, in the Atlantic SW of the Canary Islands, in position 27.59N 28.50W while on Admiralty service on a voyage from Trinidad to Gibraltar, with a cargo of 9086 tons of Admiralty furnace oil and a consignment of 732 barrels of lubricating oil and military stores, part of convoy TM 1 comprising 9 tankers. The Master, Capt Arthur Laddle, 13 crew and 3 gunners were lost. 42 crew and 1 gunner were rescued by HM destroyer *HAVELOCK* 1340/39 (H.88) (Cdr R.C. Boyle DSC) ex-Brazilian *JUTAHY* and landed at Gibraltar. Kapitänleutnant Gunther Seibicke, Knight's Cross (awarded 27.3.43) and crew of 46 were lost when U-436 was sunk on 26.5.43 in the Atlantic 290 miles W of Cape Finisterre, in position 43.49N 15.56W by HM frigate *TEST* 1370/42 (K.239) (Lt Cdr F.B. Collison) and RIN corvette *HYDERABAD* 925/41 (K.212) (Lt T. Cooper) escorting convoy KX 10 comprising 47 ships.

## BROCKLEBANK, THOS & JOHN, LIMITED – LIVERPOOL

*MANAAR* • GRT 7242 • Built 1917
6.9.39: Torpedoed and sunk by gunfire by German submarine U–38 (Liebe), in the Atlantic 70 miles SW of Cape da Roca, Portugal, in position 38.28N 10.50W while sailing independently on a voyage from Liverpool to Calcutta and Rangoon, with general cargo including agricultural and government stores. The Master, Capt Campbell Shaw, and 29 crew were rescued by Dutch ship *MARS* 1582/25 and landed at Lisbon 8.9.39, 16 crew by Portuguese ship *CARVALHO ARAUJO* 4560/30 and landed at Lisbon, and 17 crew by Italian ship *CASTELBIANCO* 4900/24. 7 crew were lost.

*MAGDAPUR* • GRT 8641 • Built 1921
10.9.39: Struck a mine, laid on 4.9.39 by German submarine U–13 (v. Eichain) and sank in the North Sea off Orford Ness, in position 52.11N 01.43W while on a voyage from South Shields to Southampton, in ballast. The Master, Capt Arthur George Dixon, and 74 crew were rescued by the Aldeburgh lifeboat and coasters. 6 crew were lost.

*MALABAR* • GRT 7976 • Built 1938
29.10.39: Torpedoed and sunk by German submarine U–34 (Rollman), in the Atlantic 180 miles W of Lands End, in position 49.57N 07.37W while on a voyage from Philadelphia and Boston, Mass. to London and Avonmouth via Halifax NS 17.10.39, with general cargo including lumber and tobacco, part of convoy HX 5 comprising 16 ships. The Master, Capt Henry Herbert Armstrong, Commodore Rear Admiral G.W. Taylor RNR, naval staff and 66 crew were rescued by HM destroyer *GRAFTON* 1335/35 (H.89) (Cdr M.S. Thomas) and landed at Plymouth. 5 crew were lost.

*MANIPUR* • GRT 8652 • Built 1920
17.7.40: Torpedoed and sunk by German submarine U–57 (Topp), in the Atlantic 8 miles NW of Cape Wrath, in position 58.41N 05.14W while on a voyage from Baltimore, Maryland, to London via Halifax NS, with general cargo including iron, steel, lumber, copper and zinc slabs, part of convoy HX 55A comprising 23 ships. The Master, Capt Raymond Mallett, and 64 crew were rescued by HMCS destroyer *SKEENA* 1337/30 (D.59) (Cdr H.T.W. Grant) and landed at Rosyth. 14 crew were lost.

*MATHERAN* • GRT 7653 • Built 1919
19.10.40: Torpedoed and sunk by German submarine U–38 (Liebe), in the Atlantic 120 miles WSW of Rockall, in position 57.00N 17.00W while on a voyage from New York to Liverpool via Halifax NS 8.10.40, with a cargo of 3000 tons of iron, 1200 tons of zinc, grain, machinery and general cargo, part of convoy HX 79 comprising 49 ships. The Master, Capt John Greenhall, and 8 crew were lost. 72 crew were rescued by British ship *LOCH LOMOND* 5452/34. On 20.10.40 *LOCH LOMOND* was sunk by German submarine U–100 (Schepke). The crew from both ships were rescued by HM sloop *JASON* 835/37 (N.99) (Lt-Cdr R.E. Terry) and landed at Methil.

*MAHRONDA* • GRT 7926 • Built 1925
11.6.42: Torpedoed and sunk by Japanese submarine I–20 (Yamada), in the Mozambique Channel N of Mozambique, in position 14.37S 40.58E while sailing independently on a

voyage from Liverpool and Durban 7.6.42 to Karachi, with 3 passengers and a cargo of government stores and general. The Master, Capt William Hill, 141 crew, 12 gunners and passengers were landed at Mozambique. 1 crew was taken prisoner.

**MANAAR** • GRT 8007 • Built 1942
18.4.43: Torpedoed and sunk by gunfire by Italian submarine *LEONARDO DA VINCI* (Gazzana), in the Indian Ocean about 130 miles ESE of Durban, in position 30.59S 33.00E while sailing independently on a voyage from Mombasa and Beira 14.4.43 to Durban and the UK, with 2 passengers and a cargo of 4400 tons of copper and cotton. The Master, Capt Raymond Mallett OBE, 80 crew, 10 gunners and passengers landed at Port St Johns, South Africa. The 2nd Officer was taken prisoner. 4 crew were lost.

## MOWT

**TASMANIA** • GRT 6405 • Built 1935
30.10.42: Torpedoed and damaged by German submarine U-659 (Stock), part of the 'Streitaxt' (Battleaxe) patrol group of eight U-boats later sunk by German submarine U-103 (Janssen), in the Atlantic N of Madeira, in position 36.06N 16.59W while on a voyage from Calcutta to Glasgow via Freetown 16.10.42, with 1 DBS and a cargo of 8500 tons of foodstuffs, tea, jute, 2000 tons of pig iron and 400 tons of ore, part of convoy SL 125 comprising 40 ships. The Master, Capt Hans Christian Roder, 35 crew, 7 gunners and DBS were rescued by Norwegian ship *ALASKA* 5681/18 which was later damaged by German submarine U-510 (Neitzel). 24 survivors were rescued by British ship *BARON ELGIN* 3942/33 and landed at Madeira, and 20 survivors by British ship *MANO* 1415/25 and landed at Greenock 9.11.42. 1 crew and 1 gunner were lost. U-659, commanded by Kapitänleutnant Hans Stock, part of the 'Drossel' (Thrush) patrol group of eleven U-boats, was lost on 3.5.43 when in collision with German submarine U-439, commanded by Oberleutnant zur See Helmut von Tippelskirch, in the Atlantic about 150 miles WNW of Cape Finisterre, in position 43.32N 13.20W. The commander of U-659 was lost with 43 crew. 3 crew were saved. The commander and 39 crew of U-439 were lost, and 9 crew were saved. The 12 U-boat survivors from U-439 and U-659 were rescued by HM motor gun boat No. 670 90/42 (Lt R.R.W. Ashby).

**SOLON II** ex-*SOLON* • GRT 4561 • Built 1925
3.12.42: Torpedoed and sunk by German submarine U-508 (Staats), in the Atlantic NE of Georgetown, British Guinea, in position 07.45N 56.30W while sailing independently on a voyage from Iskerderun, Turkey, and Cape Town to Baltimore, Maryland via Pernambuco and Trinidad, with a cargo of manganese ore and 2000 tons copper. The Master, Capt John Robinson, 68 crew and 6 gunners were lost. The 4th Engineer Alexander Macfarlane and 6 survivors landed at Weldad, 12 miles W of the River Berbice, British Guiana 7.12.42.

**SAMBRIDGE** ex-*JOHN E. WILKIE* • GRT 7176 • Built 1943
18.11.43: Torpedoed and sunk by Japanese submarine I-27 (Fukumura), in the Gulf of Aden SE of Aden, in position 11.25N 47.25E while sailing independently on a voyage from Madras 8.11.43 to Aden, with 365 tons of general cargo and 1000 tons of sand ballast. The Master,

Capt Alfred Stafford Bain, 36 crew and 11 gunners were rescued by British ship *TARANTIA* 7265/42 and HM frigate *TEVIOT* 1370/42 (K.222) (Cdr T. Taylor DSC) and landed at Aden. The 2nd Officer H. Scurr was taken prisoner; he was later awarded the Lloyd's War Medal for bravery at sea. 4 crew were lost.

## BROKEN HILL PROPRIETARY CO. LTD – MELBOURNE, VICTORIA

*IRON CHIEFTAIN* • GRT 4812 • Built 1937 (Australian)
3.6.42: Torpedoed and sunk by Japanese submarine I-24 (Hanabusa), in the Tasman Sea 27 miles E of Sydney NSW, in position 33.55S 151.50E while sailing independently on a voyage from Newcastle NSW 3.6.42 to Whyalla, South Australia, with a cargo of coke. The Master, Capt Lionel Haddelsey, and 11 crew were lost. 12 crew were rescued on 4.6.42 by RAN anti-submarine vessel *BINGERA* 922/36 (Lt-Cdr J.M. Little RANR), and 24 crew and 1 gunner landed on the beach at Tuggerag Lakes, NSW.

*IRON KNIGHT* • GRT 4812 • Built 1937 (Australian)
8.2.43: Torpedoed and sunk by Japanese submarine I-21 (Matsumra), in the Tasman Sea 21 miles NE of Montague Island (NSW), in position 35.51S 150.38E while on a voyage from Whyalla to Newcastle, NSW, with a cargo of iron ore, part of convoy OC 68 comprising 10 ships escorted by RAN minesweeping sloops *TOWNSVILLE* 650/41 (J.205) (Lt A. Farquhar–Smith) and *MILDURA* 650/41 (J.207) (Lt J. Hare). The Master, Capt Donald Ross, and 35 crew were lost. 14 crew were rescued by the French destroyer *LE TRIOMPHANT* 3230/34. Lt-Cdr H. Inada and crew were lost on 5.2.44 when I-21 was sunk in the Pacific NW of Jaluit Island, Marshall Islands, in position 06.48N 168.08E by US destroyer *CHARRETTE* 2050/42 (DD-581) (Cdr E.S. Karpe) and US destroyer escort *FAIR* 1140/43 (DE-35) (Lt-Cdr D.S. Crocker USNR).

## BROOMHILL STEAMSHIPS LTD – LONDON
**MOS**

*IRENE MARIA* • GRT 1860 • Built 1922
27.11.40: Torpedoed and sunk by German submarine U-95 (Schreiber), in the Atlantic SW of Rockall, while on a voyage from Southampton and Milford Haven to Bridgewater, Novia Scotia, in ballast, a straggler from convoy OB 248 comprising 46 ships. The Master, Capt Alfred Peter Evers, and crew of 24 were lost.

## BROWN ATKINSON, WILLIAM & CO. LTD – HULL
**Sea SS Co. Ltd**

*CHELSEA* • GRT 4804 • Built 1925
30.8.40: Torpedoed and sunk by German submarine U-32 (Jenisch), in the Atlantic 58 miles WNW of Cape Wrath, in position 58.48N 06.49W while on a voyage from Montreal to Methil and London via Halifax NS 16.8.40, with a cargo of 7600 tons of maize, part of convoy HX 66 comprising 51 ships. The Master, Capt Robert Harrison, 22 crew and 1 gunner were lost. 11 crew were rescued by HM trawler *LORD CECIL* 228/16 and landed at Scrabster, Caithness.

## BRUCE, JOHN & CO. – GLASGOW
Mossgiel Steamship Co. Ltd

*ALHAMA* • GRT 1352 • Built 1938
24.10.41: Torpedoed and sunk by German submarine U-564 (Suhren), part of the 'Breslau' patrol group of six U-boats in the Atlantic 600 miles W of Gibraltar, in position 35.42N 10.58W while on a voyage from Seville and Valencia to Belfast, with a cargo of 180 tons of tartaric acid, 1730 tons of onions, wines, cork and 27 tons of general cargo, part of convoy HG 75 comprising 17 ships. The Master, Capt Alexander Cameron, crew of 25 and 7 gunners were rescued by Free French sloop *COMMANDANT DUBOC* 630/38 and transferred to HM destroyer *LAMERTON* 1050/40 (L.88) (Lt-Cdr H.C. Simms). 18 survivors were transferred to HM destroyer *HESPERUS* 1340/39 (H.57) ex-HMS *HEARTY* (Lt-Cdr A.A. Tait) and landed at Liverpool, and 15 survivors were transferred to HM sloop *ROCHESTER* 1045/31 (L.50) (Cdr C.B. Allen) and landed at Londonderry 3.11.41. One of the escorts, HM destroyer *COSSACK* 1870/37 (F.03) (Capt E.L. Berthon), was torpedoed and damaged by German submarine U-563 (Bargsten) on 24.10.41 in the Atlantic, W of Gibraltar, in position 35.56N 10.04W, and later sank under tow on 27.10.41. HMS *COSSACK* (Capt Philip L. Vian) was famous for the daring rescue on 16.2.40 of 299 British prisoners from nine British merchant ships, the *AFRICAN SHELL* 706/39 (Capt P.G.G. Dove), *ASHLEA* 4222/29 (Capt C.A. Pottinger), *CLEMENT* 5051/34 (Capt F.C.P. Harris), *DORIC STAR* 10086/21 (Capt W. Stubbs), *HUNTSMAN* 8196/21 (Capt A.H. Brown), *NEWTON BEACH* 4651/25 (Capt J. Robinson OBE), *STREONSHALH* 3895/28 (Capt J.J. Robinson), *TAIROA* 7983/20 (Capt W.B.S. Starr) and *TREVANION* 5299/37 (Capt J.N. Edwards), sunk by German pocket battleship *ADMIRAL GRAF SPEE* 10000/34 (Kapitän zur See Hans Langsdorff) from German supply tanker *ALTMARK* ex-*UCKERMARK* 7021/30 (Kapitän zur See Heinrich Dau) in Jössingfjord, Norway. The German naval tanker *UCKERMARK* blew up and was destroyed in Yokohama harbour on 30.12.42.

## BULLARD KING & CO. LTD – LONDON
Natal Line

*UMONA* • GRT 3767 • Built 1910
30.3.41: Torpedoed and sunk by German submarine U-124 (Schulz), in the Atlantic 90 miles SW of Freetown while sailing independently on a voyage from Durban to London via Walvis Bay 20.3.41 and Freetown, with 7 passengers, 7 DBS and a cargo of 47 tons of jam, 1549 tons of maize and 50 tons of pulses. The Master, Capt Frederick Arthur Baden Peckham, 81 crew, 7 gunners, 6 DBS and passengers were lost. 1 gunner and 1 passenger were rescued after 13 days in an open boat by the British ship *LORCA* 4875/31 and landed at Freetown 13.4.41; 3 crew were rescued S of Freetown, in position 07.25N 13.55W on 7.4.41 and landed at Freetown on 8.4.41 by HM destroyer *FOXHOUND* 1350/34 (H.69) (Cdr G.H. Peters), part of the escort of convoy WS 7 comprising 24 ships. The Commodore of the convoy was Vice-Admiral R. Eliot CBE. Gunner Edward Gordon Elliott RN was awared the Lloyd's War Medal for bravery at sea.

*UMTATA* • GRT 8141 • Built 1935
7.7.42: Torpedoed and sunk by German submarine U-571 (Möhlmann), part of the 'Endrass' (named after a U-boat commander) patrol group of five U-boats, in the Florida Strait NE of

Key West, in position 25.35N 80.02W while under tow by US tug *EDMUND J. MORAN* 336/40 to Port Everglades via San Juan, Puerto Rico, and Key West, with a cargo of 2000 tons of mineral ore loaded at St Lucia, BWI. The Master, Capt R. Owen Jones, and crew of 91 were rescued by the *EDMUND J. MORAN* 336/40, transferred to the US coastguard cutter *THETIS* 337/31 (WPC.115) and landed at Miami. Kapitänleutnant Hellmut Möehlmann was awarded the Knight's Cross (16.4.43). Oberleutnant zur See Gustav Lüssow and crew of 51 were lost on 28.1.44 when U-571, part of the 'Hinein' patrol group of six U-boats, was sunk in the Atlantic 200 miles WNW of Fastnet, in position 52.41N 14.27W by Sunderland 'D' EK577, pilot F/L R.D. Lucas RAAF, No. 461 Squadron RAAF, based at Pembroke Dock. The pilot was awarded the DFC.

### *UMVUMA* • GRT 4419 • Built 1914
7.8.43: Torpedoed and sunk by German submarine U-181 (Lüth), in the Indian Ocean SW of Port Louis, Mauritius, in position 19.55S 57.20E while sailing independently on a voyage from London to Port Louis via Freetown and Durban 29.7.43, with 12 passengers and 800 tons of military stores, 2000 tons of sugar and 2000 tons of general cargo, dispersed from convoy DN 54. The Master, Capt John Newby Gibson, 72 crew, 8 gunners and 8 passengers were rescued by the Port Louis harbour salvage tug *MAURICE* 208/26 and landed at Port Louis. 17 crew, 1 gunner and 4 passengers were lost.

## BURIES MARKES, LIMITED – LONDON

### *LA ESTANCIA* • GRT 5185 • Built 1940
19.10.40: Torpedoed and sunk by German submarine U-47 (Prien), in the Atlantic 90 miles SW of Rockall, in position 57.00N 17.00W while on a voyage from Mackay, Queensland, to Methil and Middlesbrough via Panama and Halifax NS 8.10.40, with 1 passenger and 8333 tons of sugar, part of convoy HX 79 comprising 49 ships. The Master, Capt John Meneely, 24 crew and passenger were rescued by HM corvette *COREOPSIS* 925/40 (K.32) (Lt-Cdr A.H. Davies) and landed at Gourock, and 7 crew by British ship *INDUNA* 5086/25 and landed at Methil. 1 crew was lost.

### *LA CORDILLERA* • GRT 5185 • Built 1940
5.11.42: Torpedoed and sunk by German submarine U-163 (Engelmann), in the Atlantic 85 miles E of Barbados, in position 12.02N 58.04W while sailing independently on a voyage from Suez and Cape Town 15.10.42 to New York via Trinidad, in ballast. The Master, Capt John Meneely, 32 crew and 5 gunners landed at Carlist Bay, Barbados. 1 crew and 2 gunners were lost.

## BURNETT STEAMSHIP CO. LTD – NEWCASTLE
Burnett SS Co. Ltd

### *HOLMSIDE* • GRT 3433 • Built 1930
19.7.41: Torpedoed and sunk by German submarine U-66 (Zapp), in the Atlantic NE of the Cape Verde Islands, in position 19.00N 21.30W while sailing independently on a voyage from Hull to Pepel, in ballast, dispersed from convoy OG 67 comprising 51 ships. The Master, Capt Norman Caulfield, 13 crew and 2 gunners were rescued by Portuguese ship *SETE CIDADES* 2035/06 and landed at Lisbon 1.8.41. 18 crew and 3 gunners were lost.

**WALLSEND • GRT** 3157 • Built 1937
3.12.42: Torpedoed and sunk by German submarine U-552 (Popp), in the Atlantic N of the Cape Verde Islands, in position 20.08N 25.50W while sailing independently on a voyage from Liverpool and Glasgow 15.11.42 to Freetown, with a cargo of 450 tons of cement, 320 tons of coal, 15 aircraft and mail, dispersed from convoy ON146 comprising 39 ships. The Master, Capt Norman Caulfield OBE, was taken prisoner, landed at St Nazaire 15.12.42 and taken to Milag Nord. 30 crew and 6 gunners landed at Tarrafal Bay, Cape Verde Islands. 4 crew were lost.

## MOWT

**LEISE MAERSK** ex-*SVENDBORG* • GRT 3136 • Built 1921
23.11.40: Torpedoed and sunk by German submarine U-100 (Schepke), in the Atlantic 120 miles W of Rockall, in position 55.30N 11.00W while on a voyage from Three Rivers to Sharpness via Sydney CB 9.11.40, with a cargo of 4500 tons of grain and general, part of convoy SC 11 comprising 33 ships. The Master, Capt Peter Konge Mortensen, and 16 crew were lost. 7 crew were rescued by a Dutch salvage tug and landed at Campbeltown.

## BURNS PHILP & CO. LTD – SYDNEY, NEW SOUTH WALES, AUSTRALIA

**MAMUTU • GRT 300 • Built 1938**
7.8.42: Sunk by gunfire by Japanese submarine RO–33 (Kuriyama), in the Gulf of Papua 30 miles W of Bramble Bay, in position 09.11S 144.12E while sailing independently on a voyage from Port Moresby 6.8.42 to Daru, Papua, carrying 103 passengers and general cargo. The Master, crew of 38 and 102 passengers were lost when the survivors in the water, men, women and children, were machine-gunned by RO-33. 1 passenger (William Griffin) landed at the mouth of the River Fly, Papua 10.8.42 and was brought to Port Moresby 28.8.42. Lt Shigeshi Kuriyama and crew were lost on 29.8.42 when RO-33 was sunk in the Coral Sea 120 miles SE of New Guinea, in position 09.30S 147.25E by RAN destroyer *ARUNTA* 1927/40 (I.30) (Cdr J.C. Morrow DSO).

**TULAGI • GRT 2281 • Built 1938**
27.3.44: Torpedoed and sunk by German submarine U-532 (Junker), in the Indian Ocean NE of Cape Comorin, India, in position 11.00S 78.40E while on a voyage from Sydney NSW 10.3.44 to Colombo, with a cargo of 1850 tons of flour and 380 bags of mail. The Master, Capt James Ferguson Thomsen, 37 crew and 5 gunners were lost. The Chief Engineer John Ward and 6 crew drifted 1500 miles on a raft for 59 days and landed on Alphonse Island, Seychelles, in position 07.05S 52.50E. The survivors were brought to Port Victoria, Seychelles, on 16.6.44. The *TULAGI* sank in less than half a minute.

## CAIRNS, NOBLE & CO. LTD – NEWCASTLE
### Cairn Line of Steamships Ltd

**CAIRNMONA • GRT 4666 • Built 1918**
30.10.39: Torpedoed and sunk by German submarine U-13 (v. Eichhain), in the North Sea 15 miles N by E of Peterhead, in position 57.38N 01.45W while on a voyage from Montreal

and Halifax NS 17.10.39 to Newcastle and Leith, with general cargo including copper and grain, dispersed from convoy HX 5 comprising 16 ships. The Master, Capt Frederick William Fairley, and 41 crew were rescued by HM drifter *RIVER LOSSIE* 203/20 (4.246) (Skipper J.C. Spence RNR). 3 crew were lost.

### *CAIRNROSS* • GRT 5494 • Built 1921
17.1.40: Struck a mine laid on 6.1.40 by German submarine U-30 (Lemp) and sunk in the Irish Sea 7/8 miles from the Liverpool Bar Lightvessel while on a voyage from the Tyne, Leith and Liverpool to St John, New Brunswick, with general cargo including coal and earthenware, part of convoy OB 74 comprising 19 ships. The Master, Capt Laurence Halcrow, and crew of 47 were rescued by HM destroyer leader *MACKAY* 1800/18 (D.70) ex-HMS *CLAVERHOUSE* (Cdr G.H. Stokes) and landed at Liverpool.

## MOS

### *EMPIRE BRIGADE* ex-*ELIOS* • GRT 5154 • Built 1912
19.10.40: Torpedoed and sunk by German submarine U-99 (Kretschmer), in the Atlantic 100 miles ESE of Rockall, in position 57.12N 10.43W while on a voyage from Montreal to the Tyne and Leith via Sydney CB 5.10.40, with general cargo including 750 tons of copper, 129 tons of ferro alloys and 980 tons of steel, part of convoy SC 7 comprising 35 ships. The Master, Capt Sydney Wyman Parks, and 34 crew were rescued by HM sloop *FOWEY* 1105/30 (L.15) (Lt C.G. de L. Bush) and landed at Greenock. 5 crew and 1 gunner were lost. The Italian *ELIOS* was taken as a prize on 10.6.40 at Newcastle.

### *BLACK OSPREY* ex-*WAR ARROW* • GRT 5589 • Built 1918
18.2.41: Torpedoed and sunk by German submarine U-96 (Lehmann-Willenbrock), in the North Atlantic S of Iceland, in position 61.30N 18.10W while on a voyage from Baltimore to Newport, Mon. via Halifax NS, with a cargo of 4500 tons of steel and trucks, a straggler from convoy HX 107 comprising 21 ships. The Master, Capt Sydney Wyman Parks, and 24 crew were lost. 11 crew were rescued by U-96, commanded by Korvettenkapitän Heinrich Lehmann-Willenbrock (Knight's Cross 26.2.41, with Oak Leaves 31.12.41), later transferred to Norwegian ship *MOSDALE* 3022/39 and landed at Barry Roads.

## MOWT

### *EMPIRE SAILOR* ex-*CELLINA* • GRT 6140 • Built 1926
21.11.42: Torpedoed and sunk by German submarine U-518 (Wissmann), in the Atlantic 200 miles S of Placentia Bay, Newfoundland, in position 43.53N 55.12N while on a voyage from Liverpool 10.11.42 to St John, New Brunswick, with 2700 tons of general cargo including 270 tons of phosgene bombs and 26 tons of mustard gas in 68 drums, part of convoy ON 145 comprising 35 ships. The Master, Capt Frederick William Fairley, 35 crew, 2 gunners, 2 Canadian signalmen and 2 Canadian army personnel were rescued by HMCS corvette *TIMMINS* 925/41 (K.223) (Lt J.A. Brown) and HMCS minesweeper *MINAS* 672/41 (J.165) (Lt J.C. Barbour) and landed at Halifax NS. 19 crew, 3 gunners and 1 Canadian army personnel were lost. Oberleutnant zur See Hans Offermann and crew of 55 were lost on 22.4.45 when U-518, part of the 'Seewolf' (Seawolf) patrol group of six U-boats, was sunk in

the Atlantic 390 miles NW of Flores, Azores, in position 43.26N 38.23W by US destroyer escorts *CARTER* 1240/44 (DE-112) (Lt-Cdr F.J.T. Baker) and *NEAL A. SCOTT* 1240/44 (DE-769) (Lt-Cdr P.D. Holden) of the Task Group 22.5. The Italian *CELLINA* was taken as a prize on 10.6.40 at Gibraltar.

## CANADA STEAMSHIP LINES – MONTREAL

**MAGOG** ex-*JOHN C. HOWARD* • GRT 2053 • Built 1923 (Canadian)
5.7.40: Torpedoed and damaged by gunfire by German submarine U-99 (Kretschmer), in the Atlantic about 58 miles WSW of Fastnet, in position 50.31N 11.05W. It later sank on 8.7.40, in position 50.32N 11.20W while on a voyage from Halifax NS 21.6.40 to Preston, with a cargo of 512 standards of timber, a straggler from convoy HX 52 comprising 29 ships. The Master, Capt T. Swales Doughty, and crew of 22 were rescued by the Swedish ship *FIDRA* 1483/39 and landed at Queenstown (Cork).

**LENNOX** ex-*GLENLINNIE* • GRT 1904 • Built 1923 (Canadian)
23.2.42: Torpedoed and sunk by German submarine U-129 (Clausen), in the Atlantic NE of Barima, Venezuela, in position 09.15N 58.30W while sailing independently on a voyage from Paramaribo, Dutch Guiana, to Port of Spain, Trinidad, with a cargo of bauxite. The Master, Capt Daniel Percy Nolan, and 17 crew were rescued by British tanker *ATHELRILL* 7398/16 and landed at Port of Spain, Trinidad. 2 crew were lost.

**DONALD STEWART** • GRT 1781 • Built 1923 (Canadian)
3.9.42: Torpedoed and sunk by German submarine U-517 (Hartwig), in the Gulf of St Lawrence NE of Cape Whittle, in position 50.16N 59.04W while on a voyage from Quebec to Goose Bay, Labrador, with 1 passenger and a cargo of aviation gasoline in drums and cement, part of convoy LN 7 of 4 ships. The Master, Capt Daniel Percy Nolan, 15 crew and passenger were rescued by RCN corvettes *SHAWINIGAN* 925/41 (K.136) (Lt C.P. Balfry) and *TRAIL* 925/40 (K.174) (Lt G.S. Hall) and landed at Quebec. 3 crew were lost.

**NORFOLK** ex-*GLENBUCKIE* • GRT 1901 • Built 1923 (Canadian)
18.9.42: Torpedoed and sunk by German submarine U-175 (Bruns), in the Atlantic NE of Georgetown, British Guinea, in position 08.36N 59.20W while sailing independently on a voyage from Paramaribo to Trinidad, with a cargo of 3055 tons of bauxite. The Master, Capt Thomas Arthur Edge, and 5 crew were lost. 13 crew were rescued by Spanish ship *INDAUCHA* 3126/20 and landed at Port of Spain, Trinidad 19.9.42.

## CANADIAN GOVERNMENT – OTTAWA
**Merchant Marine Ltd**

**CAROLUS** • GRT 2245 • Built 1919 (Canadian)
9.10.42: Torpedoed and sunk by German submarine U-69 (Gräf), in the Gulf of St Lawrence near Bic Island, in position 48.47N 68.10W while en route to Montreal, part of convoy NL 9 comprising 4 ships. The Master, Capt William Broman, 16 crew and 2 gunners were rescued by RCN corvettes *HEPATICA* 925/40 (K.159) (Lt-Cdr T. Gilmour) and *ARROWHEAD* 925/40 (K.145) (Lt-Cdr E.G. Skinner) and landed at Quebec. 11 crew were lost.

**BIC ISLAND** ex-*CAPO NOLI* ex-*MUNARDAN* • GRT 4000 • Built 1917 (Canadian)
29.10.42: Torpedoed and sunk by German submarine U-224 (Kosbadt), part of the 'Puma' patrol group of thirteen ships in the Atlantic SW of Rockall, in position 55.05N 23.27W while on a voyage from Halifax NS to Liverpool, with a cargo of 4430 tons of foodstuffs and government stores, a straggler from convoy HX 212 comprising 45 ships. The Master, Capt James Brown, 35 crew, 8 gunners also 31 crew and 13 armed guards rescued from US tanker *GURNEY E. NEWLIN* 8225/42 sunk the previous day by U-606 (Döhler) and 26 crew, 31 passengers, 16 DBS and 4 gunners rescued from the British whale factory *SOURABAYA* 10107/15 sunk on 27.10.42 by U-436 (Seibicke), were lost. U-224 commanded by Oberleutnant zur See Hans-Carl Kosbadt was sunk on 13.1.43 in the Mediterranean 90 miles W of Algiers, in position 38.28N 00.42E while shadowing convoy TE 13 comprising 15 ships by HMC corvette *VILLE DE QUEBEC* 925/41 (K.242) ex-HMCS *QUEBEC* (Lt-Cdr A.R.E. Coleman). The U-boat commander and 43 crew were lost. The sole survivor was taken prisoner by HMC corvette *PORT ARTHUR* 925/41 (K.233) (Lt T. Simmons) and landed at Bône. The Italian *CAPO NOLI* was captured in the Gulf of St Lawrence by HMC trawler *BRAS D'OR* 221/01 (Lt Charles A. Hornsby) on 10.6.40.

**CHR. J. KAMPMANN** • GRT 2281 • Built 1924 (Canadian)
3.11.42: Torpedoed and sunk by German submarine U-160 (Lassen), in the Atlantic NW of Grenada, BWI, in position 12.06N 62.42W while on a voyage from Demerara, British Guiana, to New York via Trinidad, with a cargo of sugar and rum, part of convoy TAG 18 comprising 25 ships. 8 crew were rescued by US four-stack destroyer *LEA* 1090/18 (DD.118), transferred to US submarine chaser No. 495 280/42 and landed at Curacao. 17 crew and 2 gunners were lost.

## MOWT

**VANCOUVER ISLAND** ex-*WESER* ex-*YAKIMA STAR* ex-*SUL AMERICANO*
GRT 9472 • Built 1929 (Canadian)
15.10.41: Torpedoed and sunk by German submarine U-558 (Krech), in the Atlantic W of Ireland, in position 53.37N 25.37W while on a voyage from Montreal to Belfast and Cardiff via Sydney CB, with 32 passengers and a cargo of 3132 tons of general goods, 751 tons of aluminium, 993 tons of copper, 450 tons of zinc, 87 tons of steel and 357 tons of asbestos. a straggler from convoy SC 48 comprising 50 ships. The Master, Capt Eric Lacey Roper, crew of 64, 8 gunners and passengers were lost. The German *WESER* was captured by HMCS armed merchant cruiser *PRINCE ROBERT* 6892/30 (F.56) (Cdr C.T. Beard) off the coast of EC Mexico on 25.9.40.

## CANADIAN LAKE CARRIERS, LIMITED – MONTREAL

**TREVISA** • GRT 1813 • Built 1915 (Canadian)
16.10.40: Torpedoed and sunk by German submarine U-124 (Schulz), in the Atlantic 218 miles W of Rockall, in position 57.28N 20.30W while on a voyage from Parrsboro, Nova Scotia to Aberdeen via Sydney CB 5.10.40, with a cargo of 460 standards of lumber, a straggler of convoy SC 7 comprising 35 ships. The Master, Capt Robert C. Stonehouse, and 13 crew were rescued by HM corvette *BLUEBELL* 925/40 (K.80) (Lt-Cdr Robert E. Sherwood RNR) and landed at Gourock. 7 crew were lost.

## CANADIAN NATIONAL STEAMSHIPS LIMITED – MONTREAL
Lady Somers Ltd

*LADY SOMERS* • GRT 8194 • Built 1929
15.7.41: Torpedoed and sunk by Italian submarine *MOROSINI* (Fraternale), in the
Atlantic SE of the Azores in position 37.12N 20.32W. Lost while employed by the
Admiralty as an Ocean Boarding Ship (F.109). Cdr George L. Dunbar and crew of 174
were rescued by Spanish tanker *CAMPECHE* 6382/34 and transferred to British ship
*PROCRIS* 1033/24.

**Lady Hawkins Ltd**

*LADY HAWKINS* • GRT 7988 • Built 1928 (Canadian)
19.1.42: Torpedoed and sunk by German submarine U-66 (Zapp), part of 'Operation
Paukenschlag' (Drumbeat), the first wave of five U-boats, in the Atlantic about 150 miles
from Cape Hatteras, North Carolina, in position 35.00N 72.30W while sailing
independently on a voyage from Halifax NS and Boston, Mass. to Bermuda, with 212
passengers and 2908 tons of general cargo. The Master, Capt Huntly Osborne Giffen, 85
crew, 1 gunner, 2 DBS and 162 passengers were lost. The Chief Officer, 21 crew and 49
passengers were rescued after 5 days by US ship *COAMO* 7057/25 and landed at Puerto
Rico 28.1.42. The Chief Officer Percy A. Kelly was awarded the MBE and the Lloyd's War
Medal for bravery at sea.

**Lady Drake Ltd**

*LADY DRAKE* • GRT 7985 • Built 1928 (Canadian)
5.5.42: Torpedoed and sunk by German submarine U-106 (Rasch), in the Atlantic about 90
miles N of Bermuda, in position 35.43N 64.43W while sailing independently on a voyage
from Bermuda 4.5.42 to St John's, Newfoundland, with 147 passengers. The Master, Capt
Percy A. Kelly, 114 crew and 141 passengers were rescued by US minesweeper *OWL* 840/18
(AM.2) and landed at Bermuda. 6 crew and 6 passengers were lost.

**Canadian Transporter Ltd**

*CORNWALLIS* ex-*CANADIAN TRANSPORTER* • GRT 5458 • Built 1921 (Canadian)
3.12.44: Torpedoed and sunk by German submarine U-1230 (Hilbig), in the Bay of
Fundy NW of Yarmouth, Nova Scotia, in position 43.59N 68.20W while sailing
independently on a voyage from Barbados, BWI to St John, New Brunswick, with a cargo
of bagged sugar and molasses in barrels. The Master, Capt Emerson Horace Robinson, 35
crew and 7 gunners were lost. 5 survivors were rescued by the fishing boat *NOTRE DAME*
and landed at Rockland, Maine. U-1230, under the command of Kapitänleutnant Hans
Hilbig, surrendered at Wilhelmshaven on 9.5.45. U-1230 sailed from Cairnryan, Loch
Ryan, on 17.12.45, towed by HM frigate *CUBITT* 1300/43 (K.512) (Lt G.D. Gregory),
and was sunk by gunfire the same day in the Atlantic WNW of Bloody Foreland, in
position 55.50N 10.05W, one of 116 U-boats disposed of by the Royal Navy in
'Operation Deadlight'.

## CANADIAN PACIFIC LIMITED – MONTREAL

*BEAVERBURN* • GRT 9874 • Built 1927
5.2.40: Torpedoed and sunk by German submarine U-41 (Mugler), in the Atlantic 150 miles
S of Berehaven, Co. Cork, in position 49.20N 10.07W while on a voyage from London to St
John, New Brunswick, with general cargo, part of convoy OB 84 comprising 20 ships. The
Master, Capt Thomas Jones, and 75 crew were rescued by British motor tanker
*NARRAGANSET* 10389/36 and landed at Falmouth. 1 crew was lost. Kapitänleutnant
Gustav-Adolf Mugler and crew of 48 were lost on the same day when U-41 was sunk in the
Atlantic 170 miles WSW of Land's End, in position 49.21N 10.40W by one of the convoy's
escort HM destroyer *ANTELOPE* 1350/29 (H.36) (Lt-Cdr T. White).

*EMPRESS OF BRITAIN* • GRT 42348 • Built 1931
26.10.40: Attacked by Focke-Wulf 200 Condor, pilot Oberleutnant Bernard Jope of 2/KG 40
Bomber Group based at Bordeaux-Merignac, France, bombed and set on fire in the Atlantic
about 70 miles NW of Aran Island, Co. Donegal, in position 55.16N 09.05W while sailing
independently on government service on a voyage from Port Tewfik, Egypt, and Cape Town
to Liverpool, carrying 419 crew, 224 military personnel and their families, 300 tons of sugar
and 300 tons of government stores. Taken in tow by ORP destroyer *BURZA* 1540/29, and
later joined by Admiralty tugs *MARAUDER* 840/38 (Lt W.J. Hammond) and *THAMES*
624/38 on passage to the Clyde. On 28.10.40 while under tow she was torpedoed and sunk
by German submarine U-32 (Jenisch), NW of Bloody Foreland, Co. Donegal in position
55.16N 09.50W. The Master, Capt Charles Havard Sapsworth, 390 crew, 2 gunners and 185
passengers were rescued by HM destroyer *ECHO* 1375/34 (H.23) (Cdr H.K. Spurgeon
RAN). 25 crew and 20 passengers were lost. This was the largest British merchant ship sunk
during the Second World War. U-32, commanded by Oberleutnant zur See Hans Jenisch
(Knight's Cross 7.10.40), was sunk on 30.10.40 in the Atlantic 200 miles W by N of Bloody
Foreland, in position 55.37N 12.20W by HM destroyers *HARVESTER* 1340/39 (H.87) ex-
HMS *HANDY* (Lt-Cdr M. Thornton) and *HIGHLANDER* 1340/39 (H.44) (Cdr W.A.
Dallmeyer). The U-boat commander and 28 crew were taken prisoner by *HARVESTER* and 4
crew by *HIGHLANDER* and landed at Greenock. 9 crew were lost.

*FORFAR* ex-*MONTROSE* laid down as *MONTMORENCY* • GRT 16402 • Built 1922
2.12.40: Torpedoed and sunk by the German submarine U-99 (Kretschmer), in the Atlantic
500 miles W of Ireland in position 54.35N 18.18W while employed as an Armed Merchant
Cruiser (F.30) escorting convoy HX 90 comprising 35 ships. Capt N.A.C. Walker, 35 officers
and 136 naval ratings were lost. 20 crew were rescued by HMCS destroyer *ST LAURENT*
1375/31 (H.83) ex-HMS *CYGNET* (Cdr H.G. De Wolf), 200 crew by HM destroyer
*VISCOUNT* 1325/17 (G.24) (Lt-Cdr M.S. Townsend OBE DSC) and 89 crew by British ship
*DURSLEY* 3862/29 and landed at Oban.

*BEAVERDALE* • GRT 9957 • Built 1928
1.4.41: Torpedoed and sunk by gunfire by German submarine U-48 (Schultze), in the North
Atlantic SE of Cape Farewell, in position 60.50N 29.29W while on a voyage from St John,
New Brunswick to Liverpool via Sydney CB, with general cargo, part of convoy SC 36
comprising 40 ships. The Master, Capt Charles Draper, and survivors landed at

Ondverdarnes, Iceland and the second boat with survivors was rescued by Icelandic trawler *GULLTOPPUR* 405/28, landed at Reykjavik, transferred to British ships *ROYAL SCOT* 1444/30 and *ROYAL ULSTERMAN* 3244/36 and landed at Greenock 17.4.41. 20 crew and 1 gunner were lost.

### PRINCESS MARGUERITE • GRT 5875 • Built 1925 (Canadian)

17.8.42: Torpedoed and sunk by German submarine U-83 (Kraus), in the Mediterranean NW of Port Said, in position 32.03N 32.47E while on government service on a voyage from Port Said to Famagusta, Cyprus, with 998 troops. The Master, Capt Richard Avery Leicester, 119 crew and 954 troops were rescued by HM destroyers *HERO* 1340/36 (H.99) (Lt M.W. Antrobus) and *KELVIN* 1690/39 (F.37) (Cdr M.S. Townsend OBE DSC) and landed at Port Said. 5 crew and 44 troops were lost. Kapitänleutnant Ulrich Worisshöfer and crew of 49 were lost on 4.3.43 when U-83 was sunk in the Mediterranean 80 miles NE of Oran, in position 37.10N 00.05E by Hudson 'V', pilot Sgt G. Jackimov of No. 500 'County of Kent' Squadron RAuxAF, based at Blida, Algeria.

### DUCHESS OF ATHOLL • GRT 20119 • Built 1928

10.10.42: Torpedoed and sunk by German submarine U-178 (Ibbeken), in the South Atlantic about 200 miles ENE of Ascension Island, in position 07.03S 11.12W while sailing independently on government service on a voyage from Durban and Cape Town 3.10.42 to the UK, with 534 passengers including women and children. The Master, Capt Arthur Henry Allinson Moore, 267 crew, 25 gunners and 534 passengers were rescued by HM ocean boarding vessel *CORINTHIAN* 3196/38 (F.103) (Cdr E.J.R. Pollitt), landed at Freetown 14.10.42, transferred to Union Castle liner *CAERNARVON CASTLE* 20122/26 and sailed 15.10.42 en route for Glasgow. 5 crew were lost.

### WINNIPEG II ex-*PAIMPOL* ex-*WINNIPEG* ex-*JACQUES CARTIER*
### GRT 8379 • Built 1918

22.10.42: Torpedoed and sunk by German submarine U-443 (v. Puttkamer), part of the 'Puma' patrol group of thirteen U-boats, in the Atlantic W of Ireland, in position 49.51N 27.58W while on a voyage from Liverpool 15.10.42 to St John, New Brunswick, with 68 passengers and 3000 tons of general cargo, part of convoy ON 139 comprising 38 ships. The Master, Capt Oswald Franklin Pennington DSC, crew of 113, 10 gunners and 68 passengers were rescued by HMCS corvette *MORDEN* 925/41 (K.170) (Lt Jack J. Hodgkinson) and landed at St John's, Newfoundland 25.10.42.

### EMPRESS OF CANADA • GRT 21517 • Built 1922

14.3.43: Torpedoed and sunk by Italian submarine *LEONARDO DA VINCI* (Gazzana), in the South Atlantic about 420 miles SSW of Cape Palmas, in position 01.13S 09.57W while sailing independently on government service on a voyage from Durban to Takoradi and the UK, with 1528 passengers including military personnel and Italian prisoners-of-war. The Master, Capt George Goold OBE, 273 crew, 26 gunners and 1188 passengers were rescued by HM destroyer *BOREAS* 1360/30 (H.77) (Lt-Cdr E.L. Jones DSC), HM ocean boarding vessel *CORINTHIAN* 3198/38 (F.103) (Cdr E.J.R Pollitt), HM corvettes *CROCUS* 925/40 (K.49) (Lt J.H. Holm DSC RNZNR) and *PETUNIA* 925/40 (K.79) (Lt G.E. Newey) and landed at Freetown. 44 crew and 348 passengers were lost.

## MOWT

**FORT RICHEPANSE** ex-*BELFAST* • GRT 3485 • Built 1936
3.9.41: Torpedoed and sunk by German submarine U-567 (Fahr), in the Atlantic 450 miles SW of Bloody Foreland, in position 52.15N 21.10W while sailing indpendently on a voyage from Montreal to Liverpool, with 12 passengers and 2890 tons of general cargo including eggs and mail. The Master, Capt Charles Draper, 35 crew and 5 passengers were lost. 10 crew, 5 gunners and 7 passengers were rescued by ORP destroyers *GARLAND* 1335/35 (H.37) and *PIORUN* 1690/40 ex-HMS *NERISSA*, and landed at Greenock. Kapitänleutnant Engelbert Endrass was awarded the Knight's Cross (5.9.40) with Oak Leaves (10.6.41). Crew of 46 were lost on 21.12.41 when U-567 was pursuing convoy HG 76 comprising 32 ships and was sunk in the Atlantic 500 miles W by N of Cape Finisterre, in position 44.02N 20.10W by HM sloop *DEPTFORD* 990/35 (L.53) (Lt Cdr H.C. White) and HM corvette *SAMPHIRE* 925/41 (K.128) (Lt-Cdr F.T. Renny).

**EMPIRE THRUSH** ex-*LORAIN* • GRT 6160 • Built 1919
14.4.42: Torpedoed and sunk by German submarine U-203 (Mützelburg), part of 'Operation Paukenschlag' (Drumbeat), the fourth wave of eleven U-boats, in the Atlantic near Cape Hatteras, in position 35.08N 75.18W while sailing independently on a voyage from Tampa, Florida, to the Mersey via Halifax NS, with a cargo of 5000 tons of rock phosphate, 740 tons of TNT and 2800 tons of citrus pulp. The Master, Capt G. Frisk, crew of 47 and 7 gunners were rescued by US ship *EVELYN* 3140/12 and landed at Norfolk, Virginia.

**EMPIRE REINDEER** ex-*CLAIRTON* • GRT 6259 • Built 1922
10.8.42: Torpedoed and sunk by German submarine U-660 (Baur), in the Atlantic S of Iceland, in position 57.00N 22.30W while on a voyage from Montreal to Hull via Sydney CB 31.7.42, with 5950 tons of general cargo and government stores, part of convoy SC 94 comprising 30 ships. The Master, Capt William Edward Bacon, crew of 55 and 9 gunners were rescued by HM corvettes *DIANTHUS* 925/40 (K.95) (Lt-Cdr C.E. Bridegman) and *NASTURTIUM* 925/40 (K.107) (Lt C.D. Smith DSC) ex-French *LA PAIMPOLAISE* and landed at Liverpool 14.8.42.

**EMPIRE UNION** ex-*MYRICA* ex-*SISTIANA* ex-*SALVORE* • GRT 5952 • Built 1924
27.12.42: Torpedoed and sunk by German submarine U-356 (Ruppelt), part of the 'Spitz' (Sharp) patrol group of ten U-boats, in the Atlantic NNE of the Azores, in position 47.30N 24.30W while on a voyage from London to St John, New Brunswick via Loch Ewe 19.12.42, with a part cargo of 940 tons general including government stores, part of convoy ONS 154 comprising 45 ships. The Master, Capt Hubert Arthur MacCallum, 4 crew and 1 gunner were lost. 59 crew and 4 gunners were rescued by rescue ship *TOWARD* 1571/23 (Capt Gordon K. Hudson) and landed at Halifax NS 9.1.43. The Italian *SISTIANA* was taken as a prize on 10.6.40 at Table Bay by the South African Navy.

## CAPPER, ALEXANDER & CO. LTD – LONDON
**Alexander Shipping Co. Ltd**

**LEDBURY** ex-*ODESSA* ex-*PODESTA* • GRT 3528 • Built 1912
24.10.39: Torpedoed and sunk by German submarine U-37 (Hartmann), in the Atlantic 100 miles W of Gibraltar, in position 36.01N 07.22W while sailing independently on a voyage

from Toulon to Burntisland, with a cargo of 5800 tons of bauxite. The Master, Capt Norman Rice, and crew of 30 were rescued by US ship *CROWN CITY* 5433/20 and landed at Gibraltar.

*AYLESBURY* • GRT 3944 • Built 1932
9.7.40: Torpedoed and sunk by German submarine U-43 (Ambrosius), in the Atlantic about 200 miles SW of Ireland, in position 48.39N 13.55W while sailing independently on a voyage from Buenos Aires to Avonmouth, with general cargo and grain. The Master, Capt Theodore Pryser, and crew of 34 were rescued by HM destroyers *HARVESTER* 1340/39 (H.19) (Lt-Cdr M. Thornton) and *HAVELOCK* 1340/39 (H.88) (Capt E.B.K. Stevens DSC) ex-Brazilian *JUTAHY*, and landed at Liverpool.

*WOODBURY* • GRT 4434 • Built 1936
18.7.40: Torpedoed and sunk by German submarine U-99 (Kretschmer), in the Atlantic about 300 miles W of Land's End, in position 50.46N 13.56W while sailing independently on a voyage from Uriburu, Argentina, to Manchester, with a cargo of 3000 tons of tinned meat, 2500 tons of wheat and 2500 tons of general cargo. The Master, Capt Norman Rice, and 18 crew landed at Castletown Berehaven, Co. Cork and 16 crew landed at Cahiriveen, Co. Kerry 19.7.40.

*BIBURY* • GRT 4616 • Built 1929
2.9.40: Torpedoed and sunk by German submarine U-46 (Endrass), in the Atlantic SSW of Rockall, in position 55.14N 16.40W while sailing independently on a voyage from Cardiff to Buenos Aires, with a cargo of coal, dispersed on 30.8.40 from convoy OB 205 comprising 33 ships. The Master, Capt James Ellerby Hunter, and crew of 35 were lost.

*TEWKESBURY* ex-*GLOCLIFFE* • GRT 4601 • Built 1927
21.5.41: Torpedoed and sunk by gunfire by German submarine U-69 (Metzler), in the Atlantic SW of Monrovia, in position 05.49N 24.09W while sailing independently on a voyage from Rosario and Montevideo to Oban via St Vincent, with 7477 tons of general cargo including tinned meat and wheat. The Master, Capt Theodore Pryse OBE, and 19 crew were rescued by US ship *EXHIBITOR* 6736/40, transferred to HM armed merchant cruiser *CILICIA* 11100/38 (F.54) (Capt V.B. Cardwell) and landed at Freetown. 22 crew were rescued by US ship *KNOXVILLE CITY* 5686/21 and landed at Cape Town. Korvettenkapitän Jost Metzler (Knight's Cross 28.7.41) also sank on 21.5.41 the unarmed US merchant ship *ROBIN MOOR* ex-*EXMOOR* 4999/19 (Capt Edward W. Myers) while en route from New York to Cape Town, with 5100 tons of general cargo. This was the first US ship to be sunk by a U-boat before the United States of America declared war on Germany on 11.12.41.

*NEWBURY* • GRT 5102 • Built 1927
15.9.41: Torpedoed and sunk by German submarine U-94 (Ites), in the Atlantic SE of Cape Farewell, in position 54.39N 28.04W while on a voyage from Cardiff to Buenos Aires, with a cargo of 6800 tons of coal, a straggler from convoy ON 14 comprising 47 ships. The Master, Capt Theodore Pryse OBE, crew of 38 and 6 gunners were lost.

*CHARLBURY* • GRT 4836 • Built 1940
28.5.42: Torpedoed and sunk by gunfire by Italian submarine *BARBARIGO* (Grossi), in the South Atlantic NE of Recife, in position 06.22S 29.44W while sailing independently on a

voyage from Cardiff 5.5.42 and Belfast Lough 9.5.42 to Buenos Aires, with a cargo of 8518 tons of coal, dispersed on 17.5.42 from convoy ON 93 comprising 25 ships. The Master, Capt William Laidler, crew of 36 and 5 gunners were rescued on 1.6.42 by Panamanian ship *OMAHA* ex-*FRODE* 2114/18 and landed at Recife 1.6.42. 2 crew were lost. Lt Roberto Rigoli and crew were lost when the *BARBARIGO* was sunk on 18.6.43 in the Bay of Biscay 100 miles NW of Cape Ortegal by two Whitleys 'J' and 'L' LA814, pilots P/O Orr and P/O H. Martin of No. 10 OTU, RAF Bomber Command, based at St Eval.

**SHAFTESBURY** • GRT 4284 • Built 1923
12.7.42: Torpedoed and sunk by German submarine U-116 (v. Schmidt), part of the 'Hai' (Shark) patrol group of six U-boats, in the Atlantic 430 miles 115° from Las Palmas, Canary Islands, in position 31.42N 25.30W while sailing independently on a voyage from Newport, Mon. 29.6.42 and Belfast Lough 2.7.42 to Buenos Aires, with a cargo of 5700 tons of coal, dispersed from convoy OS 33 comprising 41 ships. The Master, Capt Uriel Eynon, was taken prisoner, landed at Lorient 23.8.42 and was then taken to Milag Nord. The Chief Officer and 20 survivors landed at Villa Cisneros, Spanish Sahara, and were brought to Las Palmas. The 2nd Officer and 22 survivors were rescued on 23.7.42 in position 28.15N 22.15W by Blue Star ship *TUSCAN STAR* 11449/30, transferred to HM sloop *FOLKESTONE* 1045/30 (L.22) (Cdr J.G.C. Gibson OBE) and landed at Freetown. U-116, commanded by Oberleutnant zur See Wilhelm Grimme, and crew of 54 were lost sometime after 6.10.42 W of the Bay of Biscay by an unknown cause.

**KINGSBURY** • GRT 4898 • Built 1937
17.3.43: Torpedoed and sunk by German submarine U-338 (Kinzel), part of the 'Stürmer' (Attacker) patrol group of eighteen U-boats, in the Atlantic W of Ireland, in position 51.55N 32.41W while on a voyage from Port Harcourt to London via New York 5.3.42, with 2 passengers and a cargo of West African produce and 2000 tons of bauxite, part of convoy SC 122 comprising 51 ships. The Master, Capt William Laidler, 36 crew, 6 gunners and 1 passenger were rescued by rescue ship *ZAMALEK* 1567/21 (Capt Owen Charles Morris DSO) and landed at Gourock 22.3.43. 3 crew and 1 passenger were lost.

**HOLMBURY** ex-*WIRRAL* • GRT 4566 • Built 1925
5.5.43: Torpedoed and sunk by German submarine U-123 (v. Schroeter), in the Atlantic about 170 miles W of Cape Palmas, in position 04.30N 10.20W while sailing independently on a voyage from Buenos Aires and Montevideo 17.4.43 to the UK via Freetown, with 7798 tons of general cargo. The Master, Capt John Bryce Lawson, was taken prisoner, landed at Lorient 8.6.43 and taken to Milag Nord. 37 crew and 6 gunners landed at Tradetown, Liberia. 2 crew were lost.

## CARRICK F. & CO. LTD – NEWCASTLE UPON TYNE
## MOWT

**EMPIRE THUNDER** • GRT 5965 • Built 1941
6.1.41: Torpedoed and sunk by German submarine U-124 (Schulz), in the Atlantic NNE of Rockall, in position 59.14N 12.43W while sailing independently on a voyage from Sunderland to William Head, Washington via Oban, in ballast, dispersed from convoy OB

269 comprising 26 ships owing to engine breakdown. The Master, Capt William Dowell, and 29 crew were rescued by HM armed boarding ship *KINGSTON ONYX* 357/28 (Lt R. Walgate) and landed at Stornoway, Hebrides 8.1.41. 9 crew were lost.

## CEREAL TRADE & SHIPPING CO. LTD – LONDON

*START POINT* ex-*BRETWALDA* • GRT 5293 • Built 1919
10.11.42: Torpedoed and sunk by German submarine U–128 (Heyse), in the Atlantic SW of the Cape Verde Islands, in position 13.12N 27.25W while sailing independently on a voyage from Barry Dock to Freetown via Milford Haven 22.10.42, with a cargo of 6280 tons of coal, dispersed from convoy ON 141 comprising 59 ships. The Master, David George Evans, 38 crew and 7 gunners were rescued after 12 days by British ship *ESKDALEGATE* 4250/30 and landed at Pernambuco. The Chief Officer and Chief Engineer were taken prisoner, landed at Lorient 15.1.43 and taken to Milag Nord. 2 crew were lost.

## CHAMBERS, JAMES & CO. LTD – LIVERPOOL
**Lancashire Shipping Co. Ltd**

*WRAY CASTLE* • GRT 4253 • Built 1938
3.5.41: Torpedoed and sunk by German submarine U–103 (Schütze), in the Atlantic 110 miles SSW of Freetown, in position 06.48N 13.55W while sailing independently on a voyage from Port Louis, Mauritius, to the UK via Cape Town and Freetown, with a cargo of 6800 tons of sugar. The Master, Capt Gerald T. Dobson, 49 crew and 6 gunners were rescued by Portuguese ship *ANGOLA* 7884/12, landed at St Thomas, Gulf of Guinea, and later brought to Freetown by Portuguese ship *LOURENCO MARQUES* 6281/05. 1 crew was lost.

*MUNCASTER CASTLE* • GRT 5853 • Built 1928
30.3.42: Torpedoed and sunk by German submarine U–68 (Merten), in the Atlantic SSW of Monrovia, in position 02.02N 12.02W while sailing independently on government service on a voyage from Glasgow to Colombo via Freetown 28.3.42 and Cape Town, with 265 passengers, 2 naval signalmen and 3000 tons of government stores. The Master, Capt Harold William Harper, 69 crew, 11 gunners, naval signalmen and 246 passengers were rescued by HM corvette *AUBRIETIA* 925/40 (K.96) (Lt-Cdr V.F. Smith DSO) and Greek ship *ANN STATHATOS* 5685/18 and landed at Freetown. 4 crew, 1 gunner and 19 passengers were lost. Capt H.W. Harper was awarded the Lloyd's War Medal for bravery at sea.

## MOWT

*FORT LONGUEUIL* • GRT 7128 • Built 1942
19.9.43: Torpedoed and sunk by German submarine U–532 (Junker), part of the 'Monsun' (Monsoon) patrol group of nine U-boats, in the Indian Ocean SW of Chagos Archipelago, in position 10.00S 68.00E while sailing independently on a voyage from Kosseir, Egypt, and Aden to Fremantle, Port Kemble and Newcastle NSW, with a cargo of 8475 tons of phosphate. The Master, Capt George Cardno Edward, 46 crew and 10 gunners were lost. Two Indian crewmen on a life raft drifted ashore after 134 days on an unknown island on 1.2.44 and were taken prisoner by the Japanese.

## CHAPMAN, R. & SONS – NEWCASTLE UPON TYNE

*CLEARTON* • GRT 5219 • Built 1919

1.7.40: Torpedoed and sunk by German submarine U–102 (v. Klot-Heydenfeldt), in the Atlantic 180 miles W of Ushant, in position 47.53N 09.30W while on a voyage from Rosario to Manchester via Freetown 15.6.40, with a cargo of 7320 tons of cereals, a straggler from convoy SL 36 comprising 41 ships. The Master, Capt John Edward Elsdon, 24 crew and 1 gunner were rescued by HM destroyer *VANSITTART* 1120/19 (D.64) (Lt-Cdr R.G. Knowling) and landed at Plymouth. 8 crew were lost. Kapitänleutnant Harro von Klot-Heydenfeldt and crew of 42 were lost when U–102 was sunk in the Atlantic 210 miles W of Ushant, in position 48.33N 10.26W on the same day by *VANSITTART*.

*TIBERTON* • GRT 5225 • Built 1920

14.2.40: Torpedoed and sunk by German submarine U–23 (Kretschmer), in the North Sea E of the Orkney Islands, in position 58.55N 01.53W while sailing independently on a voyage from Narvik to Middlesbrough, with a cargo of iron ore. The Master, Capt Hugh Mason, and crew of 32 were lost.

*MABRITON* • GRT 6694 • Built 1920

25.9.40: Torpedoed and sunk by German submarine U–32 (Jenisch), in the Atlantic WSW of Rockall, in position 56.12N 23.00W while on a voyage from the Tyne to Father Point, New Brunswick, for orders, in ballast, dispersed on 23.9.40 from convoy OB 216 comprising 27 ships. The Master, Capt Reginald Patrick, 23 crew and 1 gunner were rescued: the Master and 17 survivors by HM survey ship *JASON* 835/37 (Lt-Cdr R.E. Terry) and 7 more survivors on 30.9.40 by HM sloop *ROCHESTER* 1105/31 (L.50) (Cdr G.E. Renwick) and landed at Londonderry. 12 crew were lost.

*CARLTON* • GRT 5162 • Built 1924

20.12.40: Torpedoed and sunk by Italian submarine *PIETRO CALVI* (Caridi), in the Atlantic NW of Rockall, in position 58.30N 18.30W while on a voyage from Newport, Mon. to Buenos Aires, with a cargo of 6545 tons of coal, dispersed on 19.12.40 from convoy OB 260 comprising 27 ships. The Master, Capt William Learmount, 29 crew and 1 gunner were lost. 4 crew were rescued by British ship *ANTIOPE* 4545/30.

*KORANTON* • GRT 6695 • Built 1920

27.3.41: Torpedoed and sunk by German submarine U–98 (Gysae), in the Atlantic SSW of Reykjavik, in position 59.00N 27.00W while on a voyage from Philadelphia to Hull via Sydney CB, with general cargo, a straggler from convoy SC 25 comprising 32 ships. The Master, Capt Charles Edward Howard, and crew of 33 were lost.

*EARLSTON* • GRT 7195 • Built 1941

5.7.42: Damaged by bombs from Ju-88s of 111/KG 30 Bomber Group based at Banak, North Cape, later torpedoed and sunk by German submarine U–334 (Siemon), in the Barents Sea NE of North Cape, in position 74.54N 37.40E while on government service on a voyage from Glasgow to Archangel via Reykjavik 27.6.42, with 5 passengers and a cargo of 2005 tons military stores and 195 vehicles, 33 aircraft and a steam launch on deck, dispersed from the ill-fated convoy PQ 17 comprising 36 ships. The Master, Capt Hilmar John Stenwick DSC, and 3 gunners were taken prisoner. The 2nd Officer and 20 survivors landed on the Rabachi Peninsula after 7 days; the Chief Officer and 26 survivors landed on Norwegian-occupied territory. U-334 commanded by Oberleutnant zur See Heinz Ehrich and crew of 46 were lost on 14.6.43 in the Atlantic 750 miles W of the Butt of Lewis, in position 58.16N 28.20W sunk by HM frigate *JED* 1370/42 (K.235) (Lt-Cdr R.C. Freaker) and HM sloop *PELICAN* 1200/38 (L.86) (Cdr J.G. Gould), part of the 1st Support Group, escorting convoy ON 10 comprising 73 ships.

### PETERTON • GRT 5221 • Built 1919
17.9.42: Torpedoed and sunk by German submarine U-109 (Bleichrodt), in the Atlantic NW of the Cape Verde Islands, in position 18.45N 29.15W while sailing independently on a voyage from London, Hull and Oban to Buenos Aires via Oban 1.9.42, with a cargo of 5758 tons of coal, dispersed from convoy OG 80 comprising 29 ships. Capt Thomas William Marrie was taken prisoner, landed at Lorient 6.10.42 and taken to Milag Nord. 22 crew were adrift for 49 days in an open boat rescued by HM trawler *CANNA* 545/40 (T.161) (Lt W.N. Bishop-Laggett) and landed at Freetown, and 12 further crew were rescued by British ship *EMPIRE WHIMBREL* 5983/19 and landed at Buenos Aires 11.10.42. 8 crew were lost. Korvettenkapitän Heinrich Bleichrodt was awarded the Knight's Cross (24.10.40) with Oak Leaves (23.9.42). U-109, commanded by Oberleutnant zur See Joachim Schramm, and crew of 51 were lost while shadowing convoy HX 236 comprising 46 ships on 4.5.43, sunk in the Atlantic 600 miles WSW of Cape Clear, in position 47.22N 22.40W by Liberator 'P' FL955, pilot P/O J.C. Green of No. 86 Squadron RAF, based at Aldergrove, Co. Antrim, part of 15 Group.

## MOWT

### EMPIRE DEW • GRT 7005 • Built 1941
12.6.41: Torpedoed and sunk by German submarine U-48 (Schultze), in the Atlantic N of the Azores, in position 51.09N 30.16W while sailing independently on a voyage from the Tyne to Father Point, New Brunswick, for orders, in ballast, dispersed from convoy OG 64 comprising 52 ships. The Master, Capt John Edward Elsdon, 16 crew and 2 gunners were rescued by the RNoN destroyer *ST ALBANS* 1060/18 (I.15) ex-US four-stack *THOMAS* and landed at Liverpool. 23 crew were lost. Kapitänleutnant Herbert Schultze (Knight's Cross 1.3.40; with Oak Leaves 12.6.41) returned to Kiel on 22.6.41. U-48 was then decommissioned after her twelfth patrol having sunk fifty-five British, Allied and Neutral ships: a total of 307,515 gross tonnage. U-48 was later scuttled on 3.5.45 at Neustadt, Baltic Sea, and was the most successful German submarine of the Second World War, in terms of the number of ships and tonnage sunk.

### FORT GOOD HOPE • GRT 7130 • Built 1942
11.6.42: Torpedoed and sunk by German submarine U-159 (Witte), in the Atlantic NNW of Colon, Panama, in position 10.N 80.16W while sailing independently on a voyage from Vancouver BC and Cristobal 10.6.42 to Garston via Key West, with a cargo of 9250 tons of wheat, timber, lead and zinc. The Master, Capt Horatio Gentles, 40 crew and 4 gunners were rescued by the US gunboat *ERIE* 1900/36 (PG.50) and landed at Cristobal. 2 crew were lost.

## CHARLTON, McALLUM & CO. LTD – NEWCASTLE UPON TYNE
Charlton SS Co. Ltd

*HAZELSIDE* • GRT 4646 • Built 1928
24.9.39: Torpedoed and sunk by German submarine U-31 (Habekost), in the Atlantic SE of Fastnet, in position 51.17N 09.22W while sailing independently on a voyage from Tacoma, Washington, to Garston and Liverpool, with a cargo of timber, pulp and wheat. The Master, Capt Charles Henry Davis, and 11 crew were lost. 22 crew landed at Schull near Baltimore, Co. Cork.

*HAZELSIDE* • GRT 5297 • Built 1940
28.10.41: Torpedoed and sunk by German submarine U-68 (Merten), in the South Atlantic 600 miles SE of St Helena, in position 23.10S 01.36E while sailing independently on a voyage from Cardiff to Alexandria via Durban, carrying 3476 tons of general cargo including military stores. The Master, Capt Charles Knight Evans, 37 crew and 6 gunners were rescued by British ship *MALAYAN PRINCE* 8593/26 and landed at Cape Town. 2 crew were lost. Capt C.K. Evans was awarded the Lloyd's War Medal for bravery at sea.

*HOLLINSIDE* • GRT 4172 • Built 1930
3.9.42: Torpedoed and sunk by German submarine U-107 (Gelhaus), in the Atlantic near Setubal, Portugal, in position 38.00N 09.00W while on a voyage from Lisbon 2.9.42 to Almeria, in ballast, part of an unescorted convoy of 5 ships. The Master, Capt Edgar Campling, 33 crew, 8 gunners and 6 crew from British ship *AVILA STAR* 14443/23 were rescued by Spanish trawlers and landed at Lisbon. 3 crew were lost.

## MOWT

*FORT RAMPART* • GRT 7134 • Built 1943
17.4.43: Torpedoed and damaged by German submarine U-628 (Hasenchar), later sunk by *coups de grâce* from U-628 and U-226 (Borchers), in the Atlantic 900 miles ENE of the Azores, in position 47.22N 21.58W while on a voyage from Port Alberni BC to Hull via Panama and New York 6.4.43, with a cargo of 8700 tons of lumber and generals, part of convoy HX 233 comprising 54 ships. The Master, Capt William Henry Stein, 40 crew, 6 gunners and 3 DBS were rescued by HMCS corvette *ARVIDA* 925/40 (K.113) (Lt D.G. King) and landed at Greenock. 6 crew were lost. Oberleutnant zur See Albrecht Gänge and crew of 51 were lost on 6.11.43 when U-226, part of the 'Tirpitz' group of twenty-two U-boats, was sunk in the Atlantic 500 miles E by S of Cape Race, in position 44.49N 41.13W by HM sloops *KITE* 1350/42 (U.87) (Cdr W.E.R. Segrave), *STARLING* 1350/42 (U.66) (Capt Frederic John Walker CB DSO DSC) and *WOODCOCK* 1250/42 (U.90) (Lt-Cdr C. Gwinner).

*FORT YALE* • GRT 7134 • Built 1942
23.8.44: Torpedoed and sunk by German submarine U-480 (Förster), in the English Channel 17 miles SE of St Catherine's Point, Isle of Wight, in position 50.23N 00.55W while under tow from Juno beach, Normandy, to Portsmouth by HM tug *HUDSON* 294/39 (W.02) and US tug *FARALLON* 1117/43, having previously sustained mine damage while part of convoy

ETC 72. The Master, Capt George William Mortimer, crew of 57 and 8 gunners were rescued by 3 Landing Craft Infantry and landed at Portsmouth. 1 naval signalman was lost.

## CHELLEW NAVIGATION CO. LTD – CARDIFF

*PENSILVA* ex-*BRN-Y-MOR* • GRT 4258 • Built 1929
19.11.39: Torpedoed and sunk by gunfire by German submarine U-49 (v. Gossler), in the Atlantic NW of Cape Ortegal, in position 46.51N 11.36W while on a voyage from Durban to Rouen and Dunkirk via Gibraltar, with a cargo of 6985 tons of maize, part of convoy HG 7 comprising 32 ships. The Master, Capt Alfred Montague Brockwell, and crew were rescued by HM destroyer *ECHO* 1375/34 (H.23) (Cdr S.H.K. Spurgeon RAN), transferred to HM destroyer *WANDERER* 1100/19 (D.74) (Cdr R.F. Morice) and landed at Plymouth. U-49, commanded by Kapitänleutnant Kurt von Gossler, was sunk on 15.4.40 in the North Sea in the entrance to Vaags Fjord, Norway, in position 68.53N 16.59E by HM destroyers *BRAZEN* 1360/30 (H.80 (Lt-Cdr M. Culme-Seymour) and *FEARLESS* 1375/34 (H.67) (Cdr K.L. Harkness). The U-boat commander and 39 crew were taken prisoner by *FEARLESS* and *BRAZEN*, transferred to HM cruiser *AURORA* 5270/36 (12) (Capt L.H.K. Hamilton DSO) and finally transferred to HM battleship *VALIANT* 32700/14 (02) (Capt H.B. Rawlings OBE). 2 crew were lost.

*PENROSE* • GRT 4393 • Built 1928
3.9.42: Torpedoed and sunk by German submarine U-107 (Gelhaus), in the Atlantic 3 miles off Cape Sines, Portugal, in position 38.00N 09.00W while on a voyage from Lisbon to Gibraltar, in ballast, part of a convoy of 5 unescorted ships. The Master, Capt Dudley Allan Nicholls, and crew of 49 were rescued by a Spanish trawler and landed at Lisbon.

*PENOLVER* • GRT 3721 • Built 1928
17.10.43: Struck a mine, laid on 9.10.43, by German submarine U-220 (Barber) and sank in the Atlantic W of St John's, Newfoundland, in position 47.19N 52.27W while on a voyage from Wabana, Conception Bay 19.10.43, to Sydney CB, with a cargo of 5300 tons of iron ore, part of convoy WB 65 comprising 7 ships. The Master, Capt George H. Naish, 12 crew and 1 gunner were rescued by HM trawler *MISCOU* 545/42 (T.277) ex-HMS *BOWELL* ex-HMS *CAMPENIA* and landed at St John's. 23 crew and 3 gunners were lost. Oberleutnant zur See (Reserve) Bruno Barber and crew of 50 were lost on 28.10.43 when U-220 was sunk by an Avenger, pilot Lt Franklin M. Murray and a Wildcat, pilot Ensign Harold L. Hanshuh of US Navy Composite Squadron VC-1 from US escort carrier *BLOCK ISLAND* 10900/43 (CVE.21) (Capt L.C. Ramsay), in the Atlantic 565 miles N by W of Flores, Azores, in position 48.53N 33.30W.

## MOWT

*EMPIRE DRUM* • GRT 7244 • Built 1942
24.4.42: Torpedoed and sunk by German submarine U-136 (Zimmermann), in the Atlantic N of Bermuda, in position 37.00N 69.15W while sailing independently on a voyage from New York 23.4.42 to Alexandria via Cape Town, with a cargo of government stores. The Master, Capt John Robert Miles, 32 crew and 6 gunners were

rescued by Swedish ship *VENEZIA* 1673/38 and landed at New York; 2 crew were rescued by a USN destroyer and landed at Norfolk, Virginia. Kapitänleutnant Heinrich Zimmermann and crew of 44 were lost while attacking convoy OS 33 comprising 41 ships on 11.7.42 when U-136 was sunk by HM frigate *SPEY* 1370/41 (K.246) (Cdr H.G. Boys-Smith), HM sloop *PELICAN* 1200/38 (L.86) (Cdr J.G. Gould) and Free French destroyer *LEOPARD* 2126/40 (Capt J. Evenou), in the Atlantic 295 miles N by W of Madeira, in position 33.30N 22.52W.

### OCEAN HONOUR • GRT 7174 • Built 1942
16.9.42: Torpedoed and sunk by gunfire by Japanese submarine I-29 (Izu), in the Gulf of Aden W of Socotra Island, in position 12.48N 50.50E while sailing independently on a voyage from Liverpool to Aden and Alexandria via Durban 3.9.42, with a cargo of 6000 tons of government stores including motor vehicles. The Master, Capt Percy Bond, 29 crew and 3 gunners landed on an isolated island, were rescued by RAF aircraft and brought to Aden. 15 crew and 5 gunners were lost.

## CHELLEW STEAMSHIP MANAGEMENT COMPANY – LONDON

### JUSTITIA • GRT 4562 • Built 1935
23.11.40: Torpedoed and sunk by German submarine U-100 (Schepke), in the Atlantic about 160 miles W of Bloody Foreland, Co. Donegal, in position 55.00N 13.10W while on a voyage from Savannah, Georgia, to London via Sydney CB 9.11.40, with a cargo of 7749 tons of timber, steel, turpentine and generals, part of convoy SC 11 comprising 33 ships. The Master, Capt David L. Davies, and 12 crew were lost. 25 crew and 1 gunner were rescued by HM sloop *ENCHANTRESS* 1190/34 (L.56) ex-HMS *BITTERN* (Cdr A.K. Scott-Moncrieff) and landed at Liverpool.

## CHINA NAVIGATION CO. LTD – LONDON

### SHUNTIEN • GRT 3059 • Built 1934
23.12.41: Torpedoed and sunk by German submarine U-559 (Heidtmann), in the Mediterranean NE of Tobruk, in position 32.06N 24.46E while on Admiralty service in convoy on a voyage from Tobruk to Alexandria, with 1100 German and Italian prisoners-of-war. On board were the Master, Capt William L. Shinn, crew of 69 and 18 gunners. The Master and 47 crew and an unknown number of gunners and prisoners were lost as rescue ship HM corvette *SALVIA* 925/40 (K.97) (Lt-Cdr J.I. Miller DSO DSC) was torpedoed and sunk by German submarine U-568 (Preuss) on 24.12.41 100 miles W of Alexandria, in position 31.46N 28.00E. A number of survivors were rescued by HM destroyer *HEYTHORP* 1050/40 (L.85) (Lt-Cdr R.S. Stafford).

### KWANGTUNG • GRT 2626 • Built 1921
5.1.42: Sunk by gunfire by Japanese submarine I-156 (Ohashi), in the Indian Ocean SE of Pangul, Java, in position 09.12S 111.10E while sailing independently on a voyage from Hong Kong and Sourabaya, Java, to Colombo, carrying 35 military personnel. The Master, Capt Frank N. Booth, and 49 survivors were rescued on 6.1.42 by Greek ship *HELLAS* 2081/16 and landed at Sourabaya. 48 crew and military personnel were lost.

*KAYING* • GRT 2626 Gt. • Built 1922
18.3.43: Torpedoed and sunk by German submarine U-593 (Kelbling), in the Mediterranean near Derna, Tripolitania, in position 32.59N 22.21E while on government service on a voyage from Benghazi 9.3.43 and Tripoli to Alexandria, in ballast. The Master, Capt R.H. Fairley, and 67 crew were rescued and landed at Alexandria. 7 crew and gunners were lost.

*HOIHOW* • GRT 2798 • Built 1933
2.7.43: Torpedoed and sunk by German submarine U-181 (Lüth), in the Indian Ocean 105 miles WNW of Mauritius, in position 19.30S 56.00E while sailing independently on government service on a voyage from Mauritius to Tamatave, Madagascar, with 48 passengers. The Master, Capt William Mackensie Christie, 90 crew, 7 gunners and 47 passengers were lost. 3 crew and 1 passenger were rescued by US ship *MORMACSWAN* 7194/40 and landed at Montevideo 25.7.43.

## CHINE SHIPPING CO. LTD – SWANSEA

*CANFORD CHINE* ex-*BRYNTAWE* • GRT 3364 • Built 1917
10.2.41: Torpedoed and sunk by German submarine U-52 (Salman), in the Atlantic W of the Hebrides, while on a voyage from Cardiff to Buenos Aires and Uriburu, with a cargo of coal, a straggler from convoy OG 52 comprising 45 ships. The Master, Capt Neil MacDonald, and crew of 34 were lost. U-52 was scuttled at Kiel on 3.5.45.

## MOWT

*INGER TOFT* ex-*ELPHINSTONE* ex-*VAN DYCK* • GRT 2190 • Built 1920
16.3.45: Torpedoed and sunk by German submarine U-722 (Reimers), in the Atlantic 3 miles 270° from Neirst Point, Isle of Skye, in position 57.25N 06.52W while on a voyage from Reykjavik to London, with a cargo of 885 tons of herring meal and cod liver oil in drums, part of convoy RU 156 comprising 6 ships. The Master, Capt N.M. Brinck, and crew of 29 were rescued by HM trawler *GRENADIER* 750/42 (Lt A.G. Day) and landed at Loch Ewe. Oberleutnant zur See Hans Reimers and crew of 42 were lost on 27.3.45 when U-722 was sunk by HM frigates *FITZROY* 1300/43 (K.553) (Lt-Cdr A.J.M. Miller), *REDMILL* 1300/43 (K.554) (Lt G. Pitt) and *BYRON* 1300/43 (K.508) (Lt J.B. Burfield), part of the 21st Escort Group, in the Minches, 23 miles SW of Dunvegan, Isle of Skye, in position 57.09N 06.55W.

## CLAN LINE OF STEAMERS LIMITED (CAYZER, IRVINE & CO. LTD) – LONDON

*CLAN CHISHOLM* • GRT 7256 • Built 1937
17.10.39: Torpedoed and sunk by German submarine U-48 (Schultze), in the Atlantic 150 miles NW of Cape Finisterre, in position 45.00N 15.00W while on a voyage from Calcutta to Liverpool and Glasgow, with a cargo of 9550 tons of generals including pig iron, jute and tea, part of convoy HG 3 comprising 25 ships. The Master, Capt Francis T. Stenson, and 41 crew were rescued by Swedish motor ship *BARDALAND* 2595/36 and landed at Kirkwall, 17 crew by Norwegian whaler *SKUDD* I 247/29 and 15 more after four days by British liner

*WARWICK CASTLE* 17383/39. 4 crew were lost. This was the first Clan Line ship lost in the Second World War.

**CLAN MENZIES** • GRT 7336 • Built 1938
29.7.40: Torpedoed and sunk by German submarine U-99 (Kretschmer), in the Atlantic 150 miles W of Loop Head, Co. Clare, in position 54.10N 12.00W while sailing independently on a voyage from Sydney NSW and Melbourne to Liverpool via Panama, with 8240 tons of general cargo including wheat, zinc and dried fruit. The Master, Capt William John Hughes, and 87 crew landed at Enniscrone, Co. Sligo. 6 crew were lost.

**CLAN MACPHEE** • GRT 6628 • Built 1911
16.8.40: Torpedoed and sunk by German submarine U-30 (Lemp), in the Atlantic 350 miles W of North Uist, Outer Hebrides, in position 57.30N 17.14W while on a voyage from Glasgow and Liverpool to Bombay and the coast of Malabar, with 6700 tons of general cargo, part of convoy OB 197 comprising 54 ships. The Master, Capt Thomas Philip B. Cranwell, and 66 crew were lost. 41 survivors were rescued by Hungarian ship *KELET* 4295/13. The *KELET* was sunk on 19.8.40 by German submarine UA (Cohausz) and 35 survivors from the *CLAN MACPHEE* were rescued by Norwegian ship *VAREGG* 943/10 and landed at Galway 26.8.40.

**CLAN OGILVY** • GRT 5802 • Built 1914
21.3.41: Torpedoed and sunk by German submarine U-105 (Schewe), in the Atlantic 182 miles 350° from St Antonio Island, Cape Verde Islands, in position 20.04N 25.45W while on a voyage from Chittagong to London and Glasgow via Freetown 13.3.41, with 5000 tons of general cargo including pig iron, groundnuts and tea, part of convoy SL 68 comprising 59 ships. The Master, Capt Edward Gough, and 3 crew were rescued by British ship *BATNA* 4399/28 and landed at Takoradi, and 20 further survivors rescued by Spanish ship *CABO VILLANO* 3755/20 landed at Santos. 61 crew were lost.

**CLAN MACDOUGALL** • GRT 6843 • Built 1929
31.5.41: Torpedoed and sunk by German submarine U-106 (Oesten), in the Atlantic N of the Cape Verde Islands, in position 16.50N 25.10W while sailing independently on a voyage from Glasgow to East London, South Africa, with 7500 tons of general cargo. The Master, Capt Cyril H. Parfitt, 74 crew and 10 gunners landed at San Antonio, Cape Verde Islands. 2 crew were lost.

**CLAN ROSS** • GRT 5897 • Built 1914
2.4.42: Torpedoed and sunk by Japanese submarine I-6 (Inaba), in the Arabian Sea 300 miles SW of Bombay, in position 15.55N 68.26E while sailing independently on a voyage from Liverpool 29.1.42 to Bombay and Cochin via Durban 19.3.42, with 3655 tons of general cargo and 1027 tons of explosives. The Master, Capt Gavin McColl, and 36 survivors were rescued by the Norwegian ship *L A CHRISTENSEN* 4362/25 and landed at Durban 20.4.42; 33 more survivors were rescued and landed at Bombay. 11 crew were lost.

**CLAN SKENE** ex-*HALOCRATES* ex-*CLAN SKENE* ex-*WAR ADDER* • GRT 5214 • Built 1919
10.5.42: Torpedoed and sunk by German submarine U-333 (Cremer), in the Atlantic 300 miles SE of Cape Hatteras, in position 31.43N 70.43W while sailing independently on a

voyage from Beira, Portuguese East Africa and Cape Town 15.4.42 to New York, with a part cargo of 2006 tons of chrome ore. The Master, Capt Edward Gough, and 72 survivors were rescued by US naval transport *McKEAN* 1020/18 (APD.5) and landed at San Juan, Puerto Rico. 9 crew were lost. Kapitänleutnant Hans Fiedler and crew of 44 were lost when U-333 was sunk on 31.7.44 by HM sloop *STARLING* 1350/42 (U.66) (Cdr N.A. Duck) and HM frigate *LOCH KILLIN* 1435/43 (K.391) (Lt-Cdr S. Darling) in the Atlantic 50 miles WSW of the Scilly Isles, in position 49.39N 07.28W. This was the first U-boat to be sunk by a 'Squid', a battery of three mortar type weapons. U-333 had previously been commanded by Kapitänleutnant Peter Erich Cremer, holder of the Knight's Cross (awarded 5.6.42), from August 1941 to October 1942 and June 1943 to June 1944.

### CLAN MACQUARRIE • GRT 6471 • Built 1913
13.6.42: Torpedoed and sunk by gunfire by Italian submarine *LEONARDO DA VINCI* (Longanesi-Cattani), in the Atlantic SW of Freetown, in position 05.30N 23.30W while sailing independently on a voyage from Bombay and Durban 28.5.42 to New York, in ballast. The Master, Capt Ronald Douglas, 82 crew and 6 gunners were saved. The Master and 60 survivors were rescued by French ship *DÉSIRADE* 9645/21 and landed at Cape Town, and 28 further survivors rescued by Norwegian tanker *CLARONA* 9412/28 landed at Port of Spain, Trinidad.

### CLAN MACNAUGHTON • GRT 6008 • Built 1921
1.8.42: Torpedoed and sunk by German submarine U-155 (Piening), in the Atlantic about 180 miles E of Tobago, in position 11.54N 54.25W while sailing independently on a voyage from Alexandria to New York via Freetown 22.7.42 and Trinidad, with a cargo of 10670 bales of cotton. The Master, Capt Robert John Wylie Bennett, and 28 survivors in his boat landed on Tobago Island; the Chief Officer and 24 survivors were rescued by British ship *EMPIRE BEDE* 6959/42 and landed at Port of Spain, Trinidad 5.8.42; the 3rd Mate and 22 survivors landed at Trinidad. 4 crew and 1 gunner were lost.

### CLAN MACWHIRTER ex-WILLCASINO ex-HALIZONES ex-YPRESVILLE
GRT 5941 • Built 1918
27.8.42: Torpedoed and sunk by German submarine U-156 (Hartenstein), part of the 'Eisbär' (Polarbear) patrol group of five U-boats, in the Atlantic 200 miles NW of Madeira, in position 35.45N 18.45W while on a voyage from Bombay, Durban and Bathurst 14.8.42 to Hull via Freetown, with a cargo of 2000 tons of manganese ore, 3500 tons of linseed, 2200 tons of pig iron and generals, a straggler from convoy SL 119 comprising 30 ships. The Master, Capt Roderick Sutherland Masters, 8 crew and 2 gunners were lost. 68 crew and 7 gunners were rescued by Portuguese sloop *PEDRO NUNES* 1090/35 (A.528) and landed at Funchal.

### CLAN MACTAVISH • GRT 7631 • Built 1921
8.10.42: Torpedoed and sunk by German submarine U-159 (Witte), part of the 'Eisbär' (Polarbear) patrol group of five U-boats, in the Indian Ocean 250 miles E of Cape of Good Hope, in position 34.55S 16.48E while sailing independently on a voyage from Beira and Durban 4.10.42 to New York via Trinidad, carrying 35 survivors from British ship *BORINGIA* 5821/30 and a cargo of 4597 tons of copper, 1180 tons of extract and 280 tons of generals. The Master, Capt Ernest Edwin Arthur, 51 crew, 2 gunners and 7 survivors from

the *BORINGIA* were lost. 36 crew, 3 gunners and 28 survivors were rescued by British ship *MATHERAN* 8007/42 and landed at Cape Town.

**CLAN MACTAGGART** • GRT 7622 • Built 1920
16.11.42: Torpedoed and sunk by German submarine U-92 (Oelrich), part of the 'Westwall' patrol group of thirteen U-boats, in the Atlantic about 50 miles SW of Cadiz, in position 36.08N 07.23W while on government service on a voyage from Gibraltar 15.11.42 to the Clyde, carrying 55 naval personnel, part of convoy MKS 1X comprising 29 ships. The Master, Capt Joseph Henry Crellin, 97 crew, 17 gunners and 54 naval personnel were rescued by HM corvette *COREOPSIS* 925/40 (K.32) (Lt A.H. Davies). The survivors were distributed by HMS *COREOPSIS* to HM escort sloops *LANDGUARD* 1546/30 (Y.56) (Lt-Cdr T.S.L. Fox Pitt) ex-USCG *SHOSHONE*, and *LULWORTH* 1546/28 (Y.60) (Lt-Cdr C. Gwinner DSO) ex-USCG *CHELAN* and landed at Londonderry. 34 lascars rescued by *LULWORTH* were transferred to British ship *HAVILDAR* 5407/40, sailing in the same convoy. 2 crew and 1 naval personnel were lost.

**CLAN MACFAYDEN** • GRT 6191 • Built 1923
27.11.42: Torpedoed and sunk by German submarine U-508 (Staats), in the Atlantic 95 miles SE of Galeota Point, Trinidad, in position 08.57N 59.48W while sailing independently on a voyage from Port Louis, Mauritius, to the UK via Cape Town, Pernambuco 17.11.42 and Trinidad, with a cargo of 6705 tons of sugar and 5 tons of hemp and rum. The Master, Capt Percy Edgar Williams, 82 crew and 7 gunners were lost. 3 crew and 1 gunner were rescued from a raft by British schooner *HARVARD* 114/91 and landed at Port of Spain 31.11.42.

**CLAN ALPINE** • GRT 5442 • Built 1918
13.3.43: Torpedoed and damaged by German submarine U-107 (Gelhaus), part of the 'Robbe' (Seal) patrol group of five U-boats, later sunk by HM sloop *SCARBOROUGH* 1045/30 (L.25) (Lt-Cdr E.B. Carnduff) in the Atlantic 190 miles W of Cape Finisterre, in position 42.45N 13.31W while on a voyage from Liverpool 6.3.43 to Walvis Bay, South West Africa and Port Sudan, Sudan, with 11,317 tons of general cargo including army and naval stores, part of convoy OS 44 comprising 48 ships. The Master, Capt Joseph Henry Crellin, 59 crew and 9 gunners were rescued by HMS *SCARBOROUGH*, transferred to British ship *PENDEEN* 4174/23 and landed at Gibraltar.

**CLAN MACPHERSON** • GRT 6940 • Built 1929
1.5.43: Torpedoed and sunk by German submarine U-515 (Henke), in the Atlantic 75 miles SW of Freetown, in position 07.58N 14.14W while on a voyage from Calcutta, Durban and Takoradi 26.4.43 to the UK via Freetown and Trinidad, with 8440 tons of general cargo including 2750 tons of pig iron, linseed, tea, jute, mica and groundnuts, part of convoy TS 37 comprising 19 ships. The Master, Capt Edward Gough, 126 crew, 7 gunners and 2 naval signalmen were rescued by HM trawler *ARRAN* 545/40 (T.06) (Lt D.S. Hutton) and landed at Freetown 1.5.43. 4 crew were lost.

**CLAN MACARTHUR** • GRT 10528 • Built 1936
11.8.43: Torpedoed and sunk by German submarine U-181 (Lüth), in the Indian Ocean 350 miles E of Farafangan, Madagascar, in position 23.00S 53.11E while sailing independently on a voyage from Glasgow to Port Louis, Mauritius via Durban 5.8.43, carrying 6 passengers and 6346 tons of general cargo including 5500 tons of military stores, dispersed from convoy DN

55 comprising 6 ships. The Master, Capt John Drayton Matthews, 70 crew and 6 passengers were rescued by Free French sloop *SAVORGNAN DE BRAZZA* 1969/31 and landed at Port Louis. 52 crew and 1 gunner were lost. U-181 was commanded by Kapitänleutnant Wolfgang Lüth, the first member of the U-boat arm to be awarded on 9.8.43 Diamonds to his Knight's Cross (24.10.40), Oak Leaves (13.11.42) and the Swords (15.4.43). The *CLAN MACARTHUR* was his last victim.

## CLARK & SERVICE – GLASGOW
### Ardan SS Co.

*ARDANBHAN* • GRT 4930 • Built 1929
26.12.40: Torpedoed and damaged by German submarine U-38 (Liebe) later sunk the same day by Italian submarine *ENRICO TAZZOLI* (Raccanelli), in the Atlantic 235 miles WNW of Rockall, in position 59.16N 20.27W while on a voyage from Hull to Mar del Plata, Argentine, with a cargo of about 6000 tons of coal, a straggler from convoy OB 263 comprising 26 ships. The Master, Capt William Alexander Mulveny, crew of 36 and 2 gunners were lost.

## CLAYMORE SHIPPING CO. LTD – CARDIFF

*DAYDAWN* • GRT 4768 • Built 1940
21.11.40: Torpedoed and sunk by German submarine U-103 (Schütze), in the Atlantic 250 miles W of Bloody Foreland, Co. Donegal, in position 56.30N 14.10W while on a voyage from Barry to Rio Santiago, Argentina, with a cargo of 6860 tons of coal, part of convoy OB.244 comprising 46 ships. The Master, Capt James Horsfield, and 20 crew were rescued by HM corvette *RHODODENDRON* 925/40 (K.78) (Lt-Cdr W.N.H. Faichney). 2 crew were lost.

*DAYROSE* • GRT 4113 • Built 1928
15.1.42: Torpedoed and sunk by German submarine U-552 (Topp), in the Atlantic W of Cape Race, in position 46.32N 53.00W while sailing independently on a voyage from St John's, Newfoundland to Portland, Maine via Halifax, in ballast. The Master, Capt Arthur Frederick Newman, 31 crew and 6 gunners were lost. 4 crew were rescued by US destroyers *ERICSSON* 1620/40 (DD-440) and *STOCKTON* 1620/41 (DD-646) and landed at Argentia, Newfoundland.

## MOWT

*EMPIRE SKY* • GRT 7455 • Built 1941
6.11.42: Torpedoed and sunk by German submarine U-625 (Benker), in the Greenland Sea S of Spitzbergen, in position 76.20N 17.30E while sailing independently on government service on a voyage from Hull to Archangel via Reykjavik, with a cargo of government stores. The Master, Capt Thomas Morley, and crew of 40 were lost.

## CLYDE SHIPPING CO. LTD – GLASGOW

*TOWARD* • GRT 1571 • Built 1923
7.2.43: Torpedoed and sunk by German submarine U-402 (v. Forstner), part of the 'Pfeil' (Arrow) patrol group of twelve U-boats, in the Atlantic SE of Cape Farewell, in

position 54.55N 26.05W while on government service on a voyage from Halifax NS to Greenock, acting as the convoy's rescue ship for SC 118 comprising 61 ships. The Master, Capt Gordon K. Hudson, 21 crew, 5 gunners and 1 signalman were rescued by HM corvette *MIGNONETTE* 925/41 (K.38) (Lt H.H. Brown) and landed at Londonderry. 29 crew, 11 gunners, 1 naval surgeon, 1 sick bay attendant, 2 signalmen and 2 passengers were lost.

## COAST LINES LIMITED – LIVERPOOL

*CARMARTHEN COAST* ex-*NORA* ex-*LANGFJORD* • GRT 961 • Built 1921
9.11.39: Struck a mine, laid on 27.10.39 by German submarine U-24 (Jeppener-Haltenhoff), and sank in the North Sea 3 miles E of Seaham Harbour while on a voyage from Methil to London, with 1000 tons of general cargo. The Master, Capt J.O. Rowlands, and survivors were rescued by the Seaham Lifeboat. 2 crew were lost. U-24 commanded by Oberleutnant-zur-see Dieter Lenzmann was scuttled on 25.8.44 at Constanza Roads, Roumania, in position 44.12N 28.41E.

*MUNSTER* • GRT 4305 • Built 1938
7.2.40: Struck a mine laid on 6.1.40 by German submarine U-30 (Lemp), and sank in the Irish Sea, in position 53.36N 03.24W while on a voyage from Belfast to Liverpool, carrying 190 passengers and general cargo. The Master, Capt William James Paisley, crew of 44 and passengers were rescued by British coaster *RINGWALL* ex-*MARY SUMMERFIELD* 407/21 and landed at Liverpool.

*NORMANDY COAST* • GRT 1428 • Built 1916
11.1.45: Torpedoed and sunk by German submarine U-1055 (Meyer), in the Irish Sea W of Anglesey, in position 53.19N 04.48W while on a voyage from London to Liverpool, with a cargo of 266 tons of steel plates, dispersed from coastal convoy T.98A. The Master, Capt Frederick Mara, 5 crew and 2 gunners were rescued by HM patrol ship PC 74 694/18 and landed at Holyhead 12.1.45. 18 crew and 1 gunner were lost. The *NORMANDY COAST* sank within 2 minutes.

*NORFOLK COAST* • GRT 646 • Built 1937
28.2.45: Torpedoed and sunk by German submarine U-1302 (Herwatz), in the St George's Channel SW of Strumble Head, in position 51.58N 05.25W while on a voyage from Cardiff to Liverpool, with general cargo. The Master, Capt Thomas Humphreys, 4 crew and 1 gunner were rescued by HMCS corvette *MOOSEJAW* 925/41 (K.164) (Lt A. Harvey) and landed at Fishguard. 6 crew and 1 gunner were lost.

*MONMOUTH COAST* ex-*GRANIA* • GRT 878 • Built 1924
24.4.45: Torpedoed and sunk by German submarine U-1305 (Christiansen), in the Atlantic 80 miles from Sligo, while on a voyage from Sligo to Liverpool, with a cargo of 841 tons of barytes (sulphate). The Master, Capt Albert Henry Standen, 13 crew and 2 gunners were lost. The sole survivor, messroom boy Derek Cragg, was rescued by Irish fishermen. U-1305 was surrendered at Loch Eriboll, Sutherlandshire, on 10.5.45, and later transferred to Russia as a war prize.

## MOWT

**BOSTON** • GRT 4989 • Built 1924
25.9.42: Torpedoed and sunk by German submarine U-216 (Schultz), part of the 'Pfeil' (Arrow) patrol group of ten U-boats, in the Atlantic SE of Cape Farewell, in position 54.23N 27.54W while on a voyage from New York and St John's, Newfoundland 21.9.42, to Londonderry, in ballast, part of convoy RB 1 comprising 8 ships. The Master, Capt Robert Cook Smith Young, 54 crew and 10 gunners were rescued by HM destroyer *VETERAN* 1120/19 (D.72) (Lt H.A.A. Clogstown). *VETERAN* was sunk the following day by U-404 (v. Bülow) with the loss of her crew and 63 survivors from the *BOSTON*. 2 crew were rescued by US ship *NEW BEDFORD* 1595/28. Kapitänleutnant Karl Otto Schultz and crew of 44 were lost on 20.10.42 when U-216, part of the 'Wotan' (god of the Vikings) patrol group of fourteen U-boats was sunk in the Atlantic 550 miles W of Cape Ortegal, in position 48.21N 19.25W by Liberator 'H' FL910, pilot F/O D.M. Sleep of No. 224 Squadron RAF, based at Beaulieu, Hampshire, part of 19 Group. The pilot was awarded the DFC.

**NEW YORK** • GRT 4989 • Built 1924
25.9.42: Torpedoed and sunk by German submarine U-96 (Hellriegel), part of the 'Vorwärts' (Forward) patrol group of ten U-boats, in the Atlantic SE of Cape Farewell, in position 54.34N 25.44W while on a voyage from New York and St John's, Newfoundland 21.9.42, to Londonderry, in ballast, part of convoy RB 1 comprising 8 ships. The Master, Capt Chilion Mayers, 53 crew and 10 gunners were lost. U-96 commanded by Oberleutnant-zur-See Robert Rix was sunk on 30.3.45 by USAAF aircraft at Wilhelmshaven, in position 53.31N 08.10E.

**YORKTOWN** • GRT 1547 • Built 1928
26.9.42: Torpedoed and sunk by German submarine U-619 (Makowski), part of the 'Vorwärts' (Forward) patrol group of ten U-boats, in the Atlantic 550 miles W of Butt of Lewis, in position 55.10N 18.50W while on a voyage from Baltimore and St John's 21.9.42 to Londonderry, in ballast, a straggler from convoy RB 1 comprising 8 ships. The Master, Capt William Paul Boylan, 33 crew and 8 gunners were rescued on 28.9.42 by HM destroyer *SARDONYX* 905/19 (H.54) (Lt-Cdr A.F.C. Gray) and landed at Londonderry 29.9.42. 16 crew and 2 gunners were lost. Kapitänleutnant Kurt Makowski and 43 crew were lost on 5.10.42 when U-619, part of the 'Luchs' (Lynx) patrol group of seventeen U-boats, while shadowing convoy ONS 136 comprising 36 ships, was sunk in the Atlantic 550 miles W of the Butt of Lewis, in position 58.41N 22.58W by Hudson 'N', pilot F/O J. Markham of No. 269 Squadron RAF, based at Reykjavik. The pilot was awarded the DFC.

## COCKERLINE W.H. & COMPANY – HULL

**ALBIONIC** • GRT 2468 • Built 1924
11.9.40: Torpedoed and sunk by German submarine U-99 (Kretschmer), in the Atlantic SSE of Rockall, while sailing independently on a voyage from Wabana 31.8.40 to Liverpool with a cargo of 3500 tons of iron ore. The Master, Capt Harry Thompson, crew of 23 and 1 gunner were lost.

**PACIFIC** • GRT 6034 • Built 1915
2.3.41: Torpedoed and sunk by German submarine U-95 (Schreiber), in the Atlantic 180 miles WSW of Syderö, Faroe Islands, while on a voyage from New York to Grangemouth via

Halifax NS 13.2.41, with a cargo of 9000 tons of steel and scrap, part of convoy HX 109 comprising 37 ships. The Master, Capt Alan Francis King, and 33 crew were lost. 1 crew was rescued by Icelandic trawler *DORA* 101/13 and landed at Fleetwood 5.3.41. U-95 commanded by Kapitänleutnant Gerd Schreiber was sunk on 28.11.41 in the Mediterranean 60 miles east of Gibraltar, in position 36.24N 03.20W by the RNeN submarine 0 21 962/40 (Lt-Cdr J.F. van Dulm). The U-boat commander and 10 crew were taken prisoner by submarine 0 21. 35 crew were lost.

### GERMANIC • GRT 5352 • Built 1936
29.3.41: Torpedoed and sunk by German submarine U-48 (Schultze), in the North Atlantic S of Iceland, in position 61.18N 22.05W while on a voyage from Halifax NS to Liverpool, with a cargo of 7982 tons of wheat, part of convoy HX 115 comprising 32 ships. The Master, Capt Richard Mortimer, and 34 crew were rescued by HM corvette *DIANELLA* 925/40 (K.07) ex-*DAFFODIL* (Lt J.G. Rankin) and landed at Londonderry.

### ATHENIC • GRT 5351 • Built 1937
3.4.41: Torpedoed and sunk by German submarine U-73 (Rosenbaum), in the Atlantic SSW of Reykjavik, in position 58.32N 20.13W while on a voyage from Portland, Maine, to London via Sydney CB, with a cargo of 8400 tons of wheat, part of convoy SC 26 comprising 24 ships. The Master, Capt Ernest William Agnes, crew of 37 and 2 gunners were rescued by HM corvette *ARBUTUS* 925/40 (K.86) (Lt A.L. Warren) and landed at Liverpool.

### CORINTHIC • GRT 4823 • Built 1924
13.4.41: Torpedoed and sunk by German submarine U-124 (Schulz), in the Atlantic SW of Freetown, in position 08.10N 14.40W while sailing independently on a voyage from Rosario to the UK via Freetown, with a cargo of 7710 tons of grain. The Master, Capt Townson Ridley, 36 crew and 2 gunners were rescued by the Dutch tanker *MALVINA* 8245/32 and landed at Freetown. 2 crew were lost.

## COMBEN LONGSTAFF & CO. LTD – LONDON
### Williamstown Shipping Co. Ltd

### GASRAY ex-SPRINGFAL ex-UHTI ex-WHITWORTH ex-WAR CHAR • GRT 1406 • Built 1919
5.4.45: Torpedoed and sunk by German submarine U-2321 (Barschkis), in the North Sea 2 miles N ¾ E (mag) from St Abbs Head while on a voyage from Grangemouth to Blyth, in ballast. The Master, Capt R.E. Baker, 11 crew and 4 gunners were rescued, 5 survivors were rescued by St Abbs Lifeboat and 10 survivors by the British coaster *CLOVA* 310/35 and landed at St Abbs. 6 crew and 2 gunners were lost. U-2321 commanded by Oberleutnant zur See Hans-Heinrich Barschkis surrendered at Kristiansand, Norway, on 9.5.45. On 27.11.45 left Cairnryan, Loch Ryan, towed by HM frigate *CUBITT* 1085/43 (K.512) (Lt G.D. Gregory) ex-USN frigate *DE-83* and was sunk by gunfire by HM destroyer *ONSLOW* ex-HMS *PAKENHAM* 1550/41 (G.17) (Lt-Cdr E.C.F. Coxwell) and ORP destroyer *BLYSKAWICA* 2144/36 (H.34) in the Atlantic NW of Bloody Foreland, in position 56.10N 10.05W. This was one of 116 U-boats disposed of by the Royal Navy in 'Operation Deadlight'.

## COMMON BROTHERS – NEWCASTLE UPON TYNE
### Hindustan Steam Shipping Co. Ltd

*PUKKASTAN* • GRT 5809 • Built 1929
7.9.39: Torpedoed and sunk by gunfire by German submarine U-34 (Rollman), in the Atlantic SW of the Bishop Rock, in position 49.23N 07.49W while sailing independently on a voyage from Cape Town to Rotterdam, with a cargo of maize. The Master, Capt John Strachan Thomson, and crew were rescued by Dutch ship *BILDERDIJK* 6856/22.

*KAFIRISTAN* • GRT 5193 • Built 1924
17.9.39: Torpedoed and sunk by German submarine U-53 (Heinicke), in the Atlantic 350 miles W of Cape Clear, in position 50.16N 16.55W while sailing independently on a voyage from Jucaro, Cuba, to Liverpool, with a cargo of 8870 tons of sugar. The Master, Capt John Busby, and 28 crew were rescued by US ship *AMERICAN FARMER* 7430/20 and landed at New York. 6 crew were lost. Korvettenkapitän Harold Grosse and crew of 41 were lost on 23.2.40 when U-53 was sunk by HM destroyer *GURKHA* 1870/37 (F.20) (Cdr A.W. Buzzard), in the Atlantic S of the Faröe Islands, in position 60.32N 06.14W.

*DAGHESTAN* (tanker) • GRT 5742 • Built 1921
25.3.40: Torpedoed and sunk by German submarine U-57 (Korth), in the North Sea 9 miles E of Copinsay, Orkneys while on government service on a voyage from Scapa Flow to Sullom Voe, Shetlands, with a cargo of 7600 tons of crude oil. The Master, Capt John Rutherford, and 28 crew were rescued by HM trawlers *NORTHERN DAWN* 655/36 (FY.146) (Lt G.P.S. Lowe) and *BRONTES* 428/34 (FY.118) (Cdr T. St V. Tyler) and landed at Lyness, Orkneys. 2 crew and 1 gunner were lost.

*KURDISTAN* • GRT 5844 • Built 1928
10.12.41: Torpedoed and sunk by German submarine U-130 (Kals), in the Atlantic W of Rockall, in position 56.51N 16.36W while on a voyage from New York to Manchester, with 6534 tons of general cargo including foodstuffs, base metals and textiles, part of convoy SC 57 comprising 33 ships. The Master, Capt William Fearon McMillan, Commodore R. Gill CBE RNR RD, 45 crew, 5 gunners and 4 naval staff were rescued by HM corvette *KINGCUP* 925/40 (K.33) (Lt-Cdr R.A.D. Cambridge) and landed at Londonderry. 7 crew, 1 gunner and 2 naval staff were lost.

*WAZIRISTAN* • GRT 5135 • Built 1924
2.1.42: Torpedoed and sunk by German submarine U-134 (Schendel), part of the 'Ulan' patrol group of three U-boats in the Greenland Sea NW of Jan Mayen Island, in position 74.09N 19.10E while on a voyage from New York to Murmansk, USSR, with a cargo of military supplies. She crossed the Atlantic in convoy SC 60 comprising 22 ships and left near Iceland and proceeded to Hvalfiordur, Iceland, and sailed from there on 26.12.41 in company with the Panamanian ship *COLD HARBOUR* 5010/20, part of convoy PQ 7A comprising 2 ships escorted by HM trawlers *HUGH WALPOLE* 498/37 (FY.102) (Lt P.O. Elliott) and *OPHELIA* 545/40 (T.05) (Lt A.J. Southgate). The escorts left on 27.12.41. The *WAZIRISTAN* was in company with the *COLD HARBOUR* when on 1.1.42 bad weather separated the two ships; the next day the *WAZIRISTAN*, stranded on an ice ledge, was attacked by enemy

aircraft and later sunk by U-134. The Master, Capt Reynold Tate, crew of 36 and 10 gunners were lost. Kapitänleutnant Hans-Georg Brosin and 47 crew were lost on 24.8.43 when U-134, part of the 'Stürmer' (Attacker) group of eighteen U-boats, was sunk in the Atlantic 40 miles W by S of Vigo, in position 42.07N 09.30W by a Leigh Light-equipped Wellington XIV 'J', pilot F/O Donald F. McRae RCAF, of No. 179 Squadron RAF, based at Gibraltar. The pilot was awarded the DFC. U-134 had the unique distinction of shooting down the US Navy blimp K-74 (Lt Nelson G. Grills), sunk on 19.6.43 about 30 miles off Key West, Florida. Lt Grills and 8 crew were rescued off North Elbow Cay by the US four-stack destroyer *DAHLGREN* 1190/18 (DD.187). 1 crew was lost.

### GOOLISTAN • GRT 5851 • Built 1929
23.11.42: Torpedoed and sunk by German submarine U-625 (Benker), in the Greenland Sea W of Bear Island, in position 75.50N 16.45E while on a voyage from Archangel, USSR 17.11.42 to Manchester via Loch Ewe, in ballast, part of convoy QP 15 comprising 28 ships. The Master, Capt William Thomson, and crew of 41 were lost. Oberleutnant zur See Siegfried Straub and crew of 52 were lost on 10.3.44 when U-625, part of the 'Preussen' (Prussian) patrol group of sixteen U-boats, was sunk in the Atlantic 400 miles W by N of Cape Clear, in position 52.35N 20.19W by Sunderland 'U' EK591, pilot F/Lt Sidney W. Butler of No. 422 'Snowy Owl' Squadron RCAF, based at Castle Archdale, Co. Fermanagh, part of 15 Group. The pilot was awarded the DFC.

### SELVISTAN • GRT 5136 • Built 1924
5.5.43: Torpedoed and sunk by German submarine U-266 (v. Jessen), part of 'Amsel 2' (Blackbird) patrol group of five U-boats, in the Atlantic S of Cape Farewell, in position 53.10N 44.40W while on a voyage from the Tyne to Halifax NS, in ballast, part of convoy ONS 5 comprising 42 ships. The Master, Capt George Edward Miles, 38 crew and 1 gunner were rescued by HM frigate *TAY* 1370/42 (K.232) (Lt-Cdr Robert E. Sherwood) and landed at St John's, Newfoundland. 1 crew and 5 gunners were lost.

## Northumbrian Shipping Co. Ltd

### HOLYSTONE • GRT 5462 • Built 1927
14.2.41: Torpedoed and sunk by German submarine U-101 (Mengersen), in the Atlantic W of Ireland, while on a voyage from Hull to Halifax NS via Oban, in ballast, part of convoy OB 284 comprising 35 ships. The Master, Capt John Stewart Bain, crew of 35, 2 gunners and 2 passengers were lost.

## MOWT

### EMPIRE BURTON • GRT 6966 • Built 1941 (Catapult Armed Merchantman)
20.9.41: Torpedoed and sunk by German submarine U-74 (Kentrat), part of the 'Brandenburg' (district of Berlin) patrol group of eleven U-boats, in the North Atlantic E of Cape Farewell, in position 61.34N 35.05W while on a voyage from Halifax NS to Liverpool via Sydney CB 11.9.41, carrying 6 RAF personnel and a cargo of 9106 tons of wheat, part of convoy SC 44 comprising 54 ships. The Master, Capt John Mitchell, 47 crew, 4 gunners and RAF personnel were rescued by HM corvette *HONEYSUCKLE* 925/40 (K.27) (Lt-Cdr G.W.

Gregorie) and landed at Reykjavik. 1 crew and 1 gunner were lost. One of the escorts to the convoy HMCS corvette *LÉVIS* 925/40 (K.115) (Lt C.W. Gilding) of 19th Escort Group was sunk on the same day by U-74 in the North Atlantic E of Cape Farewell, in position 60.07N 38.37W. 91 survivors were rescued by HMCS corvette *MAYFLOWER* 925/40 (K.191) (Lt-Cdr G. Stephen). 18 crew were lost.

**TENNESSEE** ex-*FREDENSBRO* • GRT 2342 • Built 1921
23.9.42: Torpedoed and sunk by German submarine U-617 (Brandi), part of the 'Pfeil' (Arrow) patrol group of seven U-boats, in the Atlantic SE of Cape Farewell, in position 58.40N 33.41W while on a voyage from Three Rivers, Quebec, to the Tyne via Sydney CB 13.9.42, with a cargo of 3438 tons of wheat, a straggler from convoy SC 100 comprising 20 ships. The Master, Capt Aage Henry Albrechtsen, 9 crew and 5 gunners were lost. 9 crew and 3 gunners were rescued by HM corvette *NASTURTIUM* 925/40 (K.107) (Lt C.D. Smith DSC) ex-French *LA PAIMPOLAISE* landed at Londonderry, the 2nd Officer and 7 crew rescued by USCG cutter *INGHAM* 2216/36 (WPG.35) and landed at Reykjavik 2.10.42. U-617, commanded by Kapitänleutnant Albrecht Brandi (Knight's Cross 21.1.43, Oak Leaves 11.4.43, with the Swords 9.5.44, and Diamonds 23.11.44), was damaged on 11.9.43 in the Mediterranean 25 miles W by N of Cape Tres Forcas, Spanish Morocco, in position 35.13N 03.29W by Leigh Light-equipped Wellington 'J', pilot P/O W.H. Brunini and Leigh Light-equipped Wellington 'P', pilot S/Ldr D. Hodgkinson (Canadian) of No. 179 Squadron RAF, based at Gibraltar. 12.9.43: U-617 was beached and scuttled by her crew SW of Cape Tres Forcas. The wreck of U-617 was destroyed by gunfire by HM corvette *HYACINTH* 925/40 (K.84) (Cdr R.T. White), HM trawler *HAARLEM* 431/38 (FY.306) (Lt J.R.T. Brown) and RAN minesweeping sloop *WOOLONGOOG* 650/41 (J.172) (Lt T.H. Smith). The U-boat commander and crew of 48 survived and were later repatriated to Germany by the Spanish authorities. KL Albrecht Brandi was in command of U-380 from November 1943 to March 1944 when she was sunk by USAAF aircraft at Toulon.

**EMPIRE PORTIA** • GRT 7058 • Built 1942
29.6.44: Torpedoed and damaged by German submarine U-988 (Dobberstein), in the English Channel off Selsey Bill, in position 50.33N 00.35W while on government service on a voyage from the Normandy beaches to Portsmouth, in ballast, part of convoy FMT 22. Taken in tow by LST 416 1625/43 the tow parted and she grounded on Peel Bank near Ryde, Isle of Wight, and her back was broken. The two halves were later refloated and the forward section was towed to Falmouth, the aft section to Briton Ferry, South Wales, and subsequently broken up. The Master, Capt Thomas Kirby Suttie, and 41 crew were saved. 5 crew were lost. Oberleutnant zur See Erich Dobberstein and crew of 49 were lost when U-988 was sunk on the same day in the English Channel 40 miles S of Start Point, in position 49.37N 03.41W by HM frigates *ESSINGTON* 1085/43 (K.353) (Lt-Cdr W. Lambert), *DUCKWORTH* 1085/43 (K.351) (Cdr R.G. Mills), *DOMETT* 10865/43 (K.473) (Lt-Cdr S. Gordon), and *COOKE* 1085/43 (K.471) (Lt-Cdr L.C. Hill) of the 3rd Escort Group and Liberator 'L', pilot F/Lt John W. Barling of No. 224 Squadron RAF, based at St Eval, part of 19 Group.

**EMPIRE GOLD** (tanker) • GRT 8028 • Built 1941
18.4.45: Torpedoed and sunk by German submarine U-1107 (Parduhn), in the Atlantic W of the Bay of Biscay, in position 47.47N 06.26W while on a voyage from Philadelphia and New

York to Antwerp, with a cargo of 10278 tons of motor spirit, part of convoy HX 348 comprising 82 ships. The Master, Capt Henry Cecil Cansdale, 37 crew and 5 gunners were lost. 4 crew were rescued by rescue ship *GOTHLAND* 1286/32 (Capt James Murray Hadden OBE) and landed at Greenock 21.4.45. Kapitänleutnant Fritz Parduhn and crew of 35 were lost on 25.4.45 when U-1107 was sunk by Catalina 'R', pilot Lt Frederick G. Lake of US Navy Patrol Squadron VP-63 in the Bay of Biscay 30 miles SW of Ushant, in position 48.12N 05.42W. The *EMPIRE GOLD* was allocated the name *EPPINGDALE* but was not taken over by the Admiralty. This was the last *EMPIRE* ship to be lost through enemy action.

## CONNELL & GRACE LIMITED – NEWCASTLE UPON TYNE
## Quayside Shipping Co. Ltd

### AKENSIDE ex-*BURNHOPE* • GRT 2694 • Built 1917
22.9.39: Torpedoed and sunk by German submarine U-7 (Heydel), in the North Sea 15 miles W by N of Marsten Island, in position 59.10N 04.50E while sailing independently on a voyage from Blyth to Bergen, with a cargo of coal. The Master, Capt John Thomas Nelson, and 25 crew were rescued by the Norwegian torpedo boat *STORM* and the Marsten Pilot Boat and landed at Bergen.

### FELLSIDE ex-*BLAIRBEG* ex-*WYNBURN* ex-*CLIFFTOWER* • GRT 3509 • Built 1917
17.7.40 Torpedoed and sunk by German submarine U-43 (Ambrosius), in the Atlantic 135 miles NW of Bloody Foreland, Co. Donegal, in position 56.09N 12.30W while on a voyage from Middlesbrough to Sydney CB, in ballast, a straggler from convoy OA 184 comprising 43 ships. The Master, Capt John Thomas Nelson, and 20 crew were rescued and landed at Liverpool. 12 crew were lost.

## MOWT

### EMPIRE NOMAD • GRT 7167 • Built 1942
13.10.42: Torpedoed and sunk by German submarine U-159 (Witte), part of 'Eisbar' (Polarbear) patrol group of five U-boats, in the Indian Ocean 250 miles S of Cape Point, Cape Colony, in position 37.57S 18.26E while on a voyage from Beirut to New York via Durban 9.10.42 and Trinidad, in ballast. The Master, Capt John Thomas Nelson, 19 crew and 5 gunners were rescued by Panamanian motor tanker *ELISHA WALKER* 7007/20, transferred to RAN destroyer *NORMAN* 1690/40 (G.49) (Cdr H.M. Burrell) and landed at Cape Town; 19 crew rescued by British ship *TYNEBANK* 4651/34 landed at Rio de Janeiro. 7 crew and 3 gunners were lost.

## CONSETT IRON CO. LTD – NEWCASTLE UPON TYNE

### LEADGATE ex-*SEVEN SEAS SOUND* ex-*CHILTON* • GRT 2125 • Built 1925
8.3.43: Torpedoed and sunk by German submarine U-642 (Brünning), part of 'Ostmark' (East German mark) patrol group of nine U-boats, in the Atlantic W of the Hebrides, in position 58.00N 15.00W while on a voyage from New York 23.2.43 to the UK, with general cargo, a straggler from convoy SC 121 comprising 57 ships. The Master, Capt Ernest Hay Halliday, and crew of 25 were lost. U-642, commanded by Kapitänleutnant Herbert Brünning, was sunk on 5.7.44 by a Liberator of the USAAF at Toulon, in position 43.07N 05.55E.

## CONSTANTINE SS LINE LIMITED – MIDDLESBROUGH

*BALMORALWOOD* • GRT 5834 • Built 1937
14.6.40: Torpedoed and sunk by German submarine U-47 (Prien), in the Atlantic 70 miles SSW of Cape Clear, in position 50.19N 10.28W while on a voyage from Sorel, Quebec, to Falmouth via Halifax NS, with a cargo of 8730 tons of wheat and 4 aircraft on deck, a straggler from convoy HX 48 comprising 40 ships. The Master, Capt Frank H. Chilton, crew of 40 and 1 gunner were rescued by British ship *GERMANIC* 5352/36 and landed at Liverpool.

*BROOKWOOD* • GRT 5082 • Built 1929
24.8.40: Torpedoed and sunk by gunfire by German submarine U-37 (Oehrn), in the Atlantic S of Iceland, in position 54.40N 27.57W while sailing independently on a voyage from London to Sydney CB via Methil, in ballast, dispersed on 20.8.40 from convoy OA 200 comprising 40 ships. The Master, Capt Frank H. Chilton, 34 crew and 1 gunner were rescued after 5 days by Clan ship *CLAN MACBEAN* 5052/18, landed at Freetown and brought by Union Castle ship *GLOUCESTER CASTLE* 7612/11 to the UK. 1 crew was lost.

*YORKWOOD* • GRT 5401 • Built 1936
8.1.43: Torpedoed and sunk by German submarine U-507 (Schacht), in the South Atlantic NW of Ascension Island, in position 04.10S 35.30W while sailing independently on a voyage from Durban and Cape Town to the UK via Pernambuco, with general cargo. The Master, Capt Frank Herbert Fenn, was taken prisoner and lost. 38 crew and 8 gunners landed at Macau, Brazil. 1 crew was lost. Korvettenkapitän Harro Schacht (Knight's Cross 9.1.43) and crew of 54 were lost on 13.1.43 in the South Atlantic 150 miles NW of Ceara, Brazil, in position 01.38S 39.52W when U-507 was sunk by Catalina P–10, pilot Lt L. Ludwig of US Navy Squadron VP-83. Capt Donald MacCallum of the *BARON DECHMONT*, a prisoner on board the submarine, also lost his life.

*KINGSWOOD* • GRT 5055 • Built 1929
17.12.43: Torpedoed and sunk by German submarine U-515 (Henke), in the Bight of Benin, SW of Kotonu, Dahomey, in position 05.57S 01.43E while sailing independently on a voyage from Forcados and Lagos 12.12.43 to Takoradi and the UK, with a cargo of 7400 tons of cotton and groundnuts. The Master, Capt Frederick H. Parmee, crew of 40 and 7 gunners landed 10 miles W of Dahomey 19.12.43.

## MOWT

*FORT LA REINE* • GRT 7133 • Built 1942
17.8.42: Torpedoed and sunk by German submarine U-658 (Senkel), in the Windward Passage SW of Mole St Nicolas, Haiti, in position 18.80N 75.20W while on a voyage from Vancouver to the UK via Cristobal 13.8.42, Guantanamo Bay and Halifax NS, with 9300 tons of general cargo including grain and lumber, part of convoy PG 6 comprising 23 ships. The Master, Capt Percy William Pennock, 37 crew and 3 gunners were rescued; 29 survivors were rescued by HM corvette *PIMPERNEL* 925/40 (K.71) (Lt-Cdr F.H. Thornton) and landed at Guantanamo Bay and 12 survivors rescued by a US patrol boat landed at New Orleans. 2 crew and 1 gunner were lost. Kapitänleutnant Hans Senkel and crew of 47 crew were lost on 30.10.42 when U-658, part of the 'Veilchen' (Violet) patrol group of eleven U-boats, was sunk in the Atlantic

120 miles E of St John's, Newfoundland, in position 50.32N 46.32W by Hudson 'Y', pilot F/O E.L. Robinson of No. 145 Squadron RCAF, based at Tor Bay, Newfoundland.

**FORT BUCKINGHAM** • GRT 7122 • Built 1943
20.1.44: Torpedoed and sunk by German submarine U-188 (Lüdden), part of the 'Monsun' (Monsoon) patrol group of eleven U-boats, in the Indian Ocean NW of the Maldive Islands, in position 08.19N 66.40E while sailing independently on a voyage from Bombay to Buenos Aires via Durban, in ballast. The Master, Capt Murdo Macleod DSC, 30 crew and 7 gunners were lost. 28 crew and 9 gunners were rescued on 5.2.44 by the Norwegian ship ORA 9537/37, transferred to HM destroyer REDOUBT 1705/42 (H.41) (Lt-Cdr N.E.G. Ropner) and landed at Bombay 9.2.44, 8 survivors rescued by the Norwegian tanker KONGSDAL 9959/37 landed at Melbourne 22.2.44 and 6 survivors rescued by British ship MOORBY 4992/36 landed at Fremantle 29.1.44. The FORT BUCKINGHAM sank in about five minutes.

## CONSTANTINE SHIPPING CO. LTD – MIDDLESBROUGH

**WINDSORWOOD** • GRT 5395 • Built 1936
25.6.40: Torpedoed and sunk by German submarine U-51 (Knorr), in the Atlantic about 370 miles WSW of Land's End, in position 48.24N 15.05W while on a voyage from the Tyne to Freetown, with a cargo of 7100 tons of coal, part of convoy OA 172 comprising 56 ships. The Master, Capt George Albert Norton, and crew of 39 were rescued by British ship AINDERBY 4860/25 and landed at Barry.

**KIRNWOOD** • GRT 3829 • Built 1928
10.12.41: Torpedoed and sunk by German submarine U-130 (Kals), in the Atlantic W of Rockall, in position 56.57N 16.35W while on a voyage from Albany, New York, to Ipswich via Sydney CB, with a cargo of 5500 tons of grain, part of convoy SC 57 comprising 33 ships. The Master, Capt George Albert Norton, and 11 crew were lost. 29 crew and 4 gunners were rescued by rescue ship DEWSBBURY 1631/10 (Capt Arthur James Elvin Snowden OBE), transferred to HM corvette KINGCUP 925/40 (K.33) (Lt-Cdr R.A.D. Cambridge) and landed at Londonderry.

## MOWT

**ERNA III** ex-ERNA • GRT 1590 • Built 1930
22.9.41: Torpedoed and sunk by German submarine U-562 (Hamm), in the North Atlantic NW of Cape Farewell, in position 61.45N 35.15W while on a voyage from Swansea to Montreal, in ballast, dispersed from convoy ON 16 comprising 42 ships. The Master, Capt Knud Christian Sorensen, and crew of 22 were lost.

## CONSTANTS, HALFORD LIMITED – LONDON
### Constants (South Wales) Ltd

**HEMINGE** ex-ROCHESTER ex-WAR CURRANT • GRT 2595 • Built 1919
30.9.40: Torpedoed and sunk by German submarine U-37 (Oehrn), in the Atlantic W of Ireland, in position 53.26N 18.33W while on a voyage from the Tyne to Tenerife, with a

cargo of 3300 tons of coal, a straggler from convoy OB 220 comprising 30 ships. The Master, Capt Trevor Thomas, 23 crew and 1 gunner were rescued by British ship *CLAN CUMMING* 7264/38 landed at Liverpool. 1 crew was lost.

**HAWINGE** ex-*PENTREATH* • GRT 2475 • Built 1924
27.7.41: Torpedoed and sunk by German submarine U-203 (Mützelburg), in the Atlantic 800 miles SW of Fastnet, in position 44.55N 17.44W while on a voyage from Glasgow to Lisbon, with a cargo of 2806 tons of coal, part of convoy OG 69 comprising 27 ships. The Master, Capt Walter Aron Isaksson, and 5 crew were rescued by HM corvette *SUNFLOWER* 925/40 (K.41) (Lt-Cdr J.T. Jones) and landed at Londonderry; 7 crew and 3 gunners were rescued by HM destroyer *VANCO* 1090/17 (H.33) (Lt-Cdr S.G.W. Deneys DSO) and landed at Liverpool. 13 crew and 2 gunners were lost.

**WROTHAM** ex-*FIRTREE* ex-*RAMSHOPE* • GRT 1884 • Built 1927
28.7.41: Torpedoed and sunk by German submarine U-561 (Bartels), in the Atlantic W of Cape Finisterre, in position 43.00N 17.00W while on a voyage from Ardrossan to Huelva, Spain, in ballast, part of convoy OG 69 comprising 27 ships. The Master, Capt James Gordon Davies, crew of 22 and 3 gunners were rescued by HM corvettes *FLEUR DE LYS* 925/40 (K.122) (Lt A. Collins) and *RHODODENDRON* 925/40 (K.78) (Sub-Lt R.H. Towersey) and landed at Gibraltar. Oberleutnant zur See Fritz Henning was lost on 12.7.43 when U-561 was sunk by HM motor torpedo boat No. 81 47/41 (Lt L.V. Strong) in the Tyrrhenian Sea SW of Lipari Island, in position 38.16N 15.39E. The U-boat commander and 4 crew were rescued by Axis craft. 42 crew were lost.

**RUCKINGE** • GRT 2869 • Built 1939
19.12.41: Torpedoed and damaged by German submarine U-108 (Scholtz), part of the 'Seeräuber' (Pirate) patrol group of five U-boats, in the Atlantic W of Lisbon, in position 38.20N 17.15W while on a voyage from Lisbon to Oban for orders, with 2129 tons of general cargo including foodstuffs, chemicals, base metal and wood, part of convoy HG 76 comprising 32 ships. Later sunk by gunfire by HM corvette *SAMPHIRE* 925/41 (K.128) (Lt-Cdr F.T. Renay). The Master, Capt Walter Albert Ross, Chief Officer and 12 crew were rescued by HM sloop *STORK* 1190/36 (L.81) (Cdr Frederic John Walker CB DSO DSC) and landed at Devonport; 18 crew, 3 DBS and 4 gunners were rescued by US ship *FINLAND* 6495/06. 3 crew were lost. Two escorts of the convoy were sunk. HM escort carrier *AUDACITY* ex-*EMPIRE AUDACITY* ex-*HANOVER* 11000/39 (Cdr D.W. Mackendrick) was sunk 500 miles W of Cape Finisterre, in position 44.00N 20.00W by German submarine U-751 (Bigalk) on 21.12.41. The survivors from *AUDACITY* were rescued by HM corvettes *CONVOLVULUS* 925/40 (K.45) (Lt R.S. Connell), *MARIGOLD* 925/40 (K.87) (Lt W.S. Macdonald) and *PENSTEMON* 925/41 (K.61) (Lt-Cdr J. Byron). HM destroyer *STANLEY* 1190/19 (I.73) (Lt-Cdr D.B. Shaw) ex-USN four-stack *McCALLA* (DD 253) was sunk 330 miles W of Cape Sines, Portugal, in position 38.12N 17.23W by German submarine U-574 (Gengelach) on 19.12.41. U-574 commanded by Oberleutnant zur See Dietrich Gengelbach was sunk on the same day by HM sloop *STORK* of the 36th Escort Group, in the Atlantic 330 miles W of Cape Sines, in position 38.12N 17.23W. The commander of the U-boat and 27 crew were lost. 16 crew were taken prisoner by *STORK* and *SAMPHIRE*. U-434, commanded by Kapitänleutnant Wolfgang Heyda, was sunk on 18.12.41 while attacking this convoy by HM destroyers *STANLEY* 1190/19 (I.73) (Lt-Cdr D.B. Shaw) and *BLANKNEY* 1050/40 (L.30) (Lt-Cdr M.V. Thorburn) in the Atlantic 270 miles WSW of Cape St Vincent. The

U-boat commander and 41 crew were taken prisoner by *BLANKNEY, STANLEY* and HM destroyer *EXMOOR* 1050/41 (L.08) (Lt-Cdr L. St G. Rich) ex-*BURTON* 1050/41 (L.08). 3 crew were lost. The German *HANOVER* was captured on 7.3.40 by HM cruiser *DUNEDIN* 4850/18 (I.93) (Capt C.E. Lambe CVO) and HMCS destroyer *ASSINIBOINE* 1390/31 (D.18) ex-HMS *KEMPENFELT* (Cdr E.R. Mainguy) in the Great Antilles.

**GARLINGE** ex-*PETWORTH* • GRT 2012 • Built 1918
10.11.42: Torpedoed and sunk by German submarine U-81 (Guggenberger), in the Mediterranean 21 miles N of Cape Ivi, Algeria, in position 37.00N 02.00E while on government service on a voyage from Greenock to Algiers via Gibraltar 7.11.42, with a cargo of 2700 tons of coal. The Master, Capt William Charles Barnes, 6 crew and 8 gunners were rescued by HM examination ship *MINNA* 390/39 (Lt W.E. Bady RANVR) and landed at Algiers. 18 crew and 7 gunners were lost.

## COOK, JAMES & CO. LTD – LONDON
**Bulk Oil SS Co. Ltd**

**PASS OF BALMAHA** (tanker) • GRT 758 • Built 1933
17.10.41: Torpedoed and sunk by German submarine U-97 (Heilmann), in the Mediterranean about 50 miles W of Alexandria, in position 31.14N 28.50E while on a voyage from Alexandria to Tobruk, with a cargo of motor spirit, escorted by HM whaler *KOS XIX* 258/32. The Master, Capt Stanley Kirby Hardy, crew of 15 and 2 gunners were lost.

## CORY, JOHN & SONS LIMITED – CARDIFF
**British Steam Shipping Co.**

**RUPERRA** • GRT 4548 • Built 1925
19.10.40: Torpedoed and sunk by German submarine U-46 (Endrass), in the Atlantic 90 miles SW of Rockall, in position 57.00N 16.00W while on a voyage from New York to Greenock and Leith, with a cargo of steel billets, scrap iron and aircraft, part of convoy HX 79 comprising 49 ships. The Master, Capt David Thomas Davies, 29 crew and 1 gunner were lost. 7 crew were rescued by British ship *INDUNA* 5086/25 and landed at Methil.

**RAMILLIES** • GRT 4553 • Built 1927
8.5.41: Torpedoed and sunk by German submarine U-97 (Heilmann), in the Atlantic SE of Cape Farewell, in position 48.05N 32.26W while on a voyage from the Tyne to Baltimore via Oban, with a cargo of 3074 tons of coke, dispersed from convoy OB 317 comprising 23 ships. The Master, Capt William Henry Macey, 25 crew and 3 gunners were lost. 11 crew and 1 gunner were rescued by British ship *GEDDINGTON COURT* 6903/28 and landed at Halifax NS.

## MOWT

**EMPIRE VOLUNTEER** ex-*PROCIDA* ex-*CANADIAN TRAVELLER* • GRT 5319 • Built 1921
15.9.40: Torpedoed and sunk by German submarine U-48 (Bleichrodt) in the Atlantic 65 miles W of Rockall, in position 56.43N 15.17W while on a voyage from Wabana to Glasgow, with a cargo of 7700 tons of iron ore, part of convoyy SC 3 comprising 47 ships. The Master, Capt Benjamin Pearson, and 6 crew were rescued by Norwegian ship *FIDO* 1857/18 and

landed at Belfast; 26 crew were rescued by Norwegian ship *GRANLI* 1577/35 and landed at Glasgow. One of the convoy's escorts HM sloop *DUNDEE* 1060/32 (L.84) (Capt O.M.F. Stokes) was sunk the same day by U-48, W of Ireland, in position 56.45N 14.14W. The Italian *PROCIDA* was taken as a prize on 10.6.40 at Cardiff.

**EMPIRE SUN** • GRT 6952 • Built 1941 (CAM ship)
7.2.42: Torpedoed and sunk by German submarine U-751 (Bigalk), in the Atlantic S of Halifax NS, in position 43.55N 64.22W while sailing independently on a voyage from Portland, Maine, to the UK via Halifax NS, with 8 RAF personnel and a cargo of 9000 tons of grain. The Master, Capt Lloyd Evans, 34 crew, 12 gunners and 7 RAF personnel landed at Liverpool, Novia Scotia. 8 crew, 2 gunners and 1 RAF personnel were lost. Kapitänleutnant Gerhard Bigalk (Knight's Cross 26.12.41) and crew of 44 were lost on 17.7.42 when U-751 was sunk in the Atlantic 200 miles WNW of Cape Ortegal, in position 45.14N 12.22W by Whitley 'H', pilot P/O A.R.A. Hunt of No. 502 'Ulster' Squadron RAuxAF, based at St Eval and Lancaster 'F', pilot F/L Peter R. Casement of No. 61 Squadron RAF, based at Syerston, Nottinghamshire.

**FORT BATTLE RIVER** • GRT 7133 • Built 1942
6.3.43: Torpedoed and sunk by German submarine U-410 (Fenski), part of the 'Robbe' (Seal) patrol group of five U-boats, in the Atlantic W of Gibraltar, in position 36.33N 10.22W while on government service on a voyage from Liverpool to Bougie, Algeria, with 9 army personnel and 3000 tons of government stores, part of convoy KMS 10 comprising 57 ships. The Master, Capt Albert Victor Parkinson Turnbull, crew of 45, 10 gunners and army personnel were rescued by HMCS corvette *SHEDIAC* 925/41 (K.110) (Lt J.E. Clayton) and British ship *EMPIRE FLAMINGO* 4994/20, and landed at Gibraltar.

**FORT LAMY** ex-*PORTFIELD* • GRT 5242 • Built 1919
8.3.43: Torpedoed and sunk by German submarine U-527 (Uhlig), part of the 'Westmark' (West German mark) patrol group of seventeen U-boats, in the Atlantic SE of Cape Farewell, in position 58.30N 31.00W while on a voyage from Philadelphia and New York 23.2.43 to Liverpool, with 6333 tons of general cargo, explosives and deck cargo of one 291 ton landing craft tank No. 2480, a straggler from convoy SC 121 comprising 57 ships. The Master, Capt William Evans, 39 crew and 6 gunners were lost. 3 crew and 2 gunners were rescued after 12 days by HM corvette *VERVAIN* 925/41 (K.190) ex-HM *BROOM* (Lt H.P. Crail) and landed at St John's, Newfoundland. U-527 commanded by Kapitänleutnant Herbert Uhlig was sunk on 23.7.43 in the Atlantic 200 miles S of the Azores, in position 35.25N 27.56W by an Avenger, pilot Lt Robert L. Stearns of US Navy Composite Squadron VC-9 from US escort carrier *BOGUE* 9800/42 (CVE-9) (Capt J.B. Dunn). The U-boat commander and 13 crew were rescued by the US four-stack destroyer *CLEMSON* 1190/18 (DD 186), transferred to USS *BOGUE* and landed at Casablanca. 40 crew were lost. The pilot was awarded the US Navy Cross.

**FORT ST NICOLAS** • GRT 7154 • Built 1943
15.2.44: Torpedoed and sunk by German submarine U-410 (Fenski), in the Tyrrhenian Sea E of the island of Capri, in position 40.34N 14.37E while on government service on a voyage from Hull to Augusta and Naples, with 4 passengers and a cargo of 4000 tons of military stores. The Master, Capt Kenneth Howard Pengelly, crew of 48, 14 gunners and passengers

were rescued by a RAF Crash Launch and landed at Salerno. Oberleutnant zur See Horst-Arno Fenski (Knight's Cross 26.11.43) was lost on 4.5.44 when U-371 was attacking convoy GUS 38 comprising 107 ships in the Mediterranean off Cavallo Point, Gulf of Bougie, in position 37.49N 05.39E by USN destroyer escorts *PRIDE* 1200/43 (DE-323) (Cdr R.R. Curry) *JOSEPH E. CAMPBELL* 1140/43 (DE-70) (Lt J.M. Robertson), USN minesweeper *SUSTAIN* 890/42 (AM-119), FFS destroyer *L'ALCYON* 1378/26, FFS frigate *SÉNÉGALAIS* 1300/43 (Capt P. Poncet) and HM destroyer *BLANKNEY* 1050/40 (L. 30) (Lt B.H. Brown). The U-boat commander and 45 crew were taken prisoner by USS *JOSEPH CAMPBELL* and *SUSTAIN* and landed at Algiers. 3 crew were taken prisoner by FFS *SÉNÉGALAIS* and landed at Bougie. 3 crew were lost.

## COUNTIES SHIP MANAGEMENT CO. LTD – LONDON

***MILL HILL*** ex-*GRACECHURCH* ex-*PEEBLES* • GRT 4318 • Built 1930
30.8.40: Torpedoed and sunk by German submarine U-32 (Jenisch), in the Atlantic 58 miles WNW of Cape Wrath, in position 58.48N 06.49W while on a voyage from Boston, Mass. to Middlesbrough via Halifax NS 16.8.40, with a cargo of 6755 tons of pig iron and steel, part of convoy HX 66 comprising 51 ships. The Master, Capt Robert Du Buisson, and crew of 33 were lost.

***BROCKLEY HILL*** • GRT 5207 • Built 1919
24.6.41: Torpedoed and sunk by German submarine U-651 (Lohmeyer), in the Atlantic SE of Cape Farewell, in position 58.30N 38.20W while on a voyage from Montreal 12.6.41 to London via Sydney NS 16.6.41, with a cargo of 7000 tons of grain, part of convoy HX 133 comprising 57 ships. The Master, Capt James Howard Williams, crew of 37 and 4 gunners were rescued by British ship *SAUGOR* 6303/28 and landed at Loch Ewe.

### Bury Hill Shipping Co. Ltd

***MICHAEL E*** • GRT 7628 • Built 1941 (CAM ship)
2.6.41: Torpedoed and sunk by German submarine U-108 (Scholtz), in the Atlantic SW of Cape Clear, in position 48.50N 29.00W while sailing independently on a voyage from Belfast to Halifax NS, in ballast, dispersed on 1.6.41 from convoy OB 327 comprising 41 ships. The Master, Capt Murdo Macleod, 44 crew, 2 gunners and 12 RAF personnel were rescued by Dutch ship *ALCINOUS* 6189/25 and landed at Halifax NS. 1 crew and 2 gunners were lost.

### Dorset Shipping Co. Ltd

***LULWORTH HILL*** • GRT 7628 • Built 1940
19.3.43: Torpedoed and sunk by Italian submarine *LEONARDO DA VINCI* (Gazzana), in the South Atlantic 940 miles W by S of Loanda, Portuguese West Africa, in position 10.10S 01.00E while sailing independently on a voyage from Port Louis, Mauritius, to Liverpool via Cape Town and Freetown, with a cargo of 10097 tons of sugar and 413 tons of rum and fibre. The Master, Capt William Ernest McEwan, 36 crew and 6 gunners were lost. Carpenter K. Cooke and Able Seaman Colin H. Armitage were rescued after 50 days (7.5.43) from a raft about 400 miles S of Liberia by HM destroyer *RAPID* 1705/42 (H.32) (Lt-Cdr

M.W. Tomkinson DSC) and landed at Freetown. The survivors were awarded the George Cross and the Lloyd's War Medal for bravery at sea. 1 gunner was taken prisoner.

## Leith Hill Shipping Co. Ltd

*MARIETTA E* • GRT 7628 • Built 1940
4.3.43: Torpedoed and sunk by German submarine U-160 (Lassen), part of the 'Seehund' (Seal) group of five U-boats, in the Indian Ocean ENE of East London, in position 32.04S 31.05E while on a voyage from New York to Aden and Alexandria via Durban, with a cargo of 4865 tons of government and commercial stores, part of convoy DN 21 comprising 11 ships. The Master, Capt James Howard Williams, 33 crew and 6 gunners were rescued by SAAF Crash Launch R.8 and landed at Durban. 4 crew and 1 gunner were lost.

## Putney Hill Shipping Co. Ltd

*KINGSTON HILL* • GRT 7628 • Built 1940
7.6.41: Torpedoed and sunk by German submarine U-38 (Liebe), in the Atlantic SW of the Cape Verde Islands, in position 09.35N 29.40W while on a voyage from Cardiff and Glasgow to Cape Town and Alexandria, with a cargo of 8300 tons of coal and 400 tons of general cargo, part of convoy OB 288 comprising 46 ships. The Master, Capt William Edwin Niven, and 13 crew were lost. 16 crew were rescued by HM destroyer *ACHATES* 1350/29 (H.12) (Lt-Cdr Viscount Jocelyn) and landed at Greenock; 26 crew and 6 gunners were rescued by US tanker *ALABAMA* 2840/01 and landed at Cape Town. U-38 commanded by Korvettenkapitän George Peters was scuttled at Wesermünde on 5.5.45.

*PUTNEY HILL* • GRT 5216 • Built 1940
26.6.42: Torpedoed and sunk by German submarine U-203 (Mützelburg), in the Atlantic 450 miles ENE of Puerto Rico, in position 24.20N 63.16W while sailing independently on a voyage from Haifa to New York via Cape Town 1.6.42, in ballast. The Master, Capt Donald McWilliam Hughson, 29 crew and 5 gunners were rescued after 10 days by HM corvette *SAXIFRAGE* 925/41 (K.04) (Lt-Cdr R.P. Chapman) and landed at San Juan, Puerto Rico. 2 crew and 1 gunner were lost.

*PRIMROSE HILL* • GRT 7628 • Built 1941
29.10.42: Torpedoed and sunk by German submarine UD-5 ex-Dutch 0–27 (Mahn), in the Atlantic NW of the Cape Verde Islands, in position 18.58N 28.40W while sailing independently on a voyage from Glasgow 16.10.42 to Takoradi and Apapa, with 4796 tons of general cargo including coal and 11 aircraft, dispersed from convoy ON 139 comprising 38 ships. The Master, Capt Maxwell Dunnett Mackenzie, 37 crew and 8 gunners were rescued by British ship *SANSU* 5446/39 and landed at Freetown. 3 crew were lost.

## Tower Shipping Co. Ltd

*TOWER GRANGE* • GRT 5226 • Built 1940
18.11.42: Torpedoed and sunk by German submarine U-154 (Schuch), in the Atlantic 250 miles NE of Cayenne, French Guiana, in position 06.20N 49.10W while sailing independently from

Calcutta to the UK via Cape Town 27.10.42 and Trinidad, with 8332 tons of general cargo including manganese ore. The Master, Capt William Henry Williamson, and 29 survivors were rescued by British ship *CASTALIA* 6601/06 and landed at Trinidad 27.11.42; the Chief Officer and 10 survivors were rescued by British ship *BARON BELHAVEN* 6591/25 and landed at Trinidad. 4 crew were lost. Oberleutnant zur See Gerth Gemeiner and crew of 57 were lost on 3.7.44 in the Atlantic 125 miles NW by N of Madeira, in position 34.00N 19.30W when U-154 was sunk by USN escort destroyers *FROST* 1200/43 (DE-144) (Lt-Cdr John H. McWhorter) and *INCH* 1200/43 (DE-146) (Lt-Cdr C.W. Frey), part of USN Task Group 22.5 (Capt Vest).

## MOWT

**EVEROJA** ex-*BRIGHT WINGS* ex-*DELIA* ex-*MIDDLEHAM CASTLE* • GRT 4530 • Built 1910
3.11.41: Torpedoed and sunk by German submarine U-203 (Mütelburg), part of the 'Raubritter' (Robber Knight) patrol group of fourteen U-boats, in the Atlantic 80 miles E of Belle Island, Newfoundland, in position 52.18N 53.05W while on a voyage from St John, New Brunswick, to Dublin, with a cargo of 6401 tons of of wheat, part of convoy SC 52 comprising 35 ships. The Master, Capt Alfred Kirschfeloths, 40 crew and 5 gunners were rescued by HM corvette *NASTURTIUM* 925/40 (K.107) (Lt-Cdr R.C. Freaker DSO) ex-French *LA PAIMPOLAISE* and landed at St John's, Newfoundland.

**EMPIRE TOWER** ex-*TOWER FIELD* ex-*ROXBURGH* • GRT 4378 • Built 1935
5.3.43: Torpedoed and sunk by German submarine U-130 (Keller), in the Atlantic about 250 miles W of Cape Finisterre, in position 43.50N 14.46W while on a voyage from Huelva to Middlesbrough, with a cargo of 6532 tons of iron ore, part of convoy XK 2 comprising 20 ships. The Master, Capt David John Williams OBE, 35 crew and 6 gunners were lost. 3 crew were rescued by HM trawler *LOCH OSKAIG* 534/37 (FY.175) (Lt G.F.S. Clampitt) and landed at Londonderry. The *EMPIRE TOWER* sank in 60 seconds.

## CRAVOS, CHARLES & COMPANY – CARDIFF
Ampleforth SS Co.

**AMPLEFORTH** ex-*GLOFIELD* • GRT 4576 • Built 1929
19.8.40: Torpedoed and sunk by German submarine U-101 (Frauenheim), in the Atlantic W of the Hebrides, in position 56.10N 10.40W while on a voyage from Hull to Jacksonville, Florida, in ballast, a straggler from convoy OA 199 comprising 29 ships. The Master, Capt Harry Binham, and 28 crew were rescued by HM destroyer *WARWICK* 1120/17 (D.25) (Lt-Cdr M.A.G. Child) and landed at Liverpool. 9 crew were lost.

## CRAWFORD SHIPPING CO. LTD – LONDON

**GOGOVALE** • GRT 4586 • Built 1927
4.8.40: Torpedoed and sunk by German submarine U-52 (Salman), in the Atlantic 250 miles NW of Ireland, in position 56.59N 17.38W while on a voyage from Montreal to London, with a cargo of 6386 tons of flour, part of convoy HX 60 comprising 60 ships. The Master, Capt Frank S. Passmore, and crew of 36 were rescued by HM destroyer *VANOC* 1090/17 (H.33) (Lt-Cdr J.G.W. Deneys) and landed at Liverpool.

**GRETAVALE** • GRT 4586 • Built 1928
3.11.41: Torpedoed and sunk by German submarine U-202 (Linder), part of the 'Raubritter' (Robber Knight) patrol group of fourteen U-boats, in the Atlantic NE of Notre Dame Bay, Newfoundland, in position 51.21N 51.45W while on a voyage from Baltimore, Maryland to Loch Ewe via Sydney CB 29.10.41, with a cargo of 6700 tons of steel and 17 lorries, part of convoy SC 52 comprising 35 ships. The Master, Capt Frank S. Passmore, 31 crew and 6 gunners were lost. 6 crew were rescued by HMCS corvette *WINDFLOWER* 925/40 (K.155) (Lt John Price) and landed at St John's, Newfoundland.

## CREST SHIPPING CO. LTD – LONDON

**FIRCREST** ex-*PRERADOVIC* ex-*RIVOL* • GRT 5394 • Built 1907
25.8.40: Torpedoed and sunk by German submarine U-124 (Schulz), in the Atlantic N of the Isle of Lewis, in position 58.52N 06.34W while on a voyage from Wabana, Conception Bay, to Middlesbrough via Halifax NS, with a cargo of 7900 tons of iron ore, part of convoy HX 65 comprising 51 ships. The Master, Capt Russell Helton Tuckett OBE, and crew of 38 were lost.

**YEWCREST** ex-*IVO RACIC* • GRT 3774 • Built 1907
25.8.40: Sunk by gunfire by German submarine U-37 (Oehrn), in the Atlantic SW of Iceland, in position 55.10N 25.02W while on a voyage from Cardiff and Liverpool to Wabana, in ballast, a straggler from convoy OB 201 comprising 31 ships. The Master, Capt Cyril Lionel Doughty, 36 crew and 1 gunner were rescued by HM destroyer *HIGHLANDER* 1340/39 (H.44) ex-Brazilian *JAGUARIBE* (Cdr W.A. Dallmeyer). 1 crew was lost.

**OAKCREST** ex-*KORANA* • GRT 5407 • Built 1929
23.11.40: Torpedoed and sunk by German submarine U-123 ( Moehle), in the Atlantic about 250 miles W of Rockall, in position 53.00N 17.00W while on a voyage from Liverpool to New York, in ballast, a straggler from convoy OB 244 comprising 46 ships. The Master, Capt Samuel George Dyer, and 34 crew were lost. 6 survivors landed on Barra Island, Hebrides.

**ASHCREST** ex-*ZRINSKI* ex-*ERLE* • GRT 5652 • Built 1920
8.12.40: Torpedoed and sunk by German submarine U-140 (Hinsch), in the Atlantic W of Ireland, in position 54.35N 09.20W while on a voyage from Philadelphia to Middlesbrough, with a cargo of steel, a straggler from convoy SC 13 comprising 32 ships. The Master, Capt Herbert Mant, and crew of 36 were lost. U-140 commanded by Oberleutnant zur See Wolfgang Scherfling was scuttled at Wilhelmshaven on 2.5.45.

**BELCREST** ex-*TREHERBERT* ex-*GARDEPEE* • GRT 4517 • Built 1925
14.2.41: Torpedoed and sunk by Italian submarine *MICHELE BIANCHI* (Giovannini), in the Atlantic S of Iceland, in position 54.00N 21.00W while on a voyage from Halifax NS to Newport, Mon. with a cargo of steel and general cargo, a straggler from convoy SC 21 comprising 38 ships. The Master, Capt Norman Cecil Brockwell, and crew of 35 were lost.

## CROSBY SON & COMPANY – STOCKTON ON TEES
## MOWT

*EMPIRE GULL* ex-*BRAVE COEUR* • GRT 6058 • Built 1919
12.12.42: Torpedoed and sunk by German submarine U-177 (Gysae), in the Mozambique Channel W of Maputo, Portuguese East Africa, in position 26.15S 34.40E while sailing independently on a voyage from Port Sudan 23.11.42 and Aden 27.11.42 to Baltimore via Lourenco Marques, in ballast. The Master, Capt William James Escudier, and 43 crew were rescued by HM destroyer *INCONSTANT* 1360/41 (H.49) (Lt-Cdr W.S. Clouston) ex-Turkish *MUAVENET* and HM corvette *FREESIA* 925/40 (K.43) (Lt R.A. Cherry) and landed at Durban 16.12.42. 2 crew were lost.

## CUNARD – WHITE STAR LIMITED – LIVERPOOL

*BOSNIA* • GRT 2407 • Built 1928
5.9.39: Torpedoed and sunk by gunfire by German submarine U-47 (Prien), in the Atlantic 120 miles NNW of Cape Ortegal, in position 45.29N 09.45W while sailing independently on a voyage from Licata, Sicily, to Manchester, with a cargo of sulphur. The Master, Capt Walter Henry Poole, and survivors were rescued by Norwegian tanker *EIDANGER* 9432/38 and landed at Lisbon 6.9.39. 1 crew was lost.

*CARINTHIA* • GRT 20277 • Built 1925
6.6.40: Torpedoed and sunk by German submarine U-46 (Endrass), in the Atlantic W of Galway Bay, in position 53.13N 10.40W. 4 crew were lost. Lost while on government service employed as an Armed Merchant Cruiser (F.) (Capt J.F.B. Barrett).

*ANDANIA* • GRT 13950 • Built 1922
16.6.40: Torpedoed and sunk by German submarine UA (Cohausz), in the North Atlantic about 230 miles WNW of the Faröes Islands, in position 62.36N 15.09W. Lost while on government service employed as an Armed Merchant Cruiser (F.) (Capt D.K. Bain).

*LAURENTIC* • GRT 18724 • Built 1927
3.11.40: Torpedoed and sunk by German submarine U-99 (Kretschmer), in the Atlantic W of Black Rock, in position 54.09N 13.44W. Lost while on government service employed as an Armed Merchant Cruiser (F.51) (Capt E.P. Vivian). 368 survivors were rescued by HM destroyer *HESPERUS* 1340/39 (H.57) ex-HMS *HEARTY* (Lt-Cdr D.G.F.W. Macintyre).

*LACONIA* • GRT 19695 • Built 1922
12.9.42: Torpedoed and sunk by German submarine U-156 (Hartenstein), part of the 'Eisbär' (Polarbear) patrol group of five U-boats, in the South Atlantic 360 miles NE of Ascension Island, in position 05.10S 11.25W while sailing independently from Suez to the UK, carrying 766 passengers, 1793 Italian prisoners-of-war and 200 tons of general cargo. The Master, Capt Rudolph Sharp OBE, 138 crew, 551 passengers and 1378 prisoners were lost. 453 crew, 215 passengers and 415 prisoners were rescued by German submarines U-156 (Hartenstein), U-506 (Würdemann), U-507 (Schach) and Italian submarine *CAPPELLINI* (Revedin). A number of survivors were taken on board the submarines and the lifeboats were towed to rendezvous

on 17.9.42 with Vichy French warships, the cruiser *GLORIA* 7600/35, the sloop *DUMONT D'URVILLE* 1969/31 and the minesweeper *ANNAMITE* 647/39; the warships took 1083 survivors to Dakar. 668 survivors from the *LACONIA* sailed from Dakar on the *GLORIA* and arrived at Casablanca 26.9.42. The survivors on the *GLORIA* were 1 RN officer and 178 men, 17 army officers and 87 men, 9 RAF officers and 70 men, 80 Merchant Navy officers and 178 men, 1 Polish officer and 69 men, and 50 women and children.

## MOWT

**EMPIRE BARRACUDA** ex-*BLACK HERON* ex-*SACANDAGA* • GRT 4972 • Built 1918
15.12.41: Torpedoed and sunk by German submarine U-77 (Schonder), in the Atlantic 34 miles 310° from Cape Trafalgar, Spain, in position 35.30N 06.17W while on government service on a voyage from Gibraltar to Suez via Cape Town, with a cargo of 5800 tons of naval and military stores including munitions, part of convoy HG 76 comprising 32 ships. The Master, Capt Frederick Ridley, 37 crew and 1 gunner were rescued by HM corvette *COLTSFOOT* 925/41 (K.140) (Lt-Cdr Hon W.K. Rous) and landed at Gibraltar. 9 crew and 4 gunners were lost. Kapitänleutnant Heinrich Schonder (Knight's Cross 19.8.42) and 61 crew were lost on 24.6.43 when U-200 was sunk in the Atlantic 345 miles S by W of Reykjanes, in position 58.15N 25.25W by Liberator 'H' AM929, pilot F/L A.W. Fraser DFC (Australian) of No. 120 Squadron RAF, based at Reykjavik. U-200 sailed from Kiel on 12.6.43 on her first patrol to join the 'Monsun' (Monsoon) patrol group in the Arabian Sea.

**EMPIRE HAWK** ex-*BLACK TERN* ex-*COAHOMA COUNTY* • GRT 5033 • Built 1919
12.12.42: Torpedoed and sunk by gunfire by Italian submarine *ENRICO TAZZOLI* (Fecia di Cossato), in the Atlantic N of Recife, Brazil, in position 05.56N 39.50W while sailing independently on a voyage from New York to Alexandria via Trinidad 5.12.42 and Cape Town, with 6989 tons of general cargo including army stores and coal. The Master, Capt John Stampe, crew of 44 and 6 gunners were saved. The Master and 19 survivors were towed in the life boats by Amazon Indians in their craft, landed at Bragancia, Para, brought to Belem where they arrived 25.12.42. 31 survivors were rescued on 17.12.42 by the British ship *CAPE BRETON* 6044/40 and landed at Recife 21.12.42.

**SAMBO** ex-*EDWIN JOSEPH O'HARA* (Liberty) • GRT 7219 • Built 1943
10.11.43: Torpedoed and sunk by Japanese submarine I-27 (Fukumura), in the Red Sea SE of Hodeida, Yemen, in position 12.28N 43.31E while on a voyage from Iquique, Peru, and Wellington to Aden 10.11.43 and Suez, with a cargo of 8850 tons of nitrate and 366 tons of general cargo. The Master, Capt John Diack Smith, 33 crew and 1 gunner were rescued by Norwegian ship *HELGÖY* 5614/20 and landed at Aden. 3 crew and 9 gunners were lost.

**CUBA** • GRT 11420 • Built 1923
6.4.45: Torpedoed and sunk by German submarine U-1195 (Cordes), in the English Channel SE of Brighton, in position 50.36N 00.57W while on government service on a voyage from Le Havre to Southampton, in ballast, part of UK coastal convoy VWP 16. The Master, Capt J. Cailloce, 221 crew, 29 gunners, 10 army staff and 3 signallers were rescued by HM frigate *NENE* 1370/42 (K.270) (Lt-Cdr R.F.J. Maberley) and landed at Portsmouth. 1 crew was lost. Kapitänleutnant Ernest Cordes and 30 crew were lost when U-1195 was sunk on the same

day in the English Channel 15 miles E of St Catherine's Point, Isle of Wight, in position 50.33N 00.55W by HM destroyer *WATCHMAN* 1300/17 (G.23) (Lt-Cdr J.R. Clarke). 18 crew were taken prisoner by the French frigate *L'ESCARMOUCHE* 1370/43 ex-HMS *FROME*, transferred to HM frigate *HOSTE* 1085/43 (K.566) (Lt P.J.H. Hoare) ex-USN *MITCHELL* (DE.43) and landed at Portsmouth.

## CURRIE LINE LIMITED – LEITH

*COURLAND* • GRT 1325 • Built 1932
9.2.41: Torpedoed and sunk by German submarine U-37 (Clausen), in the Atlantic 160 miles SW of Cape St Vincent, Portugal, in position 35.53N 13.13W while on a voyage from Lisbon to London, with 1395 tons of general cargo, part of convoy HG 53 comprising 21 ships. The Master, Capt Robert Cecil Smith, and 25 crew were lost. 2 crew and 2 gunners were rescued by HM sloop *DEPTFORD* 990/35 (L.53) (Lt-Cdr G.A. Thring DSO) and landed at Liverpool.

*BRANDENBURG* • GRT 1473 • Built 1910
10.2.41: Torpedoed and sunk by German submarine U-37 (Clausen), in the Atlantic W of Gibraltar, in position 36.10N 16.38W while on a voyage from Vila Real, Portugal, to Leith, with a cargo of 1800 tons of pyrites and sulphur, part of convoy HG 53 comprising 21 ships. The Master, Capt William Henderson, and crew of 22 were lost. U-37 under the command of Kapitänleutnant Eberhard von Wended was scuttled in Sonderborg Bay, Denmark, on 5.5.45, later raised and scrapped. U-37 sank a total of 51 ships (190, 477 GRT) and was the second highest scoring U-boat, only exceeded by U-48.

*LAPLAND* ex-*HONNOR* • GRT 1330 • Built 1936
28.7.41: Torpedoed and sunk by German submarine U-203 (Mützelburg), in the Atlantic NW of Cape Finisterre, in position 40.36N 15.30W while on a voyage from London to Lisbon, with a cargo of 950 tons of tinplate and general cargo, part of convoy OG 69 comprising 27 ships. The Master, Capt James Stuart Brown, crew of 22 and 3 gunners were rescued by HM corvette *RHODODENDRON* 925/40 (K.78) (Sub-Lt R.H. Towersey) and landed at Gibraltar.

*RHINELAND* ex-*ALTENGAMME* • GRT 1381 • Built 1922
21.9.41: Torpedoed and sunk by German submarine U-201 (Schnee), in the Atlantic 800 miles NNE of the Azores, in position 47.00N 22.00W while on a voyage from the Clyde to Lisbon and Gibraltar, with a cargo of 912 tons coal and bags of mail, part of convoy OG 74 comprising 22 ships. The Master, Capt John Thorburn Gilroy, crew of 22 and 3 gunners were lost.

*HENGIST* • GRT 984 • Built 1928
8.3.42: Torpedoed and sunk by German submarine U-569 (Hinsch), in the Atlantic NW of Cape Wrath, in position 59.31N 10.15W while sailing independently on a voyage from Reykjavik 6.3.42 to Scrabster and Grimsby, with a cargo of 700 tons of fish. The Master, Capt Arthur Jamieson, 24 crew and 4 gunners were rescued by French trawler *GROENLAND* 1179/30 and landed at Loch Ewe. 2 crew and 1 gunner were lost. U569 commanded by Oberleutnant zur See (Reserve) Hans Johannsen was lost on 22.5.43 when U-569, part of the

'Mosel' (German river) patrol group of twenty-one U-boats was sunk in the Atlantic about 600 miles SSE of Cape Farewell, in position 50.40N 35.21W while shadowing convoy ON 184 comprising 32 ships by two Avengers, pilots Lt William F. Chamberlain and Lt Howard S. Roberts of US Navy Composite Squadron VC-9 from US escort carrier *BOGUE* 9800/42 (CVE-9) (Capt G.E. Short) of the 6th Support Group. The U-boat commander and 24 crew were taken prisoner by HMCS destroyer *ST LAURENT* 1375/31 (H.83) ex-HMS *CYGNET* (Lt-Cdr George H. Stephen). 21 crew were lost. U-569 was the first U-boat to be sunk by the US Navy's hunter-killer groups operating from escort carriers.

### KIRKLAND • GRT 1361 • Built 1934

23.4.42: Torpedoed and sunk by German submarine U-565 (Franken), in the Mediterranean 35 miles ENE of Sidi Barrâni, Egypt, in position 31.51N 26.37E while in convoy on government service on a voyage from Tobruk 22.4.42 to Alexandria, in ballast. The Master, Capt James Stuart Brown, 15 crew and 6 gunners were rescued by HM trawler *FALK* 307/37 (Lt H.S. Upperton) and landed at Mersa Matruh. 1 crew was lost. U-565, commanded by Kapitänleutnant Fritz Henning, was damaged on 24.9.44 by USAAF at Salamis, Greece, in position 37.52N 23.34E.

### ZEALAND • GRT 1433 • Built 1936

28.6.42: Torpedoed and sunk by German submarine U-97 (Bürgel), in the Mediterranean 15 miles S of Cape Carmel, Palestine, in position 32.27N 34.43E while on government service on a voyage from Port Said to Famagusta, Cyprus, with a cargo of cased benzine, part of convoy (codenamed Metril) comprising 3 ships. The Master, Capt Lancelot James Branagan, 12 crew and 6 gunners were rescued by HM trawler *ISLAY* 545/41 (T.172) (Lt C.H.L. Clarke) and landed at Haifa. 10 crew and 4 gunners were lost.

## DALGLIESH, R.S. LIMITED – NEWCASTLE UPON TYNE

### ASHWORTH • GRT 5227 • Built 1920

13.10.42: Torpedoed and sunk by German submarine U-221 (Trojer), part of the 'Leopard' patrol group of eight U-boats, in the Atlantic NE of St John's, Newfoundland, in position 53.05N 44.06W while on a voyage from Trinidad to Belfast via Halifax NS, with a cargo of 7300 tons bauxite, part of convoy SC 104, comprising 47 ships. The Master, Capt William Mouat, crew of 41 and 7 gunners were lost.

## Watergate Steamship Co. Ltd

### WENTWORTH ex-*WAR PHLOX* • GRT 5212 • Built 1919

5.5.43: Torpedoed and damaged by German submarine U-264 (Looks), part of the 'Fink' (Finch) patrol group of twenty-eight U-boats, HM corvette *LOOSESTRIFE* 925/41 (K.105) (Lt H.A. Stonehouse) failed to sink the *WENTWORTH*, which was finally sunk by gunfire by German submarine U-628 (Hasenschar), in the Atlantic S of Cape Farewell, in position 53.59N 43.55W while on a voyage from Middlesbrough to Macoris, Cuba via Oban 22.4.43 and New York, in ballast, part of convoy ONS 5 comprising 46 ships. The Master, Capt Reginald Gilbert Phillips, 35 crew and 6 gunners were rescued by *LOOSESTRIFE*. 5 crew were lost. Kapitänleutnant Heinrich Hasenschar and crew of 48 were lost on 3.7.43 when U-

628 was sunk in the Atlantic 60 miles WNW of Cape Ortegal, in position 44.11N 08.45W by Liberator 'J' FL963, pilot S/Ldr Peter J. Cundy DFC of No. 224 Squadron RAF, based at St Eval, part of 19 Group.

## DAWSON, FRANK S. LIMITED – CARDIFF
### Coronation SS Co. Ltd

*THOMAS WALTON* ex-*PORTGWARRA* • GRT 4460 • Built 1917
7.12.39: Torpedoed and sunk by German submarine U-38 (Liebe), in the North Sea S of Svolvaer, Norway, in position 67.52N 14.28E while sailing independently on a voyage from Port Talbot to Narvik, in ballast. The Master, Capt Percy Dudley Townsend, and 20 crew were rescued by German ship *SEBU* 1894/21 and landed at Bodo, Norway. 13 crew were lost.

### Edwardian SS Co. Ltd

*LEO DAWSON* ex-*ROSEDEN* • GRT 4330 • Built 1918
4.2.40: Torpedoed and sunk by German submarine U-37 (Hartmann), in the North Sea NE of Fair Isle, in position 60.10N 00.39W while sailing independently on a voyage from Narvik to Immingham, with a cargo of iron ore. The Master, Capt Charles Edwin Underwood, and crew of 34 were lost.

### MOWT

*GRAVELINES* ex-*ROI ALBERT* • GRT 2491 • Built 1925
31.5.41: Torpedoed and damaged by German submarine U-147 (Wetjen), in the Atlantic NW of Bloody Foreland, in position 56.00N 11.13W while on a voyage from St John, New Brunswick, to London via Halifax NS, with a cargo of 1101 standards of timber, a straggler from convoy HX 127 comprising 56 ships. The afterpart of the ship sank and the forepart was towed to the Clyde and beached at Kames Bay. The Master, Capt Jean Soulé, and 10 crew were lost. 23 crew and 2 gunners were rescued by HM sloop *DEPTFORD* 990/35 (L.53) (Lt-Cdr H.R. White) and landed at Liverpool. Oberleutnant zur See Eberhard Wetjen and crew of 25 were lost on 2.6.41 when U-147 was sunk in the Atlantic 150 miles W of Skerryvore, in position 56.38N 10.24W by HM destroyer *WANDERER* 1300/19 (D.74) (Cdr A.F. St G. Orpen) and HM corvette *PERIWINKLE* 925/40 (K.55) (Lt-Cdr P.C. MacIver) escorting convoy OB 329 comprising 41 ships.

## DENE MANAGEMENT CO. LTD – LONDON
### Elmdene Shipping Co. Ltd

*ELMDENE* • GRT 4853 • Built 1939
8.6.41: Torpedoed and sunk by German submarine U-103 (Schütze), in the Atlantic 200 miles WSW of Freetown, in position 08.47N 16.37W while on a voyage from the Tyne 16.5.41 and Loch Ewe 20.5.41 to Alexandria via Freetown, with a cargo of 5000 tons of coal, 1000 tons of munitions and 20 aircraft, dispersed on 27.5.41 from convoy OB 324 comprising 35 ships. The Master, Capt Ernest Fear, and crew of 35 were rescued by an unknown ship.

## Eskdene Shipping Co. Ltd

*ESKDENE* • GRT 3829 • Built 1934
8.4.41: Torpedoed and sunk by gunfire by German submarine U-107 (Hessler), in the Atlantic SE of the Azores, in position 34.43N 24.21W while on a voyage from Hull to Buenos Aires, with a cargo of 5167 tons of coal and general, part of convoy OG 57 comprising 37 ships. The Master, Capt William Joshua Thomas, and crew of 38 were rescued on the same day by British ship *PENHALE* 4071/24 and landed at Pernambuco 22.4.41.

## Glendene Shipping Co. Ltd

*GLENDENE* • GRT 4412 • Built 1929
8.10.42: Torpedoed and sunk by German submarine U-125 (Folkers), in the Atlantic SW of Freetown, in position 04.29N 17.41W while sailing independently on a voyage from Buenos Aires 20.9.42 to the Mersey via Freetown, with 6900 tons of general cargo. the Master, Capt Ernest Fear, and 4 crew were lost. 30 crew and 6 gunners were rescued by Holt's ship *AGAPENOR* 7392/29. The *AGAPENOR* was sunk on 11.10.42 by German submarine U-87 (Berger), the survivors from the *GLENDENE* were rescued by HM corvette *PETUNIA* 925/40 (K.79) (Lt-Cdr J.M. Rayner), landed at Freetown, embarked on the Union Castle liner *CAERNARVON CASTLE* 20122/26 on 15.10.42 and sailed for Glasgow. Kapitänleutnant Ulrich Folkers (Knight's Cross 27.3.43) and crew of 53 were lost on 6.5.43 when U-125, part of the 'Fink' (Finch) patrol group of thirty U-boats, was sunk while attacking convoy ONS 5 comprising 42 ships in the Atlantic about 400 miles NE of Cape Race, in position 52.31N 44.50W. She was rammed by HM destroyer *ORIBI* 1540/41 (G.66) ex-HMS *OBSERVER* (Lt-Cdr J.C.A. Ingram) and sunk by gunfire by HM corvette *SNOWFLAKE* 925/41 (K.211) (Lt Harold G. Chesterman).

## Oakdene Shipping Co. Ltd

*OAKDENE* • GRT 4255 • Built 1936
6.5.41: Torpedoed and sunk by German submarine U-105 (Schewe), in the Atlantic NW of St Paul Rocks, in position 06.19N 27.55W while sailing independently on a voyage from Cardiff to Buenos Aires, with a cargo of 6222 tons of coal, dispersed from convoy OG 59 comprising 43 ships. The Master, Capt Ernest Hart, crew of 31 and 3 gunners were rescued by HM cruiser *DORSETSHIRE* 9975/29 (40) (Capt B.S.C. Martin). *DORSETSHIRE* (Capt A.W.S. Agar VC DSO) was lost on 5.4.42, sunk by Japanese carrier-borne aircraft from Japanese carriers *AKAGI* 36500/ 27, *SORYU* 15900/37 and *HIRYU* 17300/39 in the Indian Ocean near Colombo, Ceylon.

## DENHOLM J. & J. LIMITED – GLASGOW
## The Denholm Line of Steamers Ltd

*EARLSPARK* • GRT 5186 • Built 1929
12.6.40: Torpedoed and sunk by German submarine U-101 (Frauenheim), part of the 'Rösing' (named after a U-boat commander) patrol group of five U-boats, in the Atlantic NW of Cape Finisterre, in position 42.26N 11.33W while sailing independently on a voyage

from Sunderland to Bordeaux, with a cargo of 7500 tons of coal. The Master, Capt Evan James Williams, and 6 crew were lost. 31 crew were rescued by HM sloop *ENCHANTRESS* 1190/34 (L.56) ex-HMS *BITTERN* (Cdr A.K. Scott-Moncrieff).

**DENPARK** • GRT 3491 • Built 1928
13.5.42: Torpedoed and sunk by German submarine U-128 (Heyse), in the Atlantic 300 miles NW of the Cape Verde Islands, in position 22.28N 28.10W while on a voyage from Takoradi 24.4.42 to the Clyde and Workington via Freetown 4.5.42, with a cargo of 5000 tons of manganese ore, part of convoy SL 109 comprising 31 ships. The Master, Capt John McCreadie, 15 crew and 5 gunners were lost. 22 crew and 3 gunners were rescued by Danish ship *NORDLYS* 3726/16 and British ship *CITY OF WINDSOR* 7247/23 and landed at Clyde.

**BROOMPARK** • GRT 5136 • Built 1939
25.7.42: Torpedoed and damaged by German submarine U-552 (Topp), part of the 'Wolf' patrol group of ten U-boats, in the Atlantic E of Newfoundland, in position 49.02N 40.26W while on a voyage from the Tyne to New York, in ballast, part of convoy ON 113 comprising 35 ships. The Master, Capt John Leask Sinclair, and 3 crew were lost. Taken in tow by US ship *CHEROKEE* 5896/25 but sank at 06.00 hours 28.7.42 after 4 days towing about 50 miles SW of St John's, Newfoundland, in position 47.41N 51.50W. 38 crew and 7 gunners were rescued by HMCS corvette *BRANDON* 925/41 (K.149) (Lt J.C. Littler) and landed at St John's.

**HOLMPARK** • GRT 5780 • Built 1927
24.10.42: Torpedoed and sunk by German submarine U-516 (Wiebe), in the Atlantic 900 miles E of Barbados, in position 13.11N 47.00W while sailing independently on a voyage from Lourenco Marques to Philadelphia via Cape Town 30.9.42 and Trinidad, in ballast. The Master, Capt Alfred Cromarty, 40 crew and 8 gunners landed at Port Dennery, St Lucia. 1 crew was lost. Capt A. Cromarty was awarded the Lloyd's War Medal for bravery at sea.

**GRANGEPARK** • GRT 5132 • Built 1919
20.11.42: Torpedoed and sunk by German submarine U-263 (Nölke), part of the 'Westwall' patrol group of thirteen U-boats, in the Atlantic W of Gibraltar, in position 35.55N 10.14W while on government service on a voyage from Barry 3.11.42 and the Clyde 8.11.42 to Oran, carrying 10 US army personnel and a cargo of 2000 tons of government stores, part of convoy KMS 3 comprising 56 ships. The Master, Capt John Scott Webster, 40 crew, 16 gunners, 1 signalman and 9 US army personnel were rescued by HM sloop *FOWEY* 1045/30 (L.15) (Cdr L.B.A. Majendie) and landed at Gibraltar. 3 crew and 1 US army personnel were lost. Kapitänleutnant Kurt Nölke and crew of 50 were lost on 20.1.44 when U-263 struck a mine in the Bay of Biscay S of La Pallice, in position 46.10N 01.14W.

**MOWT**

**EMPIRE BREEZE** • GRT 7457 • Built 1941
25.8.42: Torpedoed and sunk by German submarines U-176 (Dierksen) and U-438 (Franzius), part of the 'Lion' patrol group of thirteen U-boats, in the Atlantic SE of Cape Farewell, in position 49.22N 35.52W while on a voyage from Manchester 15.8.42 to Hampton Roads, in ballast, part of convoy ON 122 comprising 36 ships. The Master, Capt

Robert Thomson, 41 crew and 6 gunners were rescued by Irish ship *IRISH WILLOW* 2009/18 and landed at Dunmore, Ireland. 1 crew was lost.

**FORT HALKETT** • GRT 7133 • Built 1942
6.8.43: Torpedoed and sunk by German submarine U-185 (Maus), in the South Atlantic about 600 miles SE of Natal, Brazil, in position 09.30S 25.50W while sailing independently on a voyage from Bona to Rio de Janeiro via Freetown 28.7.43, in ballast. The Master, Capt William Walker DSO, and 23 survivors landed S of Natal. The Chief Officer and 23 survivors were rescued by the US four-stack destroyer *GOLDSBOROUGH* 1190/18 (DD-188) and landed at Recife; the 2nd Officer and 10 survivors landed at Cabadello, Brazil. U-185, commanded by Kapitänleutnant August Maus (Knight's Cross 21.9.43), was sunk on 24.8.43 in the Atlantic about 800 miles SW by S of the Azores, in position 27.00N 37.06W by an Avenger, pilot Lt Robert P. Williams and a Wildcat, pilot Lt Martin G. O'Neill of US Navy Composite Squadron VC-13 from US escort carrier *CORE* 9800/42 (CVE-13) (Capt M.R. Greer), part of US Navy Task Force 66. The U-boat commander and 26 crew were taken prisoner by the US four-stack destroyer *BARKER* 1190/19 (DD-213). 15 crew were lost.

# DODD, THOMPSON & CO. LTD – LONDON
## King Line Ltd

**KING ALFRED** ex-*WAR AZALEA* • GRT 5275 • Built 1919
4.8.40: Torpedoed and sunk by German submarine U-52 (Salman), in the Atlantic 300 miles WNW of Bloody Foreland, in position 56.59N 17.38W while on a voyage from St John's, Newfoundland, to Methil via Halifax NS, with a cargo of 6750 tons pit props, part of convoy HX 60 comprising 60 ships. The Master, Capt Richard Storm, and 33 crew were rescued by HM destroyer *VANOC* 1090/17 (H.33) (Lt-Cdr J.G.W. Deneys) and landed at Liverpool. 7 crew were lost.

**KING IDWAL** ex-*KERAMIES* ex-*WAR CORONET* • GRT 5115 • Built 1920
23.11.40: Torpedoed and sunk by German submarine U-123 (Moehle), in the Atlantic 158 miles W of Rockall, in position 56.44N 19.13W while on a voyage from Liverpool to Baltimore, Maryland, in ballast, part of convoy OB 244 comprising 46 ships. The Master, Capt Richard Storm, and 27 crew were rescued by HM sloop *SANDWICH* 1045/28 (L.12) (Cdr M.J. Yeatman) and landed at Liverpool 27.1.40. 12 crew were lost.

**KING LUD** • GRT 5224 • Built 1928
8.6.42: Torpedoed and sunk by Japanese submarine I-10 (Kayahara), in the Mozambique Channel 350 miles E of Beira, in position 20.00S 40.00E while sailing independently on a voyage from New York to Bombay via Cape Town, with 5 military personnel and a cargo of government stores. The Master, Capt Benjamin Roderick Evans, crew of 33 and the military personnel were lost.

**KING ARTHUR** • GRT 5228 • Built 1928
15.11.42: Torpedoed and sunk by German submarine U-67 (Müller-Stöckheim), in the Atlantic W of Trinidad, in position 10.30N 59.50W while sailing independently on a voyage from Alexandria and Port Elizabeth 15.10.42 to the UK via Trinidad, with a cargo of 5200

tons of cotton and general. The Master, Capt Angus MacNeil, crew of 32 and 7 gunners were rescued by a USN patrol ship and landed at Trinidad. U-67, commanded by Kapitänleutnant Gunther Müller-Stöckheim (Knight's Cross 27.11.42), and 47 crew were lost on 16.7.43 in the Atlantic 960 miles SW by S of Flores, Azores, in position 30.05N 44.17W sunk by an Avenger, pilot Lt Robert P. Williams of the US Navy Composite Squadron VC-13 from the US Navy escort carrier *CORE* 9800/42 (CVE-13) (Capt M.R. Greer), part of Task Group 21.16. One officer and two ratings were taken prisoner by the US Navy four-stack destroyer *McCORMICK* 1190/20 (DD-223).

**KING EDWARD** ex-*GORALA* ex-*WAR TERRIER* • GRT 5217 • Built 1919
27.12.42: Torpedoed and sunk by German submarine U-356 (Ruppelt), part of the 'Spitz' (Sharp) patrol group of ten U-boats, in the Atlantic NNE of the Azores, in position 47.25N 25.20W while on a voyage from Hull and Loch Ewe 18.12.42 to New York, in ballast, part of convoy ONS 154 comprising 47 ships. The Master, Capt James Herbert Ewens, 15 crew and 4 gunners were rescued by rescue ship *TOWARD* 1571/23 (Capt Gordon K. Hudson) and landed at Halifax NS 9.1.43; 5 crew by RCN corvette *NAPANEE* 925/41 (K.118) (Lt S. Henderson) and landed at St John's, Newfoundland. 19 crew and 4 gunners were lost. Oberleutnant zur See Günther Ruppelt and crew of 45 were lost on the same day in the Atlantic N of the Azores, in position 45.30N 25.40W when U-356 was sunk by RCN destroyer *ST LAURENT* 1375/31 (H.83) (Lt-Cdr Guy S. Windmeyer DSC), RCN corvettes *CHILLIWACK* 925/40 (K.131) (A/Lt-Cdr L.F. Foxall), *BATTLEFORD* 925/41 (K.165) (Lt F.A. Beck) and *NAPANEE* 925/40 (K.118) (Lt S. Henderson) of the Escort Group C1.

**KING GRUFFYDD** ex-*AMBATIELOS* ex-*WAR TROOPER* • GRT 5063 • Built 1919
17.3.43: Torpedoed and sunk by German submarine U-338 (Kinzel), part of the 'Stürmer' (Attacker) patrol group of eighteen U-boats, in the Atlantic SE of Cape Farewell, in position 51.55N 32.41W while on a voyage from New York 5.3.42 to Loch Ewe and Hull, with a cargo of 5000 tons of steel, 500 tons of tobacco and 493 tons of high explosives, part of convoy SC 122 comprising 51 ships. The Master, Capt Hywell Griffiths, 21 crew and 2 gunners were lost. 18 crew and 7 gunners were rescued by the rescue ship *ZAMALEK* 1567/21 (Capt Owen Charles Morris DSO) and landed at Gourock 22.3.43.

**KING FREDERICK** ex-*TRIALOS* ex-*WAR SCEPTRE* • GRT 5106 • Built 1919
19.7.44: Torpedoed and sunk by German submarine U-181 (Freiwald), in the Arabian Sea in the Nine Degree Channel, in position 09.29N 111.45E while sailing independently on a voyage from Haifa and Aden to Colombo and Calcutta, with 2 military personnel and 6600 tons of salt and mail. The Master, Capt Richard John Esslemont, 27 crew and 1 gunner were rescued by the US Liberty ship *SHAMSHEE* 7176/44 and landed at Aden. 20 crew, 5 gunners and the military personnel were lost. U-181 was transferred to Japan and renamed I-501 at Singapore on VJ Day 14.8.45.

**KING EDGAR** • GRT 4536 • Built 1927
2.3.45: Torpedoed and sunk by German submarine U-1302 (Herwatz), in the St George's Channel, in position 52.05N 05.42W while on a voyage from Victoria, BC to Swansea and London via Panama and Halifax NS, with a cargo of 1667 standards of lumber, 2038 tons of plywood and 500 tons of lead and zinc, part of convoy SC 167 comprising 39 ships. The

Master, Capt Arthur Warren Wheeler, 32 crew and 9 gunners were rescued by HM frigate *NYSALAND* 1318/43 (K.587) (Lt-Cdr J. Scott) ex-USN *HOSTE* and landed at Milford Haven. 2 crew and 2 gunners were lost. Kapitänleutnant Wolfgang Herwatz and crew of 48 were lost on 7.3.45 when U-1302 was sunk in St George's Channel, 26 miles N of St David's Head, in position 52.19N 05.23W by HMCS frigates *LA HULLOISE* 1370/43 (K.668) (Lt-Cdr John Brock), *STRATHADAM* 1370/44 (K.682) (A/Lt-Cdr H.L. Quinn) and *THETFORD MINES* 1370/43 (K.459) (Lt-Cdr J.A.R. Allen), part of the 25th Escort Group.

## Scottish Steamship Co. Ltd

**KING ROBERT** ex-*CITTA DI MESSINA* • GRT 5886 • Built 1920
29.1.41: Torpedoed and sunk by German submarine U-93 (Korth), in the Atlantic S of Rockall, in position 56.00N 15.23W while on a voyage from St John, New Brunswick, to Cardiff via Sydney CB, with a cargo of 7942 tons of grain, a straggler from convoy SC 19 comprising 27 ships. The Master, Capt Leslie Trail, and 21 crew were rescued by HM destroyer *ANTHONY* 1350/29 (H.40) (Lt-Cdr V.C.F. Clark) and landed at Gourock; 20 crew rescued by HM trawler *LADY MADELINE* 581/39 (FY.283) (Lt P.H. Potter) also landed at Greenock.

**KING MALCOLM** • GRT 5064 • Built 1925
31.10.41: Torpedoed and sunk by German submarine U-106 (Rasch), in the Atlantic SE of St John's, Newfoundland, in position 47.04N 51.50W while on a voyage from Haifa to Belfast and Garston via Sydney CB, with a cargo of potash, a straggler from convoy SC 50 comprising 40 ships. The Master, Capt James Wilson, crew of 33 and 4 gunners were lost.

## MOWT

**EMPIRE COMET** • GRT 6914 • Built 1941
17.2.42: Torpedoed and sunk by German submarine U-136 (Zimmermann), in the Atlantic W of Rockall, in position 58.15N 17.10W while on a voyage from Bombay 12.11.41 to Manchester via Table Bay 16.12.41 and Halifax NS 7.2.42, with 8672 tons of general cargo including manganese ore, linseed, tea and groundnuts, a straggler from convoy HX 174 comprising 27 ships. The Master, Capt Hector Raymond Willis, crew of 37 and 8 gunners were lost.

**OCEAN CRUSADER** • GRT 7178 • Built 1942
26.11.42: Torpedoed and sunk by German submarine U-262 (Franke), part of the 'Drachen' (Dragon) patrol group of seven U-boats, in the Atlantic NE of St John's, Newfoundland, in position 50.30N 45.30W while on a voyage from Portland, Maine, to Avonmouth via Panama and New York 19.11.42 with 8891 tons of general cargo, a straggler from convoy HX 216 comprising 42 ships. The Master, Capt Ellis Wynne Parry, and crew of 44 were lost. U-262 commanded by Kapitänleutnant Karl-Heinz Laudahn was damaged beyond repair in December 1944 in an air attack on the port of Gotenhafen (Gdynia).

**FORT FRANKLIN** • GRT 7135 • Built 1942
16.7.43: Torpedoed and sunk by German submarine U-181 (Lüth), in the Indian Ocean SW of Reunion, in position 22.36S 51.22E while sailing independently on a voyage from Port

Said and Aden 1.7.43 to Lourenco Marques and Durban, with 1500 tons of salt as ballast. The Master, Capt Thomas Witney Trott, 43 crew and 9 gunners landed at Manajara, Madagascar. 2 crew were lost.

### EMPIRE HOUSMAN • GRT 7359 • Built 1943
30.12.43: Torpedoed and damaged by German submarine U-545 (Mannesmann), part of the 'Rugen 3' (German island) patrol group of three U-boats, in the North Atlantic S of Iceland, in position 60.03N 24.34W; on 3.1.44 she was torpedoed and sunk by German submarine U-744 (Blischke) of the same patrol group, S of Iceland, in position 60.50N 22.07W while on a voyage from the Tyne to New York via Loch Ewe 24.12.43 for orders, in ballast, a straggler from convoy ON 217 comprising 70 ships. The Master, Capt David John Lewis, 37 crew and 7 gunners were rescued by HM trawler *ELM* 530/39 (T.105) (Lt K.A. Grant) and HM rescue tug *EARNER* 700/43 (W.143) ex-HMS *EARNEST* and landed at Reykjavik. 1 crew was lost. Kapitänleutnant Gert Mannesmann was lost on 10.2.44 when U-545, part of the 'Igel' (Hedgehog) patrol group of fourteen U-boats, was sunk in the Atlantic 40 miles NNE of Rockall, in position 58.17N 13.22W by Wellington 'O', pilot P/O Max H. Painter, RAAF of No. 612 'County of Aberdeen' Squadron RAuxAF, based at Limavady, Co. Londonderry, part of 15 Group. The pilot was awarded the DFC. Kapitänleutnant Mannesmann and 47 crew were rescued by U-714 (Schwebcke) and landed at St Nazaire 25.2.44. U-744 commanded by Oberleutnant zur See Heinz Blischke was sunk on 6.3.44 in the Atlantic 480 miles W of Cape Clear while shadowing convoy HX 280 comprising 45 ships by RCN frigate *ST CATHERINES* 1370/42 (K.325) (Lt-Cdr A.F. Pickard), RCN corvettes *CHILLIWACK* 925/40 (K.131) (Lt-Cdr C.R. Coughlin) and *FENNEL* 925/40 (K.194) (Lt-Cdr W.P. Moffat), RCN destroyers *GATINEAU* 1375/34 (H.61) (Lt-Cdr H.V.W. Groos) and *CHAUDIERE* 1340/36 (H.99) (Lt-Cdr C.P. Nixon), HMS *ICARUS* 1370/36 (D.03) (Lt-Cdr R. Dyer) and HM corvette *KENILWORTH CASTLE* 1010/43 (K.420) (Lt J.J. Allon) of the Escort Group C2. The U-boat commander and 11 crew were lost. 22 crew were taken prisoner by HMCS *CHAUDIERE* and 17 crew by HMCS *FENNEL* and landed at Londonderry. U-744 was destroyed after a 32 hour hunt. Kapitänleutnant Hans-Joachim Schwebcke and crew of 50 were lost on 14.3.45 when U-714 was sunk in the North Sea N of St Abb's Head, in position 55.57N 01.57W by SAN frigate *NATAL* 1435/44 (K.430) ex-HMS *LOCH CREE* (Lt-Cdr D.A. Hall).

## DOMINION SHIPPING CO. LTD – HALIFAX, NOVA SCOTIA

### LORD STRATHCONA • GRT 7335 • Built 1915
5.9.42: Torpedoed and sunk by German submarine U-513 (Rüggeberg), in the Atlantic while at anchor in Wabana Roads, Conception Bay, Newfoundland, in position 47.35N 52.59W with a cargo of iron ore en route to Sydney CB. The Master, Capt Charles Stewart, and crew of 43 were rescued by a Customs launch and landed at Lana Bay, Bell Island. U-513, commanded by Kapitänleutnant Friedrich Guggenberger (Knight's Cross 10.12.41, with Oak Leaves 8.1.43), was sunk on 19.7.43 in the South Atlantic off Paranuagua, Brazil, in position 27.17S 47.32W by a Mariner, pilot Lt Roy S. Whitcomb of US Navy Patrol Squadron VP–74 based at Aratu, Brazil. The U-boat commander and 6 crew were taken prisoner by the US seaplane tender *BARNEGAT* 1766/41 (AVP.10) and landed at Rio de Janeiro. 46 crew were lost. U-81, under the command of K/L Guggenberger, sank HM

aircraft carrier *ARK ROYAL* 22600/37 (91) (Capt L.E.H. Maund) on 13.11.41 in the Mediterranean E of Gibraltar, in position 36.06N 05.07E.

## Rose Castle Shipping Co. Ltd

*ROSE CASTLE* • GRT 7803 • Built 1915 (Canadian flag)
2.11.42: Torpedoed and sunk by German submarine U-518 (Wissmann), in the Atlantic while lying at anchor off Bell Island, Conception Bay, in position 47.36N 52.58W, waiting to sail with convoy WB-9 on a voyage from Wabana to Sydney CB, with a cargo of 10200 tons of iron ore. The Master, Capt Walter J. MacDonald, 17 crew and 2 gunners were rescued by RCN motor launches. 22 crew and 1 gunner were lost.

## DONALDSON BROTHERS LIMITED – GLASGOW
## Anglo-Newfoundland Steamship Co. Ltd

*GERALDINE MARY* • GRT 7244 • Built 1924
4.8.40: Torpedoed and sunk by German submarine U-52 (Salman), in the Atlantic 270 miles WNW of Bloody Foreland, in position 56.58N 15.55W while on a voyage from Botwood, Newfoundland, to Manchester via Halifax NS 23.7.40, with 5 passengers and a cargo of 6112 tons of newsprint and 494 tons of sulphite pulp, part of convoy HX 60 comprising 60 ships. The Master, Capt George McCartney Sime, and 27 survivors were rescued by HM ship and landed at Methil 8.8.40, 6 survivors were rescued and landed at Liverpool and 14 survivors landed at Uig, Isle of Lewis. 2 crew and 1 passenger were lost.

*ESMOND* ex-*TRAPRAIN LAW* • GRT 4976 • Built 1930
9.5.41: Torpedoed and sunk by German submarine U-110 (Lemp), in the North Atlantic E of Cape Farewell, in position 60.45N 33.02W while on a voyage from the Tyne to Sydney CB, in ballast, part of convoy OB 318 comprising 38 ships. The Master, Capt James Bernard McAulay Macaffert, crew of 44 and 5 gunners were rescued: 22 survivors were rescued by Norwegian ship *BORGFRED* 2183/20, 27 by British ship *AELYBRYN* 5986/38 and landed at Sydney CB 18.5.41, and 1 by HM corvette *AUBRIETIA* 925/40 (K.96) (Lt-Cdr V.F. Smith) and landed at Reykjavik.

*ROTHERMERE* • GRT 5366 • Built 1938
20.5.41: Torpedoed and sunk by German submarine U-98 (Gysae), in the Atlantic SE of Cape Farewell, in position 57.48N 41.36W while on a voyage from Botwood, Newfoundland, to London via Halifax NS, with 1 passenger and a cargo of 1998 tons of steel and 4750 tons of newsprint and paper pulp, part of convoy HX 126 comprising 29 ships. The Master, Capt George McCartney, and 20 crew were lost. 30 crew, 4 gunners and the passenger were rescued by Icelandic ship *BRUARFOSS* 1579/27 and landed at Reykjavik.

## Donaldson Brothers & Black Limited

*ATHENIA* • GRT 13465 • Built 1923
3.9.39: Torpedoed and sunk by German submarine U-30 (Lemp), in the Atlantic about 250 miles W of Donegal, in position 56.44N 14.05W while sailing independently on a voyage

from Glasgow and Liverpool to Montreal, with 1103 passengers including women, children and general cargo. The Master, Capt James Cook, and many survivors were rescued: 364 by Norwegian ship *KNUTE NELSON* 5749/26 were landed at Galway 5.9.39; Swedish motor yacht *SOUTHERN CROSS* 734/30 rescued 376 survivors who were later transferred to US ship *CITY OF FLINT* 4963/18 and landed at a port in the USA; 300 survivors were rescued by HM destroyer *ESCORT* 1375/34 (H.66) (Lt–Cdr J. Bostock); about 200 survivors by HMS *ELECTRA* 1375/34 (H.27) (Lt–Cdr S.A. Buss) and landed at Greenock 5.9.39. 18 crew and 93 passengers were lost. The survivors were rescued from the *ATHENIA*'s twenty–six lifeboats. This was the first British merchantman to be sunk by a U–boat in the Second World War.

### *SULAIRIA* • GRT 5802 • Built 1929
25.9.40: Torpedoed and sunk by German submarine U-43 (Ambrosius), in the Atlantic 356 miles W of Achill Head, Co. Mayo, in position 53.43N 20.10W while on a voyage from Glasgow to Montreal, with 540 tons of general cargo and livestock, a straggler from convoy OB 217 comprising 38 ships. The Master, Capt Robert Clarke Young, and 55 crew were rescued by RCN destroyer *OTTAWA* 1375/31 (H.60) ex-HMS *CRUSADER* (Cdr E.R. Mainguy) and landed at Gourock 27.9.40. 1 crew was lost.

### *GREGALIA* • GRT 5802 • Built 1929
9.5.41: Torpedoed and sunk by German submarine U-201 (Schnee), in the North Atlantic ENE of Cape Farewell, in position 60.24N 32.37W while on a voyage from Glasgow to Buenos Aires via Halifax NS, in ballast, part of convoy OB 318 comprising 38 ships. The Master, Capt Alexander Bankier, crew of 57 and 8 gunners were rescued by HM trawler *DANEMAN* 516/37 (FY.123) (Lt A.H. Ballard); the Master and 51 survivors were transferred to British ship *AELYBRYN* 5986/38 and 14 survivors to Norwegian ship *BORGFRED* 2183/20 and landed at Sydney CB 18.5.41.

## Donaldson South America Line Ltd

### *CORRIENTES* • GRT 6863 • Built 1920
20.9.40: Torpedoed and damaged by German submarine U-32 (Jenisch), in the Atlantic 608 miles W of Achill Head, Co. Mayo, in position 53.49N 24.19W and sunk on 28.9.40 by torpedo and gunfire by German submarine U-37 (Oehrn), while sailing independently on a voyage from Glasgow to Montreal via Halifax NS with 1800 tons of general cargo, dispersed from convoy OB 217 comprising 38 ships. The Master, Capt Thomas Halliday Young Stewart, and crew of 49 were rescued by Swedish ship *KOLSNAREN* 2465/23 and landed at Philadelphia.

### *CORTONA* • GRT 7093 • Built 1921
12.7.42: Torpedoed and damaged by German submarine U-116 (v. Schmidt) and sunk by a *coup de grâce* by German submarine U-201 (Schnee), in the Atlantic S of the Azores, in position 32.45N 24.45W while on a voyage from Liverpool 1.7.42 to Buenos Aires, with 2400 tons of general cargo, dispersed from convoy OS 33 comprising 41 ships. The Master, Capt Matthew McKirdie Brown, 18 crew and 4 gunners were rescued after 10 days in an open boat by HM destroyer *PATHFINDER* 1540/41 (G.04) ex-HMS *ONSLOW* (Cdr E.A. Gibbs) and landed at Londonderry. 29 crew and 2 gunners were lost.

**CORINALDO** • GRT 7173 • Built 1921
30.10.42: Torpedoed and damaged by German submarine U-509 (Witte), two attempted *coups de grâce* by submarine U-659 (Stock) and finally sunk by torpedo and gunfire by submarine U-203 (Kottmann), part of the 'Streitaxt' (Battleaxe) patrol group of eight U-boats, in the Atlantic N of the Canary Islands, in position 33.20N 18.12W while on a voyage from Buenos Aires to Glasgow via Freetown 16.10.42, with a cargo of 5141 tons of frozen meat, part of convoy SL 125 comprising 40 ships. The Master, Capt William Anderson, 41 crew and 8 gunners were rescued by HM corvette *COWSLIP* 925/41 (K.196) (Sub-Lt J.S.N. Swift) and landed at Gibraltar. 7 crew and 1 gunner were lost. U-203, commanded by Kapitänleutnant Herman Kottmann, was lost on 25.4.43 when U-203, part of the 'Meise' (Titmouse) patrol group of twenty-eight U-boats, shadowing convoy ONS 4 comprising 32 ships, was sunk in the Atlantic 290 miles SSE of Cape Farewell, in position 55.05N 42.25W by Fairey Swordfish 'L' of No. 811 Naval Air Squadron from HM escort carrier *BITER* 8200/40 (D.97) (Capt E.M.C. Abel-Smith) and HM destroyer *PATHFINDER* 1540/41 (G.10) (Cdr E.A. Gibbs) of the 5th Escort Group. The U-boat commander and 38 crew were taken prisoner by HMS *PATHFINDER*. 11 crew were lost.

**CORACERO** • GRT 7252 • Built 1923
17.3.43: Torpedoed and sunk by German submarine U-384 (v. Rosenberg-Gruszcynski), part of the 'Stürmer' (Attacker) patrol group of eighteen U-boats in the Atlantic NE of St John's, Newfoundland, in position 51.04N 33.20W while on a voyage from Buenos Aires to Liverpool via New York 8.3.43, with a cargo of 5758 tons of refrigerated meat and mail, part of convoy HX 229 comprising 40 ships. The Master, Capt Robert Clarke Young, 44 crew, 7 gunners and 1 DBS were rescued by HM destroyer *MANSFIELD* 1090/18 (G.76) (Lt-Cdr L.C. Hill OBE) ex-USN four-stack *EVANS* and landed at Gourock. 5 crew were lost. Oberleutnant zur See Hans-Achim von Rosenberg-Gruszcynski and crew of 46 were lost on 20.3.43 when U-384 was sunk in the Atlantic 640 miles W of Malin Head, in position 54.18N 26.15W by Fortress 'B' FK208, pilot P/O Leslie G. Clark of No. 206 Squadron RAF, based at Benbecula, Hebrides, part of 15 Group.

**MOWT**

**EMPIRE SPRING** • GRT 6946 • Built 1941 (CAM ship)
14.2.42: Torpedoed and sunk by German submarine U-576 (Heinicke), in the Atlantic SE of Sable Island, in position 42.00N 55.00W while sailing independently on a voyage from Manchester to Halifax NS, in ballast, dispersed on 13.2.42 from convoy ON 63 comprising 31 ships. The Master, Capt Alexander McKechan, Commodore A.D.H. Dibben OBE RNR, 41 crew, 5 gunners and 5 naval staff were lost. Kapitänleutnant Hans-Dieter Heinicke and 44 crew were lost on 15.7.42 when U-576 was attacking the US convoy KS 520 comprising 19 ships; she was damaged in the Atlantic 50 miles E of Cape Hatteras, North Carolina, in position 34.51N 75.22W by two US Navy Kingfisher aircraft, pilots Ensign Frank C. Lewis and Ensign Charles D. Webb from US Navy Scouting Squadron VS-9 based at Cherry Point, North Carolina, then rammed and sunk by gunfire by the USN ship *UNICOI* 5873/20 (IX.216) (Lt M.K. Amos).

**EMPIRE REDSHANK** ex-*BRADDOCK* • GRT 6615 • Built 1919
22.2.43: Torpedoed and damaged by German submarine U-606 (Döhler), later sunk by gunfire by RCN corvette *TRILLIUM* 925/40 (K.172) (Lt P.C. Evans), in the Atlantic E of St

John's, Newfoundland, in position 47.00N 34.30W while on a voyage from Cardiff and Belfast Lough to Galveston, in ballast, part of convoy ON 166 comprising 48 ships. The Master, Capt John Houston Clinton, crew of 39 and 7 gunners were rescued by HMCS *TRILLIUM* and landed at St John's, Newfoundland. U-606 commanded by Oberleutnant zur See Hans Döhler was sunk on the same day in the Atlantic 540 miles W by N of Fayal, Azores, in position 47.44N 33.43W by the convoy's escorts US coastguard cutter *CAMPBELL* 2216/36 (PG-32) (Cdr James A. Hirshfield) and ORP destroyer *BURZA* 1540/29 (Lt-Cdr F. Pitulko) of the Escort Group A3 commanded by Capt Paul R. Heineman USN. The U-boat commander and 35 crew were lost. 12 crew were taken prisoner by USCG *CAMPBELL* and ORP *BURZA*. Oberleutnant zur See Hermann Schröder and crew of 46 were lost on 21.2.43 in the Atlantic 800 miles WSW of Cape Clear, in position 48.08N 29.37W when U-623, part of the 'Ritter' (Knight) patrol group of twelve U-boats, was sunk while shadowing convoy ON 166 by Liberator III 'T' FK223, pilot S/Ldr Desmond J. Isted DFC of No. 120 Squadron RAF, based at Aldergrove, Co. Antrim, part of 15 Group.

**EMPIRE WHALE** ex-*WINONA COUNTY* • GRT 6159 • Built 1919
29.3.43: Torpedoed and sunk by German submarine U-662 (Müller), in the Atlantic 425 miles NW of Cape Finisterre, in position 46.44N 16.38W while on a voyage from Pepel to Methil and the Tyne via Freetown 12.3.43, with 3 RAF personnel and a cargo of 7870 tons of iron ore, part of convoy SL 126 comprising 36 ships. The Master, Capt James Thompson Davitt, 41 crew, 4 gunners and 1 RAF personnel were lost. 7 crew, 1 gunner and 2 RAF personnel were rescued by HM frigate *SPEY* 1370/41 (K.246) (Cdr H.G. Boys-Smith DSO) and landed at Londonderry. U-662, commanded by Kapitänleutnant Heinz–Eberhard Müller, was sunk on 21.6.43 while pursuing convoy TF 2 by two US Navy Catalina flying boats, pilots Lt Stanley E. Auslander and Lt R.H. Howland of US Navy Patrol Squadron VP–94 based at Amapa, Brazil, in the Atlantic 210 miles E by S of Cayenne, French Guiana, in position 03.36N 48.46N. The U-boat commander and 3 crew were taken prisoner some days later by US Navy submarine chaser PC 494 280/42. 46 crew were lost.

## DOREY, ONESIMUS & SONS LTD – GUERNSEY, CHANNEL ISLANDS

**PORTELET** ex-*LOCHEE* • GRT 1064 • Built 1918
2.2.40: Torpedoed and sunk by German submarine U-59 (Jürst), in the North Sea ¾ mile SW by W of Smith's Knoll Lightship, in position 52.40N 02.13E while on a voyage from Ipswich to Sunderland, in ballast. The Master, Capt Alexander Welsh, and 8 crew were rescued by the Finnish ship *OSCAR MIDLING* 2287/89 and landed at Immingham 4.2.40. 2 crew were lost.

## DORNOCH SHIPPING COMPANY – LONDON

**COULTARN** • GRT 3759 • Built 1938
30.3.41: Torpedoed and sunk by German submarine U-69 (Metzler), in the North Atlantic SW of Iceland, in position 60.18N 29.28W while on a voyage from Hull to Mobile, in ballast, part of convoy OB 302 comprising 32 ships. The Master, Capt Harold Cecil Lewis Phillips, 34 crew and 4 gunners were rescued by HM armed cruiser *CALIFORNIA* 16799/23 (Capt C.J. Pope RAN). 3 crew were lost.

## DOUGLAS & RAMSAY – GLASGOW

*DARCOILA* • GRT 4084 • Built 1928
26.9.40: Torpedoed and sunk by German submarine U–32 (Jenisch), in the Atlantic W of Ireland, in position 53.32N 26.00W while sailing independently on a voyage from Barry to Philadelphia, in ballast, dispersed from convoy OB 217 comprising 38 ships. The Master, Capt William Anderson, and crew of 30 were lost.

### Lochinver Limited

*WILHELMINA* • GRT 6725 • Built 1909
2.12.40: Torpedoed and sunk by German submarine U–94 (Kuppish), in the Atlantic 265 miles W of Bloody Foreland, in position 55.43N 15.06W while on a voyage from New Westminster BC to Liverpool via Panama and Halifax NS 21.11.40, with a cargo of 6365 tons of general cargo including fish and wood pulp, part of convoy HX 90 comprising 35 ships. The Master, Capt James Black Rue, and 33 crew were rescued by HM corvette *GENTIAN* 925/40 (K.90) (Lt-Cdr R.O. Yemans) and landed at Gourock. 4 crew and 1 gunner were lost.

## MOWT

*EMPIRE ELAND* ex-*WEST KEDRON* • GRT 5613 • Built 1920
15.9.41: Torpedoed and sunk by German submarine U–94 (Ites), in the Atlantic SE of Cape Farewell, in position 54.00N 28.00W while on a voyage from Liverpool to Mobile and Tampa, in ballast, a straggler from convoy ON 14 comprising 47 ships. The Master, Capt Donald Cameron Sinclair, crew of 32 and 5 gunners were lost.

## DOUGLAS SHIPPING CO. LTD – HONG KONG

*HAICHING* • GRT 2182 • Built 1898
2.10.43: Torpedoed and sunk by German submarine U–168 (Pich), in the Arabian Sea 80 miles WSW of Bombay, in position 18.46N 71.55E while sailing independently from Calcutta and Cochin to Karachi. The Master, Capt Charles E. Steuart, 55 crew and 2 gunners were rescued by Indian dhow *MAHADRO PRASAD* and landed at Bombay. 12 crew were lost. U–168 commanded by Kapitänleutnant Helmuth Pich was sunk on 5.10.44 in the Java Sea, 80 miles WNW of Sourabaya, in position 06.20S 111.28E by RNeN submarine *ZWAARDVISCH* 1093/43 (Lt-Cdr H.A.W. Goosens) ex-HMS *TALENT.* The U-boat commander and 26 crew were rescued by a fishing boat. 23 crew were lost.

## DOVER NAVIGATION COMPANY – TRING

*SEA VENTURE* • GRT 2327 • Built 1930
20.10.39: Torpedoed and sunk by gunfire by German submarine U–34 (Rollman), in the North Sea 50 miles NE of the Shetland Islands, in position 61.00N 00.48E while sailing independently on a voyage from the Tyne to Tromso, Norway, with a cargo of 3000 tons of coal. The Master, Capt Charles Swanson Tate, and crew of 24 were rescued by the Lerwick lifeboat and landed at Lerwick, Shetland Islands.

*SEA GLORY* • GRT 1964 • Built 1919

6.7.40: Torpedoed and sunk by German submarine U-99 (Kretschmer), in the Atlantic S of Fastnet, while sailing independently on a voyage from Fowey to Philadelphia, with a cargo of china clay. The Master, Capt Stanley Winston Harvey, crew of 27 and 1 gunner were lost.

## DUNLOP T. & SONS – GLASGOW
### Cadogan SS Co. Ltd

*QUEEN ANNE* • GRT 4937 • Built 1937

10.2.43: Torpedoed and sunk by German submarine U-509 (Witte), in the Indian Ocean 8 miles SSW of Cape Agulhas, South Africa, in position 34.57S 19.46E while on a voyage from Manchester to Aden, Alexandria and Beirut via Cape Town, with 6126 tons of government cargo and 698 tons of general cargo including explosives, part of convoy CA 11 comprising 6 ships. The Master, Capt Charles Hicking Radford, and 17 survivors were rescued by HM trawler *ST ZENO* 608/40 (FY.280) (Lt J.K. Craig) and landed at Cape Town; 22 survivors landed at Bredasdorp, near Cape Agulhas. 3 crew and 2 gunners were lost.

### The Dunlop Steam Ship Co. Ltd

*QUEEN MAUD* • GRT 4976 • Built 1936

5.5.41: Torpedoed and sunk by German submarine U-38 (Liebe), in the Atlantic W of Freetown, in position 07.54N 16.41W while sailing independently on a voyage from Cardiff to Alexandria via Freetown, with a cargo of 7320 tons of coal and government stores, dispersed from convoy OB 209 comprising 42 ships. The Master, Capt Robert John McDonald, 38 crew and 4 gunners were rescued by the Portuguese ship *MIRANDELLA* 5179/06, transferred to HM light cruiser *DRAGON* 4850/17 (I.46) (Capt R.J. Shaw MBE) and landed at Freetown 8.5.41. 1 crew was lost.

*QUEEN VICTORIA* • GRT 4957 • Built 1936

28.6.42: Torpedoed and sunk by Japanese submarine I-10 (Kayahara), in the Mozambique Channel S of Beira, in position 21.15S 40.30E while sailing independently on a voyage from the Tyne to Aden via Cape Town, with a cargo of military stores. The Master, Capt Roderick Macleod, and crew of 38 were lost.

## MOWT

*FORT MISSANABIE* • GRT 7147 • Built 1943

19.5.44: Torpedoed and sunk by German submarine U-453 (Lührs), in the Mediterranean S of Taranto, in position 38.20N 16.28E while on government service on a voyage from Taranto to Augusta, in ballast, part of convoy HA 43 comprising 40 ships. The Master, Capt Charles Robert Williamson, 10 crew and 1 gunner were lost. 35 crew and 13 gunners were rescued by Norwegian ship *SPERO* 3619/19 and Italian corvette *URANIA* 565/42 and landed at Augusta, Sicily. U-453 commanded by Oberleutnant zur See Dierk Lührs was sunk on 21.5.44 in the Mediterranean 20 miles S of Punto Stilo, Italy, in position 38.13N 16.36E by HM destroyers *TERMAGANT* 1710/43 (R.89) (Lt-Cdr J.P. Scatchard), *TENACIOUS* 1710/43 (R.45) (Lt-Cdr D.F. Townsend) and *LIDDESDALE* 1050/40 (L.100) (Lt C.J. Batemen). The

U-boat commander and 14 crew were taken prisoner by HMS *TERMAGANT* and HMS *TENACIOUS* and landed at Taranto; 34 crew were taken prisoner by HMS *LIDDESDALE* and landed at Palermo. 1 crew was lost. The *FORT MISSANABIE* was the last victim of U-boats in the Mediterranean.

## E.R. MANAGEMENT CO. LTD (EVANS & REID) – CARDIFF
### Bantham Steamship Co. Ltd

**NAILSEA COURT** • GRT 4946 • Built 1936
10.3.43: Torpedoed and sunk by German submarine U-229 (Schetelig), part of the 'Ostmark' patrol group of eleven U-boats, in the Atlantic S of Reykjavik, in position 58.45N 21.57W while on a voyage from Beira to New York 23.2.43 and London, with 2 passengers and 7661 tons of general cargo including 650 tons of copper bars, 800 tons of nickel ore and asbestos, part of convoy SC 121 comprising 57 ships. The Master, Capt Robert James Lee, 33 crew, 9 gunners and passengers were lost. 1 crew was rescued by the rescue ship *MELROSE ABBEY* 1908/29 (Capt Ralph Good OBE) and landed at Gourock 13.3.43; 3 crew by RCN corvette *DAUPHIN* 925/40 (K.157) (Lt M.H. Wallace) and landed at Londonderry 13.3.43. Oberleutnant zur See Robert Schetelig and crew of 49 were lost on 22.9.43 when U-229, part of the 'Leuthen' patrol group of nineteen U-boats, was sunk while attacking convoy ON 202 comprising 38 ships in the Atlantic 430 miles ESE of Cape Farewell, in position 54.36N 36.25W by HM destroyer leader *KEPPEL* 1750/20 (D.84) (Cdr M.J. Evans) of Escort Group B.

**NAILSEA MEADOW** • GRT 4952 • Built 1937
11.5.43: Torpedoed and sunk by German submarine U-196 (Kentrat), in the Indian Ocean 40 miles S of Port St Johns, Cape Colony, in position 32.04S 29.13E while sailing independently on a voyage from Hampton Roads and New York to Durban, Bombay and Karachi via Trinidad and Cape Town 8.5.43, with a cargo of 7104 tons of war materials, general cargo and mail. The Master, Capt Eric William Lambert, 34 crew and 7 gunners were rescued by SAAF Crash Launch R 6 and landed at East London 12.5.43. 2 crew were lost.

### Nailsea Steamship Co. Ltd

**NAILSEA LASS** ex-*SPECIALIST* ex-*SANTILLE* • GRT 4289 • Built 1917
24.2.41: Torpedoed and sunk by German submarine U-48 (Schultze), in the Atlantic 60 miles SW of Fastnet, while on a voyage from Calcutta to London via Cape Town, Freetown 30.1.41 and Oban, with 2632 tons of general cargo including charcoal, pig iron and iron, a straggler from convoy SLS 64 comprising 28 ships. The Master, Capt Thomas Llewellyn Bradford, and the Chief Officer were taken prisoner, landed at St Nazaire 27.2.40 and taken to Milag Nord. The 2nd Officer E.J. Knight and 18 crew landed at Ballyoughtraugh, Co. Kerry and the 3rd Officer and 9 crew landed near Berehaven, Co. Cork. 5 crew were lost.

**NAILSEA MANOR** • GRT 4926 • Built 1937
10.10.41: Torpedoed and sunk by German submarine U-126 (Bauer), in the Atlantic NE of the Cape Verde Islands, in position 18.45N 21.18W while on a voyage from Newport, Mon. and Belfast Lough to Suez via Freetown, with a cargo of 6000 tons of military stores

including 1000 tons of ammunition and deck cargo of a tank landing craft, a straggler from convoy OS 7 comprising 41 ships. The Master, Capt John Herbert Hewitt, crew of 36 and 5 gunners were rescued by HM corvette *VIOLET* 925/40 (K.35) (Lt-Cdr K.M. Nicholson), transferred to the British ship *CITY OF HONG KONG* 9606/24 and landed at Freetown 14.10.41.

## Strath Steamship Co. Ltd

*HELMSPEY* • GRT 4764 • Built 1931
11.2.43: Torpedoed and sunk by German submarine U-516 (Wiebe), in the Indian Ocean 11 miles S of Cape St Francis, Cape Colony, in position 34.17S 25.04E while sailing independently on a voyage from Colombo and East London to the UK, with 2 naval ratings and 2772 tons of tea, 2000 tons of manganese ore, 1457 tons of rubber and 464 tons of general cargo. The Master, Capt Harry Jones, 32 crew, 7 gunners and passengers were rescued by SAAF Crash Launch R 4 and landed at Port Elizabeth. 3 crew and 1 gunner were lost. U-516 commanded by Kapitänleutnant Friedrich Petran surrendered at Lough Eriboll, Sutherlandshire to the 21st Escort Group on 14.5.45. U-516 sailed from Lishally, Loch Foyle, on 2.1.46 towed by HM destroyer *QUANTOCK* 907/40 (L.58) (Lt J.G. Brookes), foundered in the Atlantic SE of Rockall and sank on 3.1.46 by gunfire by the ORP destroyer *PIORUN* 1690/40 ex-HMS *NERISSA,* in position 56.06N 09.00W, part of 'Operation Deadlight', the disposal of 116 U-boats by the Royal Navy.

## MOWT

*VULCAIN* ex-*ROUEN* • GRT 4362 • Built 1911
24.5.41: Torpedoed and sunk by German submarine U-38 (Liebe), in the Atlantic 160 miles NW of Freetown, in position 09.20N 15.35W while on a voyage from Newport, Mon. and Barry to Freetown, with a cargo of 4617 tons of coal, part of convoy OG 59 comprising 43 ships. The Master, Capt Jack Reginald Lewis, and 38 crew landed at Boffa, French Colonial Territory, and were interned by the Vichy French authorities. 7 crew were lost. Capt J.R. Lewis was awarded the Lloyd's War Medal for bravery at sea.

*P L M 22* • GRT 5646 • Built 1921
27.6.41: Torpedoed and sunk by German submarine U-123 (Hardegen), in the Atlantic WSW of the Canary Islands, in position 25.43N 22.47W while on a voyage from Pepel to Middlesbrough via Freetown 18.6.41, with a cargo of 7600 tons of iron ore, part of convoy SL 78 comprising 25 ships. The Master, Capt Yves Le Bitter, Médaille Militaire and Chevalier du Mérite Maritime, and 32 crew were lost. 10 crew and 2 French naval gunners were rescued by HM corvette *ARMERIA* 925/41 (K.187) (Lt-Cdr H.M. Russell), transferred to HM corvette *ASPHODEL* 925/40 (K.56) (Lt-Cdr K.W. Steward) and landed at Freetown 4.7.41.

*RADCHURCH* ex-*VID* ex-*ISTINA* • GRT 3547 • Built 1910
9.8.42: Torpedoed and sunk by German submarine U-176 (Dierksen), in the Atlantic SE of Cape Farewell, in position 56.15N 32.00W while on a voyage from Wabana, Conception Bay to Barry via Sydney CB 31.7.42, with a cargo of iron ore, a straggler from convoy SC 94

comprising 30 ships. The Master, Capt John Lewin, and 39 crew were rescued by RCN corvette *BATTLEFORD* 925/41 (K.165) (Lt R.J. Roberts) and landed at Greenock. 2 crew were lost. The *RADCHURCH* had been abandoned in the heat of the battle by her crew with the exception of the Master on 8.8.42.

**GAZCON** • GRT 4224 • Built 1932
2.9.42: Torpedoed and sunk by Japanese submarine I-29 (Izu), in the Gulf of Aden W of Socotra Island, in position 13.01N 50.41E while sailing independently on a voyage from New York to Suez via Durban and Aden, with a cargo of 8116 tons of military stores. The Master, Capt Thomas James Jones, 10 crew and 1 gunner were lost. 33 crew and 4 gunners were rescued by British ship *GRAINTON* 6341/29 and landed at Aden 4.9.42.

## EAGLE OIL SHIPPING CO. LTD – LONDON

**SAN ALBERTO** (tanker) • GRT 7397 • Built 1935
9.12.39: Torpedoed and damaged by German submarine U-48 (Schultze), in the Atlantic 120 miles S of Cape Clear, in position 49.20N 09.45W while on a voyage from the Clyde to Trinidad, in ballast, part of convoy OB 48 comprising 13 ships. The damaged tanker was sunk by gunfire on 12.12.39 by HM destroyer leader *MACKAY* 1530/18 (D.70) ex-HMS *CLAVERHOUSE* (Cdr G.H. Stokes). The Master, Capt George Waite OBE, and 35 crew were rescued by the Belgian tanker *ALEXANDRE ANDRÉ* 5322/28, transferred to HMS *MACKAY* and landed at Plymouth. 1 crew was lost.

**SAN TIBURCIO** (tanker) • GRT 5995 • Built 1921
4.5.40: Struck a mine, laid on 9.2.40 by German submarine U-9 (Lüth) and sank in the Moray Firth 4 miles SE of Tarbet Ness while on government service on a voyage from Scapa Flow, Orkney, to Invergordon, with a part cargo of 2193 tons of fuel oil and aircraft floats. The Master, Capt Walter Frederick Fynn, and crew of 39 were rescued by HM trawler *LEICESTER CITY* 422/34 (FY.223) (Lt A.R. Cornish) and landed at Invergordon.

**SAN FERNANDO** (tanker) • GRT 13056 • Built 1919
21.6.40: Torpedoed and sunk by German submarine U-47 (Prien), part of the 'Prien' patrol group of seven U-boats, in the Atlantic 50 miles SSW of Cape Clear, in position 50.20N 10.24W while on a voyage from Curacao to Liverpool, with a cargo of 13500 tons of crude oil and 4200 tons of fuel oil, part of convoy HX 49 comprising 50 ships. The Master, Capt Arthur Richard Buckley, and crew of 48 were rescued by HM sloops *FOWEY* 1105/30 (L.15) (Cdr H.B. Ellison) and S*ANDWICH* 1043/28 (L.12) (Cdr M.J. Yeatman) and landed at Plymouth.

**SAN FLORENTINO** (tanker) • GRT 12842 • Built 1919
1.10.41: Torpedoed and damaged by gunfire by German submarine U-94 (Ites), part of 'Brandenburg' (district of Berlin) patrol group of eleven U-boats, in the Atlantic SE of Cape Farewell, in position 52.50N 34.40W, again torpedoed and damaged by U-94 on 2.10.42 in position 52.42N 34.51W and later sunk by gunfire by RCN corvette *ALBERNI* 925/40 (K.103) (Lt-Cdr G.O. Baugh) while on government service on a voyage from Glasgow to Curacao, in ballast, a straggler from convoy ONS 19 comprising 49 ships. The Master, Capt

Robert William Davis, 21 crew and 1 gunner were lost. 31 crew and 4 gunners were rescued by RCN corvette *MAYFLOWER* 925/40 (K.191) (Lt-Cdr George Stephen) and landed at St John's, Newfoundland.

*SAN ARCADIO* (tanker) • GRT 7419 • Built 1935
31.1.42: Torpedoed and sunk by gunfire by German submarine U-107 (Gelhaus), part of 'Operation Paukenschlag' (Drumbeat), the second wave of five U-boats, in the Atlantic N of Bermuda, in position 38.10N 63.50W while sailing independently on a voyage from Houston to the Mersey via Halifax NS, with a cargo of 6600 tons of gas oil and 3300 tons of lubricating oil. The Master, Capt Walter Frederick Flynn, 37 crew and 3 gunners were lost. 7 crew and 2 gunners were rescued by a Mariner flying boat from US Navy Patrol Squadron VP-74 and landed at Bermuda.

*SAN DEMETRIO* (tanker) • GRT 8073 • Built 1938
17.3.42: Torpedoed and sunk by German submarine U-404 (v. Bülow), part of 'Operation Paukenschlag' (Drumbeat), the third wave of twelve U-boats, in the Atlantic NW of Cape Charles, Virginia, in position 37.03N 73.50W while sailing independently on a voyage from Baltimore 14.3.42 to the UK via Halifax NS, with a cargo of 4000 tons of alcohol and 7000 tons of motor spirit. The Master, Capt Conrad Vidot, 26 crew and 5 gunners were rescued after 2 days by US ship *BETA* 5665/17 and landed at Norfolk, Virginia. 16 crew and 3 gunners were lost. Capt C. Vidot was awarded the Lloyd's War Medal for bravery at sea.

*SAN GERARDO* (tanker) • GRT 12915 • Built 1922
31.3.42: Torpedoed and sunk by German submarine U-71 (Flachsenberg), part of 'Operation Paukenschlag' (Drumbeat), the fourth wave of eleven U-boats, in the Atlantic SE of New York, in position 36.00N 67.00W while on government service sailing independently on a voyage from Curacao 23.3.42 to Halifax NS, with a cargo of 17000 tons of fuel oil. The Master, Capt Stanley Foley, 47 crew, 2 gunners and 1 DBS were lost. 3 crew and 3 gunners were rescued by British tanker *REGENT PANTHER* 9565/37 and landed at Halifax, Nova Scotia.

*SAN DELFINO* (tanker) • GRT 8072 • Built 1938
10.4.42: Torpedoed and sunk by German submarine U-203 (Mützelburg), part of 'Operation Paukenschlag' (Drumbeat), the fourth wave of eleven U-boats, in the Atlantic E of Cape Hatteras, in position 35.35N 75.06W while sailing independently on a voyage from Houston 3.4.42 to Hull via Halifax NS, with a cargo of 11000 tons of aviation spirit. The Master, Capt Albert Edward Gumbleton, 19 crew and 2 gunners were rescued by HM trawler *NORWICH CITY* 541/37 (FY.229) (Lt L.H. Stammers) and landed at Morhead City, North Carolina. 24 crew and 4 gunners were lost.

*SAN VICTORIO* (tanker) • GRT 8136 • Built 1942
17.5.42: Torpedoed and sunk by German submarine U-155 (Piening), in the Atlantic SW of Grenada, BWI, in position 11.40N 62.33W while sailing independently on her maiden voyage from Curacao 13.5.42 to the UK via Freetown, with 1 passenger and a cargo of about 12000 tons of benzine and paraffin. The Master, Capt Sidney Perry, crew of 43, 7 gunners and passenger were lost. The sole survivor, DEMS gunner Anthony Ryan, was rescued by US submarine chaser *TURQUOISE* ex-*ENTROPHY* 513/22 (PY 18) and landed at Trinidad.

**SAN EMILIANO** (tanker) • GRT 8071 • Built 1939
9.8.42: Torpedoed and sunk by German submarine U-155 (Piening), in the Atlantic 450 miles W of Trinidad, in position 07.22N 54.08W while sailing independently on a voyage from Curacao 29.7.42 and Trinidad 6.8.42 to Table Bay and Suez, with a cargo of 11286 tons of aviation spirit, dispersed from convoy E 7. The Master, Capt James Wilfred Tozer, 35 crew and 4 gunners were lost. 8 crew were rescued by a US army transport ship landed at Paramaribo, Dutch Guinea. The apprentice Donald Owen Clarke was awarded posthumously the George Cross and the Chief Radio Officer D.W. Dennis was awarded posthumously the George Medal, both for their outstanding bravery.

**SAN FABIAN** (tanker) • GRT 13031 • Built 1922
27.8.42: Torpedoed and sunk by German submarine U-511 (Steinhoff), in the Atlantic SE of Cape Tiburon, Haiti, in position 18.09N 74.38W while on a voyage from Curacao 25.8.42 to the UK via Key West, with a cargo of 18000 tons of fuel oil, part of convoy TAW 15 comprising 29 ships. The Master, Capt Lloyd Guy Emmott, 31 crew and 1 gunner were rescued, the Master and 23 survivors by the US four-stack destroyer *LEA* 1090/18 (DD.118), the Chief Officer and 8 further survivors by US patrol boat PC 38, landed at Guantanamo Bay, transferred to US ship *NONSUCO* 5225/38 and landed at Charleston, South Carolina 15.9.42. 23 crew and 3 gunners were lost.

**SAN ERNESTO** (tanker) • GRT 8078 • Built 1939
16.6.43: Torpedoed and damaged by gunfire by Japanese submarine I-37 (Otani), in the Indian Ocean SE of Diego Garcia, in position 09.18S 80.20E while sailing independently on a voyage from Sydney NSW to Abadan, in ballast. The derelict drifted 2000 miles before running aground on Nias Island, Sumatra, in position 01.15N 97.15E where it was dismantled by the Japanese. The Master, Capt George White, and 22 crew were rescued by US ship *ALCOA POINTER* 6711/43 and landed at Fremantle. The 2nd Mate and 11 crew were adrift for 28 days and then landed on Fanhandu Island, Maldive Islands. 2 crew and 2 gunners were lost.

**SAN ALVARO** (tanker) • GRT 7385 • Built 1935
22.2.44: Torpedoed and damaged by German submarine U-510 (Eick), in the Gulf of Aden off Majdaha, in position 13.46N 48.49E while on a voyage from Abadan and Bandar Abbas to Aden and Suez, with a cargo of 11000 tons of motor spirit and diesel oil, part of convoy PA 69 comprising 19 ships. Later sunk by gunfire and depth charges by RAN minesweeping sloop *TAMWORTH* 650/42 (J.181) (Lt F.E. Eastman). The Master, Capt George Arthur H. Knott, crew of 42, 8 gunners and 1 DBS were rescued by HMAS *TAMWORTH* and landed at Aden 23.2.44. 1 gunner was lost. Capt G.A.H. Knott was awarded the Lloyd's War Medal for bravery at sea.

## MOWT

**EMPIRE NORSEMAN** (tanker) • GRT 9811 • Built 1942
23.2.43: Torpedoed and damaged by German submarine U-382 (Juli), later sunk by a *coup de grâce* by U-558 (Krech); both U-boats were part of the 'Rochen' (Ray) patrol group of ten U-boats, in the Atlantic S of the Azores, in position 31.18N 27.20W while on a voyage from

Greenock to Curacao for orders, in ballast, part of convoy UC 1 comprising 33 ships. The Master, Capt William Sharp Smith, crew of 41 and 11 gunners were rescued by HM sloop *TOTLAND* 1546/31 (Y.88) (Lt-Cdr L.E. Woodhouse) ex-US coastguard cutter *CAYUGA*, transferred to Dutch ship *MAASKERK* 4452/29 and landed at Trinidad. U-382 commanded by Oberleutnant zur See Günther Schimmel was scuttled on 3.5.45 at Wilhelmshaven. U-558 commanded by Kapitänleutnant Gunther Krech, holder of the Knight's Cross (awarded 17.9.42) was sunk on 20.7.43 in the Atlantic 120 miles NW of Cape Ortegal, in position 45.10N 09.42W by Liberator F/19, pilot F/Lt Charles F. Gallmeier of the 19th Squadron, 479th Antisubmarine Group, USAAF, based at St Eval, and Halifax E/DT 642, pilot F/Lt Geoffrey A. Sawell of No. 58 Squadron RAF, based at St Eval, part of 19 Group. The British pilot was later awarded the DFC. The U-boat commander and 4 crew were taken prisoner after 5 days from a raft by RCN destroyer *ATHABASKAN* 1927/41 (G.07) ex-HMCS *IROQUOIS* (Capt G.R. Miles OBE). 41 crew were lost.

## EASTERN & AUSTRALIAN STEAM SHIP CO. LTD – LONDON (part of P & O)

*NELLORE* • GRT 6942 • Built 1913
29.6.44: Torpedoed and sunk by Japanese submarine I-8 (Ariizumi), in the Indian Ocean, SW of Diego Garcia, in position 07.51S 75.20E while sailing independently on a voyage from Bombay to Fremantle, Melbourne, and Sydney NSW, with 49 passengers and 2720 tons general cargo including government stores. The Master, Capt Frederick O. Colvin, 107 crew and 4 gunners were rescued on 6.7.44 near Chagos Archipelago, in position 05.48S 72.52E by HM frigate *LOSSIE* 1370/43 (K.303) (Lt-Cdr A.F. MacFie OBE) and landed at Addu Atoll 10.7.44, 2 crew were rescued by RAF aircraft and landed at Koggala, Ceylon 17.7.44 and 10 crew landed at Sambavany, Madagascar about 27.7.44. 1 gunner and 10 passengers were taken prisoner. 35 crew, 5 gunners and 39 passengers were lost. Lt-Cdr Shigeo Shinohara and crew were lost on 31.3.45 when I-8 was sunk in the Pacific SE of Okinawa, in position 25.29N 128.35E by US destroyers *MORRISON* 2050/43 (DD-560) (Cdr J.R. Hansen) and *STOCKTON* 1630/41 (DD-646) (Lt-Cdr W.R. Glennon).

*TANDA* ex-*MADRAS* ex-*TANDA* • GRT 6956 • Built 1924
15.7.44: Torpedoed and sunk by German submarine U-181 (Freiwald), in the Arabian Sea NW of Mangalore, in position 13.22N 74.09E while on a voyage from Melbourne and Colombo to Bombay, with 27 passengers and 5600 tons of general cargo including copra and tallow. The Master, Capt Thomas John Mills, 158 crew, 12 gunners and 26 passengers were rescued by RIN minesweeper *BIHAR* 672/42 (J.247) (Lt W.L. Deeble DSC) and HM corvette *MONKSHOOD* 925/41 (K.207) (Lt G.W. McGuinness) and landed at Colombo 18.7.44. 18 crew and 1 passenger were lost.

## ELDER DEMPSTER LINES, LTD – LIVERPOOL

*ACCRA* • GRT 9337 • Built 1926
26.7.40: Torpedoed and sunk by German submarine U-34 (Rollman), in the Atlantic 320 miles W of Bloody Foreland, in position 55.40N 16.28W while on a voyage from Liverpool to Freetown and West African ports, with 323 passengers and 1700 tons general cargo, part of convoy OB 188 comprising 37 ships. The Master, Capt John Joseph Smith, 153 crew and 311

passengers were rescued. British ship *HOLLINSIDE* 4172/30 rescued 215 survivors, Norwegian ship *LOKE* 2421/15 rescued 126 survivors, HM sloop *ENCHANTRESS* 1190/34 (L.56) ex-HMS *BITTERN* (Cdr A.K. Scott-Moncrieff) rescued 27 crew and 52 passengers and HM corvette *CLARKIA* 925/40 (K.88) (Lt-Cdr F.J.G. Jones) rescued 45 survivors. HMS *ENCHANTRESS* and HMS *CLARKIA* landed the survivors at Liverpool. 12 crew and 12 passengers were lost. The *ACCRA* sank in 1 hour and 15 minutes.

**BOMA** • GRT 5408 • Built 1920
4.8.40: Torpedoed and sunk by German submarine U-56 (Harms), in the Atlantic NW of Malin Head, in position 55.44N 08.04W while on a voyage from Cardiff to Lagos, with 10000 tons of coal, part of convoy OB 193 comprising 48 ships. The Master, Capt Charles Eric Anders, 47 crew and 2 gunners were rescued by Norwegian tanker *VILJA* 6672/28, transferred to HM destroyer *VISCOUNT* 1120/17 (D.92) (Lt-Cdr M.S. Townsend OBE) and landed at Liverpool. 3 crew were lost. U-56, commanded by Oberleuntnant zur See Joachim Sauerbier, was sunk in an Allied air raid on Kiel 28.4.45, in position 54.19N 10.10E.

**BASSA** ex-*WAR POINTER* • GRT 5267 • Built 1918
29.9.40: Torpedoed and sunk by German submarine U-32 (Jenisch), in the Atlantic SW of Rockall, in position 54.00N 21.00W while sailing independently on a voyage from Liverpool to New York, in ballast. The Master, Capt George Edward Anderson, and crew of 47 were lost.

**SEAFORTH** • GRT 5459 • Built 1939
18.2.41: Torpedoed and sunk by German submarine U-103 (Schütze), in the Atlantic S of Iceland, in position 58.48N 18.17W while sailing independently on a voyage from Monrovia, Liberia, to Liverpool, with 10 passengers and a cargo of West African produce. The Master, Capt Walter Minns, crew of 46, 2 gunners and passengers were lost.

**DUNKWA** • GRT 4752 • Built 1927
6.5.41: Torpedoed and sunk by German submarine U-103 (Schütze), in the Atlantic 216 miles WNW of Freetown, in position 08.49N 16.52W while sailing independently on a voyage from Glasgow to Opobo, Nigeria, with a cargo of 868 tons of government stores and 3248 tons of general cargo, dispersed from convoy OB 310 comprising 48 ships. The Master, Capt John William Andrew, 37 crew and 1 gunner were rescued by Dutch ship *POLYDORUS* 5922/24 and landed at Oban. 5 crew and 3 gunners were lost.

**ALFRED JONES** • GRT 5013 • Built 1930
1.6.41: Torpedoed and sunk by German submarine U-107 (Hessler), in the Atlantic 140 miles WSW of Freetown, in position 08.00N 15.00W while sailing independently on a voyage from Liverpool and Ellesmere Port to Freetown and Bathurst, Gambia, with 12 passengers and a cargo of RAF planes, lorries and 180 tons of steel, dispersed from convoy OB 320 comprising 16 ships. The Master, Capt Harold Harding, Commodore Vice-Admiral G.T.C.P. Swabey CB DSO RN, 38 crew, 4 gunners, 6 naval staff and passengers were rescued by HM corvette *MARGUERITE* 925/40 (K.54) (Lt-Cdr A.N. Blundell) and landed at Freetown. 14 crew were lost.

*ADDA* laid down as *ANCOBRA* • GRT 7816 • Built 1922
8.6.41: Torpedoed and sunk by German submarine U-107 (Hessler), in the Atlantic 82 miles
WSW of Freetown, in position 08.30N 14.39W while sailing independently on a voyage
from Liverpool to Freetown, Takoradi, Accra and Lagos, with 266 passengers and 613 tons of
general cargo, dispersed from convoy OB 323 comprising 34 ships. The Master, Capt John
Tate Marshall, 141 crew, 4 gunners, 5 naval staff and 264 passengers were rescued by HM
corvette *CYCLAMEN* 925/40 (K.83) (Lt H.N. Lawson) and landed at Freetown 8.6.41. The
convoy commodore W.H. Kelly CBE DSO RNR RD, 7 crew and 2 passengers were lost.

*EDWARD BLYDEN* • GRT 5003 • Built 1930
22.9.41: Torpedoed and sunk by German submarine U-103 (Winter), in the Atlantic SW of
the Canary Islands, in position 27.36N 24.29W while on a voyage from Takoradi and
Freetown 14.9.41 to Liverpool, with 12 passengers and a cargo of 5525 tons of general cargo,
part of convoy SL 87 comprising 11 ships. The Master, Capt William Exley, crew of 46, 4
gunners and passengers were rescued by HM sloop *BIDEFORD* 1045/31 (L.43) (Lt-Cdr W.J.
Moore) and landed at Londonderry 5.10.41.

*DIXCOVE* • GRT 3790 • Built 1927
24.9.41: Torpedoed and sunk by German submarine U-107 (Hessler), in the Atlantic SW of
Madeira, in position 31.12N 23.41W while on a voyage from Port Harcourt to Liverpool via
Freetown 14.9.41, with 6 passengers and a cargo of 3046 tons of West African produce, part
of convoy SL 87 comprising 11 ships. The Master, Capt Richard Jones, 36 crew, 8 gunners
and passengers were rescued by British ship *ASHBY* 4868/27, transferred to HM escort sloop
*GORLESTON* 1546/29 (Y.92) (Cdr R.W. Keymer) ex-US coastguard cutter *ITASCA*,
transferred to Dutch ship *FAUNA* 1254/12, transferred to HM escort sloop *LULWORTH*
1546/28 (Y.60) (Lt-Cdr C. Gwinner) ex-US coastguard cutter *CHELAN* and landed at
Londonderry 4.10.41. 2 crew were lost. Korvettenkapitän Günther Hessler was awarded the
Knight's Cross (24.6.41). Günther Hessler was the son-in-law of Grand Admiral Karl Dönitz,
Commander-in-Chief U-boats.

*NEW BRUNSWICK* ex-*WAR LIBERTY* • GRT 6529 • Built 1920
21.5.42: Torpedoed and sunk by German submarine U-159 (Witte), in the Atlantic ESE of
the Azores, in position 36.53N 22.55W while on a voyage from Glasgow 12.5.42 to Lagos,
with a cargo of 5895 tons of government stores, general cargo and 20 RAF aircraft, part of
convoy OS 28 comprising 37 ships. The Master, Capt Cyril Malcolm Whalley, 53 crew and 5
gunners were rescued; the Master and 6 crew by HM sloop *WESTON* ex-*WESTON SUPER
MARE* 1045/32 (L.72) (Cdr J.G. Sutton), 12 survivors by HM escort sloop *TOTLAND*
1546/31 (Y.88) (Lt-Cdr S.G.C. Rawson) ex-US coastguard cutter *CAYUGA,* 10 survivors by
HM sloop *WELLINGTON* 990/34 (L.65) (Lt-Cdr W.F.R. Segrave), 5 survivors by HM
corvette *WOODRUFF* 925/41 (K.53) (Lt-Cdr F.H. Gray) and 25 survivors by British ship
*INCHANGA* 7069/34 and landed at Freetown. 2 crew and 1 gunner were lost.

*MATTAWIN* ex-*EDIBA* • GRT 6919 • Built 1923
2.6.42: Torpedoed and sunk by German submarine U-553 (Thurmann), part of the
'Pfadfinder' (Pathfinder) patrol group of eight U-boats, in the Atlantic SE of New York, in
position 40.14N 66.01W while sailing independently on a voyage from New York 29.5.42 to

Cape Town, Durban and Alexandria, with 12 US military personnel and a cargo of 7000 tons of military stores. The Master, Capt Charles Herbert Sweeny, crew of 51, 7 gunners and the US military personnel were rescued, 32 crew and 5 military by Norwegian ship *TORVANGER* 6568/20 and landed at Halifax NS, and the US coastguard cutter *GENERAL GREENE* 220/27 (WPC.140) rescued 20 crew, 7 gunners and 7 military who were landed at Cape Cod, Massachusetts.

*ILORIN* ex-*SMERDIS* ex-*KIRKWYND* ex-*MARION MERRETT* • GRT 815 • Built 1920
1.9.42: Torpedoed and sunk by German submarine U-125 (Folkers), in the Atlantic off Legu, Gold Coast, in position 05.00N 01.00W while sailing independently on a voyage from Port Harcourt to Takoradi, in ballast. The Master, Capt Charles Lewis Bott, and 32 crew were lost. 4 crew were saved.

*ABOSSO* • GRT 11330 • Built 1935
29.10.42: Torpedoed and sunk by German submarine U-575 (Heydemann), in the Atlantic 700 miles NW of the Azores, in position 48.30N 28.50W while on government service sailing independently on a voyage from Cape Town 8.10.42 to Liverpool, with 207 passengers and a cargo of 3000 tons of wool and bags of mail. The Master, Capt Reginald William Tate, 148 crew, 18 gunners and 173 passengers were lost. 34 crew, 2 gunners and 17 passengers were rescued by HM sloop *BIDEFORD* 1105/31 (L.43) (Lt-Cdr W.J. Moore) and landed at Londonderry. Kapitänleutnant Gunther Heydemann was awarded the Knight's Cross (3.2.43). U-575, commanded by Oberleutnant zur See Wolfgang Boehmer, was lost on 13.3.44, sunk in the Atlantic 680 miles W by N of Cape Finisterre, in position 46.18N 27.34W while shadowing convoy ON 227 comprising 65 ships by RCN frigate *PRINCE RUPERT* 1370/43 (K.324) (Lt-Cdr R.W. Draney), US destroyers *HAVERFIELD* 1200/43 (DE-393) (Lt-Cdr Jerry A. Matthews) and *HOBSON* 1620/41 (DD-464) (Lt-Cdr Kenneth Loveland) of Task Group 21.11 and an Avenger, pilot Lt-Cdr John F. Adams of US Navy Composite Squadron VC-95 from USN escort carrier *BOGUE* 9800/42 (CVE-9) (Capt J.B. Dunn), Wellington XIV 'B' HF183, pilot F/O John P. Finnessey, No. 172 Squadron RAF, Fortress 'R' FA700, pilot F/L A. David Beaty, No. 220 Squadron RAF, and Fortress 'J', pilot F/O Wilfred R. Travell, No. 220 Squadron RAF, based at Lagens, Azores, part of 247 Group. The U-boat commander and 36 crew were taken prisoner. USS *HAVERFIELD* rescued 7 crew, USS *HOBSON* rescued the U-boat commander and 15 crew who were landed at Casablanca, and HMCS *PRINCE RUPERT* rescued 14 crew landed at St John's, Newfoundland. 19 crew were lost.

*DAGOMBA* • GRT 3845 • Built 1928
3.11.42: Torpedoed and sunk by Italian submarine *AMMIRAGLIO CAGNI* (Liannazza), in the Atlantic about 450 miles W of Freetown, in position 02.29N 19.00W while on a voyage from Forcados and Takoradi 29.10.42 to Liverpool via Trinidad, with 1 passenger and a cargo of 5000 tons of West African produce including palm oil, timber and tin ore, part of convoy TS 23 comprising 7 ships. The Master, Capt John Tate Marshall OBE, 19 crew and passenger landed at Luanda, Angola, were brought to Freetown by Portuguese sloop *BARTHOLOMEW DIAS* 1788/35 (F.471), 19 crew and 5 gunners by Vichy French sloop *ANNAMITE* 647/39 (A 73) and landed at Dakar, Senegal, and were interned, 2/3 days later US forces landed at Dakar and the survivors were brought to Bathurst, Gambia. 6 crew were lost.

**NEW TORONTO** • GRT 6568 • Built 1919

5.11.42: Torpedoed and sunk by German submarine U-126 (Bauer), in the Bight of Benin SE of Kotonu, in position 05.57N 02.30E while on a voyage from Forcados, Lagos 5.11.42 and Accra to Liverpool, with 29 cattlemen plus Kroomen and a cargo of 8000 tons of African produce including cotton, tin. palm oil, wolfram, kernels, gold and bags of mail, part of convoy TS 23 comprising 7 ships. The Master, Capt Claude James Kewley, 50 crew, 6 gunners, 28 cattlemen and 17 Kroomen were rescued by HM motor launch ML 263 65/40. 3 crew and 1 cattleman were lost. Kapitänleutnant Ernst Bauer was awarded the Knight's Cross (16.3.42). Oberleutnant zur See Siegfried Kietz and crew of 54 were lost on 3.7.43 when U-126 was sunk in the Atlantic 200 miles NW of Cape Ortegal, in position 46.02N 11.23W by Leigh Light-equipped Wellington 'R', pilot F/Sgt Alexander Coumbis (Rhodesian) of No. 172 Squadron RAF, based at Chivenor, Devon, part of 19 Group.

**HENRY STANLEY** • GRT 5026 • Built 1929

6.12.42: Torpedoed and sunk by German submarine U-103 (Janssen), part of the 'Westwall' patrol group of sixteen U-boats, in the Atlantic 580 miles NW of the Azores, in position 40.35N 39.40 W while on a voyage from Liverpool 26.11.42 to Freetown and Lagos, with 11 passengers and 4000 tons of general cargo including explosives and bags of mail, a straggler from convoy ON 149 comprising 50 ships. The Master, Capt Richard Jones, was taken prisoner, landed at Lorient 29.12.42 and taken to Milag Nord. 44 crew, 8 gunners and passengers were lost. U-103 commanded by Oberleutnant zur See Hans-Norbet Schunck was scuttled on 3.5.45 at Kiel, in position 54.19N 10.10E.

**WILLIAM WILBERFORCE** • GRT 5004 • Built 1930

9.1.43: Torpedoed and sunk by German submarine U-511 (Schneewind), in the Atlantic W of the Canary Islands, in position 29.20N 26.53W while sailing independently on a voyage from Lagos and Takoradi to Liverpool, with 12 passengers and a cargo of 5054 tons of West African produce including palm kernels, palm oil and rubber. The Master, Capt John William Andrew, 42 crew, 6 gunners and passengers were rescued by Spanish ship *MONTE ARNABAL* 2955/29 and landed at Las Palmas. 3 crew were lost. U-511 was transferred to the Japanese navy in July 1943, was commissioned as RO-500, surrendered at Maizuru, Japan, in August 1945 and was scuttled by the US Navy during April 1946.

**MARY SLESSOR** • GRT 5027 • Built 1930

7.2.43: Struck a mine, laid on 1.2.43 by German submarine U-118 (Czygan) and sank in the Strait of Gibraltar off Gibraltar, in position 35.55N 06.02W while on government service on a voyage from Algiers and Gibraltar to Liverpool, with 5 military personnel and general cargo including sardines, part of convoy MKS 7 comprising 65 ships. The Master, Capt Charles Herbert Sweeney, 32 crew, 12 gunners and 3 military personnel were rescued by HM sloop *LANDGUARD* 1546/30 (Y.56) (Lt-Cdr T.S.L. Fox-Pitt) ex-US coastguard cutter *SHOSHONE* and landed at Liverpool. 28 crew, 2 gunners and 2 military personnel were lost.

**NEW COLUMBIA** ex-*WAR PAGEANT* • GRT 6574 • Built 1920

31.10.43: Torpedoed and sunk by German submarine U-68 (Lauzemis), in the Gulf of Guinea SW of Bingerville, Ivory Coast, in position 04.25N 05.03E while sailing independently on a voyage from Matadi, Belgian Congo, and Libreville, French Equatorial

Africa 27.9.43, to Lagos, with a cargo of 5500 tons of West African produce including copper, cotton, kernels, palm oil, copra and rice. The Master, Capt Frederick Bradley Kent, crew of 54, 10 gunners and 19 Kroomen were rescued by British ship *CONAKRIAN* 4876/37 and landed at Lagos. Oberleutnant zur See Albert Lauzemis and crew of 56 were lost on 10.4.44 when U-68 was sunk in the Atlantic 85 miles WNW of Madeira, in position 33.25N 18.59W by two Avengers, pilots Lt Samuel G. Parson, Lt Helmuth E. Hoerner and a Wildcat, pilot S/Cdr Richard K. Gould of US Navy Composite Squadron VC-58 from US escort carrier *GUADALCANAL* 7800/43 (CVE-60) (Capt Daniel V. Gallery). The Kroomen, most of whom belonged to the Kroo tribe from Liberia (formerly known as the Grain Coast), were employed as cargo stevedores for loading and unloading cargoes between various West African ports traded by ships of the Elder Dempster Line.

## MOWT

**EMPIRE ABILITY** ex-*UHENFELS* • GRT 7603 • Built 1931
27.6.41. Torpedoed and sunk by German submarine U-69 (Metzler), in the Atlantic 200 miles SE of the Azores, in position 23.50N 21.10W while on a voyage from Port Louis, Mauritius, to Liverpool via Freetown 30.5.41, with 17 military personnel, 27 passengers and a cargo of 7725 tons of sugar, 238 tons of rum, 400 tons of kernels and 35 tons of fibre, part of convoy SL 76 comprising 60 ships. The Master, Capt Herbert Flowerdew, 60 crew, 2 gunners, military personnel and passengers were rescued by British ship *AMERIKA* 10219/30, transferred to HM corvette *BURDOCK* 925/40 (K.126) (Lt H.J. Fellowes *SARNVR*) and landed at Freetown. 2 crew were lost. The German *UHENFELS* was captured off Freetown 4.11.39 by HM destroyer *HEREWARD* 1340/36 (H.93) (Lt-Cdr C.W. Greening).

**MACON** ex-*POINT ANCHA* ex-*DELIGHT* • GRT 5135 • Built 1919
25.7.41: Torpedoed and sunk by Italian submarine *BARBARIGO* (Murzi), in the Atlantic SW of Madeira, in position 32.48N 26.12W while sailing independently on a voyage from Liverpool to Freetown and Port Harcourt via Porta Delgado, Azores, for boiler repairs, with 2 stowaways and 4000 tons general cargo, dispersed from convoy OB 290 comprising 42 ships. The Master, Capt Alexander English, 15 crew and 1 stowaway were rescued by HM sloop *LONDONDERRY* 990/35 (L.76) (Cdr J.S. Dalison), transferred to British ship *LIBRARIAN* 5205/36 and landed at Freetown. British ship *CLAN MACPHERSON* 6940/29 rescued 27 crew who were landed at Cape Town. 4 crew and 1 stowaway were lost.

**HAI HING** • GRT 2561 • Built 1929
4.11.42: Torpedoed and sunk by German submarine U-178 (Ibbeken), in the Mozambique Channel off Maputo, in position 25.46S 33.20S while on government service sailing independently on a voyage from Bombay to Durban diverted to Lourenco Marques, with 1400 tons general cargo. The Master, Capt Erling Reeder Hannevig, 35 crew and 6 gunners were rescued by Portuguese tug *CHAIMITE* 475/39 and landed at Lourenco Marques. 24 crew and 1 gunner were lost.

**OUED GRON** ex-*PETER* • GRT 797 • Built 1921
4.11.42: Torpedoed and sunk by German submarine U-126 (Bauer), in the Bight of Benin SW of Forcados, in position 04.53N 04.49E while sailing independently on a coastal voyage

from Takoradi and Lagos 3.11.42 to Port Harcourt, in ballast. The Master, Capt Sydney Pattinson Dodgson, and 34 crew landed on the coast at the village of Kulama, Nigeria. 5 crew were lost.

### DE LA SALLE • GRT 8400 • Built 1921

9.7.43: Torpedoed and sunk by German submarine U-508 (Staats), in the Gulf of Benin 60 miles SW of Lagos, in position 05.50N 02.22E while sailing independently on a voyage from Liverpool to Walvis Bay and East London via Freetown, with 99 passengers and 2103 tons of general and government cargo, part of convoy ST 71 comprising 12 ships. The Master, Capt J. Le Manchec, 129 crew, 12 gunners and 97 passengers were rescued by the Free French corvette COMMANDANTE DETROYAT 925/41 ex-HMS CORIANDER ex-HMS IRIS and British ship CALABAR 1932/35 and landed at Lagos. 8 crew and 2 passengers were lost.

### POINT PLEASANT PARK • GRT 7136 • Built 1943

23.2.45: Torpedoed and sunk by gunfire by German submarine U-510 (Eick), in the Atlantic 510 miles NW of Cape Town, in position 29.42S 09.58E while sailing independently on a voyage from St John, New Brunswick to Cape Town and Durban via Trinidad, with general cargo. The Master, Capt Owen Owens, and 19 crew landed at Mercury Island 2.3.45 and were brought by the fishing boat BOY RUSSELL to Luderitz, South West Africa. 29 crew, rescued by SAN trawler AFRICANA 313/30 (T.01) (Sub-Lt A.G. Merryweather) N of Spencer Bay 4.3.45 were landed at Walvis Bay, South West Africa. 9 crew were lost. U-510, commanded by Kapitänleutnant Alfred Eick (Knight's Cross 31.3.44), surrendered to the French authorities at St Nazaire 8.5.45.

## ELDERS & FYFFES LIMITED – LIVERPOOL

### CHAGRES • GRT 5406 • Built 1927

9.2.40: Struck a mine, laid on 6.1.40 by German submarine U-30 (Lemp) and sank in the Irish Sea 5½ miles 270° from the Bar lightvessel, Liverpool, while on a voyage from Victoria, Cameroons, to Garston, with a cargo of 1500 tons of bananas. The Master, Capt Hugh Roberts, and 61 crew were rescued by HM trawler LOCH MONTEITH 531/36 (Lt-Cdr F.R. Pope) and landed at Liverpool. 2 crew were lost.

### SAMALA • GRT 5390 • Built 1928

30.9.40: Torpedoed and sunk by gunfire by German submarine U-37 (Oehrn), in the Atlantic W of Ireland, in position 53.00N 18.00W while sailing independently on a voyage from Kingston, Jamaica, to Garston, with 2 passengers and a cargo of bananas. The Master, Capt Albert Edward Harvey, crew of 64, 1 gunner and passengers were lost.

### SULACO • GRT 5389 • Built 1926

20.10.40: Torpedoed and sunk by German submarine U-124 (Schulz), in the Atlantic about 360 miles W by S of Rockall, in position 57.25N 25.00W while on a voyage from Avonmouth to Victoria, Cameroons via the USA, in ballast, part of convoy OB 229 comprising 35 ships. The Master, Capt Henry Carlton Bower, 62 crew and 2 gunners were lost. The sole survivor, chief cook James Thompson Harvey, was rescued by RCN destroyer SAGUENAY 1337/30 (D.79) (Capt G.R. Miles) and landed at Greenock 23.10.40.

**MATINA** • GRT 5389 • Built 1929
26.10.40: Torpedoed and damaged by German submarine U-28 (Kuhnke), later given the *coup de grâce* by German submarine U-31 (Prellberg) in the Atlantic W of Rockall, in position 57.30N 16.31W while sailing independently on a voyage from Port Antonio, Jamaica, to Garston, with a cargo of bananas. The Master, Capt David Alexander Jack, and crew of 67 were lost. Korvettenkapitän Günter Kuhnke was awarded the Knight's Cross (14.9.40). U-28, commanded by Oberleutnant zur See Dietrich Sachse, was lost on 17.3.44 after a marine accident off Neustadt in the Baltic, in position 54.07N 10.50E. U-31, commanded by Kapitänleutnant Wilfried Prellberg, was sunk on 2.11.40 in the Atlantic 110 miles NW of Bloody Foreland, in position 56.26N 10.18W by HM destroyer *ANTELOPE* 1350/29 (H.36) (Lt-Cdr T. White). The U-boat commander and 43 crew were taken prisoner by HMS *ANTELOPE*. 2 crew were lost.

**CASANARE** • GRT 5376 • Built 1925
3.11.40: Torpedoed and sunk by German submarine U-99 (Kretschmer), in the Atlantic 240 miles WSW of Bloody Foreland, in position 53.58N 14.13W while on a voyage from Victoria, Cameroons, to Garston via Halifax NS 24.10.40, with a cargo of 1500 tons of bananas, part of convoy HX 83 comprising 37 ships. The Master, Capt John Allan Moore, and 53 crew were rescued by HM destroyer *BEAGLE* 1360/30 (H.30) (Lt-Cdr R.H. Wright) and landed at Greenock. 9 crew were lost.

**ARACATACA** • GRT 5378 • Built 1925
30.11.40: Torpedoed and sunk by German submarine U-101 (Mengersen), in the Atlantic WNW of Rockall, in position 57.08N 20.50W while on a voyage from Port Antonio, Jamaica, to Avonmouth via Halifax NS 21.11.40, with 2 passengers and a cargo of 1600 tons of bananas, part of convoy HX 90 comprising 35 ships. The Master, Capt Samuel Brown, 16 crew and 1 passenger were rescued by the Royal Mail ship *POTARO* 5416/40 and landed at Buenos Aires 23.12.40; 14 crew, 1 gunner and 1 passenger rescued by British ship *DJURDJURA* 3460/22 were landed at St John's, Newfoundland. 36 crew were lost.

**MANISTEE** • GRT 5360 • Built 1921
23.2.41: Torpedoed and sunk by German submarine U-107 (Hessler), in the Atlantic S of Iceland, in position 58.13N 21.33W while escorting convoy OB 288 comprising 46 ships. She was lost while on government service employed as an Ocean Boarding Vessel (F.104) (Cdr E.H. Smith).

**CAMITO** • GRT 6611 • Built 1915
6.5.41: Torpedoed and sunk by German submarine U-97 (Heilmann), in the Atlantic WSW of Cape Clear, in position 50.42N 21.20W. Lost while on government service employed as an Ocean Boarding Vessel (F.77) (Cdr A.A. Barnet) escorting Italian tanker *SANGRO* 6466/25 to the UK taken as a prize while sailing from Brazil to France. The *SANGRO* was also sunk by U-97. The survivors from the *CAMITO* were rescued by HM corvette *ORCHIS* 925/40 (K.76) (Lt H. Vernon) and landed at Greenock.

**CRISTALES** • GRT 5389 • Built 1926
12.5.42: Torpedoed and damaged by German submarine U-124 (Mohr), part of the 'Hecht' (Pike) patrol group of six U-boats, in the Atlantic SE of Cape Farewell, in position 52.55N

29.50W while on a voyage from Newport, Mon. and Milford Haven to Montreal, with 10 passengers, general cargo and china clay, part of convoy ON 92 comprising 42 ships. She was sunk by gunfire by HMCS *SHEDIAC* 925/41 (K.110) (Lt J.E. Clayton) on 12.5.42. The Master, Capt Hugh Roberts OBE, crew of 64, 7 gunners and passengers were rescued, 37 survivors including 7 passengers by HMCS *SHEDIAC* 925/41 (K.110) and landed at St John's, Newfoundland 16.5.42; 45 survivors and 3 passengers by US Coastguard cutter *SPENCER* 2216/37 (WPG.36) and landed at Boston, Mass.

**NICOYA** • GRT 5364 • Built 1929
12.5.42: Torpedoed and sunk by German submarine U-553 (Thurmann), in the Gulf of the St Lawrence, S of Anticosti Island, in position 49.19N 64.51W while sailing independently on a voyage from Montreal 10.5.42 to Avonmouth, with 10 passengers and 3800 tons of general cargo including aircraft. The Master, Capt Ernest Henry Brice, 62 crew, 9 gunners and passengers landed at Fame Point Lighthouse, Gaspé Peninsula, New Brunswick. 5 crew and 1 gunner were lost.

**TUCURINCA** • GRT 5412 • Built 1926
10.3.43: Torpedoed and sunk by German submarine U-221 (Trojer), part of the 'Neuland' (New Territory) patrol group of eleven U-boats, in the Atlantic SE of Cape Farewell, in position 51.00N 30.10W while on a voyage from Halifax NS to Avonmouth, with 10 RCAF officers and 4000 tons of general cargo including foodstuffs and mail, part of convoy HX 228 comprising 60 ships. The Master, Capt John Allen Moore, 65 crew, 2 gunners and the RCAF officers were rescued by the Free French corvette *ROSELYS* 925/41 (K.57) ex-HMS *SUNDEW* and landed at Gourock. The 3rd Engineer was lost. One of the escorts of Escort Group B3, HM destroyer *HARVESTER* 1340/39 (H.19) ex-HMS *HANDY* (Cdr A.A. Tait) ex-Brazilian *JURUA* was torpedoed and sunk by German submarine U-432 (Eckhardt) of the 'Neuland' group on 11.3.43 in position 51.23N 28.40W. Prior to the sinking of HMS *HARVESTER* she had rescued Capt James Calvin Ellis and 59 crew from the US liberty ship *WILLIAM C. GORAS* 7176/43 which had been sunk by U-444 (Langeld). On the sinking, her commander and an unknown number of officers and ratings and 48 crew from the *WILLIAM C. GORAS* were lost. The survivors from HMS *HARVESTER* and USS *WILLIAM C. GORAS* were rescued by Free French corvette *ACONIT* 925/41 (K.58). U-432, commanded by Kapitänleutnant Hermann Eckhardt, was lost soon after the sinking of *HARVESTER* when she was herself sunk by FFS *ACONIT* (Capt Jean Levasseur FFN) on the same day in the Atlantic about 600 miles W of Valentia Island, in position 51.35N 28.20W. The U-boat commander and 19 crew were lost. 20 crew were taken prisoner by *ACONIT* and landed at Greenock 14.3.43. Oberleutnant zur See Albert Langfeld was lost on 11.3.43 in the Atlantic 600 miles W of Valentia Island, in position 51.14N 29.18W when U-444 of the 'Neuland' group was depth-charged and rammed by HMS *HARVESTER* and later rammed by FFS *ACONIT* and sunk. The U-boat commander and 30 crew were lost. 21 crew were rescued by *ACONIT* and landed at Greenock 14.3.43.

**MOWT**

**ROSENBORG** ex-*FAGERNES* • GRT 1512 Gt. • Built 1919
8.6.42: Sunk by gunfire by German submarine U-504 (Poske), in the Atlantic E of the Yucatan Peninsula, Mexico, in position 18.47N 85.05W while sailing independently on a

voyage from Trinidad 29.5.42 to Mobile, Alabama, with a cargo of 1970 tons of bauxite. The Master, Capt William Jennings, and 3 crew were lost. 23 crew were rescued by Norwegian ship *GEISHA* 5113/21 and landed at Cristobal, Panama.

## ELLERMAN LINES, LIMITED – LIVERPOOL
### City Line, Ltd

**CITY OF MANDALAY** • GRT 7049 • Built 1925
17.10.39: Torpedoed and sunk by German submarine U-46 (Sohler), in the Atlantic 360 miles WNW of Cape Finisterre, in position 44.57N 13.36W while on a voyage from Saigon, Singapore, Port Swettenham and India for Le Havre, London, Dunkirk and Glasgow, with 1 passenger and general cargo, part of the unescorted convoy HG 3 comprising 25 ships. The Master, Capt Alexander Graham Melville, 76 crew and passenger were rescued by US ship *INDEPENDENCE HALL* 5050/20 and landed at Bordeaux. 2 crew were lost.

**CITY OF BENARES** • GRT 11081 • Built 1936
18.9.40: Torpedoed and sunk by German submarine U-48 (Bleichrodt), in the Atlantic 253 miles WSW of Rockall, in position 56.43N 21.15W while on a voyage from Liverpool 13.9.40 to Quebec and Montreal, with 191 passengers, part of convoy OB 213 comprising 19 ships. The Master, Capt Landles Nicoll, Commodore Rear Admiral E.J.G. Mackinnon DSO RN, 3 naval staff, 121 crew and 134 pasengers including children were lost. 105 survivors were rescued by HM destroyer *HURRICANE* 1340/39 (H.06) (Lt-Cdr H.C. Simms) ex-Brazilian *JAPARUA* and landed at Greenock; 42 survivors were adrift for 8 days, then rescued by HM destroyer *ANTHONY* 1350/29 (Lt-Cdr N.J.V. Thew) (H.40) and landed at Greenock.

**CITY OF SIMLA** • GRT 10138 • Built 1921
21.9.40: Torpedoed and sunk by German submarine U-138 (Lüth), in the Atlantic 52 miles NW of Rathlin Island, in position 55.55N 08.20W while on a voyage from London and Glasgow to Cape Town and Bombay, with 167 passengers and 3000 tons of general cargo, part of convoy OB 216 comprising 27 ships. On board were the Master, Capt Herbert Percival, crew of 182 and 167 passengers. 165 crew and 153 passengers were rescued by British ship *GUINEAN* 5129/36, transferred to HM destroyer *VANQUISHER* 1090/17 (D.54) (Lt-Cdr A.P. Northey DSC) and landed at Londonderry 22.9.40; 17 crew and 12 passengers by the Belgian trawler *VAN DYKE* 352/26 were landed at Liverpool. 1 crew and 2 passengers were lost.

**CITY OF NAGPUR** • GRT 10146 • Built 1922
29.4.41: Torpedoed and sunk by German submarine U-75 (Ringelmann), in the Atlantic about 600 miles W of Valentia Island, Ireland, in position 52.30N 26.00W while sailing independently on a voyage from Glasgow to Natal, Bombay and Karachi via Freetown, with 274 passengers and 2184 tons of general cargo. The Master, Capt David Llewellyn Lloyd, 170 crew, 8 gunners and 273 passengers were rescued by HM destroyer *HURRICANE* 1340/39 (H.06) (Lt H.C. Simms) ex-Brazilian *JAPARUA* and landed at Greenock. 15 crew and 1 passenger were lost.

**CITY OF VENICE** • GRT 8762 • Built 1924
4.7.43: Torpedoed and sunk by German submarine U-375 (Könenkamp), in the Mediterranean 10 miles N of Cape Tenez, Algeria, in position 36.44N 01.31E while on

government service on a voyage from the Clyde 24.6.43 to Algiers, with 292 army personnel, 10 naval personnel and 700 tons of military equipment, part of convoy KMS 18B comprising 19 ships (Operation Husky). The Master, Capt James Wyper, 10 crew and 10 military personnel were lost. 147 crew, 22 gunners, 282 army personnel and 10 naval personnel were rescued by HM corvettes *HONEYSUCKLE* 925/40 (K.27) (Lt H.M.D. MacKillican DSC) and *RHODODENDRON* 925/40 (K.78) (Lt O.B. Medley), HM frigate *TEVIOT* 1370/42 (K.222) (Cdr T.T. Taylor DSC) and HM rescue tug *RESTIVE* 700/40 (W.39) (Lt D.M. Richards). Kapitänleutnant Jurgen Könenkamp and crew of 44 were lost on 30.7.43 when U-375 was sunk in the Mediterranean NW of Malta, in position 36.40N 12.28E by US submarine chaser PC-624 280/43 (Lt-Cdr Robert D. Lowther). 'Operation Husky' was the landing of Allied troops in Sicily on 10.7.43.

**CITY OF ORAN** • GRT 7784 • Built 1915
2.8.43: Torpedoed and damaged by German submarine U-196 (Kentrat), in the Arabian Sea about 100 miles NE of Memba Bay, Tanganyika, in position 13.31S 41.12E while on a voyage from Durban 26.7.43 to Mombasa and Colombo, with a cargo of 8005 tons of coal, part of convoy CB 21 comprising 3 ships. Later sunk by gunfire by one of the escorts, HM tug *MASTERFUL* 783/42 (W.20) ex-USN BA 6. The Master, Capt Frederick William Letton, crew of 75 and 10 gunners were rescued by HMS *MASTERFUL* and landed at Mombasa.

**MOWT**

**D'ENTRECASTEAUX** • GRT 7291 • Built 1922
8.11.42: Torpedoed and sunk by German submarine U-154 (Schuch), in the Atlantic 150 miles E of Barbados, in position 15.30N 57.00W while sailing independently on a voyage from Beira 15.9.42 and Table Bay 10.10.42 to the UK via Pernambuco 30.10.42 and St Thomas, with 6214 tons of general cargo including 1002 tons of copper. The Master, Capt William Jones, and 57 crew and 5 gunners landed on the island of Dominica 14.11.42, part of the Leeward Islands. 1 crew and 2 gunners were lost.

**CAP PADARAN** ex-*D'IBERVILLE* • GRT 8009 • Built 1922
9.12.43: Torpedoed and sunk by German submarine U-596 (Nonn), in the Mediterranean NE of Cape Spartivento, Italy, in position 39.15N 17.30E while in convoy on a voyage from Taranto 8.12.43 to Augusta, in ballast. The Master, Capt Edward Garner, 180 crew and 11 gunners were rescued by HM trawler *SHEPPEY* 545/42 (T.292) ex-HMS *RAASAY* (Sub-Lt B.F. Wimbush) and landed at Augusta, Sicily. 5 crew were lost. U-596 commanded by Oberleutnant zur See Hans Kolbus was sunk on 24.9.44 by a Liberator of the USAAF at Salamis, Greece. The *CAP PADARAN* was captured from the Vichy French by HM armed merchant cruiser *CARTHAGE* 14253/31 (F.99) (Capt B.O. Bell-Slater) and brought to Port Elizabeth 7.11.41.

**Hall Line Ltd**

**CITY OF KOBE** ex-*MALVERNIAN* • GRT 4373 • Built 1924
19.12.39: Struck a mine, laid on 17.12.39, by German submarine U-60 (Schewe) and sank in the North Sea near Cross Sand Buoy, Great Yarmouth, in position 52.35N 01.59E while on a voyage from Antwerp, the Tyne and Hull to Alexandria, Bombay and the Malabar coast, with

general cargo and coal, part of coastal convoy FS 5 comprising 53 ships. The Master, Capt William Scott Craig and 29 crew were rescued by British coasters *CORINIA* 870/28 and *FAXFLEET* 863/16 and Admiralty trawler *TUMBY* 204/18 (FY.850) (Skipper J.W. Greengrass). 1 crew was lost.

**CITY OF WINCHESTER** • GRT 7891 • Built 1917
9.5.41: Torpedoed and sunk by German submarine U–103 (Schütze), in the Atlantic about 400 miles SSW of the Cape Verde Islands, in position 08.20N 26.14W while sailing independently on a voyage from London to Cape Town and Beira, with 6500 tons of general cargo, dispersed on 28.4.41 from convoy OB 313 comprising 38 ships. The Master, Capt William Samuel Coughlan, 84 crew and 7 gunners were rescued by the Norwegian ship *HERMA* 2406/24 and landed at Takoradi. 6 crew were lost.

**CITY OF SHANGHAI** • GRT 5528 • Built 1917
11.5.41: Torpedoed and sunk by gunfire by German submarine U–103 (Schütze), in the South Atlantic off St Paul Rocks, in position 06.40S 27.50W while sailing independently on a voyage from the Tyne to Cape Town and Turkey, with 8000 tons of government cargo and deck cargo, dispersed on 28.4.41 from convoy OB 313 comprising 38 ships. The Master, Capt Arthur Frank Goring, and 27 crew were rescued by Dutch ship *STAD ARNHEM* 3819/20 and landed at Freetown, 17 crew by British ship *RICHMOND CASTLE* 7798/39 and landed at Glasgow and 22 crew by Argentinian ship *JOSEFINA* S 2166/07 and landed at Pernambuco. 6 crew were lost.

**CITY OF MANCHESTER** • GRT 8917 • Built 1935
28.2.42: Torpedoed and sunk by gunfire by Japanese submarine I–153 (Nakamura), in the Indian Ocean SE of Tjilatjap, Sumatra, in position 08.16S 108.52E while sailing independently on a voyage from Pekan, Malaya, to Tjilatjap, with 6400 tons of general cargo including military stores. The Master, Capt Harry Johnson, 126 crew, 17 gunners and 13 naval signalmen were rescued by US minesweeper *WHIPPOORWILL* 840/19 (AM.35), landed at Batavia and brought to Fremantle by Dutch liner *ZAANDAM* 10909/39. 9 crew were lost. I–153 was at Otake, Japan, on 14.8.45 VJ Day.

**CITY OF MELBOURNE** • GRT 6630 • Built 1919
13.5.42: Torpedoed and sunk by gunfire by German submarine U–156 (Hartenstein), in the Atlantic W of Barbados, in position 15.00N 54.40W while sailing independently on a voyage from Beira and Cape Town 23.4.42 to New York, with a cargo of 4000 tons of general cargo. The Master, Capt Harry George Thorne Booth, 75 crew and 10 gunners landed at Barbados. 1 crew was lost.

**CITY OF MANILA** • GRT 7463 • Built 1916
19.8.42: Torpedoed and sunk by German submarine U–406 (Dieterichs), part of the 'Blucher' patrol group of seven U-boats, in the Atlantic W of Cape Finisterre, in position 43.21N 18.20W while on a voyage from Bombay, Cochin and Cape Town to Glasgow via Freetown 4.8.42, with a cargo of 10000 tons of general cargo including pig iron and groundnuts, part of convoy SL 118 comprising 34 ships. The Master, Capt Alfred Sutton Reay, 83 crew and 11 gunners were rescued. 46 survivors were rescued by British ship

*EMPIRE VOICE* 6902/40 and landed at Loch Ewe and 49 by HM sloop *GORLESTON* 1546/29 (Y.92) (Cdr R.W. Keymer) ex-US Coastguard cutter *ITASCA* and landed at Londonderry. 1 crew was lost. U-406 part of the 'Hai' (Shark) patrol group of nineteen U-boats, was sunk on 18.2.44 in the Atlantic 570 miles WSW of Cape Clear, in position 48.32N 23.36W while shadowing convoy ONS 29 comprising 44 ships by HM frigate *SPEY* 1370/41 (K.246) (Cdr H.G. Boys-Smith). Kapitänleutnant Horst Dieterichs and 11 crew were lost and 41 crew were taken prisoner by HMS *SPEY*.

### CITY OF WELLINGTON • GRT 5733 • Built 1925
21.8.42: Torpedoed and sunk by German submarine U-506 (Würdemann), in the Atlantic SW of Freetown, in position 07.29N 14.40W while sailing independently on a voyage from Lourenco Marques and Mossel Bay, South Africa 6.8.42, to the UK via Freetown, with 7500 tons of general cargo including chrome ore and copper ore. The Master, Capt McDonald Martyn, 60 crew and 5 gunners were rescued by HM detroyer *VELOX* 1090/17 (D.34) (Lt G.B. Barston) and landed at Freetown 22.8.42. 7 crew were lost.

### CITY OF CARDIFF ex-LANGTON HALL • GRT 5661 • Built 1918
28.8.42: Torpedoed by German submarine U-566 (Remus), part of the 'Iltis' (Polecat) patrol group of seven U-boats, and sank on 30.8.42 in the Atlantic WNW of Lisbon, in position 40.20N 16.02W while on a voyage from Beira to Manchester via Freetown 14.8.42, with 7500 tons of general cargo including copper, part of convoy SL 119 comprising 30 ships. The Master, Capt Robert Leonard Stewart and 62 crew were rescued by HM sloop *ROCHESTER* 1045/31 (L.50) (Cdr C.B. Allen) and landed at Londonderry. 21 crew were lost.

### KIOTO • GRT 3297 • Built 1918
15.9.42: Torpedoed and damaged by gunfire by German submarine U-514 (Auffermann), in the Atlantic E of Tobago, in position 11.05N 60.46W while sailing independently on a voyage from Diego Suarez, Madagascar and Cape Town 22.8.42 to Baltimore via Trinidad, with a cargo of 2000 tons of chrome ore. The ship drifted ashore at Columbus Point, Tobago, a burnt-out hulk. The Master, Capt Arthur Lloyd Beckett, 65 crew and 3 gunners were rescued by the Trinidad government ship *TRINIDAD* 606/31 and landed at Scarborough, Tobago. 4 crew and 1 gunner were lost.

### CITY OF ATHENS • GRT 6558 • Built 1923
8.10.42: Torpedoed and sunk by German submarine U-179 (Sobe), in the South Atlantic 60 miles WNW of Cape Town, in position 33.32S 17.26E while sailing independently on a voyage from Glasgow and Takoradi to Cape Town and Alexandria, with 8 Admiralty staff and 5646 tons of government stores and general. The Master, Capt James Albert Kingsley, 80 crew, 9 gunners and the Admiralty staff were rescued by HM destroyer *ACTIVE* 1350/29 (H.14) (Lt-Cdr M.W. Tomkinson) and landed at Cape Town. 1 crew was lost. Korvettenkapitän Ernst Sobe and crew of 60 were lost on the same day when U-179 was sunk in the South Atlantic 80 miles NW by N of Cape Point, South Africa, in position 33.28S 17.05E by HMS *ACTIVE*.

### CITY OF JOHANNESBURG ex-MELFORD HALL • GRT 5669 • Built 1920
23.10.42: Torpedoed and sunk by German submarine U-504 (Poske), part of the 'Eisbär' (Polarbear) patrol group of five U-boats, in the Indian Ocean SE of East London, in position

33.27S 29.10E while sailing independently on a voyage from Calcutta and Colombo 6.10.42 to the UK via Cape Town, with 7750 tons of general cargo including pig iron, cotton, jute and tea. The Master, Capt Walter Armour Owen, and 12 crew were rescued by Dutch ship ZYPENBERG 5054/30 and landed at Durban, 54 crew by British ship FORT GEORGE 7130/42 and landed at Port Elizabeth and 20 crew by British ship KING EDWARD 5224/19 and landed at Cape Town. 2 crew were lost.

**CITY OF CAIRO** • GRT 8034 • Built 1915
6.11.42: Torpedoed and sunk by German submarine U-68 (Merten), part of the 'Eisbär' (Polarbear) patrol group of five U-boats, in the South Atlantic 480 miles S of St Helena, in position 23.30S 05.30W while sailing independently on a voyage from Bombay, Durban and Cape Town 1.11.42 to the UK via Pernambuco, with 100 passengers and 7422 tons of general cargo including pig iron, timber, wool and silver bullion. The Master, Capt William A. Rogerson, and 154 survivors were rescued by British ship CLAN ALPINE 5442/18 and landed on the island of St Helena, 47 survivors by British ship BENDORAN 5567/10 and landed at Cape Town, 2 survivors by the Brazilian corvette CARAVELAS 552/39 and landed at Recife and 3 survivors by the German blockade runner RHAKOTIS 6753/28 on a voyage from Japan to Bordeaux. 79 crew, 3 gunners and 22 passengers were lost. The RHAKOTIS 6753/28 (Kapitän zur See Jacobs) was torpedoed and sunk by HM cruiser SCYLLA 5450/40 (98) (Capt T.M. Browning OBE) on 1.1.43 in the Atlantic 200 miles NW of Cape Finisterre. One of the survivors from the CITY OF CAIRO died on board the RHAKOTIS and 2 survivors were rescued by German submarine U-410 commanded by Korvettenkapitän Kurt Sturm and landed at St Nazaire 4.1.43. Korvettenkapitän Karl-Friedrich Merten was awarded the Knight's Cross (13.6.42) with Oak Leaves (16.11.42).

**CITY OF CORINTH** • GRT 5318 • Built 1918
17.11.42: Torpedoed and sunk by German submarine U-508 (Staats), in the Atlantic N of Trinidad, in position 10.55N 61.01W while sailing independently on a voyage from Calcutta and Cape Town to the UK via Pernambuco 7.11.42 and Trinidad, with 8300 tons of general cargo including tea, linseed and pig iron. The Master, Capt George Johnston Law, 69 crew and 6 gunners were rescued by US submarine chaser PC 536 95/42 and landed at Port of Spain, Trinidad. 11 crew were lost.

**CITY OF BATH** • GRT 5079 • Built 1926
2.12.42: Torpedoed and sunk by German submarine U-508 (Staats), in the Atlantic NW of Georgetown, British Guinea, in position 09.29N 59.30W while sailing independently on a voyage from Mombasa to the UK via Pernambuco 23.11.42 and Trinidad, with 6800 tons of general cargo including 2000 tons of copper ingots, 500 tons of magnesite ore, 500 tons of chrome ore and mail. The Master, Capt Thomas Victor Birkett, and 27 survivors landed at Palo Seco, Trinidad 5.12.42 and 52 survivors were rescued on 3.12.42 by the Hall Line ship CITY OF DUNKIRK 5861/12 and landed at Trinidad. 3 crew were lost.

**CITY OF BOMBAY** • GRT 7140 • Built 1937
13.12.42: Torpedoed and sunk by gunfire by German submarine U-159 (Witte), in the South Atlantic S of St Paul Rocks, in position 02.43S 29.06W while sailing independently on a voyage from Liverpool and Trinidad 5.12.42 to Saldanha Bay, South Africa, and Karachi, with

14 passengers and 6500 tons of military stores. The Master, Capt Forbes Wyse Penderworthy, 122 crew and 7 gunners were rescued: 24 survivors by Egyptian ship STAR OF CAIRO 4579/24 and landed at Cape Town, 92 survivors on 19.12.42 by British ship CAPE BRETON 6044/40 and landed at Recife 21.12.42 and 14 survivors by US corvette TENACITY 925/40 (PG.71) ex-HMS CANDYTUFT and landed at Pernambuco. 9 crew and 1 gunner were lost.

**CITY OF GUILDFORD** ex-ROMEO ex-WAR MIDGE • GRT 5157 • Built 1919
27.3.43: Torpedocd and sunk by German submarine U-593 (Kelbling), in the Mediterranean off Derna, in position 33.00N 22.50E while on government service on a voyage from Alexandria to Tripoli, with 53 army personnel and 9000 tons of general cargo including cased octane spirit and ammunition. The Master, Capt Clifford Collard, 6 crew, 1 gunner and 5 army personnel were rescued by HM destroyer EXMOOR 1050/41 (L.08) ex-HMS BURTON (Lt D.T. McBarnett DSC) and landed at Benghazi. 70 crew, 11 gunners and 48 army personnel were lost. U-593, commanded by Kapitänleutnant Gerd Kelbling (Knight's Cross 19.8.43), was sunk on 13.12.43 in the Mediterranean 50 miles NNW of Cape Bougaroni, Algeria, in position 37.38N 05.58E by HM destroyer CALPE 1050/41 (L.71) (Lt-Cdr H. Kirkwood) and US destroyer WAINWRIGHT 1570/39 (DD–419) (Cdr W.B. Strohbehn). The U-boat commander and crew of 44 were taken prisoner by HMS CALPE and USS WAINWRIGHT. Prior to the sinking of U-593 her commander sank HM escort destroyers TYNEDALE 907/40 (L.96) (Lt-Cdr J.J.S Yorke DSC) off Bougie, in position 37.10N 06.05E and HOLCOMBE 1087/42 (L.56) (Lt-Cdr S.H. Pinchin DSC) off Bougie, in position 37.20N 05.50E on 12.12.43.

**CITY OF BARODA** • GRT 7129 • Built 1918
2.4.43: Torpedoed and damaged by German submarine U-509 (Witte), part of the 'Seehund' (Seal) patrol group of five U-boats, in the South Atlantic SW of Cape Town, in position 27.50S 14.48E while on a voyage from London to Walvis Bay 1.4.43, Durban, Colombo and Calcutta via Trinidad, with 203 passengers, 7000 tons of general cargo and 1500 bags of mail, part of convoy CN 9 comprising 2 ships. The Master, Capt Charles Stuart Nelson, 124 crew, 4 gunners and 196 passengers were rescued by HM trawler CAPE WARWICK 516/37 (FY.167) (Lt W.E. Goggin) and landed at Cape Town. 1 crew and 7 passengers were lost. The CITY OF BARODA was later towed to Luderitz Bay, South West Africa, and declared a CTL. Kapitänleutnant Werne Witte and crew of 53 were lost on 15.7.43 when U-509, part of the 'Monsun' (Monsoon) patrol group of nine U-boats, was sunk in the Atlantic 225 miles S of San Miguel, Azores, in position 34.02N 26.02W by an Avenger, pilot Lt Claude N. Barton and a Wildcat, pilot Ensign Jack D. Anderson of US Navy Composite Squadron VC-29 from USN escort carrier SANTEE 11400/42 (CVE-29) of the Task Group 21.11 (Capt H.F. Fick).

**CITY OF SINGAPORE** • GRT 6555 • Built 1923
1.5.43: Torpedoed and sunk by German submarine U-515 (Henke), in the Atlantic SW of Freetown, in position 07.55N 14.16W while on a voyage from Calcutta and Takoradi 26.4.43 to Liverpool via Freetown, with 9025 tons general cargo including 2700 tons of pig iron, jute, linseed, 2400 tons of groundnuts and mail, part of convoy TS 37 comprising 19 ships. The Master, Capt Alfred George Freeman, crew of 86 and 10 gunners were rescued by HM trawlers ARRAN 545/40 (T.06) (Lt D.S. Sutton) and BIRDLIP 750/41 (T.218) (Lt E.N. Groom) and landed at Freetown.

**CITY OF CANTON** • GRT 6692 • Built 1916

16.7.43: Torpedoed and sunk by German submarine U-178 (Dommes), in the Mozambique Channel NE of Beira, in position 13.40S 41.40E while sailing independently from Liverpool to Beira 14.7.43 and Mombasa, with 2000 tons of general cargo and 4500 tons of coal. The Master, Capt Edward Scrymgeour, and 74 crew were rescued by the Free French cruiser *SUFFRIN* 9938/30 and landed at Durban; 19 crew by Portuguese ship *LUABO* 1419/09 and landed at Mozambique. The 2nd Officer was taken prisoner, 8 crew were lost. Kapitänleutnant Wilhelm Dommes was awarded the Knight's Cross (2.12.42). U-178 commanded by Kapitänleutnant Wilhelm Spahr was scuttled on 20.8.44 at Bordeaux, in position 44.52N 00.34W.

**CITY OF ADELAIDE** • GRT 6589 • Built 1920

30.3.44: Torpedoed and sunk by gunfire by Japanese submarine I-8 (Ariizumi), in the Indian Ocean SE of Diego Garcia, Chagos Archipelago, in position 12.01S 80.27E while sailing independently on a voyage from Karachi to Fremantle, in ballast. The Master, Capt Richard James Ricketts, crew of 79 and 10 gunners were rescued by US Liberty ship *CAROLE LOMBARD* 7207/44 and landed at Colombo.

## ELLERMAN & BUCKNALL STEAMSHIP CO. LTD – LONDON

**CITY OF PRETORIA** • GRT 8049 • Built 1937

4.3.43: Torpedoed and sunk by German submarine U-172 (Emmermann), in the Atlantic WNW of the Azores, in position 41.45N 43.30W while sailing independently on a voyage from New York to Liverpool, with 7032 tons of general cargo. The Master, Capt Frank Deighton OBE, crew of 108, 24 gunners, 7 DBS and 5 apprentices were lost.

**CITY OF PERTH** ex-*KANDAHAR* • GRT 6415 • Built 1913

26.3.43: Torpedoed and damaged by German submarine U-431 (Schöneboom), in the Mediterrean NW of Oran, in position 35.04N 01.30W while on a voyage from Bona to Liverpool, in ballast, part of convoy MKS 10 comprising 25 ships. Taken in tow by HM trawler *MAN O'WAR* 517/36 (FY.104) (Lt G.L. Coles) and beached S of Cape Figalo, Algeria, it became a CTL. The Master, Capt John Blewitt, crew of 78 and 11 gunners were rescued by HMS *MAN O'WAR* and landed at Gibraltar 28.3.43. 2 gunners were lost. Oberleutnant zur See Dietrich Schöneboom, Knight's Cross awarded 20.10.43 and crew of 51 were lost on 21.10.43 when U-431 was sunk in the Mediterranean SE of Cartagena, in position 37.20N 00.43W by Leigh Light-equipped Wellington XIV 'Z' MP741, pilot Sgt Donald M. Cornish (Canadian) of No. 179 Squadron RAF, based at Gibraltar.

## ELLERMAN & PAPAYANNI & COMPANY – LONDON

**DARINO** • GRT 1351 • Built 1917

19.11.39: Torpedoed and sunk by German submarine U-41 (Mugler), in the Atlantic W of Cape Ortegal, in position 44.12N 11.07W while sailing independently on a voyage from Oporto to Liverpool, with 1600 tons of general cargo including wine, sardines and tin ore. The Master, Capt William James Ethelbert Colgan, and 15 crew were lost. 11 crew were rescued by U-41, later transferred to Italian steamer *CATERINA GEROLIMICH* 5430/12 and landed at Dover.

**IONIAN** • GRT 3114 • Built 1938
29.11.39: Struck a mine, laid on 22.11.39 by German submarine U-20 (Moehle) and sank in the North Sea about 4 miles N of Newarp Lightship while on a voyage from Candia, Crete to London and Hull, with general cargo including 200 tons of currants and mohair, part of coastal convoy FN 43 comprising 23 ships. The Master, Capt William Smith, and crew of 36 were rescued by HM sloop *HASTINGS* 1045/30 (L.27) (Cdr E.H. Vincent) and landed at South Shields.

**MARDINIAN** • GRT 2434 • Built 1919
9.9.40: Torpedoed and sunk by German submarine U-28 (Kuhnke), in the Atlantic 100 miles NNW of Bloody Foreland, in position 56.37N 09.00W while on a voyage from Trinidad to Methil and London via Sydney CB, with a cargo of 3500 tons of pitch, part of convoy SC 2 comprising 53 ships. The Master, Capt Joseph Every, 19 crew and 1 gunner were rescued by British trawler *APOLLO* 106/04 and landed at Belfast. 10 crew landed at Leverburgh, South Uist, and 1 crew was rescued by HM armed merchant cruiser *AURANIA* 13984/24 (F.28) (Capt J.W. Whitehorn). 6 crew were lost.

**ASSYRIAN** ex-*FRITZ* • GRT 2962 • Built 1914
19.10.40: Torpedoed and sunk by German submarine U-101 (Frauenheim), in the Atlantic about 102 miles W by N of Barra Head, Outer Hebrides, in position 57.12N 10.43W while on a voyage from New Orleans to Liverpool via Sydney CB 5.10.40, with 9 passengers and 3700 tons of grain, part of convoy SC 7 comprising 35 ships. The Master, Capt Reginald Sanderson Kearon, Commodore Vice-Admiral Lachlan D.I. Mackinnon CB CVO RN, 20 crew, 3 naval staff and passengers were rescued by HM sloop *LEITH* 990/33 (L.36) (Cdr Roland C. Allen) and landed at Liverpool. 15 crew and 2 naval staff were lost. Capt Kearon was awarded the Lloyd's War Medal for bravery at sea. Korvettenkapitän Fritz Frauenheim was awarded the Knight's Cross (29.8.40).

**FABIAN** • GRT 3059 • Built 1919
16.11.40: Torpedoed and sunk by German submarine U-65 (v. Stockhausen), in the Atlantic 350 miles SSW of Freetown, in position 02.49N 15.29W while sailing independently on a voyage from Liverpool 24.10.40 to Port Said and Istanbul via Cape Town, with 4000 tons of general cargo, dispersed from convoy OB 234 comprising 26 ships. The Master, Capt Montague Hocking, and 32 crew were rescued by British tanker *BRITISH STATESMAN* 6991/23 and landed at Freetown. 6 crew were lost.

**PALMELLA** • GRT 1578 • Built 1920
1.12.40: Torpedoed and sunk by German submarine U-37 (Clausen), in the Atlantic SW of Oporto, in position 40.30N 13.30W while sailing independently on a voyage from London to Oporto, with general cargo and mail. The Master, Capt Joseph Every, 26 crew and 1 gunner were rescued by the Spanish trawler *NAVEMAR* and landed at Lisbon. 1 crew was lost.

**FLORIAN** • GRT 3174 • Built 1939
20.1.41: Torpedoed and sunk by German submarine U-94 (Kuppisch), in the North Atlantic W of the Faröe Islands, in position 61.14N 12.05W while sailing independently on a voyage from Hull to New York, in ballast. The Master, Capt Lawrence Robert Mann, and crew of 40 were lost.

**ESTRELLANO** • GRT 1963 • Built 1920
9.2.41: Torpedoed and sunk by German submarine U-37 (Clausen), in the Atlantic 160 miles SW of Cape St Vincent, in position 35.53N 13.13W while on a voyage from Leixoes to Liverpool, with a cargo of 3110 tons of general cargo including canned fish, part of convoy HG 53 comprising 21 ships. The Master, Capt Fred Bird, 19 crew and 1 gunner were rescued by British ship *BRANDENBERG* 1473/10, transferred to HM sloop *DEPTFORD* 990/35 (L.53) (Lt-Cdr G.A. Thring DSO) and landed at Liverpool. 6 crew were lost.

**ANDALUSIAN** • GRT 3074 • Built 1918
17.3.41: Torpedoed and sunk by German submarine U-106 (Oesten), in the Atlantic N of the Cape Verde Islands, in position 14.33N 21.06W while on a voyage from Freetown 13.3.41 to Oban for orders, with a cargo of 3231 tons of cocoa, part of convoy SL 68 comprising 59 ships. The Master, Capt Harry Bourne McHugh, crew of 39 and 2 gunners landed on Boavista, Cape Verde Islands, and were brought to Funchal by Portuguese ship *NYASA* 8980/06.

**BELGRAVIAN** • GRT 3133 • Built 1937
5.8.41: Torpedoed and sunk by German submarine U-372 (Neumann), in the Atlantic W of Ireland, in position 53.03N 15.54W while on a voyage from Port Harcourt and Freetown 15.7.41 to Hull, with a cargo of 3946 tons of kernels, groundnuts and tin ore, part of convoy SL 81 comprising 18 ships. The Master, Capt Richard Sanderson Kearon OBE, 40 crew and 6 gunners were rescued by HM corvette *BLUEBELL* 925/40 (K.80) (Lt-Cdr Robert E. Sherwood RNR) and landed at Gourock. 3 crew were lost.

**SERBINO** • GRT 4099 • Built 1919
21.10.41: Torpedoed and sunk by German submarine U-82 (Rollman), in the Atlantic W of Fastnet, in position 51.10N 19.20W while on a voyage from Mombasa to Liverpool via Freetown 5.10.41, with 3500 tons of general cargo including sisal, part of convoy SL 89 comprising 23 ships. The Master, Capt Lawrence Edwin Brooks, and 50 crew were rescued by HM corvette *ASPHODEL* 925/40 (K.56) (Lt-Cdr K.W. Stewart) and landed at Gourock. 14 crew were lost.

**CITY OF OXFORD** • GRT 2759 • Built 1926
15.6.42: Torpedoed and sunk by German submarine U-552 (Topp), in the Atlantic W of Cape Finisterre, in position 43.42N 18.12W while on a voyage from Lisbon 11.6.42 to Garston, with a cargo of 2000 tons of ore and 300 tons of cork, part of convoy HG 84 comprising 23 ships. The Master, Capt Alfred Norbury, 36 crew and 6 gunners were rescued by rescue ship *COPELAND* 1526/23 (Capt W.J. Hartley DSC), transferred to HM corvette *MARIGOLD* 925/40 (K.87) (Lt J.A.S. Halcrow), transferred to HM sloop *STORK* 1190/36 (L.81) (Cdr Frederic John Walker) and landed at Liverpool. 1 crew was lost.

**EGYPTIAN** • GRT 2868 • Built 1920
7.3.43: Torpedoed and sunk by German submarine U-230 (Siegmann), part of the 'Westmark' (West German mark) patrol group of seventeen U-boats, in the Atlantic SSE of Cape Farewell, in position 56.25N 37.38W while on a voyage from Lagos to Loch Ewe for orders via New York 23.2.43, with a cargo of 6689 tons of West African produce, part of

convoy SC 121 comprising 57 ships. The Master, Capt Dominic Vincent Murphy, 36 crew and 9 gunners were lost. 3 crew were rescued by RCN corvette *ROSTHERN* 925/40 (K.169) (Lt R.J.G Johnson) and landed at Londonderry. U-230 commanded by Oberleutnant zur See Heinz-Eugen Eberbach was scuttled at Toulon 21.8.44. Oberleutnant zur See Bernard Müller and crew of 43 were lost on 10.3.43 when U-633 part of the 'Neuland' (New Territory) patrol group of sixteen U-boats was rammed and sunk in the Atlantic WNW of Rockall, in position about 58.51N 19.55W while attacking convoy SC 121 by British ship *SCORTON* 4795/39 (Capt Terrot Glover) position number 52 in the convoy. As a result of this action, Capt Glover was awarded the OBE.

*OPORTO* • GRT 2352 • Built 1928
13.3.43: Torpedoed and sunk by German submarine U-107 (Gelhaus), in the Atlantic SW of Cape Finisterre, in position 42.45N 13.31W while on a voyage from Liverpool to Seville, with a cargo of 1500 tons of sulphate of copper, 413 tons of seed potatoes and mail, part of convoy OS 44 comprising 48 ships. The Master, Capt Fred Bird, 35 crew and 7 gunners were lost. 4 crew were rescued by HM corvette *SPIRAEA* 925/40 (K.08) (Lt A.H. Pierce OBE), transferred to HM corvette *GENTIAN* 925/40 (K.90) (Lt-Cdr H.H. Russell DSC) and landed at Gibraltar.

## ELLERMAN'S WILSON LINE LTD – HULL

*TRURO* • GRT 974 • Built 1922
15.9.39: Torpedoed and sunk by gunfire by German submarine U-36 (Fröhlich), in the North Sea about 150 miles E of Kinnard Head, in position 58.20N 02.00E while sailing independently on a voyage from Hull and the Tyne to Trondheim, with 800 tons of general cargo including coal, coke, nickel and copper. The Master, Capt John Charles Egner, and crew of 19 were rescued by Belgian trawlers *NAUTILUS* 352/26 and *EDWAARD VAN FLAANEREN* 324/25, the survivors were transferred to one of the trawlers and landed at Aberdeen 17.9.39. Kapitänleutnant Wilhelm Frohlich and crew of 39 were lost on 4.12.39 when U-36 was sunk in the North Sea 85 miles SW of Lindesnes, in position 57.00N 05.20E by HM submarine *SALMON* 670/34 (N.65) (Lt-Cdr E.O. Bickford).

*KYNO* • GRT 3946 • Built 1924
28.8.40: Torpedoed and sunk by German submarine U-28 (Kuhnke), in the Atlantic 30 miles NNE of Rockall, in position 58.06N 13.26W while on a voyage from New York to Hull via Halifax NS 16.8.40, with 4499 tons of general cargo, part of convoy HX 66 comprising 51 ships. The Master, Capt William Ansdell Thompson, and 32 crew were rescued by British ship *QUEEN MAUD* 4976/36 and landed at Methil. 4 crew were lost.

*TASSO* • GRT 1586 • Built 1938
2.12.40: Torpedoed and sunk by German submarine U-52 (Salman), in the Atlantic 360 miles W of Bloody Foreland, in position 55.03N 18.04W while on a voyage from Demerara to Oban for orders via Halifax NS 21.11.40, with a cargo of 1300 tons of logs, part of convoy HX 90 comprising 35 ships. The Master, Capt Arnold Herbert, and 26 crew were rescued by HM destroyer *VISCOUNT* 1325/17 (D.92) (Lt-Cdr M.S. Townsend OBE DSC) and landed at Liverpool. 5 crew were lost.

**BASSANO** • GRT 4843 • Built 1937

9.1.41: Torpedoed and sunk by German submarine U-105 (Schewe), in the Atlantic NW of Rockall, in position 57.57N 17.42W while sailing independently on a voyage from New York to Hull, with 5 passengers and a cargo of 5000 tons of iron and steel and 600 tons of grain. The Master, Capt Dunsley Harwood Casson, 48 crew, 2 gunners and passengers were rescued by HM destroyer *WILD SWAN* 1120/19 (D.62) (Lt-Cdr C.E.L. Sclater) and landed at Liverpool. 1 crew was lost.

**ERATO** • GRT 1335 • Built 1923

27.7.41: Torpedoed and sunk by German submarine U-126 (Bauer), in the Atlantic W of Cape Finisterre, in position 43.10N 17.30W while on a voyage from Liverpool 20.7.41 to Oporto and Gibraltar, with 732 tons of general cargo, 1200 tons of military and naval stores, part of convoy OG 69 comprising 27 ships. The Master, Capt George D. Smail, 22 crew and 4 gunners were rescued by HM corvette *BEGONIA* 925/40 (K.66) (Lt T.A.R. Muir) and landed at Gibraltar. 8 crew and 1 gunner were lost.

**ARIOSTO** • GRT 2176 • Built 1940

24.10.41: Torpedoed and sunk by German submarine U-564 (Suhren), part of the 'Breslau' patrol group of six U-boats, in the Atlantic 220 miles W by S of Gibraltar, in position 36.20N 10.40W while on a voyage from Lisbon to Liverpool, with the convoy's Commodore F.L.J. Butler RNR RD, 6 naval staff, 3 passengers, 1 DBS and 650 tons of general cargo including cork and ore, part of convoy HG 75 comprising 17 ships. The Master, Capt Harold Hill, the Commodore, 31 crew, 3 gunners, 6 naval staff and passengers were rescued: 38 survivors were rescued by the Swedish ship *PACIFIC* 4978/14 and landed at Barrow and 7 survivors by HM destroyer *LAMERTON* 1050/40 (L.88) (Lt-Cdr H.C. Simms) and landed at Gibraltar. 5 crew and 1 gunner were lost.

**VOLO** • GRT 1587 • Built 1938

28.12.41: Torpedoed and sunk by German submarine U-75 (Ringelmann), in the Mediterranean 45 miles NW of Mersa Matruh, Egypt, in position 31.45N 26.48E while on government service on a voyage from Tobruk to Alexandria, in ballast, part of convoy ME 8 comprising 2 ships. The Master George Rowland Whitefield MBE, 20 crew and 3 gunners were lost. 9 crew and 5 gunners were rescued by Admiralty lighter A.11 and landed at Alexandria. U-75 commanded by Kapitänleutnant Helmuth Ringelmann was sunk on the same day in the Mediterranean 30 miles NE of Mersa Matruh, in position 31.50N 26.40E by HM destroyer *KIPLING* 1690/39 (F.91) (Cdr A. St Clair-Ford). The U-boat commander and 13 crew were lost. 21 crew were taken prisoner by HMS *KIPLING* and 9 crew by HM destroyer *LEGION* 1920/39 (F.74) (Cdr R.F. Jessel) and landed at Alexandria.

**THURSO** laid down as *WAR BRAMBLE* • GRT 2436 • Built 1919

15.6.42: Torpedoed and sunk by German submarine U-552 (Topp), part of the 'Endrass' (named after a U-boat commander) patrol group of eight U-boats, in the Atlantic about 350 miles WSW of Cape Finisterre, in position 43.41N 18.02W while on a voyage from Lisbon to Liverpool via Gibraltar 9.6.42, with 850 tons of general cargo including cork and mail, part of convoy HG 84 comprising 23 ships. The Master, Capt William Walker, 22 crew and 6 gunners were rescued by HM corvette *MARIGOLD* 925/40 (K.87) (Lt J.A.S. Halcrow) and landed at Greenock. 13 crew were lost.

**KELSO** • GRT 3956 • Built 1924
8.8.42: Torpedoed and sunk by German submarine U-176 (Dierksen), in the Atlantic SE of Cape Farewell, in position 56.30N 32.14W while on a voyage from New York to Liverpool via Sydney CB 31.7.42, with 4618 tons of general cargo including 2000 tons of ammunition, part of convoy SC 94 comprising 30 ships. The Master, Capt Alfred Hinchcliff, 34 crew and 6 gunners were rescued by RCN corvette *BATTLEFORD* 925/41 (K.165) (Lt R.J. Roberts) and landed at Gourock. 3 crew were lost.

**CITY OF RIPON** ex-*LEPANTO* • GRT 6368 • Built 1915
11.11.42: Torpedoed and sunk by German submarine U-160 (Lassen), in the Atlantic 90 miles NW of Georgetown, British Guinea, in position 08.40N 59.20W while sailing independently on a voyage from Port Said to New York via Cape Town 18.10.42 and Trinidad, in ballast. The Master, Capt John Edward Robinson, 18 crew and 3 gunners were rescued by Brazilian ship *MIDOSI* 4951/19 and landed at Port of Spain, Trinidad. 52 crew and 4 gunners were lost.

**GUIDO** • GRT 3921 • Built 1920
8.3.43: Torpedoed and probably sunk by German submarine U-526 (Möglich), part of the 'Westmark' (West German mark) patrol group of seventeen U-boats, in the Atlantic 450 miles ESE of Cape Farewell, in position 58.08N 32.20W while on a voyage from St Kitts, BWI, and New York 23.2.43 to Greenock, with 4242 tons of sugar, 35 tons of cotton and mail, a romper from convoy SC 121 comprising 57 ships. The Master, Capt George Mussared, 28 crew and 6 gunners were rescued by the US coastguard cutter *SPENCER* 2126/37 (WPG 36) and landed at Londonderry. 8 crew and 2 gunners were lost. U-526 commanded by Kapitänleutnant Hans Möglich was sunk on 14.4.43 when she hit a British mine in the Bay of Biscay, off Lorient, in position 47.41N 03.22W. The U-boat commander and 41 crew were lost. 12 crew were saved.

**RUNO** • GRT 1858 • Built 1920
11.4.43: Torpedoed and sunk by German submarine U-593 (Kelbling), in the Mediterranean about 60 miles NE of Bardia, Cyrenaica, in position 32.15N 23.55E while on government service on a voyage from Benghazi to Alexandria, in ballast. The Master, Capt C.H. Tully, 15 crew and 5 gunners were rescued and landed at Alexandria 13.4.43. 16 crew were lost.

**MOWT**

**FLORA II** ex-*FLORA* • GRT 1218 • Built 1909
2.8.42: Torpedoed and sunk by German submarine U-254 (Gilardone), in the North Atlantic 60 miles SE of Vestmannaoerne, Iceland, in position 62.45N 19.07W while on a voyage from Reykjavik 2.8.42 to Hull via Scrabster, with 1 passenger and a cargo of 358 tons of fish and ice. The Master, Capt Peter Kristjan Johanes Nielsen, crew of 24, 4 gunners and passenger were rescued by Icelandic trawler *JUNI* 328/20 and landed at Reykjavik.

**EGHOLM** ex-*PHYLLIS SEED* ex-*LANGFOND* • GRT 1317 • Built 1924
25.2.45: Torpedoed and sunk by German submarine U-2322 (Heckel), in the North Sea SE of Holy Island, in position 55.50N 01.32W while on a voyage from Leith to London, with general cargo, part of coastal convoy FS 1739. The Master, Capt K.S. Kristensen, and 20 crew landed Tyne. 2 crew and 3 gunners were lost. U-2322 commanded by Oberleutnant zur See Fridtjof Heckel surrendered at Stavanger on 9.5.45. U-2322 sailed from Cairnryan, Loch Ryan, on 27.11.45 under tow by HM rescue tug *SAUCY* 700/42 (W.131) and was sunk by gunfire on 27.11.45 by HM destroyer *ONSLOW* 1550/41 ex-HMS *PAKENHAM* (G.17) (Lt-Cdr E.C.F. Coxwell) and ORP destroyer *BLYSKAWICA* 2144/36 (H.34) in the Atlantic SW of Rockall, in position 56.10N 10.05W, part of 'Operation Deadlight', the disposal by the Royal Navy of 116 U-boats.

## EUXINE SHIPPING CO. LTD – LONDON

**HELENA MARGARETA** ex-*LARENBERG* • GRT 3316 • Built 1915
8.4.41: Torpedoed and sunk by German submarine U-107 (Hessler), in the Atlantic 330 miles W of Madeira, in position 33.00N 23.52W while sailing independently on a voyage from the Tyne to Takoradi, in ballast, dispersed from convoy OG 57 comprising 37 ships. The Master, Capt Owen Thomas Jones, 6 crew and 2 gunners were rescued 12.4.41 by Royal Fleet Auxiliary tanker *CAIRNDALE* 8129/39 (Capt Stanley Guy Kent) and landed at Gibraltar 17.4.41. 27 crew were lost. Capt O.T. Jones was awarded the Lloyd's War Medal for bravery at sea.

## MOWT

**MODESTA** • GRT 3830 • Built 1917
25.4.42: Torpedoed and sunk by German submarine U-108 (Scholtz), in the Atlantic 110 miles NE of Bermuda, in position 33.40N 63.10E while sailing independently on a voyage from Trinidad and St Thomas, Virgin Islands 17.4.42 to New York, with a cargo of 5800 tons of bauxite. The Master, Capt James Robertson Murray, 16 crew and 1 gunner were lost. 19 crew and 4 gunners were rescued by Belgian ship *BELGIAN AIRMAN* ex-*EMPIRE BALLANTYNE* 6959/42 and landed at Bermuda.

## FEDERAL STEAM NAVIGATION CO. LTD – LONDON

**CUMBERLAND** ex-*WENDLAND* • GRT 11446 • Built 1919
23.8.40: Torpedoed by German submarine U-57 (Topp), in the Atlantic 25 miles NE of Malin Head, in position 55.44N 07.32W and sank on 24.8.40 8 miles from Inishtrahull while on a voyage from Glasgow and Liverpool to Curacao and Port Chalmers, New Zealand via Panama, with 9000 tons of general cargo including metal, part of convoy OB 202 comprising 32 ships. The Master, Capt Edwin Arthur J. Williams, and 53 crew landed at Moville, Co. Donegal. 4 crew were lost.

**HUNTINGDON** ex-*MUNSTERLAND* • GRT 11509 • Built 1920
23.2.41: Torpedoed and sunk by Italian submarine *MICHELE BIANCHI* (Giovannini), in the Atlantic 240 miles WNW of Rockall, in position 58.25N 20.23W while sailing independently

from Cardiff and Swansea to Brisbane via Freetown, with 10000 tons of general cargo including tinplate, part of convoy OB 288 comprising 46 ships. The Master, Capt John Percy Styrin, crew of 59 and 2 gunners were rescued by Greek ship *PAPALEMOS* 3748/1910, landed at Horta, Azores 3.3.41, then brought by Portuguese ship *CARVALHO ARAUYO* 4560/30 to Lisbon 12.3.41.

*NORFOLK* ex-*SAUERLAND* • GRT 10973 • Built 1918
18.6.41: Torpedoed and sunk by German submarine U-552 (Topp), in the Atlantic 150 miles NW of Malin Head, in position 57.17N 11.14W while sailing independently on a voyage from Newport, Mon. to New Zealand via New York, with 4000 tons of general cargo including steel plates and mail. The Master, Capt Frederick Lougheed, 63 crew and 6 gunners were rescued by HM destroyer *SKATE* 1065/17 (F.46) (Lt F. Baker DSC) and landed at Londonderry. 1 crew was lost.

*NOTTINGHAM* • GRT 8532 • Built 1941
7.11.41: Torpedoed and sunk by German submarine U-74 (Kentrat), part of the 'Raubritter' (Robber Knight) patrol group of fourteen U-boats, in the Atlantic 550 miles SE of Cape Farewell, in position 53.24N 31.51W while sailing independently on her maiden voyage from Glasgow to New York, with general cargo. The Master, Capt Francis Cecil Pretty OBE DSC, crew of 55 and 6 gunners were lost. U-74 commanded by Oberleutnant zur See Karl Friederich and crew of 45 were lost on 2.5.42 in the Mediterranean ESE of Cartagena, in position 37.22N 00.10E damaged by Catalina 'C' AJ162, pilot F/Lt R.Y. Powell of No. 202 Squadron RAF, based at Gibraltar and later sunk the same day by HM destroyers *WISHART* 1345/19 (D.67) (Cdr E.R. Condor) and *WRESTLER* 1300/18 (G.31) (Lt R.W.B. Lacon). The pilot was awarded the DFC.

*HERTFORD* ex-*FRIESLAND* • GRT 10965 • Built 1918
29.3.42: Torpedoed and sunk by German submarine U-571 (Möhlmann), part of 'Operation Paukenschlag' (Drumbeat), the fourth wave of eleven U-boats, in the Atlantic 200 miles S of Halifax NS, in position 40.50N 63.31W while sailing independently on a voyage from Sydney NSW, Brisbane and Wellington to the UK via Colon 21.3.42 and Halifax NS, with 12103 tons of general cargo including refrigerated meat. The Master, Capt John Collier Tuckett, and 18 crew landed at Liverpool, Nova Scotia; 21 crew were rescued by British steamer *GLENSTRAE* 9640/22; 16 crew and 2 gunners by British ship *FORT TOWNSEND* 3489/19 and landed at Halifax NS. 4 crew were lost.

*WESTMORELAND* • GRT 8967 • Built 1917
1.6.42: Torpedoed and sunk by gunfire by German submarine U-566 (Borchert), part of the 'Pfadfinder' (Pathfinder) patrol group of eight U-boats, in the Atlantic 240 miles NNE of Bermuda, in position 35.55N 63.35W while sailing independently on a voyage from Wellington to Liverpool via Colon 25.5.42, with a cargo of refrigerated meat, foodstuff and wool. The Master, Capt Ernst Arthur Burton, 59 crew and 5 gunners were rescued, 45 survivors by Canadian ship *CATHCART* 3708/20 and landed at Halifax NS, and 20 survivors by US ship *HENRY R. MALLORY* 6063/16 and landed at New York. 2 crew and 1 gunner were lost.

*SURREY* • GRT 8581 • Built 1919
10.6.42: Torpedoed and sunk by German submarine U-68 (Merten), in the Atlantic 150 miles N of Cristobal, Panama, in position 12.45N 80.20W while sailing independently on a

voyage from New York and Hampton Roads 29.5.42 to Sydney NSW via Panama, with 9180 tons of general cargo including ammunition, tanks, guns and machinery. The Master, Capt Frederick Lougheed, and 34 survivors were rescued by Colombian schooner *RESOLUTE* and transferred to US destroyer *EDISON* 1620/40 (DD.439); 20 survivors by Dutch ship *FLORA* 1417/21 and Panamanian ship *POTOMAC* 3906/06 and landed at Colon, Panama. 10 crew and 2 gunners were lost.

## FRANCE, W. FENWICK & CO. LTD – LONDON

*GOODWOOD* • GRT 2796 • Built 1937
10.9.39: Struck a mine laid on 6.9.39 by German submarine U-15 (Bucholz), and sank in the North Sea 1 mile SE of Flamborough Head while on a voyage from the Tyne to Bayonne, with a cargo of coal. The Master, Capt Harold Stevendale Hewson, and 22 crew were rescued by a fishing boat and landed at Bridlington. 1 crew was lost.

## FURNESS, WITHY & CO. LTD – LONDON

*PACIFIC RANGER* • GRT 6866 • Built 1929
12.10.40: Torpedoed and sunk by German submarine U-59 (Matz), in the Atlantic 134 miles 302° from Bloody Foreland, in position 56.20N 11.43W while on a voyage from Vancouver and Seattle 27.8.40 to Manchester via Panama and Bermuda 28.9.40 with 2 naval ratings and 8235 tons of general cargo including lumber and metals, part of convoy HX 77 comprising 40 ships. The Master, Capt William Evans, crew of 52 and 2 naval ratings were rescued; the Master and 12 survivors after 9 days by Icelandic trawler *THORMODUR* 101/19 and landed at Reykjavik 21.10.40; the Chief Officer and 22 crew were landed at Glencolumbkille near Killybegs, Co. Donegal; 19 crew were rescued by HM ship. U-59, commanded by Oberleutnant zur See Herbert Walther, was scuttled at Kiel on 2.5.45.

*PACIFIC PRESIDENT* • GRT 7113 • Built 1928
2.12.40: Torpedoed and sunk by German submarine U-43 (Lüth), in the Atlantic WSW of Rockall, in position 56.04N 18.45W while on a voyage from Leith to New York, in ballast, part of convoy OB 251 comprising 33 ships. The Master, Capt James Smith Stuart, and crew of 49 were lost.

*MANAQUI* • GRT 2802 • Built 1921
16.3.42: Torpedoed and sunk by Italian submarine *MOROSINI* (Fraternale), in the Atlantic SE of Barbuda, Leeward Islands, BWI, in position 17.15N 61.00W while sailing independently on a voyage from Cardiff to Kingston, Jamaica, with general cargo, dispersed from convoy OS 20 comprising 55 ships. The Master, Capt Charles Edward Wordingham, and crew of 34 were lost.

*PACIFIC PIONEER* • GRT 6723 • Built 1928
30.7.42: Torpedoed and sunk by German submarine U-132 (Vogelsang), in the Atlantic SW of Sable Island, in position 43.40N 60.35W while on a voyage from Belfast 17.7.42 to New York, in ballast, with 4 passengers, part of convoy ON 113 comprising 35 ships. The Master, Capt Hugh Campbell, crew of 58, 8 gunners and passengers were rescued by RCN corvette *CALGARY* 925/41 (K.231) (Lt G. Lancaster) and landed at Halifax NS.

**PACIFIC GROVE** • GRT 7117 • Built 1928

12.4.43: Torpedoed and sunk by German submarine U-563 (v. Hartmann), part of the 'Lerche' (Lark) patrol group of nine U-boats, in the Atlantic SE of Cape Farewell, in position 54.10N 30.00W while on a voyage from New York 1.4.43 to Glasgow via Halifax NS, with 16 passengers and 8684 tons of general cargo including diesel oil, part of convoy HX 232 comprising 47 ships. The Master, Capt Evan William Pritchard, 38 crew, 1 gunner and passengers were rescued by HM corvette *AZALEA* 925/40 (K.25) (Lt G.C. Geddes) and landed at Gourock. 10 crew and 1 gunner were lost. Oberleutnant zur See Gustav Borchardt and crew of 48 were lost on 31.5.43 when U-563 was sunk in the Atlantic 270 miles SW of the Scilly Isles, in position 46.35N 10.40W by Halifax 'R' HR774, pilot W/Cdr Wilfred E. Oulton DSO, DFC of No. 58 Squadron RAF, based at St Eval, Sunderland 'X' DD838, pilot F/O William Maynard French DFC of No. 228 Squadron RAF, based at Pembroke Dock and Sunderland 'E' DV969, pilot F/Lt Maxwell Stanley Mainprize DFC of No. 10 Squadron RAAF, based at Mount Batten, part of 19 Group.

## MOWT

**FRED W. GREEN** ex-*CRAYCROFT* • GRT 2292 • Built 1918 (derrick ship)

31.5.42: Sunk by gunfire by German submarine U-506 (Würdmann), in the Atlantic SE of Bermuda, in position 30.20N 62.00W while sailing independently on a voyage from New York and Bermuda to Freetown, with government cargo including motor trucks. The Master, Capt A.G. Simpson, 32 crew and 3 gunners were rescued by US destroyer *LUDLOW* 1620/40 (DD.438). 4 crew and 1 gunner were lost.

**EMPIRE STANLEY** • GRT 6942 • Built 1941 (CAM ship)

17.8.43: Torpedoed and sunk by German submarine U-197 (Bartels), in the Indian Ocean SSE of Cap Sainte Marie, Madagascar, in position 27.12S 47.25E while sailing independently on a voyage from Lourenco Marques and Durban 13.8.43 to Aden and Beirut, with 1 passenger and 8890 tons of coal. The Master, Capt Arthur John Pilditch MBE, 17 crew, 6 gunners and passenger were lost. 19 crew and 1 gunner were rescued on 20.8.43 by P&O motor ship *SOCOTRA* 7840/43 and landed at Bombay 30.8.43; 8 crew and 1 gunner by HM corvette *THYME* 925/41 (K.210) (Lt H. Roach) and landed at Durban 29.8.43. Kapitän-leutnant Robert Bartels and crew of 66 were lost when U-197 was sunk on 20.8.43 in the Indian Ocean 250 miles SW by S of Cap Sainte Marie, in position 28.40S 42.36E by Catalina 'C' 259, pilot F/Lt L.O. Barnett of No. 259 Squadron RAF, based at St Lucia and Catalina 'N' 265, pilot F/O C.E. Robin of No. 265 Squadron RAF, based at St Lucia, South Africa.

## Johnston Warren Lines Ltd

**AVIEMORE** • GRT 4060 • Built 1920

16.9.39: Torpedoed and sunk by German submarine U-31 (Habekost), in the Atlantic 220 miles SW of Cape Clear, in position 49.11N 13.38W while on a voyage from Swansea to Montevideo and Buenos Aires, with a cargo of 5105 tons of tinplate and black sheets, part of convoy OB 4 comprising 9 ships. The Master, Capt Morton Forsythe, and 22 crew were lost. 11 crew were rescued by HM destroyer *WARWICK* 1100/17 (D.25) (Lt-Cdr M.A.G. Child) and landed at Liverpool 18.9.39.

*NOVA SCOTIA* • GRT 6796 • Built 1926
28.11.42: Torpedoed and sunk by German submarine U-177 (Gysae), in the Indian Ocean
SE of Lourenco Marques, in position 28.30S 33.15E while on government service sailing
independently on a voyage from Port Tewfik and Aden 18.11.42 to Durban, with 6
passengers, 11 military and naval personnel, 130 South African guards and 780 Italian
internees. The Master, Capt Alfred Hender, 96 crew, 10 gunners, 8 military and naval
personnel, 5 passengers, 88 South African Guards and 650 Italian internees were lost. 17 crew,
1 gunner, 3 military and naval personnel, 1 passenger, 42 South African guards and 130 Italian
internees were rescued by Portuguese frigate *ALFONSO DE ALBUQUERQUE* 1788/35.

## Norfolk and North American Steamship Co. Ltd

*PACIFIC RELIANCE* • GRT 6717 • Built 1927
4.3.40: Torpedoed and sunk by German submarine U-29 (Schuhart), in the Atlantic N of
Land's End, in position 50.23N 05.49W while on a voyage from New Westminster and Los
Angeles to London, Liverpool and Manchester via Halifax NS 7.2.40, with the convoy
commodore and 4 naval staff, general cargo and aircraft parts, part of convoy HX 19
comprising 44 ships. The Master, Capt Evan Owen Evan, Commodore R.P. Galer CBE
RNR RD, crew of 47 and naval staff were rescued by British ship *MACVILLE* 666/15 and
landed at Newlyn, Cornwall.

## Prince Line Ltd

*WESTERN PRINCE* • GRT 10926 • Built 1929
14.12.40: Torpedoed and sunk by German submarine U-96 (Lehmann–Willenbrock), in the
Atlantic 400 miles 280° from Cape Wrath, in position 59.32N 17.47W while on a voyage
from New York to Liverpool via Halifax NS 29.11.40, with 61 passengers and 5759 tons of
general cargo including base metal and foodstuffs, part of convoy HX 92 comprising 24 ships.
The Master, Capt John Reed, 7 crew and 6 passengers were lost. 99 crew and 55 passengers
were rescued by British ship *BARON KINNARD* 3355/27 and 1 crew by HM destroyer
*ACTIVE* 1350/29 (H.14) (Lt-Cdr E.C.L. Turner) and landed at Gourock.

*SIAMESE PRINCE* • GRT 8456 • Built 1929
17.2.41: Torpedoed and sunk by German submarine U-69 (Metzler), in the Atlantic SW of
the Faröe Islands, in position 59.53N 12.12W while sailing independently on a voyage from
New York to Liverpool, with 8 passengers and general cargo. The Master, Capt Edgar
Litchfield, crew of 47, 1 gunner and passengers were lost.

*JAVANESE PRINCE* • GRT 8593 • Built 1926
20.5.41: Torpedoed and sunk by German submarine U-138 (v. Gramitzky), in the Atlantic
155 miles NW of the Butt of Lewis, Outer Hebrides, in position 59.46N 10.45W while on a
voyage from Cardiff to New York, in ballast, with 4 passengers, part of convoy OB 322
comprising 38 ships. The Master, Capt George Gillanders, crew of 45, 8 gunners and
passengers were rescued by HM destroyer leader *FAULKNOR* 1475/34 (H.62) (Capt A.F. de
Salis), HM destroyer *LINCOLN* 1090/18 (G.42) (Lt R.J. Hanson) ex-USN four-stack
*YARNALL* and HM tug *ASSURANCE* 700/40 (W.59) (Sub-Lt E.E. Litts). The survivors were

transferred to rescue ship *TOWARD* 1571/23 (Capt Arthur James Knell) and landed at Gourock 28.5.41. 1 crew was lost. U-138, commanded by Oberleutnant zur See Franz Gramitzky, was sunk on 18.6.41 in the Atlantic 100 miles W of Cape Trafalgar, in position 36.04N 07.29W by HM destroyer leader *FAULKNOR* 1475/34 (H.62) (Capt A.F. de Salis), HM destroyers *FEARLESS* 1375/34 (H.67) (Cdr A.F. Pugsley), *FORESTER* 1350/34 (H.74) (Lt-Cdr E.B. Tancock), *FORESIGHT* 1350/34 (H.68) (Cdr J.S.C. Salter) and *FOXHOUND* 1350/34 (H.69) (Cdr G.H. Peters) of the 13th Destroyer Flotilla. The U-boat commander and crew of 26 were taken prisoner by HMS *FAULKNOR*.

### CHINESE PRINCE • GRT 8593 • Built 1926
12.6.41: Torpedoed and sunk by German submarine U-552 (Topp), in the Atlantic S of Rockall, in position 56.12N 14.18W while sailing independently on a voyage from Port Said to Liverpool via Cape Town, with 9167 tons of general cargo including potash, currants and magnesite. The Master, Capt Wilma Finch, 15 crew and 3 gunners were rescued by HM corvettes *ARBUTUS* 925/40 (K.86) (Lt A.L.W. Warren) and *PIMPERNEL* 925/40 (K.71) (Lt F.H. Thornton) and landed at Londonderry. 45 crew were lost.

### CINGALESE PRINCE • GRT 8474 • Built 1929
20.9.41: Torpedoed and sunk by German submarine U-111 (Kleinschmidt), in the South Atlantic ESE of St Paul Rocks, in position 02.00S 25.30W while sailing independently on a voyage from Bombay to Liverpool via Cape Town and Trinidad, with 11156 tons of general cargo including manganese ore and pig iron. The Master, Capt John Smith, 48 crew and 8 gunners were lost. 15 crew and 3 gunners were rescued after 12 days by Spanish ship *CASTILLO MONTJUICH* 6581/20 and landed at St Vincent, Cape Verde Islands, 1 crew was rescued by HM sloop *WESTON* 1045/32 (L.72) ex-HMS *WESTON SUPER MARE* (Cdr J.G. Sutton) and 1 officer by HM sloop *LONDONDERRY* 990/35 (L.76) (Cdr J.S. Dalison) and landed at Londonderry 3.11.41. U-111, commanded by Kapitänleutnant Wilhem Kleinschmidt, was sunk on 4.10.41 in the Atlantic 140 miles SW of Palma, Canary Islands, in position 27.15N 20.27W by HM trawler *LADY SHIRLEY* 472/37 (Lt A.H. Gallaway). The U-boat commander and 8 crew were lost. 44 crew were taken prisoner by *LADY SHIRLEY* and landed at Gibraltar.

### SCOTTISH PRINCE • GRT 4917 • Built 1938
17.3.42: Torpedoed and sunk by gunfire by German submarine U-68 (Merten), in the Atlantic about 180 miles W of Takoradi, in position 04.10N 08.00W while sailing independently on a voyage from Calcutta to the UK via Cape Town 5.3.42 and Freetown, with a cargo of 6000 tons of palm kernels, 600 tons of castor seed and 900 tons of pig iron. The Master, Capt William Raymond Milner Hill, 34 crew and 3 gunners landed at Cape Palmas, Ivory Coast and were brought to Freetown by RCN corvette *WEYBURN* 925/41 (K.173) (Lt Thomas M.W. Golby). 1 crew was lost.

### NORMAN PRINCE • GRT 1931 • Built 1940
29.5.42: Torpedoed and sunk by German submarine U-156 (Hartenstein), in the Atlantic 60 miles W of St Lucia, BWI, in position 14.40N 62.15W while sailing independently on a voyage from Liverpool to Barranquilla, Colombia 24.5.42 and St Lucia, in ballast. The Master, Capt William Richard Harries, 24 crew and 7 gunners were rescued by French ship

*ANGOULEME* 2415/19, landed at Martinique and were interned by the Vichy French authorities. The Radio Officer Hubert John Tanner was rescued after 2½ days by US Coastguard cutter *UNALGA* 1181/12 (WPG.53). 14 crew and 2 gunners were lost.

**LANCASTRIAN PRINCE** • GRT 1914 • Built 1940
12.4.43: Torpedoed and sunk by German submarine U-404 (v. Bülow), part of the 'Adler' (Eagle) patrol group of nine U-boats, in the Atlantic E of Newfoundland, in position 50.18N 42.48W while on a voyage from Partington to Boston, Mass, in ballast, part of convoy ON 176 comprising 44 ships. The Master, Capt Frederick Randell Elliott, crew of 37 and 7 gunners were lost. One of the convoy's escorts, HM destroyer *BEVERLEY* 1190/19 (H.64) (Lt-Cdr R.A. Price) ex-USN four-stack *BRANCH*, was sunk by German submarine U-188 (Lüdden) in the Atlantic SW of Iceland, in position 52.28N 40.32W on 11.4.43. Korvettenkapitän Otto von Bülow was awarded the Knight's Cross (20.10.42) with Oak Leaves (25.4.43). Oberleutnant zur See Adolf Schoenberg and crew of 49 were lost on 28.7.43 when U-404 was sunk in the Atlantic 140 miles NNW of Cape Ortegal, in position 45.53N 09.25W by Liberator W/224, pilot F/O Robert V. Sweeny DFC of No. 224 Squadron RAF, based at St Eval, part of 19 Group, Liberator Y/4, pilot Major Stephen D. McElroy and Liberator N/4, pilot Lt Arthur J. Hammer of the 4th Squadron, 479th Antisubmarine Group, USAAF, based at St Eval.

## GALBRAITH, PEMBROKE & CO. LTD – LONDON

**MARLENE** ex-*NOGOYA* ex-*HIGHLAND WARRIOR* • GRT 6507 • Built 1920
4.4.41: Torpedoed and sunk by German submarine U-124 (Schulz), in the Atlantic SW of Freetown, in position 08.15N 14.19W while sailing independently on a voyage from Calcutta and Walvis Bay, South West Africa, to the UK via Freetown, with 8700 tons of general cargo including 1500 tons of pig iron. The Master, Capt Henry Ellison Lascelles, and 46 crew landed at False Cape, Sierra Leone. 13 crew were lost.

**LORNASTON** • GRT 4934 • Built 1925
8.3.45: Torpedoed and sunk by German submarine U-275 (Wehrkamp), in the English Channel NW of Fécamp, in position 50.35N 00.30W while on a voyage from Blyth to Casablanca, with a cargo of 6002 tons of coal, part of the combined convoy OS115/KMS 89 comprising 18 ships. The Master, Capt David Cownie, crew of 40 and 7 gunners were rescued by HM frigate *HOLMES* 1318/43 (Lt-Cdr P.S. Boyle) and HM tug *PALENCIA* 95/16 and landed at Newhaven. Oberleutnant zur See Helmut Wehrkamp and crew of 47 were lost on 10.3.45 when U-275 hit a mine in the British minefield 'Brazier E' and sank in the English Channel 12 miles SSW of Beachy Head, in position 50.36N 00.04E.

### Austin Friars Steamship Co. Ltd

*FREDERIKA LENSEN* 20.7.42
20.7.42: Torpedoed and damaged by German submarine U-132 (Vogelsang), in the Gulf of St Lawrence near Anticosti Island, in position 49.22N 65.12W while on a voyage from Montreal to Sydney CB, in ballast, part of convoy QS 19. Towed by HMCS corvette *WEYBURN* 925/41 (K.173) (Lt Thomas M.W. Golby) it was beached at Grande Vallée Bay

and declared a total loss. The Master, Capt Bryan Ewart Russell, and 35 crew were rescued by HMCS *WEYBURN* and landed at Sydney CB, and 6 crew landed at Grande Vallée Bay, Quebec. 4 crew were lost.

## GARDINER, JAMES & COMPANY – GLASGOW
## MOWT

*ANNEBERG* ex-*FARMSUM* • GRT 2544 • Built 1902
8.8.42: Torpedoed and damaged by German submarine U-379 (Kettner), part of the 'Steinbrinck' patrol group of eight U-boats, later sunk by depth charges by RCN corvette *BATTLEFORD* 925/41 (K.165) (Lt R.J. Roberts), in the Atlantic ESE of Cape Farewell, in position 56.30N 32.14W while on a voyage from Sheet Harbour 24.7.42 and Sydney CB 31.7.42 to Ellesmere Port, with a cargo of 3200 tons of pulp, part of convoy SC 94 comprising 30 ships. The Master, Capt Charles Leslie Bullock, crew of 33 and 4 gunners were rescued, 17 survivors by HMCS *BATTLEFORD* and landed at Greenock, 14 survivors by HM corvette *NASTURTIUM* 925/40 (K.107) (Lt C.D. Smith DSC) ex-French *LA PAIMPOLAISE* and landed at Liverpool and 7 survivors by HM corvette *PRIMROSE* 925/41 (K.91) (Lt-Cdr A. Ayre) and landed at Londonderry 13.8.42. U-379 commanded by Kapitänleutnant Paul Hugo Kettner was sunk on the same day in the Atlantic 550 miles SW by S of Reykjanes, Iceland, in position 57.11N 30.57W by HM corvette *DIANTHUS* 925/40 (K.95) (Lt-Cdr C.E. Bridgemen). The U-boat commander and 35 crew were lost. 5 crew were taken prisoner by HMS *DIANTHUS*.

## GDYNIA AMERICA SHIPPING LINES (LONDON) LIMITED – LONDON

*KINROSS* • GRT 4956 • Built 1935
24.6.41: Torpedoed and sunk by German submarine U-203 (Mützelburg), in the Atlantic SE of Cape Farewell, in position 55.23N 38.49W while on a voyage from Dundee to Father Point via Sydney CB, in ballast, part of convoy OB 336 comprising 24 ships. The Master, Capt James Robson Reed, and crew of 36 were rescued by RCN corvette *ORILLA* 925/40 (K.119) (Lt-Cdr W. Edward S. Briggs) and landed at Reykjavik.

*DUMFRIES* • GRT 5149 • Built 1935
23.12.44: Torpedoed and sunk by German submarine U-772 (Rademacher), in the English Channel S of St Catherine's Point, Isle of Wight, in position 50.23N 01.43W while on a voyage from Bona to Tyne, with 2 passengers and a cargo of 8258 tons of iron ore, part of convoy MKS 71 comprising 24 ships. The Master, Capt Robert Blackey, crew of 48, 8 gunners and passengers were rescued, the Master and 7 crew by HM corvette *BALSAM* 925/42 ex-HMS *CHELMER* (K.72) (Lt-Cdr Sir J.H.S. Fayer DSC) and landed at Portsmouth, and 41 crew, 8 gunners and passengers by HM trawler *PEARL* 649/34 (T.22) ex-HMS *DERVISH* and landed at Southampton.

## GENERAL STEAM NAVIGATION CO. LTD – LONDON

*STORK* • GRT 787 • Built 1937
23.8.41: Torpedoed and sunk by German submarine U-201 (Schnee), in the Atlantic NW of Lisbon, in position 40.43N 11.39W while on government service on a voyage from Preston

to Gibraltar, with a cargo of cased motor spirit, part of convoy OG 71 comprising 21 ships. The Master, Capt Evan Atterbury Morris Williams, 16 crew and 2 gunners were lost. 1 crew and 2 gunners were rescued by HM corvette *WALLFLOWER* 925/40 (K.44) (Lt-Cdr I.J. Tyson) and landed at Gibraltar.

*PETREL* • GRT 1354 • Built 1920
26.9.41: Torpedoed and sunk by German submarine U-124 (Mohr), in the Atlantic NNE of the Azores, in position 47.40N 23.28W while on a voyage from Oporto to Bristol, with 1 passenger and general cargo of 403 tons including 275 tons of cork, part of convoy HG 73 comprising 25 ships. The Master, Capt John William Klemp, 26 crew, 3 gunners and passenger were rescued by British ship *LAPWING* 1348/20. 20 crew and 3 gunners were lost when the *LAPWING* was torpedoed on the same day, the survivors from the *PETREL* being the Master, 7 crew and passenger who landed at Slyne Bay, Co. Galway 9.10.41. Capt J.W. Klemp was awarded the Lloyd's War Medal for bravery at sea.

*LAPWING* • GRT 1348 • Built 1920
26.9.41: Torpedoed and sunk by German submarine U-124 (Mohr), in the Atlantic NNE of the Azores, in position 47.40N 23.30W while on a voyage from Lisbon to Glasgow, with a cargo of 750 tons of cork and pyrites, part of convoy HG 73 comprising 25 ships. The Master, Capt Thomas James Hyam, 20 crew and 5 gunners were lost. 8 crew together with the survivors from the *PETREL* landed at Slyne Bay, Co. Galway 9.10.40.

## GERMAN, SIR JAMES & CO. LTD – CARDIFF
**Arlon SS Co. Ltd**

*ARLETTA* ex-*VANDUARA* • GRT 4870 • Built 1925
5.8.42: Torpedoed and sunk by German submarine U-458 (Diggins), in the Atlantic SSW of Cape Race, in position 44.44N 55.22W while on a voyage from Grangemouth to Halifax NS via Loch Ewe 24.7.42, in ballast, a straggler from convoy ON.115 comprising 41 ships. The Master, Capt George William Stockton Rogers, 29 crew and 6 gunners were lost. The 1st Officer William H. Duncan and 4 crew were rescued after 15 days by US coastguard cutter *MENEMSHA* ex-*JOHN GEHN* 1991/18 (AG.39) and landed at Boston, Mass. 25.8.42. U-458 commanded by Kapitänleutnant Kurt Diggins was sunk on 22.8.43 while shadowing convoy MKF 22 comprising 11 ships in the Mediterranean SE of Pantellaria, in position 36.25N 12.39E by HM destroyer *EASTON* 1087/42 (L.09) (Lt C.D. Newton) and RHN destroyer *PINDOS* 1087/41 ex-HMS *BOLEBROKE*. The U-boat commander and 42 crew were taken prisoner by HMS *EASTON*. 8 crew were lost.

**Oregon SS Co. Ltd**

*OREGON* ex-*OAKRIDGE* ex-*ANNA E. MORSE* • GRT 6008 • Built 1920
10.8.42: Torpedoed and damaged by German submarines U-660 (Baur), later sunk by U-438 (Franzius), in the Atlantic S of Iceland, in position 57.05N 22.41W while on a voyage from Baltimore to Liverpool via Sydney CB 31.7.42, with 8107 tons of general cargo including foodstuffs and steel, part of convoy SC 94 comprising 30 ships. The Master, Capt Stanley Edmondson, 29 crew, 6 gunners and 1 DBS were rescued by HM corvette *DIANTHUS*

925/40 (K.95) (Lt-Cdr C.E. Bridgeman) and 3 crew by HM corvette *NASTURTIUM* 925/40 (K.107) (Lt C.D. Smith DSC) ex-French *LA PAIMPOLAISE* and landed at Liverpool. 2 crew were lost. U–438, commanded by Kapitänleutnant Heinrich Heinsohn, and crew of 47 were lost on 6.5.43, part of the 'Specht' (Woodpecker) patrol group of eighteen U-boats, while shadowing convoy ONS 5 comprising 46 ships. She was sunk in the Atlantic 400 miles E of Belle Ile, in position 52.00N 45.10W by HM sloop *PELICAN* 1200/38 (L.86) (Cdr G. Brewer) of the 1st Support Group.

## MOWT

**EMPIRE CELT** (tanker) • GRT 8032 • Built 1941
24.2.42: Torpedoed and sunk by German submarine U–558 (Krech), in the Atlantic 420 miles SSE of St John's, in position 43.50N 43.38W while on a voyage from Greenock to New York via Halifax NS, in ballast, with 2 passengers, part of convoy ON 67 comprising 37 ships. The Master, Capt Edward McCready, and 22 survivors were rescued by the Canadian government rescue ship *CITADELLE* 431/32 and 24 survivors by HM trawler *ST ZENO* 608/40 (FY.280) (Lt J.K. Craig) and landed at St John's, Newfoundland 27.2.42. 4 crew and 2 gunners were lost.

## GIBBS & COMPANY – CARDIFF
### West Wales Steamship Co.

**WEST WALES** • GRT 4353 • Built 1925
29.1.41: Torpedoed and sunk by German submarine U–94 (Kuppisch), in the Atlantic SSW of Rockall, in position 56.00N 15.23W while on a voyage from New York to Newport, Mon. via Halifax NS, with a cargo of 7147 tons of steel, a straggler from convoy SC 19 comprising 27 ships. The Master, Capt Frederick Charles Nicholls, and 14 crew were lost. 17 crew were rescued by HM destroyer *ANTELOPE* 1350/29 (H.136) (Lt-Cdr R.T. White DSO) and 4 crew by HM destroyer *ANTHONY* 1350/29 (H.40) (Lt-Cdr V.C.F. Clark) and landed at Gourock.

**EAST WALES** • GRT 4358 • Built 1925
16.12.42: Torpedoed and sunk by German submarine U–159 (Witte), in the Atlantic near St Paul Rocks, in position 00.24N 31.27W while sailing independently on a voyage from New York to Alexandria via Trinidad 9.12.42 and Durban, with a cargo of about 7000 tons of government stores and coal. The Master, Capt Stephen Archibald Rowland, 11 crew and 5 gunners were lost. 26 crew and 2 gunners were rescued by Swedish ship *GULLMAREN* 3400/38 and landed at Natal, Brazil.

## MOWT

**P L M 27** • GRT 5633 • Built 1922
2.11.42: Torpedoed and sunk by German submarine U–518 (Wissmann), in the Atlantic lying at anchor off Bell Island, Conception Bay, in position 47.36N 52.28W, waiting to sail with convoy WB-9 on a voyage from Wabana to the UK via Sydney CB, with a cargo of iron ore. The Master, Capt Jean Baptiste, 35 crew and 6 gunners swam to the shore. 7 crew were lost.

## GIBSON, GEORGE & CO. LTD – LEITH

**BORTHWICK** • GRT 1124 • Built 1920
9.3.40: Torpedoed and sunk by German submarine U-14 (Wohlfarth), in the North Sea N of Zeebrugge, in position 51.44N 03.22E while sailing independently on a voyage from Antwerp and Rotterdam to Leith, with 700 tons of general cargo. The Master, Capt G. Simpson, and crew of 20 were rescued by the Flushing Pilot Boat No. 9 and landed at Flushing 10.3.40.

**ABBOTSFORD** ex-*CYRILLE DANEELS* • GRT 1585 • Built 1924
9.3.40: Torpedoed and sunk by German submarine U-14 (Wohlfarth), in the North Sea N of Zeebrugge, while sailing independently on a voyage from Ghent to Grangemouth, with a cargo of steel and flax. The Master, Capt Alexander John Watson, and crew of 17 were lost.

**GLENDINNING** ex-*BRAMWELL* ex-*SHEAF GARTH* • GRT 1927 • Built 1921
5.7.44: Torpedoed and sunk by German submarine U-953 (Marbach), in the English Channel off Cap d'Antifer, in position 50.32N 00.22W while on government service on a voyage from Arromanches beach, Normandy, to London, in ballast, part of convoy ETC 27 (codenamed Magnesium) comprising 18 ships. The Master, Capt John William Cromarty, 20 crew, 7 gunners and 1 naval signalman were rescued by HM Motor Launch No. 250 (Lt-Cdr J.D.S. Header) (in command and SO of 19th ML Flotilla), transferred to HM escort destroyer *FERNIE* 907/40 (L.11) (Lt J.A. Tricker) and landed at Sheerness. 2 crew and 2 gunners were lost. U-953 commanded by Kapitänleutnant Erich Steinbrink surrendered at Trondheim on 9.5.45 and was broken up in the UK 6.1949.

## MOWT

**CATHERINE** ex-*PEETER* ex-*MUNCOVE* ex-*COVEDALE* • GRT 2727 • Built 1919
17.6.41: Torpedoed and sunk by German submarine U-43 (Lüth), in the Atlantic about 250 miles SW of Cape Clear, in position 49.30N 16.00W while on a voyage from Pepel to Barrow via Freetown 30.5.41, with a cargo of 3700 tons of manganese ore, part of convoy SL 76 comprising 60 ships. The Master, Capt Johannes Teng, and 23 crew were lost. 3 crew were rescued after 33 days in an open boat by British trawler *BOREAS* 184/07 and landed at Valentia, Co. Cork.

## GLEN & CO. LTD – GLASGOW
### Clydesdale Shipowners Co. Ltd

**ORSA** • GRT 1478 • Built 1925
21.10.39: Struck a mine laid on 5.9.39 by German submarine U-15 (Buchholz) and sank in the North Sea 27 miles S of Flamborough Head while sailing independently on a voyage from the Tyne to Bordeaux, with a cargo of 2100 tons of coal. The Master, Capt Alexander Simpson, and 3 crew were rescued by HM destroyer *WOOLSTON* 1120/18 (L.49) (Lt-Cdr W.J. Phipps) and landed at Rosyth. 11 crew were lost. U-15 commanded by Oberleutnant zur See Peter Frahm and crew of 24 were lost when accidentally rammed and sunk on

30.1.40 by German torpedo boat *ILTIS* 800/27 in the Baltic SE of Rugen, in position 54.19N 14.47E.

### ALVA • GRT 1584 • Built 1934

19.8.41: Torpedoed and sunk by German submarine U-559 (Heidtmann), in the Atlantic about 600 miles W of Ushant, in position 49.00N 17.00W while on a voyage from Glasgow to Lisbon, with a cargo of 2300 tons of coal, part of convoy OG 71 comprising 21 ships. The Master, Capt Cyril Spenser Palmer, 9 crew and 4 gunners were rescued by British ship *CLONLARA* 1203/26. The Master and 13 survivors were lost on 22.8.41 when the *CLONARA* was sunk by U-564 (Suhren). 11 crew were rescued by British tug *EMPIRE OAK* 482/41, transferred to HM corvette *CAMPANULA* 925/40 (K.18) (Lt-Cdr R.V.E. Case DSC), transferred to HM destroyer *VELOX* 1090/17 (D.34) (Lt-Cdr E.G. Ropner DSC) and landed at Gibraltar 25.8.41.

### LISSA • GRT 1511 • Built 1927

21.9.41: Torpedoed and sunk by German submarine U-201 (Schnee), in the Atlantic NNE of the Azores, in position 47.00N 22.00W, while on a voyage from Barry to Lisbon, with a cargo of coal, part of convoy OG 74 comprising 22 ships. The Master, Capt Donald MacQuarrie, crew of 20 and 5 gunners were lost.

### RUNA • GRT 1525 • Built 1930

21.9.41: Torpedoed and sunk by German submarine U-201 (Schnee), in the Atlantic NNE of the Azores, in position 46.20N 22.23W while on a voyage from Barry to Lisbon, with a cargo of 2200 tons of coal, a straggler from convoy OG 74 comprising 22 ships. The Master, Capt Hugh McLarty, 7 crew and 1 gunner were rescued by HM sloop *DEPTFORD* 990/35 (L.53) (Lt H.P. White) and landed at Gibraltar. 12 crew and 2 gunners were lost.

## Scottish Navigation Co. Ltd

### ULEA • GRT 1574 • Built 1936

28.10.41: Torpedoed and sunk by German submarine U-432 (Schultze), in the Atlantic ENE of the Azores, in position 41.17N 21.40W while on a voyage from Huelva to the Clyde, with 3 passengers and a cargo of 2393 tons of copper pyrites, part of convoy HG 75 comprising 17 ships. The Master, Capt Frederick Osborn Ambrose, 12 crew, 3 gunners and passengers were lost. 4 crew and 1 gunner were rescued by HM corvette *LA MALOUINE* 925/40 (K.46) (Lt V.D. Bidwell) and 2 crew by HM corvette *BLUEBELL* 925/40 (K.80) (Lt-Cdr Robert E. Sherwood) and landed at Liverpool.

### FIDRA • GRT 1574 • Built 1936

5.3.43: Torpedoed and sunk by German submarine U-130 (Keller), in the Atlantic W of the Azores, in position 43.50N 14.46W while on a voyage from Almeria to Barrow, with a cargo of 2300 tons of iron ore, part of convoy XK 2 comprising 20 ships. The Master, Capt Hugh McLarty, 13 crew and 3 gunners were lost. 9 crew and 3 gunners were rescued by HM corvette *COREOPSIS* 925/40 (K.32) (Lt R.C. Hamilton), transferred to HM trawler *LOCH OSKAIG* 534/37 (FY.175) (Lt G.F.S. Clampitt) and landed at Londonderry.

## GLOVER BROTHERS – LONDON
### MOWT

*EMPIRE LYNX* ex-*MAINE* • GRT 6379 • Built 1917
4.11.42: Torpedoed and sunk by German submarine U-132 (Vogelsang), part of the 'Veilchen' (Violet) patrol group of thirteen U-boats, in the Atlantic S of Cape Farewell, in position 55.20N 40.01W while on a voyage from New York 24.10.42 to Liverpool, with 7850 tons of general cargo, part of convoy SC 107 comprising 42 ships. The Master, Capt Thomas Herbert Muitt, 34 crew and 8 gunners were rescued by Dutch ship *TITUS* 1712/30 and landed at Liverpool 10.11.42.

## GONNEVILLE, H. LIMITED – CARDIFF
### MOWT

*HENRI MORY* ex-*MARTIME* ex-*THORIUM* • GRT 2564 • Built 1920
26.4.41: Torpedoed and sunk by German submarine U-110 (Lemp), in the Atlantic 330 miles WNW of Blaskets Islands, near Achill Head, Co. Kerry, while sailing independently on a voyage from Pepel to Barrow via Freetown, with a cargo of 3150 tons of iron ore, dispersed from convoy SL 68 comprising 59 ships. The Master, Capt Joseph Havard, and 2 crew were rescued by HM destroyer *HURRICANE* 1340/39 (H.06) (Lt M. Ridler) ex-Brazilian *JAPARUA* and landed at Gourock 1.5.41. 1 crew was rescued after 8 days by British ship *LYCAON* 7350/13. 26 crew and 2 gunners were lost.

## GOULD, W.T. & CO. LTD – CARDIFF
### Cardigan Shipping Co. Ltd

*GRELHEAD* ex-*BEACHY HEAD* • GRT 4274 • Built 1915
2.12.41: Torpedoed and sunk by German submarine U-562 (Hamm), in the Mediterreanean 2 miles N of Point Negri, Morocco, while sailing independently on a voyage from Melilla, Spanish Morocco, to the UK, with a cargo of 6900 tons of iron ore. The Master, Capt Charles John Pirie, 34 crew and 6 gunners were lost. 2 crew were rescued and landed at Tangiers.

### MOWT

*EMPIRE BANNER* • GRT 6699 • Built 1942
7.2.43: Torpedoed and sunk by German submarine U-77 (Hartmann), in the Mediterranean W of Algiers, in position 36.48N 01.32E while on government service on a voyage from Penarth to Bona, with 10 army personnel and 3800 tons of military supplies including tanks and transport, part of convoy KMS 8 comprising 55 ships. The Master, Capt Jeffrey James Bedford OBE, crew of 46, 15 gunners and the army personnel were rescued by RCN corvette *CAMROSE* 925/40 (K.154) (Lt L.R. Pavillard) and landed at Algiers.

## GOW, HARRISON & COMPANY – GLASGOW
### Venetia SS Co. Ltd

*VENETIA* • GRT 5778 • Built 1927
16.3.41: Torpedoed and sunk by German submarine U-99 (Kretschmer), in the North Atlantic WSW of the Faröe Islands, in position 61.00N 12.36W while on a voyage from

Baltimore to London via Halifax NS 1.3.41, with a cargo of 7052 tons of maize, part of convoy HX 112 comprising 41 ships. The Master, Capt Alexander Mitchell, crew of 37 and 2 gunners were rescued by HM corvette *BLUEBELL* 925/40 (K.80) (Lt-Cdr Robert E. Sherwood) and landed at Greenock. U-99, commanded by Korvettenkapitän Otto Kretschmer (Knight's Cross 4.8.40, with Oak Leaves 4.11.40, and the Swords 26.12.42), was sunk on 17.3.41 in the North Atlantic 240 miles NW of the Butt of Lewis, Hebrides, in position 61.10N 11.48W by one of convoy's escort HM destroyer *WALKER* 1300/17 (G.22) (Capt Donald F.G. Macintyre). The U-boat commander and 39 crew were taken prisoner by HMS *WALKER* and landed at Liverpool. 3 crew were lost. K/K Otto Kretschmer was the top U-boat 'ace' of the Second World War, sinking 44 ships totalling 266,629 gross tonnage.

**Vimeira SS Co. Ltd**

*VIMEIRA* (tanker) • GRT 5728 • Built 1927
11.8.42: Torpedoed and sunk by gunfire by German submarine U-109 (Bleichrodt), in the Atlantic SW of the Cape Verde Islands, in position 10.03N 28.55W while sailing independently on a voyage from Curacao and Trinidad to Freetown, with a cargo of 8100 tons of gas oil and fuel oil. The Master, Capt Norman Ross Caird, was taken prisoner, landed at Lorient 6.10.42 and taken to Milag Nord. The 2nd Mate D. Campbell and 19 survivors were rescued on the same day by Norwegian ship *SIRANGER* 5393/39, transferred on 19.8.42 to British cable ship *LADY DENISON PLENDER* 1984/20 and landed at Takoradi. 17 survivors were rescued 1200 miles W of Freetown by HM corvette *CROCUS* 925/40 (K.49) (Lt J.F. Holm RNR) and transferred to British ship *SYLVIA DE LARRINAGA* 5218/25. The Chief Officer, 5 crew and 1 gunner were lost. On 14.8.42 the *SYLVIA DE LARRINAGA* was sunk by Italian submarine *REGINALDO GIULIANA* (Bruno) and the 17 survivors from the *VIMEIRA* were rescued by British ship *PORT JACKSON* 9687/37 and landed at Liverpool.

**GOWAN SHIPPING CO. LTD – LONDON**

*WHITFORD POINT* ex-*BENHOLM* • GRT 5026 • Built 1928
20.10.40: Torpedoed and sunk by German submarine U-47 (Prien), in the Atlantic 90 miles SW of Rockall, in position 56.38N 16.00W while on a voyage from Baltimore to London via Halifax NS 8.10.40, with a cargo of 7840 tons of steel, part of convoy HX 79 comprising 49 ships. The Master, Capt John Edward Young, and 35 crew were lost. 3 crew were rescued by HM trawler *STURDEE* 202/19 ex-*MICHAEL BRION* and landed at Londonderry.

**GULF LAKE NAVIGATION CO. LTD – MONTREAL**

*OAKTON* • GRT 1727 • Built 1923 (Canadian)
7.9.42: Torpedoed and sunk by German submarine U-517 (Hartwig), in the Gulf of St Lawrence S of Anticosti Island, in position 48.50N 63.46W while on a voyage from Sandusky, Ohio, to Corner Brook, Newfoundland, with a cargo of 2289 tons of coal, part of convoy QS 33 comprising 8 ships. The Master, Capt Alfred Edward Brown, and 16 crew were rescued by RCN motor launch *Q 083*. 3 crew were lost. The *OAKTON* sank within 2 minutes. One of the escorts to the convoy, RCN armed yacht *RACCOON* 358/31 (Lt-Cdr J.N. Smith), was sunk on 6.9.42, in position 49.01N 67.17W by U-165 (Hoffmann).

Korvettenkapitän Eberhard Hoffmann and crew of 49 were lost in the Bay of Biscay, SW of Lorient on 27.9.42 by an unknown cause, probably hitting a British mine. Kapitänleutnant Paul Hartwig was sunk on 21.11.42 in the Atlantic 300 miles WNW of Cape Ortegal, in position 46.16N 17.09W by a Fairey Albacore torpedo bomber of No. 817 Naval Air Squadron from HM aircraft carrier *VICTORIOUS* 23000/39 (38) (Capt H.C. Bovell). The U-boat commander and 50 crew were taken prisoner by HM destroyer *OPPORTUNE* 1540/42 (G.80) (Cdr J. Lee-Barber). 1 crew was lost.

## GYPSUM PACKET CO. LTD – WINDSOR, NOVA SCOTIA

*GYPSUM QUEEN* • GRT 3915 • Built 1927
11.9.41: Torpedoed and sunk by German submarine U-82 (Rollman), in the North Atlantic S of Cape Farewell, in position 63.05N 37.50W while on a voyage from New Orleans to Glasgow via Sydney CB 30.8.41, with a cargo of 5500 tons of sulphur, part of convoy SC 42 comprising 65 ships. The Master, Capt Alban Jason Chapman, 22 crew and 3 gunners were rescued by Norwegian ship *VESTLAND* 1934/16 and landed at Belfast. 9 crew and 1 gunner were lost.

*GYPSUM EXPRESS* • GRT 4034 • Built 1929
3.11.42: Torpedoed and sunk by German submarine U-160 (Lassen), in the Atlantic W of Grenada, in position 12.27N 64.04W while on a voyage from Demerara to New York via Trinidad, with a cargo of 6200 tons of bauxite, part of convoy TAG 18 comprising 25 ships. The Master, Capt John Smyth Rodgers, crew of 31, 4 gunners and 4 signalmen were rescued by Spanish tanker *GOBEO* 3365/21 and landed at Trinidad 3.11.42.

## HADLEY SHIPPING CO. LTD – LONDON

*CERINTHUS* (tanker) • GRT 3878 • Built 1930
10.11.42: Torpedoed and sunk by gunfire by German submarine U-128 (Heyse), in the Atlantic 180 miles SW from the Cape Verde Islands, in position 12.27N 27.45W while sailing independently on a voyage from London to Freetown via Oban 24.10.42, in ballast, dispersed from convoy ON 141 comprising 59 ships. The Master, Capt James Chadwick, 16 crew and 3 gunners were lost. The sole survivor, donkeyman William Colbon from the Master's boat (which originally contained 20 crew, but when found contained 6 bodies) was rescued by US ship *KENTUCKIAN* 5200/10 at 14.30 hours on 24.1.43, in position 11.22N 38.56W and landed at Port of Spain, Trinidad 31.1.43. The Chief Officer Hawkins, 15 crew and 3 gunners were rescued by HM sloop *BRIDGEWATER* 1045/28 (L.01) (Cdr N.W. Weekes OBE) on 1.12.42 and landed at Freetown 6.12.42.

## MOWT

*EMPIRE AMETHYST* (tanker) • GRT 8032 • Built 1941
13.4.42: Torpedoed and sunk by German submarine U-154 (Kölle), in the Atlantic 40 miles S of Haiti, in position 17.40N 74.50W while sailing independently on a voyage from New Orleans to the UK via Freetown, with a cargo of 12000 tons of motor spirit. The Master, Capt Geoffrey Durbridge Potter, and 40 crew were lost. 5 crew were rescued by Norwegian tanker *INNEROY* 8260/36 and landed at Halifax NS.

**EMPIRE COMMERCE** (tanker) • GRT 3722 Blt 1943
1.10.43: Torpedoed and damaged by German submarine U-410 (Fenski), in the Mediterranean E of Bougie, in position 37.19N 06.40E while on a voyage from Bona 30.9.43 to Algiers, with 4 service personnel, in ballast, a straggler from convoy MKS 26 comprising 21 ships. The Master, Capt James Leo Fitzpatrick, crew of 39, 7 gunners and service personnel were rescued by HM corvette *ALISMA* 925/40 (K.185) (Lt G. Lanning RANVR) and landed at Algiers. The *EMPIRE COMMERCE* completely burnt out and drifted ashore 8 miles E of Philippeville, Algeria.

**RADBURY** ex-*BOR* ex-*IZRADA* ex-*POLDENNIS* ex-*IZRADA* • GRT 3614 • Built 1910
13.8.44: Torpedoed and sunk by German submarine U-862 (Timm), in the Mozambique Channel W of Madagascar, in position 24.20S 41.45E while sailing independently on a voyage from Lourenco Marques to Mombasa, with a cargo of 4/5000 tons of coal. The Master, Capt John H. Gregory, 18 crew and 1 gunner were lost. 30 crew and 5 gunners landed on the uninhabited island of Europa in the Mozambique Channel on 16.8.44; of these survivors 3 crew and 1 gunner left on a raft, and only 1 crew reached Quelimane, Portuguese East Africa 1.11.44. The other survivors were rescued on 27.10.44 by HM corvette *LINARIA* 980/42 (K.282) (Lt-Cdr R.H. Jameson) ex-USS *CLASH* (PG.91) and landed at Kilindine, Kenya 3.11.44.

## HAIN STEAMSHIP COMPANY – LONDON

**TREGENNA** ex-*WAR BULLDOG* • GRT 5242 • Built 1919
17.9.40: Torpedoed and sunk by German submarine U-65 (v. Stockhausen), in the Atlantic 78 miles NW of Rockall, in position 58.22N 15.42W while on a voyage from Philadelphia to Newport, Mon. via Halifax NS 5.9.40, with a cargo of 8000 tons of steel, part of convoy HX 71 comprising 34 ships. The Master, Capt W.T. Clare, and 32 crew were lost. 4 crew were rescued by British ship *FILLEIGH* 4856/28 and landed at Avonmouth.

**TRECARREL** ex-*WAR LILAC* • GRT 5272 • Built 1919
4.6.41: Torpedoed and sunk by German submarine U-101 (Mengersen), in the Atlantic W of Cape Race, in position 47.10N 31.00W while sailing independently from Hull to Father Point, New Brunswick, in ballast, dispersed on 1.6.41 in position 52.42N 22.18W from convoy OB 327 comprising 46 ships. The Master, Capt Gordon George Barrett, 38 crew and 4 gunners were rescued by British ship *CORNERBROOK* 5767/25 and landed at Halifax NS. 4 crew were lost.

**TREGARTHEN** • GRT 5201 • Built 1936
6.6.41: Torpedoed and sunk by German submarine U-48 (Schultze), in the Atlantic NNW of the Azores, in position 46.17N 36.20W while sailing independently from Cardiff to Kingston, Jamaica, with a cargo of 7800 tons of coal, dispersed on 5.6.41 in position 51.48N 20.48W from convoy OB 329 comprising 41 ships. The Master, Capt Lionel Daniel, and crew of 44 were lost.

**TREVARRACK** ex-*WAR LAUREL* • GRT 5270 • Built 1919
8.6.41: Torpedoed and sunk by German submarine U-46 (Endrass), part of the 'West' patrol group of fifteen U-boats, in the Atlantic SW of Cape Clear, in position 48.46N 29.14W while sailing independently from Glasgow to Montreal, in ballast, with 7 passengers, dispersed

on 5.6.41 in position 51.48N 20.48W from convoy OB 329 comprising 41 ships. The Master, Capt William Hanbly Freeman, crew of 37 and passengers were lost.

**TRESILLIAN** • GRT 4743 • Built 1925
13.6.41: Torpedoed and sunk by German submarine U-77 (Schonder), part of the 'West' patrol group of fifteen U-boats, in the Atlantic SE of Cape Race, in position 44.40N 45.30W while sailing independently from Immingham to the Gulf of St Lawrence, in ballast, dispersed on 7.6.41 from convoy OB 330 comprising 38 ships. The Master, Capt Ernest George Old, and crew of 44 were rescued by US Coastguard cutter *DUANE* 2216/36 (WPG.33) and landed at St John's, Newfoundland.

**TREMODA** ex-*NIMODA* • GRT 4736 • Built 1927
27.8.41: Torpedoed and sunk by German submarine U-557 (Paulshen), in the Atlantic W of Achill Island, in position 53.36N 16.40W while on a voyage from London to Duala, Cameroons, with a cargo of war stores and general, part of convoy OS 4 comprising 34 ships. The Master, Capt James Sincock Bastian, 25 crew and 6 gunners were lost. 20 crew and 1 gunner were rescued by Free French sloop *CHEVREUIL* 647/39 and landed at Kingston, Jamaica.

**TREVERBYN** ex-*WAR AIRMAN* laid down as *WAR MAPLE* • GRT 5218 • Built 1920
21.10.41: Torpedoed and sunk by German submarine U-82 (Rollman), part of the 'Schlagetot' (Strike Dead) patrol group of ten U-boats, in the Atlantic SW of Cape Clear, in position 51.00N 19.00W while on a voyage from Pepel to Cardiff via Freetown 5.10.41, with a cargo of 6900 tons of iron ore, part of convoy SL 89 comprising 23 ships. The Master, Capt Henry Edwards OBE, crew of 35 and 10 gunners were lost.

**TREDINNICK** • GRT 4597 • Built 1920
29.3.42: Torpedoed and sunk by Italian submarine *PIETRO CALVI* (Olivieri), in the Atlantic SE of Bermuda, in position 27.15N 49.15W while sailing independently on a voyage from New York to Bombay via Cape Town, with a cargo of government stores and general. The Master, Capt Gordon George Barrett, crew of 45 and 6 gunners were lost. *PIETRO CALVI* commanded by Lt-Cdr Primo Longobardo was sunk by gunfire on 14.7.42 by HM escort sloop *LULWORTH* 1546/41 (Y.60) (Lt-Cdr G. Gwinner) ex-US coastguard cutter *CHELAN* in the Atlantic 500 miles S of the Azores, in position 30.35N 25.58E. The commander of *PIETRO CALVI* and 42 crew were lost. 35 crew were taken prisoner by HMS *LULWORTH*, HM sloops *BIDEFORD* 1105/31 (L.43) (Lt-Cdr W.J. Moore) and *LONDONDERRY* 990/35 (L.76) (Cdr J.S. Dalison) and landed at Londonderry.

**TREMINNARD** ex-*MIN* • GRT 4694 • Built 1923
2.8.42: Torpedoed and sunk by German submarine U-160 (Lassen), in the Atlantic 200 miles E of Trinidad, in position 10.40N 57.07W while on a voyage from Alexandria to Trinidad via Durban 3.7.42, in ballast, part of a convoy of 8 ships. The Master, Capt W.T. Evans, crew of 28 and 9 gunners were rescued by Argentinian ship *RIO SAN JUAN* 2328/36 and landed at Pernambuco.

**TREHATA** • GRT 4817 • Built 1927
8.8.42: Torpedoed and sunk by German submarine U-176 (Dierksen), in the Atlantic SE of Cape Farewell, in position 56.30N 32.14W while on a voyage from Hampton Roads to

Manchester via Sydney CB 31.7.42, with the convoy commodore, 6 naval staff and a cargo of 3000 tons of steel, 1000 tons of manufactured goods and 3000 tons of foodstuffs, part of convoy SC 94 comprising 30 ships. The Master, Capt John Lawrie DSO with bar and DSC, Commodore Vice-Admiral D.F. Moir DSO RN, 19 crew, 4 gunners and naval staff were lost. 21 crew and 4 gunners were rescued by Norwegian ship *INGER LISE* 1582/39 and landed at Preston.

**TREVILLEY** • GRT 5296 • Built 1940
12.9.42: Torpedoed and sunk by gunfire by German submarine U-68 (Merten), in the South Atlantic ENE of Ascension Island, in position 04.30S 07.50W while sailing independently on a voyage from Middlesbrough and Oban 20.8.42 to Cape Town and Beira, with 2 passengers and a cargo of 6000 tons of general and military cargo, dispersed from convoy OS 38 comprising 31 ships. On board were the Master, Capt Richard Harvey, crew of 42 and 8 gunners. 14 survivors in the torpedoed British liner *LACONIA* were rescued by the Vichy French cruiser *GLORIA* 7600/35, landed at Dakar 21.9.42 and were interned by the Vichy French authorities, 12 survivors landed near Half Assini, Gold Coast 25.9.42 and 23 survivors were rescued by Portuguese ship *CUBANGO* 5899/03. The Master and Chief Officer were taken prisoner, later transferred to U-459 (Wilamowitz-Möllendorf), landed at St Nazaire 4.11.42 and taken to Milag Nord. 1 crew and 1 passenger were lost.

**TREKIEVE** ex-*WAR MALLARD* • GRT 5244 • Built 1919
4.11.42: Torpedoed and sunk by Germans submarine U-178 (Ibbeken), in the Mozambique Channel E of Maputo, in position 25.55S 33.35E while sailing independently on a voyage from Bombay and Mahe, Seychelles 27.10.42, to the UK via Durban, with a cargo of 2500 tons of manganese ore, 1700 tons of nuts, 1650 tons of copra and general. The Master, Capt Edwin Aubrey Grant Jenkins, 38 crew, 6 gunners and 2 DBS landed at Inhaca Island, Portuguese East Africa. 3 crew were lost.

**TREVALGAN** • GRT 5299 • Built 1937
2.12.42: Torpedoed and sunk by German submarine U-508 (Staats), in the Atlantic SE of Trinidad, in position 09.40N 59.15W while sailing independently on a voyage from Suez to New York via Cape Town 7.11.42 and Trinidad, in ballast. The Master, Capt Alfred Guy Williams, crew of 33 and 9 gunners were rescued by US submarine chaser PC.572 280/41 and landed at Trinidad 3.12.42.

**TREWORLAS** • GRT 4692 • Built 1922
28.12.42: Torpedoed and sunk by German submarine U-124 (Mohr), in the Atlantic about 50 miles E of Port of Spain, Trinidad, in position 10.52N 60.45W while sailing independently on a voyage from Massowah, Eritrea, to Baltimore via Cape Town 30.11.42, with a cargo of 3000 tons of manganese ore. The Master, Capt Thomas Harold Stanbury, 32 crew and 5 gunners were lost. 7 crew and 2 gunners were rescued by US submarine chaser PC.609 280/41 and landed at Trinidad 1.1.43.

**TREFUSIS** ex-*WAR ACONITE* • GRT 5299 • Built 1918
5.3.43: Torpedoed and sunk by German submarine U-130 (Keller), in the Atlantic W of Cape Finisterre, in position 43.50N 14.46W while on a voyage from Pepel to London via

Javanese Prince

(J. Clarkson)

Corrientes

(J. Clarkson)

Melbourne Star                                                              (J. Clarkson)

Lynton Grange                                                              (J.K. Byass)

Canonsea                                                      (J.K. Byass)

San Demetrio                                                  (J.K. Byass)

Linaria                                                                    (*J. Clarkson*)

Duchess of Atholl                                                 (*World Ship Photo Library*)

Trevarrack                                                    (*J. Clarkson*)

Centaur                                                       (*J. Clarkson*)

Tymeric                                                                    (J. Clarkson)

Bullmouth                                                      (World Ship Photo Library)

British Chivalry
(*World Ship Photo
Library*)

Charlbury
(*World Ship Photo
Library*)

Clan Chisholm
(*World Ship Photo
Library*)

Pukkastan

(*World Ship Photo Library*)

Laconia

(*World Ship Photo Library*)

Nailsea Manor                                                    (*World Ship Photo Library*)

Athenia                                                         (*World Ship Photo Library*)

Accra
(*World Ship Photo
Library*)

Beacon Grange
(*World Ship Photo
Library*)

Cerinthus
(*World Ship Photo
Library*)

Fanad Head                                              (*World Ship Photo Library*)

Tresillian                                              (*World Ship Photo Library*)

Aracataca                                              (*World Ship Photo Library*)

Glenshiel
(*World Ship Photo
Library*)

Sylvafield
(*World Ship Photo
Library*)

Lassell
(*World Ship Photo
Library*)

Anglo Canadian
(*World Ship Photo Library*)

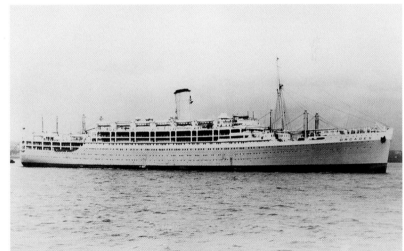

Orcades
(*World Ship Photo Library*)

Protesilaus
(*J. Clarkson*)

Nalgora
(*World Ship Photo
Library*)

Port Gisborne
(*World Ship Photo
Library*)

Sedgepool
(*World Ship Photo
Library*)

Siris
(*World Ship Photo
Library*)

Orangemoor
(*World Ship Photo
Library*)

Ceramic
(*World Ship Photo
Library*)

St Lindsay
(*World Ship Photo
Library*)

Dunvegan Castle
(*World Ship Photo
Library*)

Dartford
(*World Ship Photo
Library*)

Gibraltar, with a cargo of 7400 tons of iron ore, part of convoy XK 2 comprising 20 ships. The Master, Capt Robert Tyrer Browne, 37 crew and 6 gunners were rescued by HM corvette *COREOPSIS* 925/40 (K.32) (Lt R.C. Hamilton), transferred to HM trawler *LOCH OSKAIG* 534/37 (FY.175) (Lt G.F.S. Clampitt) and landed at Londonderry. 3 crew were lost.

## MOWT

### EMPIRE BEDE • GRT 6959 • Built 1942
18.8.42: Torpedoed and damaged by German submarine U-553 (Thurmann), sunk by gunfire by HM corvette *PIMPERNEL* 925/40 (K.71) (Lt-Cdr F.H. Thornton), in the Atlantic N of Jamaica, in position 19.41N 76.50W while on a voyage from Alexandria to New York via Trinidad 12.8.42 and Key West, with a cargo of cotton, part of convoy TAW 13 comprising 13 ships. The Master, Capt Thomas Edward Daniel, 34 crew, 6 gunners and 2 signalman were rescued by HMS *PIMPERNEL* and landed at Santiago de Cuba. 2 crew were lost.

### OCEAN JUSTICE • GRT 7173 • Built 1942
7.11.42: Torpedoed and sunk by German submarine U-505 (Zschech), in the Atlantic E of Trinidad, in position 10.06N 60.00W while sailing independently on a voyage from Karachi to New York via Durban 6.10.42 and Trinidad, with 600 tons of manganese ore, as ballast. The Master, Capt William Venables, crew of 44, 9 gunners and 2 crew from Belgian ship *BELGIAN FIGHTER* 5403/21 were rescued by HM MTBs and landed at Port of Spain, Trinidad. U-505, commanded by Oberleutnant zur See Harald Lange, was captured and crew of 58 were taken prisoner on 4.6.44 in the Atlantic 120 miles SW of Cap Blanco, French West Africa, in position 21.30N 19.20W by US escort carrier *GUADALCANAL* 7800/43 (CVE-60) (Capt Daniel V. Gallery), US destroyer escorts *PILLSBURY* 1200/43 (DE-133) (Lt-Cdr George W. Casselman), *POPE* 1200/43 (DE-134) (Lt-Cdr Edwin H. Headland), *FLAHERTY* 1200/43 (DE-135) (Lt-Cdr Means Johnson), *CHATELAIN* 1200/43 (DE-149) (Lt-Cdr Dudley S. Knox) and *JENKS* 1400/43 (DE-665) (Lt-Cdr Julius F. Way) of Task Group 22.3. U-505 is now an exhibit at the Chicago Museum of Science & Industry.

### OCEAN COURAGE • GRT 7173 • Built 1942
15.1.43: Torpedoed and sunk by German submarine U-182 (Clausen), in the Atlantic 200 miles S of the Cape Verde Islands, in position 10.52N 23.28W while sailing independently on a voyage from Pepel to the UK via Freetown and Trinidad, with a cargo of 9000 tons of iron ore and mail. The Master, Capt Thomas Harold Kemp, 41 crew, 2 gunners and 2 stowaways were lost. 6 crew and 1 gunner were rescued by British ship *SILVERWALNUT* 6770/30 and landed at Norfolk, Virginia.

### FORT CEDAR LAKE • GRT 7134 • Built 1942
17.3.43: Torpedoed and damaged by German submarine U-338 (Kinzel), later sunk by a *coup de grâce* by German submarine U-665 (Haupt), part of the 'Stürmer' (Attacker) patrol group of eighteen U-boats, in the Atlantic SE of Cape Farewell, in position 52.14N 32.15W while on her maiden voyage from Vancouver to Belfast Lough via Panama and New York 5.3.43, with general cargo, part of convoy SC 122 comprising 51 ships. The Master, Capt Charles Lloyde Collings, 42 crew and 7 gunners were rescued by rescue ship *ZAMALEK* 1567/21 (Capt Owen Charles Morris DSO) and landed at Gourock 22.3.43.

Kapitänleutnant Manfred Kinzel and crew of 50 were lost on 20.9.43 while shadowing convoy ONS 18 comprising 27 ships when U-338 was sunk in the Atlantic 430 miles SW by S of Reykjanes, Iceland, in position 57.40N 29.48W by Liberator 'F' AM917, pilot F/Lt John K. Moffatt, DFC of No. 120 'Punjab' Squadron RAF, based at Reykjavik, part of 15 Group. Oberleutnant zur See (Reserve) Hans-Jurgen Haupt and crew of 45 were lost on 22.3.43 when U-665 on her maiden voyage was sunk in the Atlantic, SW of Bishop Rock, in position 48.04N 10.26W by Whitley 'Q' Z6950, pilot Sgt J.A. Marsden of No. 10 OTU, RAF, based at St Eval.

### EMPIRE BOWMAN • GRT 7031 • Built 1942
30.3.43: Torpedoed and sunk by German submarine U-404 (v. Bülow), in the Atlantic 425 miles NW of Cape Finisterre, in position 47.26N 15.53W while on a voyage from Karachi and Mormugao to Hull via Durban and Freetown 12.3.43, with a cargo of 8471 tons of general including 2500 tons of manganese ore, part of convoy SL.126 comprising 36 ships. The Master, Capt Charles Henry Cranch OBE, 39 crew and 6 gunners were rescued by HM frigate WEAR 1370/42 (K.230) (Lt G.D. Edwards) and landed at Liverpool. 4 crew were lost.

### FORT JEMSEG • GRT 7134 • Built 1942
23.9.43: Torpedoed and sunk by German submarine U-238 (Hepp), part of the 'Leuthen' patrol group of nineteen U-boats, in the Atlantic SSE of Cape Farewell, in position 53.18N 40.24W while on a voyage from Hull to New York via Loch Ewe 15.9.43, in ballast, part of convoy ON 202 comprising 38 ships. The Master, Capt Leslie Joseph White, 22 crew and 7 gunners were rescued by HM trawler NORTHERN FOAM 655/36 (4.76) (Lt H.G. Ross) and 22 crew by Norwegian ship ROMULUS 3708/21 and landed at New York 2.10.43. 1 crew was lost. The Canadian 9th Support Group lost two warships while escorting this convoy on 20.9.43 HM frigate ITCHEN 1370/42 (K.227) (Cdr J.D. Birch) was sunk by German submarine U-666 (Engel), S of Greenland, in position 53.25N 39.42W and RCN destroyer ST CROIX 1190/19 (I.81) (Lt-Cdr A.N. Dobson) ex-USN four-stack McCOOK was sunk by German submarine U-305 (Bahr), SW of Iceland, in position 57.30N 31.10W. The Escort Group C2 (Cdr P.W. Burnett) also lost two warships. HM corvette POLYANTHUS 925/40 (K.47) (Lt J.G. Aitken) was sunk by German submarine U-952 (Curio), SW of Iceland, in position 57.00N 31.10W on 21.9.43 and HM frigate LAGAN 1370/42 (K.259) (Lt-Cdr C.E. Bridgeman) was severely damaged by German submarine U-270 (Otto) on 20.9.43. She was towed by HM rescue tug DESTINY 783/42 (W.115) ex-USS BAT 9 to the UK, arrived 24.9.43 but was never repaired and broken up at Troon during 1946. U-952, commanded by Kapitänleutnant Oscar Curio, was sunk on 6.8.44 by a USAAF daylight raid on Toulon. U-270, commanded by Oberleutnant zur See Heinrich Schreiber, was sunk on 13.8.44 in the Bay of Biscay 60 miles SSW of St Nazaire, in position 46.19N 02.56W by Sunderland 'A' ML735, pilot F/O Donald A. Little of No. 461 Squadron RAAF, based at Pembroke Dock, part of 19 Group. The U-boat commander and 70 crew were taken prisoner by RCN destroyers OTTAWA 1335/35 (H.31) ex-HMS GRIFFIN (Cdr H.F. Pullen) and ST LAURENT 1375/311 ex-HMS CYGNET (H.83) (Lt-Cdr G.H. Stephens DSC). 10 crew were lost. The pilot was awarded the DFC. Kapitänleutnant Horst Hepp and crew of 49 were lost on 9.2.44 when U-238, part of the 'Igel 2' (Hedgehog) patrol group of twelve U-boats, was sunk in the Atlantic 270 miles WSW of Cape Clear, in position 49.44N 16.07W by HM sloops KITE 1350/42 (U.87) (Lt-Cdr W.E.R. Segrave), MAGPIE 1350/43 (U.82) (Lt-Cdr R.S. Abram)

and *STARLING* 1350/42 (U.66) (Capt Frederic John Walker). Oberleutnant zur See Ernst-August Wilberg and crew of 50 were lost on 11.2.44 when U-666 was sunk in the Atlantic 260 miles W by N of Slyne Head, Co. Galway, in position 53.56N 17.16W while shadowing convoy ON 223 comprising 54 ships by Swordfish 'A', pilot S/Lt W.H. Thompson of 842 Naval Air Squadron from escort carrier HMS *FENCER* 11420/42 (D.64) (Capt W.W.R. Bentinck) ex-USS *CROATAN*.

### FORT BELLINGHAM • GRT 7153 • Built 1943
26.1.44: Torpedoed and damaged by German submarine U-360 (Becker), part of the 'Isegrim' patrol group of ten U-boats, later sunk by a *coup de grâce* by German submarine U-957 (Schaar), part of the 'Werewolf' patrol group of fifteen U-boats, in the Barents Sea N of North Cape, in position 73.25N 25.10E while on government service on a voyage from London to Murmansk via Loch Ewe 12.1.44 and Akureyre, Iceland 21.1.44, with the convoy's commodore, 6 naval staff and 4900 tons of military including 5 tons of cordite and general stores, part of convoy JW 56A comprising 20 ships. The Master, Capt James Ninian Maley, Commodore I.W. Whitehorn RN, 22 crew, 7 gunners and 4 naval staff were rescued by HM destroyer *OFFA* 1540/41 (G.29) (Lt-Cdr R.F. Leonard) and landed at Murmansk. 20 crew, 16 gunners and 2 naval staff were lost. Kapitänleutnant Klaus Becker and crew of 51 were lost on 2.4.44 when U-360 was sunk in the Barents Sea 120 miles WSW of Bear Island, in position 73.28N 13.04E by HM destroyer leader *KEPPEL* 1750/20 (D.84) (Cdr I.J. Tyson). U-957, commanded by Oberleutnant zur See Gerd Schaar (Knight's Cross 1.10.44), was decommissioned at Narvik 21.10.44.

## HALDIN & PHILIPS & CO. LTD – LONDON
### Court Line

### KENSINGTON COURT • GRT 4863 • Built 1927
18.9.39: Sunk by gunfire by German submarine U-32 (Büchel), in the Atlantic 120 miles W of Land's End, in position 50.31N 08.27W while sailing independently on a voyage from Rosario to Birkenhead, with a cargo of 8000 tons of cereals. The Master, Capt Joseph Schofield, and crew of 34 were rescued by a Sunderland, pilot F/Lt Thurston M.W. Smith of No. 228 Squadron RAF, based at Pembroke Dock, and Sunderland 'E' L5802, pilot F/Lt John Barrett of No. 204 Squadron RAF, based at Mount Batten. The pilots were each awarded the DFC on 2.11.39 for their feat.

### ARLINGTON COURT • GRT 4915 • Built 1924
16.11.39: Torpedoed and sunk by German submarine U-43 (Ambrosius), in the Atlantic 320 miles 248° from Start Point while on a voyage from Rosario to Hull via Freetown 31.10.39, with a cargo of 7340 tons of maize, a straggler from convoy SL 7 comprising 39 ships. The Master, Capt Charles Hurst, and 21 crew were rescued by Dutch steamer *ALGENIB* 5483/37 and landed at Queenstown (Cork), and 6 crew were rescued by Norwegian tanker *SPINANGER* 7429/27 and landed at Dover. 7 crew were lost.

### ILVINGTON COURT ex-IOLCOS ex-MEANDROS • GRT 5187 • Built 1919
26.8.40: Torpedoed and sunk by Italian submarine *DANDOLO* (Boris), in the Atlantic NE of the Azores, in position 37.14N 21.52W while sailing independently on a voyage from Pepel

to Glasgow, with a cargo of 7350 tons of iron ore. The Master, Capt John Horne, and crew of 38 landed at Santa Maria Island, Azores.

### DARLINGTON COURT • GRT 4974 • Built 1936

20.5.41: Torpedoed and sunk by German submarine U-556 (Wohlfarth), in the Atlantic S of Cape Farewell in position 57.28N 41.07W while on a voyage from New York to Liverpool via Halifax NS, with 3 passengers and a cargo of 8116 tons of wheat and aircraft, part of convoy HX 126 comprising 29 ships. The Master, Capt Charles Hurst, 10 crew and 1 gunner were rescued by rescue ship HONTESTROOM 1857/21 and landed at Reykjavik 27.5.41. 22 crew, 3 gunners and passengers were lost. U-556, commanded by Kapitänleutnant Herbert Wohlfarth (Knight's Cross 15.5.41), was sunk while attacking convoy HX 133 comprising 31 ships on 27.6.41 in the Atlantic 300 miles SW of Reykjavik, in position 60.24N 29.00W by HM corvettes NASTURTIUM 925/40 (K.107) (Lt-Cdr R.C. Freaker) ex-French LA PAIMPOLAISE, CELANDINE 925/40 (K.75) (Lt-Cdr A. Stannard) and GLADIOLUS 925/40 (K.34) (Lt-Cdr Harry M.C. Sanders). The U-boat commander and 39 crew were taken prisoner by HMS GLADIOLUS. 5 crew were lost.

### LAVINGTON COURT • GRT 5372 • Built 1940

19.7.42: Torpedoed and damaged by German submarine U-564 (Suhren), in the Atlantic N of the Azores, in position 42.38N 25.28W while on a voyage from Leith via Oban 11.7.42 to Cape Town and the Middle East, with 3 military personnel and 6000 tons of government stores including deck cargo of 2 naval launches, part of convoy OS 34 comprising 35 ships. The Master, Capt John William Sutherland, 33 crew, 5 gunners and 2 military personnel were rescued by HM sloop WELLINGTON 990/34 (L.65) (Lt-Cdr F.R. Segrave) and landed at Londonderry. 5 crew, 1 gunner and 1 military personnel were lost. The LAVINGTON COURT sank while under tow on 1.8.42 in the Atlantic SW of Ireland, in position 49.40N 18.04W.

### CRESSINGTON COURT • GRT 4971 • Built 1929

19.8.42: Torpedoed and sunk by German submarine U-510 (Neitzel), in the Atlantic NE of Belem, in position 07.58N 46.00W while sailing independently on a voyage from Philadelphia to Cape Town, Durban and Alexandria via Trinidad 14.8.42, with a cargo of 7362 tons of government stores and general. The Master, Capt William James Pace, and 7 crew were lost. 26 crew and 10 gunners were rescued by Dutch tanker WOENSDRECHT 4668/26. The WOENSDRECHT was damaged by German submarine U-515 (Henke) on 12.9.42 in the Atlantic SW of Trinidad, in position 10.27N 60.17W while on a voyage from Matadi and Takoradi to Trinidad, in ballast. The forepart of the WOENSDRECHT was towed to Trinidad. The survivors of the CRESSINGTON COURT were rescued by a US patrol boat and landed at Port of Spain, Trinidad.

### PENNINGTON COURT ex-ROCHDALE • GRT 6098 • Built 1924

9.10.42: Torpedoed and sunk by German submarine U-254 (Loewe), part of the 'Panther' patrol group of thirty U-boats, in the Atlantic SE of Cape Farewell, in position 58.18N 27.55W while on a voyage from St John, New Brunswick, to Belfast, with a cargo of 8494 tons of grain including trucks, a straggler from convoy SC 103 comprising 48 ships. The Master, Capt John Horne, and crew of 39 were lost. U-254 commanded by Kapitänleutnant Hans Gilardone was rammed and badly damaged on 8.12.42 in the Atlantic SE of Greenland, in position 58.20N 33.25W by U-221 (Trojer), part of the 'Draufgänger' (Daredevil) patrol group of eleven U-boats. The damaged U-boat was attacked the same day by Liberator 'H' AM929, pilot S/Ldr Terry M. Bulloch DFC of No. 120 Squadron RAF, based at Reykjavik and sank 300 miles SE of Cape Discord, Greenland, in position 57.25N 35.19W. The U-boat commander and 40 crew were lost. 2 crew were rescued by U-221 and landed at St Nazaire 23.12.42.

**ALDINGTON COURT** • GRT 4891 • Built 1929
31.10.42: Torpedoed and sunk by German submarine U-172 (Emmermann), part of the 'Eisbär' (Polarbear) patrol group of five U-boats, in the South Atlantic W of Port Nolloth, South West Africa, in position 30.10S 02.00W while sailing independently on a voyage from Philadelphia to Saldanha Bay, South Africa, and Alexandria via Trinidad 8.10.42, with a cargo of 6614 tons of government stores, coal and general. The Master, Capt Alfred Stuart, 24 crew and 9 gunners were lost. 7 crew and 3 gunners were rescued by British ship *CITY OF CHRISTIANIA* 4940/21 and landed at Montevideo 25.11.42.

**DORINGTON COURT** • GRT 5281 • Built 1938
24.11.42: Torpedoed and sunk by gunfire by German submarine U-181 (Lüth), in the Mozambique Channel 105 miles ESE of Inhaca Island, in position 26.20S 34.40E while sailing independently on a voyage from Calcutta and Madras 4.11.42 to the UK via Lourenco Marques and Durban, with a cargo of 9261 tons of general. The Master, Capt Ernest Douglas Aynge Gibbs, 33 crew and 5 gunners landed at Inhaca Island near Lourenco Marques. 4 crew were lost.

## HALL BROTHERS – NEWCASTLE

**ROYAL SCEPTRE** • GRT 4853 • Built 1937
5.9.39: Torpedoed and sunk by gunfire by German submarine U-48 (Schultze), in the Atlantic 300 miles NW of Cape Finisterre, in position 46.53N 14.59W while sailing independently on a voyage from Rosario to Belfast, with a cargo of wheat and maize. The Master, Capt James William Gair, and crew were rescued by British ship *BROWNING* 5332/19 and landed at Bahia, Brazil 26.9.39. 1 crew was lost.

**EMBASSAGE** • GRT 4954 • Built 1935
27.8.41: Torpedoed and sunk by German submarine U-557 (Paulsen), in the Atlantic 100 miles W of Achill Island, in position 54.00N 13.00W while on a voyage from Hull to Bathurst and Pepel, with 8540 tons of general cargo including lorries and aircraft, part of convoy OS 4 comprising 34 ships. The Master, Capt Edward Kiddie, 32 crew and 6 gunners were lost. 3 crew were rescued after four days by RCN destroyer *ASSINIBOINE* 1390/31 (D.18) ex-HMS *KEMPENFELT* (Capt G.C. Jones) and landed at Greenock.

**WHITE CREST** • GRT 4365 • Built 1928
24.2.42: Torpedoed and sunk by German submarine U-162 (Wattenburg), in the Atlantic SE of St John's, Newfoundland, in position 43.45N 42.15W while on a voyage from Cardiff to Buenos Aires, with a cargo of coal, part of convoy ONS 67 comprising 37 ships. The Master, Capt Gordon Joures, and crew of 40 were lost.

**BRETWALDA** • GRT 4906 • Built 1939
18.12.42: Torpedoed and sunk by German submarine U–563 (v. Hartmann), in the Atlantic about 330 miles WNE of Cape Finisterre, in position 44.35N 16.28W while on a voyage from Philippeville and Algiers 9.12.42 to Belfast, in ballast, part of convoy MKS 3Y comprising 23 ships. The Master, Capt William Stanley Dunstan, crew of 39 and 15 gunners were rescued by ORP destroyer *KRAKOWIAK* 1050/40 (L.115) ex-HMS *SILVERTON* and landed at Milford Haven 22.12.42. 1 gunner was lost.

## MOWT

**FLYNDERBORG** • GRT 1999 • Built 1930
3.11.41: Torpedoed and sunk by German submarine U–202 (Linder), part of the 'Raubritter' (Robber Knight) patrol group of fourteen U-boats, in the Atlantic NE of Notre Dame Bay, Newfoundland, in position 51.21N 51.45W while on a voyage from Parrsboro, Novia Scotia, to London via Sydney CB 29.10.41, with a cargo of 2125 tons of lumber, part of convoy SC 52 comprising 35 ships. The Master, Capt P. Petersen, 18 crew and 2 gunners were rescued by RCN corvette *WINDFLOWER* 925/40 (K.155) (Lt John Price) and landed at St John's, Newfoundland. 3 crew were lost.

**EMPIRE WEBSTER** • GRT 7043 • Built 1942
7.2.43: Torpedoed and sunk by gunfire by German submarine U–77 (Hartmann), in the Mediterranean 80 miles W of Algiers, in position 36.47N 01.37E while on government service on a voyage from Glasgow to Bona, with 8 army personnel and a cargo of 3000 tons of coal and military stores, part of convoy KMS 8 comprising 55 ships. The Master, Capt Alexander Roderick Duncan, 49 crew, 1 gunner and army personnel were rescued by RCN corvette *CAMROSE* 925/40 (K.154) (Lt L.R. Pavillard) and landed at Algiers. 3 crew and 1 gunner were lost.

## HALL CORPORATION OF CANADA – MONTREAL

**MONT LOUIS** • GRT 1905 • Built 1927 (Canadian)
9.5.42: Torpedoed and sunk by German submarine U–162 (Wattenberg), in the Atlantic SW of Trinidad, in position 08.23N 58.48W while sailing independently on a voyage from Paramaribo to Trinidad, with a cargo of bauxite. The Master, Capt Walter Bowen, and 7 crew were rescued by British schooner *MONA MARIE* 126/20 and landed at Georgetown 10.5.42. 13 crew were lost.

## HARRIS & DIXON LIMITED – LONDON
### Refast SS Co. Ltd

**REFAST** ex-*NANTUCKET CHIEF* ex-*GULFLIGHT* (tanker) • GRT 5189 • Built 1914
26.1.42: Torpedoed and sunk by German submarine U–582 (Schulte), part of the 'Ziethen' (German Town) patrol group of twelve U-boats, in the Atlantic S of St John's, Newfoundland, in position 42.41N 53.02W while sailing independently from London 3.1.42 to Baton Rouge via Loch Ewe 12.1.42, in ballast, dispersed on 16.1.42 from convoy ON 56 comprising 36 ships. The Master, Capt Arthur Ernest Wilson, 27 crew and 4 gunners were rescued by British

ship *MARIPOSA* 4940/21 and landed at Halifax NS 27.1.42. 10 crew were lost. As US tanker *GULFLIGHT,* she was the first US ship to be attacked prior to the United States of America entering the First World War on 6.4.17. On 1.5.15 at 12.50pm she was torpedoed and damaged by German submarine U–30 (v. Rosenburg) in the approaches to the English Channel while on a voyage from Port Arthur to Rouen with a cargo of motor spirit.

## MOWT

*EMPIRE LYTTON* (tanker) • GRT 9807 • Built 1942
9.1.43: Torpedoed and damaged by German submarine U–442 (Hesse), part of the 'Delphin' (Dolphin) patrol group of sixteen U–boats, an attempt by HM destroyer *HAVELOCK* 1340/39 (H.88) (Cdr Richard C. Boyle DSC) to sink the tanker by gunfire failed and she was later given a *coup de grâce* by U–522 (Schneider), in the Atlantic W of the Canary Islands, in position 28.08N 28.20W while on a voyage from Curacao and Trinidad to Gibraltar, with a cargo of 12500 tons of aviation spirit, part of convoy TM 1 comprising 9 tankers, escorted by HM destroyer *HAVELOCK*, HM corvettes *PIMPERNEL* 925/40 (K.71) (Lt-Cdr F.H. Thornton), *SAXIFRAGE* 925/41 (K.04) (Lt N.L. Knight) and *GODETIA* 925/40 (H.72) (Lt A.H. Pierce OBE) of the Escort Group B5. The Master, Capt John William Andrews, 30 crew and 3 gunners were rescued by HMS *SAXIFRAGE* and landed at Gibraltar. The Chief Officer, 12 crew and 1 gunner were lost. Korvettenkapitän Hans Joachim Hesse and crew of 47 were lost on 12.2.43 when U–442 was sunk while pursuing convoy KMS 9 comprising 46 ships in the Atlantic 145 miles W of Cape St Vincent, in position 37.32N 11.56W by Hudson 'F', pilot F/Lt Geoffrey Richard Mayhew of No. 48 Squadron RAF, based at Gibraltar. The pilot was awarded the DFC.

## HARRISON, J. & C. LIMITED – LONDON

*HARPALYCE* • GRT 5169 • Built 1940
25.8.40: Torpedoed and sunk by German submarine U–124 (Schulz), in the Atlantic 23 miles N of the Butt of Lewis, Hebrides, in position 58.52N 06.34W while on a voyage from Baltimore to Hull via Halifax NS, with a cargo of 8000 tons of steel, part of convoy HX 65 comprising 51 ships. The Master, Capt William John Rees, commodore Vice-Admiral B.G. Washington CMG DSO RN, 36 crew and 4 naval staff were lost. 4 crew were rescued by British trawler *FORT DEE* 212/29 and landed at Kirkwall, Orkney Isles.

*HARBLEDOWN* • GRT 5414 • Built 1933
4.4.41: Torpedoed and sunk by German submarine U–94 (Kuppish), in the Atlantic SSW of Iceland in position 58.30N 23.00W while on a voyage from Portland, Maine, to London via Sydney CB, with a cargo of 94157 bushels of wheat, part of convoy SC 26 comprising 24 ships. The Master, Capt Griffith Jones, 23 crew and 1 DBS were rescued by HM destroyer *VETERAN* 1120/19 (D.72) (Cdr W.T. Conchman OBE) and landed at Liverpool. 14 crew and 2 gunners were lost.

*HARPATHIAN* • GRT 4671 • Built 1930
9.4.41: Torpedoed and sunk by German submarine U–107 (Hessler), in the Atlantic SE of the Azores, in position 32.22N 22.53W while on a voyage from Middlesbrough and the Clyde to

Freetown, with a cargo of RAF stores, part of convoy OG 57 comprising 37 ships. The Master, Capt John Wharton MBE, 36 crew and 2 gunners landed at Hierro, Canary Islands. 3 crew and 1 gunner were lost.

**HARPAGUS** • GRT 5173 • Built 1940
20.5.41: Torpedoed and sunk by German submarine U-109 (Fischer), in the Atlantic about 250 miles SSE of Cape Farewell, in position 56.47N 40.55W while on a voyage from Baltimore to Barry Roads via Halifax NS, with 3 passengers and a cargo of 8250 tons of grain, part of convoy HX 126 comprising 29 ships. The Master, Capt James Valentine Stewart, and 17 crew were rescued by HM destroyer *BURNHAM* 1190/19 (H.82) (Cdr J. Bostock) ex-USN four-stack *AULICK* and landed at Reykjavik. 25 crew, 4 gunners and passengers were lost.

**HARLINGEN** • GRT 5415 • Built 1933
5.8.41: Torpedoed and sunk by German submarine U-75 (Ringelmann), in the Atlantic W of Ireland, in position 53.26N 15.40W while on a voyage from Lagos and Freetown 15.7.41 to Liverpool, with a cargo of 8000 tons of West African produce, part of convoy SL 81 comprising 18 ships. The Master, Capt Jack Willingham, 34 crew and 4 gunners were rescued by HM corvette *HYDRANGEA* 925/40 (K.39) (Lt J.E. Woolfenden) and landed at Gourock. 3 crew were lost.

**HARPAGON** • GRT 5719 • Built 1935
20.4.42: Torpedoed and sunk by German submarine U-109 (Bleichrodt), in the Atlantic 150 miles NNW of Bermuda, in position 34.35N 65.50W while sailing independently on a voyage from New York 17.4.42 to Bombay via Cape Town, with 8017 tons of general cargo including explosives, aircraft and tanks. The Master, Capt Robert William Edward Laycock, 34 crew and 6 gunners were lost. 8 crew were rescued by Argentinian ship *RIO DIAMANTE* 5159/18 and landed at Buenos Aires.

**HARTLEBURY** • GRT 5082 • Built 1934
7.7.42: Torpedoed and sunk by German submarine U-355 (La Baume), in the Arctic Sea 17 miles 180° from Britwin Lighthouse, Novaya Zemlya, in position 72.30N 52.00E while sailing independently on a voyage from Sunderland to Archangel via Reykjavik 27.6.42, with a cargo of 6 vehicles, 36 tanks, 7 aircraft and 2409 tons of military stores, dispersed from the ill-fated convoy PQ 17 comprising 36 ships. The Master, Capt George Willbourne Stephenson, and 12 survivors landed at Pomorski Bay, Novaya Zemlya. 7 survivors were found on US ship *WINSTON-SALEM* 6223/20 aground at North Gusini Shoal, Novaya Zemlya, were rescued by a Russian survey ship and transferred to British ship *EMPIRE TIDE* 6978/41, part of convoy PQ 17 at anchor in Pomorski Bay, later transferred to HM corvette *LA MALOUINE* 925/40 (K.46) (Lt V.D.H. Bidwell) and landed at Archangel 25.7.42. 29 crew, 7 gunners and 2 naval signalmen were lost. Kapitänleutnant Gunter La Baume and crew of 51 were lost on 1.4.44 when U-355, part of the 'Blitz' (Lightning) patrol group of four U-boats was shadowing convoy JW 58 comprising 49 ships was damaged in the Greenland Sea 120 miles E by S of Bear Island, in position 73.07N 10.21E by rockets fired by Avenger 'H' of No. 846 Naval Air Squadron from HM escort carrier *TRACKER* 11420/42 (D.24) (Capt J.H. Huntley) and sunk by HM destroyer *BEAGLE* 1360/30 (H.30) (Lt-Cdr N.R. Murch).

**HARTISMERE** • GRT 5498 • Built 1933

8.7.42: Torpedoed and sunk by gunfire by Japanese submarine I-10 (Kayahara), in the Mozambique Channel W of Madagascar, in position 18.00S 41.22E while sailing independently on a voyage from Philadelphia to Alexandria via Lourenco Marques 4.7.42, with 8000 tons of general cargo. The Master, Capt Kenneth Carrick Lone, crew of 39 and 7 gunners landed at Caldera Point Lighthouse, Portuguese East Africa.

**HARBOROUGH** • GRT 5415 • Built 1932

14.9.42: Torpedoed and sunk by gunfire by German submarine U-515 (Henke), in the Atlantic 40 miles E of Galera Point, Trinidad, in position 10.03N 60.20W while sailing independently on a voyage from Buenos Aires and Rio de Janeiro 29.8.42 to Trinidad and New York, with 1 passenger and 8000 tons of general cargo and bags of mail. The Master, Capt Frank Norman Hibbert, 38 crew, 5 gunners and passenger landed at Pembroke Beach, Tobago. 2 crew and 3 gunners were lost.

**HARTINGTON** • GRT 5496 • Built 1932

2.11.42: Torpedoed and damaged by German submarines U-522 (Schneider) and sunk after an additonal torpedo hit by U-438 (Franzius) and a *coup de grâce* by U-521 (Bargsten), part of the 'Veilchen' (Violet) patrol group of thirteen U-boats, in the Atlantic about 450 miles E of Belle Ile, in position 52.30N 45.30W while on a voyage from Halifax NS 27.10.42 to Belfast, with a cargo of 8000 tons of wheat and 6 tanks, part of convoy SC 107 comprising 42 ships. The Master, Capt Maurice James Edwards, 21 crew and 2 gunners were lost. 17 crew and 7 gunners were rescued by HM destroyer *WINCHELSEA* 1120/17 (D.46) (Lt-Cdr G.W. Gregorie) and landed at St John's, Newfoundland. Kapitänleutnant Volkmar Schwartzkopff and crew of 52 were lost on 30.10.42 when U-520, shadowing convoy SC 107, was sunk by a Douglas Digby torpedo/dive bomber '742', pilot F/O D.F. Raynes, No. 10 Squadron RCAF, in the Atlantic E of Conception Bay, in position 47.47N 49.50W. U-521, commanded by Kapitänleutnant Klaus Bargsten (Knight's Cross 3.4.43), was sunk on 2.6.43 in the Atlantic 140 miles E of Hampton Roads, Virginia, in position 37.43N 73.16W by US submarine chaser PC-565 280/43 (Lt Walter T. Flynn). The U-boat commander was taken prisoner by PC-565 and the crew of 51 were lost. Kapitänleutnant Heinrich Heinsohn and crew of 47 were lost while attacking convoy ONS 5 comprising 42 ships when U-438, part of the 'Fink' (Finch) patrol group of thirty U-boats, was sunk on 6.5.43 in the Atlantic E of Belle Ile, in position 52.00N 45.10W by HM sloop *PELICAN* 1200/38 (L.86) (Cdr G.N. Brewer) of the 1st Escort Group.

**HARMALA** • GRT 5730 • Built 1935

7.2.43: Torpedoed and sunk by German submarine U-614 (Sträter), in the Atlantic SE of Cape Farewell, in position 55.14N 26.37W while on a voyage from Rio de Janeiro to Middlesbrough via Trinidad, New York and Halifax NS, with a cargo of 8500 tons of iron ore, part of convoy SC 118 comprising 61 ships. The Master, Capt Harry Chessman Walker, 31 crew, 10 gunners and 1 naval signalman were lost. 11 crew were rescued by Free French corvette *LOBÉLIA* 925/41 (K.05) (Capt P. de Morsier) and landed at Greenock. Kapitänleutnant Wolfgang Sträter and crew of 48 were lost on 29.7.43 when U-614 was sunk in the Atlantic 245 miles NW by N of Cape Ortegal, in position 46.42N 11.03W by Wellington 'G', pilot W/Cdr Rowland Gascoigne Musson of No. 172 Squadron RAF, based at Chivenor, part of 19 Group. Kapitänleutnant Ralph Münnich and 18 crew were lost on 4.2.43 when U-187, part of the 'Pfeil' (Arrow) patrol group of ten U-boats, was sunk in the Atlantic 600 miles SE of Cape Farewell, in position 50.12N 36.34W while shadowing convoy SC 118 by HM destroyers *BEVERLEY* 1190/19 H.64) (Lt-Cdr R.A. Price) ex-USN four-stack *BRANCH* and *VIMY* 1090/17 (D.33) ex-HMS *VANCOUVER* (Lt-Cdr J.N.K. Knight). 45 crew were taken prisoner by HMS *BEVERLEY* and HMS *VIMY.*

### HARBURY • GRT 5081 • Built 1933

5.5.43: Torpedoed and damaged by German submarine U-628 (Hasenschar) and later sunk by U-264 (Looks), part of the 'Fink' (Finch) patrol group of thirty U-boats, in the Atlantic 500 miles S of Cape Farewell, in position 55.01N 42.59W while on a voyage from Swansea to St John, New Brunswick, with a cargo of 6129 tons of anthracite, a straggler from convoy ONS 5 comprising 42 ships. The Master, Capt Walter Edward Cook, 33 crew and 8 gunners were rescued by HM trawler *NORTHERN SPRAY* 655/36 (FY.129) (Lt F.A.J. Downer) and landed at St John's, Newfoundland. 6 crew and 1 gunner were lost. U-264, part of the 'Hai' (Shark) patrol group of nineteen U-boats, commanded by Kapitänleutnant Hartwig Looks, was sunk on 19.2.44 in the Atlantic 510 miles WSW of Cape Clear, in position 48.31N 22.05W while shadowing convoy ON 224 comprising 80 ships by HM sloops *WOODPECKER* 1300/42 (U.08) (Cdr H.L. Pryse) and *STARLING* 1350/42 (U.66) (Capt Frederic John Walker CB DSO DSC). The U-boat commander and 50 crew were taken prisoner by HMS *STARLING,* HMS *WOODPECKER* and HM sloop *WILD GOOSE* 1300/42 (U.90) (Lt-Cdr D.E.G. Wemyss DSC) of the 2nd Escort Group. U-264 was the first operational U-boat to be fitted with snorkel equipment.

### HARPERLEY • GRT 4586 • Built 1930

5.5.43: Torpedoed and sunk by German submarine U-264 (Looks), part of the 'Fink' (Finch) patrol group of thirty U-boats, in the Atlantic 500 miles S of Cape Farewell, in position 55.00N 42.58W while on a voyage from Newport, Mon. and Milford Haven 20.4.43 to Buenos Aires, with a cargo of 6005 tons of coal and bags of mail, part of convoy ONS 5 comprising 46 ships. The Master, Capt Joseph Ernest Turgoose, 32 crew and 6 gunners were rescued by HM trawler *NORTHERN SPRAY* 655/36 (FY.129) (Lt F.A.J. Downer) and landed at St John's, Newfoundland. 9 crew and 1 gunner were lost.

### HARMONIC • GRT 4558 • Built 1930

15.7.43: Torpedoed and sunk by German submarine U-172 (Emmermann), in the South Atlantic 620 miles E of Rio de Janeiro, in position 23.00S 33.00W while sailing independently on a voyage from Rosario and Buenos Aires 7.7.43 to the UK via Freetown, with a cargo of 7368 tons of linseed oil. The Master, Capt Roland Stott, 38 crew and 6 gunners were rescued on 22.7.43 by Portuguese ship *INHAMBANE* 6051/12 and landed at Bahia, Brazil 24.7.43. 1 crew was lost.

### MOWT

### EMPIRE STORM • GRT 7290 • Built 1941

29.5.41: Torpedoed and sunk by German submarine U-557 (Paulshen), part of the 'West' patrol group of fifteen U-boats, in the Atlantic S of Cape Farewell, in position 55.00N 39.50W while on a voyage from Montreal to the UK, with a cargo of 6494 tons of grain and

2983 tons of flour, a straggler from convoy HX 128 comprising 42 ships. The Master, Capt George Willbourne Stephenson, 35 crew and 4 gunners were rescued by Norwegian ship *MITRA* 1186/21 and landed at St John's, Newfoundland 4.6.41. 3 crew were lost.

**EMPIRE BYRON** • GRT 6645 • Built 1941
5.7.42: Torpedoed and damaged by a Heinkel 111 of the II/KG 26 Group, later torpedoed and sunk by German submarine U-703 (Bielfeld), in the Barents Sea, in position 76.18N 33.30E while sailing independently on government service on a voyage from Hull to Archangel via Reykjavik 27.6.42, with 2 passengers and a cargo of 6 vehicles, 30 tanks, 15 aircraft and 2455 tons of military stores, dispersed from the ill-fated convoy PQ 17 comprising 36 ships. The Master, Capt John Wharton MBE, 45 crew and 16 gunners were rescued by HM corvette *DIANELLA* 925/40 (K.07) (Lt J. Rankin) and landed at Archangel 16.7.42. 3 crew, 3 gunners and 1 passenger were lost. Capt J. Rimington REME was taken prisoner and landed at Narvik 15.7.42.

**RADHURST** ex-*SAVIA* ex-*NEREIDE* • GRT 3454 • Built 1910
20.2.43: Torpedoed and sunk by German submarine U-525 (Drewitz), part of the 'Haudegen' (Adventure) patrol group of twenty-one U-boats, in the Atlantic NW of St John's, Newfoundland, in position 49.50N 41.50W while on a voyage from the Tyne to New York, in ballast, a straggler from convoy ONS 165 comprising 32 ships. The Master, Capt Charles Faulkner Linton, and crew of 37 were lost. Kapitänleutnant Hans Joachim Drewitz and crew of 53 were lost on 11.8.43 when U-525 was sunk in the Atlantic 410 miles WNW of Flores, Azores, in position 41.29N 38.55W by an Avenger, pilot Lt Charles G. Hewitt and a Wildcat, pilot Ensign Jack H. Stewart of US Navy Composite Squadron VC-1 from US escort carrier *CARD* 9800/42 (CVE-11) (Capt Arnold J. Isbell), part of the Task Force 64.

## HARRISON, THOMAS & JAMES – LIVERPOOL
### Charente SS Co. Ltd

**COUNSELLOR** • GRT 5068 • Built 1926
9.3.40: Struck a mine laid on 7.3.40 by German submarine U-32 (Jenisch) and sank in the Irish Sea off the Liverpool Bar Lightship, in position 53.38N 03.23W while on a voyage from New Orleans to Liverpool via Halifax NS, with general cargo including cotton, part of convoy HX 22 comprising 35 ships. The Master, Capt Harold Coates, Commodore Rear Admiral H.G.C. Franklin RN, crew of 69 and 7 naval staff were rescued by HM destroyer *WALPOLE* 1300/18 (F.150) (Lt C.H.G. Bowerman) and landed at Liverpool.

**ASTRONOMER** • GRT 8401 • Built 1917
1.6.40: Torpedoed and sunk by German submarine U-58 (Kuppish), in the North Sea 30 miles SE of Wick, in position 58.01N 02.12W while on government service on a voyage from Rosyth to Scapa Flow, with 48 naval officers and ratings and a cargo of 2/3000 tons of naval stores. The Master, Capt John James Egerton, 51 crew, 1 gunner and an unknown number of naval officers and ratings were rescued by HM trawlers *STOKE CITY* 422/35 (FY.232) (Lt-Cdr N.C.H. Scallan) and *LEICESTER CITY* 422/34 (FY.223) (Lt A.R. Cornish) and landed at Rosyth. 4 crew and a number of naval ratings were lost. *ASTRONOMER* was lost while on government service employed as a boom defence carrier.

**SCHOLAR** • GRT 3940 • Built 1922

22.9.40: Torpedoed and damaged by German submarine U–100 (Schepke), in the Atlantic 340 miles W of Bloody Foreland, in position 55.11N 17.58W while on a voyage from Galveston to Manchester via Halifax NS, with a cargo of 5484 bales of cotton and 3284 tons of general cargo including steel, wood pulp and lumber, part of convoy HX 72 comprising 47 ships. Taken in tow by HM tug *MARAUDER* 840/38 (W.98) (Lt W.J. Hammond) in position 55.10N 17.49W, tow later abandoned then sunk by HM destroyer *SKATE* 1065/17 (F.46) (Lt F.P. Baker DSC) on 24.9.40 in position 54.38N 16.40W. The Master, Capt William Robert Mackenzie, crew of 44 and 1 gunner were rescued by HMS *SKATE* and landed at Londonderry.

**PLANTER** • GRT 5887 • Built 1927

16.11.40: Torpedoed and sunk by German submarine U–137 (Wohlfarth), in the Atlantic 30 miles NNW of Bloody Foreland, in position 55.38N 08.28W while on a voyage from Suez to Manchester via Freetown, with a cargo of Egyptian produce, a romper from convoy SLS 53 comprising 6 ships. The Master, Capt Dennis Henry Bryant, 58 crew and 1 gunner were rescued by HM destroyer *CLARE* 1190/20 (I.14) (Lt-Cdr C. Gwinner) and landed at Liverpool. 12 crew and 1 DBS were lost.

**DIPLOMAT** • GRT 8240 • Built 1921

27.11.40: Torpedoed and sunk by German submarine U–104 (Jürst), in the Atlantic 128 miles WNW of Bloody Foreland, in position 55.42N 11.37W while on a voyage from New Orleans to Liverpool via Bermuda, with a cargo of 4484 tons of cotton and 4303 tons of general cargo including steel, a straggler from convoy HX 88 comprising 53 ships. The Master, Capt William Augustus Hansen, and 13 crew were lost. 40 crew were rescued by HM destroyer *ACTIVE* 1350/29 (H.14) (Cdr E.C.L. Turner) and landed at Greenock. Kapitänleutnant Harald Jurst and crew of 48 were lost on 28.11.40 in the Atlantic NW of Malin Head, in position 55.30N 08.00W when U–104 probably hit a British mine.

**COLONIAL** • GRT 5108 • Built 1926

27.5.41: Torpedoed and sunk by German submarine U–107 (Hessler), in the Atlantic 200 miles WNW of Freetown, in position 09.13N 15.09W while sailing independently on a voyage from Liverpool to Beira via Freetown, with 3500 tons of cargo, dispersed from convoy OB 318 comprising 38 ships. The Master, Capt Joseph Devereaux, Commodore Rear Admiral W.B. Mackenzie RN, crew of 88, 6 naval staff and 4 gunners were rescued by HM battleship *CENTURION* 25000/11 (I.50) (Lt-Cdr R.W. Wainwright) and landed at Freetown.

**AUDITOR** • GRT 5444 • Built 1924

4.7.41: Torpedoed and sunk by German submarine U–123 (Hardegen), in the Atlantic 600 miles NW of the Cape Verde Islands, in position 25.33N 28.23W while sailing independently on a voyage from London to Cape Town and Beira, with 5300 tons of general cargo and 10 aircraft, dispersed on 28.6.41 in position 48.17N 20.40W from convoy OB 337 comprising 51 ships. The Master, Capt Edwin Bennett, and 50 crew landed at St Michael Island, Azores and 20 crew and 4 gunners landed at Taffafal Bay, San Antonio Island, Cape Verde Islands, and were brought to Bathurst, Gambia, by HM sloop *GORLESTON* 1546/29 (Y.92) (Cdr R.W. Keymer) ex-US Coastguard cutter *ITASCA*. 1 gunner was lost.

**DESIGNER** • GRT 5945 • Built 1928
9.7.41: Torpedoed and sunk by German submarine U-98 (Gysae), in the Atlantic NNW of the Azores, in position 42.59N 31.40W while sailing independently on government service on a voyage from Ellesmere Port to Cape Town, with a cargo of military stores and mail, dispersed on 6.7.41 in position 48.30N 26.30W from convoy OB 341 comprising 45 ships. The Master, Capt Donald Archibald McCallum, and 66 crew were lost. 10 crew and 1 gunner were rescued by Portuguese sailing ship *SOUTA PRINCESCA* and landed at Leixoes.

**TRAVELLER** • GRT 3963 • Built 1922
26.1.42: Torpedoed and sunk by German submarine U-106 (Rasch), part of 'Operation Paukenschlag' (Drumbeat), the second wave of five U-boats, in the Atlantic E of New York, in position 40.00N 61.45W while sailing independently on a voyage from New Orleans and Hampton Roads to Holyhead and Liverpool via Halifax NS, with general cargo including 600 tons of explosives. The Master, Capt Harold M. Fitz-Simons, and crew of 49 were lost.

**DAYTONIAN** • GRT 6434 • Built 1922
13.3.42: Torpedoed and sunk by gunfire by Italian submarine *ENRICO TAZZOLI* (di Cossato), in the Atlantic 120 miles E of Bahamas, in position 26.33N 74.43W while sailing independently on a voyage from Mobile to Liverpool, with general cargo. The Master, Capt John James Egerton, 55 crew and 1 gunner were rescued by Dutch tanker *ROTTERDAM* 8968/25 and landed at Nassau, Bahama Islands 15.3.42. 1 crew was lost.

**OBSERVER** • GRT 5881 • Built 1928
16.12.42: Torpedoed and sunk by German submarine U-176 (Dierksen), in the Atlantic 350 miles E of Cabo Sao Roque, Brazil, in position 05.30S 31.00W while sailing independently on a voyage from Mersin, Turkey, to Baltimore via Cape Town 29.11.42 and Trinidad, with a cargo of 3000 tons of chrome ore. The Master, Capt John Davidson, 57 crew and 8 gunners were lost. 14 crew and 1 gunner landed at Fortaleza. Korvettenkapitän Reiner Dierksen and crew of 52 were lost when U-176 was sunk on 15.5.43 in the Florida Strait 100 miles NE of Havana, in position 23.21N 80.18W by a Vought-Sikorsky OS2U-3 Kingfisher seaplane from US Navy Scouting Squadron VS-62 based at Guantanamo Bay, Cuba, and Cuban submarine chaser CS-13.

**CONTRACTOR** • GRT 6003 • Built 1930
7.8.43: Torpedoed and sunk by German submarine U-371 (Mehl), in the Mediterranean 75 miles SW of Sardinia, in position 37.15N 07.21E while on a voyage from Glasgow and Gibraltar 4.8.43 to Bombay, Trincomalee and Calcutta, with 6110 tons of general cargo including 3500 tons of government stores and mail, part of convoy GTX 5. The Master, Capt Andrew Brims, and 3 crew were lost. 68 crew and 11 gunners were rescued by HM minesweepers *BYMS 11* 215/42 (Lt L. Hutchinson), *BYMS 14* 215/42 (Sub-Lt R.R. Macintosh), *BYMS 24* 215/42 (Skipper J. Hunt) and *BYMS 209* 215/42 (Lt J.G. Reeve) and landed at Malta.

**DIRECTOR** • GRT 5107 • Built 1926
15.7.44: Torpedoed and sunk by German submarine U-198 (v. Waldegg), in the Mozambique Channel SE of Inhambane, Portuguese East Africa, in position 24.30S 35.44E while sailing independently on a voyage from Middlesbrough and Durban to Beira and the

Seychelles, with a part cargo of 500 tons of generals. The Master, Capt William Weatherall, 50 crew and 6 gunner were rescued, the Master and 14 crew by Portuguese sloop *GONCALVES ZARCO* 1436/32 and landed at Lourenco Marques, and the Chief Officer's boat with 34 crew and and 6 gunners landed at Kosi Bay, Portuguese East Africa. 1 crew was lost.

**WAYFARER** • GRT 5068 • Built 1925
19.8.44: Torpedoed and sunk by German submarine U-862 (Timm), in the Mozambique Channel N of Mozambique, in position 14.30S 42.20E while sailing independently on a voyage from Colombo and Beira to Port Said and the UK, with a cargo of 3000 tons of copper and 2000 tons of coal. The Master, Capt John Wales, 44 crew, 5 gunners and 1 DBS were lost. 9 crew and 2 gunners landed on an uninhabited island in the Mozambique Channel, in approximate position 11.00S 40.30E, were rescued by a dhow and landed at Palfa, Portuguese East Africa. U-862 transferred to Japan and was renamed I-502 at Singapore on 14.8.45 (VJ Day).

**MOWT**

**EMPIRE EXPLORER** ex-*INANDA* • GRT 5345 • Built 1925
9.7.42: Torpedoed and sunk by gunfire by German submarine U-575 (Heydemann), in the Atlantic W of Tobago, in position 11.40N 60.55W while sailing independently from Demerara to Barbados and the UK via Trinidad 8.7.42, with a cargo of 4000 tons of sugar, 1000 tons of pitch and mail. The Master, Capt Edgar Buckingham Stephens, 66 crew and 8 gunners were rescued by HM motor torpedo boat No. 337 32/41 and landed at Tobago. 3 crew were lost.

**ARICA** ex-*ZENON* • GRT 5390 • Built 1921
6.11.42: Torpedoed and sunk by German submarine U-160 (Lassen), in the Atlantic 8 miles N of Galera Point, Trinidad, in position 10.58N 60.52W while on a voyage from London and Trinidad 6.11.42 to Demerara, with 7000 tons of general cargo and mail, part of convoy T 24 comprising 8 ships. The Master, Capt Beaconsfield Worthington, 47 crew and 7 gunners were rescued by HM trawler *LADY ELSA* 518/37 (FY.124) (Lt S.G. Phillips DSC) and landed at Port of Spain, Trinidad. 11 crew and 1 gunner were lost.

**HAY, J. & SONS – GLASGOW**

**THE MONARCH** • GRT 824 • Built 1930
19.6.40: Torpedoed and sunk by German submarine U-52 (Rösing), in the Bay of Biscay 60 miles W of Belle Ile, in position 47.20N 04.40W while sailing independently on a voyage from Tonney-Charente, France, to Falmouth, in ballast. The Master, Capt John McNeill, and crew of 11 were lost.

**HEADLAM & SON – WHITBY**

**SNEATON** • GRT 3677 • Built 1925
14.10.39: Torpedoed and sunk by gunfire by German submarine U-48 (Schultze), in the Atlantic 150 miles SW of Cape Clear, in position 49.05N 13.05W while sailing

independently on a voyage from Cardiff to Rio de Janeiro, with a cargo of 4300 tons of coal. The Master, Capt Thomas Granger, and crew were rescued by Belgian tanker *ALEXANDRIA ANDRÉ* 5322/28 and landed at Weymouth. 1 crew was lost.

*SCORESBY* • GRT 3843 • Built 1923
17.10.40: Torpedoed and sunk by German submarine U-48 (Bleichrodt), in the Atlantic 178 miles NW of Rockall, in position 59.14N 17.51W while on a voyage from Francis Harbour, Labrador, to the Clyde via Sydney CB 5.10.40, with a cargo of 1685 fathoms of pit props, part of convoy SC 7 comprising 35 ships. The Master, Capt Lawrence Zebedee Weatherill, and crew of 38 were rescued by HM corvette *BLUEBELL* 925/40 (K.80) (Lt-Cdr Robert E. Sherwood) and landed at Gourock 20.10.40.

*SANDSEND* • GRT 3612 • Built 1925
18.10.40: Torpedoed and sunk by German submarine U-48 (Bleichrodt), in the Atlantic 254 miles WNW of Rockall, in position 58.12N 21.29W while on a voyage from Port Talbot to Quebec, with a cargo of 4350 tons of anthracite, a straggler from convoy OB 228 comprising 47 ships. The Master, Capt William Armstrong, and 33 crew were rescued by HM corvette *HIBISCUS* 925/40 (K.24) (Lt-Cdr R. Phillips) and landed at Methil. 5 crew were lost.

*BARNBY* • GRT 4813 • Built 1940
22.5.41: Torpedoed and sunk by German submarine U-111 (Kleinschmidt), part of the 'West' patrol group of fifteen U-boats, in the North Atlantic SW of Iceland, in position 60.30N 34.12W while on a voyage from St John, New Brunswick, to Hull via Halifax NS, with a cargo of 7250 tons of flour, a straggler from convoy HX 126 comprising 29 ships. The Master, Capt Arthur John Gale, 35 crew and 8 gunners landed at Reykjavik. 1 crew was lost.

*LARPOOL* • GRT 3872 • Built 1924
2.11.41: Torpedoed and sunk by German submarine U-208 (Schlieper), in the Atlantic about 200 miles ESE of Cape Race while on a voyage from London to Barbados and Demerara, with 3991 tons of general cargo, a straggler from convoy ON 27 comprising 61 ships. The Master, Capt Charles Patton, and 5 crew landed at Burin, Newfoundland 10.11.41, and 11 crew were rescued by RCN corvette *BITTERSWEET* 925/40 (K.182) (Lt-Cdr J.A. Woods) and landed at Halifax NS. 22 crew were lost. Kapitänleutnant Alfred Schlieper and crew of 44 were lost on 11.12.41 when U-208 was sunk in the Atlantic 70 miles W of Gibraltar, in position 35.51N 07.45W by HM destroyers *HARVESTER* 1340/39 (H.19) ex-HMS *HANDY* (Lt-Cdr M. Thornton) ex-Brazilian *JURUA* and *HESPERUS* 1340/39 (H.57) ex-HMS *HEARTY* (Lt-Cdr A.A. Tait).

**MOWT**

*EMPIRE EVE* • GRT 5979 • Built 1941 (CAM Ship)
18.5.43: Torpedoed and sunk by German submarine U-414 (Huth), in the Mediterranean NE of Mostaganem, Algeria, in position 36.37N 01.01E while on government service on a voyage from Cardiff and Milford Haven 4.5.43 to Algiers, with 13 service personnel, a cargo of 6500 tons of coal and 250 tons of lubricating oil, part of combined convoy KMS 14/UGS 8 comprising 42 ships. The Master, Capt Lawrence Zebedee Weatherill, 55 crew, 12 gunners,

naval and RAF personnel were rescued by HM boom defence ship *BARFOIL* 730/42 (Z.194) (Lt G.F. Williams) and a Tank Landing Craft and landed at Algiers. 5 crew were lost. Oberleutnant zur See Walter Huth and crew of 46 were lost on 25.5.43 when U–414 was sunk while attacking convoy GTX 1 in the Mediterranean 30 miles W of Cape Tenes, Algeria, in position 36.01N 00.34E by HM corvette *VETCH* 925/41 (K.132) (Lt K.M.B. Menzies).

## HECTOR WHALING LIMITED – LONDON
### Hektoria Limited

*HEKTORIA* (Whaling factory) • GRT 13797 • Built 1899
12.9.42: Torpedoed and damaged by German submarine U–211 (Hauser) and sunk by *coup de grâce* by German submarine U–608 (Struckmeimer), part of the 'Vorwärts' (Forward) patrol group of ten U-boats, in the Atlantic W of Ireland, in position 48.55N 33.38W while on a voyage from Liverpool 4.9.42 to New York, in ballast, part of convoy ON 127 comprising 32 ships. The Master, Capt Frederick Arthur Gjertsen, 76 crew and 8 gunners were rescued by RCN corvette *ARVIDA* 925/40 (K.113) (Lt A.I. McKay) and landed at St John's, Newfoundland 15.9.42. 1 crew was lost.

## HENDERSON, P. & COMPANY – GLASGOW
### British & Burmese Steam Navigation Co. Ltd

*KANBE* • GRT 6244 • Built 1941
9.5.43: Torpedoed and sunk by German submarine U–123 (v. Schroeter), in the Atlantic 60 miles S of Monrovia, while sailing independently on a voyage from Alexandria and Takoradi to the UK via Freetown, with general cargo including 3500 tons of copper, a straggler from convoy TS 38. The Master, Capt John Frederick Thomas Burke, 57 crew and 3 gunners were lost. 5 crew were rescued by Spanish ship *RIO FRANCOLI* 2337/09 and landed at Santa Isabel, Fernando Po. U–123, commanded by Oberleutnant zur See Horst von Schroeter (Knight's Cross 1.6.44), was scuttled at Lorient on 19.8.44.

*YOMA* • GRT 8131 • Built 1928
17.6.43: Torpedoed and sunk by German submarine U–81 (Krieg), in the Mediterranean NW of Derna in position 33.03N 22.04E while on government service on a voyage from Tripoli 16.6.43 to Alexandria, with 134 British army officers, 994 British troops, 22 Free French naval officers and 643 Free French naval ratings, part of convoy GTX 2 comprising 14 ships. The Master, Capt George Paterson MBE, 29 crew, 3 gunners and 451 service personnel were lost. 130 crew, 5 gunners and 1342 service personnel were rescued by HM minesweepers *LISMORE* 650/40 (J.145) (Lt L.C.G. Lever) and *GAWLER* 650/41 (J.188) ex-HMS *GAMBUI* (Lt-Cdr W.J. Seymour), HM minesweepers No. 102 165/41 (Sub-Lt R.L. Simpson RNZNVR), and No. 105 165/41 (Lt W. Henderson), and British ship *FORT MAUREPAS* 7130/42 and landed at Derna.

*HENZADA* • GRT 4161 • Built 1934
24.7.43: Torpedoed and sunk by German submarine U–199 (Kraus), in the Atlantic 100 miles SW of Rio de Janeiro, in position 25.30S 44.00W while sailing independently on a voyage from Ellesmere Port 16.6.43 to Santos, with a cargo of 2095 tons of chemicals. The Master, Capt William Innes McIntosh, crew of 55 and 6 gunners were rescued by Panamanian tanker

*BALTIC* 8805/20 and landed at Montevideo 28.7.43. 2 gunners were lost. U-199, commanded by Kapitänleutnant Hans-Werner Kraus (Knight's Cross 19.6.42), was sunk on 31.7.43 in the South Atlantic SW of Rio de Janeiro, in position 23.54S 42.54W by a Mariner, pilot Lt William F. Smith of US Navy Patrol Squadron VP-74 based at Bahia, Brazil, a Hudson, pilot Lt S.C. Schnoor and a Catalina, pilot Cadet A.M. Torres of the Brazilian Air Force. The U-boat commander and 11 crew were taken prisoner by US seaplane tender *BARNEGAT* 1766/41 (AVP.10). 49 crew were lost.

## Henderson Line

*KATHA* • GRT 4357 • Built 1938
2.4.43: Torpedoed and sunk by German submarine U-124 (Mohr), in the Atlantic W of Oporto, in position 41.02N 15.39W while on a voyage from London, Hull via Oban 26.3.43 to Durban, Colombo and Calcutta, with a cargo of 7000 tons of naval and miliary stores including general and 16 aircraft, part of convoy OS 45 comprising 42 ships. The Master, Capt Samuel Thomson, 53 crew and 4 gunners were rescued by British ships *DANBY* 4258/37, *GOGRA* 5181/19 and HM corvette *LA MALOUINE* 925/40 (K.46) (Lt V.D.H. Bidwell), transferred to Canadian ship *NEW NORTHLAND* 3445/26 and landed at Freetown. 1 crew and 5 gunners were lost.

## MOWT

*EMPIRE CITIZEN* ex-*WAHEHE* • GRT 4683 • Built 1922
3.2.41: Torpedoed and sunk by German submarine U-107 (Hessler), in the Atlantic SW of Iceland, in position 58.12N 23.22W while on a voyage from Liverpool to Rangoon, with 12 passengers and general cargo, a straggler from convoy OB 279 comprising 39 ships. The Master, Capt Edward Charles Hughes, 64 crew, 1 gunner and passengers were lost. 4 crew and 1 gunner were rescued by HM corvette *CLARKIA* 925/40 (K.88) (Lt-Cdr F.J.G. Jones) and landed at Londonderry. The German *WAHEHE* was intercepted on 21.2.40 SE of Iceland by HM cruiser *MANCHESTER* 9100/37 (15) (Cdr J.N. Sparks) and HM destroyer *KIMBERLEY* 1690/39 (F.50) (Lt-Cdr R.G.K. Knowling), boarded by a prize crew and taken to Kirkwall.

*BOTWEY* ex-*MANCHESTER PRODUCER* ex-*START POINT* • GRT 5106 • Built 1916
26.7.41: Torpedoed and sunk by German submarine U-141 (Schüler), in the Atlantic 365 miles 270° from Bloody Foreland, in position 55.42N 09.53W while on a voyage from Ellesmere Port to Port Sulphur, in ballast, part of convoy OS 1 comprising 58 ships. The Master, Capt Ebenezer Gordon, crew of 48 and 4 gunners were rescued by rescue ship *COPELAND* 1526/23 (Capt W.J. Hartley DSC) and landed at Greenock 28.7.41. U-141, commanded by Kapitänleutnant Heinrich-Dietrich Hoffmann, was scuttled at Wilhelmshaven on 5.5.45.

## HENRY, A.F. & McGREGOR LIMITED – EDINBURGH

*MARWICK HEAD* ex-*ALLANWATER* • GRT 496 • Built 1920
12.12.39: Struck a mine laid on 11.12.39 by German submarine U-59 (Jürst) and sunk in the North Sea ½ mile off Caister while on a voyage from Bo'ness to London, with a cargo of coal. The Master, Capt J.J. Thain, and 4 crew landed at Great Yarmouth. 5 crew were lost.

## HEYN, G. & SONS LIMITED – BELFAST
### Head Line

*FANAD HEAD* • GRT 5200 • Built 1917
14.9.39: Torpedoed and sunk by gunfire by German submarine U–30 (Lemp), in the Atlantic about 200 miles W of the Hebrides, in position 56.43N 15.21W while sailing independently on a voyage from Montreal to Belfast, with 8 passengers and general cargo including grain. The Master, Capt George Pinkerton, crew of 41 and passengers were rescued by HM destroyer *TARTAR* 1870/37 (F.43) (Capt G.H. Warner DSC) and landed at Mallaig.

*DUNAFF HEAD* • GRT 5877 • Built 1918
7.3.41: Torpedoed and sunk by German submarine UA (Eckermann), in the North Atlantic S of Iceland, in position 60.38N 18.50W while on a voyage from Glasgow to St John, New Brunswick, in ballast, part of convoy OB 293 comprising 37 ships. The Master, Capt R. Dicks, 34 crew and 4 gunners were rescued by HM destroyer *VERITY* 1325/19 (F.36) (Cdr R.H. Mills) and landed at Loch Ewe. 5 crew were lost. UA ex-Turkish submarine *BATIRAY*, commanded by Oberleutnant zur See Ulrich-Philipp Graf von zu Arco-Zinneberg, was scuttled at Kiel 3.5.45.

*BENGORE HEAD* • GRT 2609 • Built 1922
9.5.41: Torpedoed and sunk by German submarine U–110 (Lemp), in the North Atlantic SE of Cape Farewell, in position 60.45N 33.02W while on a voyage from Belfast to Montreal, with a cargo of 1200 tons of coal and binder twine, part of convoy OB 318 comprising 38 ships. The Master, Capt Maurice Kennedy, 35 crew and 4 gunners were rescued, 16 crew by Norwegian ship *BORGFRED* 2183/20 and landed at Sydney CB 18.5.41, and 24 crew by HM corvette *AUBRIETIA* 925/40 (K.96) (Lt-Cdr V.F. Smith) and landed at Reykjavik. 1 crew was lost. U–110 was captured the same day when depth-charged and forced to the surface in the Atlantic 550 miles SW of Reykjanes, Iceland, in position 60.31N 33.10W by HM corvette *AUBRIETIA* 925/40 (K.96), HM destroyers *BULLDOG* 1360/30 (H.91) (Capt Addison Joe Baker-Cresswell) and *BROADWAY* 1190/43 (Lt T. Taylor) of the 3rd Escort Group. U–110 was boarded by Sub-Lt David E. Balme and 8 crew from HMS *BULLDOG* and the code books and an Enigma cypher machine were captured. U–110 was taken under tow by HMS *BULLDOG* but sank the following day. U–110, commanded by Kapitänleutnant Fritz–Julius Lemp (Knight's Cross 14.8.40), sank the liner *ATHENIA* on the first day of the war. Kapitänleutnant Fritz-Julius Lemp and 14 crew were lost. 32 crew were taken prisoner by HMS *AUBRIETIA*.

*MELMORE HEAD* • GRT 5319 • Built 1918
28.12.42: Torpedoed and sunk by German submarine U–225 (Leimkühler), part of the 'Spitz' (Sharp) patrol group of ten U-boats, in the Atlantic N of the Azores, in position 43.27N 27.15W while on a voyage from Newport, Mon. and Belfast Lough 18.12.42 to St John, New Brunswick, in ballast, part of convoy ONS 154 comprising 45 ships. The Master, Capt William John Leinster, 30 crew and 4 gunners were rescued by RCN corvette *SHEDIAC* 925/41 (K.110) (Lt J.E. Clayton) and landed at Ponta Delgada, Azores. 13 crew and 1 gunner were lost.

## HILL, CHARLES & SONS – BRISTOL
**Bristol City Line**

*TORONTO CITY* • GRT 2486 • Built 1925
1.7.41: Torpedoed and sunk by German submarine U–108 (Scholtz), in the Atlantic N of the Azores, in position 47.03N 30.00W while on passage from St John's, Newfoundland. The Master, Capt Edwin John Garlick, and crew of 34 were lost. *TORONTO CITY* was on government service employed as a weather observation ship in the Atlantic.

*MONTREAL CITY* ex-*PINAR DEL RIO* • GRT 3066 • Built 1920
21.12.42: Torpedoed and sunk by German submarine U–591 (Zetzsche), part of the 'Ungestüm' (Impetuous) patrol group of eleven U-boats, in the Atlantic NE of Cape Race, in position 50.23N 38.00E while on a voyage from Bristol and Milford Haven to New York, with 1800 tons of general cargo including china clay, a straggler from convoy ONS 152 comprising 15 ships. The Master, Capt Edward Roylands W. Chanter, crew of 31 and 7 gunners were lost.

*BRISTOL CITY* • GRT 2864 • Built 1920
5.5.43: Torpedoed and sunk by German submarine U–358 (Manke), part of the 'Fink' (Finch) patrol group of thirty U-boats, in the Atlantic S of Cape Farewell, in position 54.00N 43.55W while on a voyage from Bristol and Milford Haven 21.4.43 to New York, with 2500 tons of general cargo including china clay, part of convoy ONS 5 comprising 42 ships. The Master, Capt Arthur Llewellyn Webb, 26 crew and 7 gunners were rescued by HM corvette *LOOSESTRIFFE* 925/41 (K.105) (Lt H.A. Stoneham) and landed at St John's, Newfoundland. 11 crew and 4 gunners were lost. Kapitänleutnant Rolf Manke and crew of 49 were lost on 1.3.44 when U–358, part of the 'Preussen' (Prussian) patrol group of sixteen U-boats, was sunk in the Atlantic 665 miles N by W of Cape Clear, in position 45.46N 23.16W by HM frigates *AFFLECK* 1300/43 (K.462) (Cdr C. Gwinner), *GARLIES* 1085/43 (K.475) (Lt R.F. Caple) and *GORE* 1085/43 (K.481) (Lt-Cdr J.V. Reeves-Brown), part of the 1st Support Group. During the search U–358 torpedoed HMS *GOULD* 1085/43 (K.476) (Lt D.E.W. Ungoed), 480 miles NNE of the Azores, in position 45.46N 23.10W; the survivors were rescued by HMS *AFFLECK*. This was probably the longest recorded U-boat hunt lasting over 38 hours.

## HOGARTH, H. & SONS LIMITED – GLASGOW
**Hogarth Shipping Co. Ltd**

*BARON LOVAT* • GRT 3395 • Built 1926
6.6.41: Torpedoed and sunk by Italian submarine *GUGLIELMO MARCONI* (Pollina), in the Atlantic SW of Cape St Vincent, in position 35.30N 11.30W while on a voyage from the Tyne and Oban to Huelva, with a cargo of 3245 tons of coke, part of convoy OG 63 comprising 39 ships. The Master, Capt John Norman Garrett, crew of 34 and 2 gunners were rescued by HM sloop *WELLINGTON* 990/34 (L.65) (Lt-Cdr W.F.R. Segrave) and landed at Gibraltar. *GUGLIELMO MARCONI*, commanded by Lt Mario Paolo Pollina, and crew were lost in the Atlantic by an unknown cause during the latter half of November 1941.

**BARON NEWLANDS** • GRT 3386 • Built 1928
16.3.42: Torpedoed and sunk by German submarine U-68 (Merten), in the Atlantic 6 miles S of Cape Palmas, Liberia, in position 04.35N 08.32W while sailing independently on a voyage from Takoradi to Freetown, with a cargo of 4800 tons of manganese ore. The Master, Capt William Lindsay Ewing, 17 crew and 2 gunners landed at Grande Sesters and Piccaninai Cess, near Cape Palmas. 14 crew and 4 gunners were lost.

**BARON OGILVY** • GRT 3391 • Built 1926
29.9.42: Torpedoed and sunk by German submarine U-125 (Folkers), in the Atlantic SW of Cape Palmas, in position 02.30N 14.30W while sailing independently on a voyage from Rio de Janeiro 18.9.42 to the UK via Freetown, with a cargo of 5150 tons of iron ore. The Master, Capt John Steven, 28 crew and 4 gunners were rescued by Portuguese ship *MOUZINHO* 8410/07 and landed at Cape Town. 4 crew and 4 gunners were lost.

**BARON COCHRANE** • GRT 3385 • Built 1927
29.12.42: Torpedoed and sunk by German submarine U-123 (Schroeter), part of the 'Spitz' (Sharp) patrol group of ten U-boats, in the Atlantic NW of the Azores, in position 43.23N 27.14W while on a voyage from Cardiff and Belfast Lough 19.12.42 to Pernambuco and Rio de Janeiro, with a cargo of 4376 tons of coal, a straggler from convoy ONS 154 comprising 45 ships. The Master, Capt Leslie Anderson, 36 crew and 5 gunners were rescued by HM destroyer *MILNE* 1935/41 (G.14) (Capt I.M.R. Campbell) and landed at Ponta Delgada, Azores. 1 crew and 1 gunner were lost.

**BARON DECHMONT** • GRT 3675 • Built 1929
3.1.43: Torpedoed and sunk by German submarine U-507 (Schacht), in the South Atlantic NW of Cape San Roque, Brazil, in position 03.11S 38.41W while sailing independently on a voyage from Barry and Milford Haven to Pernambuco, with a cargo of 4630 tons of coal and coke. The Master, Capt Donald MacCallum, was taken prisoner and later lost when U-507 was sunk on 13.1.43. 28 crew and 8 gunners landed at Fortalaza. 7 crew were lost.

**BARON KINNAIRD** • GRT 3355 • Built 1927
11.3.43: Torpedoed and sunk by German submarine U-621 (Kruschka), part of the 'Raubgraf' (Robber Baron) patrol group of thirteen U-boats, in the Atlantic NW of Belle Ile, in position 53.00N 44.00W while on a voyage from Middlesbrough and Loch Ewe to Macoris, in ballast, a straggler from convoy ONS 169 comprising 37 ships. The Master, Capt Leslie Anderson, crew of 35 and 6 gunners were lost. Oberleutnant zur See Herman Stuckmann (Knight's Cross 11.8.44) and crew of 53 were lost on 18.8.44 when U-621 was sunk in the Bay of Biscay 65 miles W by N of the mouth of the River Gironde, in position 45.52N 02.36W by RCN destroyers *OTTAWA* 1335/35 (H.31) ex-HMS *GRIFFIN* (Cdr J.S. Douglas Prentice DSO), *KOOTENAY* 1375/32 (H.31) ex-HMS *DECOY* (A/Lt Cdr William H. Willson) and *CHAUDIERE* 1340/36 (H.99) (A/Lt Cdr C. Patrick Nixon) ex-HMS *HERO* of the 11th Escort Group.

**BARON JEDBURGH** • GRT 3656 • Built 1936
10.3.45: Torpedoed and sunk by German submarine U-532 (Junker), in the South Atlantic NE of Bahia, in position 10.02S 25.00W while sailing independently from New York to

Cape Town and Durban via Trinidad, with 7000 tons general cargo including 3000 tons of tinplate and lubricating oil. The Master, Capt Eric Alexander Brown, crew of 52 and 5 gunners were rescued: the Master and 31 crew landed at Cabedello, Brazil 22.3.45 and 25 crew were rescued on 16.3.45 by the Union Castle ship *SANDOWN CASTLE* 7607/21 and landed at Montevideo 26.3.45. 1 gunner was lost. U-532, commanded by Freggattkapitän Ottoheinrich Junker, surrendered at Liverpool on 10.5.45. U-532 sailed from Cairnryan, Loch Ryan 9.12.45 in tow of HM rescue tug *MASTERFUL* 783/42 (W.20) (Sub-Lt W. Mackenzie) ex-USN BAT.6 and was sunk by HM submarine *TANTIVY* 1090/43 (Lt P.H. May) ex-P.319 ex-P.99 in the Atlantic NW of Malin Head, in position 56.08N 10.07W, part of 'Operation Deadlight', the disposal by the Royal Navy of 116 U-boats.

## MOS

**EMPIRE CONVEYOR** ex-*GLORIA* ex-*MOUNT PENTELIKON* ex-*ILLINOIS* ex-*FARNWORTH*
GRT 5911 • Built 1917
20.6.40: Torpedoed and sunk by German submarine U-122 (Looff), in the Atlantic about 50 miles S of Barra Head, Hebrides, in position 56.16N 08.10W while sailing independently on a voyage from Montreal to Manchester, with a cargo of 7966 tons of wheat. The Master, Capt Finlay Black MacIntyre, and 37 crew were rescued by HM destroyer leader *CAMPBELL* 1800/18 (D.60) (Lt T.F. Taylor) and landed at Liverpool. 3 crew were lost. Korvettenkapitän Hans-Günther Looff and crew of 47 were lost on 21.6.40 in the Atlantic by an unknown cause. The German *GLORIA* was captured on 21.10.39 in the Atlantic SE of Iceland by HM cruiser *SHEFFIELD* 9100/36 (24) (Capt E. de Renouf CVO) with a prize crew and taken to Leith.

## MOWT

**WESTERN CHIEF** • GRT 5759 • Built 1918
14.3.41: Torpedoed and sunk by Italian submarine *EMO* (Roselli-Lorenzini), in the Atlantic about 600 miles S of Reykjavik, in position 58.52N 21.13W while on a voyage from New York to Newport, Mon. via Halifax NS, with a cargo of 7400 tons of steel, a straggler from convoy SC 24 comprising 28 ships. The Master, Capt Eric Alexander Brown, and 20 crew were rescued by US Liberty ship *VENUS* ex-*WILLIAM WILLIAMS* 7181/42 and landed at Ponta Delgada, Azores 26.3.41. 22 crew were lost. Lt Giuseppe Franco and a number of crew were lost when the *EMO* was sunk on 10.11.42 in the Mediterranean NW of Algiers, in position 36.50N 02.50E by HM armed trawler *LORD NUFFIELD* 466/37 (FY.221) (Lt S.H. Williams). The survivors were taken prisoner by HMS *LORD NUFFIELD* and landed at Algiers.

**EMPIRE PROGRESS** ex-*MUGNONE* ex-*ANDREA* ex-*ANOMIA* ex-*WAR EXPERT*
GRT 5249 • Built 1918
13.4.42: Torpedoed and sunk by German submarine U-402 (v. Forstner), in the Atlantic S of Cape Race, in position 40.29N 52.35W while on a voyage from Glasgow 28.3.42 to Tampa, Florida, in ballast, part of convoy ON 80 comprising 26 ships. The Master, Capt Thomas S. Hewitt, 7 crew and 4 gunners were lost. 32 crew and 6 gunners were rescued by Norwegian ship *OLAF FOSTENES* 2994/36 and landed at Halifax NS. The Italian *MUGNONE* was taken as a prize on 10.6.40 at Newcastle.

**SUPETAR** ex-*MARIA N. ROUSSOS* ex-*CATERINO* • GRT 3748 • Built 1909
13.6.42: Torpedoed and sunk by Japanese submarine I-16 (Yamada), in the Mozambique
Channel about 100 miles S of Beira, Portuguese East Africa, in position 21.49S 35.50E while
sailing independently on a voyage from Durban 6.6.42 to Aden, with a cargo of 5250 tons of
coal. The Master and crew of 32 were rescued. Survivors in 2 lifeboats landed at Vilanculos,
Portuguese East Africa, and other survivors were rescued by a Greek ship and landed at Beira
16.6.42. Lt Cdr K. Yamada and crew were lost on 19.5.44 when I-16 was sunk in the Pacific
200 miles E of Buka Island, Solomon Islands, in position 05.10S 158.10E by US destroyer
escort *ENGLAND* 1400/43 (DE-635) (Lt-Cdr Walton B. Pendleton).

**FORT CHILCOTIN** • GRT 7133 • Built 1942
24.7.43: Torpedoed and sunk by German submarine U-172 (Emmermann), in the South
Atlantic 420 miles ESE of Bahia, in position 15.03S 32.35W while sailing independently
on a voyage from Rio de Janeiro 19.7.43 to the UK via Freetown, with a cargo of 9103
tons of rock crystal and iron ore, dispersed from convoy JT 2. The Master, Capt John
Kerr, 41 crew and 11 gunners were rescued on 29.7.43 by the Argentinian tanker
*TACITO* 8331/24 and landed at Rio de Janeiro 1.8.43. 4 crew were lost. Kapitänleutnant
Carl Emmermann was awarded the Knight's Cross (27.11.42) with Oak Leaves (4.7.43).
U-172 commanded by Oberleutnant zur See Hermann Hoffmann was sunk on 12.12.43
in the Atlantic 600 miles NNW of the Cape Verde Islands, in position 26.19N 29.58W
by an Avenger, pilot Lt Elisha C. Gaylord of US Navy Composite Squadron VC-19 from
US escort carrier *BOGUE* 9800/42 (CVE-9) (Cdr Joseph B. Dunn), US four-stack
destroyers *GEORGE E. BADGER* 1090/18 (DD-126) (Lt E.M. Higgins), *DUPONT*
1090/18 (DD-152) (Cdr J.G. Marshall), *CLEMSON* 1190/18 (DD-186) (Lt-Cdr E.W.
Yancey) and *OSMOND INGRAM* 1190/19 (DD-255) (Lt-Cdr R.F. Miller). The U-boat
commander and 45 crew were taken prisoner by the US destroyers and landed at
Norfolk, Virginia. 13 crew were lost.

**ANADYR** ex-*REDSEA* • GRT 5277 • Built 1930
6.5.44: Torpedoed and sunk by German submarine U-129 (v. Harpe), in the South Atlantic
about 600 miles SSE of Recife, Brazil, in position 10.55S 27.30W, while sailing
independently on a voyage from New York to Cape Town and Port Elizabeth via Trinidad,
with 7791 tons of general cargo including government stores, dispersed from convoy TJ 30.
The Master, Capt J. Bouteiller, and 7 survivors landed at Porto de Galhinas near Recife and
39 survivors landed 20 miles S of Recife. 4 crew and 2 gunners were lost. U-129,
commanded by Oberleutnant zur See Richard von Harpe, was scuttled at Lorient on
19.8.44.

## Kelvin Shipping Co. Ltd

**BARON LOUDOUN** • GRT 3164 • Built 1925
19.6.40: Torpedoed and sunk by German submarine U-48 (Rösing), in the Atlantic WNW
of Cape Oretgal, in position 45.00N 11.21W while on a voyage from Bona to Barrow, with a
cargo of 5050 tons of iron ore, part of convoy HGF 34 comprising 21 ships. The Master,
Capt Joseph Henderson Johnson, and 29 crew were rescued by HM sloop *SCARBOROUGH*
1045/30 (L.25) (Cdr C.T. Addis) and landed at Liverpool. 3 crew were lost.

**BARON BLYTHSWOOD** • GRT 3668 • Built 1929
21.9.40: Torpedoed and sunk by German submarine U-99 (Kretschmer), in the Atlantic S of Iceland, in position 56.00N 23.00W while on a voyage from Wabana, Conception Bay, to Port Talbot via Halifax NS, with a cargo of iron ore, part of convoy HX 72 comprising 47 ships. The Master, Capt John Maclarly Robertson Davies, and crew of 33 were lost. The crew of U-99 later stated that the *BARON BLYTHSWOOD* sank in 40 seconds.

**BARON NAIRN** • GRT 3164 • Built 1925
7.6.41: Torpedoed and sunk by German submarine U-108 (Scholtze), part of the 'West' patrol group of fifteen U-boats, in the Atlantic W of Cape Race, in position 47.36N 39.02W while sailing independently on a voyage from Barrow to Nuevitas, Cuba, in ballast, dispersed on 2.6.41 from convoy OB 328 comprising 26 ships. The Master, Capt John Kerr, and 20 crew were rescued after 19 days in an open boat and landed at Galway, Co. Galway 27.6.41; 18 crew were rescued by RCN corvette *CHAMBLY* 925/40 (K.116) (Cdr J.D. Prentice) and landed at St John's, Newfoundland. 1 crew was lost. Capt J. Kerr was awarded the Lloyd's War Medal for bravery at sea.

**BARON PENTLAND** • GRT 3410 • Built 1927
10.9.41: Torpedoed and damaged by German submarine U-652 (Fraatz), part of the 'Markgraf' patrol group of fourteen U-boats, in the Atlantic NE of Cape Farewell, in position 61.15N 41.05W, and later sunk on 19.9.41 by German submarine U-372 (Neuman), while on a voyage from St John, New Brunswick, to Hartlepool via Sydney CB 30.8.41, with a cargo of 1512 standards of timber, a straggler from convoy SC 42 comprising 65 ships. The Master, Capt Alexander Bleasby Campbell, 30 crew and 8 gunners were rescued by RCN corvette *ORILLA* 925/40 (K.119) (Lt-Cdr W. Edward S. Briggs) and landed at Reykjavik, part of the 24th Escort Group. 2 crew were lost.

**BARON KELVIN** ex-*WAR MAPLE* • GRT 3081 • Built 1924
19.10.41: Torpedoed and sunk by German submarine U-206 (Opitz), in the Strait of Gibraltar 14 miles 100° from Tarifa, Spain, while sailing independently on a voyage from Lisbon to Gibraltar and Melilla, in ballast. The Master, Capt William Lindsay Ewing, 12 crew and 2 gunners were rescued by Spanish ship *UROLA* 3675/98 and landed at Gibraltar and 1 crew by HM destroyer leader *DUNCAN* 1400/32 (D.99) (Lt-Cdr A.N. Rowell) also landed at Gibraltar. 19 crew and 7 gunners were lost. Kapitänleutnant Herbert Opitz and crew of 45 were lost when U-206 was sunk in the British minefield 'Beech' on 29.11.41 in the Bay of Biscay SW of St Nazaire, in position 47.05N 02.40W.

**BARON ERSKINE** • GRT 3657 • Built 1930
6.1.42: Torpedoed and sunk by German submarine U-701 (Degen), in the Atlantic N of Rockall, in position 59.15N 18.30W, while on a voyage from Tampa to Loch Ewe and Garston, with a cargo of phosphates, a straggler from convoy SC 62 comprising 28 ships. The Master, Capt George Sharp Cumming, and crew of 39 were lost. U-701, commanded by Kapitänleutnant Horst Degen, was sunk on 7.7.42 by Hudson 9-29, pilot Lt Harry J. Kane of 396th Medium Bombardment Squadron, USAAF, based at Cherry Point, North Carolina, in the Atlantic W of Cape Hatteras, in position 34.50N 74.55W. The U-boat commander and 6 crew were found on 9.7.42 by US Navy airship K-8 and taken prisoner by a US Coastguard

flying boat and landed at Norfolk, Virginia. 36 crew were lost. This was the first sinking of a U-boat by the USAAF.

**BARON VERNON** • GRT 3642 • Built 1929
30.10.42: Torpedoed and sunk by German submarine U-604 (Höltring), part of the 'Streitaxt' (Battleaxe) patrol group of eight U-boats, in the Atlantic N of Madeira, in position 36.06N 16.59W while on a voyage from Pepel to Belfast Lough and Port Talbot via Freetown 16.10.42, with a cargo of 5500 tons of iron ore, part of convoy SL 125 comprising 40 ships. The Master, Capt Peter Liston, crew of 42 and 6 gunners were rescued by Hogarth's ship *BARON ELGIN* 3942/33 and landed at Madeira.

**BARON SEMPLE** • GRT 4573 • Built 1939
2.11.43: Torpedoed and sunk by German submarine U-848 (Rollman), in the South Atlantic NW of Ascension Island, in position 05.00S 21.00W while sailing independently on a voyage from Rio de Janeiro to the UK via Freetown, with a cargo of iron ore. The Master, Capt Philip Jarvis Carnie, and crew of 61 were lost. Korvettenkapitän Wilhelm Rollmann (Knight's Cross 31.7.40) and crew of 62 were lost when U-848 was sunk on 5.11.43 in the South Atlantic 275 miles WSW of Ascension Island, in position 10.09S 18.00W by three Liberators, pilots Lt Charles A. Baldwin, Lt William R. Ford and Lt William E. Hill of US Navy Bombing Squadron VB-107 and three North American B-25 Mitchell aircraft of the 1st Composite Squadron USAAF based at Ascension Island.

## HOLT, ALFRED & COMPANY (BLUE FUNNEL LINE) – LIVERPOOL
### China Mutual Steam Navigation Co.

**PATROCLUS** • GRT 11314 • Built 1923
4.11.40: Torpedoed and sunk by German submarine U-99 (Kretschmer), in the Atlantic SW of Bloody Foreland, in position 53.43N 14.41W. *PATROCLUS* was lost while employed by the Admiralty as an Armed Merchant Cruiser (Capt G.C. Wynter) escorting convoy HX 83 comprising 37 ships. The survivors were rescued by HM destroyer *BEAGLE* 1360/30 (H.30) (Lt C.R.H. Wright) and landed at Greenock. 76 officers and ratings were lost.

**MEMNON** • GRT 7506 • Built 1931
11.3.41: Torpedoed and sunk by German submarine U-106 (Oesten), in the Atlantic 200 miles W of Cape Blanco, French West Africa, in position 20.41N 21.00W while on government service sailing independently on a voyage from Port Pirie, South Australia 28.1.41 to Avonmouth and Swansea via Freetown, with 6 RAF personnel and 7629 tons of general cargo including wheat and zinc concentrates. The Master, Capt John Parry Williams, and 21 survivors landed at Yoff near Dakar 21.3.41 from No. 1 boat and were detained by the Vichy French authorities, were later released and went to Bathurst. The Chief Officer R.J. McCarth and 40 survivors landed at Bathurst 24.3.41 from No. 5 boat. 1 gunner and the RAF personnel were taken prisoner. 3 crew were lost.

**IXION** • GRT 10229 • Built 1912
7.5.41: Torpedoed and sunk by German submarine U-94 (Kuppish), in the North Atlantic 200 miles SW of Reykjavik, in position 61.29N 22.40W while on a voyage from Glasgow to

New York, with 2900 tons of general cargo including whisky, part of convoy OB 318 comprising 38 ships. The Master, Capt Walter Francis Dark, and 18 crew were rescued by HM corvette *MARIGOLD* 925/40 (K.87) (Lt W.S. Macdonald) and landed at Greenock; 68 crew and 9 gunners by British ship *NAILSEA MOOR* 4926/37 and landed at Sydney CB.

### *ULYSSES* • GRT 14499 • Built 1913

11.4.42: Torpedoed and sunk by German submarine U-160 (Lassen), part of 'Operation Paukenschlag' (Drumbeat), the fourth wave of eleven U-boats, in the Atlantic 45 miles S of Cape Hatteras, North Carolina, in position 34.23N 75.35W while sailing independently on a voyage from Sydney NSW to Liverpool via Panama and Halifax NS, with 95 passengers and 9544 tons general cargo including 4000 tons of pig iron. The Master, Capt James Appleton Russell, crew of 189, 5 gunners and passengers were rescued by US four-stack destroyer *MANLEY* 1190/17 (DD.74) and landed at Charleston, South Carolina.

### *STENTOR* • GRT 6634 • Built 1926

27.10.42: Torpedoed and sunk by German submarine U-509 (Witte), part of the 'Streitaxt' (Battleaxe) patrol group of eight U-boats, in the Atlantic NW of the Canary Islands, in position 29.13N 20.53W while on a voyage from Lagos and Freetown to Liverpool, with 125 passengers including 26 army personnel, 11 nursing sisters and 6 naval staff, with about 6000 tons of West African produce, part of convoy SL 125 comprising 40 ships. The Master, Capt William Williams, Vice-Commodore Capt R.H. Garstin RNR, 21 crew, 3 army personnel, 4 nursing sisters and 16 passengers were lost. 93 crew, 7 gunners, 6 naval staff, 101 passengers including the remaining nurses and army personnel were rescued by HM corvette *WOODRUFF* 925/41 (K.53) (Lt-Cdr F.H. Gray); 100 survivors were transferred to HM destroyer *RAMSAY* 1190/19 (G.60) (Lt-Cdr R.B. Stannard VC) ex-USN four-stack *MEADE* and landed at Liverpool 6.11.42. The survivors on HMS *WOODRUFF* landed at Milford Haven.

### *MARON* • GRT 6487 • Built 1930

13.11.42: Torpedoed and sunk by German submarine U-81 (Guggenberger), in the Mediterranean NW of Oran, Algeria, in position 36.27N 00.55W while in convoy on government service on a voyage from Algiers 12.11.42 to Gibraltar, in ballast. The Master, Capt David Hey, crew of 67 and 13 gunners were rescued by HM corvette *MARIGOLD* 925/40 (K.87) (Lt J.A.S. Halcrew) and landed at Gibraltar. Kapitänleutnant Friedrich Guggenberger was awarded the Knight's Cross (10.12.41) with Oak Leaves (8.1.43).

### *PERSEUS* • GRT 10286 • Built 1923

16.1.44: Torpedoed and sunk by Japanese submarine I-165 (Shimizu), in the Bay of Bengal NE of Pondicherry, in position 12.00N 80.14E while sailing independently on a voyage from Liverpool to Trincomalee and Calcutta, with a cargo of 2800 tons of government stores including 500 tons of munitions. The Master, Capt George Gordon Rundle, crew of 107 and 8 gunners were rescued by HM trawler *HOXA* 545/41 (T.16) (Lt P.A. Johnson) and three HM motor torpedo boats and landed at Madras.

### *TROILUS* • GRT 7422 • Built 1921

1.9.44: Torpedoed and sunk by German submarine U-859 (Jebsen), in the Arabian Sea, 300 miles NE of Socotra Island, in position 14.10N 61.04E while sailing independently from

Colombo to Aden and the UK, with 18 passengers and a cargo of 2700 tons of coconut oil, 2300 tons of tea, and 2000 tons of copra. The Master, Capt Evan Williams, 66 crew, 12 gunners and 16 passengers were rescued by HM frigates *NADDER* 1370/43 (K.392) (Lt-Cdr P.E. Kitto) and *TAFF* 1370/43 (K.367) (Cdr G.A.G. Ormsby DSO) and landed at Aden 10.9.44. 4 crew and 2 passengers were lost. U–859, commanded by Kapitänleutnant Johann Jebsen, was lost on 23.9.44 in the Strait of Malacca NE of Pulo Penang, Malaya, in position 05.46N 100.04E, torpedoed by HM submarine *TRENCHANT* 1090/43 (P.331) (Lt-Cdr Arthur R. Hezlet). The U–boat commander and 46 crew were lost. 18 crew were saved: 8 were rescued by the Japanese and 10 were taken prisoner by HMS *TRENCHANT* and landed at Trincomalee.

**Glen Line**

***GLENSHIEL*** • GRT 9415 • Built 1924
3.4.42: Torpedoed and sunk by gunfire by Japanese submarine I-7 (Nagi), in the Indian Ocean E of Addu Atoll, Maldive Islands, in position 00.48S 78.33E while sailing independently on a voyage from Bombay and Karachi 24.3.42 to Fremantle, with 12 passengers and 1000 tons of general cargo. The Master, Capt Ramsay Brown DSC, crew of 79 and passengers were rescued by HM destroyer *FORTUNE* 1350/30 (H.70) (Lt-Cdr R.D.H.S. Pankhurst) and landed at Colombo. Lt-Cdr Katsuhiko Nagui and crew were lost on 22.6.43 when I-7 was sunk in the Bering Sea, SE of Kiska Island, Aleutian Islands, in position 51.55N 177.36E by US destroyer *MONAGHAN* 1395/35 (DD.354) (Lt-Cdr P.H. Horns).

**NSM Oceaan – Dutch flag**

***LAERTES*** • GRT 5868 • Built 1919
3.5.42: Torpedoed and sunk by German submarine U-109 (Bleichrodt), in the Atlantic SE of Cape Canaveral, Florida, in position 28.21N 80.23W while sailing independently on a voyage from New York and Hampton Roads to Cape Town and Bombay, with 5230 tons of general cargo including military stores. The Master, Capt Casparos Johannes van Heel, and 47 crew landed at Cape Canaveral, Florida. 18 crew were lost.

***POLYPHEMUS*** • GRT 6269 • Built 1930
27.5.42: Torpedoed and sunk by German submarine U-578 (Rehwinkel), in the Atlantic 340 miles N of Bermuda, in position 38.12N 63.22W while sailing independently on a voyage from Sydney NSW 16.4.42 to Liverpool via Panama and Halifax NS, with a cargo of 5936 tons of wheat and 790 tons of wool. The Master, Capt C. Koningstein, 45 crew and 14 survivors from Norwegian tanker *NORLAND* 8134/41 (Capt Eugen Christoffersen) sunk on 20.5.42 by U-108 (Scholtz) were rescued by unknown ships and landed at New Bedford and Nantucket Island, Connecticut. 15 Chinese crew were lost. Korvettenkapitän Ernst-August Rehwinkel and crew of 48 were lost on 10.8.42 when U-578 was sunk in the Atlantic 180 miles W by N of Cape Ortegal, in position 45.59N 07.44W by Wellington 'H' HF922, pilot F/O Josef Nyvlt of No. 311 (Czech) Squadron RAF, based at Talbenny, Pembrokeshire, part of 19 Group.

***POLYDORUS*** • GRT 6256 • Built 1924
27.11.42: Torpedoed and sunk by German submarine U-176 (Dierksen), in the Atlantic NW of Freetown, in position 09.01N 25.38W while sailing independently on a voyage from

Liverpool 8.11.42 to Freetown, with 2 passengers and a cargo of 8657 tons of military stores, dispersed from convoy ON 145 comprising 35 ships. The Master, Capt H. Bronwer, 66 crew, 11 gunners and passengers were rescued by Spanish ship *EOLO* 4409/29 (Capt Urgelles) and landed at Las Palmas 5.12.42. 1 crew was lost. The *POLYDOROS* was sunk after a chase lasting 50 hours, the longest recorded pursuit by a U-boat in the Second World War.

## Ocean SS Co

*PROTESILAUS* • GRT 9547 • Built 1910
21.1.40: Struck a mine laid on 13.11.40 by German submarine U-28 (Kuhnke) and was damaged in the Bristol Channel SW of Swansea, in position 51.31N 04.04W while on a voyage from Liverpool to Barry, in ballast. The Master, Capt Alfred Henry Dennistoun Shand, and crew were rescued by HM trawler *PARAMOUNT* 95/11 (FY.954) (Skipper C.E. Blowers) and landed at Swansea. Beached at Swansea Bay, later refloated and while being towed by British tug *EMPIRE HENCHMAN* 243/30 and French tug *ABEILLE* 22 433/19 to Scapa Flow for use as a blockship, she sprung a leak and was sunk on 13.9.40 by gunfire about 5 miles from Skerryvore Lighthouse, Argyllshire.

*PYRRHUS* • GRT 7615 • Built 1914
17.2.40: Torpedoed and sunk by German submarine U-37 (Hartmann), in the Atlantic NW of Cape Finisterre, in position 44.02N 10.18W while sailing independently on a voyage from Glasgow and Liverpool to Manila, with about 4000 tons general cargo including whisky, dispersed from convoy OG 18 comprising comprising 44 ships. The Master, Capt William Thomas Spencer, Vice-Commodore Rear-Admiral R.A. Hamilton RN, 5 naval staff and 72 crew were rescued by British ships *USKSIDE* 2706/37 and *SINNINGTON COURT* 6910/28 and landed at Gibraltar. 8 crew were lost.

*TITAN* • GRT 9035 • Built 1906
4.9.40: Torpedoed and sunk by German submarine U-47 (Prien), in the Atlantic 80 miles SW of Rockall, in position 58.14N 15.50W while on a voyage from London to Sydney NSW, in ballast, part of convoy OA 207 comprising 15 ships. The Master, Capt Walter Francis Dark, and 89 crew were rescued by HMCS destroyer *ST LAURENT* 1375/31 (H.83) ex-HMS *CYGNET* (Cdr H.G. DeWolf) and landed at Rosyth 9.9.40. 6 crew were lost. Capt W.F. Dark was awarded the Lloyd's War Medal for bravery at sea.

*EURYMEDON* • GRT 6223 • Built 1924
25.9.40: Torpedoed and sunk by German submarine U-29 (Schuhart), in the Atlantic 366 miles W of Achill Head, in position 53.34N 20.23W while sailing independently on a voyage from Liverpool 21.2.40 to Cape Town and Java, with 31 passengers and 3000 tons of general cargo, dispersed from convoy OB 217 comprising 38 ships. The Master, Capt John Faulkner Webster, 41 crew and 22 passengers were rescued by RCN destroyer *OTTAWA* 1375/31 (H.60) ex-HMS *CRUSADER* (Cdr E.R. Mainguy) and landed at Greenock 27.9.40. 20 crew and 9 passengers were lost. Capt J.F. Webster was awarded the Lloyd's War Medal for bravery at sea. Korvettenkapitän Otto Schuhart was awarded the Knight's Cross (16.5.40). U-29 sank HM aircraft carrier *COURAGEOUS* 22500/16 (50) on 19.9.40 in the Atlantic SW of Ireland, in position 50.10N 14-45W, with the loss of Capt W.T. Makeig-Jones and 518 officers and

ratings. 741 survivors were saved by US ship *COLLINGSWORTH* 5101/20 and Dutch liner *VEENDAM* 15450/23. U-29, commanded by Oberleutnant zur See Ulrich-Philipp Graf von zu Arco-Zinneberg, was scuttled at Kupfermühlen Bay in the Baltic on 4.5.45.

**EUMAEUS** • GRT 7472 • Built 1921
14.1.41: Torpedoed and sunk by gunfire by Italian submarine *COMMANDANTE CAPPELLINI* (Todaro), in the Atlantic 120 miles WNW of Freetown, in position 08.55N 15.03W while sailing independently on a voyage from Liverpool to Singapore and Shanghai, with 400 service personnel and general cargo. The Master, Capt John E. Watson, 83 crew and 247 service personnel were rescued by HM trawlers *BENGALI* 455/37 (FY.165) (Lt-Cdr E.E. Barnes) and *SPANIARD* 455/37 (FY.144) (Lt-Cdr F.J. Webster) and landed at Freetown. 18 crew, 15 gunners and 153 service personnel were lost. Capt J.E. Watson was awarded the Lloyd's War Medal for bravery at sea.

**CALCHAS** • GRT 10304 • Built 1921
21.4.41: Torpedoed and sunk by German submarine U-107 (Hessler), in the Atlantic 550 miles N of the Cape Verde Islands, in position 23.50N 27.00W while sailing independently on a voyage from Sydney NSW to Liverpool via Freetown, with 9 passengers and 9000 tons of general cargo including wheat, butter, flour and steel billets. The Master, Capt William Richard Fielding Holden, 21 crew, 1 gunner and 1 passenger were lost. 33 survivors landed at Sal Maria Island, Cape Verde Islands 4.5.41, 23 survivors landed at Boavista Island, Cape Verde Islands and 33 survivors landed at St Louis, Senegal, after sailing 650 miles in 16 days in No. 5 lifeboat.

**CYCLOPS** • GRT 8998 • Built 1906
12.1.42: Torpedoed and sunk by German submarine U-123 (Hardegen), part of 'Operation Paukenschlag' (Drumbeat), the first wave of five U-boats, in the Atlantic 125 miles SE of Cape Sable, Nova Scotia, in position 41.51N 63.48W while sailing independently on a voyage from Hong Kong, Auckland and Cristobal 2.1.42 to the UK via Halifax NS, with 78 passengers, 1 DBS and 6905 tons general cargo. The Master, Capt Leslie Webber Kersley, 55 crew, 6 gunners, 1 DBS and 32 passengers were rescued by RCN minesweeper *RED DEER* 672/41 (J.255) (Lt A. Moorhouse) and landed at Halifax, Nova Scotia. 40 crew, 46 passengers and 1 gunner were lost.

**HELENUS** • GRT 7555 • Built 1913
3.3.42: Torpedoed and sunk by German submarine U-68 (Merten), in the Atlantic about 200 miles S of Freetown, in position 06.01N 12.02W while sailing independently on a voyage from Penang, Malaya and Cape Town 20.2.42 to Liverpool via Freetown, with 2 passengers and general cargo including 4248 tons of rubber and 1350 tons of copper. The Master, Capt Philip Walter Savery, 73 crew, 1 gunner and 1 passenger were rescued by British ship *BEACONSFIELD* 4635/38 and landed at Freetown 5.3.42. 1 crew, 4 gunners and 1 passenger were lost.

**PEISANDER** • GRT 6225 • Built 1925
17.5.42: Torpedoed and sunk by German submarine U-653 (Feiler), in the Atlantic about 350 miles SE of Nantucket Island, in position 37.24N 65.38W while sailing independently

on a voyage from Newcastle NSW to Liverpool via Panama, with a cargo of 6590 tons of wheat, 97 tons of tungsten and wool. The Master, Capt Angus Shaw, crew of 57 and 3 gunners were rescued by US patrol boat *GENERAL GREENE* 220/27 (WPC.140) and landed at Newport, Rhode Island. Oberleutnant zur See Hans–Albrecht Kandler and crew of 50 were lost on 15.3.44 when U-653 was sunk in the Atlantic 500 miles W by N of Cape Clear, in position 53.46N 24,35W by Swordfish 'A', pilot Sub-Lt P. Cumberland of No. 825 Squadron FAA from HM escort carrier *VINDEX* 13455/43 (D.15) (Capt H.T.T. Bayliss), and HM sloops *STARLING* 1350/42 (U.66) (Capt Frederic John J. Walker) and *WILD GOOSE* 1300/42 (U.45) (Lt-Cdr R.W. Trethewey) of Support Group 2.

**MENTOR** • GRT 7585 • Built 1914
28.5.42: Torpedoed and sunk by German submarine U-106 (Rasch), in the Gulf of Mexico N of Cabo Catoche, Mexico, in position 24.11N 87.02W while sailing independently on a voyage from New Orleans 26.5.42 to Bombay via Cape Town, with 8600 tons of general cargo, including government stores and 400 tons of sulphur. The Master, Capt Alexander Pope, 74 crew and 7 gunners were rescued after three days by Holt's ship *ANTILOCHUS* 8954/06 and landed at Key West, Florida. The 4th Engineer and 3 crew were lost.

**MEDON** • GRT 5915 • Built 1923
10.8.42: Torpedoed and sunk by gunfire by Italian submarine *REGINALDO GIULIANI* (Bruno), in the Atlantic NE of Para, in position 09.26N 38.28W while sailing independently on a voyage from Port Louis, Mauritius, to New York via Cape Town 24.7.42 and Trinidad, in ballast. The Master, Capt Samuel Roland Evans, and 14 survivors were rescued by Panamanian ship *ROSEMONT* 4956/38 and landed at Cape Town; the Chief Officer and 12 survivors by Portuguese ship *LUSO* 6207/12 (Capt Botto) and landed at Buenos Aires 26.8.42; the 2nd Officer and 15 survivors on 13.9.42 by British ship *REEDPOOL* 4838/24. A week later this ship was sunk by German submarine U-515 (Henke) and the survivors from the *MEDON* were rescued by the schooner *MILLIE M. MASHER* (Capt F. Barnes) and landed at Georgetown, British Guinea 14.9.42. 21 survivors were rescued by Norwegian ship *TAMERLANE* 6778/36 (Capt Krafft) and landed at New York.

**MYRMIDON** • GRT 6663 • Built 1930
5.9.42: Torpedoed and sunk by German submarine U-506 (Würdemann), in the Atlantic SE of Cape Palmas, in position 00.45N 06.27W while on a voyage from Glasgow to Cape Town, Bombay and Colombo via Freetown 1.9.42, with 129 passengers and 4000 tons general cargo including government stores and explosives, escorted by HM destroyer *BRILLIANT* 1360/30 (H.84) (Lt-Cdr A.G. Poe) and HM boom carrier *FERNMOOR* 4972/36 (Z.208) (Lt-Cdr C.J. Linder). The Master, Capt Alexander Mann Caird, crew of 105, 10 gunners and passengers were rescued by HMS *BRILLIANT* and landed at Pointe Noire, French Congo.

**AGAPENOR** • GRT 7587 • Built 1914
11.10.42: Torpedoed and sunk by German submarine U-87 (Berger), in the Atlantic 180 miles S of Freetown, in position 06.53N 15.23W while sailing independently on a voyage from Karachi and Cape Town 29.9.42 to the UK via Freetown, with 6500 tons general cargo and 750 tons of copper. The Master, Capt Philip William Savery, 73 crew and 14 gunners were rescued by HM corvette *PETUNIA* 925/40 (K.79) (Lt-Cdr J.M. Rayner), landed at

Freetown, transferred to Union Castle liner *CARNARVON CASTLE* 20122/26 which sailed 15.10.42 for Glasgow. 7 crew were lost. Kapitänleutnant Joachim Berger and crew of 48 were lost while shadowing convoy KMS 10 comprising 34 ships on 4.3.43 when U-87 was sunk in the Atlantic 200 miles W of Oporto, in position 41.36N 13.31W by RCN destroyer *ST CROIX* 1190/19 (I.81) (Lt-Cdr A.H. Dobson DSC HMCSR) ex-USN four-stack *McCOOK* and RCN corvette *SHEDIAC* 925/41 (K.110) (Lt J.E. Clayton).

**RHEXENOR** • GRT 7957 • Built 1922
3.2.43: Torpedoed and sunk by gunfire by German submarine U-217 (Reichenbach–Klinke), in the Atlantic SE of Bermuda, in position 24.59N 43.37W while sailing independently on a voyage from Takoradi and Freetown 26.1.43 to St John, New Brunswick, with 4 passengers and 7000 tons of cocoa beans. The Master, Capt Leonard Eccles, and 19 survivors reached Guadeloupe in No. 1 boat after 19 days, Chief Officer M.J. Case and 19 survivors after 19 days landed 60 miles N of St John's, Antigua in No. 4 boat, and 2nd Mate W.M. Thomas and 17 survivors were rescued after 21 days by HM armed yacht *CONQUEROR* 900/11 (Lt-Cdr E.M. McCausland) and landed at St Thomas, Virgin Islands. 3rd Mate S.A.G. Cook and 10 survivors landed on Jost van Dyke Island in the Tobago group after 20 days in the No. 5 boat. The 4th Mate C.W.G. Allen was taken prisoner by U-217, landed at Brest on 23.2.43 and was taken to Milag Nord. 3 crew were lost. Kapitänleutnant Kurt Reichenbach-Klinke and crew of 49 were lost while shadowing convoy UGS 9 comprising 76 ships on 5.6.43 when U-217, part of the 'Trutz 3' (Defiant) patrol group of five U-boats, was sunk in the Atlantic 1300 miles WSW of the Azores, in position 30.18N 42.50W by an Avenger, pilot Lt Alexander C. McAuslan and a Wildcat, pilot Ensign Richard S. Rogers of US Navy Composite Squadron VC-9 from US escort carrier *BOGUE* 9800/42 (CVE-9) (Cdr G.E. Short).

**DOLIUS** • GRT 5507 • Built 1924
5.5.43: Torpedoed and sunk by German submarine U-638 (Staudinger), part of the 'Fink' (Finch) patrol group of thirty U-boats, in the Atlantic NE of Belle Ile, in position 54.00N 43.35W while on a voyage from Avonmouth to New York, in ballast, part of convoy ONS 5 comprising 42 ships. The Master, Capt Gilbert Robert Cheetham, 57 crew and 8 gunners were rescued by HM corvette *SUNFLOWER* 925/40 (K.41) (Lt J. Plomer RCNVR) and landed at St John's, Newfoundland. 3 crew and 1 gunner were lost. Kapitänleutnant Oskar Staudinger and crew of 43 were lost on the same day when U-638 was sunk in the Atlantic about 400 miles NE of Cape Race, in position 54.12N 44.05W by HMS *SUNFLOWER.* Oberleutnant zur See Werner Happe and crew of 54 were lost on 5.5.43 when U-192, part of the 'Fink' patrol group, was sunk while attacking convoy ONS 5 in the Atlantic about 400 miles NE of Cape Race, in position 53.06N 45.02W by HM corvette *PINK* 925/42 (K.137) (Lt R. Atkinson). Kapitänleutnant Herbert Neckel and crew of 53 were lost on 6.5.43 when U-531, also part of the 'Fink' patrol group, was damaged while attacking convoy ONS 5 in the Atlantic about 400 miles NE of Cape Race, in position 52.31N 44.40W by HM corvette *SNOWFLAKE* 925/41 (K.211) ex-HMS *ZENOBIA* (Lt-Cdr Harold G. Chesterman) and later sunk by HM destroyer *VIDETTE* 1090/18 (D.48) (Lt R. Hart). This was the first U-boat to be destroyed by a 'Hedgehog', a battery of twenty-four projectiles. U-209, commanded by Kapitänleutnant Heinrich Brodd,a and crew of 45 were lost in the Atlantic sometime after 6.5.43 while pursuing convoy ONS 5. On 4.5.43 she was badly damaged by depth charges by

Canso 'W' pilot S/Ldr B.H. Moffitt of No. 5 (RCAF) Squadron, based at Gander, Newfoundland, in the Atlantic 270 miles S of Cape Farewell, in position 55.50N 43.30W.

*CENTAUR* • GRT 3222 • Built 1921
14.5.43: Torpedoed and sunk by Japanese submarine I-177 (Nakagawa), in the Pacific Ocean E of Brisbane, in position 21.17S 154.05E while on a voyage from Sydney NSW 12.5.43 to Cairns, Queensland and New Guinea, with 257 medical personnel of the 2/12th Field Ambulance including 65 doctors and nurses. The Master, Capt George Alexander Murray, 44 crew and 223 service personnel, 18 doctors and 12 nurses were lost. 29 crew and 34 medical personnel were rescued by US destroyer *MUGFORD* 1500/36 (DD.389) (Lt-Cdr H.J. Corey USN) and landed at Brisbane 15.5.43. The *CENTAUR* caught fire and sank within two or three minutes. The ship was on loan to the Australian government and converted into a Hospital Ship, and when sunk she was fully illuminated and painted in Red Cross colours. The commander of the submarine, Lt Hiroshi Nakagawa, was to meet his fate when in command of Japanese submarine RO-109 which was sunk on 25.4.45 by US high speed transport *HORACE A. BASS* 1020/44 (APD.124) E of Formosa, in position 21.58N 129.35E. Lt Katsuji Watanabe and crew were lost on 19.11.44 when I-177 was sunk in the Pacific 35 miles NNW of Angaur, Palau Islands, in position 08.07N 134.16E by US destroyer escorts *CONKLIN* 1350/44 (DE-439) (Lt-Cdr E.L. McGibbon USNR) and *McCOY REYNOLDS* 1350/44 (DE-440) (Lt-Cdr E.K. Winn USNR). The USS *MUGFORD* was used by the US government as a target ship for the testing of nuclear weapons at Bikini Atoll, Marshall Islands, in July 1946 and was sunk in March 1948.

*PHEMIUS* • GRT 7406 • Built 1921
20.12.43: Torpedoed and sunk by German submarine U-515 (Henke), in the Atlantic 30 miles S of Accra, Gold Coast, in position 05.01N 00.47E while sailing independently on a voyage from Liverpool and Glasgow to Takoradi 19.12.43, Lagos and Beira, with 33 passengers and 4544 tons of government stores and generals including mail. The Master, Capt Thomas Arthur Kent OBE, 68 crew, 10 gunners and 12 passengers were rescued by Free French corvette *COMMANDANT DROGOU* 925/41 ex-HMS *CHRYSANTHEMUM* (K.195) and landed at Takoradi 20.12.43. 4 crew, 1 gunner and 21 passengers were lost.

**MOWT**

*MENDOZA* • GRT 8233 • Built 1919
1.11.42: Torpedoed and sunk by German submarine U-178 (Ibbeken), in the Indian Ocean 70 miles ENE of The Bluff, near Durban, in position 29.13S 32.13E while sailing independently on government service on a voyage from Mombasa 26.10.42 to Durban, with 253 military including naval personnel and 287 bags of mail. The Master, Capt Basil T. Batho, 19 crew, 3 gunners and 3 passengers were lost. 127 crew, 3 gunners and 250 passengers were rescued by the SAN whaler *NIGEL* ex-*UNI II* 250/30 (T.40) and US ship *CAPE ALAVA* 6751/41 and landed at Durban.

*PETER MAERSK* • GRT 5476 • Built 1932
7.12.42: Torpedoed and sunk by German submarine U-185 (Maus), part of the 'Westwall' patrol group of sixteen U-boats, in the Atlantic W of the Azores, in position 39.47N 41.00W

while sailing independently on a voyage from Liverpool to Saldanha Bay, South Africa, Aden and Alexandria via Cape Town, with 2 passengers and 5244 tons of government stores and general cargo. The Master, Capt Otto Aggerholm, crew of 56, 8 gunners and passengers were lost.

**VILLE DE ROUEN** • GRT 5083 • Built 1919
28.12.42: Torpedoed and damaged by German submarine U-591 (Zetzsche), part of the 'Ungestüm' (Impetuous) patrol group of eleven U-boats, given the *coup de grâce* on 29.12.42 by German submarine U-662 (Müller), part of the same patrol group in the Atlantic W of Cape Finisterre, in position 43.25N 27.15W while on a voyage from Glasgow 18.12.42 to Ascension Island and Beira, with 5500 tons of general cargo, part of convoy ONS 154 comprising 45 ships. The Master, Capt Herbert Colin Skinns, crew of 61 and 9 gunners were rescued by RCN corvette *SHEDIAC* 925/41 (K.110) (Lt J.E. Clayton) and landed at Ponta Delgada, Azores.

**FORT McLEOD** • GRT 7127 • Built 1942
3.3.44: Torpedoed and sunk by gunfire by Japanese submarine I-162 (Doi), in the Indian Ocean SW of the Maldive Islands, in position 02.01N 77.06E while sailing independently on a voyage from Cochin and Colombo to Durban, with a part cargo of 700 tons of generals. The Master, Capt William Alderton, crew of 48 and 12 gunners were rescued by HM trawler *SLUNA* 545/41 (T.117) (Lt C.J. Pilbeam) and HM rescue tug *INTEGRITY* 783/42 (W.14) ex-USS *BAT.4* and landed at Colombo 8.3.44. I-162 was at Sasebo on 14.8.45 (VJ Day).

**EMPIRE LANCER** • GRT 7037 • Built 1942
16.8.44: Torpedoed and sunk by German submarine U-862 (Timm), in the Mozambique Channel E of Mozambique, in position 15.00S 45.00E while sailing independently on a voyage from Durban to Majunga, Tamatave and Aden to the UK, with a cargo of 2000 tons of copper and 1000 tons of military stores. The Master, Capt Maximes Jollivet, 36 crew and 5 gunners were lost. 34 crew and 3 gunners landed 60 miles S of Lumbo, Portuguese East Africa 26.8.44.

## HOLT, JOHN & COMPANY (LIVERPOOL) LTD – LIVERPOOL

**JONATHAN HOLT** • GRT 4973 • Built 1938
24.2.41: Torpedoed and sunk by German submarine U-97 (Heilmann), in the North Atlantic SW of the Faröe Islands, in position 61.10N 11.55W while on a voyage from Liverpool to West Africa, with 12 passengers and general cargo, part of convoy OB 289 comprising 25 ships. The Master, Capt William Stephenson, 38 crew, 2 gunners and 10 passengers were lost. 2 crew and 1 passenger were rescued by HM corvette *PETUNIA* 925/40 (K.79) (Lt-Cdr G.V. Legassick) and landed at Stornoway. 2 crew and 1 passenger were rescued by rescue ship *COPELAND* 1526/23 (Capt W.J. Hartley DSC) and landed at Greenock.

**ROBERT L. HOLT** • GRT 2918 • Built 1926
4.7.41: Sunk by gunfire by German submarine U-69 (Metzler), in the Atlantic NW of the Canary Islands, in position 34.15N 20.00W while sailing independently on a voyage from Liverpool to Warri, in ballast, dispersed from convoy OB 337 comprising 44 ships. The

Master, Capt John Alexander Kendall, Commodore Vice-Admiral N.A. Wodehouse CB RN, crew of 41 and 6 naval staff were lost. Korvettenkapitän Jost Metzler was awarded the Knight's Cross (28.7.41).

**JOHN HOLT** • GRT 4975 • Built 1938
24.9.41: Torpedoed and sunk by German submarine U-107 (Hessler), in the Atlantic 350 miles WNW of the Canary Islands, in position 31.12N 23.32W while on a voyage from Duala to Liverpool, with 9 passengers and a cargo of 4560 tons of West African produce, part of convoy SL 87 comprising 11 ships. The Master, Capt Cecil Gordon Hime, Commodore A. MacRae DSC RNR, crew of 45, 7 gunners, 5 naval staff and passengers were rescued by HM sloop *GORLESTON* 1546/29 (Y.92) (Cdr R.W. Keymer) ex-US coastguard cutter *ITASCA* and landed at Ponta Delgada, Azores. 1 gunner was lost.

**JOHN HOLT** • GRT 4964 • Built 1942
5.3.44: Torpedoed and sunk by German submarine U-66 (Seehausen), in the Gulf of Guinea 60 miles S of the Opobo River, in position 03.56N 07.36E while sailing independently on a voyage from London and Lagos to Duala and Warri, with 4 passengers, 2600 tons of cement and 100 tons of general cargo including mail. The Master, Capt William Stephenson, and 1 passenger were taken prisoner; they were later lost when U-66 was sunk on 6.5.44. 41 crew, 9 gunners, 3 passengers and 40 Krooboys were rescued by British tanker *EMPIRE RUBY* 667/41 and landed at Port Harcourt.

## HONEYMAN & COMPANY – GLASGOW
### Carslogie Steamship Co. Ltd

**CARSBRECK** ex-*COULBEG* • GRT 3670 • Built 1936
24.10.41: Torpedoed and sunk by German submarine U-564 (Suhren), in the Atlantic 300 miles W of Gibraltar, in position 36.20N 10.50W while on a voyage from Almeria to Barrow, with a cargo of 6000 tons of iron ore, part of convoy HG 75 comprising 17 ships. The Master, Capt John Dugald Muir, 19 crew and 4 gunners were lost. 16 crew and 2 gunners were rescued by Free French sloop *COMMANDANT DUBOC* 630/38, transferred to HM auxiliary fighter catapult ship *ARIGUANI* 6746/26 (F.105) (Cdr R.A. Thornburn) later damaged by U-83 (Kraus), reboarded and towed to Gibraltar; the survivors of the *CARSBRECK* were rescued by HM corvette *CAMPION* 925/41 (K.108) (Lt-Cdr A. Johnson), transferred to HM destroyer *VIDETTE* 1090/18 (D.48) (Lt-Cdr E.N. Walmsley) and landed at Gibraltar.

## HOULDER BROTHERS & CO. LTD – LONDON
### British Empire Steam Navigation Co. Ltd

**CARONI RIVER** (tanker) • GRT 7807 • Built 1928
20.1.40: Struck a mine laid the same day by German submarine U-34 (Schultz) and sank in the English Channel in position 50.06N 05.01W while carrying out paravane trials and defensive armament tests in Falmouth Bay. The Master, Capt Robert Stanley Grigg, crew of 42, Cdr J.G. Bradshaw RN and 11 naval personnel were rescued by the Falmouth lifeboat and a naval cutter and landed at Falmouth.

## Furness-Houlder Argentine Lines Ltd

*CANONSEA* ex-*WAR MINERVA* • GRT 8286 • Built 1920
21.9.40: Torpedoed and sunk by German submarine U-100 (Schepke), in the Atlantic 340 miles W of Bloody Foreland, in position 54.55N 18.25W while on a voyage from Montreal to Liverpool via Halifax NS, with 11107 tons of general cargo including foodstuffs, part of convoy HX 72 comprising 47 ships. The Master, Capt Frederick Stephenson, 60 crew and 1 gunner were rescued by HM corvette *LA MALOUINE* 925/40 (K.46) (Lt-Cdr R.W. Keymer). 1 crew was lost.

## Houlder Line Ltd

*ROYSTON GRANGE* ex-*SALADO* ex-*AUSTRALIER* ex-*WAR BISON* • GRT 5144 • Built 1918
25.11.39: Torpedoed and sunk by German submarine U-28 (Kuhnke), in the Atlantic about 50 miles SW of Land's End, in position 49.01N 09.16W while sailing independently on a voyage from Buenos Aires to Liverpool via Freetown, with general cargo and grain, dispersed from convoy SL 8 comprising 28 ships. The Master, Capt Arthur George Phelps-Mead, and crew were rescued by British trawler *ROMILLY* 214/05 and landed at Swansea.

*UPWEY GRANGE* • GRT 9130 • Built 1925
8.8.40: Torpedoed and sunk by German submarine U-37 (Oehrn), in the Atlantic W of Ireland, in position 54.20N 15.28W while sailing independently on a voyage from Buenos Aires to London, with 11 passengers and a cargo of 5380 tons of frozen meat and cases of tinned meat. The Master, Capt William Ernest Williams, 32 crew and 3 passengers were lost. 42 crew, 1 DBS and 7 passengers were rescued by British trawler *NANIWA* 340/31, transferred to HM destroyer *VANQUISHER* 1090/17 (D.54) (Lt-Cdr A.P. Northey DSC) and landed at Liverpool.

*BEACON GRANGE* • GRT 10119 • Built 1938
27.4.41: Torpedoed and sunk by German submarine U-552 (Topp), in the Atlantic S of Iceland, in position 62.05N 16.20W while sailing independently on a voyage from the Tyne and Loch Ewe to Buenos Aires, in ballast. The Master, Capt Alfred Byford Friend, 73 crew and 8 gunners were rescued by Belgian trawler *EDOUVARD ANSEELE* 351/26, transferred to HM corvette *GLADIOLUS* 925/40 (K.34) (Lt-Cdr H.M.C. Sanders DSC) and landed at Londonderry. 2 crew were lost.

*HARDWICKE GRANGE* • GRT 9005 • Built 1921
12.6.42: Torpedoed and sunk by gunfire by German submarine U-129 (Witt), in the Atlantic N of Puerto Rico near the Tropic of Cancer, in position 25.45N 65.45W while sailing independently on a voyage from Newport News 8.6.42 to Trinidad and Buenos Aires, with 700 tons of refrigerated cargo. The Master, Capt Timothy McNamara, and 19 survivors landed at Monte Cristi, Dominican Republic; 23 survivors were rescued by British tanker *ATHELPRINCE* 8782/26 and landed at Nuevitas, Cuba; 16 survivors landed at Môle St Nicolas, Republic of Haiti; the 1st Officer, 2nd Engineer and 14 crew were rescued by an unknown ship and landed at Jamaica. The Master was awarded the OBE for bravery at sea. 3 crew were lost.

**LYNTON GRANGE** • GRT 5029 • Built 1937

29.12.42: Torpedoed and sunk by German submarine U-225 (Leimkühler), part of the 'Spitz' (Sharp) patrol group of ten U-boats, in the Atlantic N of the Azores, in position 43.23N 27.14W while on a voyage from Swansea and Belfast Lough 18.12.42 to Saldanha Bay, Cape Town and the Middle East, with a cargo of 5997 tons of government stores and general, a straggler from convoy ONS 154 comprising 45 ships. The Master, Capt Robert Stanley Grigg OBE, crew of 41 and 10 gunners were rescued by HM destroyer *MILNE* 1920/41 (G.14) (Capt I.M.R. Campbell) and landed at Ponta Delgada, Azores. Oberleutnant zur See Wolfgang Leimkühler and crew of 45 were lost while shadowing convoy SC 119 comprising 39 ships on 15.2.43 when U-225, part of the 'Ritter' (Knight) patrol group of twelve U-boats, was sunk in the Atlantic 570 miles SSW of Reykjanes, Iceland, in position 55.45N 31.09W by Liberator 'S' FK232, pilot F/O Reginald Thomas Frederick Turner of No. 120 Squadron RAF, based at Reykjavik. The pilot was awarded the DFC.

## MOWT

**ANGLO MAERSK** ex-*ANGLO SWEDE* (tanker) • GRT 7705 • Built 1930

26.10.42: Torpedoed and damaged by German tanker U-509 (Witte), part of the 'Streitaxt' (Battleaxe) patrol group of eight U-boats, later sunk by a *coup de grâce* by German submarine U-604 (Höltring), part of the same patrol, in the Atlantic W of the Canary Islands, in position 27.15N 17.55W while on a voyage from Pointe Noire, French Congo, to Glasgow via Freetown 16.10.42, in ballast, a straggler from convoy SL 125 comprising 40 ships. The Master, Capt K.N. Valsberg, crew of 32 and 2 gunners landed at Hierro Island, Canary Islands 27.10.42.

**EMPIRE STARLING** ex-*NOCKUM* • GRT 6025 • Built 1919

21.11.42: Torpedoed and sunk by German submarine U-163 (Engelmann), in the Atlantic 180 miles NE of Barbados, in position 13.05N 56.20W while sailing independently on a voyage from La Plata and Rio de Janeiro 31.10.42 to the UK via Trinidad, with a cargo of 5500 tons of frozen meat including corned beef and general cargo. The Master, Capt Eric Monckton MBE, was taken prisoner, landed at Lorient 6.1.43 and was taken to Milag Nord. 46 crew, 7 gunners and 1 DBS landed at Speightstown, Barbados, and Pointe du Vieux Fort, Guadeloupe. Korvettenkapitän Kurt Eduard Engelmann and crew of 56 were lost on 21.3.43 when U-163, shadowing convoy MKS 9 comprising 34 ships, was depth-charged and sunk in the Atlantic NW of Cape Finisterre, in position 45.05N 15.00W by RCN corvette *PRESCOTT* 925/41 (K161) (Lt-Cdr Wilfred McIsaac).

**EMPIRE SHACKLETON** • GRT 7068 • Built 1941

28.12.42: Torpedoed and damaged by German submarine U-406 (Dieterichs), on 29.12.42 was again damaged by U-123 (v. Schroeter) and sunk by gunfire by U-435 (Strelow), part of the 'Spitz' (Sharp) patrol group of ten U-boats, in the Atlantic N of the Azores, in position 43.20N 27.18W while on a voyage from Liverpool 18.12.42 to Halifax NS, with 2000 tons of general cargo, 1000 tons of ammunition and aircraft, a straggler from convoy ONS 154 comprising 45 ships. The Master, Capt Henry Ellington Jones, Commodore Vice-Admiral Wion de Malpas Egerton DSO RN, 36 crew, 11 gunners, 6 naval staff and a wireless mechanic were rescued by HM special service ship *FIDELITY* 2456/20 (D.57) (Cdr Langlais) on 30.12.42. HMS *FIDELITY* was torpedoed and sunk by U-435 (Strelow), N of the Azores, in position 43.23N 27.07W. The Master, 4 crew and 2 gunners were rescued by RCN corvette *SHEDIAC* 925/41 (K.110) (Lt J.E. Clayton) and landed at Ponta Delgada, Azores, and 6 crew and 2 gunners by British ship *CALGARY* 7206/21 and landed at Freetown. The Vice-Admiral, 32 crew, 7 gunners, wireless mechanic and 6 naval staff were lost. Kapitänleutnant Siegfried Strelow (Knight's Cross 27.10.42) and crew of 47 were lost on 9.7.43 when U-435, part of the 'Trutz' (Defiant) patrol group of five U-boats, was sunk in the Atlantic 250 miles W by S of Cape Roca, Portugal, in position 39.48N 14.22W by Wellington 'R', pilot F/O E.J. Fisher of No. 179 Squadron RAF, based at Gibraltar.

*JASPER PARK* • GRT 7129 • Built 1942 (Canadian)
6.7.43: Torpedoed and sunk by German submarine U-177 (Gysae), in the Indian Ocean SSW of Cap Sainte Marie, Madagascar, in position 32.58S 42.15E while sailing independently on a voyage from Calcutta and Cochin 22.6.43 to St John, New Brunswick via Durban with 6500 tons general cargo including jute and tea. The Master, Capt William Buchanan, 44 crew and 6 gunners were rescued by RAN destroyers *QUIBERON* 1705/42 (G.81) (Cdr W.H. Hartington DSO) and *QUICKMATCH* 1705/42 (G.92) (Lt-Cdr O.H. Becher DSC) and landed at Durban. 4 crew were lost.

## HOUSTON LINE LIMITED – LONDON
### British & South American Steam Navigation Co. Ltd

*HARMODIUS* • GRT 5229 • Built 1919
8.3.41: Torpedoed and sunk by German submarine U-124 (Schulz), in the Atlantic NNE of the Cape Verde Islands, in position 20.35N 20.40W while on a voyage from Cochin and Cape Town to London and Glasgow via Freetown 1.3.41, with 2000 tons of pig iron and 3930 tons of general cargo, part of convoy SL 67 comprising 56 ships. The Master, Capt Robert Jones Parry, 59 crew and 1 gunner were rescued by HM destroyer leader *FAULKNOR* 1457/34 (H.620) (Capt A.F. de Salis), transferred to HM destroyer *FORESTER* 1350/34 (H.74) (Lt-Cdr B. Tancock DSC) and landed at Gibraltar 16.3.41. 13 crew and 1 gunner were lost.

*HARMONIDES* • GRT 5237 • Built 1920
25.8.42: Torpedoed and sunk by Japanese submarine I-165 (Torisu), in the Indian Ocean 250 miles S of Ceylon, in position 01.47N 77.27E while sailing independently on a voyage from Calcutta and Trincomalee 22.8.42 to Lourenco Marques and the USA, with 6000 tons of general cargo including pig iron, tea, castor and linseed oil. The Master, Capt Herbert Evans, 64 crew and 6 gunners were rescued by HM sloop *SHOREHAM* 1045/30 (L.32) (Cdr G.P. Claridge) and landed at Colombo. 12 crew and 2 gunners were lost.

*BANFFSHIRE* ex-*CLAN MACRAE* • GRT 6479 • Built 1912
29.9.43: Torpedoed and sunk by German submarine U-532 (Junker), in the Indian Ocean NW of the Maldive Islands, in position 09.26N 71.20E while on a voyage from Colombo 27.9.43 to Aden and the UK, with a cargo of 4700 tons of coconut oil, copra, plumbago, rubber and tea. The Master, Capt Herbert Evans, 88 crew and 10 gunners were rescued by RIN minesweeper *RAJPUTANA* 672/41 (J.197) ex-HMS *LYME REGIS* (Lt W.G. Coltham) and landed at Colombo. 1 crew was lost.

## HOWARD SMITH LIMITED – MELBOURNE
**Australian Steamship Pty**

*KOWARRA* • GRT 2125 • Built 1916
24.4.43: Torpedoed and sunk by Japanese submarine I-26 (Yokota), in the Pacific Ocean 35 miles NE of Sandy Cape, Queensland, in position 24.26S 153.44E while sailing independently on a voyage from Bowen, Queensland to Brisbane, with a cargo of sugar. The Master, Capt Donald MacPherson, 19 crew and 1 gunner were lost. 11 crew were rescued by USN submarine chaser SC 747. Lt Chuichi Nishiuchi and crew were lost on 17.11.44 when I-26 was sunk in the Philippine Sea 500 miles ENE of Leyte Island, Philippines, in position 12.44N 130.42E by aircraft of US Navy Composite Squadron VC-82 from US escort carrier *ANZIO* 7800/43 (CVE-57) and US destroyer escort *LAWRENCE C. TAYLOR* 1350/44 (DE-415) (Cdr R. Cullinan Jr).

## HUNT, WILLIAM & COMPANY – SHANGHAI
**China Foreign SS Corporation**

*BETTY* ex-*BETTY WEEMS* ex-*LAKE AGOMAK* • GRT 2339 • Built 1918
14.8.40: Torpedoed and sunk by German submarine U-59 (Matz), in the Atlantic 35 miles N of Tory Island, in position 55.52N 08.14W while sailing independently on a voyage from Saigon, Indo-China, to Liverpool, with a cargo of 2726 tons of rice. The Master, Capt Thomas H. Sessions, and 29 crew were lost. 4 crew were rescued by HM trawler *MAN O' WAR* 517/36 (FY.104) (Lt A.D. White) and landed at Belfast.

## HUNTING & SON – NEWCASTLE UPON TYNE
**Northern Petroleum Tank Steamship Co.**

*CREOFIELD* ex-*ATHELSTAN* (tanker) • GRT 838 • Built 1928
2.2.40: Torpedoed and sunk by German submarine U-59 (Jürst), in the North Sea E of Lowestoft, in position 52.33N 02.25E while on a voyage from London to Middlesbrough, with a cargo of creosote. The Master, Capt Charles Fred Carlin, and crew of 15 were lost.

*GRETAFIELD* (tanker) • GRT 10191 • Built 1928
14.2.40: Torpedoed and damaged by German submarine U-57 (Korth), in the North Sea SE of Noss Head, in position 58.27N 02.33W while on a voyage from Curacao to Invergordon via Halifax NS, with a cargo of 13000 tons of fuel oil, a straggler from convoy HX 18 comprising 43 ships. The Master, Capt Ernst Derricks, and 30 crew were rescued by HM trawlers *PEGGY NUTTEN* 493/07 (4.450) (Skipper J.C. Taylor) and *STRATHALLADALE* 199/08 (4.458) and landed at Wick. 10 crew were lost. On fire the *GRETAFIELD* drifted ashore at Dunbeath, Caithnessshire, broke in two on 19.3.40 and was declared a CTL.

*SYLVAFIELD* (tanker) • GRT 5709 • Built 1925
15.8.40: Torpedoed and sunk by German submarine U-51 (Knorr), in the Atlantic 190 miles WNW of Rockall, in position 56.39N 11.16W while on government service on a voyage from Curacao to Glasgow via Halifax NS, with a cargo of 7860 tons of fuel oil, a straggler from convoy HX 62 comprising 77 ships. The Master, Capt James Edmund King, and 19 crew were rescued by Belgian trawler *RUBENS* 320/37 and landed at Fleetwood; 16 crew by

HM trawler *NEWLAND* 235/03 and landed at Tobermory, Isle of Mull. 3 crew were lost. Kapitänleutnant Dietrich Knorr and crew of 42 were lost on 20.8.40 when U–51 was torpedoed and sunk in the Bay of Biscay 50 miles WSW of Belle Ile, in position 47.06N 04.51W by HM submarine *CACHALOT* 1520/37 (N.83) (Lt-Cdr J. David Luce).

**DUFFIELD** (tanker) • GRT 8516 • Built 1938
9.4.41: Torpedoed and sunk by German submarine U–107 (Hessler), in the Atlantic WSW of Madeira, in position 31.13N 23.24W while on government service on a voyage from Curacao to Gibraltar, with a cargo of 11700 tons of fuel oil, part of convoy OG 57 comprising 35 ships. The Master, Capt Mariston Manthorpe, 25 crew and 2 gunners landed at Hierro Island, Canary Islands. 25 crew were lost.

**OILFIELD** (tanker) • GRT 8516 • Built 1938
28.4.41: Torpedoed and sunk by German submarine U–96 (Lehmann–Willenbrock), in the North Atlantic S of Iceland, in position 60.05N 17.00W while on a voyage from Aruba to London via Halifax NS, with a cargo of 11700 tons of benzine, part of convoy HX 121 comprising 48 ships. The Master, Capt Lawrence Robert Andersen (Commodore of Hunting's fleet), 44 crew and 2 gunners were lost. 6 crew and 2 gunners were rescued by HM trawler *ST ZENO* 608/40 (Lt J.K. Craig) and landed at Londonderry.

**WELLFIELD** (tanker) • GRT 6054 • Built 1923
5.6.41: Torpedoed and sunk by German submarine U–48 (Schultze), part of the 'West' patrol group of fifteen U-boats, in the Atlantic SE of Cape Farewell, in position 48.34N 31.34W while on government service on a voyage from Liverpool to Curacao, in ballast, part of convoy OB 328 comprising 26 ships. The Master, Capt James Edward Smith, and 7 crew were lost. 19 crew were rescued by British tanker *BRITISH ARDOUR* 7124/28 and landed at New York; 15 crew by Norwegian ship *HEINA* 4028/25 and landed at Halifax, Nova Scotia.

## IMPERIAL OIL SHIPPING CO. – TORONTO, CANADA

**MONTROLITE** (tanker) • GRT 11309 • Built 1926 (Canadian)
5.2.42: Torpedoed and sunk by German submarine U–109 (Bleichrodt), part of 'Operation Paukenschlag' (Drumbeat), the first wave of five U-boats, in the Atlantic NE of Bermuda, in position 35.14N 60.05W while sailing independently from Trinidad to Halifax NS, with a cargo of crude oil. The Master, Capt John White, 26 crew and 1 gunner were lost. 17 crew and 3 gunners were rescued by British ship *WINKLEIGH* 5468/40 and landed at Halifax NS 10.2.42.

**VICTOLITE** (tanker) • GRT 11410 • Built 1928 (Canadian)
11.2.42: Torpedoed and sunk by German submarine U–564 (Suhren), in the Atlantic NNW of Bermuda, in position 36.12N 67.14W while sailing independently on a voyage from Halifax NS to Las Piedras, Venezuela, in ballast. The Master, Capt Peter McLean Smith, crew of 44 and 2 gunners were lost.

**CALGAROLITE** (tanker) • GRT 11941 • Built 1929 (Canadian)
9.5.42: Torpedoed and sunk by gunfire by German submarine U–125 (Folkers), in the Caribbean Sea 50 miles SW of Grand Cayman Island, in position 19.24N 82.30W while

sailing independently on a voyage from New York 30.4.42 to Cartagena, Colombia, in ballast. The Master, Capt Thomas J. Mountain, and 21 crew landed at Isla de Pinos, Cuba 13.5.42 and the Chief Officer and 22 crew landed at Isla Mujeres, Mexico 12.5.42.

## INDO-CHINA STEAM NAVIGATION COMPANY – HONG KONG

*CHAK SANG* • GRT 2358 • Built 1917
21.1.42: Torpedoed and sunk by gunfire by Japanese submarine I-166 (Yoshitome), in the Bay of Bengal SW of Bassein, Burma, in position 15.42N 95.02E while sailing independently on a voyage from Madras to Rangoon, in ballast. The Master, Capt George W.F. Edwards, and 60 crew were saved. 5 crew were lost.

*KUMSANG* ex-*BARRYMORE* • GRT 5447 • Built 1920
30.9.42: Torpedoed and sunk by German submarine U-125 (Folkers), in the Atlantic 300 miles S of Freetown, in position 04.07N 13.40W while sailing independently on a voyage from Colombo, Cape Town and Walvis Bay, South West Africa, to the UK via Freetown, with 7000 tons of general cargo. The Master, Capt William J. Lawrence, 101 crew and 8 gunners landed at Cape Mount, Liberia, and were brought to Freetown by HM motor launches No. 302 and No. 2771. 4 crew were lost.

## INTERSTATE STEAMSHIP PROPRIETARY – SYDNEY, NEW SOUTH WALES

*IRON CROWN* ex-*EUROA* • GRT 3353 • Built 1922 (Australian)
4.6.42: Torpedoed and sunk by Japanese submarine I-27 (Yoshimura), in the Pacific Ocean, SE of Cape Howe, in position 38.17S 149.44E while sailing independently on a voyage from Whyalla, South Australia 30.5.42 to Port Kembla NSW, with a cargo of 5500 tons of iron ore. The Master, Capt Archibald A. McLellan, 36 crew and 1 gunner were lost. 5 crew were rescued by British India ship *MULBERA* 9100/22 and landed at Sydney NSW.

## JACOBS, JOHN I. & CO. LTD – LONDON
### Oil & Molasses Tankers Ltd

*ELMWOOD* • GRT 7167 • Built 1942
27.7.42: Torpedoed and sunk by German submarine U-130 (Kals), in the Atlantic NE of St Paul Rocks, in position 04.48N 22.00W while sailing independently on a voyage from New York to Abadan and Kuwait via Trinidad 16.7.42 and Cape Town, with 1 RAF personnel, 7000 tons of general cargo and military equipment including tanks. The Master, Capt Edward Lewis James Herbert, crew of 43, 6 gunners and passenger were saved: the Master and 19 survivors landed at Freetown, the 2nd Officer and 11 survivors landed about 200 miles further along the coast at Bissao, Portuguese Guinea 11.8.42, and the Chief Officer and 18 survivors were rescued by US Libery ship *DAVY CROCKETT* 7176/42 and landed at Cape Town.

*BEECHWOOD* • GRT 4897 • Built 1940
26.8.42: Torpedoed and sunk by German submarine U-130 (Kals), in the Atlantic S of Monrovia, in position 05.30N 14.04W while sailing independently on a voyage from Haifa to the UK via Lourenco Marques 3.8.42 and Freetown, with 3209 tons of general

cargo and 5000 tons of potash. The Master, Capt Samuel James Dring, was taken prisoner, landed at Lorient 12.9.42 and then taken to Milag Nord. 36 crew, 5 gunners and 1 stowaway were rescued by Royal Fleet Auxiliary tanker *FORTOL* 4900/17 (Capt Herbert Walker Flint) and landed at Freetown. 1 crew was lost. Korvettenkapitän Ernst Kals was awarded the Knight's Cross (1.9.42)

**ROSEWOOD** ex-*STEGG* (tanker) • GRT 5989 • Built 1931
9.3.43: Torpedoed and damaged by German submarine U-409 (Massmann), part of the 'Westmark' (West German mark) patrol group of seventeen U-boats, later sunk by gunfire by US Coastguard cutter *BIBB* 2216/37 (WPG.31), in the Atlantic S of Iceland, in position 58.37N 22.32W while on government service on a voyage from New York to the Clyde, with a cargo of fuel oil, part of convoy SC 121 comprising 57 ships. The Master, Capt Robert Taylor, crew of 32 and 9 gunners were lost. U-409 commanded by Oberleutnant zur See Hans-Ferdinand Massmann was sunk while shadowing convoy MKF 19A (F) comprising 6 ships on 12.7.43 in the Mediterranean 60 miles NE of Cape Caxine, Algeria, in position 37.12N 04.00E by HM destroyer *INCONSTANT* 1360/41 (H.49) (Lt-Cdr W.S. Clouston). The U-boat commander and 31 crew were taken prisoner by HMS *INCONSTANT.* 14 crew were lost.

**MOWT**

**LANGUEDOC** ex-*ACTOR* (tanker) • GRT 9512 • Built 1937
17.10.40: Torpedoed and sunk by German submarine U-48 (Bleichrodt), in the Atlantic 158 miles NW of Rockall, in position 59.14N 17.51W while on government service on a voyage from Trinidad to the Clyde via Sydney CB 5.10.40, with a cargo of 13700 tons of fuel oil, part of convoy SC 7 comprising 35 ships. The Master, Capt John Thomson, and crew of 38 were rescued by HM corvette *BLUEBELL* 925/40 (K.80) (Lt-Cdr Robert E. Sherwood) and landed at Gourock 20.10.40.

**JAMAICA BANANA PRODUCERS STEAMSHIP CO. LIMITED – LONDON**

*JAMAICA PROGRESS* • GRT 5475 • Built 1932
31.7.40: Torpedoed and sunk by German submarine U-99 (Kretschmer), in the Atlantic 40 miles SW of Barra Head, in position 56.26N 08.30W while sailing independently on a voyage from Kingston, Jamaica, to Avonmouth, with 4 passengers and a cargo of 2179 tons of fruit including bananas. The Master, Capt Alfred McColm, 24 crew, 1 gunner and passengers were rescued by HM trawler *NEWLAND* 235/03 and landed at Fleetwood; the Chief Officer and 16 crew landed at Barra, Hebrides. 6 crew and 1 gunner were lost.

*JAMAICA PIONEER* • GRT 5349 • Built 1931
25.8.40: Torpedoed and sunk by German submarine U-100 (Schepke), in the Atlantic E of Rockall, in position 57.05N 11.02W while sailing independently on a voyage from Kingston, Jamaica, to Avonmouth, with cargo of 1900 tons of bananas. The Master, Capt Thomas Elwyn Maurice Jenkins, 52 crew and 2 gunners were rescued; some by HM destroyer *ANTHONY* 1350/29 (H.40) (Lt-Cdr N.J.V. Threw) were landed at Greenock, and others by HM destroyer *WANDERER* 1220/19 (D.74) (Cdr J.H. Ruck-Keene) were landed at Belfast. 2 crew were lost.

## JONES, RICHARD W. & COMPANY – NEWPORT, MONMOUTHSHIRE
**Uskside Steamship Co. Ltd**

*USKMOUTH* • GRT 2483 • Built 1928
25.11.39: Torpedoed and sunk by gunfire by German submarine U-43 (Ambrosius), in the
Atlantic 120 miles WNW of Cape Finisterre, in position 43.22N 11.27W while sailing
independently on a voyage from Sunderland to Monaco, with a cargo of 3900 tons of coal.
The Master, Capt Henry Hunter, and 22 crew were rescued by Italian ship *JUVENTUS*
4920/20 and landed at Ramsgate 30.11.39. 2 crew were lost.

*USKBRIDGE* • GRT 2715 • Built 1940
17.10.40: Torpedoed and sunk by German submarine U-93 (Korth), in the North Atlantic 265
miles NNW of Rockall, in position 60.40N 15.50W while on a voyage from Swansea to Montreal,
with a cargo of 4000 tons of anthracite, part of convoy OB 228 comprising 47 ships. The Master,
Capt Wilfred Breckon Smith, and 27 crew were rescued by Dutch ship *KATWIJK* 1589/21,
transferred to British ship *CRISTALES* 5389/26 and landed at Bermuda. 2 crew were lost.

## KAYE, SON & CO. LTD – LONDON
**Coolham SS Co. Ltd**

*KAYESON* • GRT 4606 • Built 1929
2.10.40: Torpedoed and sunk by German submarine U-32 (Jenisch), in the Atlantic W of
Ireland, in position 51.12N 24.22W while sailing independently on a voyage from Liverpool
to Montevideo, with 2802 tons general cargo and 3901 tons of coal. The Master, Capt
William Ayres, and crew of 37 were lost.

**Kaye Transport Co. Ltd**

*MARYLYN* • GRT 4555 • Built 1930
31.10.42: Torpedoed and sunk by German submarine U-174 (Thilo), in the South Atlantic
450 miles WSW of St Paul Rocks, in position 00.46S 32.42W while sailing independently on
a voyage from Buenos Aires 10.10.42 and Montevideo to the UK via Trinidad, with 6600
tons of general cargo. The Master, Capt Thomas Collier Townsend, and 6 survivors were
rescued by British ship *PUNDIT* 5305/19 and landed at Trinidad; the Chief Officer and 19
survivors were rescued on 10.11.42 by British ship *ETTRICKBANK* 5138/37 and landed at
Port of Spain, Trinidad. 10 crew and 5 gunners were lost.

*MARCELLA* • GRT 4592 • Built 1928
13.3.43: Torpedoed and sunk by German submarine U-107 (Gelhaus), in the Atlantic W of
Cape Finisterre, in position 42.45N 13.31W while on a voyage from Manchester and the Clyde
to Freetown and Cape Town, with 7200 tons of commercial cargo and stores, part of convoy OS
44 comprising 46 ships. The Master, Capt Richard Downie, crew of 34 and 9 gunners were lost.

**Marconi SS Co. Ltd**

*MARCONI* • GRT 7402 • Built 1917
20.5.41: Torpedoed and sunk by German submarine U-94 (Kuppisch), in the Atlantic SSE of
Cape Farewell, in position 58.00N 41.00W while on a voyage from Manchester to Rio

Grande and the River Plate, in ballast, part of convoy OB 322 comprising 38 ships. The Master, Capt Frederick Emanuel Hailstone, 54 crew and 1 gunner were rescued by US patrol ship *GENERAL GREENE* 220/27 (WPC.140) and landed at St John's, Newfoundland. 19 crew and 3 gunners were lost.

### The 'K' SS Co. Ltd

*MARINA* • GRT 5088 • Built 1935
18.9.40: Torpedoed and sunk by German submarine U-48 (Bleichrodt), in the Atlantic 253 miles WSW of Rockall, in position 56.46N 21.15W while on a voyage from Glasgow to the River Plate, with 5700 tons of general cargo including coal, part of convoy OB 213 comprising 19 ships. The Master, Capt Richard Townshend Payne, and 16 crew were rescued after eight days by British ship *CARLINGFORD* 345/08 and landed at Londonderry; 17 crew and 3 gunners by HM destroyer *HURRICANE* 1340/39 (H.06) (Lt-Cdr H.C. Simms) ex-Brazilian *JAPARUA* and landed at Gourock. 2 crew were lost. Capt R.T. Payne was awarded the George Medal and the Lloyd's War Medal for bravery at sea.

### Walmar SS Co. Ltd

*MARSLEW* • GRT 4542 • Built 1926
24.2.41: Torpedoed and sunk by German submarine U-95 (Schreiber), in the Atlantic about 300 miles NNW of Rockall, in position 59.18N 21.30W while sailing independently on a voyage from Glasgow and Liverpool to Montevideo and Villa Constitucion, Argentina, with 6000 tons of general cargo, dispersed from convoy OB 288 comprising 46 ships. The Master, Capt H.R. Watkins, and 12 crew were lost. 21 crew and 2 gunners were rescued by British ship *EMPIRE CHEETAH* 5506/18.

*MARGOT* • GRT 4542 • Built 1926
23.5.42: Torpedoed and sunk by gunfire by German submarine U-588 (Vogel), in the Atlantic SE of Philadelphia, in position 39.00N 68.00W while sailing independently on a voyage from New York 22.5.42 to Alexandria via Trinidad, with 5500 tons of general cargo and military stores. The Master, Capt Henry Bell Collins, 38 crew and 5 gunners were rescued by Swedish ship *SAGOLAND* 3243/39 and landed at New York. 1 crew was lost. Kapitänleutnant Viktor Vogel and crew of 45 were lost when U-588 was sunk while shadowing convoy ON 115 comprising 41 ships on 31.7.42 in the Atlantic 700 miles ENE of St John's, Newfoundland, in position 49.59N 36.36W by RCN destroyer *SKEENA* 1337/30 (D.59) (A/Lt-Cdr Kenneth L. Dyer) and RCN corvette *WETASKIWIN* 925/40 (K.1750 (Lt-Cdr Guy S. Windeyer) of the Escort Group C3.

### MOWT

*EMPIRE MERCHANT* ex-*POMONA* • GRT 4864 • Built 1938
16.8.40: Torpedoed and sunk by German submarine U-100 (Schepke), in the Atlantic 186 miles W of Bloody Foreland, in position 55.23N 13.24W while on a voyage from Avonmouth to Kingston, Jamaica, with 8 passengers and 200 tons of general cargo and mail, part of convoy OA 198 comprising 12 ships. The Master, Capt Benjamin Walton Smith, 38

crew, 1 gunner and passengers were rescued by HM rescue tug *SALVONIA* 571/39 (Lt G.M.M. Robinson) and landed at Greenock. 6 crew and 1 gunner were lost. The German *POMONA* was taken as a prize on 3.9.39 in the London Docks.

**EMPIRE PRAIRE** • GRT 7010 • Built 1941
10.4.42: Torpedoed and sunk by German submarine U-654 (Forster), in the Atlantic E of Philadelphia, in position 35.00N 60.00W while sailing independently on a voyage from Halifax NS to Cape Town and Alexandria, with 9022 tons of general cargo. The Master, Capt Richard Townsend Payne, crew of 43 and 5 gunners were lost. Oberleutnant zur See Ludwig Forster and crew of 43 were lost on 22.8.42 when U-654 was sunk in the Atlantic 150 miles N of Colon, in position 12.00N 79.56W by a Douglas B-18 aircraft, pilot Lt P.A. Koening of the 45th Bombardment Squadron, based at France Field, Panama.

**EMPIRE TURNSTONE** ex-*WESTERN CITY* laid down as *WAR ARROW*
GRT 5828 • Built 1918
23.10.42: Torpedoed and sunk by German submarine U-621 (Schünemann), in the Atlantic SW of Iceland, in position 54.40N 28.00W while on a voyage from the Tyne and Loch Ewe to Port Sulphur, Louisiana, in ballast, a straggler from convoy ONS 136 comprising 36 ships. The Master, Capt Henry Bell Collins, crew of 38 and 7 gunners were lost.

## LAGO SHIPPING CO. LTD (ESSO) – LONDON

**ORANJESTAD** (tanker) • GRT 2396 • Built 1927
16.2.42: Torpedoed and sunk by German submarine U-156 (Hartenstein), in the Caribbean Sea in San Nicholas harbour, Aruba, in position 12.25N 69.55W. 10 crew were rescued by harbour craft. 15 crew were lost.

**SAN NICOLAS** (tanker) • GRT 2391 • Built 1926
16.2.42: Torpedoed and sunk by German submarine U-502 (v. Rosenstiel), in the Gulf of Venezuela 25 miles SW of Punta Macolla while on a voyage from Lake Maracaibo to Aruba, with a cargo of crude oil. 19 crew were rescued and landed at Maracaibo. 7 crew were lost.

**TIA JUANA** (tanker) • GRT 2395 • Built 1928
16.2.42: Torpedoed and sunk by German submarine U-502 (v. Rosentiel), in the Gulf of Venezuela 25 miles SW of Punta Macolla, Venezuela, while on a voyage from Lake Maracaibo to Aruba, with a cargo of crude oil. The Master, Capt George Milbanke, and 8 crew were rescued and landed at Maracaibo. 17 crew were lost.

## LAMBERT BROTHERS LIMITED – LONDON

**TEMPLE MOAT** • GRT 4427 • Built 1928
23.2.41: Torpedoed and sunk by German submarine U-95 (Schreiber), in the Atlantic S of Iceland, in position 59.27N 20.20W while on a voyage from Blyth to Buenos Aires, with a cargo of 6130 tons of coal, a straggler from convoy OB 288 comprising 46 ships. The Master, Capt Thomas Ludlow MBE, crew of 39 and 2 gunners were lost.

## MOWT

### EMPIRE CROMWELL • GRT 5970 • Built 1941

28.11.42: Torpedoed and sunk by German submarine U-508 (Staats), in the Atlantic 160 miles SE of Galeota Point, Trinidad, in position 09.00N 58.30W while sailing independently on a voyage from Haifa to New York via Cape Town 4.11.42 and Trinidad, with a cargo of 1000 tons of chrome ore. The Master, Capt Philip Dent, 20 crew and 3 gunners were lost. 19 crew and 6 gunners were rescued on 30.11.42 by HM motor torpedo boats and landed at Port of Spain, Trinidad.

## LAMPORT & HOLT LIMITED – LIVERPOOL
### Liverpool, Brazil and River Plate Steam Navigation Co. Ltd

### BRONTE ex-WAR CONEY • GRT 5317 • Built 1919

27.10.39: Torpedoed and damaged by German submarine U-34 (Rollman), in the Atlantic 180 miles W of Land's End, in position 49.30N 12.15W while on a voyage from Liverpool 26.10.39 to Rosario via Halifax NS, with general cargo including chemicals, part of convoy OB 25 comprising 17 ships. Taken in tow but later sunk on 30.10.39 in position about 50.07N 10.36W by gunfire from the escorts HM destroyers WALPOLE 1140/18 (D.41) (Lt-Cdr A.F. Burnell-Nugent) and WHIRLWIND 1300/17 (H.41) (Lt-Cdr M.B. Ewart-Wentworth). The Master, Capt Samuel James Connolly and crew of 41 were rescued by HM destroyer WALPOLE and landed at Liverpool 31.10.39.

### BONHEUR • GRT 5327 • Built 1920

15.10.40: Torpedoed and sunk by German submarine U-138 (Lüth), in the Atlantic 38 miles NW of Butt of Lewis, in position 57.10N 08.36W while on a voyage from Liverpool to Rosario, with 5200 tons of general cargo, part of convoy OB 228 comprising 47 ships. The Master, Capt Leon Otto Everett, and crew of 38 were rescued by HM trawler SPHENE 412/34 (FY.249) (Skipper W.J.J. Tucker) and landed at Belfast.

### LASSELL • GRT 7417 • Built 1922

30.4.41: Torpedoed and sunk by German submarine U-107 (Hessler), in the Atlantic about 300 miles SW of the Cape Verde Islands, in position 12.55N 28.56W while sailing independently on a voyage from Liverpool to Rio de Janeiro and Buenos Aires, with 1 passenger and 7000 tons of general cargo, dispersed on 19.4.41 in position 50.00N 23.50W from convoy OB 309 comprising 49 ships. The Master, Capt Alfred Ryder Bibby, 2nd Officer, 26 crew and passenger were rescued after nine days in an open boat by Ben Line ship BENVRACKIE 6434/1922 on 9.5.41; she was sunk on 13.5.41 by U-105 (Schewe). 15 survivors from the LASSELL were lost. Capt A.R. Bibby and 9 survivors were adrift in an open boat for 13 days before rescue by British hospital ship OXFORDSHIRE 8648/12 and landed at Freetown. The Chief Officer, H.W. Underhill, 4 officers, 13 crew and 8 gunners were rescued on 10.5.41 in position 10.57N 29.13W by the Elder Dempster ship EGBA 6681/14 and landed at Freetown 15.5.41. 17 crew were lost. U-107, commanded by Korvettenkapitän Gunther Hessler (Knight's Cross 24.6.41), sank 14 ships of 86699 gross tonnage on this patrol, the most successful U-boat patrol of the Second World War.

**PHIDIAS** • GRT 5623 • Built 1913
9.6.41: Sunk by gunfire by German submarine U-46 (Endrass), part of the 'West' patrol group of fifteen U-boats, in the Atlantic N of the Azores in position 48.25N 26.12W while sailing independently on government service on a voyage from Greenock to Cape Town, with a cargo of about 3500 tons of stores including ammunition and 14 aircraft, dispersed from convoy OB 330 comprising 38 ships. The Master, Capt Ernest Holden Parks, and 7 crew were lost. 40 crew and 3 gunners were rescued by British ship *EMBASSAGE* 4954/35 and landed at Sydney CB. Kapitänleutnant Engelbert Endrass was awarded the Knight's Cross (5.9.40) with Oak Leaves (10.6.41). U-46, commanded by Oberleutnant zur See Erich Jewinski, was scuttled on 4.5.45 at Kupfermuhlen Bay in the Baltic, in position 54.50N 09.29E.

**BIELA** ex-*WAR MASTIFF* • GRT 5298 • Built 1918
15.2.42: Torpedoed and sunk by German submarine U-98 (Gysae), in the Atlantic 400 miles SW of Cape Race, in position 42.55N 45.40W while sailing independently on a voyage from Liverpool 1.2.42 to Buenos Aires, with general cargo, dispersed from convoy ON 62 comprising 34 ships. The Master, Capt David Anderson, crew of 43 and 5 gunners were lost. Oberleutnant zur see Kurt Eichmann and crew of 45 were lost on 15.11.42 when U-98, part of the 'Westwall' patrol group of sixteen U-boats, was sunk in the Atlantic 90 miles W of Tarifa Point, Spain, in position 36.09N 07.42W by HM destroyer *WRESTLER* 1120/18 (D.35) (Lt-Cdr R.W.B. Lacon).

**BRUYERE** ex-*WAR MOLE* • GRT 5335 • Built 1919
23.9.42: Torpedoed and sunk by German submarine U-125 (Folkers), in the Atlantic SW of Freetown, in position 04.55N 17.16W while sailing independently on a voyage from Buenos Aires and Rio de Janeiro to the UK via Freetown, with 6729 tons of foodstuffs and general cargo. The Master, Capt Thomas William Major, crew of 44 and 6 gunners were rescued by HM corvette *PETUNIA* 925/40 (K.79) (Lt-Cdr J.M. Rayner) and HM trawler *SIR WISTAN* 564/37 (4.105) (Lt W.H. Forster) and landed at Freetown.

**LAPLACE** • GRT 7327 • Built 1919
29.10.42: Torpedoed and sunk by German submarine U-159 (Witte), in the Indian Ocean SE of Cape Agulhas, South Africa, in position 40.39S 21.52E while sailing independently on a voyage from Port Said and Lourenco Marques 24.10.42 to Buenos Aires, with 2 passengers and 6988 tons of coal. The Master, Capt Alexander MacKellan, crew of 55, 5 gunners and passengers were rescued, some survivors by Brazilian ship *PORTO ALEGRE* 5187/21 which was sunk on 3.11.42 by German submarine U-504 (Poske) while on a voyage from Rio de Janeiro to Cape Town and Durban, with general cargo. 11 survivors landed at Port Elizabeth from *PORTO ALEGRE* boats, one ship's boat was rescued by SAAF crash boat and landed at Port Elizabeth and the 3rd Officer's boat was rescued by US liberty ship *GEORGE GALE* 7176/42 and landed at Aden. Kapitänleutnant Helmut Witte was awarded the Knight's Cross (22.10.42).

**BROWNING** ex-*WAR MARTEN* • GRT 5332 • Built 1919
12.11.42: Torpedoed and sunk by German submarine U-593 (Kelbing), in the Mediterranean near Mostaganem, Algeria, in position 35.52N 00.45E while on government service on a

voyage from Barrow to Oran, with a cargo of US military stores including TNT and a deck cargo of four bulldozers, part of convoy KMS 2 comprising 56 ships. The Master, Capt Thomas J. Sweeney, 42 crew, 16 gunners and 2 naval signalmen were rescued by HM trawler *FLUELLEN* 545/40 (Lt H.N. Rogers) and landed at Oran. 1 crew was lost.

### DEVIS • GRT 7761 • Built 1938

5.7.43: Torpedoed and sunk by German submarine U-593 (Kelbling), in the Mediterranean NE of Cap Bengut, in position 37.01N 04.10E while on a voyage from the Clyde 24.6.43 to Sicily, with the convoy commodore Rear Admiral H.T. England RN, 6 naval staff, 289 Canadian troops, 4000 tons of government stores and a deck cargo of two landing craft, part of convoy KMS 18B comprising 19 ships. The Master, Capt Walter Denson, the Commodore, crew of 38, 8 gunners, naval staff and 237 troops were rescued by HM destroyer *CLEVELAND* 907/40 (L.46) (Lt J.K. Hamilton) and landed at Bougie. 52 Canadian troops were lost. Kapitänleutnant Gerd Kelbling was awarded the Knight's Cross (19.8.43).

## MOWT

### COCKAPONSET • GRT 5995 • Built 1919

20.5.41: Torpedoed and sunk by German submarine U-556 (Wohlfarth), in the Atlantic SSE of Cape Farewell, in position 57.28N 41.07W while on a voyage from Houston to Holyhead and Cardiff via Halifax NS, with a cargo of 2719 tons of steel, 1924 tons of carbon black, 250 tons of TNT, 223 tons of trucks and 1162 tons of generals, part of convoy HX 126 comprising 29 ships. The Master, Capt Benjamin Green, and crew of 40 were rescued by rescue ship *HONTESTROOM* 1857/21 and landed at Reykjavik 27.5.41.

### WILLIMANTIC • GRT 4857 • Built 1918

24.6.42: Sunk by gunfire by German submarine U-156 (Hartenstein), in the Atlantic SE of Bermuda, in position 25.55N 51.58W while sailing independently on a voyage from Durban and Cape Town 30.5.42 to Charleston, Virginia and Baltimore, in ballast. The Master, Capt Leon Otto Everett, was taken prisoner, landed at Lorient 7.7.42, and was taken to Milag Nord. The Chief Officer's boat and 14 crew landed after 12 days at St Martin's Island, Lesser Antilles; they were brought by Dutch ship *BARALT* 780/21 to St Thomas, Virgin Islands. The 2nd Officer, 13 crew and 2 gunners were rescued after 6 days by Norwegian ship *TAMERLANE* 6778/36 and landed at Rio de Janeiro. 3 officers and 3 crew were lost.

## LARRINAGA & CO. LTD – LIVERPOOL

### JOSE DE LARRINAGA ex-LOCH TAY • GRT 5303 • Built 1920

7.9.40: Torpedoed and sunk by German submarine U-47 (Prien), in the Atlantic NW of Rockall, in position 58.30N 16.10W while on a voyage from New York to Newport, Mon. via Sydney CB, with a cargo of 5303 tons of steel and linseed oil, part of convoy SC 2 comprising 53 ships. The Master, Capt Arthur Townshend Gass, crew of 38 and 1 gunner were lost.

### ENA DE LARRINAGA • GRT 5200 • Built 1925

5.4.41: Torpedoed and sunk by German submarine U-105 (Schewe), in the Atlantic 205 miles E of St Paul Rocks, in position 01.10N 26.00W while sailing independently on a voyage from Hull to Buenos Aires, with 2 military, 2 naval gunners, 5607 tons of coal and general cargo, dispersed from convoy OB 276 comprising 34 ships. The Master, Capt Richard Sharpe Craston, and 18 survivors were rescued after 13 days and landed at Rio de Fogo near Toures, Brazil; the Chief Officer and 18 survivors were rescued by Brazilian ship *ALMIRANTE ALEXANDRINO* 5786/00 and landed at Pernambuco. 4 crew and 1 gunner were lost. Capt R.S. Craston was awarded the Lloyd's War Medal for bravery at sea.

### *RUPERT DE LARRINAGA* • GRT 5358 • Built 1930
14.7.41: Torpedoed and sunk by Italian submarine *MOROSINI* (Fraternale), in the Atlantic W of Madeira, in position 36.18N 21.11W while sailing independently on a voyage from the Tyne and Oban to Las Palmas, with a cargo of 7098 tons of coal and general, dispersed from convoy OG 67 comprising 51 ships. The Master, Capt Harold James Kay, and crew of 43 were rescued by Spanish tanker *CAMPECHE* 6382/34, transferred to HM armed trawlers *IMPERIALIST* 520/39 (FY.126) (Lt W.SS Fowler RCNVR) and *LOCH OSKAIG* 534/37 (FY.175) (Lt-Cdr S. Darling RANR) and landed at Gibraltar.

### *NICETO DE LARRINAGA* • GRT 5591 • Built 1916
22.9.41: Torpedoed and sunk by German submarine U–103 (Winter), in the Atlantic W of the Canary Islands, in position 27.32N 24.26W while on a voyage from Lagos and Freetown 14.9.41 to London, with a cargo of 3866 tons of palm kernels, 2000 tons of manganese ore, 2482 tons of groundnuts and 622 tons of general cargo, part of convoy SL 87 comprising 11 ships escorted by HM sloops *BIDEFORD* 1045/31 (L.43) (Lt-Cdr W.J. Moore), *GORLESTON* 1546/29 (Y.92) (Cdr R.W. Keymer) ex-US Coastguard cutter *ITASCA*, *LULWORTH* 1546/28 (Y.60) (Lt-Cdr C. Gwinner) ex-US Coastguard cutter *CHELAN*, HM corvette *GARDENIA* 925/40 (K.99) (Lt-Cdr H. Hill) and Free French corvette *COMMANDANT DUBOC* 630/38 of Escort Group 40. The Master, Capt Frederick Moulton Milnes, 43 crew, 5 gunners and 4 DBS were rescued. 11 survivors were rescued by HMS *GARDENIA* and landed at Azores and 42 crew by HMS *LULWORTH* and landed at Londonderry 4.10.41. 2 crew were lost.

### *SYLVIA DE LARRINAGA* • GRT 5218 • Built 1925
14.8.42: Torpedoed and sunk by Italian submarine *REGINALDO GIULIANI* (Bruno), in the Atlantic SW of the Cape Verde Islands, in position 10.49N 33.35W while sailing independently on a voyage from Durban and Cape Town to Baltimore and New York, with a cargo of 2000 tons of manganese ore, as ballast. The Master, Capt Alfred Grant Howe, 39 crew and 10 gunners were rescued; the Master's boat with 23 survivors was rescued by Port Line ship *PORT JACKSON* 9687/37 and landed at Liverpool, the Chief Officer's boat with 25 survivors by the Italian tankers *ARCOLA* 6349/29 and *TAIGETE* 4672/08 and landed at Curacao 6.9.42. 3 crew were lost. The *REGINALDO GIULIANI* was captured by the Germans at Singapore and renamed UIT–23. Korvettenkapitän Heinrich Schaffer was lost on 14.2.44 when UIT-23 was sunk in the Strait of Malacca, in position 04.25N 100.09E by HM submarine *TALLY HO* 1090/42 (P.317) (Lt-Cdr L.W.A. Bennington). The U-boat commander and 13 crew were rescued by the Japanese. 26 crew were lost.

## MOWT

**EMPIRE BLANDA** ex-*RIO GRANDE* ex-*SOKOL* ex-*NILE* • GRT 5693 • Built 1919
19.2.41: Torpedoed and sunk by German submarine U-69 (Metzler), in the Atlantic SW of the Faröe Islands, in position 58.50N 12.12W while on a voyage from Baltimore to Grangemouth via Halifax NS, with a cargo of scrap iron and steel, a straggler from convoy HX 107 comprising 26 ships. The Master, Capt George Allan Duncan, crew of 36 and 3 gunners were lost.

**OCEAN VENTURE** • GRT 7174 • Built 1941
8.2.42: Torpedoed and sunk by German submarine U-108 (Scholtz), part of 'Operation Paukenschlag' (Drumbeat), the second wave of five U-boats, in the Atlantic near Cape Hatteras, in position 37.05N 74.46W while sailing independently on a voyage from Vancouver BC and Cristobal to Hampton Roads, with a cargo of 9115 tons of foodstuffs and aircraft on deck. The Master, Capt Reginald Sharpe Craston, and 13 crew were rescued by US destroyer *ROE* 1570/39 (DD.418) and landed at Norfolk, Virginia. 29 crew and 2 gunners were lost.

**EMPIRE HAIL** • GRT 7005 • Built 1941
24.2.42: Torpedoed and sunk by German submarine U-94 (Ites), part of 'Operation Paukenschlag' (Drumbeat), the third wave of twelve U-boats, in the Atlantic E of St John's, Newfoundland, in position 44.48N 40.21W while on a voyage from Leith to Baltimore, in ballast. part of convoy ON 66 comprising 19 ships. The Master, Capt Robert Jones, crew of 41 and 7 gunners were lost.

**EMPIRE CLOUGH** • GRT 6147 • Built 1942
10.6.42: Torpedoed and sunk by German submarine U-94 (Ites), part of the 'Hecht' (Pike) patrol group of six U-boats, in the the Atlantic NE of St John's, Newfoundland, in position 51.50N 35.00W while on her maiden voyage from the Tyne to Boston and New York via Loch Ewe 2.10.42, in ballast, part of convoy ONS 100 comprising 38 ships. The Master, Capt Felix de Bastarrechea, 38 crew and 5 gunners were rescued. 32 survivors were rescued by HM corvette *DIANTHUS* 925/40 (K.95) (Lt-Cdr C.E. Bridgeman) and landed at St John's, Newfoundland, and 12 survivors were rescued by Portuguese trawler *ARGUS* 696/39, landed at Greenland 26.6.42 and were transferred on 30.6.42 to a US Navy patrol boat. 4 crew and 1 gunner were lost.

**OCEAN VOICE** • GRT 7174 • Built 1941
22.9.42: Torpedoed and sunk by German submarine U-435 (Strelow), in the North Atlantic W of Jan Mayen Island, in position 71.23N 11.03W while on government service on a voyage from Archangel 13.9.42 to the UK via Loch Ewe, with 25 Russian passengers, 858 standards of timber and 1121 tons of sulphite pulp, part of convoy QP 14 comprising 20 ships. The Master, Capt Harold James Kay, Commodore John C.K. Dowding CBE DSO RNR RD, 47 crew, 10 gunners. 5 naval staff and passengers were rescued, the Master, Commodore, 31 crew, 5 naval staff and Russian passengers by HM minesweeper *SEAGULL* 815/37 (N.85) (Lt-Cdr C.H. Pollock) and landed at Scapa Flow, Shetlands. 16 crew and 10 gunners were rescued by rescue ship *ZAMALEK* 1567/21 (Capt Owen Charles Morris DSO) and landed at Glasgow 27.9.42.

**EMPIRE MERSEY** ex-*RAMON DE LARRINAGA* • GRT 5791 • Built 1920

14.10.42: Torpedoed and sunk by German submarine U-618 (Baberg), part of the 'Wotan' (god of the Vikings) patrol group of ten U-boats, in the Atlantic SSE of Cape Farewell, in position 54.00N 40.15W while on a voyage from New York 3.10.42 to Manchester, with a cargo of 8400 tons of government stores, part of convoy SC 104 comprising 47 ships. The Master, Capt Felix de Bastarrechea, 13 crew and 2 gunners were lost. 37 crew and 2 gunners were rescued by rescue ship *GOTHLAND* 1286/32 (Capt James Murray Hadden OBE) and landed at Gourock 21.10.42.

**FORT CONCORD** • GRT 7138 • Built 1942

11.5.43: Torpedoed and sunk by German submarines U-403 (Clausen) and U-456 (Teichert), part of the 'Rhein' (Rhine) patrol group of twelve U-boats, in the Atlantic about 350 miles N of the Azores, in position 46.05N 25.20W while on a voyage from St John, New Brunswick and Halifax NS 3.5.43 to Manchester, with a cargo of 8500 tons of grain and 700 tons of military stores, a straggler from convoy HX 237 comprising 46 ships. The Master, Capt Francis Prideaux Ryan, 28 crew and 8 gunners were lost. The Chief Officer J.B. Tunbridge, 17 crew and 1 DBS were rescued by HMCS corvette *DRUMHELLER* 925/41 (K.167) (Lt-Cdr Leslie P. Denny) and landed at Londonderry. Kapitänleutnant Max-Martin Teichert and crew of 48 were lost when U-456, part of the 'Drossel' (Thrush) patrol group of eleven U-boats was sunk by a Fido air-dropped acoustic homing torpedo on 12.5.43 while shadowing convoy HX 237 in the Atlantic 500 miles N by E of Terceira, Azores, in position 46.40N 26.20W by Liberator 'B' FK229, pilot F/Lt John Wright of No. 86 Squadron RAF, based at Aldergrove, Co. Antrim, part of 15 Group. Korvettenkapitän Alfred Manhardt von Mannstein and crew of 46 were lost on 13.5.43 in the Atlantic 550 miles WSW of Cape Clear, in position 48.37N 22.39W when U-753, shadowing convoy HX 237, was attacked on the surface by Sunderland 'G' W6006, pilot F/Lt John Musgrave of No. 423 Squadron RCAF, based at Castle Archdale, Co. Fermanagh, part of 15 Group and finally sunk by HM frigate *LAGAN* 1370/42 (K.259) (Lt-Cdr A. Ayre) and RCN corvette *DRUMHELLER* 925/41 (K.167) (Lt-Cdr Leslie P. Denny). The commander of U-753, von Mannstein, was the son of the famous Panzer General Field-Marshal Erich von Mannstein of Stalingrad fame.

## LAWTHER, LATTA & COMPANY – LONDON
### Nitrate Producers SS Co. Ltd

**ANGLO-PERUVIAN** • GRT 5457 • Built 1926

24.2.41: Torpedoed and sunk by German submarine U-96 (Lehmann-Willenbrock), in the Atlantic SW of Iceland, in position 59.30N 21.00W while on a voyage from the Tyne and Loch Ewe to Boston, Mass, with a cargo of 3015 tons of coal, part of convoy OB 288 comprising 46 ships. The Master, Capt Cyril Mervyn Quick, 26 crew and 2 gunners were lost. 17 crew were rescued by British ship *HARBERTON* 4558/30 and landed at Halifax NS 4.3.41.

**ANGLO-CANADIAN** • GRT 5268 • Built 1928

25.6.42: Torpedoed and sunk by German submarine U-153 (Reichmann), in the Atlantic 800 miles NE of Antigua, in position 25.12N 55.31W while sailing independently on a voyage from Vizagapatam and Ascension to Baltimore via Cape Town 3.6.42, in ballast. The Master, Capt

David John Williams OBE, 38 crew and 10 gunners landed on St Kitts, Windward Islands. 1 crew was lost. U-153 commanded by Korvettenkapitän Wilfried Reichmann was attacked on 5/6.7.42 off Aruba by US Army Douglas B-18 of the 59th Bombardment Squadron based at Curacao. On 13.7.42, U-153 was forced to the surface by US submarine chaser PC-458 280/42 (also known as US *EVELYN R.*) and later sunk in the Atlantic 60 miles W of Colon, Panama, in position 09.56N 81.29W by US destroyer *LANSDOWNE* 1620/42 (DD-486) (Lt-Cdr William R. Smedberg III). The U-boat commander and crew of 51 were lost.

## MOWT

**EMPIRE SUNRISE** • GRT 7459 • Built 1941
2.11.42: Torpedoed and damaged by German submarine U-402 (v. Forstner) and later sunk by a *coup de grâce* by German submarine U-84 (Uphoff), part of the 'Veilchen' (Violet) patrol group of thirteen U-boats, in the Atlantic 500 miles E of Belle Ile, in position 51.50N 46.25W while on a voyage from Three Rivers to Belfast via Sydney CB 28.10.42, with a cargo of 10000 tons of steel and timber, part of convoy SC 107 comprising 42 ships. The Master, Capt Arthur William Hawkins, crew of 45 and 5 gunners were rescued by rescue ship *STOCKPORT* 1683/11 (Capt Thomas Ernest Fea OBE) and landed at Reykjavik 8.11.42. Kapitänleutnant Horst Uphoff and crew of 45 were lost on 24.8.43 when U-84 was sunk in the Atlantic 750 miles SW by S of the Azores, in position 27.09N 37.03W by an Avenger aircraft, pilot Lt William A. Felter of US Navy Composite Squadron VC-13 from US escort carrier *CORE* 9800/42 (CVE-13) of the Task Group 21.16.

## LEITH, HULL AND HAMBURG STEAM PACKET COMPANY – LEITH

**RUTLAND** • GRT 1437 • Built 1935
31.10.40: Torpedoed and sunk by German submarine U-124 (Schulz), in the Atlantic SW of Rockall, in position 57.14N 16.00W while on a voyage from Port Antonio, Jamaica, to Garston, with a cargo of bananas, a straggler from convoy HX 82 comprising 39 ships. The Master, Capt Robert N. Sinclair, and crew of 23 were lost.

## LIMERICK SS CO. LTD – LIMERICK

**LUIMNEACH** ex-*FAIRFIELD* • GRT 1074 • Built 1915
4.9.40: Sunk by gunfire by German submarine U-46 (Endrass), in the Bay of Biscay WSW of the Scilly Isles, in position 47.50N 09.12W while sailing independently on a voyage from Huelva to Drogheda, with a cargo of 1250 tons of pyrites. The Master, Capt Eric Septimus Jones, and 8 crew were rescued by a French fishing boat, transferred to a Spanish trawler and landed at Pasajes, Spain 13.9.40. 6 crew were lost. 3 crew were taken prisoner and landed at Lorient 6.9.40.

**CLONLARA** • GRT 1203 • Built 1926
22.8.41: Torpedoed and sunk by German submarine U-564 (Suhren), in the Atlantic W of Aveiro, Portugal, in position 40.43N 11.39W while on a voyage from Cardiff to Lisbon, with a cargo of 1000 tons of coal, part of convoy OG 71 comprising 21 ships. The Master, Capt Joseph Reynolds, and 12 crew were rescued by HM corvette *CAMPION* 925/41 (K.108) (Lt-Cdr A. Johnson) and landed at Gibraltar 24.8.41. 6 crew were lost.

## LONDON & EDINBURGH SHIPPING CO. LTD – EDINBURGH

*ROYAL ARCHER* • GRT 2266 • Built 1928
24.2.40: Struck a mine laid on 3.11.39 by German submarine U-21 (Frauenheim) and sank in the North Sea off the Firth of Forth, in position 56.06N 02.55W while on a voyage from London to Leith, with 630 tons of general cargo, dispersed from coastal convoy FN 100 comprising 39 ships. The Master, Charles A. Piper, and crew of 26 were rescued by HM sloop *WESTON* 1060/32 ex-HMS *WESTON SUPER MARE* (L.72) (Lt-Cdr S.C. Tuke) and landed at Rosyth.

## LONDON & NORTH EASTERN RAILWAY COMPANY – LONDON

*STOCKPORT* • GRT 1683 • Built 1911
23.2.43: Torpedoed and sunk by German submarine U-604 (Höltring), part of the 'Knappen' (Shieldbearer) patrol group of four U-boats, in the Atlantic E of Cape Race, in position 47.22N 34.10W while on government service on a voyage from Greenock to St John's, Newfoundland, acting as a rescue ship for convoy ON 166 comprising 48 ships. The Master, Capt Thomas Ernest Fea OBE, crew of 51, 9 gunners, 4 naval personnel and 91 crew from other sunken ships on board were lost. U-604, commanded by Kapitänleutnant Horst Höltring, was scuttled on 11.8.43 as result of attacks on 3.8.43 by Ventura, pilot Lt-Cdr T.D. Davies and Liberator, pilot Lt-Cdr Bertram Prueher of US Navy Bombing Squadrons VB–129 and VB-107 based at Natal and US destroyer *MOFFETT* 1850/35 (DD-362) (Lt Gilbert H. Richards) in the South Atlantic 240 miles E by N of Bahia, in position 09.10S 29.43W. Kapitänleutnant Horst Höltring and crew were rescued by U-185, commanded by Kapitänleutnant August Maus (Knight's Cross 21.9.43). Later U-172, commanded by Kapitänleutnant Carl Emmermann, rendezvoused with U-185, took on board 23 of U-604's crew and returned to Lorient 7.9.43. U-185 was sunk on 24.8.43 with loss of 14 crew from U-604 and 9 crew were taken prisoner by US four-stack destroyer *BARKER* 1090/19 (DD.213).

## LONDON POWER CO. LTD – LONDON

*ALEXANDER KENNEDY* • GRT 1313 • Built 1932
22.2.45: Torpedoed and sunk by German submarine U-1004 (Hinz), in the English Channel SE of Falmouth, in position 50.06N 04.50W while on a voyage from Barry to London, with a cargo of coal, part of coastal convoy BTC 76 comprising 12 ships. The Master, Capt John William Johnson, 15 crew and 2 gunners were rescued by British ships *ESKWOOD* 791/11 and *GATESHEAD* 744/19 and landed at Plymouth. 1 crew was lost. Capt J.W. Johnson was awarded the Lloyd's War Medal for bravery at sea. On the same day U-1004 sank one of the escorts, RCN corvette *TRENTONIAN* 925/43 (K.368) (Lt Colin S. Glassco), in the English Channel 12 miles E of Falmouth, in position 50.06N 04.50W. U-1004, commanded by Oberleutnant zur See Rudolf Hinz, surrendered at Bergen on 9.5.45. U-1004 sailed from Cairnryan, Loch Ryan, on 1.12.45 in tow of HM rescue tug *BUSTLER* 1120/41 (W.72) and was sunk by gunfire by HM destroyer *ONSLAUGHT* ex-HMS *PATHFINDER* 1540/41 (G.04) (Lt C.W. Eason) and ORP destroyer *PIORUN* 1690/40 (G.65) ex-HMS *NERISSA* in the Atlantic SW of Barra, Hebrides, in position 56.10N 10.05W, part of 'Operation Deadlight', the disposal of 116 U-boats by the Royal Navy.

## LYLE SHIPPING CO. LTD – GLASGOW

*CAPE NELSON* ex-*KNIGHT OF ST MICHAEL* • GRT 3807 • Built 1929
24.2.41: Torpedoed and sunk by German submarine U–69 (Metzler), in the Atlantic SW of Iceland, in position 59.30N 21.00W while on a voyage from Hull to New York, in ballast, part of convoy OB 288 comprising 46 ships. The Master, Capt Kenneth Malcolm Mackenzie, and 3 crew were lost. 34 crew were rescued by British ship *HARBERTON* 4558/30 and landed at Halifax NS 4.3.41.

### Cape of Good Hope Motor Co. Ltd

*CAPE RODNEY* • GRT 4512 • Built 1940
5.8.41: Torpedoed and and damaged by German submarine U–75 (Ringelmann), in the Atlantic W of Ireland, in position 53.26N 15.40W while on a voyage from Lagos and Freetown 15.7.41 to London, with a cargo of 7320 tons of palm kernels, groundnuts and manganese ore, a straggler from convoy SL 81 comprising 18 ships; on 7.8.41 she was taken in tow by Admiralty tug *ZWARTE ZEE* 793/33 (W.163) in position 52.11N 14.42W and later foundered on 9.8.41 W of Ushant in position 52.44N 11.41W. The Master, Capt Peter Allan Wallace, crew of 31 and 4 gunners were rescued by HM corvette *HYDRANGEA* 925/40 (K.39) (Lt J.E. Woolfenden) and landed at Gourock and 3 crew by HM corvette *ZINNIA* 925/40 (K.98) (Lt-Cdr C.G. Cuthbertson) and landed at Londonderry.

*CAPE OF GOOD HOPE* • GRT 4963 • Built 1925
11.5.42: Torpedoed and sunk by gunfire by German submarine U–502 (v. Rosenstiel), in the Atlantic NE of the Virgin Islands, in position 22.48N 58.43W while sailing independently on a voyage from New York 5.5.42 to Basrah, Bandar Shapur and Abadan via Cape Town, with a cargo of 7500 tons of general and military cargo. The Master, Capt Alexander Campbell's boat with 18 survivors landed on Tortola, Virgin Islands 24.5.42, the Chief Officer's boat with 19 survivors landed after 18 days at Burgentra near Puerto Plata, Dominican Republic 28.5.42. Kapitänleutnant Jurgen von Rosenstiel and crew of 51 were lost on 6.7.42 when U–502 was sunk in the Bay of Biscay 130 miles NE of Cape Ortegal, in position 46.10N 06.40W by a Leigh Light-equipped Wellington 'H', pilot P/O Wiley B. Howell (American) of No. 172 Squadron RAF, based at Chivenor, Devon, part of 19 Group. The pilot was awarded the DFC. This was the first successful attack by a Leigh Light-equipped aircraft, and the first by a Wellington.

*CAPE VERDE* • GRT 6914 • Built 1941
9.7.42: Torpedoed and sunk by German submarine U–203 (Mützelburg), in the Atlantic E of Grenada, in position 11.32N 60.17W while sailing independently from Suez to Baltimore and New York via Cape Town and Trinidad, with general cargo including cotton, silicon and 1500 tons of chrome ore. The Master, Capt John Rankin McIntyre, 31 crew and 8 gunners landed at the Bay of St Vincent, Windward Islands 14.7.42. 1 crew and 1 gunner were lost. Kapitänleutnant Rolf Mützelburg was awarded the Knight's Cross (17.11.41) with Oak Leaves (15.7.42).

*CAPE RACE* ex-**KNIGHT OF ST JOHN** • GRT 3807 • Built 1930
10.8.42: Torpedoed and sunk by German submarine U–660 (Baur), in the Atlantic S of Iceland, in position 56.45N 22.50W while on a voyage from Boston, Mass. to Manchester via

Sydney CB 31.7.42, with a cargo of 1230 standards of timber (3979 tons) and 1040 tons of steel, part of convoy SC 94 comprising 30 ships. The Master, Capt James Barnetson, crew of 45, 5 gunners and 12 crew from Port Line ship *PORT NICHOLSON* 8402/19 were rescued: 24 survivors by HM corvettes *NASTURTIUM* 925/40 (K.107) (Lt C.D. Smith DSC) ex-French *LA PAMPOLAISE* and 39 by *DIANTHUS* 925/40 (K.95) (Lt-Cdr C.E. Bridgeman) and landed at Liverpool. U-210 commanded by Kapitänleutnant Rudolf Lemcke was sunk on 6.8.42 in the Atlantic 650 miles NE of Cape Race, in position 54.25N 39.37W while pursuing convoy SC 94 by RCN destroyer *ASSINIBOINE* 1390/31 (D.18) ex-HMS *KEMPENFELT* (Lt-Cdr John H. Stubbs). The U-boat commander and 5 crew were lost. 11 crew were taken prisoner by HMCS *ASSINIBOINE* and 28 crew by HMS *DIANTHUS*. Lt-Cdr J.H. Stubbs was awarded the DSO. U-660, commanded by Kapitänleutnant Gotz Bauer, was sunk on 12.11.42 in the Mediterranean 20 miles N of Cape Caxine, Algeria, in position 36.07N 01.00W by the escorts of convoy TE 3 comprising 17 ships, HM corvettes *LOTUS* 925/42 (K.93) (Lt-Cdr J. Hall) and *STARWORT* 925/41 (K.20) (Lt A.H. Kent). The U-boat commander and 44 crew were taken prisoner by HMS *STARWORT*. 2 crew were lost.

## MOWT

### EMPIRE BUFFALO ex-*EGLANTINE* • GRT 6404 • Built 1919
6.5.42: Torpedoed and sunk by German submarine U-125 (Folkers), in the Atlantic W of the Cayman Islands, BWI, in position 19.14N 82.34W while sailing independently on a voyage from Kingston, Jamaica, to New Orleans, in ballast. The Master, Capt John Hill, 7 crew and 5 gunners were lost. 28 crew and 1 gunner were rescued by US ship *CACIQUE* 2718/18 and landed at Kingston.

### EMPIRE DAY • GRT 7242 • Built 1941
7.8.44: Torpedoed and sunk by German submarine U-198 (v. Waldegg), in the Indian Ocean 200 miles E of Dar es Salaam, in position 07.06S 42.00E while sailing independently on a voyage from Lourenco Marques to Aden and Port Said, with a cargo of 8226 tons of coal. The Master, Capt Charles Gordon Mallett, 33 crew and 8 gunners landed on the island of Zanzibar. The Chief Officer R.C. Selfe was taken prisoner. U-198, commanded by Oberleutnant zur See Burkhard Heusinger von Waldegg, was attacked on 10.8.44 by an Avenger of No. 857 Naval Air Squadron from HM escort carrier *SHAH* 11420/43 (D.21) (Capt W.J. Yendell), again attacked on 12.8.44 by a Catalina and an Avenger from HM escort *BEGUM* 11420/42 (D.38) (Capt J.E. Broomer DSO) and sunk in the Indian Ocean 180 miles WNW of the Seychelles, in position 03.35S 52.49E by HM frigates *FINDHORN* 1370/42 (K.301) (Lt-Cdr J.C. Dawson) and *PARRET* 1370/43 (K.304) (Lt-Cdr T. Hood), and RIN sloop *GODAVARI* 1050/41 (U.52) (Cdr J.N. Jefford). The U-boat commander, crew of 65 and the Chief Officer of the *EMPIRE DAY* were lost.

## MACANDREWS & CO. LTD – LONDON

### PIZARRO • GRT 1367 • Built 1923
31.1.41: Torpedoed and sunk by Italian submarine *DANDOLO* (Boris), in the Atlantic SW of Cape Clear, in position 49.03N 19.40W while sailing independently on a voyage from London to Seville, with general cargo. The Master, Capt John Gillanders, and 26 crew were rescued by British ship *MACBRAE* 2117/24 and landed at Lisbon. 21 crew were lost.

**CISCAR** • GRT 1809 • Built 1919
19.8.41: Torpedoed and sunk by German submarine U-201 (Schnee), in the Atlantic 400 miles SW of Ireland, in position 49.10N 17.40W while on a voyage from Bristol to Gibraltar, with 1400 tons of general cargo and government stores, part of convoy OG 71 comprising 21 ships. The Master, Capt Edward Lenton Hughes, 29 crew and 5 gunners were rescued by British ship *PETREL* 1354/20 and landed at Lisbon. 9 crew and 4 gunners were lost.

**CORTES** • GRT 1374 • Built 1919
26.9.41: Torpedoed and sunk by German submarine U-203 (Mützelburg), in the Atlantic N of the Azores, in position 47.48N 23.45W while on a voyage from Lisbon to London, with 6 passengers and general cargo including potash and cork, part of convoy HG 73 comprising 25 ships. The Master, Capt Donald Ray McRae, crew of 35 and passengers were lost.

**CERVANTES** • GRT 1810 • Built 1919
26.9.41: Torpedoed and sunk by German submarine U-201 (Schnee), in the Atlantic NNE of the Azores, in position 48.37N 20.01W while on a voyage from Lisbon to Liverpool, with a cargo of 500 tons of potash and 400 tons of cork, part of convoy HG 73 comprising 25 ships. The Master, Capt Henry Austin Fraser, 27 crew, 3 gunners and 1 DBS were rescued by HM sloop *STARLING* 1350/42 (U.66) (Cdr Frederic John Walker) and landed at Liverpool. 3 crew, 2 gunners and 3 DBS were lost.

**PELAYO** • GRT 1346 • Built 1927
15.6.42: Torpedoed and sunk by German submarine U-552 (Topp), in the Atlantic 400 miles WNW of Corunna, in position 43.18N 17.38W while on government service on a voyage from Gibraltar 10.6.42 to Swansea, with 755 tons of government stores and scrap iron, part of convoy HG 84 comprising 23 ships. The Master, Capt Robert Hughes Williams, 24 crew, 2 gunners and 3 naval staff were rescued by rescue ship *COPELAND* 1526/23 (Capt W.J. Hartley DSC) and landed at Gourock 20.6.42. The convoy's commodore H.T. Hudson RNR RD, 11 crew, 3 gunners and 2 naval staff were lost.

**PINTO** • GRT 1346 • Built 1928
8.9.44: Torpedoed and sunk by German submarine U-482 (v. Matuschka), in the Atlantic NNE of Tory Island, in position 55.27N 08.01W while on a voyage from Halifax NS to Greenock, in ballast. *PINTO* was on government service acting as the rescue ship for convoy HXF 305 comprising 100 ships. The Master, Capt Lawrence Stanley Boggs MBE, 6 crew, 8 gunners, 1 signalman and 2 crew from the tanker *EMPIRE HERITAGE* 15702/30 were lost. 29 crew, 8 gunners, 1 surgeon, 2 sick bay attendants and 1 signalman were rescued by HM trawler *NORTHERN WAVE* 655/36 (FY.153) (Lt F.J.R. Storey) and landed at Londonderry. Kapitänleutnant Hartmut Graf von Matuschka and crew of 47 were lost on 16.1.45 when U-482 was sunk in the North Channel NW of Machrihanish, Mull of Kintyre, in position 55.30N 05.53W by HM sloops *PEACOCK* 1350/43 (U.96) (Lt-Cdr Richard B. Stannard VC), *HART* 1350/43 (U.58) (Cdr M.B. Sherwood), *STARLING* 1350/42 (U.66) (Cdr G.W.E. Castens DSO), *LOCH CRAGGIE* 1435/44 (K.609) (Lt-Cdr C.L.L. Davies) and *AMETHYST* 1350/43 (U.16) (Lt N. Scott-Elliot) of the 22nd Escort Group.

## MACLAY & McINTYRE – GLASGOW

*LOCH MADDY* • GRT 4996 • Built 1934
21.2.40: Torpedoed and damaged by German submarine U-57 (Korth), later sunk by a *coup de grâce* by German submarine U-23 (Kretschmer) in the Atlantic 92 miles SSW of Rockall, while sailing independently on a voyage from Vancouver and Victoria, British Columbia to Leith via Panama and Halifax NS 7.2.40, with a cargo of 2000 tons of wheat, 6000 tons of timber and aircraft, dispersed from convoy HX 19 comprising 44 ships. The Master, Capt William James Park, and 34 crew were rescued by HM destroyer *DIANA* 1375/32 (H.49) (Lt-Cdr E.G. Le Geyt) and landed at Scapa Flow. 4 crew were lost. The stern section of *LOCH MADDY* was taken in tow by HM rescue tug *ST MELLONS* 860/18 (W.81) (Lt H. King) to Inganess Bay, Orkneys Islands, for the salvage of the cargo. U-23 commanded by Oberleutnant zur See Rudolf Arendt was scuttled on 10.9.44 in the Black Sea N of Agra, Turkey, in position 41.11N 30.00E. The U-boat commander and crew were interned by the Turkish authorities at Beyschir.

*UGANDA* • GRT 4966 • Built 1927
19.10.40: Torpedoed and sunk by German submarine U-38 (Liebe), in the Atlantic 250 miles WNW of Bloody Foreland, in position 56.37N 17.15W while on a voyage from Montreal to Milford Haven via Halifax NS 8.10.40, with a cargo of 6200 tons of lumber and 2006 tons of steel, part of convoy HX 79 comprising 49 ships. The Master, Capt Charles Mackinnon, and crew of 39 were rescued by HM sloop *JASON* 835/37 (N.99) (Lt-Cdr R.E. Terry) and landed at Methil.

*LOCH LOMOND* • GRT 5452 • Built 1934
20.10.40: Torpedoed and sunk by gunfire by German submarine U-100 (Schepke), in the Atlantic SW of Rockall, in position 56.00N 14.30W while on a voyage from Montreal to Immingham via Halifax NS 8.10.40, with a cargo of 6000 tons of lumber and 1858 tons of steel, a straggler from convoy HX 79 comprising 49 ships. The Master, Capt William James Park, and 38 crew were rescued by HM sloop *JASON* 835/37 (N.99) (Lt-Cdr R.E. Terry) and landed at Methil. 1 crew was lost.

*INDUNA* • GRT 5086 • Built 1925
30.3.42: Torpedoed and sunk by German submarine U-376 (Marks), in the Barents Sea NE of Kola Inlet, in position 70.55N 37.18E while sailing independently on a voyage from New York to Murmansk via Reykjavik 20.3.42, with a cargo of 2700 tons of war material and gasoline, dispersed from convoy PQ 13 comprising 19 ships. The Master, Capt William Norman Collins, 20 crew and 6 gunners were lost. 19 crew and 4 gunners were rescued by a Russian minesweeper and landed at Murmansk. Kapitänleutnant Friedrich Marks and crew of 46 were lost on 10.4.43 when U-376 was sunk in the Atlantic 190 miles WSW of Ushant, in position 46.48N 09.00W by a Leigh Light-equipped Wellington XII 'C', pilot P/O G.H. Whitely of No. 172 Squadron RAF, based at Chivenor, Devon, part of 19 Group.

*LOCH DON* • GRT 5249 • Built 1937
1.4.42: Torpedoed and sunk by German submarine U-202 (Linder), part of 'Operation Paukenschlag' (Drumbeat), the fourth wave of eleven U-boats, in the Atlantic 500 miles

NNE of Bermuda, in position 37.05N 61.40W while sailing independently on a voyage from New York 29.3.42 to Cape Town, with 6000 tons of general cargo. The Master, Capt Malcolm Wright Anderson, 37 crew and 6 gunners were rescued by Canadian auxiliary schooner *HELEN FURSEY* 167/29 and landed at Burin, Newfoundland. 3 crew were lost. U-202 commanded by Kapitänleutnant Günter Poser was sunk on 1.6.43 in the Atlantic about 315 miles SE of Cape Farewell, in position 56.12N 39.52W by HM sloops *STARLING* 1350/42 (U.66) (Capt Frederic John Walker CB DSO DSC RN), *WILD GOOSE* 1250/42 (U.45) (Lt-Cdr D.E.G. Wemyss) and *KITE* 1350/42 (U.87) (Lt-Cdr W.F. Segrave) of the 2nd Support Group. The U-boat commander and 17 crew were taken prisoner by HMS *STARLING* and 12 crew by HMS *WILD GOOSE*. 18 crew were lost.

*JANETA* • GRT 5312 • Built 1929
1.5.44: Torpedoed and sunk by German submarine U-181 (Freiwald), in the South Atlantic 900 miles S by W of Ascension Island, in position 18.14S 20.00W while sailing independently on a voyage from Algiers and Gibraltar 15.4.44 to Rio de Janeiro and the River Plate, in ballast. The Master, Capt John Cameron, 31 crew and 3 gunners were rescued; the Master, 3rd Officer and 8 survivors were rescued and landed at Bahia 14.5.44. 25 more survivors were rescued 150 miles S of Bahia by Swedish ship *FREJA* 1497/38 and landed at Rio de Janeiro. 10 further survivors were rescued on 12.5.44 by US escort destroyer *ALGER* 1240/43 (DD.101) and landed at Bahia. 9 crew and 4 gunners were lost.

**MOWT**

*OCEAN MIGHT* • GRT 7173 • Built 1942
3.9.42: Torpedoed and sunk by German submarine U-109 (Bleichrodt), in the Atlantic SW of Takoradi, in position 00.57N 04.11W while sailing independently on a voyage from Liverpool 9.8.42 to Cape Town and the Middle East, with a cargo of 7000 tons of military stores, dispersed from convoy OS 37 comprising 33 ships. The Master, Capt William James Park, 40 crew and 9 gunners landed 35 miles E of Accra at Ningo, Gold Coast. 3 crew and 1 gunner were lost.

**MAGEE, SON & COMPANY – WEST HARTLEPOOL**
**Hartlepool SS Co.**

*EDENCRAG* • GRT 1592 • Built 1940
14.12.42: Torpedoed and sunk by German submarine U-443 (v. Puttkamer), in the Mediterranean W of Algiers, in position 35.49N 01.25W while on government service on a voyage from Gibraltar to North Africa, with 800 tons of military stores, part of convoy TE 9. The Master, Capt James Gentles, 10 crew and 2 gunners were lost. 9 crew and 2 gunners were rescued by HM corvette *SAMPHIRE* 925/41 (K.128) (Lt-Cdr F.T. Renny) and landed at Algiers. Oberleutnant zur See Konstantin von Puttkamer and crew of 47 were lost on 23.2.43 when U-443 was sunk in the Mediterranean 35 miles W of Algiers, in position 36.55N 02.25E by HM escort destroyers *BICESTER* 1050/41 (L.34) (Lt-Cdr S.W.F. Bennett), *LAMERTON* 1050/40 (L.88) (Lt-Cdr C.R. Purse) and *WHEATLAND* 1050/41 (L.122) (Lt-Cdr P. de L. Brooke).

## MANCHESTER LINERS LIMITED – MANCHESTER

*MANCHESTER BRIGADE* • GRT 6021 • Built 1918
26.9.40: Torpedoed and sunk by German submarine U–137 (Wohlfarth), in the Atlantic W of Malin Head, in position 54.53N 10.22W while on a voyage from Manchester to Montreal, with a cargo of 1147 tons of government and general goods, part of convoy OB 218 comprising 25 ships. The Master, Capt Frederick L. Clough, Commodore Vice-Admiral Humphrey Hugh Smith DSO RNR, 47 crew, 1 gunner and 6 naval staff were lost. 4 crew were rescued by French hospital ship *CANADA* 9684/12 and landed at Gibraltar.

*MANCHESTER MERCHANT* • GRT 7264 • Built 1940
25.2.43: Torpedoed and sunk by German submarine U–628 (Hasenschar), part of the 'Ritter' (Knight) patrol group of twelve U-boats in the Atlantic 410 miles ESE of Cape Race, in position 45.10N 43.23W while on a voyage from Manchester to New York via Halifax NS and St John, New Brunswick, in ballast, part of convoy ON 166 comprising 48 ships. The Master, Capt Frederick Struss DSC, 27 crew and 4 gunners were rescued by HM destroyer *MONTGOMERY* 1090/18 (G.95) (Lt-Cdr W.L. Puxley) ex-USN four-stack *ICKES* and RCN corvette *ROSTHERN* 925/40 (K.160) (Lt P.B. Cross) and landed at St John's, Newfoundland. 29 crew and 6 gunners were lost. The *MANCHESTER MERCHANT* sank in 90 seconds.

*MANCHESTER CITIZEN* • GRT 5328 • Built 1925
9.7.43: Torpedoed and sunk by German submarine U–508 (Staats), in the Atlantic SE of Lagos in position 05.50N 02.22E while sailing independently on a voyage from Freetown 3.7.43 to Lagos, in ballast, part of convoy ST 71 comprising 12 ships. The Master, Capt George Stanley Swales, 44 crew, 8 gunners and 23 Krooboys were rescued by Free French corvette *COMMANDANTE DETROYAT* 925/40 ex-HMS *CORIANDER* ex-HMS *IRIS* and landed at Lagos. 12 crew, 2 gunners and 14 Krooboys were lost.

## MARGULIES, O. – LONDON
**Pallas Oil & Trading Co. Ltd**

*STRATFORD* ex-*LUMINOUS* (tanker) • GRT 4753 • Built 1913
26.9.40: Torpedoed and sunk by German submarine U–137 (Wohlfarth), in the Atlantic 85 miles WSW of Bloody Foreland, in position 54.50N 10.40W while on a voyage from Liverpool 24.9.40 to Aruba, in ballast, part of convoy OB 218 comprising 25 ships. The Master, Capt James Robertson Murray, and 14 crew were rescued by HM corvette *GLOXINA* 925/40 (K.22) (Lt-Cdr A.J.C. Pomeroy) and 17 crew were rescued by HM trawler *WOLVES* 422/34 (FY.158) (Skipper B. Pile). 2 crew were lost.

## MARITIME NAVIGATION COMPANY – NASSAU, BAHAMAS

*WESTERN HEAD* ex-*CUMBERLAND* • GRT 2599 • Built 1899
29.5.42: Torpedoed and sunk by German submarine U–107 (Gelhaus), in the Windward Passage 50 miles E of Guantanamo Bay, Cuba, in position 19.57N 74.18W while sailing independently on a voyage from Port Antonio and Kingston, Jamaica to Sydney CB, with a

cargo of 3710 tons of sugar. The Master, Capt Thurlow W. Bagnell, and 5 crew were rescued by a US Navy patrol ship and landed at Guantanamo Bay. 24 crew were lost.

## MARITIME SHIPPING & TRADING CO. LTD – CARDIFF
## MOWT

**EMPIRE LEOPARD** ex-*ONOMEA* ex-*MARIAN OTIS CHANDLER* ex-*WEST HAVEN*
GRT 5676 • Built 1917
2.11.42: Torpedoed and sunk by German submarine U–402 (v. Forstner), part of the 'Veilchen' (Violet) patrol group of thirteen U-boats, in the Atlantic 500 miles E of Belle Ile in position 52.26N 45.22W while on a voyage from Botwood and St John's, Newfoundland 29.10.42 via Sydney CB to Belfast and Avonmouth, with a cargo of 7410 tons of zinc concentrates and munitions, part of convoy SC 107 comprising 42 ships. The Master, Capt John Evan Evans, 31 crew and 7 gunners were lost. 3 crew were rescued by rescue ship *STOCKPORT* 1637/11 (Capt Thomas Ernest Fea OBE) and landed at Reykjavik 8.11.42.

## MARKLAND SHIPPING CO. LTD – LIVERPOOL, NOVA SCOTIA
## Liverpool Packet Shipping Co. Ltd

**LIVERPOOL PACKET** ex-*SONIA* ex-*DELSON* ex-*NIDARNES* • GRT 1188 • Built 1926
31.5.42: Torpedoed and sunk by German submarine U–432 (Schultze), in the Atlantic 15 miles W of Seal Island, Nova Scotia, in position 43.20N 66.20W while sailing independently on a voyage from New York to Halifax NS, with a cargo of 1945 tons of US government stores. The Master, Capt Norman Emmons Smith, and 18 crew landed at Seal Island, near Cape Sable. 2 crew were lost. Kapitänleutnant Heinz Otto Schultze was awarded the Knight's Cross (9.7.42).

## Vineland Shipping Co. Ltd

**VINELAND** ex-*SAPINERO* • GRT 5587 • Built 1919
20.4.42: Torpedoed and sunk by gunfire by German submarine U–154 (Kölle), in the Atlantic N of Cap Haitien, Haiti, in position 23.05N 72.20W while sailing independently on a voyage from Portland, Maine to St Thomas, Virgin Islands, in ballast. The Master, Capt Robert A. Williams, and 35 crew landed at Turks Island, BWI. 1 crew was lost.

## MARSHALL, S. & COMPANY – SUNDERLAND
## Brinkburn SS Co. Ltd

**BRINKBURN** • GRT 1598 • Built 1924
21.6.43: Torpedoed and sunk by German submarine U–73 (Dechert), in the Mediterranean W of Algiers, in position 36.53N 02.22E while on government service on a voyage from Swansea to Gibraltar 18.6.43 and Philippeville, with a cargo of 2500 tons of government stores including 800 tons of ammunition, part of convoy TE 22 comprising 2 ships, 15 landing craft and 12 fishing vessels. The Master, Capt Norman Johnson, 21 crew and 5 gunners were lost. 1 crew and 5 gunners were rescued by landing craft and a fishing vessel and landed at Algiers. U–73, commanded by Oberleutnant zur See Horst Deckert, was sunk

while attacking convoy GUS 24 comprising 72 ships on 16.12.43 in the Mediterranean 30 miles NNW of Oran, in position 36.07N 00.50W by US destroyers *TRIPPE* 1500/38 (DD-403) (Lt-Cdr C.M. Dalton) and *WOOLSEY* 1620/41 (DD-437) (Lt-Cdr H.R. Weir). The U-boat commander and 33 crew were taken prisoner by the US destroyers and landed at Oran. 16 crew were lost.

## MASSEY, W.A. & SONS LIMITED – HULL

*FRANCES MASSEY* • GRT 4212 • Built 1927
7.6.40: Torpedoed and sunk by German submarine U-48 (Rösing), in the Atlantic 14 miles NW of Tory Island, in position 55.33N 08.26W while sailing independently on a voyage from Wabana, Conception Bay to Glasgow, with a cargo of 7500 tons of iron ore. The sole survivor, Master Capt Walter Whitehead, was rescued by HM destroyer *VOLUNTEER* 1120/19 (D.71) (Lt-Cdr N. Lanyou). 33 crew and 1 gunner were lost. The *FRANCES MASSEY* sank in 30 seconds.

## McCOWEN & GROSS LIMITED – LONDON

*DERRYMORE* • GRT 4799 • Built 1938
13.2.42: Torpedoed and sunk by Japanese submarine I-25 (Tagami), in the Java Sea NW of Jakarta, Sumatra, in position 05.18S 106.20E while sailing independently on a voyage from Singapore to Jakarta, with 209 RAAF personnel and a cargo of 7000 tons of military stores including explosives and aircraft. The Master, Capt Richard Doyle, crew of 34, 4 gunners and 200 RAAF personnel were rescued by RAN minesweeper *BALLARAT* 650/40 (J.184) (Lt A.D. Barling). 9 RAAF personnel were lost. Lt Masaru Obiga and crew were lost on 12.7.43 when I-25 was sunk in the Pacific E of Kolombangara, Solomon Islands, in position 08.00S 157.19E by US destroyer *TAYLOR* 2050/42 (DD-468) (Lt-Cdr Benjamin Katz).

*DERRYHEEN* • GRT 7217 • Built 1942
22.4.42: Torpedoed and sunk by German submarine U-201 (Schnee), in the Atlantic SE of Cape Hatteras, in position 31.20N 70.35W while sailing independently on a voyage from Philadelphia and Hampton Roads 19.4.42 to the Middle East via Cape Town, with 1 passenger and 11036 tons general cargo including nitrates and motor trucks. The Master, Capt Harold Richardson, crew of 41, 8 gunners and passenger were rescued by British ship *LOBOS* 6479/21 and landed at Havana, Cuba.

## MOWT

*FORT A LA CORNE* • GRT 7133 • Built 1942
30.3.43: Torpedoed and sunk by German submarine U-596 (Jahn), in the Mediterranean W of Algiers, in position 36.52N 01.47E while on government service on a voyage from Bona 28.3.43 to Gibraltar, in ballast, part of convoy ET 16 comprising 20 ships. The Master, Capt Reginald A. Grove, crew of 43 and 10 gunners were rescued by HM ship and landed at Gibraltar. Kapitänleutnant Gunter Jahn was awarded the Knight's Cross (30.4.43).

## MEDOMSLEY STEAMSHIP CO. LTD – NEWCASTLE UPON TYNE

*LANGLEEFORD* • GRT 4622 • Built 1925
14.2.40: Torpedoed and sunk by German submarine U–26 (Scheringer), in the Atlantic 70 miles NW of Fastnet while on a voyage from Boston, Mass. to the Tyne via Halifax NS, with a cargo of 6800 tons of wheat, a straggler from convoy HX 18 comprising 43 ships. The Master, Capt H. Thompson, and 29 crew landed at Ross, Co. Clare. 4 crew were lost.

## MELDRUM & SWINSON LIMITED – LONDON
### Essex Line Limited

*ESSEX LANCE* ex-*GLENSANDA* ex-*WAR COURAGE* • GRT 6625 • Built 1918
15.10.43: Torpedoed and sunk by German submarine U–426 (Reich), in the Atlantic SE of Cape Farewell, in position 57.53N 28.00W while on a voyage from Swansea and Milford Haven 8.10.42 to Halifax NS, with a cargo of 4000 tons of anthracite, a straggler from convoy ONS 20 comprising 51 ships. The Master, Capt Arthur Henry Dean, crew of 43 and 8 gunners were rescued by rescue ship *ACCRINGTON* 1678/10 and landed at Halifax NS 26.10.43. Oberleutnant zur See Christian Reich and crew of 50 were lost on 8.1.44 when U–426 was sunk in the Atlantic 225 miles NW by N of Cape Ortegal, in position 46.47N 10.42W by Sunderland 'U' EK586, pilot F/O J.P. Roberts (Australian) of No. 10 Squadron RAAF, based at Mount Batten, part of 19 Group. The pilot was awarded the DFC. Oberleutnant zur See Günther Grave was lost on 16.10.43 when U–470 was sunk while shadowing convoy ONS 20 in the Atlantic 390 miles SW by S of Rejkanes, in position 58.20N 29.20W by Liberator 'E', pilot F/L Harold F. Kerrigan (Canadian) and Liberator 'Z', pilot F/L Barry E. Peck of No. 120 Squadron RAF, based at Reykjavik and Liberator 'C' FL973, pilot P/O Wesley G. Loney of No. 59 Squadron RAF, based at Ballykelly, Co. Londonderry, part of 15 Group. The U-boat commander and 1 crew were taken prisoner by HM destroyer *DUNCAN* 1400/32 (D.99) (Lt-Cdr Peter Gretton). 46 crew were lost. Oberleutnant zur See Emmo Hummerjohan and 46 crew were lost on 16.10.43 when U–964 was sunk in the Atlantic 420 miles SSW of Rejkanes, in position 57.27N 28.17W while shadowing convoy ONS 20 by Liberator 'Y' FK241, pilot F/O George D. Gamble DFC BEM of No. 86 Squardon RAF, based at Ballykelly. 3 crew were rescued by U–231 (Wenzel). Kapitänleutnant Lorenz Kasch and crew of 54 were lost on 17.10.42 when U–540, part of the 'Schlieffen' patrol group of fifteen U–boats, was sunk in the Atlantic 375 miles E by S of Cape Farewell, in position 58.38N 31.56W while shadowing convoy ONS 20 by Liberator 'D' BZ712, pilot F/L Eric Knowles DFM of No. 59 Squadron RAF, based at Meeks Field, Iceland and Liberator 'H' AM929, pilot W/O Bryan W. Turnbull (New Zealander) of No. 120 Squadron RAF, based at Reykjavik.

## METCALF, T.J. – LONDON

*ELLEN M* • GRT 498 • Built 1938
1.2.40: Torpedoed and sunk by German submarine U–59 (Jürst), in the North Sea NE of Lowestoft, in position 52.33N 02.15E while on a voyage from Immingham to London, with a cargo of coal. The Master, Capt Kenneth Mann, and crew of 6 were lost.

## MITCHELL COTTS & COMPANY – LONDON
### Sun Shipping Co. Ltd

*CAPE ST ANDREW* • GRT 5094 • Built 1928
13.11.40: Torpedoed and damaged by German submarine U-137 (Wohlfarth), in the Atlantic
WNW of Aran Island, in position 55.14N 10.29W while on a voyage from Middlesbrough to
Bombay via Oban 10.11.40, in ballast, a straggler from convoy OB 240 comprising 57 ships.
Taken in tow by HM rescue tug *SALVONIA* 571/39 (Lt G.M.M. Robinson) and escorted by
HM destroyer *HURRICANE* 1340/39 (H.06) (Lt-Cdr H.C. Simms) ex-Brazilian *JAPARUA*
she sank the same day. The Master, Capt Albert Roy Bebb, 13 crew and 1 gunner were lost.
52 crew and 1 gunner were rescued by HMS *SALVONIA* and landed at Greenock.

### Thesens SS Co.

*HARRIER* • GRT 193 • Built 1892
7.6.43: Torpedoed and sunk by German submarine U-181 (Lüth), in the Indian Ocean 200
miles E. of Durban, in position 25.50S 33.20E while sailing independently on a voyage from
Durban to Dar es Salaam, with a cargo of explosives. The captain and crew were lost.

## MOWT

*EMPIRE MAHSEER* ex-*LIBERTY BELL* • GRT 5087 • Built 1919
4.3.43: Torpedoed and sunk by German submarine U-160 (Lassen), in the Indian Ocean
ENE of East London, in position 32.03S 30.33E while on a voyage from Fanara and Durban
to Baltimore via Bahia and Trinidad, with a cargo of 2000 tons of manganese ore, part of
convoy DN 21 comprising 11 ships. The Master, Capt Morgan Williams, 29 crew and 6
gunners were rescued by HM trawler *NORWICH CITY* 541/37 (FY.229) (Lt L.H. Stammers)
and landed at Durban. 17 crew and 1 gunner were lost.

*EMPIRE IMPALA* ex-*OAKMAN* ex-*CLEMENCE C. MORSE* ex-*BOSHBISH*
GRT 6113 • Built 1920
7.3.43: Torpedoed and sunk by German submarine U-591 (Zetzsche), part of the 'Westmark'
(West German mark) patrol group of seventeen U-boats, in the Atlantic SE of Cape Farewell,
in position 58.00N 15.00W while on a voyage from New York 23.2.42 to Hull, with general
cargo, a straggler from convoy SC 121 comprising 57 ships. The Master, Capt Thomas Henry
Munford, and crew of 40 were lost. She was attacked while rescuing survivors from British
ship *EGYPTIAN* 2868/20. U-591, commanded by Oberleutnant zur See Reimar Ziesmer,
was sunk in the South Atlantic SE of Recife, in position 08.36S 34.34W on 30.7.43 by a
Ventura, pilot Lt Walter C. Young of US Navy Bombing Squadron VB-127. The U-boat
commander and 27 crew were taken prisoner by US corvette *SAUCY* 925/40 (PG.65) ex-
HMS *ARABIS*. 19 crew were lost.

*EMPIRE TOURIST* • GRT 7062 • Built 1943
4.3.44: Torpedoed and sunk by German submarine U-703 (Brünner), in the Barents Sea near
the Kola Inlet, in position 73.25N 22.11E while on government service on a voyage from
Murmansk to Loch Ewe, with a cargo of 400 standards of timber and 600 tons of coal, part of

convoy RA 57 comprising 33 ships. The Master, Capt Hugh McCracken, crew of 41, 23 gunners, 2 signalmen and 1 naval personnel were rescued by HM minesweeper sloop *GLEANER* 815/37 (N.83) (Lt-Cdr J.G. Hewitt DSC) and landed at Aultbea, Loch Ewe. Oberleutnant zur See Joachim Brunner and crew of 53 were lost on 30.9.44 in the Atlantic SE of Iceland when U-703 probably hit a mine and sank.

## MOGUL LINE – BOMBAY

*RAHMANI* • GRT 5463 • Built 1928 (Indian flag)
12.7.43: Torpedoed and sunk by Japanese submarine I-29 (Izu), in the Gulf of Aden N of Socotra Island, in position 14.52N 52.06E while sailing independently on a voyage from Bombay 4.7.43 to Aden, Port Sudan and Jeddah, with 191 native passengers and a cargo of 5000 tons of general and government stores. The Master, Capt Peter McNab Mirlees, and 248 survivors landed E of Ras Fartak, Aden Protectate and were brought to Aden in HM trawler *VICTORIAN* 447/35 (FY.114) (Skipper A. Craig DSC) and HM whaler *SIGFRA* 356/37 (Lt H.G. Gabriel). 30 of the crew with local guides walked to Aden, a distance of some 300 miles, which took 13 days, to obtain help from the RAF station at Robat. 6 crew and 49 native passengers were lost. Lt Takaichi Kinashi and crew were lost on 26.7.44 when I-29 was sunk in the Pacific north of Luzon, Philippine Islands, in position 20.10N 121.50E by the US submarine *SAWFISH* 1525/42 (SS-276) (Lt-Cdr E.T. Sands).

## MOLLER & COMPANY – SHANGHAI

*LILIAN MOLLER* ex-*VALHALL* ex-*CAMBRIAN DUCHESS* ex-*NOVGOROD*
GRT 4866 • Built 1913
18.11.40: Torpedoed and sunk by Italian submarine *MAGGIORE FRANCESCO BARACCA* (Bertarelli), in the Atlantic 300 miles W of Ireland, in position 57.00N 17.00W while on a voyage from Calcutta to London via Cape Town, Freetown 25.10.40 and Oban, with 6000 tons of general cargo, part of convoy SLS 53 comprising 6 ships. The Master, Capt William Simon Stewart Fowler, crew of 50 and 1 gunner were lost. *MAGGIORE FRANCESCO BARACCA*, commanded by Lt Giorgio Vianni, was sunk on 8.9.41 in the Atlantic 270 miles NE of San Miguel, Azores, in position 40.30N 21.15W by HM destroyer *CROOME* 1050/41 (L.62) (Lt-Cdr J.D. Hayes).

*MARILYSE MOLLER* ex-*TSEANG TAH* • GRT 768 • Built 1915
1.7.42: Torpedoed and sunk by German submarine U-97 (Bürgel), in the Mediterranean NE of Port Said, in position 31.22N 33.44E while on a voyage from Beirut to Port Said and Alexandria, with a cargo of cased benzine, part of convoy (codenamed Nugget). The Master, Capt Douglas Stuart Pethick, and 30 crew were lost. 4 crew were rescued by HM trawler *BURRA* 545/41 (T.158) (Lt W.J. Harrison) and landed at Port Said.

*LOUISE MOLLER* ex-*BALTO* ex-*BJORNEFJORD* ex-*RIVER PLATE* • GRT 3764 • Built 1907
13.11.42: Torpedoed and sunk by German submarine U-178 (Ibbeken), in the Indian Ocean 240 miles E by S of Durban, in position 30.37S 35.44E while sailing independently on a voyage from Durban to Mombasa, with a cargo of coal. The Master, Capt George Alexander Angus, 20 crew and 2 gunners were rescued by British ship *HOPECREST* 5099/35 and landed

at East London, the Chief Officer and 28 crew were rescued by HM destroyer leader *DOUGLAS* 1800/18 (D.90) (Lt-Cdr R.B.S. Tennant) and landed at Durban. 11 crew were lost.

**DAISY MOLLER** ex-*WILFRED* ex-*HUNTSCAPE* ex-*PINDOS* • GRT 4087 • Built 1911
14.12.43: Torpedoed and sunk by Japanese submarine RO-110 (Ebato), in the Indian Ocean SE of Kakinada, India, in position 16.21N 82.13E while sailing independently on a voyage from Bombay and Colombo to Chittagong, with 2 passengers and military stores including guns and ammunition. The Master, Capt Reginald James Weeks, 13 crew and 2 gunners landed near Masulipatnam, WC India. 49 crew, 4 gunners and passengers were killed by the ramming and strafing of their rafts and lifeboats by RO-110. Lt Kazuo Ebato and crew were lost on 11.2.44 when RO-110 was attacking Blue Funnel ship *ASPHALION* 6274/24, part of convoy JC 36 from Colombo to Calcutta. RO-110 was sunk in the Bay of Bengal off Vizagapatnam, in position 17.25N 83.21E by escorts RIN sloop *JUMNA* 1300/40 (U.21) (Cdr I.B.W. Beauly), RAN minesweeping sloops *LAUNCESTON* 650/41 (J.179) (Lt P.G. Collins) and *IPSWICH* 650/41 (J.186) (Lt R.H. Creasey DSC RANR).

**NANCY MOLLER** ex-*ROWENA* ex-*NORFOLK* • GRT 3916 • Built 1907
18.3.44: Torpedoed and sunk by Japanese submarine I-165 (Shimizu), in the Indian Ocean SW of Colombo, in position 02.14N 78.25E while sailing independently from Durban to Colombo, with a cargo of coal. The Master, Capt James B. Hansen, 27 crew and 4 gunners were rescued after 4 days by HM cruiser *EMERALD* 7550/20 (I.66) (Capt F.J. Wylie) and landed at Port Louis, Mauritius 26.3.44. 30 crew and 2 gunners were lost. 1 gunner was taken prisoner. I-165, commanded by Lt Yasushi Ono, was sunk in the Pacific E of Saipan, in position 15.28N 153.39E on 27.6.45 by US aircraft from US Patrol Bombing Squadron VPB-142.

**HELEN MOLLER** ex-*SIERENTZ* ex-*WAR CATERAN* • GRT 5259 • Built 1918
5.6.44: Torpedoed and sunk by German submarine U-183 (Schneewind), in the Indian Ocean 400 miles SE of Colombo, in position 04.28S 74.45E while sailing independently on a voyage from Colombo to Fremantle, in ballast. The Master, Capt Charles Frederick Paull, 61 crew and 7 gunners were rescued, the Master and 25 survivors on 8.6.44 by British ship *EMPIRE CONFIDENCE* 5023/35 and landed at Colombo 11.6.44, and 43 survivors on 12.6.44 by HM auxiliary patrol ship *OKAPI* 246/29 (Paymaster Lt A.M.H. Baker) and landed at Addu Atoll. 2 crew and 2 gunners were lost. Kapitänleutnant Fritz Schneewind and crew of 53 were lost on 23.4.45 when U-183 was torpedoed and sunk in the Java Sea NE of Sourabaja, Sumatra, in position 04.57S 112.53E by US submarine *BESUGO* 1525/44 (SS-321) (Cdr Herman E. Miller).

**MARION MOLLER** ex-*CYMRIC PRIDE* ex-*BRINKBURN* • GRT 3827 • Built 1909
6.11.44: Torpedoed and sunk by Japanese submarine RO-113 (Harada), in the Indian Ocean about 100 miles N of Trincomalee, in position 10.40N 81.10E while on a voyage from Karachi and Colombo to Calcutta, with a cargo of 5700 tons of salt and a deck cargo of 27 cases of gliders, a straggler from a JC convoy Colombo to Calcutta. The Master, Capt Reginald James Weeks, crew of 61 and 9 gunners were rescued by RAN destroyer *NORMAN* 1690/40 (G.49) (Lt-Cdr J. Plunkett–Cole), transferred to HM destroyer *ROEBUCK* 1705/42 (H.95) (Cdr J.T. Lean DSO) and landed at Trincomalee. Lt Kiyoshi Harada and crew were lost on 13.2.45 when RO-113 was sunk in the Pacific 40 miles N of Luzon, Philippine

Islands, in position 19.10N 121.23E by US submarine *BATFISH* 1525/43 (SS-310) (Lt-Cdr J.K. Fyfe). The *BATFISH* is now on static display at Pearl Harbor, Hawaii.

## MONROE BROTHERS – CARDIFF

**KYLEGLEN** ex-*SENATOR* • GRT 3670 • Built 1917
14.12.40: Torpedoed and sunk by German submarine U-100 (Schepke), in the Atlantic WSW of Rockall, in position 58.00N 25.00W while on a voyage from Middlesbrough and Oban to Baltimore, Maryland, in ballast, dispersed on 12.12.40 in position 55.04N 15.30W from convoy OB 256 comprising 30 ships. The Master, Capt Thomas Storer, and crew of 35 were lost.

## MOORINGWELL SS CO. LTD – CARDIFF

**JEANNE M** ex-*SEABANK SPRAY* ex-*SEVEN SEAS SPRAY* ex-*BARON ELIBANK* ex-*GLASSFORD*
GRT 2465 • Built 1919
2.12.40: Torpedoed and sunk by German submarine U-37 (Clausen), in the Atlantic 230 miles N of Cape Roca, Portugal, in position 39.19N 13.45W while on a voyage from Cardiff to Lisbon, with a cargo of 3200 tons of coal, part of convoy OG 46 comprising 39 ships. The Master, Capt Jonathan MacInnes, and 18 crew were rescued by HM trawler *ERIN* 394/33 (Cdr J.O. Davies). 7 crew were lost.

## MOREL, R.E. & COMPANY – CARDIFF

**BEIGNON** • GRT 5218 • Built 1939
1.7.40: Torpedoed and sunk by German submarine U-30 (Lemp), in the Atlantic 300 miles W of Ushant, in position 47.20N 10.30W while on a voyage from Fremantle to Newcastle via Freetown 15.6.40, with a cargo of 8816 tons of wheat, part of convoy SL 36 comprising 41 ships. The Master, Capt William John Croome, and 29 crew were rescued by HM destroyers *VESPER* 1300/17 (F.39) (Lt-Cdr W.F.E. Hussey DSC) and *WINDSOR* 1300/18 (F.12) (Lt-Cdr G.P. Huddart) and landed at Plymouth. 3 crew were lost.

### Nolisement SS Co. Ltd

**ALLENDE** • GRT 5081 • Built 1928
17.3.42: Torpedoed and sunk by German submarine U-68 (Merten), in the Atlantic 20 miles S of Cape Palmas, Liberia, in position 04.00N 07.44W while sailing independently on a voyage from Calcutta and Sandheads to the UK via Cape Town 3.3.42 and Freetown, with 7700 tons of general cargo. The Master, Capt Thomas James Williamson, 30 crew and 2 gunners landed at Taba, French Ivory Coast and were interned by the Vichy French authorities at Bobo Dinlassu. 6 crew were lost.

### Pontypridd SS Co. Ltd

**PONTYPRIDD** • GRT 4458 • Built 1942
11.6.42: Torpedoed and damaged by German submarine U-569 (Hinsch), and later sunk by a *coup de grâce* by German submarines U-94 (Ites) and U-569, part of the 'Hecht' (Pike) patrol

group of six U-boats, in the Atlantic NE of St John's, Newfoundland, in position 49.50N 41.37W while on a voyage from Immingham and Loch Ewe to Father Point and Sydney CB, in ballast, a straggler from convoy ONS 100 comprising 38 ships. The Master, Capt Herbert Vivian Bradley Morden, was taken prisoner, landed at La Pallice 28.6.42 and taken to Milag Nord. 42 crew were rescued by RCN corvette *CHAMBLY* 925/40 (K.116) (Lt J.D. Prentice) and landed at St John's. 2 crew were lost. U-94, commanded by Oberleutnant zur See Otto Ites (Knight's Cross 28.3.42), was sunk while shadowing convoy TAW 15 comprising 21 ships on 28.8.42 in the Caribbean Sea S of Haiti, in position 17.40N 74.30W by RCN corvette *OAKVILLE* 925/41 (K.178) (Lt-Cdr Clarence A. King DSC) and a Catalina, pilot Lt Gordon R. Fiss from US Navy Bombing Squadron VP-92 based at Guantanamo Bay, Cuba. The U-boat commander and 25 crew were taken prisoner. HMCS *OAKVILLE* rescued 5 crew and US four-stack destroyer *LEA* 1090/18 (DD 118) (Lt-Cdr J.F. Walsh) rescued the U-boat commander and 20 crew who were landed at Guantanamo Bay. 19 crew were lost.

## MORGAN, B.J. & COMPANY – CARDIFF

*ELLAROY* ex-*SAGENITE* • GRT 712 • Built 1905
21.7.40: Torpedoed and sunk by gunfire by German submarine U-30 (Lemp), in the Atlantic 180 miles W of Cape Finisterre, in position 42.30N 12.36W while sailing independently on a voyage from Lisbon to Newport, Mon, with a cargo of 800 tons of pitwood. The Master, Capt Thomas Grafton Smith, and crew of 15 landed at Vigo, Spain.

## MORRISON, JOHN & SON – NEWCASTLE UPON TYNE

*BARBARA MARIE* • GRT 4223 • Built 1928
12.6.40: Torpedoed and sunk by German submarine U-46 (Endrass), in the Atlantic 220 miles WNW of Cape Finisterre, in position 44.16N 13.54W while on a voyage from Pepel to Workington via Freetown 31.5.40, with a cargo of 7200 tons of iron ore, part of convoy SL 34 comprising 30 ships. The Master, Capt Alfred Stanley Smith, and 31 crew were lost. 5 crew were rescued by British ship *SWEDRU* 5379/37.

*ELMDALE* • GRT 4872 • Built 1941
1.11.42: Torpedoed and sunk by German submarine U-174 (Thilo), in the Atlantic 400 miles W of St Paul Rocks, in position 00.17N 34.55W while sailing independently on a voyage from Baltimore to Alexandria via Trinidad 24.10.40 and Cape Town, with a cargo of 8300 tons of coal, military stores and general, dispersed from convoy T 20. The Master, Capt Duncan McPhee, 30 crew and 5 gunners were rescued by Brazilian ship *THEREZINA M* 3874/06 and landed at Forteleza, Brazil. 5 crew and 1 gunner were lost. Oberleutnant zur See Wolfgang Grandefeld and crew of 52 were lost when U-174 was sunk on 27.4.43 in the Atlantic 420 miles E of Cape Sable, Nova Scotia, in position 43.35N 56.18W by a Ventura, pilot Lt Thomas Kinaszczuk of the US Navy Bombing Squadron VB-125 based at Argentia, Newfoundland.

### Cliffside Shipping Co. Ltd

*THORNLEA* • GRT 4261 • Built 1929
2.9.40: Torpedoed and sunk by German submarine U-46 (Endrass), in the Atlantic 200 miles W of Bloody Foreland, Co. Donegal, in position 55.14N 16.40W while on a voyage from

Swansea to Montreal, with a cargo of 6400 tons of coal, dispersed from convoy OB 206 comprising 32 ships. The Master, Capt John Robert Potts, and 18 crew were rescued by RCN destroyer *SKEENA* 1337/30 (D.59) (Lt-Cdr James C. Hibbard) and landed at Greenock, the Chief Officer and 13 crew were rescued after 18 hours by Norwegian ship *HILD* 1356/19 and landed at Sydney CB 15.9.40. 3 crew were lost.

### HOLMELEA • GRT 4223 • Built 1928

28.2.41: Sunk by gunfire by German submarine U-47 (Prien), in the Atlantic SW of Rockall, in position 54.24N 17.25W while on a voyage from Rosario to Hull via Halifax NS 13.2.41, with a cargo of 7000 tons of grain, linseed and maize, a straggler from convoy HX 109 comprising 36 ships. The Master, Capt John Robert Potts, and 26 crew were lost. 10 crew and 1 gunner were rescued by Icelandic trawler *BALDUR* 315/21 and landed at Fleetwood. Korvettenkapitän Gunther Prien (Knight's Cross 18.10.39; with Oak Leaves 20.10.40) and crew of 44 were lost while shadowing convoy OB 293 comprising 37 ships on 7.3.41 by an unknown cause in the Atlantic NW of Rockall. On 14.9.39 U-47 torpedoed and sank HM battleship *ROYAL OAK* 29150/14 (0.8) in Scapa Flow, Orkney, in position 58.55N 02.29W. Capt W.G. Benn, 833 officers and crew were lost. Korvettenkapitän Günther Prien was the first U-boat commander to receive both awards and one of the top German U-boat 'aces' of the Second World War, sinking 28 ships totalling 164,953 gross tonnage.

### EASTLEA • GRT 4267 • Built 1924

24.3.41: Torpedoed and sunk by German submarine U-106 (Oesten), in the Atlantic about 130 miles WNW of San Antonio, Cape Verde Islands, in position 16.18N 22.05W while sailing independently on a voyage from Famagusta, Cyprus to Newport News via Table Bay 15.2.41, Freetown 9.3.41 and St Vincent, Cape Verde Islands 23.3.41, with a cargo of cotton seed. The Master, Capt Malcolm Goudie Macpherson, crew of 33 and 3 gunners were lost.

### STORNEST ex-STORMS • GRT 4265 • Built 1921

12.10.42: Torpedoed and sunk by German submarine U-706 (v. Zitzewitz), part of the 'Panther' patrol group of thirty-one U-boats, in the Atlantic W of Ireland, in position 54.25N 27.42W while on a voyage from Swansea and Belfast Lough to Boston, Mass. with a cargo of about 6000 tons of coal, part of convoy ONS 136 comprising 36 ships. The Master, Capt Henry Otley Smith, crew of 37 and 10 gunners were lost. Kapitänleutnant Eberhard Bopst and crew of 48 were lost the same day in the Atlantic 460 miles SSW of Reykjanes, in position 56.50N 28.05W when U-597, part of the 'Panther' patrol group, was attacking convoy ONS 136 and was sunk by Liberator 'H' AM929, pilot S/Ldr Terry M. Bulloch DFC of No. 120 Squadron RAF, based at Reykjavik.

### GLENLEA • GRT 4252 • Built 1930

7.11.42: Torpedoed and sunk by German submarine U-566 (Remus), part of the 'Natter' (Viper) patrol group of twelve U-boats, in the Atlantic N of the Azores, in position 50.00N 30.00W while on government service on a voyage from Cardiff and Belfast Lough 28.10.42 to Durban and Suez, with 5000 tons of coal, trucks and 1000 tons of general, a straggler from convoy ONS 142 comprising 62 ships. The Master, Capt John Russell Nicol, was taken prisoner, landed at Brest 1.12.42 and taken to Milag Nord. 3 crew and 1 gunner were rescued after 21 days in an open boat by Norwegian ship *THORSTRAND* 3041/38 and landed at

New York. 39 crew and 5 gunners were lost. U–566, commanded by Kapitänleutnant Hans Hornkohl, was sunk on 24.10.43 in the Atlantic 30 miles W of Cape Mondego, Portugal, in position 41.12N 09.31W by Leigh Light-equipped Wellington 'A' HF132, pilot Sgt Donald M. Cornish (Canadian) of No. 179 Squadron, RAF, based at Gibraltar. The pilot was awarded the DFM. The U-boat commander and crew of 48 were rescued by Spanish fishing boat *FINA*, landed at Vigo and taken by the Spanish authorities and returned to France.

## MOWT

### EMPIRE CROSSBILL ex-*WEST AMARGOSA* • GRT 5463 • Built 1919
11.9.41: Torpedoed and sunk by German submarine U–82 (Rollman), part of the 'Markgraf' patrol group of fourteen U-boats, in the North Atlantic E of Cape Farewell, in position 63.14N 37.12W while on a voyage from Philadelphia to Hull via Sydney CB 30.8.41, with 1 passenger, a cargo of 6686 tons of steel and 4 tons of relief goods, part of convoy SC 42 comprising 65 ships. The Master, Capt Eric Robinson Townend, crew of 37, 10 gunners and passenger were lost.

### OCEAN VENUS • GRT 7174 • Built 1942
3.5.42: Torpedoed and sunk by German submarine U–564 (Suhren), in the Atlantic about 12 miles ESE of Cape Canaveral, Florida, in position 28.32N 80.21W while sailing independently on a voyage from Union Bay, British Columbia to the UK via Colon 27.4.42 and Halifax NS, with 9450 tons general cargo, including 4000 tons of lead, 4000 tons of lumber, 80 tons of acetone and 1000 tons of canned herrings. The Master, Capt John Park, 37 crew and 4 gunners landed at Cape Canaveral. 5 crew were lost.

### EMPIRE ZEAL • GRT 7009 • Built 1942
2.11.42: Torpedoed and sunk by Italian submarine *LEONARDO DA VINCI* (Gazzana), in the South Atlantic near St Paul Rocks, in position 00.30S 30.45W while sailing independently on a voyage from Basrah and Bahrain to New York via Durban 10.10.42 and Trinidad, in ballast. The Master, Capt William Craig Noble Macpherson, and 1 crew were taken prisoner. 43 crew and 6 gunners were rescued on 4.11.42 by US destroyer *WINSLOW* 1850/336 (DD.359) (Cdr H.R. Holcomb) and landed at Para, Brazil 9.11.42. 2 crew were lost.

### EMPIRE DABCHICK ex-*KISNOP* • GRT 6089 • Built 1919
3.12.42: Torpedoed and sunk by German submarine U–183 (Schäfer), in the Atlantic about 200 miles SE of Sable Island, Nova Scotia, in position 43.00N 58.17W while on a voyage from Liverpool to St John, New Brunswick, part of convoy ONS 146 comprising 38 ships. The Master, Capt Philip Edward Birch OBE, crew of 35 and 11 gunners were lost.

## MOSS, H.E. & COMPANY – LIVERPOOL
## MOWT

### EMPIRE LIGHT ex-*LUMEN* (tanker) • GRT 6537 • Built 1925
7.3.43: Torpedoed and damaged by German submarine U–638 (Bernbeck), on 12.3.43 U–468 (Schamong), part of the 'Raubgraf' (Robber Baron) patrol group of eight U-boats, sank the abandoned tanker by two *coups de grâce* in the Atlantic SW of Cape Farewell, in position 53.57N

46.14W while on a voyage from Manchester to New York, in ballast, a straggler from convoy ON 168 comprising 52 ships. The Master, Capt Frederick Dolton, 3 crew and 1 gunner were rescued by HM destroyer *BEVERLEY* 1190/19 (H.64) (Lt-Cdr A.R. Price) ex-USN four-stack *BRANCH* and landed at St John's, Newfoundland. 39 crew and 6 gunners were lost. U-468, commanded by Oberleutnant zur See Klemens Schamong, was sunk on 11.8.43 in the Atlantic 210 miles W by S of Bathurst, in position 12.20N 20.07W by Liberator 'D' BZ832 of No. 200 Squadron RAF, based at Yundum, Gambia. The aircraft was shot down by U-468 and the pilot, F/O Lloyd Allan Trigg DFC, a New Zealander, and 7 crew lost their lives during this action. F/O L.A. Trigg DFC RNZAF was awarded a posthumous Victoria Cross for his bravery on the evidence of the German survivors. Oberleutnant zur See Schamong and 6 crew were taken prisoner on 13.8.43 by HM corvette *CLARKIA* 925/40 (K.88) (Lt-Cdr S. Darling RANVR) and landed at Freetown 17.8.43. 39 crew were lost. The Victoria Cross awarded to F/O L.A. Trigg was auctioned in London in May 1998 and fetched a record £138,000.

## MOSS HUTCHINSON LINE LIMITED – LIVERPOOL

*KAVAK* • GRT 2782 • Built 1929
2.12.40: Torpedoed and sunk by German submarine U-101 (Mengersen), in the Atlantic 340 miles W of Bloody Foreland, in position 55.00N 19.50W while on a voyage from Demerara to Newport, Mon. via Halifax NS 21.11.40, with a cargo of 1745 tons of bauxite and 1650 tons of pitch, part of convoy HX 90 comprising 35 ships. The Master, Capt Jackson Napier, 23 crew and 1 gunner were lost. 15 crew and 1 gunner were rescued by HM destroyer *VISCOUNT* 1325/17 (D.92) (Lt-Cdr M.S. Townsend OBE DSC) and landed at Liverpool.

*HATASU* • GRT 3198 • Built 1921
2.10.41: Torpedoed and sunk by German submarine U-431 (Dommes), in the Atlantic about 600 miles E of Cape Race on a voyage from Manchester to New York, in ballast, part of convoy ONS 19 comprising 49 ships. The Master, Capt William Johnston Meek, 33 crew and 6 gunners were lost. 7 crew were rescued after 7 days in an open boat by US destroyer *CHARLES F. HUGHES* 1620/40 (DD.428) and landed at Reykjavik.

*ETRIB* ex-*BRITISH COAST* • GRT 1943 • Built 1919
15.6.42: Torpedoed and sunk by German submarine U-552 (Topp), part of the 'Endrass' (named after a U-boat Commander) patrol group of eight U-boats, in the Atlantic W of Corunna in position 43.18N 17.38W while on a voyage from Cartagena and Gibraltar 9.6.42 to Liverpool, with 2272 tons of general cargo including fruit, wine and cork, part of convoy HG 84 comprising 23 ships. The Master, Capt Baldie McMillan, 34 crew, 4 gunners and 2 DBS were rescued by HM corvette *MARIGOLD* 925/40 (K.87) (Lt J.A. Halcrew), transferred to rescue ship *COPELAND* 1520/23 (Capt J. McKellar OBE) and landed at Gourock 20.6.42. 2 crew and 2 gunners were lost.

## MOWT

*SALLY MAERSK* • GRT 3252 • Built 1923
10.9.41: Torpedoed and sunk by German submarine U-81 (Guggenberger) part of the 'Markgraf' patrol group of fourteen U-boats, in the North Atlantic ENE of Cape Farewell, in

position 61.38N 40.40W while on a voyage from Three Rivers to Sharpness via Sydney CB 30.8.41, with a cargo of 4527 tons of wheat, part of convoy SC 42 comprising 65 ships. The Master, Capt J.K. Lindberg, crew of 28 and 5 gunners were rescued by RCN corvette *KENOGAMI* 925/40 (K.125) (Lt P.J.B. Cook) and landed at Reykjavik.

**BERURY** ex-*OLEN* • GRT 4924 • Built 1919
11.9.41: Torpedoed and sunk by German submarine U-207 (Meyer), in the North Atlantic S of Cape Farewell, in position 62.40N 38.50W while on a voyage from Quonset Point, Rhode Island to Belfast via Sydney CB 30.8.41, with a cargo of 2100 tons of general including army stores, part of convoy SC 42 comprising 65 ships. The Master, Capt Francis Joseph Morgan, 36 crew and 4 gunners were rescued by RCN corvettes *KENOGAMI* 925/40 (K.125) (Lt P.J.B. Cook) and landed at Reykjavik and *MOOSEJAW* 925/41 (K.164) (Lt L.D. Quick), landed at Loch Ewe. 1 crew was lost.

**EMPIRE ANTELOPE** ex-*BANGU* ex-*ORPHIS* • GRT 4782 • Built 1919
2.11.42: Torpedoed and sunk by German submarine U-402 (v. Forstner), part of the 'Veilchen' (Violet) patrol group of thirteen U-boats, in the Atlantic 500 miles E of Belle Ile, in position 52.26N 45.22W while on a voyage from New York 24.10.42 to Glasgow via St John's, Newfoundland 30.10.42, with 5560 tons of general cargo including steel, part of convoy SC 107 comprising 42 ships. The Master, Capt William John Slade, crew of 41 and 8 gunners were rescued by rescue ship *STOCKPORT* 1637/11 (Capt Thomas Ernest Fea OBE) and landed at Reykjavik 8.11.42.

**SAMOURI** laid down as *MANASSEH CUTLER* • GRT 7219 • Built 1943
26.1.44: Torpedoed and sunk by German submarine U-188 (Ludden), part of the 'Monsun' (Monsoon) patrol group of five U-boats, in the Gulf of Aden ENE of Socotra Island, in position 13.13N 55.56E while sailing independently on a voyage from Bombay to New York via Aden, in ballast. The Master, Capt William John Slade, crew of 38 and 10 gunners were rescued by British ship *SHAHZADA* 5454/42 and landed at Aden.

## MUIR YOUNG STEAMSHIP COMPANY – LONDON
Cree SS Co. Ltd

**CREEKIRK** ex-*HYPHAESTOS* ex-*MILCOVUL* ex-*MARISTON* • GRT 3917 • Built 1912
18.10.40: Torpedoed and sunk by German submarine U-101 (Frauenheim), in the Atlantic SE of Rockall, in position 57.30N 11.10W while on a voyage from Wabana, Conception Bay to Workington via Sydney CB 5.10.40, with a cargo of 5900 tons of iron ore, part of convoy SC 7 comprising 35 ships. The Master, Capt Elie Robilliard, crew of 34 and 1 gunner were lost.

**CREE** ex-*YOH HSING* ex-*IVANHOE* ex-*WOLLERT* ex-*BILOELA* • GRT 4791 • Built 1920
22.11.40: Torpedoed and sunk by German submarine U-123 (Moehle), in the Atlantic 365 miles W of Bloody Foreland, in position 54.39N 18.50W while on a voyage from Pepel to Workington via Freetown 27.10.40, with a cargo of 5500 tons of iron ore, a straggler from convoy SL 53 comprising 24 ships. The Master, Capt Robert Herbert Twentyman, crew of 42 and 2 gunners were lost.

**GRAYBURN** • GRT 6342 • Built 1938

29.6.41: Torpedoed and sunk by German submarine U-651 (Lohmeyer), in the Atlantic S of Iceland, in position 59.30N 18.07W while on a voyage from Baltimore to Swansea via Halifax NS, with a cargo of 10300 tons of scrap and steel, part of convoy HX 133 comprising 57 ships. The Master, Capt John William Sygrove, and 16 survivors were rescued by HM corvette *VIOLET* 925/925/40 (K.35) (Lt F.C. Reynolds), transferred to rescue ship *ZAAFARAN* 1559/21 (Capt Charles Kavanagh McGowan DSC), transferred to HM trawler *NORTHERN WAVE* 655/26 (FY.153) (Lt W.G. Pardoe–Matthews) and landed at Gourock. 1 survivor rescued by HM corvette *ARABIS* landed at Londonderry. 27 crew and 8 gunners were lost. U-651 commanded by Kapitänleutnant Peter Lohmeyer was sunk on the same day in the Atlantic 200 miles NW of Rockall, in position 59.52N 18.36W by the convoy's escorts HM destroyer leader *MALCOLM* 1804/19 (D.19) (Cdr C.D. Howard-Johnston), HM corvette *VIOLET* 925/40 (K.35) (Lt F.C. Reynolds), HM destroyer *SCIMITAR* 1075/18 (H.21) (Lt R.D. Franks), HM corvette *ARABIS* 925/40 (K.73) (Lt-Cdr P. Stewart) and HM minesweeper *SPEEDWELL* 815/35 (N.87) (Lt-Cdr J.J. Young). The U-boat commander and crew of 43 were taken prisoner by HMS *MALCOLM* and HMS *SCIMITAR*.

## MOWT

**OCEAN VINTAGE** • GRT 7174 • Built 1942

22.10.42: Torpedoed and sunk by Japanese submarine I-27 (Kitamura), in the Gulf of Oman near Masirah Island, in position 21.37N 60.06E while sailing independently on a voyage from New York and Durban 5.10.42 to Abadan and Bandar Shapur, with 9300 tons of general cargo. The Master, Capt John Robinson, crew of 43 and 6 gunners were towed in the ship's boats by a RAF Crash Launch into Ras el Hadd harbour, Oman.

## MUNGO CAMPBELL & CO. – NEWCASTLE UPON TYNE
### Ayrshire Navigation Co. Ltd

**RIVER LUGAR** • GRT 5423 • Built 1937

27.6.41: Torpedoed and sunk by German submarine U-69 (Metzler), in the Atlantic 300 miles SW of the Canary Islands, in position 24.00N 21.00W while on a voyage from Pepel to Barry Roads via Freetown 30.5.41, with 2 passengers and a cargo of 9250 tons of iron ore, part of convoy SL 76 comprising 60 ships. The Master, Capt William Frame, 35 crew and passengers were lost. 6 crew were rescued by HM corvette *BURDOCK* 925/40 (K.126) (Lt H.J. Fellowes SANVR) and landed at Milford Haven.

**RIVER AFTON** • GRT 5479 • Built 1935

5.7.42: Torpedoed and sunk by German submarine U-703 (Bielfeld), in the Arctic Sea NE of Kola, in position 75.57N 43.00E while sailing independently on government service from Middlesbrough to Archangel via Reykjavik, with the convoy's commodore, 5 naval staff, 2 passengers and a cargo of 12 vehicles, 36 tanks, 7 aircraft and 2314 tons of military stores, dispersed from the ill-fated convoy PQ 17 comprising 36 ships. The Master, Capt Harold William Charlton, Commodore John C.K. Dowding CBE DSO RNR RD, 31 crew, 1 gunner, 1 passenger and 3 naval staff were rescued by HM corvette *LOTUS* 925/42 (K.93) (Lt H.J. Hall) and landed at Matochkin, Novaya Zemlya, USSR. 15 crew, 8 gunners, 1 passenger and 2 naval staff were lost.

## United Steam Navigation Co. Ltd

*DALBLAIR* • GRT 4608 • Built 1926
29.8.40: Torpedoed and sunk by German submarine U-100 (Schepke), in the Atlantic 148 miles NW of Bloody Foreland, in position 56.06N 13.33W while on a voyage from the Tyne to Philadelphia, in ballast, part of convoy OA 204 comprising 43 ships. The Master, Capt John H. Bruton, 18 crew and 1 gunner were rescued by the Swedish ship *ALIDA GORTHON* 2373/02 and 17 crew by HM corvette *CLEMATIS* 925/40 (K.35) (Cdr Y.M. Cleeves), later transferred to HM rescue tug *ENGLISHMAN* 487/37 and landed at Londonderry. 4 crew were lost. The survivors rescued by the *ALIDA GORTHON* were lost on the same day when she was sunk by U-100 (Schepke).

*DALCAIRN* • GRT 4608 • Built 1927
21.9.40: Torpedoed and sunk by German submarine U-100 (Schepke), in the Atlantic SW of Rockall, in position 55.00N 19.00W while on a voyage from Montreal to Hull via Halifax NS, with a cargo of 8000 tons of wheat, part of convoy HX 72 comprising 47 ships. The Master, Capt Edgar Brusby, crew of 46 and 1 gunner were rescued by HM corvette *LA MALOUINE* 925/40 (K.46) (Lt-Cdr R.W. Keymer) and landed at Greenock.

*DALCROY* • GRT 4558 • Built 1930
2.11.42: Torpedoed and sunk by German submarine U-402 (v. Forstner), part of the 'Veilchen' (Violet) patrol group of thirteen U-boats, in the Atlantic 500 miles E of Belle Ile, in position 52.30N 45.30W while on a voyage from St John, New Brunswick to the Tyne via Halifax NS 27.10.42, with a cargo of 1809 tons of steel and 2044 standards of timber, part of convoy SC 107 comprising 42 ships. The Master, Capt John Phillip Johnson, crew of 40 and 8 gunners were rescued by rescue ship *STOCKPORT* 1637/11 (Capt Thomas Ernest Fea OBE) and landed at Reykjavik 8.11.42.

*DALFRAM* • GRT 4558 • Built 1930
4.8.43: Torpedoed and sunk by German submarine U-181 (Lüth), in the Indian Ocean E of Madagascar, in position 20.40S 56.40E while sailing independently on a voyage from Lourenco Marques and Durban 22.7.43 to Aden and Alexandria, with a cargo of 6821 tons of coal. The Master, Capt David H. Hogg, 34 crew and 5 gunners landed after 8 days on the island of Ile Ste Marie, E of Madagascar. 3 crew were lost.

## MOWT

*EFFNA* • GRT 6461 • Built 1919
28.2.41: Torpedoed and sunk by German submarine U-108 (Scholtze), in the North Atlantic SE of Iceland, in position 61.30N 15.45W while sailing independently on a voyage from Baltimore and Halifax NS to Newport, Mon, with a cargo of 7516 tons of steel and trucks. The Master, Capt Robert Penney Robertson, and crew of 32 were lost.

*WESTPOOL* • GRT 5724 • Built 1918
3.4.41: Torpedoed and sunk by German submarine U-73 (Rosenbaum), in the Atlantic SSW of Reykjavik, in position 58.12N 27.40W while on a voyage from Baltimore to Leith via

Halifax NS, with a cargo of 7144 tons of scrap iron, part of convoy SC 26 comprising 24 ships. The Master, Capt William Stafford, and 7 crew were rescued by HM destroyer *HAVELOCK* 1340/39 (H.88) (Cdr E.H. Thomas DSC) ex-Brazilian *JUTAHY* and landed at Liverpool 9.4.41, and 2 crew by Norwegian ship *NEA* 1877/21 and landed at Reykjavik. 34 crew and 1 gunner were lost.

## MURRELL, JOSEPH E. & SON – WEST HARTLEPOOL
Murrell SS Co. Ltd

**THURSTON** ex-*VERA KATHLEEN* • GRT 3072 • Built 1918
4.3.40: Torpedoed and sunk by German submarine U-29 (Schuhart), in the Atlantic 32 miles W by N of Trevose Head, in position 50.23N 05.49W while sailing independently on a voyage from Takoradi to Workington, with a cargo of 4500 tons of manganese ore. The Master, Capt William Carr Fortune, and 25 crew were lost. 3 crew were rescued by British ship *MOYLE* 1761/07 and landed at Cardiff.

## MOWT

**EMPIRE TENNYSON** • GRT 2880 • Built 1942
1.10.42: Torpedoed and sunk by German submarine U-175 (Bruns), in the Atlantic SE of Trinidad, in position 09.27N 60.05W while sailing independently on a voyage from Demerara 30.9.42 to Trinidad, with a cargo of 3000 tons of bauxite. The Master, Capt Alfred Ernest Wright, 29 crew and 6 gunners were rescued by US Navy gunboat PG.58 1839/31 and landed at Port of Spain, Trinidad. 4 crew were lost. U-175, commanded by Kapitänleutnant Heinrich Bruns, was sunk while shadowing convoy HX 233 comprising 60 ships on 17.4.43 in the Atlantic 480 miles SW of Cape Clear, in position 48.50N 21.20W by the US coastguard cutter *SPENCER* 2216/37 (WPG-36) (Cdr Harold S. Berdine). The U-boat commander and 12 crew were lost. 19 crew were taken prisoner by USCG *SPENCER* and 22 crew by USCG *DUANE* 2216/36 (WPG 33) (Cdr H.B. Bradbury) and landed at Gourock.

## NEIL & PANDELIS LIMITED – LONDON

**MARITIMA** ex-*CLAN GRAHAM* ex-*CAMBRIAN BARONESS* ex-*PORT LINCOLN*
GRT 5801 • Built 1912
2.11.42: Torpedoed and sunk by German submarine U-522 (Schneider), in the Atlantic 500 miles NE of St John's, Newfoundland, in position 52.20N 45.40W while on a voyage from New York 24.10.42 to Glasgow via Sydney CB 29.10.42, with 7167 tons of general cargo including explosives, part of convoy SC 107 comprising 42 ships. The Master, Capt Arthur George Phelps–Mead, 28 crew and 3 gunners were lost. 22 crew and 5 gunners were rescued by RCN corvette *ARVIDA* 925/40 (K.113) (Lt A.I. MacKay) and landed at Londonderry. The *MARITIMA* sank in 4 minutes.

## NEW ZEALAND SHIPPING CO. LTD – LONDON

**HURUNUI** • GRT 9243 • Built 1920
15.10.40: Torpedoed and sunk by German submarine U-93 (Korth), in the Atlantic 120 miles W of Butt of Lewis, in position 58.58N 09.54W while on a voyage from Newcastle and

Liverpool to Auckland via Panama, in ballast, part of convoy OB 228 comprising 47 ships. The Master, Capt Benjamin Evans, 71 crew and 1 gunner were rescued by British ship *ST MARGARET* 4312/36, transferred to HM sloop *FOWEY* 1105/30 (L.15) (Lt C.G. de L. Bush) and landed at Greenock 20.10.40. 2 crew were lost.

**ROTORUA** ex-*SHROPSHIRE* • GRT 11911 • Built 1911
11.12.40: Torpedoed and sunk by German submarine U-96 (Lehmann-Willenbrock), in the Atlantic 100 miles W of St Kilda in position 58.56N 11.20W while on a voyage from Lyttelton to Avonmouth via Halifax NS 29.11.40, with 27 service personnel and 10803 tons of general cargo including refrigerated foodstuffs, part of convoy HX 92 comprising 24 ships. The Master, Capt Edgar Reginald Harrison Kemp, Commodore Rear-Admiral J.U.P. Fitzgerald CB RN, 15 crew, 2 gunners and 3 service personnel were lost. 25 survivors were rescued by HM trawler *VARANGA* 361/29 (FY.1625) (Lt G.C. Crowley), 34 survivors by HM trawler *ALSEY* 416/32 (M.51) (Lt H.A. Inglis) and 49 survivors by HM trawler *EBOR WYKE* 348/29 (FY.1601) (Skipper T.E. Olgeirsson) and landed at Stornoway. 2 crew were taken prisoner and landed at Lorient 29.12.40.

**PIAKO** ex-*WAR ORESTES* • GRT 8286 • Built 1920
18.5.41: Torpedoed and sunk by German submarine U-107 (Hessler), in the Atlantic 130 miles SW of Freetown, in position 07.52N 14.57W while sailing independently on a voyage from Albany, Western Australia to Liverpool via Freetown, with a cargo of 10100 tons of refrigerated foodstuffs including butter and meat, also 1500 tons of zinc. The Master, Capt Benjamin Evans, 62 crew and 2 gunners were rescued by HM sloop *BRIDGEWATER* 1045/28 (L.01) (Cdr H.F.C. Leftwick) and landed at Freetown. 10 crew were lost.

**OTAIO** • GRT 10048 • Built 1930
28.8.41: Torpedoed and sunk by German submarine U-558 (Krech), in the Atlantic 330 miles W by N of Fastnet Rock, in position 52.16N 17.50W while on a voyage from Liverpool 23.8.41 to Curacao and Sydney NSW, with a general cargo including stores and mail, dispersed from convoy OS 4 comprising 34 ships. The Master, Capt Gilbert Kinnell, 53 crew and 4 gunners were rescued by HM destroyer *VANOC* 1300/17 (F.84) (Lt-Cdr S.G.W. Deneys DSO) and landed at Liverpool. 12 crew and 1 gunner were lost.

**OPAWA** • GRT 10107 • Built 1931
6.2.42: Torpedoed and sunk by German submarine U-106 (Rasch), part of 'Operation Paukenschlag' (Drumbeat), the second wave of five U-boats, in the Atlantic 400 miles NNE of Bermuda, in position 38.21N 61.13W while sailing independently from Lyttelton to the UK via Cristobal and Halifax NS, with a cargo of 8575 tons of refrigerated foodstuffs, general and 3000 tons of lead. The Master, Capt Wilfred George Evans, and 14 crew were rescued by Dutch ship *HERCULES* 2317/14 and landed at New York. 53 crew and 2 gunners were lost.

**MOWT**

**EMPIRE AVOCET** ex-*COTATI* • GRT 6015 • Built 1919
30.9.42: Torpedoed and sunk by German submarine U-125 (Folkers), in the Atlantic 350 miles S of Freetown, in position 04.05N 13.23W while sailing independently on a voyage

from Buenos Aires and Rio Grande do Sol 9.9.42, Argentina to the UK via Freetown, with a cargo of 3724 tons of meat and 1225 tons general cargo. The Master, Capt Frederick Pover, 48 crew and 7 gunners were rescued by HM corvette COWSLIP 925/41 (K.196) (Sub-Lt J.S.M. Swift) and landed at Freetown. 2 crew were lost.

**EMPIRE WHIMBREL** ex-*MONASSESS* • GRT 5983 • Built 1919
11.4.43: Torpedoed and sunk by German submarine U-181 (Luth), in the Atlantic about 420 miles SW of Freetown, in position 02.31N 15.55W while sailing independently on a voyage from Buenos Aires and Rio Grande do Sol 28.3.43, Argentina to the UK via Freetown, with a cargo of 5339 tons of refrigerated and tinned meat. The Master, Capt Alfred Ernest Williams, crew of 45 and 7 gunners were rescued by HM destroyers WOLVERINE 1120/19 (D.78) (Lt T.K. Edge-Partington) and WITCH 1120/19 (D.89) (Lt-Cdr S.R.J. Woods) and landed at Freetown.

## NEWFOUNDLAND, GOVERNMENT OF – ST JOHN'S, NEWFOUNDLAND
**Newfoundland Railway Steamship Department**

**CARIBOU** (railway ferry) • GRT 2222 • Built 1925
14.10.42: Torpedoed and sunk by German submarine U-69 (Gräf), in the Cabot Strait, in position 47.19N 59.29W while on a voyage from Sydney, Cape Breton to Paux-aux-Basques, Newfoundland, with 118 service personnel and 73 passengers, part of convoy NL 9 comprising 4 ships. The Master, Capt Benjamin Taverner, 30 crew, 57 service personnel and 48 passengers were lost. 15 crew, 61 service personnel and 25 passengers were rescued by HMCS minesweeping sloop GRANDMERE 672/41 (J.258) (Lt J.S.C. Cuthbert) and landed at Sydney CB 14.10.42. Kapitänleutnant Ulrich Graf and crew of 45 were lost on 17.2.43 when U-69, part of the 'Haudegen' (Broadsword) patrol group of twenty-one U-boats, was sunk while attacking convoy ONS 165 comprising 38 ships in the Atlantic NE of St John's, Newfoundland, in position 50.36N 41.07W by HM destroyer FAME 1350/34 (H.78) (Cdr S. Heathcote), part of the Escort Group B6.

## NIGERIA, GOVERNMENT OF – LAGOS

**ROBERT HUGHES** (suction dredger) • GRT 2879 • Built 1932
4.6.41: Struck a mine laid on 27.5.41 by German submarine U-69 (Metzler), and sank at the entrance to Lagos Harbour. The Master, Capt D. Jones, and 16 crew were rescued by harbour craft. 14 crew were lost.

## NISBET, GEORGE & COMPANY – GLASGOW
**Clydesdale Navigation Co. Ltd**

**BLAIRLOGIE** ex-*GROVEDENE* ex-*PORTFIELD* • GRT 4425 • Built 1929
11.9.39: Torpedoed and sunk by gunfire by German submarine U-30 (Lemp), in the Atlantic 200 miles W of Ireland, in position 54.59N 15.08W while sailing independently on a voyage from Portland, Maine to Lands End for orders, with a cargo of scrap iron and steel. The Master, Capt Daniel Brown MacAlpine, and crew were rescued by US ship *AMERICAN SHIPPER* 7463/21 and landed at New York 18.9.39.

**BLAIRMORE** • GRT 4141 • Built 1928

25.8.40: Torpedoed and sunk by German submarine U-37 (Oehrn), in the Atlantic SE of Cape Farewell, in position 56.00N 27.30W while on a voyage from Newcastle, New Brunswick to the Tyne via Sydney CB 15.8.40, with a cargo of 1500 fathoms of timber, part of convoy SC 1 comprising 40 ships. The Master, Capt Hugh Campbell, 28 crew and 7 naval personnel from HM sloop *PENZANCE* 1045/30 (L.28) (Cdr A.J. Wavisk) sunk by U-37 on 24.8.40 W of Ireland, in position 56.16N 27.19W were rescued by Swedish ship *EKAREN* 5243/22 and landed at Baltimore. 5 crew were lost.

**BLAIRANGUS** ex-*PORTREGIS* • GRT 4409 • Built 1930

21.9.40: Torpedoed and sunk by German submarine U-48 (Bleichrodt), in the Atlantic S of Iceland, in position 55.18N 22.21W while on a voyage from Botwood, Newfoundland to Methil via Halifax NS, with a cargo of 1825 fathoms of timber, part of convoy HX 72 comprising 47 ships. The Master, Capt Hugh Mackinnon, and 27 crew were rescued by British ship *PIKEPOOL* 3683/09 and landed at St John's, Newfoundland. 6 crew were lost.

## MOWT

**EMPIRE WILDEBEESTE** ex-*WEST EKOUK* • GRT 5631 • Built 1918

24.1.42: Torpedoed and sunk by German submarine U-106 (Rasch), part of 'Operation Paukenschlag' (Drumbeat), the second wave of five U-boats, in the Atlantic E of New York, in position 39.30N 59.54W while sailing independently on a voyage from Hull and Loch Ewe to Halifax NS and Baltimore, in ballast, dispersed from convoy ON 53 comprising 26 ships. The Master, Capt Hugh Cameron Stewart, 18 crew and 3 gunners were rescued by US destroyer *LANG* 1500/38 (DD.399) (Lt-Cdr E.A. Seay) and landed at Bermuda. 8 crew and 1 gunner were lost.

**EMPIRE DELL** • GRT 7065 • Built 1941 (CAM ship)

12.5.42: Torpedoed and sunk by German submarine U-124 (Mohr), part of the 'Hecht' (Pike) patrol group of six U-boats, in the Atlantic SE of Cape Farewell, in position 53.00N 29.57W while on a voyage from Garston 6.5.42 to Halifax NS, with 7 RAF personnel, part of convoy ONS 92 comprising 41 ships. The Master, Capt Hugh Mackinnon, 40 crew and RAF personnel were saved. 25 survivors were rescued by RCN corvette *SHEDIAC* 925/41 (K.110) (Lt J.E. Clayton) and landed at St John's, Newfoundland 17.5.42; 21 survivors by rescue ship *BURY* 1634/11 (Capt Lawrence Edwin Brown OBE) and landed at St John's 16.5.42. 2 crew were lost.

**LIFLAND** • GRT 2254 • Built 1920

29.9.42: Torpedoed and sunk by German submarine U-610 (v. Freyburg), part of the 'Luchs' (Lynx) patrol group of sixteen U-boats, in the Atlantic SE of Cape Farewell, in position 56.40N 30.30W while on a voyage from Pictou, Nova Scotia to Milford Haven, with a cargo of timber, a straggler from convoy SC 101 comprising 26 ships. The Master, Capt Niels Jensen, and crew of 23 were lost. Kapitänleutnant Walter Freiherr von Freyberg-Eisenberg Allmendingen and crew of 50 were lost when U-610, part of the 'Rossbach' patrol group of twelve U-boats, attacked convoy SC 143 comprising 39 ships on 8.10.43 and was sunk in the Atlantic 380 miles WSW of Rockall, in position 55.45N 24.33W by Sunderland 'J' DD863 pilot F/O Alfred H. Russell (Canadian) from No. 423 Squadron RCAF, based at Castle Archdale, Co. Fermanagh, part of 15 Group. The pilot was awarded the DFC. One of the escorts ORP destroyer *ORKAN* 1920/42 (Cdr Stanislaw Hryniewiecki) ex-HMS *MYRMIDON* was sunk by U-378 (Mäder) on 8.10.43, SW of Iceland, in position 56.30N 26.26W. Kapitänleutnant Erich Mäder and crew of 51 were lost on 20.10.43 when U-378 was sunk in the Atlantic 490 miles N by E of Flores, Azores, in position 47.40N 28.27W by a Wildcat, pilot Lt-Cdr Charles W. Brewster and an Avenger, pilot Lt Robert W. Hayman from US Navy Composite Squadron VC-13 from US escort carrier *CORE* 9800/42 (CVE.13) (Capt J.R. Dudley).

**EMPIRE MORDRED** • GRT 7030 • Built 1942
7.2.43: Struck a mine, laid on 1.2.43 by German submarine U-118 (Czygan) and sank in the Atlantic W of Gibraltar, in position 35.58N 05.59W while on government service on a voyage from Bona and Gibraltar to the UK, in ballast, part of convoy MKS 7 comprising 66 ships. The Master, Capt Hugh Mackinnon, 41 crew and 13 gunners were rescued by HM sloop *SCARBOROUGH* 1045/30 (L.25) (Lt-Cdr E.B. Carnduff) and landed at Londonderry. 12 crew and 3 gunners were lost. U-118 commanded by Korvettenkapitän Werner Czygan was lost on 12.6.43 in the Atlantic 550 miles SW of Santa Maria, Azores, in position 30.49N 33.49W sunk by two Avengers, pilots Lt Robert L. Stearns and Lt Wilma S. Fowler and two Wildcats, pilots Lt R.J. Johnson and Lt R.J. Tennant of US Navy Composite Squadron VC-9 from US escort carrier *BOGUE* 9800/42 (CVE-9) (Capt G.E. Short), part of 14 Task Force escorting convoy UGS 9 comprising 74 ships. The U-boat commander and 42 crew were lost. 16 crew were taken prisoner by US four-stack destroyer *OSMOND INGRAM* 1190/19 (DD.225) (Lt-Cdr R.F. Miller USNR).

## NORTH COAST STEAM NAVIGATION COMPANY – SYDNEY, NEW SOUTH WALES

**WOLLONGBAR** • GRT 2239 • Built 1922 (Australian)
29.4.43: Torpedoed and sunk by Japanese submarine I-180 (Kusaka), in the Tasman Sea about 10 miles off Crescent Head NSW, in position 31.17S 153.07E while sailing independently on a voyage from Byron Bay NSW 28.4.43 to Newcastle NSW, with a cargo of frozen meat and butter. The Master, Capt Charles Benson, 30 crew and 1 gunner were lost. 5 crew were rescued by trawler *XLER* and landed at Port Macquarie. Lt-Cdr Hidenori Fujjita and crew were lost on 26.4.44 when I-180 was sunk in the Gulf of Alaska 100 miles SSE of Cape Providence, Alaska, in position 55.10N 155.40W by US destroyer escort *GILMORE* 1140/42 (DE–18) (Lt W,D, Jenckes USNR).

## NOURSE, JAMES LIMITED – LONDON

**JHELUM** • GRT 4038 • Built 1936
21.3.41: Torpedoed and sunk by German submarine U-105 (Schewe), in the Atlantic 500 miles W of Cabo Blanco, French West Africa, in position 21.00N 25.00W while on a voyage from Izmir, Turkey to Oban via Cape Town and Freetown 13.3.41, with 4896 tons general cargo including 1400 tons boracite (borax) and 1553 tons of figs, part of convoy SL 68 comprising 59 ships. The Master, Capt Leslie Walter Newman, 47 crew and 1 gunner

landed at St Louis, Senegal and were interned by the Vichy French authorities. 8 crew were lost.

*SAUGOR* • GRT 6303 • Built 1928
27.8.41: Torpedoed and sunk by German submarine U-557 (Paulsen), in the Atlantic W of Ireland, in position 53.36N 16.40W while on a voyage from London to Calcutta via Freetown, with general cargo and 28 aircraft, part of convoy OS 4 comprising 34 ships. The Master, Capt James Arthur Aitken Steel, and 22 survivors were rescued by rescue ship *PERTH* 2259/15 (Capt Keith Williamson OBE) and landed at Greenock 28.8.41. 59 crew including 7 gunners were lost. Kapitänleutnant Ottokar Paulsen and crew of 42 were lost on 16.12.41 in the Aegean Sea NW of Crete, in position 35.33N 23.14E when U-557 was accidentally rammed by Italian torpedo boat *ORIONE* 855/37 (Lt M. Gambetta).

*BHIMA* • GRT 5280 • Built 1939
20.2.42: Torpedoed and sunk by Japanese submarine I-165 (Harada), in the Arabian Sea 300 miles SW of Cape Comorin, India, in position 07.47N 73.31E while sailing independently on a voyage from Rangoon and Colombo to Durban and the West Indies, with 2 passengers and a cargo of 1300 tons of tea and rubber for Durban and 8700 tons general cargo for the West Indies. The Master, Capt Dennis Gough Jones, crew of 67 and passengers were rescued on 23.2.42 by Greek ship *CHIOS* 5463/39 and landed at Durban 9.3.42.

*SUTLEJ* • GRT 5189 • Built 1940
26.2.44: Torpedoed and sunk by Japanese submarine I-37 (Nakagaw), in the Arabian Sea W of Diego Gracia, in position 08.00S 70.00E while sailing independently on a voyage from Kosseir, Egypt and Aden to Fremantle, Western Australia, with a cargo of 9700 tons of rock phosphates and mail. The Master, Capt Dennis Gough Jones, 40 crew and 9 gunners were lost. The Chief Engineer R.H. Rees, 10 crew and 1 gunner were rescued after 46 days adrift on a raft by HM sloop *FLAMINGO* 1250/39 (L.180 (Lt-Cdr T.H.B. Pounds) and landed at Addu Atoll 14.4.44. The raft had drifted 650 miles in a north-easterly direction. The 3rd Engineer Arthur S. Bennett, 9 crew and 1 gunner were rescued after 42 days on a raft by HM whaler *SOLVRA* 433/37 (FY.334) (Lt J.C. Elder) and landed at Diego Suarez, Chagos Archipelago. The 3rd Engineer was awarded the Lloyd's War Medal for bravery at sea.

## NOVA SCOTIA STEEL & COAL CO. LTD – PICTOU, NOVA SCOTIA

*WATUKA* • GRT 1621 • Built 1918 (Canadian)
22.3.44: Torpedoed and sunk by German submarine U-802 (Schmoeckel), in the Atlantic SE of Halifax NS, in position 44.30N 62.51W while on a voyage from Louisburg, Nova Scotia to Halifax, Nova Scotia, with a cargo of 1998 tons of coal, part of convoy SH 125. The Master, 22 crew and 2 gunners were rescued by RCN trawler *ANTICOSTI* 545/42 (T.274) (Lt J.C. Boyd). 1 crew was lost. U-802 sailed from Cairnryan, Loch Ryan on 30.12.45 towed by HM escort destroyer *PYTCHLEY* 907/40 (L.92) (Lt-Cdr D.H. Foulds DSC), the tow parted and U-802 is presumed to have foundered in approximate position 55.30N 08.25W. This was one of 116 U-boats disposed of by the Royal Navy, part of 'Operation Deadlight'.

## OHLSON, SIR ERIC, BART – HULL
### Ohlson SS Co. Ltd

*MACGREGOR* ex-*BARON GARIOCH* ex-*WAR MELON* • GRT 2498 • Built 1919
27.2.42: Sunk by gunfire by German submarine U-156 (Hartenstein), in the Atlantic about 25 miles NW of Cape Viejos, Puerto Rico, in position 19.50N 69.40W while sailing independently on a voyage from the Tyne to Tampa, Florida, with a cargo of 2621 tons of coal, dispersed from convoy ON 60 comprising 45 ships. The Master, Capt William George Todman, 23 crew and 6 gunners were rescued by a San Domingo coastguard cutter and landed at Puerto Plata, Dominican Republic. 1 crew was lost.

## OHLSON, JOHNSTON & CO. LTD – HULL
### MOWT

*MARGARETA* ex-*ATLANTIC* • GRT 3103 • Built 1904
27.9.41: Torpedoed and sunk by German submarine U-201 (Schnee), in the Atlantic SW of Cape Clear, in position 50.15N 17.27W while on a voyage from Gibraltar to Glasgow, with a part cargo of 400 tons of general including scrap and cork, part of convoy HG 73 comprising 25 ships. The Master, Capt H. Pihlgrenn, and crew of 33 were rescued by HM corvette *HIBISCUS* 925/40 (K.24) (Lt-Cdr H. Roach) and landed at Gibraltar.

## ORIENT LINE – LONDON

*ORONSAY* • GRT 20043 • Built 1925
9.10.42: Torpedoed and sunk by Italian submarine *ARCHIMEDE* (Saccardo), in the Atlantic about 500 miles SW of Freetown, in position 04.29N 20.52W while on government service sailing independently on a voyage from Cape Town 30.9.42 to the UK via Freetown, with 50 RAF personnel, 20 DBS, 8 DEMS and 1200 tons of copper slabs and 3000 tons of oranges. The Master, Capt Norman Savage, 281 crew, 15 gunners, 25 RAF personnel, DBS and DEMS were rescued by HM destroyer *BRILLIANT* 1360/30 (H.84) (Lt-Cdr A.G. Poe), landed at Freetown, transferred to Union Castle liner *CAERNARVON CASTLE* 20112/21 and sailed 15.10.42 for Glasgow. 6 crew were lost. 37 crew, 1 gunner and 25 RAF personnel were taken prisoner. Lt Guido Saccardo and crew were lost on 15.4.43 when the *ARCHIMEDE* was sunk in the South Atlantic 180 miles east of Fernando do Nonoha, Brazil, in position 03.23S 30.28W by two Liberators of US Navy Bombing Squadron VP-83 based at Arata, Brazil.

*ORCADES* • GRT 23456 • Built 1937
10.10.42: Torpedoed and sunk by German submarine U-172 (Emmermann), part of the 'Eisbär' (Polarbear) patrol group of five U-boats, in the South Atlantic 280 miles NW of Cape Town, in position 35.34S 14.44E while sailing independently on government service employed as a troopship on a voyage from Suez and Cape Town 9.10.42 to the UK, with 723 passengers and 3000 tons general cargo. The Master, Capt Charles Fox, 264 crew, 34 gunners and 694 passengers were rescued by Polish ship *NARWIK* 7030/42 and landed at Cape Town 12.10.42. 26 crew, 2 gunners and 18 passengers were lost. Capt C. Fox was awarded the Lloyd's War Medal for bravery at sea.

## ORIENTAL TRADE & TRANSPORT CO. LTD – LONDON
Oriental Tankers Limited

*FREDERICK S. FALES* (tanker) • GRT 10525 • Built 1939
22.9.40: Torpedoed and sunk by German submarine U-100 (Schepke), in the Atlantic 340 miles W of Bloody Foreland, in position 55.30N 13.40W while on government service on a voyage from Curacao to the Clyde via Halifax NS, with a cargo of 13849 tons of Admiralty fuel oil, part of convoy HX 72 comprising 47 ships. The Master, Capt Frank Ramsay, 9 crew and 1 gunner were lost. 32 crew were rescued by HM corvette *LA MALOUINE* 925/40 (K.46) (Lt-Cdr R.W. Keymer) and landed at Belfast.

*W.B. WALKER* (tanker) • GRT 10468 • Built 1935
29.1.41: Torpedoed and damaged by German submarine U-93 (Korth), in the Atlantic 150 miles SW of Rockall, in position 56.00N 15.23W while on a voyage from Aruba to Avonmouth via Halifax NS, with a cargo of 13,338 tons of aviation spirit and motor spirit, part of convoy SC 19 comprising 27 ships. Taken in tow by HM destroyer *ANTHONY* 1350/29 (H.40) (Lt-Cdr V.C.F. Clark) and HM trawler *ARAB* 531/36 (FY.202) (Lt C.A. Shillan), she later sank. The Master, Capt William Barnes Simpson, and 42 crew were rescued by HM destroyers *ANTHONY* and *ANTELOPE* 1350/29 (H.36) (Lt-Cdr R.T. White DSO), transferred to HM trawler *ARAB* and landed at Gourock. 4 crew were lost.

*ARTHUR F. CORWIN* (tanker) • GRT 10516 • Built 1938
13.2.41: Torpedoed and damaged by German submarine U-103 (Schütze), later sunk by German submarine U-96 (Lehmann–Willenbrock), in the North Atlantic SE of Iceland, in position 60.25N 17.11W while on a voyage from Aruba to Avonmouth via Halifax NS, with a cargo of 14500 tons of motor spirit, a straggler from convoy HX 106 comprising 41 ships. The Master, Capt John Lawrence Gant, crew of 43 and 2 gunners were lost.

*EDWY R. BROWN* (tanker) • GRT 10455 • Built 1938
17.2.41: Torpedoed and sunk by German submarine U-103 (Schütze), in the North Atlantic SE of Iceland, in position 61.00N 18.00W while on a voyage from Aruba to Liverpool via Halifax NS, with a cargo of clean petroleum products, a straggler from convoy HX 107 comprising 21 ships. The Master, Capt Andrew Chalmers, crew of 47 and 2 gunners were lost.

## OVERSEAS OIL & TRANSPORT CO. LTD – LONDON

*CASPIA* (tanker) • GRT 6018 • Built 1928
16.4.42: Torpedoed and sunk by German submarine U-81 (Guggenberger), in the Mediterranean 10 miles S of Beirut while on a voyage from Haifa 16.4.42 to Tripoli, Syria, escorted by the Free French trawler *VIKINGS* 1150/35, with a cargo of 7000 tons of light benzine. The Master, Capt Cecil Henry Humphries, 24 crew and 2 gunners were lost. 10 crew and 1 gunner were rescued by HM motor launches No. 1023 46/40 (Lt C.S. Roberts) and No. 1032 46/40 (Lt C.D. Searle) and landed at Beirut.

## OVERSEAS TOWAGE & SALVAGE COMPANY – LONDON

*NEPTUNIA* (tug) • GRT 798 • Built 1938
13.9.39: Torpedoed and sunk by gunfire by German submarine U-29 (Schuhart), in the Atlantic SW of Ireland, in position 49.20N 14.40W while on government service en route from Falmouth for salvage work in the Atlantic. The Master, Capt Joseph Cordery, and crew of 20 were rescued by British ship *BRINKBURN* 1598/24 and landed at Falmouth 16.9.39.

## PACIFIC STEAM NAVIGATION COMPANY – LIVERPOOL

*OROPESA* • GRT 14118 • Built 1920
16.1.41: Torpedoed and sunk by German submarine U-96 (Lehmann-Willenbrock), in the Atlantic SE of Rockall, in positiom 56.28N 12.00W while sailing independently on government service on a voyage from Mombasa to the UK, with 41 passengers, about 8252 tons of general cargo including copper and maize. The Master, Capt Harry E.H. Croft, 98 crew, 1 gunner and 6 passengers were lost. 109 crew, 33 passengers and 1 gunner were rescued by HM rescue tugs *SUPERMAN* 359/33 (W.89) and *TENACITY* 700/40 (W.18) ex-HMS *DILIGENT* and HM destroyer *WESTCOTT* 1100/18 (D.47) (Lt-Cdr W.F.R. Segrave) and landed at Liverpool.

## PALESTINE MARITIME LLOYD LIMITED – TEL–AVIV, PALESTINE

*HAR ZION* ex-*RISVEGLIO* ex-*NICKERIE* ex-*ST JAN*. • GRT 2508 • Built 1907
31.8.40: Torpedoed and sunk by German submarine U-38 (Liebe), in the Atlantic NW of Bloody Foreland, in position 56.40N 11.00W while on a voyage from Liverpool to Savannah, Georgia, with a cargo of 1000 cases of spirit and 120 tons of fertiliser, a straggler from convoy OB 205 comprising 32 ships. The Master, Capt John N. Beighton, and 33 crew were lost. The sole survivor was Seaman Osman Adem.

## PANAMA TRANSPORT COMPANY (ANGLO–AMERICAN OIL COMPANY) – LONDON

*T.J. WILLIAMS* (tanker) • GRT 8212 • Built 1921
20.9.41: Torpedoed and sunk by German submarine U-552 (Topp), in the North Atlantic ENE of Cape Farewell, in position 61.34N 35.11W while on a voyage from Baltimore to Stanlow via Sydney CB 11.9.41, with a cargo of 10036 tons of motor spirit, part of convoy SC 44 comprising 54 ships. The Master, Capt Robert Thomas Charles Wright, 20 crew and 1 gunner were rescued by HM corvette *HONEYSUCKLE* 925/40 (K.27) (Lt-Cdr G.W. Gregorie) and landed at Reykjavik. 15 crew and 2 gunners were lost.

*W.C. TEAGLE* (tanker) • GRT 9552 • Built 1917
17.10.41: Torpedoed and sunk by German submarine U-558 (Krech), in the Atlantic 600 miles W of Rockall, in position 57.00N 25.00W while on a voyage from Aruba to Swansea via Sydney CB, with a cargo of 15000 tons of fuel oil, part of convoy SC 48 comprising 50 ships. The Master, Capt Harold Redvers Barlow, 38 crew and 1 gunner were lost. 10 crew were rescued by HM destroyer *BROADWATER* 1190/19 (H.81) (Lt-Cdr W.M.L. Astwood) ex-USN four-stack *MASON*

(DD 191). Two of the convoy's escorts were lost. HMS *BROADWATER* was sunk in the Atlantic, in position 57.01N 19.08W the next day by U-101 (Mengersen). 9 survivors of the *W.C. TEAGLE* were lost. The sole survivor Radio Officer N.D. Houston was rescued by HM corvette *VERONICA* 925/40 (K.37) (Lt-Cdr D.F. White) and landed at Londonderry. HM corvette *GLADIOLUS* 925/40 (K.34) (Lt-Cdr Harry M.C. Sanders DSO DSC) was torpedoed and sunk in about position 57.00N 25.00W on 17.10.41, probably by U-558.

**GEO. H. JONES** (tanker) • GRT 6914 • Built 1919
11.6.42: Torpedoed and sunk by German submarine U-455 (Giessler), in the Atlantic NNE of the Azores, in position 45.40N 22.40W while on a voyage from Aruba to Lamlash and Ardrossan via Freetown 24.5.42, with 2 passengers and a cargo of 9300 tons of fuel oil, a straggler from convoy SL 111 comprising 38 ships. The Master, Capt Frederick James Hewlett, and 19 survivors were rescued by HM sloop *LULWORTH* 1546/28 (Y.60) (Lt-Cdr C. Gwinner) ex-US Coastguard cutter *CHELAN* and landed at Freetown; 20 survivors by HM minesweeper *ORISSA* 672/41 (J.200) ex-HMS *CLYDEBANK* (Lt D. Whyte) and landed at Londonderry. 1 crew and 1 gunner were lost. U-455 commanded by Kapitänleutnant Hans-Martin Scheibe and crew of 50 were lost on 6.4.44 when U-455 probably detonated a mine in a German minefield in the Ligurian Sea S of La Spezia, in position 44.04N 09.51E.

## PATERSON STEAMSHIPS LIMITED – FORT WILLIAM, ONTARIO

**KENORDOC** ex-*GEO. R. DONOVAN* • GRT 1780 • Built 1926 (Canadian)
16.9.40: Damaged by gunfire by German submarine U-99 (Kretschmer), later sunk by HM destroyer *AMAZON* 1352/26 (D.39) (Lt-Cdr E.G. Roper), in the Atlantic 44 miles WNW of Rockall, in position 57.42N 15.02W while on a voyage from Quebec to Bristol via Sydney CB, with a cargo of 2000 tons of timber (700 standards), a straggler from convoy SC 3 comprising 47 ships. The Master, Capt Charles Ernest Brown, and 6 crew were lost. 13 crew were rescued by HM destroyer *AMAZON* and RCN destroyer *ST LAURENT* 1375/31 (H.83) ex-HMS *CYGNET* (Cdr Harry G. DeWolf) and landed at Greenock.

**PORTADOC** ex-*JAMES B. FOOTE* ex-*EUGENE C. ROBERTS*
GRT 1746 • Built 1924 (Canadian)
7.4.41: Torpedoed and sunk by German submarine U-124 (Schulz), in the Atlantic 150 miles SW of Freetown, in position 07.17N 16.53W while sailing independently on a voyage from St Lucia, BWI to Freetown, in ballast. The Master, Capt John Evan Jones, and crew of 19 landed six days later at Benty, French Guinea and were interned by the Vichy French authorities.

**SARNIADOC** • GRT 1940 • Built 1929 (Canadian)
14.3.42: Torpedoed and sunk by German submarine U-161 (Achilles), in the Caribbean Sea 200 miles W of Guadeloupe, in position 15.45N 65.00W while sailing independently on a voyage from Georgetown, British Guinea to St Thomas, Virgin Islands, in ballast. The Master, Capt William Allen Darling, and crew of 18 were lost.

**TORONDOC** • GRT 1927 • Built 1927 (Canadian)
21.5.42: Torpedoed and sunk by German submarine U-69 (Gräf), in the Atlantic 60 miles NW of Martinique, in position 14.45N 62.15W while sailing independently on a voyage

from St Thomas, Virgin Islands to Trinidad, with a cargo of bauxite. The Master, Capt François Xavier Daneau, and crew of 20 were lost.

**TROISDOC** • GRT 1925 • Built 1928 (Canadian)
21.5.42: Torpedoed and sunk by German submarine U-558 (Krech), in the Atlantic about 40 miles NW of Jamaica, in position 18.15N 79.20W while sailing independently on a voyage from Mobile to Georgetown, British Guinea, with general cargo including cement. The Master and crew of 17 were rescued by US coastguard cutter *MOHAWK* 1005/34 (WPG.78).

**PRESODOC** • GRT 1938 • Built 1929 (Canadian)
29.7.42: Torpedoed and sunk by German submarine U-160 (Lassen), in the Atlantic NW of Georgetown, British Guinea, in position 08.50N 59.05W while sailing independently on a voyage from Georgetown to Trinidad, in ballast. The Master, Capt John Charles Prowse, and 5 crew were rescued by Yugoslavian ship *PRESEDNIK KOPAJTIC* 1798/28 and landed at Port of Spain, Trinidad. 15 crew were lost.

## PENINSULAR & ORIENTAL STEAM NAVIGATION CO. LTD – LONDON

**ESTON** • GRT 1487 • Built 1919
28.1.40: Struck a mine, laid on 20.12.39, by German submarine U-22 (Jenish), and sank in the North Sea near Blyth while on a voyage from Hull to Blyth, in ballast, a straggler from coastal convoy FN 81 comprising 11 ships. The Master, Capt Herbert Roser Harris, and crew of 17 were lost. Kapitänleutnant Karl-Heinrich Jenisch and crew of 26 were lost on 25.4.40 when U-22 probably struck a mine in the Skagerrak NW of Vigsö Bay, Denmark, in position 57.00N 09.00E.

**LAHORE** • GRT 5252 • Built 1920
8.3.41: Torpedoed and sunk by German submarine U-124 (Schulz), in the Atlantic NE of the Cape Verde Islands, in position 21.03N 20.38W while on a voyage from Calcutta to London via Freetown 1.3.41, with general cargo including 1120 tons of timber, tea, pig-iron and mail, part of convoy SL 67 comprising 56 ships. The Master, Capt Geoffrey Scott Stable, and crew of 81 were rescued by HM destroyer *FORESTER* 1350/34 (H.74) (Lt-Cdr E.B. Tancock DSC) and landed at Gibraltar 16.3.41.

**RAJPUTANA** • GRT 16568 • Built 1925
13.4.41: Torpedoed and sunk by German submarine U-108 (Scholtz), in the North Atlantic W of Reykjavik, in position 64.50N 27.25W while escorting convoy HX 117 comprising 43 ships. Cdr C.T.O Richardson, 4 officers and 35 crew were lost. 283 survivors were rescued by HM destroyer *LEGION* 1920/39 (F.74) (Cdr R.F. Jessel) and landed at Reykjavik. *RAJPUTANA* was lost while on government service employed as an Armed Merchant Cruiser (F.35) (Capt F.H. Taylor DSC).

**SURAT** • GRT 5529 • Built 1938
6.5.41: Torpedoed and sunk by German submarine U-103 (Schütze), in the Atlantic NW of Freetown, in position 08.23N 15.13W while sailing independently on a voyage from Karachi and Cape Town to the UK, with a cargo of 2500 tons of pig iron and 5700 tons of peas and

rape seed. The Master, Capt Thomas Edward Daniel, 58 crew and 2 gunners were rescued by British hopper barge *FOREMOST* 102 833/40 and landed at Freetown. 4 crew were lost.

### *ALIPORE* • GRT 5273 • Built 1920

30.9.42: Torpedoed and sunk by gunfire by German submarine U-516 (Wiebe), in the Atlantic NE of Georgetown, British Guinea, in position 07.09N 54.23W while sailing independently on a voyage from Alexandria and Cape Town 6.9.42 to New York via Trinidad, with a cargo of 1500 tons of chrome ore and 400 tons of olive oil. The Master, Capt Ernest Lee, 68 crew and 4 gunners were towed in the ship's boats by fishing schooner *UNITED EAGLE* of Georgetown where they landed. 10 crew were lost.

### *NAGPORE* • GRT 5283 • Built 1920

28.10.42: Torpedoed and damaged by German submarine U-509 (Witte) later sunk by torpedo and gunfire by the German submarine U-203 (Kottmann), part of the 'Streitaxt' (Battleaxe) patrol group of eight U-boats, in the Atlantic NW of the Canary Islands, in position 31.30N 19.35W while on a voyage from Suez and Durban to Manchester via Freetown 16.10.42, with 7000 tons of general cargo including 1501 tons of copper, part of convoy SL 125 comprising 40 ships. The Master, Capt Percy Ernest Tonkin, 18 crew and 1 naval staff were lost. 23 crew, 5 gunners, Commodore Rear Admiral Sir C.N. Reyne KBE RN and 5 naval staff were rescued by HM corvette *CROCUS* 925/40 (K.49) (Lt J.F. Holm) and landed at Liverpool 9.11.42. The 4th Engineer J.J. Marshall with 18 survivors landed at La Orotave, Canary Islands 10.11.42, after being adrift in an open boat for fourteen days.

### *JEYPORE* launched as *WAR MOTH* • GRT 5318 • Built 1920

3.11.42: Torpedoed and sunk by German submarine U-89 (Lohmann), part of the 'Veilchen' (Violet) patrol group of thirteen U-boats, in the Atlantic SSE of Cape Farewell, in position 55.30N 40.16W while on a voyage from Baltimore and New York 24.10.42 to Hull, with 6200 tons of general cargo including explosives, part of convoy SC 107 comprising 42 ships. The Master, Capt Thomas Stevens, 74 crew, 8 gunners, Commodore Vice-Admiral B.C. Watson CB DSO RN and 6 naval staff were rescued by US naval tugs *UNCAS* 147/41 and *PESSACAS*, transferred to rescue ship *STOCKPORT* 1637/11 (Capt Ernest Fea OBE) and landed at Reykjavik 8.11.42. 1 crew was lost.

### *VICEROY OF INDIA* • GRT 19648 • Built 1929

11.11.42: Torpedoed and sunk by German submarine U-407 (Brüller), in the Mediterranean 34 miles NW of Oran, in position 36.26N 00.24W while on government service on a voyage from Algiers 10.11.42 to the UK via Gibraltar, in ballast, part of convoy KMF 1 comprising 39 ships. The Master, Capt Sydney Herbert French, 398 crew, 29 gunners and 22 passengers were rescued by HM destroyer *BOADICEA* 1360/30 (H.65) (Lt-Cdr F.C. Brodrick) and landed at Gibraltar. 4 crew were lost. The *VICEROY OF INDIA* was lost while on government service employed as a landing ship infantry. U-407, commanded by Oberleutnant zur See Hans Kolbus, was sunk on 19.9.44 in the Aegean Sea 15 miles S of Milos, in position 36.27N 24.33E by HM destroyers *TROUBRIDGE* 1730/42 (R.00) (Capt C.L. Firth) and *TERPSICHORE* 1710/43 (R.33) (Cdr A.C. Bohague) and ORP destroyer *GARLAND* 1335/35 (Cdr B. Biskupski). The U-boat commander and 47 crew were taken prisoner: 18 crew were taken prisoner by HM destroyer *BRECON* 1175/42 (L.76) (Lt A.M. Coke-

Hamilton), 13 by HMS *TERPSICHORE* and 17 by ORP *GARLAND*. All the prisoners were transferred to ORP *GARLAND* and landed at Alexandria 20.9.44. 5 crew were lost. This was the last U-boat to be sunk at sea in the Mediterranean.

**ETTRICK** • GRT 11279 • Built 1938
15.11.42: Torpedoed and sunk by German submarine U-155 (Piening), part of the 'Westwall' patrol group of sixteen U-boats, in the Atlantic 120 miles NW of Gibraltar, in position 36.13N 07.54W while on a voyage from Gibraltar to Glasgow, in ballast, part of convoy MKF 1 (Y) comprising 8 ships. The Master, Capt John Murray Legg, 204 crew, 41 gunners and 66 naval ratings were rescued by RNoN destroyer *GLAISSDALE* 1087/42 (L.44) and landed at Gibraltar. 6 crew and 18 naval ratings were lost. The *ETTRICK* was lost while on government service employed as an auxiliary transport. Capt J.M. Legg was awarded the OBE. Kapitänleutnant Adolf Piening was awarded the Knight's Cross (13.8.42). U-155, commanded by Oberleutnant zur See Friedrich Altmeier, sailed from Wilhelmshaven on 21.6.45 to surrender to Great Britain. U-155 sailed from Cairnryan on 21.12.45 towed by HM tug *PROSPEROUS* 700/42 (W.96); after the line parted during bad weather U-155 was sunk by gunfire by ORP destroyer *BLYSKAWICA* 2144/36 (H.34) in the Atlantic NNW of Malin Head, in position 55.35N 07.39W, part of 'Operation Deadlight', the disposal of 116 U-boats by the Royal Navy.

**STRATHALLAN** • GRT 23722 • Built 1938
21.12.42: Torpedoed and damaged by German submarine U-562 (Hamm), in the Mediterranean 40 miles N of Oran, in position 36.52N 00.34W while on government service employed as a troopship on a voyage from Glasgow 11.12.42 to Algiers, carrying 4408 British and US troops and 248 Queen Alexandra nurses, part of convoy KMF 5 comprising 12 ships. The Master, Capt John Henry Biggs CBE, 426 crew, 248 nurses, 296 army officers and 4112 warrant officers and other ranks were rescued by HM destroyers *LAFOREY* 1935/41 (F.99) (Capt R.M.J. Hutton DSO), *VERITY* 1140/19 (D.63) (Lt J.C. Rushbrooke DSC), *PANTHER* 1540/41 (G.41) (Lt-Cdr Viscount Jocelyn) and *PATHFINDER* 1540/41 (G.10) ex-HMS *ONSLAUGHT* (Cdr E.A. Gibbs) and landed at Oran. 4 crew were lost. Taken in tow by HMS *LAFOREY*, and later joined by HM rescue tug *RESTIVE* 700/40 (W.39) (Lt D.M. Richards), towing proved unsuccessful and she capsized en route to Oran and sank on 22.12.42. Capt J.H. Biggs was awarded the Lloyd's War Medal for bravery at sea. Kapitänleutnant Horst Hamm and crew of 48 were lost on 19.2.43 when U-562 was sunk in the Mediterranean 30 miles W of Ras el Hamana, Cyrenaica, in position 32.57N 20.54E by HM destroyers *ISIS* 1370/36 (D.87) (Cdr B. Jones) and *HURSLEY* 710/41 (L.84) (Lt W.J.C. Church) and Wellington 'S', pilot F/O I.B. Butler AFC of No. 38 Squadron RAF, based at Gambut, Cyrenaica.

**SHILLONG** • GRT 5529 • Built 1939
4.4.43: Torpedoed and sunk by German submarine U-630 (Winkler), part of the 'Löwenherz' (Lionhearted) patrol group of fourteen U-boats, in the Atlantic SE of Cape Farewell, in position 57.10N 35.30W while on a voyage from Port Lincoln, South Australia to Belfast Lough and Swansea via New York 25.3.43, with a cargo of 4000 tons of zinc concentrates and 3000 tons of generals including grain, part of convoy HX 231 comprising 61 ships. The Master, Capt James Harry Hollow, 67 crew and 3 gunners were lost. Apprentice David Clowe, 1 crew and 5 gunners were rescued after eight days in an open boat by British rescue ship *ZAMALEK* 1567/21 (Capt Owen Charles Morris DSO) and landed at

Halifax NS 21.4.43. Oberleutnant zur See Werner Winkler and crew of 46 were lost when U-630, part of the 'Fink' (Finch) patrol group of thirty U-boats, was sunk on 4.5.43 in the Atlantic about 400 miles NE of Cape Race, in position 52.31N 44.50W by HM destroyer *VIDETTE* 1090/18 (D.48) (Lt-Cdr Raymond Hart).

**PESHAWUR** ex-*WAR DIANE* • GRT 7934 • Built 1919
23.12.43: Torpedoed and sunk by Japanese submarine RO-111 (Nakamura), in the Indian Ocean SE of Madras, in position 11.11N 80.11E while on a voyage from Swansea and Trincomalee 22.12.43 to Calcutta, with a cargo of 2300 tons of government stores including tinplate, 150 tons of explosives, bleaching powder and 1983 tons of general cargo, part of convoy JC 30 comprising 12 ships. The Master, Capt John Clifford Mellonie, 124 crew and 9 gunners were rescued by RAN minesweeping sloop *IPSWICH* 650/41 (J.186) (Lt-Cdr J.S. McBryde) and landed at Madras 24.12.43.

**PETERSEN, WILLIAM & CO. LTD – LONDON**
**Thompson SS Co. Ltd**

**RIO CLARO** • GRT 4086 • Built 1922
6.9.39: Torpedoed and sunk by German submarine U-47 (Prien), in the Atlantic NW of Cape Ortegal, in position 46.30N 12.00W while sailing independently on a voyage from Sunderland to Montevideo, with a cargo of coal. The Master, Capt John Ainsley Robson, and crew of 40 were rescued by Dutch ship *STAD MAASTRECHT* 6552/24 and landed at Fayal 11.9.39.

**RIO AZUL** • GRT 4088 • Built 1921
29.6.41: Torpedoed and sunk by German submarine U-123 (Hardegen), in the Atlantic 200 miles SE of the Azores, in position 29.00N 25.00W while on a voyage from Pepel to Middlesbrough via Freetown 30.5.41, with a cargo of 6700 tons of iron ore, part of convoy SL 76 comprising 60 ships. The Master, Capt Thomas Vickers Sutherland, 31 crew and 1 gunner were lost. 6 crew and 3 gunners were rescued by HM armed merchant cruiser *ESPERANCE BAY* 14024/22 (F.67) (Capt G.S. Holden) and landed at Scapa Flow, Orkneys.

**RIO BLANCO** • GRT 4086 • Built 1922
1.4.42: Torpedoed and sunk by German submarine U-160 (Lassen), part of 'Operation Paukenschlag' (Drumbeat), the fourth wave of eleven U-boats, in the Atlantic 60 miles E of Cape Hatteras, in position 35.16N 74.18W while sailing independently on a voyage from St Thomas, Virgin Islands 16.3.43 to Hampton Roads and the UK, with a cargo of 6440 tons of iron ore. The Master, Capt Aiden Blackett, 9 crew and 2 gunners were rescued by HM trawler *HERTFORDSHIRE* 458/38 (FY.176) (Cdr J.A. Shater) and landed at Norfolk, Virginia, and 9 crew by RCN destroyer *NIAGARA* 1060/18 (I.57) (Lt T.J. Bellas) ex-USN four-stack *THATCHER* and landed at Halifax NS. 18 crew and 1 gunner were lost.

**MOWT**

**SUSAN MAERSK** • GRT 2355 • Built 1923
12.6.41: Torpedoed and sunk by German submarine U-553 (Thurmann), part of the 'West' patrol group of fifteen U-boats, in the Atlantic N of the Azores, in position 43.39N 28.00W

while sailing independently on a voyage from Newport, Mon. to Curacao, in ballast, dispersed from convoy OG 64 comprising 52 ships. The Master, Capt Kai Bjorn Thomsen, and crew of 21 were lost.

## PORT LINE – LONDON

*PORT GISBORNE* • GRT 8390 • Built 1927
11.10.40: Torpedoed and sunk by German submarine U-48 (Bleichrodt), in the Atlantic WSW of Rockall, in position 56.38N 16.40W while on a voyage from Auckland to Belfast and Cardiff via Halifax NS, with refrigerated and general cargo including bales of wool and sheepskin, part of convoy HX 77 comprising 40 ships. The Master, Capt Thomas Kippins OBE DSC, and 36 crew were rescued by HM rescue tug *SALVONIA* 571/39 (W.43) (Lt G.M.M. Robinson) and British ship *ALPERA* 1770/20 and landed at Greenock. 26 crew were lost. Capt T. Kippins was awarded the Lloyd's War Medal for bravery at sea.

*PORT HARDY* • GRT 8705 • Built 1923
28.4.41: Torpedoed and sunk by German submarine U-96 (Lehmann-Willenbrock), in the North Atlantic SE of Reykjavik, in position 60.14N 15.20W while on a voyage from Wellington to Ellesmere Port and Avonmouth via Panama, with 10 passengers and general cargo including 700 tons of zinc, 3000 tons of cheese, part of convoy HX 121 comprising 48 ships. The Master, Capt John Geoffrey Lewis, 82 crew, 4 gunners and passengers were rescued by rescue ship *ZAAFAREN* 1559/21 (Capt Charles Kavanagh McGowan DSC) and landed at Greenock 1.5.41. 1 crew was lost.

*PORT MONTREAL* • GRT 5882 • Built 1937
10.6.42: Torpedoed and sunk by German submarine U-68 (Merten), in the Atlantic NE of the Panama Canal, in position 12.17N 80.20W while sailing independently from Halifax NS 21.5.42 and Hampton Roads 1.6.42 to Melbourne via Panama, with a cargo of 7500 tons of ammunition and a deck cargo of 14 aircraft. The Master, Capt John Geoffrey Lewis, crew of 42 and 2 gunners were rescued by Colombian schooner *HILOA* and landed at Cristobal.

*PORT NICHOLSON* • GRT 8402 • Built 1919
16.6.42: Torpedoed and sunk by German submarine U-87 (Berger), in the Atlantic NE of Cape Cod, in position 42.11N 69.25W while on a voyage from Avonmouth, Barry and New York to Wellington via Halifax NS 14.6.42 and Panama, with a cargo of 1600 tons of automobile parts and 4000 tons of military stores, part of convoy XB 25 comprising 5 ships. The Master Harold Charles Jeffrey and 3 crew were lost. 79 crew and 4 gunners were rescued by RCN corvette *NANAIMO* 925/40 (K.101) (Lt T.J. Bellas) and landed at Boston, Mass.

*PORT HUNTER* • GRT 8437 • Built 1922
12.7.42: Torpedoed and sunk by German submarine U-582 (Schulte), part of the 'Hai' (Shark) patrol group of six U-boats, in the Atlantic W of Madeira, in position 31.00N 24.00W while sailing independently on a voyage from Liverpool 1.7.42 to Durban and Auckland via Panama, with 5 passengers and general cargo including ammunition, dispersed from convoy OS 33 comprising 41 ships. The Master, Capt John Bentham Bradley, 67 crew, 14 gunners and passengers were lost. 3 crew were rescued by HM sloop *PELICAN* 1200/38 (L.86) (Cdr G.V. Gladstone).

**PORT AUCKLAND** • GRT 8308 • Built 1922

18.3.43: Torpedoed and sunk by German submarine U-305 (Bahr), part of the 'Stürmer' (Attacker) patrol group of eighteen U-boats, in the Atlantic SW of Cape Farewell, in position 52.25N 30.15W while on a voyage from Brisbane to Belfast Lough and Avonmouth via Cristobal and Halifax NS 8.3.43, with 10 RAF personnel and 8000 tons of general cargo including 7000 tons of frozen produce and mail, part of convoy SC 122 comprising 51 ships. The Master, Capt Arthur Eric Fishwick, 87 crew, 12 gunners and RAF personnel were rescued by HM corvette *GODETIA* 925/41 (K.226) ex-HMS *DART* (Lt A.M. Larose) and landed at Gourock. 8 crew were lost. Kapitänleutnant Rudolf Bahr and crew of 50 were lost on 17.1.44 when U-305 was sunk in the Atlantic 425 miles W by S of Cape Clear, in position 49.39N 20.10W by HM destroyer *WANDERER* 1710/19 (D.74) (Lt-Cdr Reginald F. Whinney) and HM frigate *GLENARM* 1370/43 (K.258) (Cdr L.A.B. Majendie).

**PORT VICTOR** • GRT 12411 • Built 1942

1.5.43: Torpedoed and sunk by German submarine U-107 (Gelhaus), in the Atlantic NE of the Azores, in position 47.49N 22.02W while sailing independently on a voyage from Buenos Aires and Montevideo 17.4.43 to Liverpool, with 65 passengers including 23 women and children, 7600 tons refrigerated foodstuffs and 2000 tons of general cargo. The Master, Capt William Gordon Higgs, 74 crew, 10 gunners and 60 passengers were rescued by HM sloop *WREN* 1300/42 (U.28) (Lt-Cdr R.M. Aubrey) and landed at Liverpool. 12 crew, 2 gunners and 5 passengers were lost. Kapitänleutnant Harald Gelhaus was awarded the Knight's Cross (26.3.43). Kapitänleutnant Volker Simmermacher and crew of 58 were lost on 18.8.44 when U-107 was sunk in the Bay of Biscay 40 miles SW by S of Belle Ile, in position 46.46N 03.39W by Sunderland 'W' EJ150, pilot F/Lt Leslie H. Baveystock DFC DFM, of No. 201 Squadron RAF, based at Pembroke Dock, part of 19 Group. The pilot was awarded the DSO.

## RADCLIFFE, EVAN THOMAS & COMPANY – CARDIFF

**LLANARTH** • GRT 5053 • Built 1929

28.6.40: Torpedoed and sunk by German submarine U-30 (Lemp), in the Atlantic 220 miles W by S of Ushant, in position 47.30N 10.30W while sailing independently on a voyage from Melbourne to Leith and Aberdeen, with a cargo of 7980 tons of flour. The Master, Capt John James Perry, and 15 crew were rescued by HM corvette *GLADIOLUS* 925/40 (K.34) (Lt-Cdr Harry M.C. Sanders RNR) and landed at Plymouth. The Chief Officer and 18 crew were rescued by a Spanish trawler and landed at San Sebastian.

**LLANFAIR** • GRT 4966 • Built 1928

11.8.40: Torpedoed and sunk by German submarine U-38 (Liebe), in the Atlantic W of Ireland, in position 54.48N 13.46W while on a voyage from Mackay, Queensland to Avonmouth via Freetown 25.2.40, with a cargo of 7800 tons of sugar, a straggler from convoy SL 41 comprising 39 ships. The Master, Capt William Evans, and 29 crew were rescued by US ship *CALIFORNIA* 5441/20. 3 crew were lost.

**LLANOVER** • GRT 4959 • Built 1928

12.5.42: Torpedoed and damaged by German submarine U-124 (Mohr), part of the 'Hecht' (Pike) patrol group of six U-boats, sunk by RCN corvette *ARVIDA* 925/40 (K.113) in the

Atlantic SE of Cape Farewell, in position 52.50N 29.04W while on a voyage from the Tyne to Halifax NS via Loch Ewe 6.5.42, with a cargo of coal, part of convoy ONS 92 comprising 41 ships. The Master, Capt Lionel Alfred Osborne, crew of 39 and 6 gunners were rescued by rescue ship *BURY* 1634/11 (Capt Lawrence Edwin Brown OBE) and landed at St John's, Newfoundland 16.5.42.

**LLANDILO** • GRT 4966 • Built 1928
2.11.42: Torpedoed and sunk by German submarine U-172 (Emmermann), in the South Atlantic SE of St Helena, in position 27.03S 03.08W while sailing independently on a voyage from New York to Saldanha Bay and Bombay via Trinidad 9.10.42 and Durban, with a cargo of 9024 tons of US military stores. The Master, Capt William Redvers Baden Burgess, 20 crew and 3 gunners were lost. 17 crew and 3 gunners were rescued by Norwegian ship *OLAF BERGH* 5811/21 and landed at Port of Spain, Trinidad.

**LLANASHE** • GRT 4836 • Built 1936
17.2.43: Torpedoed and sunk by German submarine U-182 (Clausen), part of the 'Seehund' (Seal) patrol group of five U-boats, in the Indian Ocean S of Cape Saint Francis, Cape Colony, in position 34.00S 28.30E while sailing independently on a voyage from Basrah and Bandar Abbas to Port Elizabeth and Cape Town, with a cargo of 3500 tons of tinplate and aluminium. The Master, Capt James Parry, 27 crew and 5 gunners were lost. The Chief Officer S.P. Lloyd, 7 crew and 1 gunner were rescued after 11 days adrift by Dutch ship *TARAKAN* 8183/30, transferred to HM troopship *CARTHAGE* 14253/31 (F.99) (Capt W.H.V. Harris MVO DSC) and HM destroyer *RACEHORSE* 1705/42 (H.11) (Cdr A.F. Burness-Nugent) and landed at Cape Town 4.3.43.

**CLARISSA RADCLIFFE** ex-*WINDSOR* ex-*GWENT* • GRT 5754 • Built 1915
18.3.43 Torpedoed and sunk by German submarine U-663 (Schmid), in the Atlantic W of Boston, in position 42.00N 62.00W while on a voyage from Pepel to Barrow via New York 5.3.43, with a cargo of iron ore, a straggler from convoy SC 122 comprising 51 ships. The Master, Capt Stuart Gordon Finnes, crew of 42 and 12 gunners were lost. Kapitänleutnant Heinrich Schmid and crew of 48 were lost after 8.5.43 in the Atlantic NW of Cape Finisterre in position 46.33N 11.12W possibly by the damage inflicted on U-663 on 7.5.43 240 miles NNW of Cape Ortegal by Sunderland W/10, pilot F/Lt Geoffrey G. Rossiter of No. 10 Squadron RAAF, based at Mount Batten, part of 19 Group.

**MOWT**

**LORIENT** • GRT 4737 • Built 1921
4.5.43: Torpedoed and sunk by German submarine U-732 (Carlsen), part of the 'Specht' (Woodpecker) patrol group of eighteen U-boats, in the Atlantic S of Cape Farewell, in position 54.04N 44.18W while on a voyage from London to New York, in ballast, a straggler from convoy ONS 5 comprising 42 ships. The Master, Capt Walter John Manley, and crew of 39 were lost. U-732 commanded by Oberleutnant zur See Klaus-Peter Carlsen was attacked and damaged on 1.11.43 in the Strait of Gibraltar by HM trawler *IMPERIALIST* 520/39 (FY.126) (Lt A.R. Pelling), later in the day U-732 was sunk by HM destroyer *DOUGLAS* 1530/18 (D.90) (Lt-Cdr K.H.J.L. Phibbs), NW of Tangier, in position 35.45N 05.50W. The

U-boat commander and 8 crew were taken prisoner by HMS *DOUGLAS* and 10 crew by HM destroyer *WITHERINGTON* 1120/19 (D.76) (Lt R.B.S. Tennant). 31 crew were lost. Lt-Cdr B.H.C Rodgers was awarded the DSC.

## RAEBURN & VEREL LIMITED – GLASGOW
**Monarch SS Co. Ltd**

***BRITISH MONARCH*** • GRT 5661 • Built 1923
19.6.40: Torpedoed and sunk by German submarine U-48 (Rösing), in the Atlantic about 200 miles NNW of Corunna, in position 45.00N 11.21W while on a voyage from Bougie to Glasgow, with a cargo of 8200 tons of iron ore, part of convoy HG 34 comprising 15 ships. The Master, Capt John Ferguson Scott, and crew of 39 were lost.

***NORMAN MONARCH*** • GRT 4718 • Built 1937
20.5.41: Torpedoed and sunk by German submarine U-94 (Kuppisch), in the Atlantic about 200 miles SSE of Cape Farewell, in position 56.41N 40.52W while on a voyage from Halifax NS to Barry Roads, with a cargo of 8300 tons of wheat, part of convoy HX 126 comprising 29 ships. The Master, Capt Thomas Alexander Robertson, crew of 41 and 6 gunners were rescued by British ship *HARPAGUS* 5173/40. The Master, 19 crew and 6 gunners were lost when the *HARPAGUS* was sunk later on the same day by U-94. 22 crew were rescued by HM destroyer *BURNHAM* 1190/19 (H.82) (Cdr J. Bostock) ex-USN four-stack *AULICK* and landed at Reykjavik. Korvettenkapitän Herbert Kuppisch was awarded the Knight's Cross (14.5.41).

***SCOTTISH MONARCH*** • GRT 4719 • Built 1938
1.6.41: Torpedoed and sunk by German submarine U-105 (Schewe), in the Atlantic SW of the Cape Verde Islands, in position 12.58N 27.20W while sailing independently on a voyage from the Tyne and Loch Ewe to Freetown, with a cargo of 7000 tons of coal, dispersed from convoy OB 319 comprising 38 ships. The Master, Capt Graham Clegg Winchester, and 23 survivors were rescued on 8.6.41 by Dutch ship *ALPHARD* 5483/37 and landed at Freetown 13.6.41; the Chief Officer M. Macleod and 19 survivors were rescued on 11.6.41 by British ship *CHRISTINE MARIE* 3895/19 and landed at Freetown 19.6.41. 1 crew was lost. Kapitänleutnant Georg Schewe was awarded the Knight's Cross (23.5.41).

***CALEDONIAN MONARCH*** • GRT 5851 • Built 1928
18.1.42: Torpedoed and sunk by German submarine U-333 (Cremer), in the Atlantic SW of Iceland, in position 57.00N 26.00W while on a voyage from Halifax NS to London, with a cargo of wheat, a straggler from convoy SC 63 comprising 27 ships. The Master, Capt James Valentine Stewart, and crew of 40 were lost.

## MOWT

***EMPIRE HOWARD*** • GRT 6985 • Built 1941
16.4.42: Torpedoed and sunk by German submarine U-403 (Clausen), in the Barents Sea NW of North Cape in position 73.48N 21.32E while on government service on a voyage from the Tyne to Murmansk via Reykjavik 8.4.42, with 2 passengers, the convoy commodore, 5 naval staff and 2000 tons of war materials including army trucks, part of

convoy PQ 14 comprising 24 ships. The Master, Capt Howard John McDonald Downie, and 8 crew were rescued by HM trawler *LORD MIDDLETON* 464/36 (FY.219) (Lt R.H. Jameson) and 21 crew, 3 gunners, 2 naval staff and passengers by HM trawler *NORTHERN WAVE* 655/36 (FY.153) (Lt W.G. Pardoe-Matthews) and landed at Polarnoe, near Murmansk. The convoy Commodore E. Rees DSC RNR, 18 crew, 3 naval staff and 3 gunners were lost. The *EMPIRE HOWARD* sank in 57 seconds. Kaptiänleutnant Karl–Franz Heine and crew of 49 were lost on 17.8.43 when U-403 was sunk in the Atlantic 60 miles S by W of Dakar, in position 14.11N 17.40W while shadowing convoy SL 168 comprising 24 ships by Hudson 'O' V9220, pilot F/O P.R. Hobart of No. 200 Squadron RAF, based at Yundum, Gambia and Wellington 'HZ' HF697 of No. 697 Free French Squadron based at Dakar.

## RANKIN, GILMORE & CO. LTD – LIVERPOOL
### Saint Line Ltd

**SAINT DUNSTAN** ex-*WAR KEEP* • GRT 5681 • Built 1919
24.8.40: Torpedoed and damaged by German submarine U-57 (Topp), in the Atlantic 21 miles NNW of Malin Head, in position 55.44N 07.32W while on a voyage from Glasgow to Baltimore, Mass, in ballast, part of convoy OB 202 comprising 32 ships. The Master, Capt Thomas Gordon Cookes, and 48 crew were rescued by rescue ship *COPELAND* 1526/23 (Capt J. McKellar OBE), transferred to HM destroyer *WITCH* 1140/19 (D.89) (Lt-Cdr J.R. Barnes), later transferred to HM destroyer *WANDERER* 1120/19 (D.74) (Cdr J.H. Ruck–Keene) and landed at Belfast 25.8.40. 14 crew were lost. The *SAINT DUNSTAN* was taken in tow on 26.8.40 but sank on 27.8.40 between Pladda Point and Holy Island, Irish Sea.

**SAINT AGNES** ex-*CAPE ST AGNES* ex-*TITAN* ex-*WAR BRETON* • GRT 5199 • Built 1918
14.9.40: Torpedoed and sunk by gunfire by Italian submarine *EMO* (Liannazza), in the Atlantic 575 miles WSW of Cape Finisterre, in position 41.27N 21.50W while on a voyage from Vizagapatam to Hull via Freetown 1.9.40, with a cargo of 5500 tons of linseed in bags, 1300 tons of castor seeds and 400 tons of manganese ore, a straggler from convoy SLS 46 comprising 32 ships. The Master, Capt Edwin Harry Powell, and crew of 63 were rescued by US ship *EXOCORDA* 9359/31.

**SAINT GERMAN** ex-*EPOCA* ex-*EDOUARD GIRAND* • GRT 1044 • Built 1924
17.11.40: Torpedoed and sunk by German submarine U-137 (Wohlfarth), in the Atlantic NNW of Tory Island, in position 55.40N 08.40W while on a voyage from Leixoes, Portugal to Port Talbot, with a cargo of 1440 tons of pit props, part of convoy HG 46 comprising 51 ships. The Master, Capt Ernest Welch Bearpark, and crew of 17 were rescued by HM corvette *MALLOW* 925/40 (K.84) (Lt-Cdr W.B. Piggott) and landed at Londonderry. U-137, commanded by Oberleutnant zur See Hans-Joachim Dierks, was scuttled at Wilhelmshaven on 1.5.45.

**SAINT ANSELM** ex-*SAINT ANDREW* launched as *WAR TURRET* • GRT 5614 • Built 1919
30.6.41: Torpedoed and sunk by gunfire by German submarine U-66 (Zapp), in the Atlantic SW of Madeira, in position 31.00N 26.00W while sailing independently on a voyage from Calcutta to Hull via Freetown, with a cargo of 2150 tons of pig iron, 650 tons of linseed and 5154 tons of groundnuts, dispersed from convoy SL 78 comprising 25 ships. The Master,

Capt Thomas Ross, and 17 survivors were rescued by HM armed merchant cruiser *MORETON BAY* 14193/21 (F.11) (Capt C.C. Bell) and landed at Freetown 13.7.41; and 15 survivors rescued by Spanish ship *TOM* 3056/19 were landed at Buenos Aires. 34 men were lost.

## REES, T. BOWEN & CO. LTD – LONDON
### Egypt & Levant Steam Ship Co. Ltd

*ANTIGONE* • GRT 4545 • Built 1928
11.5.43: Torpedoed and sunk by German submarine U-402 (v. Forstner), part of the 'Elbe 2' (named after a German river) patrol group of thirteen U-boats, in the Atlantic 300 miles NW of the Azores, in position 40.30N 32.30W while on a voyage from St John, New Brunswick to Avonmouth via Halifax NS, with a cargo of 7800 tons of grain, 255 tons of general cargo and 250 trucks, part of convoy SC 129 comprising 26 ships. The Master, Capt Frederick Williams, 35 crew and 7 gunners were rescued by rescue ship *MELROSE ABBEY* 1908/29 (Capt Ralph Good OBE) and landed at Gourock 20.5.43. 3 crew were lost. Korvettenkapitän Freiherr Siegfrid von Forstner (Knight's Cross 9.2.43) and crew of 49 were lost on 13.10.43 when U-402 was sunk in the Atlantic 560 miles N by E of Flores, Azores, in position 48.56N 29.41W by an Avenger, pilot Lt-Cdr Howard M. Avery and a Wildcat, pilot Ensign B.C. Sheelah, of US Navy Composite Squadron VC-9 from US escort aircraft carrier *CARD* 9800/42 (CVE-11) of USN Task Group TG.21.14 commanded by Capt Arnold J. Isbell.

## RIDGE STEAMSHIP CO. LTD – CARDIFF

*MENIN RIDGE* ex-*PENTIRION* • GRT 2474 • Built 1924
24.10.39: Torpedoed and sunk by German submarine U-37 (Hartman), in the Atlantic 90 miles W of Gibraltar, in position 36.01N 07.22W while on a voyage from Djidjelli, Algeria to Port Talbot, with a cargo of 4200 tons of iron ore. The Master, Capt David Emlyn Powell, and 19 crew were lost. 5 crew were rescued by US ship *CROWN CITY* 5433/20 and landed at Gibraltar.

## ROBERTS, HUGH & SON – NEWCASTLE UPON TYNE
### North Shipping Co. Ltd

*NORTH BRITAIN* • GRT 4635 • Built 1940
5.5.43: Torpedoed and sunk by German submarine U-707 (Gretschel), part of the 'Specht' (Woodpecker) patrol group of eighteen U-boats, in the Atlantic S of Cape Farewell, in position 55.08N 42.43W while on a voyage from Glasgow to Halifax NS for orders, with a part cargo of 993 tons of firebricks and fire clay in bags, a straggler from convoy ONS 5 comprising 42 ships. The Master, Capt John Lamsdale Bright, 27 crew and 7 gunners were lost. 10 crew and 1 gunner were rescued by HM trawler *NORTHERN SPRAY* 655/36 (FY.129) (Lt F.A.J. Downer) and landed at St John's, Newfoundland. Oberleutnant zur See Gunther Gretschel and crew of 50 were lost while shadowing convoy MKS 29A comprising 60 ships on 9.11.43 when U-707 was sunk in the Atlantic 280 miles NE by E of San Miguel, Azores, in position 40.31N 20.17W by Flying Fortress 'J' FL459, pilot F/Lt Roderick Patrick Drummond of No. 220 Squadron RAF, based at Lagens, Azores, part of 247 Group. The pilot was awarded the DFC.

## ROBERTSON, WILLIAM – GLASGOW

*CORAL* • GRT 638 • Built 1919
20.8.44: Torpedoed and sunk by German submarine U-764 (v. Bremen) in the English
Channel SE of St Catherine's Point, Isle of Wight, in position 50.13N 00.48W while on
government service on a voyage from Arromanches, Normandy to Southampton, in ballast,
part of coastal convoy ETC 73 comprising 30 ships. The Master, Capt Donald McKinnon, 8
crew and 2 gunners were rescued by British ship *ROEBUCK* 776/25 and HM motor launch
and landed at Southampton. 4 crew, 1 gunner and 1 army storekeeper were lost. U-764,
commanded by Oberleutnant zur See Hanskurt von Bremen, surrendered at Loch Eriboll,
Sutherlandshire on 14.5.45, sailed from Lishally, Lough Foyle on 2.1.46. Towed by ORP
destroyer *KRAKOWIAK* 1050/40 ex-HMS *SILVERTON* (L.115), at 10.30 hours the sea
became too rough and she was sunk by gunfire by ORP destroyer *PIORUN* 1690/40 ex-HMS
*NERISSA* (G.65) in the Atlantic NNW of Tory Island, in position 56.06N 09.00W. She was
one of 116 U-boats disposed of by the Royal Navy in 'Operation Deadlight'.

## ROBINSON, JOSEPH & SONS – NORTH SHIELDS
**Stag Line**

*CLINTONIA* • GRT 3106 • Built 1917
19.10.40: Torpedoed and damaged by German submarine U-99 (Kretschmer) and sunk by
gunfire by German submarine U-123 (Moehle), in the Atlantic 200 miles W of St Kilda, in
position 57.10N 11.20W while on a voyage from St Francis, Nova Scotia to Manchester via
Sydney CB 5.10.40, with a cargo of 3850 tons of pulpwood, part of convoy SC 7 comprising
35 ships. The Master, Capt Thomas Hector Irvin, 33 crew and 1 gunner were rescued by
HM corvette *BLUEBELL* 925/40 (K.80) (Lt-Cdr Robert E. Sherwood) and landed at
Greenock. 1 crew was lost.

*EUPHORBIA* • GRT 3380 • Built 1924
14.12.40: Torpedoed and sunk by German submarine U-100 (Schepke), in the Atlantic
WSW of Rockall while on a voyage from Swansea and Milford Haven to Lynn, Mass, with a
cargo of 3837 tons of coal, dispersed on 12.12.40 in position 59.04N 15.30W from convoy
OB 256 comprising 30 ships. The Master, Capt Thomas Hilton, crew of 32 and 1 gunner
were lost.

*LINARIA* • GRT 3385 • Built 1924
24.2.41: Torpedoed and sunk by German submarine U-96 (Lehmann-Willembrock), in the
North Atlantic SW of Reykjavik, in position 61.00N 25.00W while sailing independently on a
voyage from the Tyne to Halifax NS, with a part cargo of coal, dispersed from convoy OB 288
comprising 46 ships. The Master, Capt Henry T. Speed, crew of 30 and 3 gunners were lost.

## MOWT

*EMPIRE HEATH* • GRT 6643 • Built 1941
11.5.44: Torpedoed and sunk by German submarine U-129 (v. Harpe), in the South Atlantic
ENE of Rio de Janeiro, in position 19.00S 31.00W while sailing independently on a voyage

from Victoria, Brazil to Loch Ewe for orders via Freetown, with a cargo of iron ore. The Master, Capt William Thompson Brown DSC, 46 crew and 9 gunners were lost. U-129, commanded by Oberleutnant zur See Richard von Harpe, was scuttled at Lorient on 19.8.44.

## ROPNER. SIR R. & CO. LTD – WEST HARTLEPOOL
## Pool Shipping Co. Ltd

### HERONSPOOL • GRT 5202 • Built 1929
12.10.39: Torpedoed and sunk by gunfire by German submarine U-48 (Schultze), in the Atlantic 260 miles SW of Cape Clear, in position 50.13N 14.48W while on a voyage from Swansea to Montreal, with a cargo of 8000 tons of coal, a straggler from convoy OB 17 comprising 11 ships. The Master, Capt Sydney Edward Batson OBE, and crew were rescued by US liner PRESIDENT HARDING 13869/22 and landed at New York.

### WILLOWPOOL • GRT 4815 • Built 1925
10.12.39: Struck a mine, laid on 9.12.39, by German submarine U-20 (Moehle), and sank in the North Sea 3 miles E of Newarp Lightship while sailing independently on a voyage from Bona to Middlesbrough, with a cargo of 7850 tons of iron ore, dispersed from convoy HG 9 comprising 53 ships. The Master, Capt Norman Joseph Oliver, and crew of 35 were rescued by the Gorleston Lifeboat. U-20, commanded by Oberleutnant zur See Karl Grafen, was scuttled on 10.9.44 in the Black Sea near Karasu, Turkey, in position 41.10N 30.47E. The U-boat commander and crew were interned by the Turkish authorities at Beyschir.

### OTTERPOOL • GRT 4867 • Built 1926
20.6.40: Torpedoed and sunk by German submarine U-30 (Lemp), in the Atlantic 130 miles W of Ushant, in position 48.45N 08.13W while on a voyage from Bona to Middlesbrough, with a cargo of 8180 tons of iron ore, part of convoy HGF 34 comprising 22 ships. The Master, Capt Thomas Prince, 21 crew and 1 gunner were lost. 16 crew were rescued by HM sloop SCARBOROUGH 1045/30 (L.25) (Cdr N.V. Dickinson) and landed at Liverpool.

### SEDGEPOOL • GRT 6530 • Built 1918
19.10.40: Torpedoed and sunk by German submarine U-123 (Moehle), in the Atlantic about 80 miles W by S from St Kilda, in position 57.20N 11.22W while on a voyage from Montreal to Manchester via Sydney CB 5.10.40, with a cargo of 8720 tons of wheat, part of convoy SC 7 comprising 35 ships. The Master, Capt Robert Bell Witten, and 2 crew were lost. 35 crew and 1 gunner were rescued by HM tug SALVONIA 571/39 (Lt G.M.M. Dickinson) and landed at Gourock.

### RUSHPOOL • GRT 5125 • Built 1928
30.1.41: Torpedoed and sunk by German submarine U-94 (Kuppisch), in the Atlantic SE of Rockall, in position 56.00N 15.42W while on a voyage from St John, New Brunswick to Belfast via Halifax NS, with a cargo of 7714 tons of grain, a straggler from convoy SC 19 comprising 27 ships. The Master, Capt William George Stewart Hewison, and crew of 39 were rescued by HM destroyer ANTELOPE 1350/29 (H.40) (Lt-Cdr R.T. White DSO) and landed at Greenock.

**MANSEPOOL** • GRT 4894 • Built 1928
24.2.41: Torpedoed and sunk by German submarine U-97 (Heilmann), in the North Atlantic SW of the Faröe Islands, in position 61.01N 12.00W while on a voyage from Cardiff to Halifax NS, in ballast, part of convoy OB 289 comprising 25 ships. The Master, Capt Harry Raymond Clark, and 19 crew were rescued by British ship *THOMAS HOLT* 3585/29, later transferred to HM corvette *PETUNIA* 925/40 (K.79) (Lt-Cdr G.V. Legassisk), and 17 crew rescued by HMS *PETUNIA* were landed at Stornoway. 2 crew were lost.

**HINDPOOL** • GRT 4897 • Built 1928
8.3.41: Torpedoed and sunk by German submarine U-124 (Schulz), in the Atlantic N of the Cape Verde Islands, in position 20.51N 20.32W while on a voyage from Pepel to Middlesbrough via Freetown, with a cargo of 7700 tons of iron ore, part of convoy SL 67 comprising 56 ships. The Master, Capt Malcolm Vernon A. Tinnock, and 27 crew were lost. 6 crew were rescued by HM destroyer leader *FAULKNOR* 1457/34 (H.62) (Capt A.F. de Salis) and landed at Gibraltar 16.3.41, and 4 crew and 2 gunners by British ship *GUIDO* 3921/20.

**ALDERPOOL** ex-*NORTHWICK* • GRT 4313 • Built 1936
3.4.41: Torpedoed and sunk by German submarine U-46 (Endrass), in the Atlantic SW of Reykajvik, in position 58.21N 27.59W while on a voyage from New York to Hull via Sydney CB, with a cargo of 7200 tons of wheat, part of convoy SC 26 comprising 24 ships. The Master, Capt Tom Valentine Frank OBE, crew of 36 and 2 gunners were rescued by Ropner's ship *THIRLBY* 4887/28 and landed at Loch Ewe.

**SWIFTPOOL** • GRT 5205 • Built 1929
5.8.41: Torpedoed and sunk by German submarine U-372 (Neumann), in the Atlantic W of Ireland, in position 53.03N 16.00W while on a voyage from Pepel to Middlesbrough via Freetown 15.7.41, with a cargo of 8000 tons of iron ore, part of convoy SL 81 comprising 18 ships. The Master, Capt Harry Raymond Clark, 36 crew and 5 gunners were lost. 2 crew were rescued by HM corvette *BLUEBELL* 925/40 (K.80) (Lt-Cdr Robert E. Sherwood) and landed at Greenock. Kapitänleutnant Heinz-Joachim Neumann was lost on 4.8.42 when U-372 was sunk in the Mediterranean 90 miles SW of Haifa, Palestine, in position 32.00N 34.00E by HM destroyers *SIKH* 1870/37 (F.82) (Capt J.A. Mickethwaite), *ZULU* 1870/37 (F.18) (Cdr R.D. White), *CROOME* 1950/41 (L.62) (Lt H.D.M. Slater) and *TETCOTT* 1050/41 (L.99) (Lt-Cdr H.R. Rycroft) and Wellington 'M', pilot F/Sgt Gray of No. 221 Squadron RAF, based at Luqa, Malta. The U-boat commander, 45 crew and an agent to be landed near Beirut, Lebanon, were taken prisoner by HM ships.

**STONEPOOL** • GRT 4803 • Built 1928
11.9.41: Torpedoed and sunk by German submarine U-207 (Meyer), in the North Atlantic E of Cape Farewell, in position 63.05N 37.50W while on a voyage from Montreal to Avonmouth via Sydney CB 30.8.41, with a cargo of 528 tons of oats, 7000 tons of grain and 115 tons of trucks, part of convoy SC 42 comprising 65 ships. The Master, Capt Albert White, 33 crew and 8 gunners were lost. 6 crew and 1 gunner were rescued by RCN corvette *KENOGAMI* 925/40 (K.125) (Lt P.J.B. Cook) and landed at Loch Ewe. Oberleutnant zur See Fritz Meyer and crew of 40 were lost on the same day when U-207 was sunk in the North Atlantic 310 miles W of Reykjanes, in position 63.59N 34.48W by HM destroyers

*LEAMINGTON* 1090/40 (G.19) (Lt-Cdr H.G. Bowerman) and *VETERAN* 1325/19 (D.72) (Cdr W.E.J. Eames). The *STONEPOOL*, dispersed from convoy OB 17 comprising 11 ships, was attacked by gunfire by U-42 (Dau) on 13.10.39 in the Atlantic S of Bantry Bay, the merchant ship returned fire and the submarine dived; U-42 later resurfaced and was then sunk 400 miles W of Land's End, in position 49.12N 16.00W by HM destroyers *ILEX* 1370/37 (D.61) (Lt-Cdr P.L. Saumarez) and *IMOGEN* 1370/36 (D.44) (Cdr E.B.K. Stevens). Kapitänleutnant Rolf Dau and 19 crew were taken prisoner by HMS *IMOGEN*. 26 crew were lost.

**REEDPOOL** • GRT 4838 • Built 1924
20.9.42: Torpedoed and sunk by German submarine U-515 (Henke), in the Atlantic 240 miles SE of Trinidad, in position 08.58N 57.34W while sailing independently on a voyage from Massowah, Eithopia to Fernandina, Florida via Cape Town 21.8.42 and Trinidad, in ballast. The Master, Capt William James Downs, was taken prisoner, landed at Lorient 14.10.42 and taken to Milag Nord. 32 crew, 4 gunners and 16 survivors from the *MEDON* 5915/23 were rescued on 21.9.42 by British schooner *MILLIE M. MASHER* and landed at Georgetown, British Guinea. 5 crew were lost.

## Ropner Shipping Co. Ltd

**FIRBY** • GRT 4868 • Built 1926
11.9.39: Torpedoed and sunk by gunfire by German submarine U-48 (Schultze), in the Atlantic 270 miles W of Hebrides, in position 59.40N 13.50W while sailing independently on a voyage from the Tyne to Port Churchill, Hudson Bay, in ballast. The Master, Capt Thomas Prince, and 33 crew were rescued by HM destroyer *FEARLESS* 1375/34 (H.67) (Cdr K.L. Harkness) and landed at Scapa Flow 12.9.39. The commander of U-48, Kapitänleutnant Herbert Schultze, after the sinking of the *FIRBY* sent the following radio message: 'Transmit to Mr. Churchill. I have sunk British steamer *FIRBY* position 59 degrees 40 minutes North 13 degrees 50 minutes West. Save the crew if you will please. German submarine.' The message was relayed by US ship *SCANPENN* 5152/19 and received by the Admiralty at Rosyth at 16.25 hours GMT 11.9.39.

**SWAINBY** • GRT 5811 • Built 1917
17.4.40: Torpedoed and sunk by German submarine U-13 (Schulte), in the North Sea 25 miles N of Muckle Flugga, Shetland Isles, in position 61.00N 05.00W while sailing independently on a voyage from Kirkwall to Malvoysund, Vaargo Island, Norway, in ballast. The Master, Capt Hugh Thompson, and crew of 37 landed at Nor Wick Bay, Shetland Isles. U-13, commanded by Kapitänleutnant Max Schulte, was sunk on 31.5.40 in the North Sea 9 miles SE of Lowestoft, in position 52.27N 02.02E by HM sloop *WESTON* 1060/32 (L.72) ex-HMS *WESTON SUPER MARE* (Lt-Cdr S.C. Tuke). The U-boat commander and crew of 25 were taken prisoner by HMS *WESTON*.

**WANDBY** • GRT 4947 • Built 1940
19.10.40: Torpedoed and damaged by German submarine U-47 (Endrass), in the Atlantic 135 miles WSW of Rockall, in position 56.45N 17.07W while on her maiden voyage from Victoria BC to Middlesbrough via Panama and Halifax NS 8.10.40, with a cargo of 1700

tons of lead and zinc and 7200 tons of lumber, part of convoy HX 79 comprising 49 ships. Abandoned by her crew she sank on 21.10.40. The Master, Capt John Kenny, and 33 crew were rescued by HM trawler *ANGLE* 531/36 (FY.201) (Lt A.N. Blundell) and landed at Belfast 26.10.40.

**SOMERSBY** • GRT 5168 • Built 1930
13.5.41: Torpedoed and sunk by German submarine U–111 (Kleinschmidt), in the North Atlantic SW of Reykjavik, in position 60.39N 26.13W while on a voyage from Halifax NS to Hull via Loch Ewe, with a cargo of 8300 tons of grain, a straggler from convoy SC 30 comprising 28 ships. The Master, Capt John William Thompson, crew of 38 and 4 gunners were rescued by Greek ship *MARIKA PROTOPAPA* 4417/15 and landed at Loch Ewe.

**AINDERBY** • GRT 4860 • Built 1925
10.6.41: Torpedoed and sunk by German submarine U–552 (Topp), in the Atlantic 130 miles W by N of Bloody Foreland, in position 55.30N 12.10W while sailing independently on a voyage from Santos to the Tyne, with a cargo of 7700 tons of iron ore. The Master, Capt George Robert Cobb, 27 crew and 1 gunner were rescued by HM destroyer *VETERAN* 1120/19 (D.72) (Cdr W.E.J. Eames) and landed at Greenock. 11 crew and 1 gunner were lost.

**ASHBY** • GRT 4871 • Built 1927
30.11.41: Torpedoed and sunk by German submarine U–43 (Lüth), in the Atlantic 170 miles SSE of Flores, Azores, in position 36.54N 29.51W while on a voyage from Middlesbrough to Pepel via Freetown, in ballast, a straggler from convoy OS 12 comprising 55 ships. The Master, Capt Tom Valentine Frank OBE, 11 crew and 5 gunners were lost. 28 crew and 5 gunners landed at Fayal, embarked on Portuguese destroyer *LIMA* 1238/33 (D.333), transferred and were brought to Lisbon by Portuguese ship *CARVALHO ARAUJO* 4560/30.

**THIRLBY** • GRT 4888 • Built 1928
23.1.42: Torpedoed and sunk by German submarine U–109 (Bleichrodt), part of 'Operation Paukenschlag' (Drumbeat), the first wave of five U-boats, in the Atlantic 12 miles 240° from Seal Island, Cape Sable, in position 43.20N 66.15W while sailing independently on a voyage from New York to Loch Ewe for orders, with a cargo of 7600 tons of maize, dispersed from convoy SC 66 comprising 29 ships. The Master, Capt Peter Edward Birch, 30 crew, 9 gunners and the US pilot were rescued by the US ship *BELLE ISLE* 1960/33 and landed at Halifax NS. 5 crew were lost.

**CARPERBY** • GRT 4890 • Built 1928
1.3.42: Torpedoed and sunk by German submarine U–588 (Vogel), in the Atlantic about 420 miles S of Newfoundland, in position 39.57N 55.40W while sailing independently on a voyage from the Tyne to St Vincent and Buenos Aires, with a cargo of 2009 tons of coal and 3262 tons of coke, dispersed from convoy ON 66 comprising 19 ships. The Master, Capt Frederick Gardiner, and crew of 39 were lost.

**DALEBY** ex-*KITTY TAYLOR* • GRT 4640 • Built 1929
4.11.42: Torpedoed and sunk by German submarine U–89 (Lohmann), part of the 'Veilchen' (Violet) patrol group of thirteen U-boats, in the Atlantic SE of Cape Farewell, in position

57.24N 35.54W while on a voyage from Halifax NS 27.10.42 to London, with a cargo of 8500 tons of grain, tanks and motor parts, part of convoy SC 107 comprising 42 ships. The Master, Capt John Edward Elsdon, crew of 39 and 7 gunners were rescued by the Icelandic ship *BRÚARFOSS* 1529/27 and landed at Reykjavik. Korvettekapitän Dietrich Lohmann and crew of 47 were lost while shadowing convoy HX 237 comprising 46 ships on 12.5.43 when U-89, part of the 'Drossel' (Thrush) patrol group of eleven U-boats was sunk in the Atlantic 480 miles N by E of Terceira, Azores, in position 46.30N 25.40W by HM destroyer *BROADWAY* 1190/43 (H.90) (Lt-Cdr E.H. Chevasse), HM frigate *LAGAN* 1370/42 (K.259) (Lt-Cdr A. Ayre) of the Escort Group C2 and and Swordfish aircraft 'B' from No. 811 Naval Air Squadron from HM escort carrier *BITER* 8200/40 (D.97) (Capt E.M.C. Abel-Smith) of the 5th Escort Group.

**ROXBY** • GRT 4252 • Built 1923
7.11.42: Torpedoed and sunk by German submarine U-613 (Köppe), part of the 'Natter' (Viper) patrol group of twelve U-boats, in the Atlantic SW of Cape Clear, in position 49.35N 30.32W while on a voyage from Cardiff and Gourock 30.10.42 to Halifax NS, with a cargo of 6400 tons of coal, part of convoy ONS 142 comprising 62 ships. The Master, Capt George Robinson, 28 crew and 5 gunners were lost. 11 crew and 2 gunners were rescued by Irish ship *IRISH BEECH* 2002/84 and landed at St John's, Newfoundland. Kapitänleutnant Helmut Köppe and crew of 48 were lost on 23.7.43 while shadowing convoy UGS 12 comprising 80 ships when U-613 was sunk in the Atlantic 185 miles S of Fayal, Azores, in position 35.32N 28.36W by US four-stack destroyer *GEORGE E. BADGER* 1190/20 (DD-196) (Lt-Cdr Thomas H. Byrd) of the USN Task Group 21.12.

**LACKENBY** • GRT 5112 • Built 1928
25.1.43: Torpedoed and sunk by German submarine U-624 (v. Soden), part of the 'Haudegen' (Broadsword) patrol group of twenty-one U-boats, in the Atlantic S of Cape Farewell, in position 55.00N 37.50W while on a voyage from Tampa to London via New York and Loch Ewe, with a cargo of 8000 tons of phosphate, a straggler from convoy SC 117 comprising 21 ships. The Master, Capt William Arthur Allon MBE, crew of 38 and 5 gunners were lost. Kapitänleutnant Ulrich Graf von Soden-Fraunhofen and crew of 44 were lost while shadowing convoy SC 118 comprising 64 ships when U-624 was sunk on 7.2.43 in the Atlantic 420 miles W by S of Rockall, in position 55.42N 26.17W by Flying Fortress II 'J' FL459, pilot P/O G. Robertson of No. 220 Squadron RAF, based at Aldergrove, Co. Antrim, part of 15 Group.

**MOWT**

**EMPIRE MERLIN** ex-*WEST ISLETA* • GRT 5763 • Built 1919
25.8.40: Torpedoed and sunk by German submarine U-48 (Rösing), in the Atlantic 90 miles E by N of Flannan Isles, in position 58.30N 10.15W while on a voyage from Port Sulphur, Louisiana to Hull, with a cargo of 6830 tons of sulphur, part of convoy HX 65 comprising 51 ships. The Master, Capt David W. Simpson OBE, 33 crew and 1 gunner were lost. The sole survivor Ordinary Seaman John Lee was rescued by HM corvette *GODETIA* 925/40 (K.72) (Lt-Cdr G.V. Lagassisk) and landed at Methil. The *EMPIRE MERLIN* sank in 35 seconds.

**EMPIRE BISON** ex-*WEST CAWTHON* • GRT 5612 • Built 1919
1.11.40: Torpedoed and sunk by German submarine U-124 (Schulz), in the Atlantic about 400 miles W of Rockall, in position 59.30N 17.40W while on a voyage from Baltimore to the Clyde for orders via Halifax NS, with 1 passenger and a cargo of 6067 tons of scrap steel and 94 trucks, a straggler from convoy HX 82 comprising 39 ships. The Master, Capt William Herbert Harland OBE, 29 crew and 1 gunner were lost. 3 crew and passenger were rescued by Danish ship *OLGA* S 2252/38 and landed at Gourock.

**EMPIRE DRYDEN** • GRT 7164 • Built 1942
20.4.42: Torpedoed and sunk by German submarine U-572 (Hirsacker), part of 'Operation Paukenschlag' (Drumbeat), the fourth wave of eleven U-boats, in the Atlantic E of Cape Hatteras, in position 34.21N 69.00W while sailing independently on a voyage from New York 17.4.42 to Alexandria via Table Bay, with 7000 tons of government and general cargo. The Master, Capt Robert Powley, 22 crew and 3 gunners were lost. 22 crew and 3 gunners were rescued by liner *MONARCH OF BERMUDA* 22424/31 and landed at Bermuda. U-572, commanded by Oberleutnant zur See Heinz Kummetat, and crew of 46 were lost on 3.8.43 when U-572 was sunk in the Atlantic 405 miles E of Trinidad, in position 11.33N 54.05W by a Mariner P-6, pilot Lt Clifford C. Cox of US Navy Patrol Squadron VP-205 based at Chaguaramas Naval Base, Trinidad. The pilot and 11 aircrew were lost during the attack on U-572.

**EMPIRE RAINBOW** • GRT 6942 • Built 1941
26.7.42: Torpedoed and sunk by German submarines U-607 (Mengersen) and U-704 (Kessler), part of the 'Wolf' patrol group of ten U-boats, in the Atlantic 300 miles E of Cape Race, in position 47.08N 42.57W while on a voyage from Avonmouth and Belfast Lough 18.7.42 to Halifax NS, in ballast, part of convoy ON 113 comprising 35 ships. The Master, Capt John Kenny, crew of 38 and 8 gunners were rescued by HM destroyer *BURNHAM* 1190/19 (H.82) (Cdr T. Taylor) ex-USN four-stack *AULICK* and RCN corvette *DAUPHIN* 925/40 (K.157) (Lt R.A.S. MacNeil) and landed at St John's, Newfoundland. Kapitänleutnant Ernst Mengersen was awarded the Knight's Cross (18.11.41). U-607 commanded by Oberleutnant zur See Wolf Jeschonneck (half-brother of the late General Hans Jeschonnek of the Luftwaffe) was sunk on 13.7.43 in the Atlantic 100 miles NE of Cape Ortegal, in position 45.02N 09.14W by Sunderland 'N' JM708, pilot F/O Reader D. Hanbury of No. 228 Squadron RAF, based at Pembroke Dock, part of 19 Group. The U-boat commander and 6 crew were taken prisoner by HM sloop *WREN* 1300/42 (U.28) (Lt-Cdr R.M. Aubrey) of the 2nd Escort Group. 45 crew were lost.

**EMPIRE ARNOLD** • GRT 7045 • Built 1942
4.8.42: Torpedoed and sunk by German submarine U-155 (Piening), in the Atlantic 500 miles NE of Trinidad, in position 10.45N 52.30W while sailing independently on a voyage from New York to Alexandria via Trinidad 1.8.42 and Cape Town, with 2 passengers and a cargo of 10,000 tons of government stores including tanks and aircraft, dispersed from convoy E 6 comprising 11 ships. The Master, Capt Frederick Tate, was taken prisoner, landed at Lorient 15.9.42 and taken to Milag Nord. 42 crew, 7 gunners and passengers were rescued after 8 days by Norwegian ship *DALVANGER* 2412/31 and landed at Georgetown, British Guinea 14.8.42. 8 crew and 1 gunner were lost.

**EMPIRE MOONBEAM** • GRT 6849 • Built 1941
11.9.42: Torpedoed and damaged by German submarines U-211 (Hause) later sunk by U-608 (Struckmeimer), part of the 'Vorwarts' (Forward) patrol group of ten U-boats, in the Atlantic SW of Cape Clear, in position 48.55N 33.38W while on a voyage from Glasgow 4.9.42 to New York and Norfolk, Virginia, with 1 passenger and in ballast, part of convoy ON 127 comprising 32 ships. The Master, Capt William George Stewart Hewison, 44 crew, 6 gunners and passenger were rescued by RCN corvette *ARVIDA* 925/40 (K.113) (Lt A.I. MacKay) and landed at St John's, Newfoundland 15.9.42. 3 crew were lost. Kapitänleutnant Karl Hause and crew of 53 were lost while shadowing convoy SL 139/MKS 30 comprising 66 ships on 19.11.43 when U-211 was sunk in the Atlantic 310 miles ENE of San Miguel, Azores, in position 40.15N 19.18W by a Leigh Light-equipped Wellington XIV 'F', pilot F/O Donald M. McRae DFC (Canadian) of No. 179 Squadron RAF, based at Azores. U-608 commanded by Oberleutnant zur See Wolfgang Reisener was sunk on 10.8.44 in the Atlantic 60 miles SW of St Nazaire, in position 46.30N 03.28W by Liberator 'C' EV877, pilot W/Cdr R.T.F. Gates AFC of No. 53 Squadron RAF, based at St Eval, part of 19 Group. The U-boat commander and crew of 50 were taken prisoner by HM sloop *WREN* 1300/42 (U.28) (Lt-Cdr S.R.J. Woods). The pilot was awarded the DFC.

**SAMSUVA** (Liberty) • GRT 7219 • Built 1944
29.9.44: Torpedoed and sunk by German submarine U-310 (Ley), part of the 'Zorn' (Anger) patrol group of twelve U-boats, in the Barents Sea N of North Cape, in position 72.58N 23.59E while on a voyage from Archangel to the UK via Loch Ewe for orders, with a cargo of 1139 fathoms (3000 tons) of pitwood, part of convoy RA 60 comprising 30 ships. The Master, Capt Clifford H. Churchill, 36 crew and 20 gunners were rescued by rescue ship *RATHLIN* 1600/36 (Capt August Banning DSO) and landed at Clyde 5.9.44. 3 crew were lost. U-310, commanded by Oberleutnant zur See Wolfgang Ley, surrendered at Trondheim on 10.5.45 and was scrapped in the UK 3.47.

## ROYAL MAIL LINE – LONDON

**LOCHAVON** • GRT 9205 • Built 1938
14.10.39: Torpedoed and sunk by German submarine U-45 (Gelhaar), in the Atlantic about 230 miles SW of Fastnet, in position 50.25N 13.10W while on a voyage from Vancouver BC to Liverpool, Glasgow and Southampton via Panama, with passengers and general cargo including 31000 cases of dried fruit, part of the unescorted convoy KJF 3 comprising 4 ships. The Master, Capt Charles Edward Ratkins RNR, crew and passengers were rescued by HM destroyers *IMOGEN* 1370/36 (D.44) (Cdr E.B.K. Stevens) and *ILEX* 1370/37 (D.61) (Lt-Cdr P.L. Saumarez) and landed at Plymouth. Kapitänleutnant Alexander Gelhaar and crew of 37 were lost on the same day when U-45 was sunk in the Atlantic 83 miles WSW of Berehaven, Co. Cork, in position 50.58N 12.57W by HM destroyer *INGLEFIELD* 1530/36 (D.02) (Capt P. Todd), HMS *IVANHOE* 1370/37 (D.16) (Cdr B. Jones), HMS *INTREPID* 1370/36 (D.10) (Cdr J.W. Josselyn) and HMS *ICARUS* 1370/36 (D.03) (Lt-Cdr C.D. Maud).

**NAVASOTA** • GRT 8803 • Built 1918
5.12.39: Torpedoed and sunk by German submarine U-47 (Prien), in the Atlantic about 150 miles W of Bishop Rock, in position 50.43N 10.16W while on a voyage from Liverpool to

Buenos Aires, in ballast, part of convoy OB 46 comprising 7 ships. The Master, Capt Charles Joseph Goble, and 36 crew were lost. 37 crew were rescued by HM destroyer *ESCAPADE* 1375/34 (H.17) (Cdr H.R. Graham); 8 crew by British ship *CLAN FARQUHAR* 7958/18 and landed at Cape Town.

**SAMBRE** ex-*WAR SWIFT* • GRT 5260 • Built 1919
27.7.40: Torpedoed and sunk by German submarine U–34 (Rollman), in the Atlantic SSW of Rockall, in position 56.37N 17.53W while on a voyage from Manchester to Philadelphia, with a part cargo of 1500 tons of generals, part of convoy OB 188 comprising 37 ships. The Master, Capt E. Bertie Ingram, and crew of 47 were rescued by HM destroyer *WINCHELSEA* 1300/17 (F.40) (Lt-Cdr W.A.F. Hawkins) and landed at Liverpool. U–34 commanded by Oberleutnant zur See Edward Aust was sunk on 5.8.43 in collision with German submarine tender *LECH* 3850/30 (K/L W.G. Schapler) during exercises in the Baltic Sea W of Memel, in position 55.42N 21.09E. 4 crew were lost and 39 rescued. U–34 was later salvaged and decommissioned at Memel 8.9.43.

**HIGHLAND PATRIOT** • GRT 14172 • Built 1932
1.10.40: Torpedoed and sunk by German submarine U–38 (Liebe), in the Atlantic 500 miles W of Bishop Rock, in position 52.20N 19.04W while sailing independently on a voyage from Buenos Aires to Glasgow, with 33 pasengers and a cargo of 5700 tons of general and refrigerated cargo. The Master, Capt Robert Henry Robinson, 135 crew and passengers were rescued by HM sloop *WELLINGTON* 990/34 (L.65) (Cdr R.E. Hyde-Smith) and landed at Greenock. 3 crew were lost.

**CULEBRA** ex-*RIPOSTO* • GRT 3044 • Built 1919
25.1.42: Sunk by gunfire by German submarine U–123 (Hardegen), part of 'Operation Paukenschlag' (Drumbeat), the first wave of five U-boats, in the Atlantic ENE of Bermuda, in position 35.30N 53.25W while sailing independently on a voyage from London to Bermuda and Kingston, Jamaica, with general cargo, dispersed from convoy ON 53 comprising 26 ships. The Master, Capt George Douglas Bonner, crew of 38 and 6 gunners were lost.

**SOMME** ex-*WAR TOUCAN* • GRT 5265 • Built 1919
18.2.42: Torpedoed and sunk by German submarine U–108 (Scholtz), part of 'Operation Paukenschlag' (Drumbeat), the second wave of five U-boats, in the Atlantic SE of Sable Island, in position 40.00N 55.00W while sailing independently from London to Bermuda and Curacao, with general cargo, dispersed on 15.2.42 from convoy ONS 62 comprising 34 ships. The Master, Capt Cornish Prosser, and crew of 47 were lost.

**SIRIS** • GRT 5242 • Built 1919
12.7.42: Torpedoed and sunk by German submarine U–201 (Schnee), part of the 'Hai' (Shark) patrol group of six U-boats, in the Atlantic S of the Azores, in position 31.20N 24.48W while sailing independently on a voyage from Hull and Oban 2.7.42 to Rio de Janeiro and Buenos Aires, with 3600 tons of general cargo, dispersed from convoy OS 33 comprising 41 ships. The Master, Capt Harwood Treweeks, 46 crew and 5 gunners were rescued after 10 days by HM corvette *JONQUIL* 925/40 (K.68) (Lt-Cdr R.E.H. Partington),

transferred to HM sloop *IBIS* 1250/40 (U.99) (Cdr H.M. Darrell-Brown) and landed at Milford Haven. 1 crew and 2 gunners were lost.

**LOCHKATRINE** • GRT 9419 • Built 1922
3.8.42: Torpedoed and sunk by German submarine U-553 (Thurmann), part of the 'Pirat' (Pirate) patrol group of twelve U-boats, in the Atlantic E of Cape Race, in position 45.52N 46.44W while on a voyage from Liverpool 23.7.42 to New York, in ballast with 18 passengers, part of convoy ON 115 comprising 41 ships. The Master, Capt Percy Cooper, 55 crew, 8 gunners and 17 passengers were rescued by RCN destroyer *HAMILTON* 1060/18 (I.24) (Lt-Cdr N.V. Clark) ex-USN four-stack *KALK* and RCN corvette *AGASSYZ* 925/40 (K.129) (Lt B D.L. Johnson) and landed at Halifax NS. 8 crew and 1 passenger were lost.

**SARTHE** • GRT 5271 • Built 1919
8.10.42: Torpedoed and sunk by German submarine U-68 (Merten), part of the 'Eisbar' (Polarbear) patrol group of five U-boats, in the South Atlantic SW of the Cape of Good Hope, in position 34.53S 18.24E while sailing independently on a voyage from Port Said, Aden and Lourenco Marques 3.10.42 to Rio de Janeiro and Buenos Aires, with a cargo of 6000 tons of bauxite and pinewood. The Master, Capt Charles Ernest Mason, crew of 48 and 8 gunners were rescued on 9.10.42 by the SAN whaler *VEREENIGING* ex-*VESTFOLD IX* 355/36 (T.62) and landed at Simonstown.

**BRITTANY** • GRT 4772 • Built 1928
30.10.42: Torpedoed and sunk by German submarine U-509 (Witte), part of the 'Streitaxt' (Battleaxe) patrol group of eight U-boats, in the Atlantic near Madeira, in position 33.29N 18.32W while on a voyage from Buenos Aires to Liverpool via Freetown 16.10.42, with 4 passengers and 7132 tons of hides, rice and cotton, part of convoy SL 125 comprising 40 ships. The Master, Capt William White Dovell, 32 crew, 7 gunners and 3 passengers were rescued by HM auxiliary patrol vessel *KELANTAN* 1282/21 (F.166) (Lt A.E. Jones) and landed at Gourock 8.11.42. 12 crew, 1 gunner and 1 passenger were lost.

**SABOR** ex-*WAR WHALE II* • GRT 5212 • Built 1920
7.3.43: Torpedoed and sunk by German submarine U-506 (Würdemann), in the South Atlantic SE of Mossel Bay, in position 34.33S 22.58E while sailing independently from Port Said, Mombasa, Tamatave and Durban to Cape Town and Rio de Janeiro, with 1100 tons of salt ballast and 63 bags of mail. The Master, Capt Peter Merrick Burrell, 41 crew and 9 gunners were rescued by SAAF crash launch No. 8 and landed at Mossel Bay. 7 crew were lost. U-506, commanded by Kapitänleutnant Erich Würdemann (Knight's Cross 14.3.43), was sunk on 12.7.43 in the Atlantic 330 miles W of Cape Finisterre, in position 42.30N 16.30W by Liberator C/1, pilot Lt Ernest Salm, of 1st A/S Squadron, 480th Antisubmarine Group, USAAF, based at Craw Field, Port Lyautey, French Morocco. The U-boat commander and 47 crew were lost. 6 crew were taken prisoner by RCN destroyer *IROQUOIS* 1927/41 (G.07) (Cdr James C. Hibbard DSC) on 15.7.43.

**NARIVA** • GRT 8723 • Built 1920
17.3.43: Torpedoed and damaged by German submarine U-600 (Zurmühlen), part of the 'Raubgraf' (Robber Baron) patrol group of thirteen U-boats, damaged by a *coup de grâce* by German submarine U-91 (Walkerling) and later sunk by gunfire by HM destroyer *MANSFIELD*

1090/18 (G.76) (Lt-Cdr L.C. Hill OBE) ex-USN four-stack *EVANS* and HM corvette *ANEMONE* 925/40 (K.48) (Lt-Cdr P.G.A. King), in the Atlantic SE of Cape Farewell, in position 55.34N 35.02W while on a voyage from Buenos Aires to Swansea via New York 8.3.43, with a cargo of 5600 tons of refrigerated foodstuffs, part of convoy HX 229 comprising 40 ships. The Master, Capt Bernard Cyril Dodds, crew of 86 and 7 gunners were rescued by HM corvette *ANEMONE* 925/40 (K.48) and landed at Gourock. U-91, commanded by Kapitänleutnant Heinz Hungerhausen, part of the 'Preussen' (Prussian) patrol group of thirty-two U-boats, was sunk on 25.2.44 in the Atlantic 590 miles W by S of Cape Clear, in position 49.45N 26.20W by HM frigates *AFFLECK* 1240/44 (K.462) (Cdr G. Gwinner), *GORE* 1240/43 (K.481) (Lt J. Reeves-Brown) and *GOULD* 1140/43 (K.476) (Lt D.W. Ungoed) of the 1st Support Group. The U-boat commander and 15 crew were taken prisoner by HMS *AFFLECK* and HMS *GORE*. 35 crew were lost.

### NAGARA • GRT 8803 • Built 1918
29.3.43: Torpedoed and damaged by German submarine U-404 (v. Bülow), in the Atlantic 425 miles NW of Cape Finisterre in position 46.50N 16.40W and taken in tow by HM rescue tug *DEXTEROUS* 700/42 (W.111) but sank on 4.4.43, in position 47.52N 14.03W while on a voyage from Buenos Aires to Cardiff via Freetown 12.3.43, with a cargo of 6069 tons of refrigerated meat, part of convoy SL 126 comprising 36 ships. The Master, Capt Percy Cooper, crew of 84 and 12 gunners were rescued by HM frigate *WEAR* 1370/42 (K.230) (Lt G.D. Edwards) and landed at Liverpool.

### PALMA • GRT 5419 • Built 1941
29.2.44: Torpedoed and sunk by German submarine U-183 (Schneewind), in the Indian Ocean 400 miles S of Ceylon, in position 05.51N 79.58E while sailing independently on a voyage from Liverpool, Cape Town and Colombo to Madras and Calcutta, with 300 tons of general cargo. The Master, Capt Alfred Robert Osburn, 41 crew and 4 gunners were rescued by HM trawler *BALTA* 545/40 (T.50) (Lt W.E. Turner) and HM whaler *SEMLA* 217/24 (4.38) (Lt S.V. Bateman) and landed at Colombo 2.3.44. 4 crew and 3 gunners were lost.

### NEBRASKA • GRT 8261 • Built 1920
8.4.44: Torpedoed and sunk by German submarine U-843 (Herwatz), in the South Atlantic SW of Ascension Island, in position 11.55S 19.52W while sailing independently on a voyage from Taranto and Gibraltar to Buenos Aires, in ballast, dispersed on 14.2.44 from the combined convoy OS 71/KMS 45 comprising 44 ships. The Master, Capt Bernard Cyril Dodds, 55 crew, 8 gunners and 2 stowaways were saved: the Master's boat with survivors landed at Bahia, the Radio Officer's boat with 20 survivors landed at Recife 22.4.44 and the remaining survivors were rescued by British ship *KINDAT* 4358/38 and landed at Freetown. 2 crew were lost. Kapitänleutnant Oskar Herwatz and 43 crew were lost when U-843 was sunk on 9.4.45 in the Kattegat 27 miles NE of Skagen Lighthouse, Denmark, in position 57.58N 11.15E by Mosquito 'A', pilot F/O A.J. Randell of No. 235 Squadron RAF, based at Banff, part of 18 Group.

## RUNCIMAN, WALTER & CO. LTD – NEWCASTLE UPON TYNE
### Barberry SS Co. Ltd

### BARBERRYS ex-AMERICAN ORIOLO ex-EASTERN GLEN • GRT 5170 • Built 1920
26.11.42: Torpedoed and sunk by German submarine U-663 (Schmid), part of the 'Drachen' (Dragon) patrol group of seven U-boats, in the Atlantic NE of St John's, Newfoundland, in

position 50.36N 47.10W while on a voyage from New York 17.11.42 to Glasgow, with 6867 tons of general cargo, part of convoy SC 110 comprising 33 ships. The Master, Capt George Halker Squires, Commodore A.H. Young RNR RD, 21 crew, 4 gunners and 5 naval staff were lost. 17 crew, 3 gunners and 1 naval staff were rescued by US Coastguard cutter *MOHAWK* 1005/34 (WPG.78) and landed at St John's, Newfoundland.

## Moor Line Limited

**ORANGEMOOR** • GRT 5775 • Built 1923
31.5.40: Torpedoed and sunk by German submarine U-101 (Frauenheim), in the English Channel SW of Roches Doures, in position 49.43N 03.23W while on a voyage from Bona to the Tyne, with a cargo of 8150 tons of iron ore, part of convoy HGF 31 comprising 29 ships. The Master, Capt Robert Edward Richardson, and 21 crew were rescued by British ship *BRANDENBERG* 1473/42 and landed at London. 18 crew were lost.

**PEARLMOOR** • GRT 4581 • Built 1923
19.7.40: Torpedoed and sunk by German submarine U-62 (Michalowski), in the Atlantic 62 miles W of Malin Head, in position 55.23N 09.18W while on a voyage from Pepel to Methil and Immingham via Freetown 1.7.40, with a cargo of 7860 tons of iron ore, a straggler from convoy SL 38 comprising 30 ships. The Master, Capt James Basil Rodgers, and 25 crew landed at Gola Island, Co. Donegal. 13 crew were lost. U-62 commanded by Oberleutnant zur See Hans-Eckart Augustin was scuttled at Wilhelmshaven on 1.5.45.

**VINEMOOR** • GRT 4359 • Built 1924
26.7.40: Torpedoed and sunk by German submarine U-34 (Rollman), in the Atlantic 320 miles W of Bloody Foreland, in position 55.43N 16.25W while on a voyage from Manchester to Naura, in ballast, part of convoy OB 188 comprising 37 ships. The Master, Capt David John Jones, and crew of 31 were rescued by HM corvette *CLARKIA* 925/40 (K.88) (Lt-Cdr F.J.G. Jones), transferred to British ship *HOLLINSIDE* 4172/30 and landed at Liverpool.

**GLENMOOR** • GRT 4393 • Built 1928
27.11.40: Torpedoed and sunk by German submarine U-103 (Schütze), in the Atlantic 167 miles NW of Slyne Head, in position 54.35N 14.31W while on a voyage from Cardiff to Alexandria, with a cargo of 7410 tons of coal, a straggler from convoy OB 248 comprising 44 ships. The Master, Capt Jack Young and 30 crew were lost. 2 crew were rescued by HM destroyers *HARVESTER* 1340/39 (H.19) ex-HMS *HANDY* (Lt-Cdr M. Thornton) ex-Brazilian *JURUA* and *HAVELOCK* 1340/39 (H.88) (Cdr E.H. Thomas) ex-Brazilian *JUTAHY* and landed at Liverpool.

**ALNMOOR** • GRT 6500 • Built 1922
15.2.41: Torpedoed and sunk by German submarine U-123 (Moehle), in the Atlantic SSE of Rockall, in position 55.00N 13.00W while on a voyage from New York to Glasgow via Sydney CB, with general cargo, a straggler from convoy SC 21 comprising 38 ships. The Master, Capt Albert Edwards, and crew of 54 were lost. Korvettenkapitän Karl-Heinz Moehle was awarded the Knight's Cross (28.2.41).

**JEDMOOR** • GRT 4392 • Built 1928
16.9.41: Torpedoed and sunk by German submarine U-98 (Gysae) part of the 'Bosemüller' patrol group of nine U-boats, in the Atlantic NW of St Kilda, in position 59.00N 10.00W while on a voyage from Santos to Glasgow via Sydney CB 30.8.41, with a cargo of 7400 tons of iron ore, a straggler from convoy SC 42 comprising 65 ships. The Master, Capt Robert Clifford Collins, 25 crew and 5 gunners were lost. 3 crew were rescued by Norwegian ship *KNOLL* 1151/16 and 2 crew by British ship *CAMPUS* 3667/25.

**EASTMOOR** • GRT 5812 • Built 1922
1.4.42: Torpedoed and sunk by German submarine U-71 (Flachsenberg), part of 'Operation Paukenschlag' (Drumbeat), the fourth wave of eleven U-boats, in the Atlantic about 600 miles E of Hampton Roads, in position 37.33N 68.18W while sailing independently on a voyage from Savannah to the UK via Halifax NS, with 7500 tons of general cargo. The Master, Capt James Basil Rodgers, 12 crew and 3 gunners were lost. 29 crew and 7 gunners were rescued by British ship *CALGARY* 7206/21 and landed at Cape Town. U-71, commanded by Oberleutnant zur See Emil Ranzau, was scuttled at Wilhelmshaven on 1.5.45.

**ZURICHMOOR** • GRT 4455 • Built 1925
23.5.42: Torpedoed and sunk by German submarine U-432 (Schultze), part of the 'Pfadfinder' (Pathfinder) patrol group of eight U-boats, in the Atlantic E of Philadelphia, in position 39.30N 66.00W while sailing independently on a voyage from Halifax NS to St Thomas, Virgin Islands, in ballast. The Master, Capt James Henry Anderson, and crew of 37 were lost.

**YORKMOOR** • GRT 4457 • Built 1925
27.5.42: Sunk by gunfire by German submarine U-506 (Würdemann), in the Atlantic NNE of Bahamas, in position 29.30N 72.29W while sailing independently on a voyage from St Thomas, Virgin Islands 23.5.42 to New York, with a cargo of 6700 tons of bauxite. The Master, Capt Thomas Harrison Matthews, crew of 40 and 5 gunners were rescued by a US Coastguard cutter and landed at Morehead City, North Carolina.

**NORTHMOOR** • GRT 4392 • Built 1928
17.5.43: Torpedoed and sunk by German submarine U-198 (Hartmann), in the Indian Ocean N of Durban, in position 28.40S 32.45E while on a voyage from Lourenco Marques 16.5.43 to Buenos Aires via Durban, with a cargo of 6912 tons of coal, part of convoy LMD 17 comprising 6 ships. The Master, Capt Arthur Peters, 20 crew, 4 gunners and 2 DBS were rescued by HM trawler *ST LOMAN* 5655/36 (FY.276) (Lt R.C. Warwick DSC) and landed at Durban. 11 crew and 1 gunner were lost.

## MOWT

**EMPIRE MOOSE** ex-*OAKWOOD* ex-*COLIN H. LIVINGSTONE* • GRT 6103 • Built 1920
29.8.40: Torpedoed and sunk by German submarine U-100 (Schepke), in the Atlantic 130 miles WNW of Bloody Foreland, in position 56.06N 13.33W while on a voyage from Hull to Port Sulphur, in ballast, a straggler from convoy OB 204 comprising 43 ships. The Master, Capt Robert Edward Richardson, and crew of 35 landed at Killybegs, Co. Donegal.

**EMPIRE ADVENTURE** ex-*ANDREA* ex-*GERMAINE L.D.* ex-*EASTNEY*
GRT 5145 • Built 1921
20.9.40: Torpedoed and damaged by German submarine U-138 (Lüth), in the Atlantic 52 miles NW of Rathlin Island, in position 55.48N 07.22W while on a voyage from the Tyne to Wabana, Conception Bay, in ballast, part of convoy OB 216 comprising 27 ships. Taken in tow by HM rescue tug *SUPERMAN* 359/33 to the Clyde but sank on 23.9.40. The Master, Capt Thomas O. Phinn, and 20 crew were lost. 18 crew were rescued by Swedish ship *INDUSTRIA* 1688/40 and landed at Belfast. The Italian *ANDREA* was taken as a prize in June 1940 at Newcastle.

**EMPIRE STATESMAN** ex-*PELLICE* ex-*ANSALDO OTTAVO* ex-*ANSALDO VIII*
GRT 5306 • Built 1920
11.12.40: Torpedoed and sunk by German submarine U-94 (Kuppisch), in the Atlantic W of Ireland while on a voyage from Pepel to Middlesbrough via Freetown, with a cargo of iron ore, a straggler from convoy SL 56 comprising 42 ships. The Master, Capt James Brown, and crew of 30 were lost. The Italian *PELLICE* was captured by the Royal Navy on 10.6.40 taken as a prize to Methil.

**EMPIRE SEAL** ex-*EMPIRE KITE* ex-*CALIFORNIAN* • GRT 7965 • Built 1922
19.2.42: Torpedoed and sunk by German submarine U-96 (Lehmann-Willenbrock), part of 'Operation Paukenschlag' (Drumbeat), the third wave of twelve U-boats, in the Atlantic SE of Sable Island, in position 43.14N 64.45W while sailing independently on a voyage from New York and Halifax NS to Belfast, with a cargo of 4500 tons of steel. The Master, Capt Arthur Charles Kyle, 43 crew, 11 gunners and the US pilot were rescued by British ship *EMPIRE FLAME* 7069/41 (CAM) and landed at Halifax NS. 1 crew was lost.

**EMPIRE HAWKSBILL** ex-*DELAWAREAN* ex-*GOLDEN COAST* ex-*WEST MIVARIA*
GRT 5724 • Built 1920
19.7.42: Torpedoed and sunk by German submarine U-564 (Suhren), in the Atlantic about 200 miles N of the Azores, in position 42.29N 25.56W while on government service on a voyage from Barry and Belfast Lough to Cape Town, with a cargo of government stores, part of convoy OS 34 comprising 35 ships. The Master, Capt Harold Theodore Lamb, crew of 37 and 9 gunners were lost.

## SAGUENAY TERMINALS LIMITED – MONTREAL, QUEBEC

**SIRE** • GRT 5664 • Built 1938
31.5.41: Torpedoed and sunk by German submarine U-107 (Hessler), in the Atlantic WSW of Freetown, in position 08.50N 15.30W while sailing independently on a voyage from Las Palmas to Pepel, in ballast, dispersed from convoy OB 320 comprising 18 ships. The Master, Capt John Thomas Bennett, and 45 crew were rescued by HM corvette *MARGUERITE* 925/40 (K.454) (Lt-Cdr A.N. Blundell) and landed at Freetown 6.6.41. 3 crew were lost.

**CORABELLA** • GRT 5682 • Built 1937
30.4.43: Torpedoed and sunk by German submarine U-515 (Henke), in the Atlantic SW of Freetown, in position 07.15N 13.49W while on a voyage from Takoradi 26.4.43 to the UK

via Freetown, with a cargo of 8065 tons of manganese ore, part of convoy TS 37 comprising 19 ships. The Master, Capt Peter Leggett, 30 crew and 8 gunners were rescued by HM trawler BIRDLIP 750/41 (T.218) (Lt E.N. Groom) and landed at Freetown. 9 crew were lost.

## SALVESEN, CHRISTIAN & COMPANY – LEITH

**GLEN FARG** • GRT 876 • Built 1937
4.10.39: Torpedoed and sunk by gunfire by German submarine U-23 (Kretschmer), in the North Sea 60 miles SSW of Sumburgh Head, in position 58.52N 01.31W while sailing independently on a voyage from Folden Fjord near Trondheim to Methil and Grangemouth, with general cargo including pulp, carbide, paper and ferro-chrome. The Master, Capt Robert Galloway Hall, and 15 crew were rescued by HM destroyer FIREDRAKE 1350/34 (H.79) (Lt-Cdr S.H. Norris) and landed at Kirkwall 5.10.39. 1 crew was lost.

**BRANDON** ex-BREDON ex-HOLBROOK • GRT 6665 • Built 1917
8.12.39: Torpedoed and sunk by German submarine U-48 (Schultze), in the Atlantic 80 miles SW of Fastnet, in position 50.28N 08.28W while on a voyage from Cardiff to Port Everglades, Florida, in ballast, a straggler from convoy OB 48 comprising 13 ships. The Master, Capt Richard Black Chisholm, and survivors were rescued by the Belgian trawlers MARIE JOSE ROSETTE 139/36 and TRITTEN and landed at Milford Haven. 9 crew were lost.

**NEW SEVILLA** ex-RUNIC (whaling factory) • GRT 13801 • Built 1900
20.9.40: Torpedoed and damaged by German submarine U-138 (Lüth), in the Atlantic 52 miles NW of Rathlin Island, in position 55.48N 07.22W while on a voyage from Liverpool to South Georgia via Aruba, in ballast, part of convoy OB 216 comprising 27 ships. Taken in tow but sank on 21.9.40 9 miles from the Mull of Kintyre, in position 55.48N 07.22W. The Master, Capt Richard Black Chisholm, and 22 crew were rescued by HM corvette ARABIS 925/40 (K.73) (Lt-Cdr A. Blewitt) and landed at Liverpool; 259 crew were rescued by Swedish ship INDUSTRIA 1688/40 and landed at Belfast. 2 crew were lost.

**SHEKATIKA** • GRT 5458 • Built 1936
18.10.40: Torpedoed and damaged by German submarines U-123 (Moehle) and U-100 (Schepke) and given a *coup de grâce* by German submarine U-123 (Moehle), in the Atlantic 90 miles ESE of Rockall, in position 57.12N 11.08W while on a voyage from Gaspé, New Brunswick to Hartlepool via Sydney CB 5.10.40, with a cargo of 2003 tons of steel and 6000 tons of pit props, a straggler from convoy SC 7 comprising 35 ships. The Master, Capt Robert Paterson, and crew of 35 were rescued by HM sloop FOWEY 1105/30 (L.15) (Lt-Cdr C.G. de L. Bush) and landed at Greenock 20.10.40.

**SIRIKISHNA** • GRT 5458 • Built 1936
24.2.41: Torpedoed and sank by German submarine U-96 (Lehmann-Willenbrock), in the Atlantic S of Iceland, in position 58.00N 21.00W while on a voyage from Barry to Halifax NS, in ballast, dispersed from convoy OB 288 comprising 46 ships. The Master, Capt Robert Paterson, commodore, Rear Admiral R.R.A. Plowden DSO RN, crew of 25 and 6 naval staff were lost.

**PEDER BOGEN** (tanker) • GRT 9741 • Built 1925
23.3.42: Torpedoed and sunk by gunfire by Italian submarine MOROSINI (Fraternale), in the Atlantic E of the West Indies, in position 24.41N 57.44W while sailing independently on government service on a voyage from Trinidad 19.3.42 to Halifax NS, with 1 passenger and a cargo of 14000 tons of fuel oil. The Master, Capt William T. Dawson, 46 crew, 5 gunners and passenger were rescued, the Master and 21 survivors by Spanish tanker GOBEO 3365/21 and landed at Lisbon; 32 survivors by an unknown ship and landed at New York. Lt Francesco d'Alessandro and crew were lost on 10.8.42 when the MOROSINI was sunk in the Bay of Biscay 140 miles N by E of Cape Ortegal by Wellington 'H' P9230, of No. 311 (Czech) Squadron RAF, based at Talbenny, Pembrokeshire, part of 19 Group.

**SAGANAGA** • GRT 5452 • Built 1935
5.9.42: Torpedoed and sunk by German submarine U-513 (Rüggeberg), in the Atlantic while at anchor off Wabana, Conception Bay, in position 47.35N 52.29W on a voyage from Wabana to Sydney CB, with a cargo of 8300 tons of iron ore. The Master, Capt Alfred William Dugald Mackay, 10 crew and 3 gunners were rescued by a Customs launch and landed at Lance Cove, Bell Island, Newfoundland. 27 crew and 3 gunners were lost.

**SOUTHERN EMPRESS** ex-SAN JERONIMO • GRT 12398 • Built 1914 (whale factory)
14.10.42: Torpedoed and damaged by German submarine U-221 (Trojer), part of the 'Wotan' (god of the Vikings) patrol group of ten U-boats, later sunk by a coup de grâce by U-221, in the Atlantic NE of St John's, Newfoundland, in position 53.40N 40.40W while on a voyage from New Orleans and New York 3.10.42 to Glasgow, with 51 DBS and a cargo of 11700 tons fuel oil and a deck cargo of 21 invasion barges, part of convoy SC 104 comprising 47 ships. The Master, Capt Olaf Hansen, 23 crew, 20 DBS and 4 gunners were lost. 44 crew, 2 gunners and 31 DBS were rescued by RNoN corvette POTENTILLA 925/41 (K.214) (Lt-Cdr Monsson), transferred to Norwegian whale factory SUDEROY 7562/13 and landed at Liverpool. U-353, part of the 'Leopard' patrol group of six U-boats, commanded by Oberleutnant zur See Wolfgang Rommer, was sunk while attacking this convoy on 16.10.42 by HM destroyer FAME 1350/34 (H.78) (Cdr R. Heathcote) in the Atlantic, 630 miles W of Blacksod Bay, in position 53.54N 29.30W. The U-boat commander and 38 crew were taken prisoner by HMS FAME and RNoN corvette ACANTHUS 925/41 (K.01) (Lt-Cdr Brunn). 6 crew were lost.

**SOURABAYA** ex-CARMARTHENSHIRE • GRT 10107 • Built 1915 (whale factory)
27.10.42: Torpedoed and sunk by German submarine U-436 (Seibicke), part of the 'Puma' patrol group of thirteen U-boats, in the Atlantic SE of Cape Farewell, in position 54.32N 31.02W while on government service on a voyage from New York 18.10.42 to Liverpool, with 55 passengers, 32 DBS and a cargo of 7800 tons of fuel oil and 200 tons of war stores, part of convoy HX 212 comprising 45 ships. The Master, Capt William Thompson Dawson, 36 crew, 4 gunners, 24 passengers and 16 DBS were rescued by RCN corvettes ALBERNI 925/40 (K.103) (Lt A.W. Ford) and VILLE DE QUEBEC 925/41 (K.242) ex-HMCS QUEBEC (Lt-Cdr D.G. Jeffrey) and landed at Liverpool 2.11.42; 26 crew, 31 passengers, 16 DBS and 4 gunners by Canadian ship BIC ISLAND 4000/17. The survivors were later lost when the BIC ISLAND was sunk on 29.10.42 by U-224 (Kosbadt).

**FINTRA** ex-*CARCAVELLOS* ex-*TUTSHILL* • GRT 2089 • Built 1918
23.2.43: Torpedoed and sunk by German submarine U-371 (Mehl), in the Mediterranean
NE of Algiers, in position 36.57N 03.41E while sailing independently on a voyage from
Philippeviile 22.2.43 to Algiers, with 1 passenger and 340 tons of ammunition and stores.
The Master, Capt Richard John Roll, 21 crew and passenger were saved. 7 crew and 5
gunners were lost.

**SOUTHERN PRINCESS** ex-*SAN PATRICIO* • GRT 12156 • Built 1915 (whale factory)
17.3.43: Torpedoed and sunk by German submarine U-600 (Zurmülen), part of the
'Raubgraf' (Robber Baron) patrol group of thirteen U-boats, in the Atlantic E of St John's,
Newfoundland, in position 50.36N 34.30W while on a voyage from New York 8.3.43 to the
Clyde, with 29 passengers, 10053 tons of heavy fuel oil and a deck cargo of 463 tons of
locomotives and invasion barges, part of convoy HX 229 comprising 40 ships. The Master,
Capt H. Neilson, 59 crew, 7 gunners and 27 passenger were rescued by British ship *TEKOA*
8531/22 and landed at Liverpool. 4 crew and 2 passengers were lost. Kapitänleutnant Bernard
Zurmuhlen and crew of 53 were lost on 25.11.43 when U-600, part of the 'Weddigen'
(named after a U-boat commander) patrol group of fifteen U-boats, was sunk while attacking
the combined convoys KMS 30/OG 95 comprising 39 ships in the Atlantic 235 miles NE of
San Miguel, Azores, in position 40.31N 22.07W by HM frigates *BAZLEY* 1085/42 (K.311)
(Lt-Cdr J.V. Brock) and *BLACKWOOD* 1085/42 (K.313) (Lt-Cdr L.T. Sly) of the 4th Support
Group (Cdr H.J.R. Paramore).

## MOWT

**CROWN ARUN** ex-*HANNAH BOGE* • GRT 2373 • Built 1938
17.9.40: Torpedoed and sunk by gunfire by German submarine U-99 (Kretschmer), in the
Atlantic N of Rockall, in position 58.02N 14.18W while on a voyage from Gaspe, New
Brunswick to Hull via Halifax NS 5.9.40, with a cargo of 2800 tons of pit props, a straggler
from convoy HX 71 comprising 34 ships. The Master, Capt Hugh Laurence Leaske, and crew
of 24 were rescued by HM destroyer *WINCHELSEA* 1100/17 (D.46) (Lt-Cdr W.A. Hawkins
DSC) and landed at Liverpool. The German *HANNAH BOGE* was captured on 3.9.39 by
HM destroyer *SOMALI* 1870/37 (F.33) (Capt R.S.G. Nicholson DSO DSC) in the Atlantic
and taken to Kirkwall by a prize crew.

**EMPIRE BRUCE** • GRT 7459 • Built 1941
18.4.43: Torpedoed and sunk by German submarine U-123 (v. Schroeter), in the Atlantic
100 miles SW of Freetown, in position 06.40N 13.17W while sailing independently on a
voyage from Buenos Aires 30.3.43 to the UK via Freetown, with a cargo of 9141 tons of
linseed. The Master, Capt J Edwards, crew of 41 and 7 gunners were rescued by HM
minesweeper 107 165/42 (Skipper H.J. Craven) and landed at Freetown 19.4.43.

**EMPIRE DUNSTAN** • GRT 2887 • Built 1942
18.11.43: Torpedoed and sunk by German submarine U-81 (Krieg), in the Gulf of Taranto
SW of Taranto, in position 39.24N 17.40E while on government service on a voyage from
Bona to Brindisi via Augusta 16.11.43, with 3 passengers and a cargo of 1550 tons of military
stores including 700 tons of land mines, dispersed from combined convoy SL 140/MKS 31

comprising 66 ships. The Master, Capt Norman Ramsay, 29 crew, 7 gunners and passengers were rescued by the Norwegian ship *LOM* 1268/20 and landed at Taranto. 2 crew were lost. U-81, commanded by Oberleutnant zur See Johann Otto Krieg, was sunk on 9.1.44 by aircraft of the USAAF at Pola, Italy. The U-boat commander and 43 crew survived. 2 crew were lost.

**EMPIRE HERITAGE** ex-*TAFELBERG* (tanker) • GRT 15720 • Built 1930
8.9.44: Torpedoed and damaged by German submarine U-482 (v. Graf), later sunk by a *coup de grâce* by U-482, in the Atlantic NNE of Tory Island, in position 55.27N 08.01W while on a voyage from New York to Liverpool and Glasgow, with a cargo of 16000 tons of fuel oil and 1942 tons of deck cargo including tanks and trucks, part of convoy HXF 305 comprising 97 ships. The Master, Capt James Campbell Jamieson OBE, 24 crew, 3 gunners, 20 DBS and 1 signalman were rescued by HM trawler *NORTHERN WAVE* 655/36 (FY.153) (Lt F.J.R. Storey) and landed at Londonderry. 52 crew, 8 gunners, 1 army storekeeper and 53 DBS were lost.

**EMPIRE KINGSLEY** • GRT 6996 • Built 1941
22.3.45: Torpedoed and sunk by German submarine U-315 (Zoller), in the Atlantic NW of Land's End in position 50.08N 05.51W while on a voyage from Ghent to Manchester, in ballast, part of coastal convoy TBC 103 comprising 13 ships. The Master, Capt David Hunter, 38 crew and 10 gunners were rescued by HM trawler *FIR* 530/40 (Lt W.H. Buley) and transferred to the Sennen lifeboat. 8 crew were lost. U-315, commanded by Oberleutnant zur See Herbert Zoller, surrendered at Trondheim on 10.5.45 and was scrapped in the UK during April 1947.

## SCINDIA STEAM NAVIGATION COMPANY – BOMBAY

*JALARAJAN* ex-*CHULMLEIGH* • GRT 5102 • Built 1925 (Indian)
15.1.42: Torpedoed and sunk by gunfire by Japanese submarine I-165 (Harada), in the Indian Ocean W of the Mentawai Islands, in position 00.12S 97.00E while sailing independently on a voyage from Singapore to Calcutta, in ballast. The Master, Capt F. de Chaumont, 70 crew and 3 gunners landed at Siberut Island, Sumatra and were brought to Batavia, Java by Dutch ships *SIBIGO* 1594/96 and *BALIKPAPAN* 1979/39. 4 crew were lost.

*JALATARANG* ex-*ELIZABETH STONER* • GRT 2498 • Built 1921 (Indian)
30.1.42: Torpedoed and sunk by gunfire by Japanese submarine I-164 (Ogawa), in the Bay of Bengal S of Madras, in position 12.59N 81.00E while sailing independently on a voyage from Cochin to Rangoon, with a part cargo of 100 tons of general. The Master, Capt Robert Craig Leitch, and 37 crew were lost. 11 crew were rescued by British ship *KEPONG* 1889/16.

*JALAPALAKA* ex-*FRANKLEY* ex-*WILLIAM WALLACE* • GRT 4215 • Built 1917 (Indian)
31.1.42: Torpedoed and sunk by gunfire by Japanese submarine I-164 (Ogawa), in the Bay of Bengal 50 miles S of Madras, in position 13.00N 81.08E while sailing indpendently on a voyage from Bombay to Rangoon, in ballast. The Master, Richard Stanford Smith, and 53 crew were rescued by RIN auxiliary patrol ship *IRRAWADI* 1243/13 (4.186) (Lt A.M. Robinson) and landed at Madras. 13 crew were lost. Lt Tsunayashi Ogawa and crew were lost

on 17.5.42 when I-164 was sunk in the Pacific SE of Kyushu, in position 29.25N 134.09E by the US submarine *TRITON* 1475/40 (SS–201) (Lt-Cdr George K. MacKenzie, Jr).

**JALABALA** • GRT 3610 • Built 1927 (Indian)
11.10.43: Torpedoed and sunk by German submarine U-532 (Junker), in the Indian Ocean W of Cape Comorin, India, in position 11.40N 75.19E while on a voyage from Colombo to Bombay and Karachi, with 2000 tons of copra and 1800 tons of general cargo, part of convoy GM 50. The Master, Capt James George Conner, 71 crew and 3 gunners landed at Calicut 12.10.43 and Mangalore, WC India 15.10.43. 5 crew were lost.

**EL MADINA** • GRT 3962 • Built 1937 (Indian)
16.3.44 Torpedoed and sunk by Japanese submarine RO-111 (Nakamura), in the Bay of Bengal at the mouth of the River Ganges, in position 20.54N 89.36E while on government sevice on a voyage from Calcutta to Chittagong, with 1161 troops and stores, part of convoy HC 44 comprising 7 ships. The Master, Capt Gerald Stuart Macwilliam, 46 crew, 6 gunners and 364 troops were lost. 78 crew, 1 gunner and 797 troops were rescued by RIN minesweeping sloop *ROHILKHAND* 656/42 (J.180) ex-HMS *PADSTOW* (Lt-Cdr H.M.S. Choudie), RIN auxiliary patrol vessel *IRRAWADI* 1243/13 (4.186) (Lt G.W.P. O'Donoghue) and Norwegian ship *LOVSTAD* 3246/21 and landed at Chittagong. Lt Naozo Nakamura and crew were lost on 10.6.44 when RO-111 was sunk in the Pacific 60 miles E of Roi Island, part of the Marshall Islands, in position 10.05N 168.22E by US destroyer escort *BANGUST* 1240/43 (DE.739) (Lt-Cdr C.F. MacNish).

## SEAGER, W.H. & COMPANY – CARDIFF
### Tempus Shipping Co. Ltd

**BEATUS** • GRT 4885 • Built 1925
18.10.40: Torpedoed and sunk by German submarine U-46 (Endrass), in the Atlantic about 100 miles W by S of Barra Head, in position 57.31N 13.10W while on a voyage from Three Rivers to the Tyne and Middlesbrough via Sydney CB 5.10.40, with a cargo of 1626 tons of steel, 5874 tons of lumber and a deck cargo of crated aircraft, part of convoy SC 7 comprising 35 ships. The Master, Capt Wilfred Leslie Brett, and crew of 36 were rescued by HM corvette *BLUEBELL* 925/40 (K.80) (Lt-Cdr Robert E. Sherwood) and landed at Gourock.

**FISCUS** • GRT 4815 • Built 1928
18.10.40: Torpedoed and sunk by German submarine U-99 (Kretschmer), in the Atlantic E of Rockall, in position 57.29N 11.10W while on a voyage from Three Rivers to the Clyde for orders via Sydney CB 5.10.40, with a cargo of steel, lumber and a deck cargo of crated aircraft, part of convoy SC 7 comprising 35 ships. The Master, Capt Ebenezer Williams, crew of 37 and 1 gunner were lost.

**AMICUS** • GRT 3660 • Built 1925
19.12.40: Torpedoed and sunk by Italian submarine *ALPINO ATTILIO BAGNOLINI* (Tosoni-Pittoni), in the Atlantic 265 miles 257° from Bloody Foreland, in position 54.10N 15.50W while sailing independently on a voyage from Tampa to Ipswich via Sydney CB, with a cargo of 5600 tons of phoshates, dispersed from convoy SC 15 comprising 21 ships. The Master, Capt

William Leyshon Harries, crew of 34 and 2 gunners were lost. *ALPINO ATTILIO BAGNOLINI* was captured by the Germans at Bordeaux on 10.9.43 and renamed UIT-22. Oberleutnant zur See Karl Wunderlich and crew of 42 were lost on 11.3.44 when UIT-22 was sunk in the South Atlantic 430 miles S of Cape of Good Hope, in position 41.28S 17.40E by Catalina 'D', pilot F/Lt Frederick T. Roddick (Canadian), Catalina 'P', pilot F/Lt E.S.S. Nash and Catalina 'A', pilot F/Lt A.H. Surridge of No. 262 Squadron RAF, based at St Lucia, Natal.

## MOWT

### OCEAN VANGUARD • GRT 7174 • Built 1941
13.9.42: Torpedoed and sunk by German submarine U-515 (Henke), in the Atlantic 45 miles E of Galera Point, Trinidad, in position 10.43N 60.11W while sailing independently on a voyage from Suez to New York via Cape Town 19.8.42 and Trinidad, in ballast. The Master, Capt Wilfred Leslie Brett, 34 crew and 5 gunners were rescued by Norwegian ship *BRAGA* 1671/38 and landed at Port of Spain, Trinidad. 10 crew and 1 gunner were lost.

### OCEAN VAGABOND • GRT 7174 • Built 1942
11.1.43: Torpedoed and sunk by German submarine U-186 (Hesemann), part of the 'Habicht' (Hawk) patrol group of eight U-boats, in the Atlantic S of Iceland, in position 57.17N 20.11W while on a voyage from Botwood and St John's, Newfoundland to Hull, with a cargo of wheat, lumber and 3165 tons of sulphite pulp, a straggler from convoy SC 115 comprising 18 ships. The Master, Capt John William Smith, 41 crew and 4 gunners were rescued by HM destroyer *WANDERER* 1120/19 (D.74) (Lt-Cdr D.H.P. Gardiner) and landed at Liverpool. 1 crew was lost.

## SHAMROCK SHIPPING CO. LTD – LARNE

### SLEMISH • GRT 1536 • Built 1909
23.12.44: Torpedoed and sunk by German submarine U-772 (Rademacher), in the English Channel about 40 miles N of Cherbourg, in position 49.45N 01.42W while on a voyage from Hull to Cherbourg via St Helen's Roads, Isle of Wight, with a cargo of 1650 tons of coal, part of coastal convoy WEG 14 comprising 5 ships. The Master, Capt J. McCarlie, 11 crew and 3 gunners were rescued by US submarine chaser PC 553 280/44 and landed at Cherbourg on 24.12.44. The survivors embarked on British hospital ship No. 53 *EL NIL* 7769/16 and landed at Southampton 25.12.44. 6 crew and 1 gunner were lost.

## SHAW, SAVILL & ALBION CO. LTD – LONDON

### WAIOTIRA • GRT 12823 • Built 1939
26.12.40: Torpedoed and damaged by German submarine U-95 (Schreiber), in the Atlantic 124 miles W by N of Rockall, in position 58.05N 17.10W, given a *coup de grâce* by German submarine U-38 (Liebe) and sank on 27.12.40, in position 58.10N 16.56W while sailing independently on a voyage from Sydney NSW to the UK via the Panama Canal, with 11 passengers and a cargo of 7000 tons refrigerated and general. The Master, Capt Arthur V. Richardson, crew of 78 and 10 passengers were rescued by HM destroyer *MASHONA* 1870/37 (F.59) (Cdr W.H. Selby) and landed at Greenock 28.12.40. 1 passenger was lost.

**ZEALANDIC** • GRT 8281 • Built 1928
16.1.41: Torpedoed and sunk by German submarine U-106 (Oesten), in the Atlantic NW of Rockall, in position 58.28N 20.43W while sailing independently on a voyage from Liverpool to Brisbane via Panama, with 6 passengers and general cargo. The Master, Capt Frederick James Ogilvie, crew of 64, 2 gunners and passengers were lost.

**WAIWERA** • GRT 12435 • Built 1934
29.6.42: Torpedoed and sunk by German submarine U-754 (Oestermann), in the Atlantic W of St John's, Newfoundland, in position 45.49N 34.29W while sailing independently on a voyage from Auckland to Liverpool via Colon 17.6.42, with 20 military personnel and 12933 tons of foodstuffs including butter, tea and beef, and 2100 bags of mail. The Master, Capt Cyril Maurice Andrews, 71 crew, 7 gunners and 18 military personnel were rescued by Norwegian ship *OREGON EXPRESS* 3642/33 and landed at New York. 6 crew and 2 military personnel were lost. Capt M.A. Andrews was awarded the Lloyd's War Medal for bravery at sea. Kapitänleutnant Johannes Oestermann and crew of 43 were lost on 31.7.42 when U-754 was sunk while shadowing convoy ON 113 comprising 33 ships in the Atlantic 30 miles SSE of Cape Sable, Nova Scotia, in position 43.02N 64.52W by Hudson 625, pilot S/Ldr N.E. Small of No. 113 Squadron RCAF, based at Yarmouth, Nova Scotia. This was the first U-boat to be sunk by an aircraft of the Royal Canadian Air Force.

**CERAMIC** • GRT 18713 • Built 1913
7.12.42: Torpedoed and sunk by German submarine U-515 (Henke), part of the 'Westwall' patrol group of seventeen U-boats, in the Atlantic W of the Azores, in position 40.30N 40.20W while sailing independently on a voyage from Liverpool 26.11.42 to St Helena, Durban and Sydney NSW, with 378 passengers including troops and 12362 tons of government stores and general cargo, dispersed from convoy ON 149 comprising 50 ships. The Master, Capt Herbert Charles Elford, crew of 295 and 377 passengers including troops were lost. The sole survivor, Sapper Eric Munday, Royal Engineers, was rescued by U-515, taken prisoner, landed at Lorient 6.1.43 and was then taken to Stalag B prisoner-of-war camp in Upper Silesia.

**MOWT**

**EMPIRE TRADER** ex-*TAINUI* • GRT 9990 • Built 1908
21.2.43: Torpedoed and damaged by German submarine U-92 (Oelrich), part of the 'Knappen' (Shieldbearer) patrol group of four U-boats, in the Atlantic N of the Azores, in position 48.25N 30.10W while on a voyage from Newport, Mon. and Belfast Lough to New York, with a cargo of 985 tons of chemicals, a straggler from convoy ON 166 comprising 48 ships. She was later sunk by one of her escort, RCN corvette *DAUPHIN* 925/40 (K.157) Lt-Cdr R.A.S. MacNeil), on 22.2.43 in the Atlantic NW of the Azores, in position 48.27N 29.47W. The Master, Capt Eric Thomas Baker, crew of 89 and 16 gunners were rescued by rescue ship *STOCKPORT* 1683/11 (Capt Thomas Ernest Fea OBE), transferred to HMCS *DAUPHIN* and landed at St John's, Newfoundland. U-92, commanded by Kapitänleutnant Wilhelm Brauel, was damaged beyond repair by aircraft of No. 6 and No. 8 Groups of RAF Bomber Command at Bergen on 4.10.44 and scrapped in 1945.

## SMITH HOGG & CO. LTD – WEST HARTLEPOOL

*ARKLESIDE* • GRT 1567 • Built 1924
16.9.39: Torpedoed and sunk by German submarine U–33 (v. Dresky), in the Atlantic 150 miles SW of Land's End, in position 48.00N 09.30W while sailing independently on a voyage from the Tyne to Gibraltar, with a cargo of 2500 tons of coal and coke. The Master, Capt Robert William Edmondson, and crew were rescued by two French fishing smacks and landed at Concarneau, 60 miles S of Ushant. U–33, commanded by Kapitänleutnant Hans-Wilhelm von Dresky, was sunk on 12.2.40 in the North Channel N of Corsewall Point, in position 55.25N 05.07W by HM minesweeper *GLEANER* 835/37 (N.83) (Lt-Cdr Hugh P. Price). The U-boat commander and 22 crew were lost. 1 officer and 4 crew were taken prisoner by HMS *GLEANER,* 2 crew by HM destroyer *KINGSTON* 1690/39 (F.64) (Lt-Cdr P. Somerville), 1 officer by trawler *FLORADORA* (GY 317) of Fleetwood (Skipper John Farquhar) was landed at Lamlash, Firth of Clyde. 2 officers and 7 crew by trawler *BOHEMIAN GIRL,* transferred to HMS *GLEANER* and landed at Greenock.

*MAGDALENA* • GRT 3118 • Built 1923
18.9.40: Torpedoed and sunk by German submarine U–48 (Bleichrodt), in the Atlantic S of Iceland, in position 57.20N 20.16W while on a voyage from St John's, Newfoundland to Holyhead and Liverpool via Sydney CB, with a cargo of 4600 tons of iron ore, part of convoy SC 3 comprising 47 ships. The Master, Capt Frederick Allen, crew of 29 and 1 gunner were lost.

## MOWT

*EMPIRE WAGTAIL* ex-*POINT LOBOS* ex-*OSSINING* • GRT 4893 • Built 1919
28.12.42: Torpedoed and sunk by German submarine U–260 (Purkhold), part of the 'Spitz' (Sharp) patrol group of ten U-boats, in the Atlantic about 900 miles W of Cape Finisterre, in position 43.17N 27.22W while on a voyage from Cardiff and Belfast Lough to Boston, Mass. via Halifax NS, with a cargo of 3857 tons of coal, part of convoy ONS 154 comprising 45 ships. The Master, Capt Gabriel Almond, 31 crew and 7 gunners were lost. U–260, commanded by Oberleutnant zur See Klaus Becker, was lost on 12.3.45 when U–260 hit a mine in the Atlantic W of Galley Head, Co. Cork, in position 51.15N 09.05W. The U-boat commander and crew of 48 landed in dinghies near Galley Head and were interned by the Irish authorities.

## SMITH, SIR WILLIAM REARDON & SONS, LIMITED – CARDIFF
**Leeds Shipping Co. Ltd**

*BRADFYNE* • GRT 4740 • Built 1928
23.11.40: Torpedoed and sunk by German submarine U–100 (Schepke), in the Atlantic SE of Rockall, in position 55.04N 12.15W while on a voyage from Montreal to Belfast via Sydney CB 9.11.40, with a cargo of 7900 tons of grain, part of convoy SC 11 comprising 33 ships. The Master, Capt Robert Greville Vanner, and 38 crew were lost. 4 crew were rescued by Norwegian ship *NORSKE KING* 5701/20 and landed at Belfast.

## Reardon Smith Line Ltd

*VANCOUVER CITY* • GRT 4739 • Built 1929
14.9.39: Torpedoed and sunk by German submarine U–28 (Kuhnke), in the Atlantic 75 miles WSW of Milford Haven, in position 51.23N 07.03W while sailing independently on a voyage from Suva, Fiji to the UK, with a cargo of sugar. The Master, Capt Hugh Charles Egerton, and 29 crew were rescued by Dutch motor tanker *MAMURA* 8245/32 and landed at Liverpool. 3 crew were lost.

*EDGEHILL* ex-*WILLAMETTE VALLEY* ex-*WEST LYNN* • GRT 4702 • Built 1928
29.6.40: Torpedoed and sunk by German submarine U–51 (Knorr), part of the 'Prien' (named after a U-boat commander) patrol group of six U-boats, in the Atlantic 240 miles SW of Fastnet. She was lost while on Admiralty service employed as a Special Service Ship (X.39).

*JERSEY CITY* • GRT 6322 • Built 1920
31.7.40: Torpedoed and sunk by German submarine U–99 (Kretschmer), in the Atlantic 70 miles NW of Tory Island, in position 55.47N 09.18W while on a voyage from Newport Mon. to Baltimore, in ballast, part of convoy OB 191 comprising 29 ships. The Master, Capt Frank Jameson Stirling, and 42 crew were rescued by British ship *GLOUCESTER CITY* 3071/19, transferred to HM destroyer *WALKER* 1120/17 (D.27) (Lt-Cdr A.A. Tait) and landed at Liverpool. 2 crew were lost.

*VICTORIA CITY* • GRT 4739 • Built 1929
2.12.40: Torpedoed and sunk by German submarine U–140 (Hinsch), in the Atlantic N of Ireland while on a voyage from New York to London via Halifax NS, with a cargo of steel, a straggler from convoy HX 90 comprising 32 ships. The Master, Capt Alfred Longstaff, and crew of 42 were lost.

*SACRAMENTO VALLEY* ex-*SKEGNESS* • GRT 4573 • Built 1924
6.6.41: Torpedoed and sunk by German submarine U–106 (Oesten), in the Atlantic W of the Cape Verde Islands, in position 17.10N 30.10W while sailing independently on a voyage from Cardiff to Pernambuco, with a cargo of 6843 tons of coal, dispersed on 27.5.41 in position 53.00N 29.30W from convoy OB 324 comprising 35 ships. The Master. Capt Harold L. Sharp, and 38 survivors were rescued by British ship *CAITHNESS* 4970/35 and landed at Freetown 14.6.41; 7 survivors were rescued on 24.6.41 by US tanker *STANVAC CAPE TOWN* 10169/41 and landed at Aruba 3.7.41. 3 crew were lost. The survivors that landed at Freetown were brought back to the UK by Union Castle liner *LLANSTEPHEN CASTLE* 11348/14 and landed at Greenock 22.7.41, British ship *MODESTA* 3830/17 and Canadian Pacific liner *EMPRESS OF AUSTRALIA* 19379/24; the former landed at Liverpool 28.7.41 and the latter 7.8.41. Kapitänleutnant Jürgen Oesten was awarded the Knight's Cross (26.3.41).

*BRADFORD CITY* • GRT 4953 • Built 1936
1.11.41: Torpedoed and sunk by German submarine U–68 (Merten), in the South Atlantic 300 miles W of Walvis Bay, South West Africa, in position 22.59S 09.49E while sailing independently on a voyage from Port Louis, Mauritius to the UK via Cape Town and

Freetown, with a cargo of 9500 tons of sugar and rum. The Master, Capt Henry Paul, crew of 36 and 8 gunners landed near Walvis Bay and were rescued by South African troops.

**BARRDALE** • GRT 5072 • Built 1925
17.5.42: Torpedoed and sunk by German submarine U-156 (Hartenstein), in the Atlantic E of Martinique, in position 15.15N 52.27W while sailing independently on a voyage from New York 9.5.42 to Basrah and Abadan via Cape Town, with 9824 tons of government and general cargo. The Master, Capt Frank Jameson Stirling, 44 crew and 7 gunners were rescued by Argentinian ship *RIO IGUAZI* 3177/28 and landed at Pernambuco. 1 gunner was lost.

**QUEBEC CITY** • GRT 4745 • Built 1927
19.9.42: Torpedoed and sunk by gunfire by German submarine U-156 (Hartenstein), in the South Atlantic NNW of the Ascension Island, in position 02.12S 17.36W while sailing independently on a voyage from Alexandria and Cape Town 3.9.42 to the UK via Freetown, with 6600 tons of general cargo and cotton. The Master, Capt William Caradoc Thomas, 37 crew and 3 gunners were rescued by HM destroyer *DECOY* 1375/32 (H.75) (Lt G.I.M. Balfour) and landed at Freetown. 5 crew were lost. Korvettenkapitän Werner Hartenstein (Knight's Cross 17.9.42) and crew of 52 were lost on 8.3.43 when U-156 was sunk in the Atlantic about 380 miles ENE of Trinidad, in position 12.38N 54.39W by Catalina 'P', pilot Lt John D. Dryden of US Navy Bombing Squadron VP-53 based at Chaguaramas Naval Station, Trinidad.

**BARRWHIN** • GRT 4998 • Built 1929
29.10.42: Torpedoed and sunk by German submarine U-436 (Seibicke), part of the 'Puma' patrol group of thirteen U-boats, in the Atlantic S of Iceland, in position 55.02N 22.45W while on a voyage from Halifax NS to London, with 60 survivors from British ship *ABOSSO* 11330/35 and Norwegian whaling factory *KOSMOS III* 16966/31 and a cargo of 8200 tons of grain and military stores, part of convoy HX 212 comprising 45 ships. The Master, Capt Thomas Sydney Dixon, 41 crew and 48 survivors were rescued by RCN corvette *KENOGAMI* 925/40 (K.125) (Lt P.J.B. Cook) and landed at Londonderry. 12 crew and 12 survivors were lost.

**QUEEN CITY** ex-*CRAGNESS* • GRT 4809 • Built 1924
21.12.42: Torpedoed and sunk by gunfire by Italian submarine *ENRICO TAZZOLI* (di Cossato), in the South Atlantic E of Para, in position 00.49S 41.34W while sailing independently on a voyage from Bombay to the UK via Cape Town 1.12.42 and Trinidad, with 7414 tons of general cargo including rubber, jute and hemp. The Master, Capt George Hornsby, 33 crew and 6 gunners landed at Maranhão near St Luiz, Brazil. 5 crew were lost and 1 crew taken prisoner. Lt-Cdr Carlo Fecia di Cossato and crew were lost on 16.5.43 when the *ENRICO TAZZOLI* was sunk in the Bay of Biscay W of La Pallice, in position 45.57N 11.40W by Halifax 'R', pilot F/O Anthony J.W. Birch of No. 58 Squadron RAF, based at St Eval, part of 19 Group.

**FRESNO CITY** • GRT 7261 • Built 1942
12.4.43: Torpedoed and damaged by German submarine U-563 (v. Hartmann), sunk by a *coup de grâce* by the German submarine U-706 (v. Zitzewitz), part of the 'Lerche' (Lark) patrol group of ten U-boats, in the Atlantic SE of Cape Farewell, in position 54.15N 30.00W while on a

voyage from Bombay to Liverpool via Cristobal and New York 1.4.43, with a cargo of 3000 tons of manganese ore and 5965 tons of general plus mail, part of convoy HX 232 comprising 47 ships. The Master, Capt Randolph Alfred Lawson, crew of 36 and 8 gunners were rescued by HM corvette *AZALEA* 925/40 (K.25) (Lt G.C. Geddes) and landed at Gourock. U-706, commanded by Kapitänleutnant Alexander von Zitzewitz, was sunk on 2.8.43 in the Atlantic 180 miles NW of Cape Ortegal, in position 46.15N 10.25W by Handley Page Hampden bomber 'A', pilot S/Ldr Charles G. Ruttan of No. 415 'Swordfish' Squadron RCAF, based at Tain, Ross & Cromarty and Liberator T/4, pilot Capt Joseph L. Hamilton of 4th Squadron, 479th Antisubmarine Group, USAAF, based at St Eval. The U-boat commander and 41 crew were lost. 4 crew were taken prisoner and landed at Plymouth by HM frigate *WAVENEY* 1370/42 (K.248) (Lt-Cdr A.E. Wilmott DSC), part of the 40th Support Group.

**VERNON CITY** • GRT 4748 • Built 1929
28.6.43: Torpedoed and sunk by German submarine U-172 (Emmermann), in the South Atlantic SSE of St Paul Rocks, in position 04.30S 27.20W while sailing independently on a voyage from the Tyne and Oban 4.6.43 to Montevideo, with a cargo of 4000 tons of coal and 3000 tons of coke, dispersed on 20.6.43 from convoy KMS 16/OS 49 comprising 76 ships. The Master, Capt Malcolm Douglas Loutit, crew of 43 and 8 gunners were rescued by Brazilian coastal tanker *AURORA M* 423/21 and landed at Recife 4.7.43.

**CORNISH CITY** • GRT 4952 • Built 1937
29.7.43: Torpedoed and sunk by German submarine U-177 (Gysae), in the Indian Ocean SE of Madagascar, in position 27.40S 52.15E while on a voyage from Lourenco Marques and Durban 22.7.43 to Aden and Suez, with a cargo of 9600 tons of coal. The Master, Capt Henry Thomas Isaac, 31 crew and 5 gunners were lost. 5 crew and 1 gunner were rescued by RAN destroyer *NIZAM* 1960/40 (G.38) (Cdr C.H. Brooks) and landed at Port Louis, Mauritius. Kapitänleutnant Robert Gysae was awarded the Knight's Cross (31.12.41; Oak Leaves 31.5.43). U-177, commanded by Kapitänleutnant Heinz Buchholz, was sunk on 6.2.44 in the South Atlantic 570 miles WNW of Ascension, in position 10.35S 23.15W by Liberator B-3, pilot Lt C.I. Pinnell of US Navy Bombing Squadron VB-107 based at Ascension. The U-boat commander and 49 crew were lost. 13 crew were taken prisoner by US light cruiser *OMAHA* 7050/20 (CL.4).

## MOWT

**EMPIRE TOUCAN** ex-*FREEPORT SULPHUR No. 5* • GRT 4421 • Built 1920
29.6.40: Torpedoed and sunk by gunfire by German submarine U-47 (Prien), in the Atlantic 190 miles SW of Fastnet, in position 49.20N 13.52W while sailing independently on a voyage from Garston to Port Sulphur, Louisiana, in ballast. The Master, Capt Hywel Tudor Thomas, and 30 crew were rescued by HM destroyer *HURRICANE* 1340/39 (H.06) (Lt-Cdr H.C. Simms) ex-Brazilian *JAPARUA* and landed at Plymouth. 3 crew were lost.

**EMPIRE JAGUAR** ex-*EASTERN GLADE* • GRT 5186 • Built 1919
9.12.40: Torpedoed and sunk by German submarine U-103 (Schütze), in the Atlantic 296 miles 248° from Slyne Head, in position 51.34N 17.35W while on a voyage from Cardiff to Philadelphia, in ballast, a straggler from convoy OB 252 comprising 44 ships. The Master, Capt Hywel Tudor Thomas, and crew of 36 were lost.

***EMPIRE CARIBOU*** ex–*DEFACTO* ex–*NORTHERN STAR* ex–*WATERBURY*
GRT 4861 • Built 1919
10.5.41: Torpedoed and sunk by German submarine U–556 (Wohlfarth), in the Atlantic 465 miles SW of Reykjanes, in position 59.28N 35.44W while on a voyage from London and Loch Ewe to Boston, Mass, with a cargo of 2020 tons of chalk, part of convoy OB 318 comprising 38 ships. The Master, Capt Bernard Edwin Duffield, 31 crew and 2 gunners were lost. 9 crew and 2 gunners were rescued by HM destroyer *MALCOLM* 1804/19 (D.19) (Cdr C.D. Howard-Johnston), landed at Reykjavik and brought to Greenock by HM destroyer *SCIMITAR* 905/18 (H.21) (Lt R.D. Frank).

***FORT MUMFORD*** • GRT 7132 • Built 1942
20.3.43: Torpedoed and sunk by Japanese submarine I–27 (Fukumura), in the Indian Ocean about 500 miles NW of Ceylon, in position 10.00N 71.00E while on her maiden voyage from Vancouver BC and Lyttelton, New Zealand to Suez and Alexandria via Colombo and Aden, with 6649 tons of military stores. The Master, Capt John Henry Reardon Smith OBE, crew of 45 and 4 gunners were lost. The sole survivor, Seaman Gunner H. Bailey, was rescued by an Arab dhow and landed at Mikindani, Tanganyika. Capt J.H.R. Smith was awarded the Lloyd's War Medal for bravery when in command of the *BOTAVON* 5848/12; she was damaged on 2.5.42 by German aircraft while on a voyage from Middlesbrough to Murmansk via Reykjavik, with a cargo of government stores, part of convoy PQ 15 comprising 26 ships. The damaged *BOTAVON* was sunk by HM destroyer *BADSWORTH* 1050/41 (L.03) (Lt G.T.S. Gray) on 3.5.42 in the Barents Sea NE of North Cape, in position 73.00N 20.22E.

## SOCONY VACUUM TRANSPORTATION CO. LTD – MONTREAL

***COIMBRA*** (tanker) • GRT 6768 • Built 1937
15.1.42: Torpedoed and sunk by German submarine U–123 (Hardegen), part of 'Operation Paukenschlag' (Drumbeat), the first wave of five U-boats, in the Atlantic 100 miles E of Long Island, in position 40.25N 72.21W while sailing independently on a voyage from New York to the UK, with a cargo of 9000 tons of lubricating oil. The Master, Capt John Patrick Barnard, 29 crew and 6 gunners were lost. 2 crew were rescued by US destroyer *ROWAN* 1500/38 (DD.405) and landed at Argentia, Newfoundland, and 8 crew by a US destroyer landed at St John's, Newfoundland.

***WINAMAC*** ex–*PULPIT POINT* (tanker) • GRT 8621 • Built 1926
31.8.42: Torpedoed and sunk by German submarine U–66 (Markworth), in the Atlantic 390 miles E of Trinidad, in position 10.36N 54.34W while sailing independently on a voyage from Trinidad 28.8.42 to Gibraltar, with a cargo of 12500 tons of fuel oil, dispersed from convoy T 3. The Master, Capt Edgar Harrison, 26 crew and 3 gunners were lost. 21 crew and 3 gunners were rescued by British ship *EMPIRE LUGARD* 7241/41 and landed at Trinidad.

## MOWT

***EOCENE*** ex–*SCHULAU* ex–*VACOIL* ex–*FORT McHENRY* (tanker) • GRT 4216 • Built 1922
20.5.42: Torpedoed and sunk by German submarine U–431 (Dommes), in the Mediterranean near Sollum, in position 31.56N 25.14E while on a voyage from Alexandria

18.5.42 to Tobruk, with 2 army engineers and a cargo of 1980 tons of benzine and 3700 tons of water, part of convoy AT 46 comprising 5 ships. The Master, Capt H.W. Wilcox, crew of 34, 6 gunners and army engineers were rescued by HM whaler *COCKER* ex-*KOS XIX* 303/39 and landed at Tobruk.

## SOUTER, W.A. & COMPANY – NEWCASTLE UPON TYNE

*NEPTUNIAN* • GRT 5155 • Built 1925
7.9.40: Torpedoed and sunk by German submarine U-47 (Prien), in the Atlantic NW of Rockall, in position 58.27N 17.17W while on a voyage from Santiago to Liverpool via Sydney CB 25.8.40, with a cargo of sugar, part of convoy SC 2 comprising 53 ships. The Master, Capt Alexander Thomas Campbell, and 35 crew were lost.

### Hebburn SS Co. Ltd

*HYLTON* • GRT 5197 • Built 1937
29.3.41: Torpedoed and sunk by German submarine U-48 (Schultze), in the North Atlantic 600 miles W of Cape Wrath in position 60.20N 18.10W while on a voyage from Vancouver BC to the Tyne via Panama and Halifax NS, with a cargo of 6900 tons of lumber and 1500 tons of wheat, part of convoy HX 115 comprising 28 ships. The Master, Capt Watson Edward O'Connell, Commodore Admiral Sir C.G. Ramsey KCB RN, crew of 34, 2 gunners, and 6 naval staff were rescued by HM corvette *DIANELLA* 925/40 (K.07) (Lt J.G. Rankin) and landed at Londonderry.

### Sheaf Steam Shipping Co. Ltd

*SHEAF MEAD* ex-*GRETASTON* • GRT 5008 • Built 1924
27.5.40: Torpedoed and sunk by German submarine U-37 (Oehrn), in the Atlantic about 180 miles from Cape Finisterre, in position 43.48N 12.32W while sailing independently on a voyage from Swansea to Philadelphia, in ballast. The Master, Capt Alexander Henderson Still, 30 crew and 1 gunner were lost. 5 crew were rescued by Greek ship *FRANGOULA B GOULANDRIS* 6701/18 and landed at Queenstown (Cork) 31.5.40.

*SHEAF MOUNT* ex-*LUCISTON* • GRT 5017 • Built 1924
25.8.42: Torpedoed and sunk by German submarine U-605 (Schütze), part of the 'Lohs' patrol group of sixteen U-boats, in the Atlantic SE of Cape Farewell, in position 48.55N 35.10W while on a voyage from Swansea and Milford Haven to Botwood, Newfoundland in ballast, part of convoy ONS 122 comprising 36 ships. The Master, Capt Ralph Sydney De Gruchy, 27 crew and 3 gunners were lost. 21 crew and 6 gunners were rescued by rescue ship *STOCKPORT* 1637/11 (Capt Thomas Ernest Fea OBE) and landed at Halifax NS 1.9.42. Kapitänleutnant Herbert Viktor Schutze (Knight's Cross awarded 18.12.40; Oak Leaves 14.7.41) and crew of 45 were lost on 14.11.42 when U-605 was sunk in the Mediterranean 40 miles NW of Cap Bougaroni, Algeria, in position 36.20N 01.01W by Hudson 'B' FH332, pilot P/O John W. Barling of No. 233 Squadron RAF, based at Gibraltar. The pilot was awarded the DFC.

## MOWT

***EMPIRE OCELOT*** ex-*SAN MARCOS* ex-*MYRTLE* ex-*WEST JENA* • GRT 5758 • Built 1919
28.9.40: Torpedoed and sunk by gunfire by German submarine U-32 (Jenisch), in the Atlantic
SW of Rockall, in position 54.37N 21.30W while sailing independently from Liverpool to
Philadelphia and Baltimore, in ballast, dispersed from convoy OB 218 comprising 25 ships. The
Master, Capt Peter Bonar, and 31 crew were rescued by HM destroyer *HAVELOCK* 1340/39
(H.88) (Capt E.B.K. Stevens DSC) and landed at Liverpool. 2 crew were lost.

***EMPIRE SPRINGBUCK*** ex-*SAN ANGELO* ex-*WILLANGLO* ex-*WESTMEAD* ordered as *WAR DIDO*
GRT 5991 • Built 1918
9.9.41: Torpedoed and sunk by German submarine U-81 (Guggenberger), in the North
Atlantic SE of Cape Farewell, in position 61.38N 40.40W, while on a voyage from Boca
Grande, Cuba to Leith and London via Sydney CB 30.8.41, with a cargo of explosives and
steel, a straggler from convoy SC 42 comprising 65 ships. The Master, Capt Walter
O'Connell, and crew of 41 were lost.

***EMPIRE GEMSBUCK*** ex-*SAN FELIPE* ex-*WILLWELLO* ex-*WESTERN GLENA* ordered as *WAR JUNO*
GRT 5959 • Built 1919
3.11.41: Torpedoed and sunk by German submarine U-203 (Mützelburg), part of the
'Raubritter' (Robber Knight) patrol group of fourteen U-boats, in the Atlantic NE of Cape
Charles, Labrador, in position 52.18N 53.05W while on a voyage from Philadelphia to
Londonderry via Sydney CB 29.10.41, with 6200 tons of general cargo including machinery,
part of convoy SC 52 comprising 35 ships. The Master, Capt Willian Stewart Anderson, crew
of 36 and 6 gunners were rescued by RCN corvette *BUCTOUCHE* 925/40 (K.179) (Lt G.N.
Downey) and landed at St John's, Newfoundland 6.11.41.

## SOUTH AFRICAN RAILWAYS & HARBOURS ADMINISTRATION –
## CAPE TOWN, SOUTH AFRICA

***ALOE*** • GRT 5047 • Built 1925
5.4.43: Torpedoed and sunk by German submarine U-182 (Clausen), in the Indian Ocean
420 miles SE of Durban, in position 32.37S 37.50E while sailing independently from
Bunbury, Western Australia, to Durban, with a cargo of 5000 tons of wheat, 1500 tons of
timber and 320 tons of lead also mail. The Master, Capt Angus Maclennan, was taken
prisoner and lost. 44 crew and 2 gunners were rescued by US liberty ship *ALEXANDER
RAMSEY* 7181/42 and landed at Cape Town. Korvettenkapitän Nicolaus Clausen (Knight's
Cross 13.3.42) and crew of 60 were lost on 16.5.43 when U-182 was sunk in the Atlantic NE
of Madeira, in position 33.55N 20.35W, after encountering convoy UGS 8 comprising 80
ships, by US destroyer *MACKENZIE* 1620/42 (DD-614) (Cdr D.B. Miller).

## SOUTH AMERICAN SAINT LINE – CARDIFF

***ST ELWYN*** • GRT 4940 • Built 1938
28.11.40: Torpedoed and sunk by German submarine U-103 (Schütze), in the Atlantic about
500 miles E of Bishop Rock, in position 55.30N 19.30W while on a voyage from Hull to

Santos, with a cargo of coal, part of convoy OB 249 comprising 54 ships. The Master, Capt Edward Thomas Alexander Daniells DSC and bar, and 23 crew were lost. 16 crew were rescued by British ship *LEEDS CITY* 4758/27 and landed at Gourock.

**SHAKESPEAR** • GRT 5029 • Built 1926
5.1.41: Sunk by gunfire by Italian submarine *COMDTE. ALFREDO CAPPELLINI* (Todaro), in the Atlantic 180 miles NE of Sal Island, Cape Verde Islands, in position 18.05N 21.10W while sailing independently on a voyage from Barry to Suez and Alexandria, with a cargo of 5300 tons of coal and 700 tons of military stores, dispersed from convoy OB 262 comprising 37 ships. The Master, Capt Charles Albert Bailey, and 22 crew landed at Sal Island and were brought to St Vincent, Cape Verde Islands, by Portuguese sloop *GONCALVES ZARRO* 1788/35. 17 crew and 2 gunners were lost.

**RIPLEY** • GRT 4997 • Built 1936
12.12.42: Torpedoed and sunk by German submarine U-161 (Achilles), in the South Atlantic SW of St Paul Rocks, in position 00.35S 32.17W while sailing independently on a voyage from Forcados, Duala and Takoradi 1.12.42 to the UK via Trinidad, with a cargo of 9000 tons of palm oil, mahogany and rubber. The Master, Capt Sydney Beeston Davis, crew of 33 and 7 gunners were rescued: 29 survivors landed at Cape Branco, Brazil, and the Chief Officer and 11 survivors were rescued by British ship *ROYAL STAR* 7900/19 and landed at Buenos Aires 23.12.42.

**ORMINSTER** ex-*CLAN KEITH* ex-*HILARIUS* ex-*CLAN KEITH* ex-*ETONIAN*
GRT 5712 • Built 1914
25.8.44: Torpedoed and sunk by German submarine U-480 (Förster), in the English Channel about 35 miles NW of Cap d'Antifer, in position 50.09N 00.44W while on a voyage from Juno Beach, Normandy to Portsmouth, in ballast, a straggler from coastal convoy FTM 1774. The Master, Capt Harold Gittins, 43 crew, 14 gunners and 1 army storekeeper were rescued by HM corvette *PENNYWORT* 925/41 (K.111) (Lt W.P. Hart) and HM trawler *DAMSAY* 530/42 (T.208) and landed at Portsmouth. 1 crew and 3 gunners were lost.

**St Quentin Shipping Co. Ltd**

**ST HELENA** • GRT 4313 • Built 1936
12.4.41: Torpedoed and sunk by German submarine U-124 (Schulz), in the Atlantic about 100 miles SW of Freetown, in position 07.50N 14.00W while sailing independently on a voyage from Rio Grande do Sul, Santos and Bahia to Hull via Freetown, with 3 passengers and a cargo of 7600 tons of grain and general including canned meat, cotton, rice and wet hides. The Master, Capt Percy John Reavley, crew of 35, 2 gunners and passengers were rescued by HM destroyer *WISHART* 1350/19 (D.67) (Cdr E.T. Cooper) and landed at Freetown.

**ST LINDSAY** ex-*CANADIAN HIGHLANDER* • GRT 5370 • Built 1921
14.6.41: Torpedoed and sunk by German submarine U-751 (Bigalk), in the Atlantic SW of Iceland, in position 51.00N 30.00W while sailing independently on a voyage from the Clyde to Trinidad and Buenos Aires, with general cargo, dispersed from convoy OG 64 comprising 52 ships. The Master, Capt Oliver John S. Hill, and crew of 43 were lost.

*ST MARGARET* • GRT 4312 • Built 1936
27.2.43: Torpedoed and sunk by German submarine U-66 (Markworth), part of the 'Rochen' (Ray) patrol group of ten U-boats, in the Atlantic SE of Bermuda, in position 27.38N 43.23W while sailing independently on a voyage from Liverpool to Pernambuco and Buenos Aires, with 7 passengers and 6000 tons of general cargo including coal, dispersed from convoy ON 156 comprising 26 ships. The Master, Capt Daniel Sydney Davies, was taken prisoner, landed at Lorient 24.3.43 and taken to Milag Nord. 34 crew, 5 gunners and passengers were rescued by US destroyer *HOBSON* 1620/41 (DD.464) and landed at Bermuda 5.3.43. 3 crew were lost. Kapitänleutnant Friedrich Markworth was awarded the Knight's Cross (8.7.43).

*ST ESSYLT* • GRT 5634 • Built 1941
4.7.43: Torpedoed and sunk by German submarine U-375 (Koenenkamp), in the Mediterranean W of Algiers, in position 36.44N 01.31E while on government service on a voyage from the Clyde 24.6.43 to Sicily, with 322 military personnel and 900 tons of military stores, part of convoy KMS 18B comprising 20 ships. The Master, Capt Stephen Diggins, 53 crew, 24 gunners and 319 military personnel were rescued by HM corvettes *HONEYSUCKLE* 925/40 (K.27) (Lt H.H.D. MacKillican DSC), and *RHODODENDRON* 925/40 (K.78) (Lt O.B. Medley) and HM tug *RESTIVE* 700/40 (W.39) (Lt D.M. Richards) and landed at Algiers. 1 crew and 1 military personnel were lost. Capt S. Diggins was awarded the Lloyd's War Medal for bravery at sea.

**Triton Steamship Co. Ltd**

*ST USK* ex-*NAILSEA BELLE* ex-*HELLENIC* • GRT 5472 • Built 1909
20.9.43: Torpedoed and sunk by German submarine U-161 (Achilles), in the South Atlantic NE of Martin Vaz Rocks, in position 16.30S 29.28W while sailing independently on a voyage from Rio Grande and Rio de Janeiro 15.9.43 to Hull via Freetown, with a cargo of 6883 tons of general including rice, tinned meat and cotton seed. The Master, Capt G.H. Moss, was taken prisoner. 43 crew and 7 gunners were rescued by Spanish ship *ALBAREDA* 3925/03 and landed at Rio de Janeiro 28.9.43. Korvettenkapitän Albrecht Achilles (Knight's Cross awarded 16.1.43), crew of 52 and Capt G.H. Moss were lost when U-161 was sunk on 27.9.43 in the South Atlantic 175 miles E by N of Bahia, in position 12.30S 35.35W by Mariner P-2, pilot Lt Harry B. Patterson of US Navy Patrol Squadron VP-74 based at Aratu, Brazil.

**MOWT**

*EMPIRE SURF* • GRT 6640 • Built 1941
14.1.42: Torpedoed and sunk by German submarine U-43 (Lüth), in the Atlantic S of Iceland, in position 58.42N 19.16W while on a voyage from Manchester to Jacksonville, Florida, in ballast, part of convoy ON 55 comprising 28 ships. The Master, Capt Albert Sandham, 37 crew and 9 gunners were lost. 6 crew were rescued by HM corvette *ALISMA* 925/40 (K.185) (Lt-Cdr M.G. Rose) and landed at Londonderry. Oberleutnant zur See Hans-Joachim Schwantke and crew of 54 were lost when U-43 was sunk on 30.7.43 in the Atlantic 315 miles SW by S of Flores, Azores, in position 34.57N 35.11W by an Avenger,

pilot Lt R.F. Richmond and a Wildcat, pilot Lt Edward van Vranken of US Navy Composite Squadron VC-29 from US escort carrier *SANTEE* 11400/42 (CVE-29) of the USN Task Group 21.11 commanded by Capt H.F. Fick.

## SOUTHERN RAILWAY – LONDON

*MAID OF ORLEANS* • GRT 2348 • Built 1918
28.6.44: Torpedoed and sunk by German submarine U-988 (Dobberstein), in the English Channel SE of St Catherine's Point, Isle of Wight, in position 50.06N 00.41W while on government service on a voyage from the Normandy beaches to Portsmouth, part of coastal convoy FXP 18. The Master, Capt Herbert L. Payne, 72 crew, 18 gunners and 2 Observer Corps personnel were rescued by HM frigate *HOTHAM* 1300/43 (K.583) (Lt-Cdr S. Ayles), HM destroyer *EGLINTON* 907/39 (Lt-Cdr F.M. Graves) and British tug *EMPIRE ROGER* 235/44 and landed at Portsmouth. 5 crew were lost.

## STANDARD TRANSPORTATION CO. LTD – HONG KONG

*VACLITE* (tanker) • GRT 5026 • Built 1928
30.1.40: Torpedoed and sunk by German submarine U-55 (Heidel), in the Atlantic 50 miles SW of the Scilly Isles, in position 49.20N 07.04W while on a voyage from London to New York, in ballast, part of convoy OA 80G comprising 27 ships. The Master, Capt George Legg, and 35 crew were rescued by Italian ship *POLLENZO* 6470/20 and landed at Barry. U-55, commanded by Kapitänleutnant Werner Heidel, was sunk on the same day in the Atlantic 120 miles W of Ushant, in position 48.37N 07.46W by the convoy's escorts HM sloop *FOWEY* 1105/30 (L.15) (Cdr H.B. Ellison), HM destroyer *WHITSHED* 1325/19 (F.A7) (Cdr E.R. Condor), French destroyer *VALMY* 2436/30 and Sunderland 'Y' N9025, pilot F/Lt Edward J. Brooks of No. 228 Squadron RAF, based at Pembroke Dock, part of 15 Group. The U-boat commander was lost. 11 crew were taken prisoner by HMS *FOWEY* and 30 by HMS *WHITSHED*. This was the first air/sea success by RAF Coastal Command and the Royal Navy.

*YARRAVILLE* (tanker) • GRT 8627 • Built 1928
21.6.40: Torpedoed and sunk by German submarine U-43 (Ambrosius), in the Atlantic SW of Figueira da Foz, Portugal, in position 39.40N 11.34W while on a voyage from Bec d'Ambes to Casablanca and Beaumont, Texas, in ballast, part of the French convoy 65 X. The Master, Capt William Alexander Beveridge, and 44 crew were rescued by escort French trawler *MARIE GILBERTE* 286/19 and landed at Gibraltar. 5 crew were lost.

## STEPHENS, SUTTON LIMITED – NEWCASTLE UPON TYNE
### The Whalton Shipping Co. Ltd

*ROTHLEY* • GRT 4996 • Built 1936
19.10.42: Torpedoed and sunk by German submarine U-332 (Liebe), in the Atlantic 300 miles E of Barbados, in position 13.34N 54.34W while sailing independently on a voyage from Durban to New York via Trinidad, in ballast. The Master, Capt Cyril John Forster, and 40 crew landed at Aruba, NWI. 1 crew and 1 gunner were lost. Oberleutnant zur See Eberhard Huttemann and crew of 44 were lost on 29.4.43 in the Atlantic 110 miles NW of

Cape Ortegal, in position 45.08N 09.33W when U-332, part of the 'Drossel' (Thrush) patrol group of eleven U-boats, was sunk by Liberator 'D', pilot F/Lt A. Russell Laughland of No. 224 Squadron RAF, based at St Eval, part of 19 Group.

## STEPHENSON, CLARKE & CO. LTD – LONDON
## MOWT

*ASHMUN J. CLOUGH* • GRT 1791 • Built 1942
26.8.44: Torpedoed and sunk by German submarine U-989 (v. Roithberg), in the English Channel N of Cherbourg, in position 50.10N 01.41W while on government service on a voyage from Avonmouth and Barry to Utah beach, Normandy, with a cargo of 1200 tons of military stores, part of coastal convoy TBC 82 comprising 4 ships. The Master, Capt Edward Dent Hodge, 11 crew and 4 gunners were lost. 15 crew and 4 gunners were rescued by HM motor launch 450 65/43 (Sub-Lt R. Freeman), transferred to HM corvette *AZALEA* 925/40 (K.25) (Lt-Cdr G.C. Geddes) and landed at Cherbourg. Kapitänleutnant Hardo Rodler von Roithberg and crew of 47 were lost on 14.2.45 when U-989 was sunk in the North Sea 48 miles N of Unst, Shetland Islands, in position 61.36N 01.35W by HM frigates *BAYNTUN* 1085/42 (K.310) (Lt-Cdr L.P. Bourke), *BRAITHWAITE* 1085/43 (K.468) (Lt-Cdr E.M. MacKay), *LOCH ECK* 1435/44 (K.422) (Lt-Cdr N. McInnes) and *LOCH DUNVEGAN* 1435/44 (K.425) (Cdr F.E. Wheeler).

## STOCKWELL REES CO. LTD – SWANSEA
## Dillwyn SS Co. Ltd

*KELLWYN* ex-*MARIE LLEWELLYN* • GRT 1459 • Built 1920
27.7.41: Torpedoed and sunk by German submarine U-79 (Kaufmann), in the Atlantic about 350 miles WNW of Cape Finisterre, in position 43.00N 17.00W while on a voyage from the Tyne and Oban to Lisbon, with a cargo of 1100 tons of coke, part of convoy OG 69 comprising 27 ships. The Master, Capt Alexander McLean, 10 crew and 3 gunners were lost. 9 crew were rescued by HM trawler *ST NECTAN* 565/36 (Lt-Cdr H.B. Phillips RNR) and landed at Gibraltar 1.8.41. U-79, commanded by Kapitänleutnant Wolfgang Kaufmann, was sunk on 23.12.41 in the Mediterranean 30 miles NE of Bardia, in position 32.15N 25.19E by HM destroyers *HASTY* 1340/36 (H.24) (Lt-Cdr L.R.K. Tyrwitt) and *HOTSPUR* 1340/36 (H.01) (Lt P.M. Whatley). The U-boat commander and 43 crew were taken prisoner by HMS *HASTY* and HMS *HOTSPUR*.

## MOWT

*KATVALDIS* ex-*ODILE* ex-*HENRY W. BREYER* ex-*HALLFRIED* ex-*MAGDALENE* ex-*DUKE OF YORK* • GRT 3206 • Built 1907
25.8.42: Torpedoed and sunk by German submarine U-605 (Schütze), part of the 'Lohs' patrol group of sixteen U-boats, in the Atlantic SE of Cape Farewell, in position 48.55N 35.10W while on a voyage from Cardiff 12.8.42 and Milford Haven to Clarke City, Quebec via Sydney CB, in ballast, part of convoy ONS 122 comprising 36 ships. The Master, Capt Ints Lejnieks, 31 crew and 8 gunners were rescued by rescue ship *STOCKPORT* 1683/11 (Capt Thomas Ernest Fea OBE) and landed at Halifax, Nova Scotia 1.9.42. 3 crew were lost.

## STONE & ROLFE – LLANELLY
## MOWT

*SAMSO* • GRT 1494 • Built 1930
1.5.41: Torpedoed and sunk by German submarine U-103 (Schütze), in the Atlantic SW of Freetown, in position 08.35N 16.17W while on a voyage from Bathurst to Freetown, with a cargo of 1316 tons of groundnuts. The Master, Capt Hefarn Madsorn, and 18 crew landed at Los Island, French Guinea 3.5.41, were taken to Conakry and thence to Freetown 16.5.41. 1 crew was lost.

*DINARIC* ex-*COATSWORTH* • GRT 2555 • Built 1919
6.7.42: Torpedoed and damaged by German submarine U-132 (Vogelsang), in the St Lawrence River S of Clarke City, Quebec, in position 49.30N 66.30W, later sank on 9.7.42, in position 49.15N 66.43W while on a voyage from Rimouski 5.7.42 and Father Point, New Brunswick to the UK via Sydney CB, with a cargo of 957 standards of timber and steel, part of convoy QS 15 comprising 12 ships. The Master, Capt Marijan Zadrijevac, 27 crew and 6 gunners were rescued by RCN minesweeping sloop *DRUMMONDVILLE* 672/41 (J.253) (Lt James P. Fraser) and landed at Sydney CB. 4 crew were lost.

## STOTT, ARTHUR & COMPANY – NEWCASTLE UPON TYNE
## Novocastria Shipping Co. Ltd

*HOPECASTLE* • GRT 5178 • Built 1937
29.10.42: Torpedoed and damaged by German submarine U-203 (Kottmann), part of the 'Streitaxt' (Battleaxe) patrol group of eight U-boats, later given a *coup de grâce* on the same day by U-509 (Witte), part of the same patrol group, in the Atlantic NW of the Canary Islands, in position 31.39N 19.35W while on a voyage from Cochin to the Mersey via Freetown 16.10.41, with a cargo of 2500 tons of magnesite and ilmenite (black ore of titanium) and 3000 tons of general cargo including tea, a straggler from convoy SL 125 comprising 40 ships. The Master, Capt Dugald McGilp, and 20 survivors were rescued by British ship *MANO* 1415/25 and landed at Greenock 9.11.42. 19 survivors landed at Funchal. 3 crew and 2 gunners were lost.

## STOTT, MANN & FLEMING – NEWCASTLE UPON TYNE
## Clive Shipping Co. Ltd

*HOPETARN* • GRT 5231 • Built 1939
29.5.43: Torpedoed and sunk by German submarine U-198 (Hartmann), in the Indian Ocean about 450 miles E of Durban, in position 31.10S 39.20E while sailing independently on a voyage from Calcutta 7.5.43 and Colombo 16.5.43 to the UK via Durban and Table Bay, with 9000 tons of general cargo. The Master, Capt Stewart Wilson, 28 crew and 7 gunners were rescued on 31.5.43 by British India ship *NIRVANA* 6031/14 and landed at Durban 3.6.43. 6 crew and 1 gunner were lost. The 2nd Officer was taken prisoner, landed at Bordeaux 24.9.43 and taken to Milag Nord.

## MOWT

*EMPIRE LUGARD* • GRT 7241 • Built 1941
13.9.42: Torpedoed and sunk by German submarine U-558 (Krech), in the Caribbean Sea W of Grenada, in position 12.07N 63.32W while on a voyage from Trinidad 12.9.42 to St John,

New Brunswick, with a cargo of 8842 tons of bauxite, part of convoy TAG 5. The Master, Capt C.K. Nielsen, crew of 35, 10 gunners and 1 signalman were rescued by Norwegian tanker *VILJA* 6672/28 and landed at Port of Spain, Trinidad. U-558, commanded by Kapitänleutnant Gunther Krech (Knight's Cross 17.9.42), was sunk on 20.7.43 in the Atlantic 120 miles NW of Cape Ortegal, in position 45.10N 09.42W by Liberator 'F', pilot F/Lt Charles F. Gallmeir of the 19th Squadron, 479th Antisubmarine Group, USAAF, based at St Eval and Halifax 'E' DT642, pilot F/Lt Geoffrey A. Sawell of No. 58 Squadron RAF, based at St Eval, part of 19 Group. The RAF pilot was awarded the DFC. The U-boat commander and 4 crew were rescued after 5 days on a raft by RCN destroyer *ATHABASKAN* ex-HMCS *IROQUOIS* 1927/41 (G.07) (Lt J.B. Caldwell). 41 crew were lost.

## STRAITS STEAMSHIP CO. LTD – SINGAPORE

*KAMUNING* • GRT 2076 • Built 1916
14.2.42: Torpedoed and damaged by gunfire by Japanese submarine I-166 (Yoshitome), in the Indian Ocean E of Trincomalee, in position 08.35N 81.44E while sailing indpendently on a voyage from Rangoon 7.2.42 to Colombo and Singapore. Later sank in position 08.35N 81.26E while being towed to Trincomalee. The Master and 62 survivors were rescued by HM trawler *BALTA* 545/40 (T.50) (Lt H.P. Price DSO) and landed at Trincomalee. 6 crew were lost.

## STRANAGHAN, J.S. & CO. LTD – CARDIFF
## MOWT

*ASTRA II* ex-*FERM* ex-*SAPHIR* • GRT 2393 • Built 1920
29.8.40: Torpedoed and sunk by German submarine U-100 (Schepke), in the Atlantic 148 miles NW of Bloody Foreland, in position 56.09N 12.14W while on a voyage from the Tyne to Rimouski, New Brunswick, in ballast, part of convoy OA 204 comprising 43 ships. The Master, Capt Carl Niels Nielson, and 19 crew were rescued by HM minesweeping sloop *GLEANER* 835/37 (N.83) (Lt-Cdr H.P. Price DSO). 4 crew and 1 gunner were lost.

*EMPIRE STREAM* • GRT 2922 • Built 1941
25.9.41: Torpedoed and sunk by German submarine U-124 (Mohr), in the Atlantic NNE of the Azores, in position 46.03N 24.40W while on a voyage from Huelva to Dundee, with a cargo of 3730 tons of potash, part of convoy HG 73 comprising 25 ships. The Master, Capt Stanley Herbert Evans, 24 crew and 2 gunners were rescued by HM corvette *BEGONIA* 925/40 (K.66) (Lt-Cdr H.B. Phillips) and landed at Milford Haven. 4 crew, 2 gunners and 2 stowaways were lost.

*ROSENBORG* • GRT 1997 • Built 1914
24.4.43: Torpedoed and sunk by German submarine U-386 (Kandler), in the North Atlantic N of Rockall, in position 61.00N 15.00W while on a voyage from Reykjavik 22.4.43 to Belfast and Swansea, in ballast, with 2 passengers, a straggler from convoy RU 71 comprising 7 ships. The Master, Capt Peter Volmar Petersen, 21 crew, 4 gunners and passengers were lost. 2 crew were rescued by rescue ship *GOODWIN* 1570/17 (Capt George Lewis Campbell OBE) and landed at Clyde 28.4.43. U-386, commanded by Oberleutnant zur See Fritz

Albrecht, was sunk on 19.2.44 in the Atlantic 540 miles WSW of Cape Clear, in position 48.51N 22.41W by HM frigate *SPEY* 1370/41 (K.246) (Cdr H.G. Boys-Smith). The U-boat commander and 18 crew were taken prisoner by HMS *SPEY.* 33 crew were lost.

## STRICK, FRANK C. & CO. LTD – LONDON
### Cory & Strick (Steamers) Ltd

*BATNA* • GRT 4399 • Built 1928
13.5.42: Torpedoed and sunk by German submarine U-94 (Ites), part of the 'Hecht' (Pike) patrol group of six U-boats, in the Atlantic SE of Cape Farewell, in position 52.09N 33.56W while on a voyage from Newport, Mon. and Milford Haven 5.5.42 to Halifax NS, with a cargo of 4988 tons of coal, part of convoy ONS 92 comprising 41 ships. The Master, Capt Robert Maxwell Potts, 34 crew and 6 gunners were rescued by rescue ship *BURY* 1634/11 (Capt Lawrence Edwin Brown OBE) and landed at St John's, Newfoundland 16.5.42. 1 crew was lost.

*HAMLA* • GRT 4416 • Built 1929
23.8.42: Torpedoed and sunk by German submarine U-506 (Würdemann), in the South Atlantic SE of Fernando Noronha, Brazil, in position 04.00S 24.00W while sailing independently on a voyage from Rio de Janeiro to the UK via Trinidad and Freetown, with a cargo of manganese ore. The Master, Capt William Ashley Shute OBE, and crew of 37 were lost.

### La Tunisienne Steam Navigation Co. Ltd

*TAFNA* • GRT 4413 • Built 1930
24.10.39: Torpedoed and sunk by German submarine U-37 (Hartmann), in the Atlantic 84 miles W of Gibraltar, in position 35.44N 07.23W while sailing independently on a voyage from Benisaf, Algeria to London, with a cargo of 6900 tons of iron ore. The Master, Capt Royal Cecil Newlands, and 30 crew were rescued by HM destroyer leader *KEPPEL* 1750/20 (D.84) (Capt F.S.W. de Winton) and landed at Gibraltar. 2 crew were lost.

*MEDJERDA* • GRT 4380 • Built 1924
18.3.41: Torpedoed and sunk by German submarine U-105 (Schewe), in the Atlantic N of the Cape Verde Islands, in position 17.00N 21.00W while on a voyage from Pepel to Middlesbrough via Freetown 13.3.41 with a cargo of 6450 tons of iron ore, part of convoy SL 68 comprising 59 ships. The Master, Capt Charles Edward Banks, 50 crew and 2 gunners were rescued by HM corvette *MARGUERITE* 925/40 (K.54) (Lt-Cdr A.N. Blundell) and landed at Bathurst. 1 crew was lost.

*GUELMA* • GRT 4402 • Built 1928
17.7.41: Torpedoed and sunk by Italian submarine *ALESSANDRO MALASPINA* (Prini), in the Atlantic S of Madeira, in position 30.44N 17.33W while on a voyage from Madeira to Pepel, with a part cargo of 500 tons of onions, dispersed on 28.6.41 from convoy OB 337 comprising 51 ships. The Master, Capt Wilfred Gillespie Taylor, crew of 35 and 5 gunners were rescued by HM submarine *THUNDERBOLT* ex-HMS *THETIS* 1090/38 (11.T) (Lt-Cdr

C.B. Crouch DSO) and landed at Gibraltar. Lt Giuliano Prini and crew were lost on 21.9.41 when the *ALESSANDRO MALASPINA* was sunk in the Atlantic possibly by HM destroyer *VIMY* 1090/17 (D.33) ex-HMS *VANCOUVER* (Lt-Cdr H.G.D. de Chair).

## Strick Line (1923) Ltd

*ARMANISTAN* • GRT 6805 • Built 1937.
3.2.40: Torpedoed and sunk by German submarine U-25 (Schütze), in the Atlantic W of the River Tagus, Portugal, in position 38.25N 11.20W while on a voyage from Antwerp to Basrah, with 8300 tons of general cargo, including sugar, zinc, chemical products and iron rails, part of convoy OG 16 comprising 37 ships. The Master, Capt Charles Rolls Knight, and crew were rescued by Spanish ship *MONTE ABRIL* 2955/30 and landed at Tenerife.

*BALTISTAN* • GRT 6803 • Built 1937
27.2.41: Torpedoed and sunk by Italian submarine *MICHELE BIANCHI* (Giovannini), in the Atlantic W of Ireland, in position 51.52N 19.55W while on government service on a voyage from Ellesmere Port to Cape Town, with 8 passengers and 6200 tons of military stores, part of convoy OB 290 comprising 42 ships. The Master, Capt John Hobson Hedley, 13 crew and 4 passengers were rescued by HM destroyer *BRIGHTON* 1060/18 (I.08) (Cdr C.W.V.T.S. Lepper) ex-USN four-stack *COWELL* and landed at Plymouth. 47 crew and 4 passengers were lost. *MICHELE BIANCHI*, commanded by Lt-Cdr Giovanni Adalbert, was sunk on 7.8.41 in the Atlantic 220 miles SW of Cape St Vincent, in position 34.38N 13.04W by HM submarine *SEVERN* 1850/34 (N.57) (Lt-Cdr A.N.G. Campbell).

*TABARISTAN* ex-*FRANKENFELS* • GRT 6251 • Built 1914
29.5.41: Torpedoed and sunk by German submarine U-38 (Liebe), in the Atlantic SW of Freetown, in position 06.32N 15.23W while sailing independently on a voyage from Basrah and Cape Town to the UK via Freetown, with a cargo of 2200 tons of pig iron, 3950 tons of groundnuts and 800 tons of general including 560 tons of manganese ore. The Master, Capt Thomas Dunn, 35 crew and 3 gunners were rescued by HM trawlers *BENGALI* 455/37 (FY.165) (Skipper F.C. Butler) and *TURCOMAN* 455/37 (FY.130) (Lt R.L. Petty-Major) and landed at Freetown. 21 crew were lost.

*SHAHRISTAN* • GRT 6935 • Built 1938
30.7.41: Torpedoed and sunk by German submarine U-371 (Driver), in the Atlantic SE of the Azores, in position 35.19N 23.53W while on a voyage from London and the Clyde to Basrah, with 68 passengers, government stores and general cargo, part of convoy OG 69 comprising 27 ships. The Master, Capt Eric Henry Wilson, 38 crew and 26 passengers were lost. 33 survivors were rescued by Spanish tanker *CAMPECHE* 6382/34, 37 survivors rescued by HM corvette *SUNFLOWER* 925/40 (K.41) (Lt-Cdr J.T. Jones) were landed at Ponta Delgada, Azores; 6 survivors were rescued by HM armed merchant cruiser *DERBYSHIRE* 11660/35 (F.78) (Capt E.A.B. Stanley DSO MVO) and landed at Greenock.

*BALUCHISTAN* • GRT 6992 • Built 1940
8.3.42: Torpedoed and sunk by gunfire by German submarine U-68 (Merten), in the Atlantic 30 miles SW of Grand Cess, Liberia, in position 04.13N 08.32W while sailing independently

on a voyage from Basrah to the UK via Cape Town 25.2.42 and Freetown, with 5 passengers and 8000 tons of general cargo including dates. The Master, Capt Thomas Huntly Farrar, crew of 61, 4 gunners and 2 passengers landed near Cape Palmas, Liberia. 3 passengers were lost.

**REGISTAN** • GRT 6008 • Built 1930
29.9.42: Torpedoed and sunk by German submarine U-332 (Liebe), in the Atlantic 140 miles E of Barbados, in position 12.37N 57.10 W while sailing independently on a voyage from Basrah to Philadelpha via Cape Town 8.9.43 and Trinidad, with a part cargo of 1319 tons of general cargo. The Master, Capt Charles Spencer Bartlett, 34 crew and 3 gunners were rescued on 30.9.42 by Argentinian ship *RIO NEUQUEN* 5696/19 and landed at Pernambuco 11.10.42. 11 crew and 5 gunners were lost.

**BANDAR SHAHPOUR** ex-*ARABISTAN* • GRT 5236 • Built 1927
30.4.43: Torpedoed and sunk by German submarine U-515 (Henke), in the Atlantic 130 miles SW of Freetown, in position 07.15N 13.49W while on a voyage from Abadan, Mormugao and Takoradi 26.4.43 to the UK via Freetown, with 8 passengers and 6768 tons of general cargo including oil seeds, 3000 tons manganese ore, rubber and copra, part of convoy TS 37 comprising 19 ships. The Master, Capt Wilfred Allinson Chappell, 61 crew, 8 gunners and 7 passengers were rescued by HM trawler *BIRDLIP* 750/41 (T.218) (Lt E.M. Groom) and landed at Freetown. 1 passenger was lost.

## MOWT

**OCEAN SEAMAN** • GRT 7178 • Built 1942
15.3.43: Torpedoed and damaged by German submarine U-380 (Röther), in the Mediterranean 60 miles W of Algiers, in position 36.55N 01.59E while on a voyage from Philippeville and Algiers to Gibraltar and Liverpool, in ballast, part of convoy ET 14 comprising 20 ships. She was towed by US four-stack destroyer *PAUL JONES* 1190/20 (DD-230) to Algiers 16.3.43, subsequently beached and declared a CTL. The Master, Capt Edward Bacon, crew of 48 and 10 gunners were rescued by HM minesweeper No. 133 165/41 and British ship *EILDON* 1447/36, and landed at Gibraltar and Oran. U-380, commanded by Kapitänleutnant Albrecht Brandi (Knight's Cross 21.1.43; Oak Leaves 11.4.43), was sunk on 11.3.44 by USAAF aircraft at Toulon.

**FORT HOWE** • GRT 7133 • Built 1942
1.10.43: Torpedoed and sunk by German submarine U-410 (Fenski), in the Mediterranean E of Bougie, in position 37.19N 06.40E while on a voyage from Salerno to the UK, in ballast, part of convoy MKS 26 comprising 21 ships. The Master, Capt William Williams, crew of 49 and 18 gunners were rescued by HM corvettes *SPIRAEA* 925/40 (K.08) (Lt A.H. Pierce OBE) (landed at Bougie) and *ALISMA* 925/40 (K.185) (Lt G. Lanning RANVR) (landed at Algiers). 2 gunners were lost. Oberleutnant zur See Horst-Arno Fenski was awarded the Knight's Cross (26.11.43).

## STRUBIN, CHARLES & CO. LTD – LONDON

**NEWTON ASH** • GRT 4625 • Built 1925
8.2.43: Torpeoded and sunk by German submarine U-402 (v. Forstner), part of the 'Pfeil' (Arrow) patrol group of ten U-boats, in the Atlantic S of Iceland, in position 56.25N 22.26W

while on a voyage from St John, New Brunswick to Hull via Halifax NS, with a cargo of 6500 tons of grain, military stores and mail, part of convoy SC 118 comprising 61 ships. The Master, Capt James Purvis, 29 crew and 4 gunners were lost. 4 crew were rescued by the US Coastguard cutter *INGHAM* 2216/36 (WPG.35) and landed at Reykjavik.

## SUTHERLAND, B. J. & CO. LTD – NEWCASTLE UPON TYNE

*INVERNESS* • GRT 4897 • Built 1940
9.7.41: Torpedoed and sunk by German submarine U-98 (Gysae), in the Atlantic NNW of the Azores, in position 42.46N 32.45W while sailing independently from Liverpool to Cape Town and the Middle East, with a cargo of 4000 tons of military stores, dispersed on 6.7.41 in position 48.30N 26.30W from convoy OB 341 comprising 35 ships. The Master, Capt James Maxwell Henderson, 31 crew and 5 gunners landed at Corvo Island, Azores. 6 crew were lost.

*ROSS* • GRT 4978 • Built 1936
29.10.42: Torpedoed and sunk by German submarine U-159 (Witte), in the Indian Ocean SE of Cape Agulhas, in position 39.05S 22.06E while sailing independently on a voyage from Port Elizabeth 27.10.42 to Trinidad, with a part cargo of 2000 tons of manganese ore. The Master, Capt John Dodds, crew of 32 and 6 gunners were rescued by HM corvette *ROCKROSE* 925/41 (K.51) (Lt E.J. Binfield) and landed at Simonstown. 1 gunner was lost.

## SUTTON, E.J. & COMPANY – NEWCASTLE UPON TYNE

*CONFIELD* • GRT 4956 • Built 1940
8.10.40: Torpedoed and damaged by German submarine U-58 (Schonder), in the Atlantic 88 miles W of Barra Head, in position 56.48N 10.17W while on a voyage from Port Alberni, British Columbia to Portishead via Halifax NS, with 5800 tons of timber, 2000 tons of grain and 300 tons of lead, a straggler from convoy HX 76 comprising 38 ships. Abandoned 9.10.40, in position 56.48N 10.17W and sunk by gunfire by HM sloop *WESTON* 1060/32 (L.72) ex-HMS *WESTON SUPER MARE* (Cdr J.G. Sutton). The Master, Capt Walter Austin Sage, and 4 crew were rescued by HMS *WESTON* and 31 crew by HM corvette *PERIWINKLE* 925/40 (K.55) (Lt-Cdr P.G. MacIver) and landed at Londonderry. 1 crew was lost. U-58, commanded by Oberleutnant zur See Richard Schulz, was scuttled at Kiel on 3.5.45.

## TAI YAN SS CO. LTD – HONG KONG

*HARELDAWINS* ex-*HARELDA* • GRT 1288 • Built 1901
10.12.41: Torpedoed and sunk by Japanese submarine I-124 (Kishigami), in the Pacific 8 miles W of Luzon Island, Philippines, while on a voyage from Hong Kong 7.12.41 to Singapore. The Master, Capt Edward Bentley, was taken prisoner. The number of crew that survived and those lost is not known. Lt Koichi Kishigami and crew were lost on 20.1.42 when I-124 was sunk in the Arfura Sea off Darwin, in position 12.24S 129.49E by US four-stack destroyer *EDSALL* 1190/20 (DD-219) (Lt Joshua J. Nix), RAN minesweeping sloops *DELORAINE* 650/41 (J.232) (Lt-Cdr D.A. Menlove), *LITHGOW* 650/40 (J.206) (Cdr A.V. Knight DSC) and *KATOOMBA* 650/41 (J.204) (Lt P.E. Begg).

## TANKERS LIMITED – LONDON

*SCOTTISH MINSTREL* (tanker) • GRT 6998 • Built 1922
16.7.40: Torpedoed and sunk by German submarine U–61 (Oesten), in the Atlantic 130 miles
NW of Bloody Foreland, in position 56.10N 10.20W while on a voyage from New York to
London via Halifax NS, with a cargo of 9200 tons of fuel oil, part of convoy HX 55 comprising
38 ships. The Master, Capt Peter Dunn, and 31 crew were rescued by HM corvette
*GARDENIA* 925/40 (K.99) (Lt-Cdr T.A.O. Ellis) and landed at Folkestone. 9 crew were lost.
U–61, commanded by Leutnant zur See Werner Zalf, was scuttled at Wilhelmshaven on 1.5.45.

*SCOTTISH MAIDEN* (tanker) • GRT 6998 • Built 1922
5.11.40: Torpedoed and sunk by German submarine U–99 (Kretschmer), in the Atlantic
about 225 miles W by S of Bloody Foreland, in position 54.40N 14.08W while on a voyage
from Curacao to Avonmouth via Halifax NS 24.10.40, with a cargo of 3000 tons of diesel oil
and 6500 tons of marine fuel oil, part of convoy HX 83 comprising 37 ships. The Master,
Capt John William Albert Gibson, and 27 crew were rescued by HM destroyer *BEAGLE*
1360/30 (H.30) (Lt-Cdr H. Wright) and landed at Liverpool. 16 crew were lost.

*SCOTTISH STANDARD* (tanker) • GRT 6999 • Built 1921
21.2.41: Damaged by bombs from a FW–200 Condor of I/KG 40 Bomber Group in the
Atlantic SE of Iceland, in position 59.19N 16.14W, and torpedoed and sunk on 22.2.41 by
German submarine U–96 (Lehmann-Willenbrock), in position 59.20N 16.12W while on
government service on a voyage from the Clyde to New York via Loch Ewe, in ballast, a
straggler from convoy OB 287 comprising 44 ships. The Master, Capt John Ward, 37 crew
and 1 gunner were rescued by HM destroyer *MONTGOMERY* 1090/18 (G.95) (Cdr H.F.
Nash) ex-USN four-stack *WICKES* and landed at Oban. 5 crew were lost.

*SCOTTISH CHIEF* (tanker) • GRT 7006 • Built 1928
19.11.42: Torpedoed and sunk by German submarine U–177 (Gysae), in the Indian Ocean
about 200 miles ESE of Durban, in position 30.50S 34.30E while sailing independently on
Admiralty service on a voyage from Bandar Mashur 28.10.42 and Bandar Abbas to Cape Town,
with a cargo of 13000 tons of Admiralty fuel oil, dispersed from a convoy of 15 ships. The
Master, Capt Thomas Thorogood, 32 crew and 3 gunners were lost. 5 survivors were rescued
by HM corvette *JASMINE* 925/41 (K.23) (Lt-Cdr C.D.B. Coventry) and 7 survivors by HM
corvette *GENISTA* 925/41 (K.200) (Lt-Cdr R.M. Pattinson DSC) and landed at Durban.

## TATEM W.J. LIMITED – CARDIFF
### Atlantic Shipping & Trading Co. Ltd

*CHULMLEIGH* • GRT 5445 • Built 1938
5.11.42: Bombed and damaged by a Ju-88 of II/KG 30 Bomber Group based at Banak, North
Cape, and beached at South Cape, Spitzbergen, then torpedoed by German submarine U–625
(Benker) and again attacked by a German Ju-88 while sailing independently from Philadelphia
to Archangel, with a cargo of government stores. The Master, Capt D.N. Williams, 3 crew and
9 gunners survived. 36 crew and 9 gunners were lost; many died of frostbite. The Master and
crew landed on an isolated part of Spitzbergen and were not rescued until 4.1.43 by troops

from the local garrison at Barentsburg. Stranded for months, the survivors were eventually rescued by HM cruisers *BERMUDA* 8000/41 (52) (Capt T.H. Back) and *CUMBERLAND* 9750/26 (57) (Capt A.H. Maxwell-Hyslop AM) and landed at Thurso 16.5.43.

*HADLEIGH* • GRT 5222 • Built 1930
16.3.43: Torpedoed and damaged by German submarine U-77 (Hartmann), in the Mediterranean NW of Oran, in position 36.10N 00.30W while on a voyage from Algiers to Gibraltar, in ballast, part of convoy ET 14 comprising 30 ships. Taken in tow by the Admiralty rescue tug *RESTIVE* 700/40 (W.39) to Oran, then to Mers el Kebir, beached and declared a CTL. The Master, Capt William Henry Gould, 41 crew and 8 gunners were rescued by HM destroyer *TYNEDALE* 907/40 (L.96) (Lt A.S. Corbould). 2 crew were lost. U-77 commanded by Kapitänleutnant Otto Hartmann was damaged on 28.3.43 by Hudson VI 'L', pilot F/O J.B. Harrop, of No. 48 Squadron RAF, based at Gibraltar. Later the same day U-77 was attacked by Hudson 'L' T9430, pilot F/O Edgar Frederick Castell of No. 233 Squadron RAF, based at Gibraltar. She sank in the Mediterranean E of Cape de Palos, Spain, in position 37.42N 00.10E. F/O Castell was awarded the DFC. The U-boat commander and 38 crew were lost. 9 crew were rescued by a Spanish fishing boat and landed at Denia, Spain. They were later repatriated to Germany.

*EVERLEIGH* • GRT 5222 • Built 1930
6.2.45: Torpedoed and sunk by German submarine U-1017 (Riecken), in the English Channel SE of Durlston Head, in position 50.30N 01.48W while on a voyage from London and Barry Roads to New York, in ballast, part of coastal convoy TBC 60 comprising 17 ships. The Master, Capt William Henry Gould, 42 crew and 7 gunners were rescued by LCI No. 33 and landed at Portland. 6 crew were lost. Oberleutnant zur See (Reserve) Werner Riecken and crew of 33 were lost on 29.4.45 when U-1017 was sunk in the Atlantic 110 miles NW of Bloody Foreland, in position 56.04N 11.06W by Liberator VIII 'Q', pilot F/O H.J. Oliver of No. 120 'Punjab' Squadron RAF, based at Ballykelly, Co. Londonderry, part of 15 Group.

*FILLEIGH* • GRT 4856 • Built 1928
18.4.45: Torpedoed and sunk by German submarine U-245 (Schumann-Hindenberg), in the North Sea 10 miles ESE of North Foreland, in position 51.19N 01.42E while on a voyage from London to Antwerp, with 6000 tons of military cargo, part of coastal convoy TAM 142. The Master, Capt Patrick McSweeney, 37 crew and 10 gunners and the Belgian pilot were rescued by HM ship and landed at Dover. 5 crew were lost. U-245, commanded by Korvettenkapitän Friedrich Schumann-Hindenberg, surrendered at Bergen on 29.5.45 and later sailed to Loch Ryan. U-245 sailed from Cairnryan on 7.12.45 towed by HM tug *ENCHANTER* 868/44 (W.178); the tow line broke in heavy weather and U-245 sank the same day NNW of Rathlin Island, in position 55.25N 06.15W, part of 'Operation Deadlight', the disposal of 116 U-boats by the Royal Navy.

## Tatem Steam Navigation Co. Ltd

*WINKLEIGH* • GRT 5055 • Built 1927
8.9.39: Torpedoed and sunk by German submarine U-48 (Schultze), in the Atlantic SW of Ireland, in position 48.06N 18.12W while sailing independently on a voyage from Vancouver

BC to Manchester via Panama, with a cargo of grain and lumber. The Master, Capt Thomas Georgeson, and crew of 36 were rescued by Dutch liner *STATENDAM* 29511/29 and landed at New York.

### LADY GLANELY • GRT 5497 • Built 1938

2.12.40: Torpedoed and sunk by German submarine U-101 (Mengersen), in the Atlantic 410 miles W of Bloody Foreland, in position 55.00N 20.00W while on a voyage from Vancouver BC to London via Panama and Bermuda, with a cargo of 2000 tons of wheat and 6125 tons of lumber, part of convoy HX 90 comprising 35 ships. The Master, Capt Alexander Hughson, crew of 30 and 1 gunner were lost.

### GOODLEIGH • GRT 5448 • Built 1938

2.12.40: Torpedoed and sunk by German submarine U-52 (Salman), in the Atlantic 367 miles W of Bloody Foreland, in position 55.02N 18.45W while on a voyage from New Westminster BC to Oban via Panama and Bermuda, with a cargo of 1000 tons of spelter and 8400 tons of lumber, part of convoy HX 90 comprising 35 ships. The Master, Capt William Wilson Quaitre, 34 crew and 1 gunner were rescued by HM destroyer *VISCOUNT* 1325/17 (D.92) (Lt-Cdr M.S. Townsend OBE DSC) and landed at Liverpool. 1 crew was lost.

## MOWT

### EMPIRE CHAUCER • GRT 5970 • Built 1942

17.10.42: Torpedoed and sunk by German submarine U-504 (Poske), part of the 'Eisbar' (Polarbear) patrol group of five U-boats, in the Indian Ocean 450 miles S of Cape Town, in position 38.12S 20.04E while sailing independently on a voyage from Calcutta and Durban 13.10.42 to the UK via Cape Town and Trinidad, with 1 passenger and 8500 tons of general cargo including 2000 tons of pig iron, tea and bags of mail. The Master, Capt Roy Jennings, and 11 survivors were rescued by British ship *EMPIRE SQUIRE* 7044/42 and landed at Trinidad, 15 survivors by Royal Mail ship *NEBRASKA* 8261/20 after 23 days in an open boat landed at Cape Town and 20 survivors landed at Bredasdorp near Simonstown after 14 days in an open boat. 3 crew were lost.

## TAYLOR, MATTHE – METHIL

### PARKHILL ex-GLENARCH ex-WHEATSHEAF • GRT 500 • Built 1915

18.11.39: Torpedoed and sunk by German submarine U-22 (Jenisch), in the North Sea NNW of Kinnairds Head, in position 58.07N 02.18W while sailing independently on a voyage from Blyth to Kirkwall, Orkney Islands, with a cargo of 449 tons of coal. The Master, Capt Eric Charles Middleton, and crew of 8 were lost.

## THOMAS, J.J. & COMPANY – CARDIFF
### Eclipse Shipping & Trading Co. Ltd

### POLZELLA • GRT 4751 • Built 1929

17.1.40: Torpedoed and sunk by German submarine U-25 (Schütze), in the North Sea 6/7 miles N of Muckle Flugga, Shetland Isles, in position 60.58N 00.55W while sailing independently on a voyage from Narvik to Middlesbrough, with a cargo of iron ore. The Master, Capt James Harburn Thompson, and crew of 35 were lost.

## THOMPSON, STANLEY & JOHN – LONDON
**Silver Line**

*SILVERPINE* • GRT 5122 • Built 1924
5.12.40: Torpedoed and sunk by Italian submarine *ARGO* (Crepas), in the Atlantic 355 miles W of Bloody Foreland, in position 54.14N 18.08W while on a voyage from Liverpool to New York, in ballast, with 2 passengers, a straggler from convoy OB 252 comprising 44 ships. The Master, Capt William Barrington Bowyer, 32 crew and passengers were lost. 19 crew were rescued by HM destroyer *HARVESTER* 1340/39 (H.19) ex-HMS *HANDY* (Lt-Cdr M. Thornton) and landed at Londonderry.

*SILVERYEW* • GRT 6373 • Built 1930
30.5.41: Torpedoed and sunk by German submarine U-106 (Oesten), in the Atlantic W of the Cape Verde Islands, in position 16.42N 25.29W while sailing independently on a voyage from Calcutta to London and Oban via Cape Town, with a cargo of 2501 tons of pig iron, 5304 tons of kernels, 500 tons of manganese ore and 382 tons of kyanite ore. The Master, Capt James Smith, 49 crew and 3 gunners landed at San Antonio, Cape Verde Islands. 1 crew was lost.

*SILVERPALM* • GRT 6373 • Built 1929
9.6.41: Torpedoed and sunk by German submarine U-101 (Mengersen), in the Atlantic N of the Azores, in position 51.00N 26.00W while sailing independently on a voyage from Calcutta to Glasgow via Cape Town, carrying 3 passengers and general cargo. The Master, Capt Richard Long Pallett, crew of 53, 11 gunners and passengers were lost. U-101 commanded Oberleutnant zur See Helmut Münster was scuttled on 3.5.45 at Neustadt, in position 54.07N 10.50E.

*SILVERBELLE* • GRT 5302 • Built 1927
22.9.41: Torpedoed and damaged by German submarine U-68 (Merten), in the Atlantic SW of the Canary Islands, in position 25.45N 24.00W while on a voyage from Durban to Liverpool via Freetown 14.9.41, with 3 passengers and a cargo of 6000 tons of phosphate, including palm oil, copper and cocoa beans, part of convoy SL 87 comprising 11 ships. Taken in tow by Free French corvette *COMMANDANT DUBOC* 630/38 but abandoned 29.9.41 in the Atlantic SW of the Canary Islands, in position 26.30N 23.14W. The Master, Capt Hilton Rowe, crew of 47, 7 gunners, 2 DBS and passengers were rescued by the *COMMANDANT DUBOC* and landed at Freetown.

*SILVERCEDAR* • GRT 4354 • Built 1924
15.10.41: Torpedoed and sunk by German submarine U-553 (Thurmann), in the Atlantic SE of Cape Farewell, in position 53.26N 29.57W while on a voyage from New York to Liverpool via Sydney CB, with 7300 tons general cargo including steel, part of convoy SC 48 comprising 50 ships. The Master, Capt Thomas Keane, 18 crew, 2 gunners and 1 DBS were lost. 19 crew and 7 gunners were rescued by Free French corvette *MIMOSA* 925/41 (K.11) and landed at Reykjavik.

**SILVERAY** • GRT 4535 • Built 1925

4.2.42: Torpedoed and sunk by German submarine U-751 (Bigalk), in the Atlantic S of Halifax NS, in position 43.54N 64.16W while on a voyage from Liverpool and Greenock to New York via Halifax NS, with 2229 tons general cargo, part of convoy ON 55 comprising 28 ships. The Master, Capt Harry Green, and 34 survivors were rescued by US coastguard cutter *CAMPBELL* 2216/36 (WPG.22) and landed at Argentia, Newfoundland; 6 survivors by fishing boat *LUCILLE M* and landed at Lockeport, Nova Scotia. 7 crew and 1 gunner were lost.

**SILVERWILLOW** • GRT 6373 • Built 1930

30.10.42: Torpedoed and damaged by German submarine U-409 (Massmann), part of the 'Streitaxt' (Battleaxe) patrol group of eight U-boats, in the Atlantic NNE of Madeira, in position 35.08N 16.44W while on a voyage from Lagos and Freetown 16.10.42 to Liverpool, with 5 passengers and 9000 tons general cargo, part of convoy SL 125 comprising 40 ships. Abandoned on 5.11.42 in position 34.07N 14.39W but foundered on 11.11.42 in position 37.24N 10.45W. The Master, Capt Reginald Charles Butler, 49 crew, 7 gunners, 1 DBS and 3 passengers were rescued by HM auxiliary patrol vessel *KELANTAN* 1106/21 (F.166) (Lt A.E. Jones) and landed at Gourock 8.11.42. 3 crew, 1 gunner and 2 passengers were lost.

**SILVERBEECH** • GRT 5311 • Built 1926

29.3.43: Torpedoed and sunk by German submarine U-172 (Emmermann), part of the 'Seeräuber' (Pirate) patrol group of seven U-boats, in the Atlantic SE of the Canary Islands, in position 25.30N 15.55W while on a voyage from Liverpool and Gibraltar to Freetown and Lagos, with 6 passengers and 5053 tons general cargo including ammunition and high explosives, part of convoy RS 4 comprising 4 ships. The Master, Capt Thomas George Hyem, 50 crew, 5 gunners and passengers were lost. 2 crew and 6 gunners were rescued by British tug *EMPIRE ACE* 275/42 and landed at Bathurst, Gambia.

**SILVERMAPLE** • GRT 5302 • Built 1927

26.2.44: Torpedoed and sunk by German submarine U-66 (Seehausen), in the Atlantic 130 miles W of Takoradi, Gold Coast, in position 04.44N 03.20W while on a voyage from Bathurst and Freetown to Takoradi, with 1 passenger and 5395 tons general cargo and mail, part of convoy STL 12 comprising 13 ships. The Master, William Candlish Brydson, 47 crew, 9 gunners and passenger were rescued by HM sloop *KILDWICK* 795/43 (5.06) (Lt P. Pannell) and landed at Takoradi 27.2.44. 5 crew and 1 gunner were lost. On 23.4.43 the *SILVERMAPLE* was torpedoed and damaged by German submarine U-954 (Loewe), in the Atlantic SW of Iceland, in position 59.05N 35.40W while on a voyage from Halifax NS to the UK, with general cargo, part of convoy HX 234 comprising 43 ships. Oberleutnant zur See Udo Loewe and crew of 46 were lost on 19.5.43 when U-954, part of the 'Donau 2' (Danube) patrol group of twelve U-boats, was sunk while attacking convoy SC 130 comprising 38 ships in the Atlantic 480 miles SE of Cape Farewell, in position 54.54N 34.19W by HM frigate *JED* 1370/42 (K.235) (Lt-Cdr R.C. Freaker) and HM escort sloop *SENNEN* 1546/41 (Y.21) (Lt-Cdr F.H. Thornton) ex-USS *CHAMPLAIN*. U-954 sailed from Kristiansund, Norway, on her first patrol on 8.4.43. One of the officers lost was Leutnant zur See Peter Dönitz, son of Grand Admiral Karl Dönitz. Kapitänleutnant Hellmut Kurrer and crew of 53 were lost on 23.4.43 when U-189, part of the 'Meise' (Titmouse) patrol group of twenty-eight U-boats, was sunk while shadowing convoy HX 234 in the Atlantic 265 miles E of Cape Farewell, in position 59.50N 34.43W by Liberator

'V' FL923, pilot F/O John K. Moffatt, No. 120 Squadron RAF, based at Reykjavik. The pilot was awarded the DFC. Oberleutnant zur See Dietrich von Carlowitz and crew of 48 were lost on 24.4.43 when U-710 was sunk in the Atlantic 170 miles SE by S of Reykjanes, in position 61.25N 19.48W while pursuing convoy HX 234 by Fortress 'D' FL451, pilot F/O Robert Leonard Cowey of No. 206 Squadron RAF, based at Benbecula, Hebrides, part of 15 Group.

### SILVERLAUREL • GRT 6142 • Built 1939

18.12.44: Torpedoed and sunk by German submarine U-486 (Meyer), in the English Channel S of the Eddystone Lighthouse, in position 50.07N 04.40W while on a voyage from Duala to Hull via Falmouth, with 9 passengers and 2949 tons of cocoa beans, 2423 tons of palm oil, 758 tons of timber, 303 tons of lumber, 317 tons of rutile (titanium dioxide), 66 tons of coffee, 30 tons of ramie (fibre) and 195 tons of rubber, part of coastal convoy BTC 10 comprising 3 ships and 2 invasion barges. The Master, Capt John Duncan OBE, crew of 45, 10 gunners and passengers were rescued by British ship *MONKSTONE* 867/23 and landed at Plymouth. Oberleutnant zur See (Reserve) Gerhard Meyer and crew of 47 were lost on 12.4.45 when U-486 was sunk in the North Sea 30 miles NW of Bergen, in position 60.44N 04.39E by HM submarine *TAPIR* 1090/44 (P.335) (Lt John C. Roxburgh).

## MOWT

### EMPIRE HUDSON • GRT 7465 • Built 1941 (CAM ship)

10.9.41: Torpedoed and sunk by German submarine U-82 (Rollman), in the North Atlantic S of Cape Farewell, in position 61.28N 39.46W while on a voyage from Halifax NS via Sydney CB 30.8.41, to Liverpool, with 9 RAF personnel and 9562 tons of wheat, part of convoy SC 42 comprising 65 ships. The Master, Capt John Campbell Cooke, 47 crew, 6 gunners and RAF personnel were rescued by British ship *BARON RAMSAY* 3650/29 and Norwegian ship *REGIN* 1386/17 and landed at Loch Ewe. 4 crew were lost.

## THOMSON, HENRY M. – EDINBURGH

### SITHONIA ex-RADNORSHIRE • GRT 6723 • Built 1919

13.7.42: Torpedoed and sunk by German submarine U-201 (Schnee), part of the 'Hai' (Shark) patrol group of six U-boats, in the Atlantic W of the Canary Islands, in position 29.00N 25.00W while on a voyage from Barry and Belfast Lough 2.7.42 to Montevideo, with a cargo of 8026 tons of coal, part of convoy OS 33 comprising 41 ships. The Master, Capt Charles Cottew Brown, and 21 crew landed at Timiris, Senegal, after 18 days in an open boat and were interned by the Vichy French authorities at Port Etienne; the Chief Officer and 25 crew were rescued after 14 days sailing about 820 miles in an open boat by a Spanish fishing vessel and landed at Las Palmas. 7 crew were lost.

### ORFOR ex-ROMSDALSHORN • GRT 6578 • Built 1921

14.12.42: Torpedoed and sunk by German submarine U-105 (Nissen), in the Atlantic NE of Barbados, in position 16.00N 50.00W while sailing independently on a voyage from Calcutta to St Thomas, Virgin Islands, Kingston, Jamaica and Ciudad Trujillo, Cuba via Cape Town 16.11.42, with a cargo of 7170 tons of gunnies (jute fibre). The Master, Capt Charles William Matthew Crone, 18 crew and 3 gunners were lost. 21 survivors landed on Desirade Island,

Guadaloupe on 26.12.42 after 11 days sailing about 600 miles in an open boat. The Chief Officer and 14 survivors were rescued by HM yacht *BLACK BEAR* ex-*XARIFA* 756/30 (FY.046) (Cdr H.B. Pilcher) and landed at Trinidad 24.12.42.

## THOMSON, WILLIAM & COMPANY – LEITH
### Ben Line Steamers Ltd

**BENLAWERS** • GRT 5943 • Built 1930
6.10.40: Torpedoed and sunk by German submarine U-123 (Moehle), in the Atlantic NE of St John's, Newfoundland, in position 53.20N 26.10W while on government service on a voyage from Swansea to Durban and Port Said, with a cargo of army stores including lorries, a straggler from convoy OB 221 comprising 35 ships. The Master, Capt W.G. Scott-Campbell, 9 crew and 1 gunner were rescued by British ship *FOREST* 4998/37 and landed at Bermuda; the 2nd Officer, 14 crew and 1 gunner by British ship *BENGORE HEAD* 2609/22. 23 crew and 1 gunner were lost.

**BENWYVIS** • GRT 5920 • Built 1929
21.3.41: Torpedoed and sunk by German submarine U-105 (Schewe), in the Atlantic N of the Cape Verde Islands, in position 20.00N 26.00W while on a voyage from Rangoon and Durban to Liverpool via Freetown 13.3.41, with general cargo including 3500 tons of rice, 500 tons of lead, 1100 tons of timber and 150 tons of wolfram, part of convoy SL 68 comprising 59 ships. The Master, Capt Henry John Small, 32 crew and 1 gunner were lost. 17 crew and 3 gunners were rescued by British ship *KING EDGAR* 4536/27 and landed at Freetown; 1 crew was rescued after 28 days in an open boat by a French ship and landed at Madagascar.

**BENVRACKIE** ex-*DARIAN* • GRT 6434 • Built 1922
13.5.41: Torpedoed and sunk by German submarine U-105 (Schewe), in the Atlantic 700 miles SW of Freetown, in position 00.49N 20.15W while sailing independently on a voyage from London and Loch Ewe to Cape Town and Beira, with 5850 tons general cargo including silver and aircraft, dispersed from convoy OB 312 comprising 25 ships. The Master, Capt William Edward Rawlings Eyton-Jones, 40 crew and 4 gunners were rescued after 13 days in open boats by British hospital ship *OXFORDSHIRE* 8648/12. 13 crew were lost. Capt W.E.R. Eyton-Jones was awarded the Lloyd's War Medal for bravery at sea.

**BENVENUE** • GRT 5920 • Built 1927
15.5.41: Torpedoed and sunk by German submarine U-105 (Schewe), in the Atlantic about 420 miles SW by W of Freetown, in position 04.27N 18.25E while sailing independently on a voyage from London, Newcastle and Loch Ewe to Gibraltar, Cape Town, Bombay and Karachi, with 6 army personnel, 5000 tons general cargo and 6 aircraft, dispersed from convoy OB 314 comprising 31 ships. The Master, Capt James Struth, 47 crew, 1 gunner and army personnel were rescued by British ship *ENGLISH TRADER* 3953/36 and landed at Freetown. 1 crew and 1 gunner were lost.

**BENMHOR** • GRT 5920 • Built 1928
5.3.42: Torpedoed and sunk by German submarine U-505 (Loewe), in the Atlantic about 210 miles SSW of Freetown, in position 06.05N 14.15W while sailing independently on a voyage

from Bombay and Durban to Oban via Freetown, with 8539 tons general cargo including silver bullion, pig iron and rubber. The Master, Capt David Boag Anderson, 51 crew and 4 gunners were rescued by a Sunderland flying boat of No. 95 Squadron RAF and landed at Freetown.

**BENLOMOND** ex-*MARIONGA J. GOULANDRIS* ex-*LONDON CORPORATION* ex-*HOOSAC* ex-*CYNTHIANA* • GRT 6630 • Built 1922
23.11.42: Torpedoed and sunk by German submarine U-172 (Emmermann), in the Atlantic 750 miles E of the River Amazon, Brazil, in position 00.30N 38.45W while sailing independently on a voyage from Port Said and Cape Town to Paramaribo and New York, in ballast. The Master, Capt John Maul, 44 crew and 8 gunners were lost. The sole survivor, 2nd Steward Poom Lim, was rescued after 133 days in an open boat east of Salinas, Brazil, by a Brazilian fisherman.

## MOWT

**EMPIRE PROTECTOR** ex-*PAMIA* ex-*SEBETO* ex-*CARIDDI* ex-*ARTENA*
GRT 6181 • Built 1921
30.5.41: Torpedoed and sunk by German submarine U-38 (Liebe), in the Atlantic SW of Freetown, in position 06.00N 14.25W while sailing independently on a voyage from Port Sudan and Cape Town to London via Freetown, with a cargo of 2250 tons of cotton, 4200 tons of cotton seed and 1252 tons of copper. The Master, Capt John Cringle, 29 crew and 3 gunners were rescued by Dutch ship *ARUNDO* 5163/30 and landed at Freetown. 5 crew were lost. The Italian *PAMIA* was captured at sea on 10.6.40 by HM trawler *LIFFEY* 520/16 (4332) ex-HMS *STONEAXE* (Lt F.S. Croughan) and taken to Methil.

**FORT QU'APPELLE** • GRT 7127 • Built 1942
17.5.42: Torpedoed and sunk by German submarine U-135 (Praetorius), in the Atlantic N of Bermuda, in position 59.50N 63.30W while sailing independently on her maiden voyage from Vancouver BC, Seattle and Kingston, Jamaica to the UK via Panama and Halifax NS, with 9200 tons general cargo including 500 tons of acetone. The Master, Capt Wilfred Alexander Murray, 12 crew and 1 gunner were lost. 10 crew and 1 gunner were rescued by RCN minesweeping sloop *MELVILLE* 590/41 (J.263) (Lt-Cdr R.T. Ingram) and landed at Shelburne, Nova Scotia 19.5.42; 22 crew by US ship *GREEN ISLAND* 1946/37 and landed at Kingston, Jamaica. U-135 commanded by Oberlautnant zur See Otto Luther was sunk while attacking convoy OS 51 comprising 61 ships on 15.7.43 in the Atlantic 50 miles N of Cape Juby, Rio de Oro, in position 28.20N 13.17W by HM sloop *ROCHESTER* 1045/31 (L.50) (Cdr C.B. Allen), HM corvettes *MIGNONETTE* 925/41 (K.38) (Lt H.H. Brown) and *BALSAM* 925/42 (K.72) (Lt J.E.L. Peters), part of the 39th Escort Group and a Catalina, pilot Lt R.J. Finnie of USN VP-92 Patrol Squadron based at Port Lyautey, French Morocco. The U-boat commander and 40 crew were taken prisoner by HMS *MIGNONETTE*. 5 crew were lost.

## TOWNSEND BROTHERS – LONDON

**MUREFTE** (ferry) • GRT 691 • Built 1941
10.9.41: Sunk by gunfire by Italian submarine *TOPAZIO* (Berengan), in the Mediterranean 60 miles W of Beirut, in position 34.12N 34.35E while sailing independently on a voyage from

Tyne to Iskenderun and Istanbul via Freetown, Durban, Mombasa, Aden, Suez and Port Said, with a part cargo of military stores. The Master, Capt Thomas Blackwood, and 16 crew were rescued by Egyptian ship *TALODI* 1578/28 and landed at Beirut 11.9.41. 1 crew was lost. The *MUREFTE* was built by Swan Hunter & Wigham Richardson – yard no: 1674 – for the Turkish government and contracted to Townsend Brothers for delivery. The *TOPAZIO* was lost on 12.9.43 off Sardinia, four days after the surrender of Italy, as a result of an identification error by British aircraft.

## TRADER NAVIGATION COMPANY – LONDON

*SCOTTISH TRADER* • GRT 4016 • Built 1938
6.12.41: Torpedoed and sunk by German submarine U-131 (Baumann), in the Atlantic S of Iceland while on a voyage from Philadelphia to Liverpool via Sydney CB, with general cargo, a straggler from convoy SC 56 comprising 42 ships. The Master, Capt George Ralph Joseph Harkness, crew of 36 and 6 gunners were lost. U-131 commanded by Korvettenkapitän Arend Baumann, part of the 'Seeräuber' (Pirate) patrol group of five U-boats, was sunk while attacking convoy HG 76 comprising 32 ships on 17.12.41 in the Atlantic 280 miles SW of Cape St Vincent, in position 34.12N 13.35W by HM escort destroyers *EXMOOR* ex-HMS *BURTON* 1050/41 (L.08) (Lt-Cdr L. St G. Rich), and *BLANKNEY* 907/40 (L.30) (Lt P.F. Powlett), HM destroyer *STANLEY* 1190/19 (I.73) Lt-Cdr D.B. Shaw), HM escort sloop *STORK* 1190/36 (L.81) (Capt Frederic John Walker), HM corvette *PENTSTEMON* 925/41 (K.61) (Lt-Cdr J. Bryon) and a Martlet, pilot Sub-Lt George R.P. Fletcher of No. 802 Naval Air Squadron from HM escort carrier *AUDACITY* 11000/39 (D.10) (Commander D.W. Mackendrick) of the 36th Escort Group. The Martlet was shot down by U-131 and the pilot was killed. The U-boat commander and crew of 54 were taken prisoner by HMS *EXMOOR* and HMS *STANLEY*.

## TRANSITUS SHIPPING LIMITED – LONDON

*TWEED* ex-*QUERCUS* • GRT 2697 • Built 1926
8.4.41: Torpedoed and sunk by German submarine U-124 (Schulz), in the Atlantic SW of Freetown, in position 07.43N 15.11W while sailing independently on a voyage from Liverpool to Pepel, in ballast, dispersed from convoy OG 57 comprising 37 ships. The Master, Capt Henry Fellingham, 25 crew and 2 gunners landed at Conarky, French Guinea. 3 crew were lost.

## TRINDER, ANDERSEN & COMPANY – LONDON
**Australind Steam Shipping Co. Ltd**

*ARDENVOHR* • GRT 5025 • Built 1940
10.6.42: Torpedoed and sunk by German submarine U-68 (Merten), in the Atlantic NE of the Panama Canal, in position 12.45N 80.20W while sailing independently on a voyage from New York 24.5.42 and Hampton Roads to Sydney NSW and Melbourne via Panama, with 8900 tons general cargo including munitions, tanks, guns and machinery. The Master, Capt Percy Edmund Crickmer, and 21 survivors were rescued by Dutch ship *FLORA* 1417/21 and 31 survivors by US destroyer *EDISON* 1620/40 (DD.439) and landed at Colon. 1 crew was lost.

## TRINIDAD LEASEHOLDS LIMITED – LONDON

*LA CARRIERE* (tanker) • GRT 5685 • Built 1938
25.2.42: Torpedoed and sunk by German submarine U-156 (Hartenstein), in the Atlantic 70 miles S by W of Guanica, Puerto Rico, in position 16.53N 67.05W while sailing independently on a voyage from New York to Trinidad, in ballast. The Master, Capt Robert Hyde Cairns, and 4 crew were rescued by a US Coastguard cutter and landed at Trinidad; 21 crew landed at Guanica 25.2.42. 11 crew and 4 gunners were lost.

## TURNBULL MARTIN CO. LTD – GLASGOW
### Scottish Shire Line Ltd

*STIRLINGSHIRE* ex-*CLAN MACDONALD* • GRT 6022 • Built 1928
2.12.40: Torpedoed and sunk by German submarine U-94 (Kuppisch), in the Atlantic 280 miles W by N of Bloody Foreland, in position 55.36N 16.22W while on a voyage from Sydney NSW and Townsville, Queensland to Liverpool via Bermuda, with a cargo of 3270 tons of sugar, 2000 tons of lead, 1900 tons of refrigerated foodstuffs and 460 tons general cargo, part of convoy HX 90 comprising 35 ships. The Master, Capt Charles Edward O'Byrne, crew of 72 and 1 gunner were rescued by British ship *EMPIRE PUMA* 7777/20 ex-*ETHAN ALLEN* and landed at Liverpool.

*BERWICKSHIRE* ex-*CLAN MACARTHUR* • GRT 7464 • Built 1912
20.8.44: Torpedoed and sunk by German submarine U-861 (Oesten), in the Indian Ocean about 400 miles ESE of Durban, in position 30.58S 38.50E while on a voyage from Liverpool to Durban and Tamatave, Madagascar, with 6000 tons general cargo and a deck cargo of 70 tons of high octane motor spirit in drums, part of convoy DN 68 comprising 6 ships. The Master, Capt James McCrone, 83 crew and 10 gunners were rescued by HM trawler *NORWICH CITY* 541/37 (FY.229) (Lt R.A. Groom) and landed at Durban. 7 crew and 1 gunner were lost. U-861, commanded by Kapitänleutnant Jurgen Oesten (Knight's Cross 26.3.41), surrendered at Trondheim, Norway, on 9.5.45. U-861 sailed from Lisahally, Lough Foyle, on 31.12.45 under tow by HM rescue tug *FREEDOM* 1360/43 (W.139) ex-USS *BATR* 19. At 14.45 hours the main engine broke down and U-861 was sunk by gunfire by ORP destroyer *BLYSKAWICA* 2144/36 in the Atlantic 1 mile S of Inishtrahull, in position 55.25N 07.15W, part of 'Operation Deadlight', the disposal of 116 U-boats by the Royal Navy. HMS *FREEDOM* was towed to Moville by HM destroyer *MENDIP* 907/40 (L.60) (Lt P.D. Davey).

## TURNBULL, SCOTT & COMPANY – LONDON

*WAYNEGATE* • GRT 4260 • Built 1931
24.2.41: Torpedoed and sunk by German submarine U-73 (Rosenbaum), in the Atlantic S of Iceland, in position 58.50N 21.47W while sailing independently on a voyage from Newport, Mon. to Freetown, with a cargo of 6200 tons of coal, dispersed from convoy OB 288 comprising 46 ships. The Master, Capt Sydney Gray Larard, crew of 41 and 2 gunners were rescued by Free French destroyer leader *LEOPARD* 2126/27 and landed at Greenock 28.2.41. The *WAYNEGATE* sank in 4 minutes.

**WIDESTONE** ex-*SANTURCE* ex-*CANADIAN RANCHER* • GRT 3192 • Built 1920
17.11.42: Torpedoed and sunk by German submarine U–184 (Dangschat), part of the 'Kreuzotter' (Viper) patrol group of nine U-boats, in the Atlantic SE of Cape Farewell, in position 54.30N 37.10W while on a voyage from Cardiff and Milford Haven to St John's, Newfoundland, with a cargo of 3400 tons of coal, part of convoy ONS 144 comprising 28 ships. The Master, Capt William Storm, crew of 34 and 7 gunners were lost. Kapitänleutnant Gunther Dangschat and crew of 49 were lost on or about 21.11.42 in the Atlantic NE of St John's, Newfoundland, in approximate position 49.00N 45.30W by an unknown cause.

## TURNER, BRIGHTMAN & COMPANY – LONDON
**'Z' Steamship Co. Ltd**

**ZOUAVE** • GRT 4256 • Built 1930
17.3.43: Torpedoed and sunk by German submarine U–305 (Bahr), part of the 'Stürmer' (Attacker) patrol group of eighteen U-boats, in the Atlantic about 900 miles W of Fastnet, in position 52.25N 30.15W while on a voyage from Pepel to Middlesbrough via Curacao and Halifax NS 8.3.43, with a cargo of 7100 tons of iron ore, part of convoy SC 122 comprising 51 ships. The Master, Capt William Hunter Cambridge, 24 crew and 5 gunners were rescued by HM corvette *GODETIA* 925/41 (K.226) (Lt A.M.F. Larose) and landed at Gourock. 12 crew and 1 gunner were lost.

## MOWT

**EMPIRE GILBERT** • GRT 6640 • Built 1941
2.11.42: Torpedoed and sunk by German submarine U–586 (v. Esch) in the North Atlantic E of Iceland, in position 70.15N 13.50W while on government service sailing independently on a voyage from the Tyne and Loch Ewe to Archangel via Reykjavik, with a cargo of war material. The Master, Capt William Williams, 46 crew and 17 gunners were lost. 1 crew and 2 gunners were taken prisoner and landed at Skjomenfjord, Norway 5.11.42. U–586, commanded by Oberleutnant zur See Herbert Göetz, was sunk on 5.7.44 by USAAF aircraft at Toulon.

## TYNE & WEAR SHIPPING COMPANY – NEWCASTLE UPON TYNE
## MOWT

**JUTLAND** • GRT 6153 • Built 1928
3.5.42: Torpedoed and damaged by German torpedo aircraft of I/KG 26 Bomber Group, the wreck was torpedoed and sunk by German submarine U–251 (Timm), in the Arctic Sea S of Bear Island, in position 73.02N 19.46E while on a voyage from Dundee to Murmansk via Reykjavik, with 9 passengers and a cargo of 1560 tons of military stores including 500 tons of cordite and 300 tons of ammunition, part of convoy PQ 15 comprising 26 ships. The Master, Capt John Henderson, crew of 53 and 8 passengers were rescued by HM destroyer *BADSWORTH* 1050/41 (L.03) (Lt G.T.S. Gray) and landed at Murmansk 6.5.42. 1 passenger was lost. U–251 commanded by Oberleutnant zur See Joachim Sauerbier and crew of 38 were lost when U–251 was sunk on 19.4.45 in the Kattegat 10 miles SE of Anholt Island, Denmark, in position 56.37N 11.51E by Mosquitos of Nos 143, 235, 248 Squadrons RAF and No. 333 Squadron RNAF, based at Banff, Banffshire, part of 18 Group.

## TYNE TEES STEAM SHIPPING CO. LTD – NEWCASTLE UPON TYNE

*AKELD* ex-*THE EARL* ex-*MAYFIELD* • GRT 643 • Built 1922
9.3.40: Torpedoed and sunk by German submarine U-14 (Wohlfarth), in the North Sea NE of Zeebrugge, in position 51.44N 03.22E while sailing independently on a voyage from Rotterdam to Newcastle, with general cargo. The Master, Capt David Lambert, and crew of 11 were lost. U-14 commanded by Oberleutnant zur See Hans-Joachim Dierks was scuttled on 1.5.45 at Wilhelmshaven.

## UNION CASTLE MAIL STEAMSHIP CO. LTD – LONDON

*DUNVEGAN CASTLE* • GRT 15007 • Built 1936
27.8.40: Torpedoed and sunk by German submarine U-46 (Endrass), in the Atlantic 120 miles SW of Cape Clear, in position 55.05N 11.00W while escorting convoy SL 43 comprising 47 ships. Lost while employed on government service as an Armed Merchant Cruiser (F). Capt H. Adriff, 249 officers and ratings were rescued. 27 ratings were lost.

*RICHMOND CASTLE* • GRT 7798 • Built 1939
4.8.42: Torpedoed and sunk by German submarine U-176 (Dierksen), in the Atlantic SE of Cape Farewell, in position 50.25N 25.05W while sailing independently on a voyage from Buenos Aires and Montevideo 18.7.42 to Avonmouth, with a cargo of 5250 tons of frozen meat. The Master, Capt Thomas Goldstone, 44 crew and 5 gunners were rescued: the Master and 14 survivors by Irish ship *IRISH PINE* 5621/19 and landed at Kilrush, the Chief Officer W. Gibb and 16 survivors were rescued after 12 days by HM corvette *SUNFLOWER* 925/40 (K.41) (Lt-Cdr J.T. Jones) and landed at Londonderry, the 2nd Officer F.J. Pye and 17 survivors by British ship *HORORATER* 13945/42 and landed at Liverpool. 14 crew were lost.

*WARWICK CASTLE* • GRT 20445 • Built 1931
14.11.42: Torpedoed and sunk by German submarine U-413 (Poel), in the Atlantic NW of Cape Espichel, Portugal, in position 38.44N 13.00W while on government service on a voyage from Gibraltar 11.11.42 to Glasgow, with 165 service personnel, part of convoy MKF 1(X) comprising 11 ships. The Master, Capt Henry Richard Leepman-Shaw, and 61 crew were lost. 201 crew, 29 gunners, 5 naval personnel and 131 service personnel were rescued by HM destroyers *ACHATES* 1350/29 (H.12) (Lt-Cdr A.H.T. Jones) and *VANSITTART* 1120/19 (D.64) (Lt-Cdr T. Johnstone), RCN corvette *LOUISBURG* 925/41 (K.143) (Lt-Cdr W.F.C. Campbell) and British ship *LEINSTER* 4303/37 and landed at Greenock. Kapitänleutnant Gustav Poel was awarded the Knight's Cross (21.3.44). HMS *ACHATES* was sunk in the Barents Sea in position 73.18N 30.06E on 31.12.42 by gunfire from German cruiser *ADMIRAL HIPPER* 18500/39 (Kapitän zur See Hans Hartmann) while escorting convoy JW 51B comprising 15 ships.

*LLANDAFF CASTLE* • GRT 10799 • Built 1926
30.11.42: Torpedoed and sunk by German submarine U-177 (Gysae), in the Indian Ocean SE of Lourenco Marques, in position 27.20S 33.20E while sailing independently on government service on a voyage from Mombasa and Dar es Salaam 26.11.42 to Durban, with 150 passengers including 6 Russian diplomats with wives and children and 70 military officers with families, and 300 tons of general cargo. The Master, Capt Cornwallis Jasper Clutterbuck

OBE, 155 crew, 4 gunners and passengers were rescued on 2.12.42 by HM destroyer *CATTERICK* 1087/41 (L.81) (Lt A. Tyson) and landed at Durban. 3 crew were lost.

**ROXBURGH CASTLE** • GRT 7801 • Built 1937
22.2.43: Torpedoed and sunk by German submarine U–107 (Gelhaus), part of the 'Robbe' (Seal) patrol group of eight U-boats, in the Atlantic N of the Azores, in position 38.12N 26.22W while sailing independently on a voyage from Glasgow to Buenos Aires, with a cargo of 1030 tons of chemicals and mail. The Master, Capt George Henry Mayhew, 55 crew and 8 gunners landed at Ponta Delgada, Azores, and were taken to Lisbon by Portuguese ship *SERPA PINO* 8267/15.

## MOWT

**CHARLES L.D.** • GRT 5273 • Built 1933
9.12.42: Torpedoed and sunk by German submarine U–553 (Thurmann), part of the 'Draufganger' (Daredevil) patrol group of eleven U-boats, in the Atlantic SE of Cape Farewell, in position 59.02N 30.45W while on a voyage from Karachi 8.9.42 and New York 27.11.42 to Glasgow, with 6517 tons general cargo, part of convoy HX 217 comprising 26 ships. The Master, Capt Diego Emmanuel Canoz, and 11 crew were rescued by rescue ship *PERTH* 2208/15 (Capt Keith Williamson OBE) and landed at Clyde 13.12.42. 36 crew were lost. Korvettenkapitän Karl Thurman (Knight's Cross 24.8.42) and crew of 46 were lost when U-553, part of the 'Landsknecht' (Mercenary) patrol group of twenty U-boats, was lost in the Atlantic after 22.1.43 by an unknown cause.

## UNION GOVERNMENT OF SOUTH AFRICA – CAPE TOWN

**COLUMBINE** ex-*SURIYOTHAI NAWA* ex-*ADMIRAL LAWS* ex-*SUNUGENTCO*
GRT 3268 • Built 1921 (South African)
16.6.44: Torpedoed and sunk by German submarine U–198 (v. Waldegg), in the South Atlantic 25 miles NW of Cape Castle, South West Africa, in position 32.44S 17.22E while sailing independently on a voyage from the Congo River and Luanda to Cape Town, with 3 passengers and a cargo of timber. The Master, Capt Andre Reidar Simensen, crew of 19 and passengers were lost.

## UNION OIL OF CALIFORNIA – LOS ANGELES

**LA BREA** (tanker) • GRT 6665 • Built 1916 (British)
24.8.40: Torpedoed and sunk by German submarine U–48 (Rösing), in the Atlantic WNW of Rockall, in position 57.24N 11.21W while on a voyage from Aruba to Dundee, with a cargo of 9410 tons of fuel oil, a straggler from convoy HX 65 comprising 51 ships. The Master, Capt George Edward Firth, and 1 crew were lost. 14 crew landed at Islivig Bay, Isle of Lewis and 17 crew landed at South Uist.

## UNION STEAMSHIP COMPANY OF NEW ZEALAND – LONDON

**KALINGO** • GRT 2051 • Built 1927
16.1.43: Torpedoed and sunk by Japanese submarine I–21 (Matsumura), in the Tasman Sea about 110 miles E of Sydney NSW, in position 34.07S 153.15E while sailing independently

on a voyage from Sydney NSW 17.1.43 to New Plymouth, New Zealand, with 2 passengers and general cargo. The Master, Capt Robert Duncan, 28 crew, 1 gunner and passengers landed at Sydney NSW 19.1.43. 2 crew were lost.

**LIMERICK** • GRT 8724 • Built 1925
25.4.43: Torpedoed and sunk by Japanese submarine I-177 (Nakagawa), in the Tasman Sea 20 miles SE of Cape Bryon, in position 28.54S 153.54E while on a voyage from Sydney NSW 24.4.43 to Brisbane, Queensland, with 2 passengers and general cargo, part of convoy GP 48 comprising 5 ships. The Master, Capt Frank L.G. Jaunay, 61 crew, 6 gunners and passengers were rescued by RAN minesweeping sloop *COLAC* 650/41 (J.242) (Lt W.S. Reynolds). 2 crew were lost.

## UNION WHALING COMPANY – LONDON

**UNIWALECO** ex-*FRATERNITAS* ex-*SIR JAMES CLARK ROSS* (Whaling factory)
GRT 9775 • Built 1905 (South African)
7.3.42: Torpedoed and sunk by German submarine U-161 (Achilles), in the Atlantic 45 miles W of St Vincent Passage, BWI, in position 13.23N 62.04W while sailing independently on a voyage from Curacao to Freetown via Trinidad, with a cargo of 8800 tons of fuel oil. The Master, Capt Johannes Marins Bernard Rosvik, and 32 crew landed on the Island of St Vincent. 18 crew were lost.

## UNITED AFRICA CO. LTD – LONDON

**CONGONIAN** • GRT 5065 • Built 1936
18.11.40: Torpedoed and sunk by German submarine U-65 (v. Stockhausen), in the Atlantic WSW of Freetown, in position 08.21N 16.12W while sailing independently on a voyage from Liverpool to Freetown, in ballast. The Master, Capt George Washington Irvin, and 34 crew were rescued by British ship *DEVONSHIRE* 11275/39 and landed at Freetown 29.11.40. 1 crew was lost.

**KUMASIAN** • GRT 4922 • Built 1935
5.8.41: Torpedoed and sunk by German submarine U-74 (Kentrat), in the Atlantic W of Ireland, in position 53.26N 15.40W while on a voyage from Lagos and Freetown 15.7.41 to London, with 9 passengers and 7000 tons general cargo, part of convoy SL 81 comprising 18 ships. The Master, Capt William Edward Pelissier, 43 crew, 6 gunners and passengers were rescued by HM corvette *LA MALOUINE* 925/40 (K.46) (Lt V.D.H. Bidwell RNR) and landed at Liverpool. 1 crew was lost.

**NIGERIAN** • GRT 5423 • Built 1936
8.12.42: Torpedoed and sunk by German submarine U-508 (Staats), in the Atlantic 130 miles SE of Trinidad, in position 09.17N 59.00W while sailing independently on a voyage from Port Harcourt and Takoradi 22.11.42 to the UK via Trinidad, with 12 passengers and 4200 tons of palm oil seed, 1300 tons of timber, 1000 tons of cocoa and 750 tons of peanut oil in bulk. The Master, Capt Edward Robert Owen, 35 crew, 8 gunners and 7 passengers were rescued, The Master and 28 survivors were rescued on 11.12.42 by US submarine chaser

No. 624 280/42 and landed at Moruga Bay, Trinidad, the Chief Officer and 15 survivors landed at Georgetown and the 2nd Officer and six survivors were rescued by Panamanian ship *MARAVI* 2802/21. 4 crew and 1 passenger were lost. 4 British military officers were taken prisoner and landed at Lorient 6.1.43.

### *LAGOSIAN* ex-*MELMAY* • GRT 5449 • Built 1930

28.3.43: Torpedoed and sunk by German submarine U-159 (Witte), part of the 'Seeräuber' (Pirate) patrol group of seven U-boats, in the Atlantic SE of the Canary Islands, in position 25.35N 15.43W while on a voyage from Algiers and Gibraltar to Takoradi, in ballast, part of convoy RS 3 comprising 4 ships. The Master, Capt George Washington Irvin, 24 crew and 10 gunners were rescued by British tug *EMPIRE DENIS* 275/43 and landed at Bathurst. 11 crew were lost. U-159, commanded by Kapitänleutnant Heinz Beckmann, and crew of 52 were lost on 28.7.43, sunk in the Caribbean Sea 160 miles W of Dominica, in position 15.57N 68.30W by Mariner P-10, pilot Lt D.C. Pinholster of US Navy Bombing Squadron VP-32 based at Guantanamo Bay, Cuba.

### *ASHANTIAN* • GRT 4917 • Built 1935

21.4.43: Torpedoed and sunk by German submarine U-415 (Neide), part of the 'Meise' (Titmouse) patrol group of twenty-eight U-boats, in the Atlantic NE of St John's, Newfoundland, in position 55.50N 44.00W while on a voyage from Liverpool and Belfast 6.4.43 to New York and Philadelphia, in ballast, with the convoy's commodore, 6 naval staff and 3 passengers, part of convoy ONS 3 comprising 18 ships. The Master, Capt Charles Carter Taylor, Commodore Vice-Admiral J. Elliot CBE RN, 13 crew and 1 gunner were lost. 40 crew, 9 gunners, naval staff and passengers were rescued by HM trawler *NORTHERN GIFT* 655/36 (4.50) (Lt-Cdr A.J. Clemence) and landed at St John's, Newfoundland.

### *MATADIAN* (tanker) • GRT 4275 • Built 1936

21.3.44: Torpedoed and sunk by German submarine U-66 (Seehausen), in the Bight of Benin SE of Lagos, in position 05.07N 04.47E while sailing independently on a voyage from Port Harcourt and Lagos to the UK, with 5380 tons of palm oil. The Master, Capt Cyril Gordon Silwyn Shorter, crew of 38 and 8 gunners were rescued by HM motor launch ML282 (Sub-Lt D.R. Pearson), transferred to HM motor launch ML1016 and landed at Lagos. U-66, commanded by Oberleutnant zur See Gerhard Seehausen, was sunk on 6.5.44 in the Atlantic 385 miles W of San Antonio, Cape Verde Islands, in position 17.17N 32.29W by an Avenger, pilot Lt Jimmie J. Sellars of US Navy Composite Squadron VC–55 from US escort carrier *BLOCK ISLAND* 9800/42 (CVE-21) (Capt F.M. Hughes) and US destroyer escort *BUCKLEY* 1400/43 (DE-51) (Lt-Cdr Brent M. Abel) of the Task Group 21.11. The U-boat commander and 23 crew were lost. 36 crew were taken prisoner by USS *BUCKLEY.*

### *DAHOMIAN* • GRT 5277 • Built 1929

1.4.44: Torpedoed and sunk by German submarine U-852 (Eck), in the South Atlantic 10 miles WSW of Cape Point, South Africa, in position 34.25S 18.19E while sailing independently on a voyage from New York 6.2.44 to Cape Town via Trinidad, with 5198 tons of general cargo including 17 aircraft and mail. The Master, Capt William Logan Taylor, 41 crew and 7 gunners were rescued by SAN whalers *KRUGERSDORP* ex-*UNI V* 198/23 (T.48) and *NATALIA* 238/25 (T.02) and landed at Simonstown. 2 crew were lost. U-852, commanded by Kapitänleutnant Heinz-Wilhelm Eck, was attacked and badly damaged in the Arabian Sea 150 miles S by W of Cape Guardafui, Somaliland, in position 09.32N 50.59E on 2.5.44 by Wellington 'E' JA107, pilot F/O H. Roy Mitchell DFC of No. 8 Squadron RAF, and Wellington 'T', pilot W/C P.G. Green of No. 621 Squadron RAF, both based at Khormaksar, Aden. U-852 later beached at Ras Hafun, Somaliland, and was blown up by her crew. The U-boat commander and 58 crew were taken prisoner by HM sloop *FALMOUTH* 1045/32 (L.34) (Lt-Cdr E.A. Woodhead) and landed at Aden 6.5.44. 7 crew were lost. Kapitänleutnant Heinz-Wilhelm Eck, Leutnant zur See August Hoffman (2WO) and Oberstabsarzt Walter Weisspfennig (medical officer) were sentenced to death by a British military court in Hamburg in November 1945 for firing on the survivors of Greek ship *PELEUS* 4695/28, sunk by U-852 on 13.3.44 in the South Atlantic. Eck was the only German U-boat commander to be executed for war crimes. The *PELEUS* was on passage from Algiers to Buenos Aires via Freetown, in ballast, with her Master, Capt Minas Mavris, crew of 34 and 6 gunners. 3 survivors were rescued on 20.4.44 after 37 days on a raft by Portuguese ship *ALEXANDRE SILVA* 1699/43 and landed at Lobito, Angola.

## Elmina Limited

*LAFIAN* • GRT 4876 • Built 1937
24.9.41: Torpedoed and sunk by German submarine U-107 (Hessler), in the Atlantic WNW of the Canary Islands, in position 31.21N 23.32W while on a voyage from Port Harcourt to Liverpool via Freetown 14.9.41, with 4 passengers and 5724 tons of palm kernels, 1128 tons of timber, 810 tons of palm oil and bullion, part of convoy SL 87 comprising 11 ships. The Master, Capt Evan Llewellyn Phillips, 37 crew, 5 gunners and passengers were rescued by HM sloop *GORLESTON* 1546/29 (Y.92) (Cdr R.W. Keymer) ex-US Coastguard cutter *ITASCA* and landed at Ponta Delgada, Azores.

*ZARIAN* • GRT 4871 • Built 1938
29.12.42: Torpedoed and sunk by German submarine U-591 (Zetzsche), in the Atlantic N of the Azores, in position 43.23N 27.14W while on a voyage from Leith and Loch Ewe 18.12.42 to Takoradi, with 4 passengers and 7500 tons of general stores plus government cargo, a straggler from convoy ONS 154 comprising 45 ships. The Master, Capt William Edward Pelissier, 37 crew, 7 gunners and passengers were rescued by HM destroyer *MILNE* 1935/41 (G.14) (Capt I.M.R. Campbell) and landed at Ponta Delgada, Azores. 4 crew were lost.

## MOWT

*ST CLAIR II* ex-*ST CLAIR* • GRT 3753 • Built 1929
24.9.41: Torpedoed and sunk by German submarine U-67 (Müller-Stockheim), in the Atlantic WNW of the Canary Islands, in position 30.25N 23.35W while on a voyage from Lagos and Freetown 14.9.41 to Liverpool, with a cargo of 4032 tons of palm kernels and palm oil, part of convoy SL 87 comprising 11 ships. The Master, Capt Harry Readman, 26 crew and 4 gunners were saved, 26 survivors were rescued by HM sloop *GORLESTON* 1546/29 (Y.92) (Cdr R.W. Keymer) ex-US Coastguard cutter *ITASCA* and landed at Ponta Delgada, Azores, and 5 survivors by HM sloop *LULWORTH* 1546/28 (Y.60) (Lt-Cdr C. Gwinner) ex-USCG *CHELAN* and landed at Londonderry 4.10.41. 12 crew and 1 gunner were lost.

## UNITED BALTIC CORPORATION – LONDON
### Anglo-Lithuanian Shipping Co. Ltd

*BALTANGLIA* ex-*LANGFOND* • GRT 1523 • Built 1921
23.1.40: Torpedoed and sunk by German submarine U-19 (Schepke), in the North Sea SE of the Farne Islands, in position 55.35N 01.27W while sailing independently on a voyage from Homelvik, Norway to the Tyne and Rochester, with general cargo. The Master, Capt George Edward Thomas, and crew of 27 landed at Seahouses, Northumberland. U-19, commanded by Oberleutnant zur See Hubert Verpoorten, was scuttled on 11.9.44 in the Black Sea N of Zonguldak, Turkey, in position 41.34N 31.50E. The U-boat commander and crew were interned by the Turkish authorities at Beyschir.

*BALTALLINN* ex-*STARLING* • GRT 1303 • Built 1920
20.9.41: Torpedoed and sunk by German submarine U-124 (Mohr), in the Atlantic NNE of the Azores, in position 48.07N 22.07W while on a voyage from Preston and Oban to Gibraltar, with 442 tons of government stores, part of convoy OG 74 comprising 22 ships. The Master, Capt Charles Walter Browne, 22 crew and 5 gunners were rescued by rescue ship *WALMER CASTLE* 906/36 (Capt Gerald Lewis Clarke). 7 crew were lost. The *WALMER CASTLE* was destroyed by enemy aircraft on 21.9.41 and 10 crew and 1 gunner from the *BALTALLINN* were lost. The Master, Capt C.W. Brown, 12 crew and 4 gunners were rescued by HM sloop *DEPTFORD* 990/35 (L.53) (Lt-Cdr H.R. White) and landed at Gibraltar 28.9.41. Capt G.L. Clarke was posthumously awarded the Lloyd's War Medal for bravery at sea.

*BALTONIA* ex-*BUENA VISTA* • GRT 2013 • Built 1925
7.2.43: Struck a mine laid on 1.2.43 by German submarine U-118 (Czygan), and sank in the Atlantic NW of Tangiers, in position 35.58N 05.59W while on a voyage from Seville and Gibraltar to Belfast Lough for orders, with a cargo of 1215 tons of oranges and 6 tons general cargo, part of convoy MKS 7 comprising 65 ships. The Master, Capt Jack Ames Prosser, 42 crew and 9 gunners were rescued by British ship *KINGSLAND* 3669/30, transferred to RCN corvette *ALBERNI* 925/40 (K.103) (Lt A.W. Ford) and landed at Londonderry. 9 crew and 1 gunner were lost.

## MOWT

*MALAYA II* ex-*DA MALAYA* • GRT 8651 • Built 1921
27.6.41: Torpedoed and sunk by German submarine U-564 (Suhren), in the Atlantic E of Cape Farewell, in position 59.56N 30.35W while on a voyage from Montreal to Cardiff via Halifax NS, with a cargo of 3698 tons of metal, 2143 tons of wheat and 413 tons of TNT, part of convoy HX 133 comprising 51 ships. The Master, Capt W. Kragelund, 38 crew and 4 gunners were lost. 6 crew were rescued by RCN corvette *COLLINGWOOD* 925/40 (K.180) (Lt-Cdr W. Woods) and landed at Reykjavik.

*PERU* • GRT 6961 • Built 1916
13.11.41: Torpedoed and sunk by German submarine U-126 (Bauer), in the Atlantic SW of Cape Palmas, in position 01.30N 13.20W while sailing independently on a voyage from

Calcutta to the UK via Cape Town and Freetown, with a cargo of 3001 tons of pig iron, 4184 tons of groundnuts and 2082 tons general cargo. The Master, Capt C.V. Frederiksen, crew of 42 and 7 gunners were rescued by South African tanker *UNIWALECO* 9755/05 and landed at Freetown 16.11.41.

**CHILE** • GRT 6956 • Built 1915
7.6.42: Torpedoed and sunk by Italian submarine *LEONARDO DA VINCI* (Longanesi-Cattani), in the Atlantic SW of Freetown, in position 04.17N 13.48W while sailing independently on a voyage from Calcutta and Cape Town 23.5.42 to the Mersey, with a cargo of 2500 tons of pig iron, 6302 tons of groundnuts and 800 tons of cotton seed. The Master, Capt N.E. Bom, 37 crew and 1 gunner were rescued by HM trawler *SPANIARD* 453/37 (FY.144) (Lt J.D. Love) and landed at Freetown. 5 crew were lost.

**DANMARK** • GRT 8391 • Built 1925
30.7.42: Torpedoed and sunk by gunfire by German submarine U-130 (Kals), in the Atlantic S of the Cape Verde Islands, in position 07.00N 24.19W while sailing independently on a voyage from Durban to the UK via Trinidad and Halifax NS, in ballast. The Master, Capt E. Honore Christensen, crew of 37 and 8 gunners were rescued by the Norwegian tanker *MOSLI* 8291/35 and landed at Freetown.

**SIAM II** ex-*SIAM* • GRT 6637 • Built 1913
30.9.42: Torpedoed and sunk by German submarine U-506 (Würdemann), in the Atlantic SW of Monrovia, in position 03.25N 15.46W while sailing independently on a voyage from Alexandria and Cape Town 13.9.42 to the UK via Freetown, with 9000 tons general cargo and grain including 3502 tons of cotton. The Master, Capt Aage Larsen, crew of 36 and 2 gunners were rescued on 1.10.42 by P & O ship *NAGPORE* 5283/20 and landed at Freetown.

**BORINGIA** • GRT 5821 • Built 1930
7.10.42: Torpedoed and sunk by German submarine U-159 (Witte), in the South Atlantic 200 miles WSW of Cape Town, in position 35.09S 16.32E while sailing independently on a voyage from Haifa and Cape Town 7.10.42 to the UK via Hampton Roads, with a cargo of 3000 tons of potash, 2967 tons of cotton and 490 tons of gum. The Master, Capt Sofus Heinrick Konard Kolls, 27 crew and 4 gunners were lost. 27 crew and 1 gunner were rescued by British ship *CLAN MACTAVISH* 7631/21. The *CLAN MACTAVISH* was sunk next day by U-159; 7 crew from the *BORINGIA* were lost and 20 crew and 1 gunner were rescued by British ship *MATHERAN* 8007/42 and landed at Cape Town.

**AFRIKA** • GRT 8597 • Built 1920
7.2.43: Torpedoed and sunk by German submarine U-402 (v. Forstner), part of the 'Pfeil' (Arrow) patrol group of ten U-boats, in the Atlantic SE of Cape Farewell, in position 55.12N 26.31W while on a voyage from Halifax NS to Liverpool, with 2 passengers and 11457 tons of government and general cargo including 5000 tons of steel, part of convoy SC 118 comprising 61 ships. The Master, Capt Emanuel Broholm Jensen, 18 crew and 4 gunners were lost. 29 crew, 6 gunners and passengers were rescued by HM corvettes *CAMPANULA* 925/40 (K.18) (Lt-Cdr B.A. Royes) and *MIGNONETTE* 925/41 (K.38) (Lt H.H. Brown) and landed at Liverpool.

**AMERIKA** • GRT 10219 • Built 1930
22.4.43: Torpedoed and sunk by German submarine U-306 (v. Trotha), part of the 'Meise' (Titmouse) patrol group of twenty-eight U-boats, in the Atlantic S of Cape Farewell, in position 57.30N 42.50W while on a voyage from Halifax NS 14.4.43 to Liverpool, with 53 RCAF personnel and 8844 tons general cargo including metal, flour, meat and 200 bags of mail, a straggler from convoy HX 234 comprising 43 ships. The Master, Capt Christian Nielsen, 29 crew, 8 gunners and 16 RCAF personnel were rescued by HM corvette *ASPHODEL* 925/40 (K.56) (Lt H.P. Carse DSC) and landed at Greenock. 42 crew, 7 gunners and 37 RCAF personnel were lost. Capt C. Nielsen was awarded the Lloyd's War Medal for bravery at sea. Kappitänleutnant Claus von Trotha and crew of 50 were lost when U-306, part of the 'Schill' patrol group of ten U-boats, was shadowing the combined convoy SL 138/KMS 28 comprising 60 ships and was sunk on 31.10.43 in the Atlantic 525 miles WNW of Cape Finisterre, in position 46.N 20.44W by HM escort destroyer *WHITEHALL* 1120/19 (D.94) (Lt-Cdr P.J. Cowell) and HM corvette *GERANIUM* 925/40 (K.22) (Lt R.J. Tilston), part of the 39th Escort Group commanded by Lt-Cdr P.G.A. King RNR.

## UNITED TOWING & SALVAGE COMPANY – PORT ARTHUR, ONTARIO

**MAPLECOURT** ex-*NORTH WEST* • GRT 3388 • Built 1894 (Canadian)
6.2.41: Torpedoed and sunk by German submarine U-107 (Hessler), in the Atlantic SSW of Rockall, in position 55.39N 15.56W while on a voyage from Montreal to Preston via Sydney CB, with 3604 tons general cargo including 1540 tons of steel, a straggler from convoy SC 20 comprising 42 ships. The Master, Capt Emrys Herbert Humphreys, and crew of 36 were lost.

## UNITED TOWING CO. LTD – HULL
## MOWT

**EMPIRE OAK** (tug) • GRT 482 • Built 1941
22.8.41: Torpedoed and sunk by German submarine U-564 (Suhren), in the Atlantic W of Ireland, in position 40.43N 11.39W, while on a voyage from Methil Roads to Gibraltar, part of convoy OG 71 comprising 21 ships. The Master, Frederick Edward Christian, 3 crew and 4 gunners were rescued by HM corvette *CAMPANULA* 925/40 (K.18) (Lt-Cdr R.V.E. Case DSC), transferred to HM destroyer *VELOX* 1090/17 (D.34) (Lt-Cdr E.G. Ropner DSC) and landed at Gibraltar 25.8.41. 13 crew were lost. During the attack on this convoy two escorts of the 5th Escort Group were lost: HM corvette *ZINNIA* 925/40 (K.98) (Lt-Cdr C.G. Cuthbertson) was sunk by U-564 on 23.8.41, in the Atlantic W of Portugal, in position 40.43N 11.39W and RNoN destroyer *BATH* 1060/18 (I.17) (Lt-Cdr Frederick Melsom) ex-USN four-stack *HOPEWELL* was sunk by U-204 (Kell) on 19.8.41 in the Atlantic 400 miles SW of Ireland, in position 49.00N 17.00W. Lt-Cdr F. Melsom and 82 crew were lost.

## UNITED WHALERS LIMITED – LONDON

**TERJE VIKEN** (Whaling factory) • GRT 20638 • Built 1936
7.3.41: Torpedoed and damaged by German submarine U-47 (Prien) and then attacked by German submarine U-99 (Kretschmer), in the North Atlantic SE of Iceland, in position

60.00N 12.50W while on a voyage from Glasgow to Curacao, in ballast, part of convoy OB 293 comprising 37 ships. Later abandoned and sunk on 14.3.41 by gunfire by HM salvage tug. The Master, Capt O. Borchgrevink, crew of 99 and 5 gunners were rescued by HM destroyer *HURRICANE* 1340/39 (H.06) (Lt-Cdr H.C. Simms) ex-Brazilian *JAPARUA* and landed at Greenock. The *TERJE VIKEN* was the largest whaling factory ship at that time in the world.

## UPPER LAKES & ST LAWRENCE TRANSPORTATION CO. LTD – TORONTO

*GEORGE L. TORIAN* • GRT 1754 • Built 1926 (Canadian)
22.2.42: Torpedoed and sunk by German submarine U-129 (Clausen), in the Atlantic 120 miles SSE of Trinidad, in position 09.13N 59.04W while sailing independently on a voyage from Paramaribo to Trinidad, with a cargo of bauxite. 4 crew were rescued by a US Navy flying boat landed at Trinidad. The Master, Capt John Allan, and 14 crew were lost.

*FRANK B. BAIRD* • GRT 1748 • Built 1923
22.5.42: Sunk by gunfire by German submarine U-158 (Rostin), in the Atlantic ESE of Bermuda, in position 28.03N 58.50W while sailing independently on a voyage from Demerara, British Guinea to Sydney CB, with a cargo of 2457 tons of bauxite. The Master, Capt Charles Swanson Tate, and crew of 22 were rescued by Norwegian ship *TALISMAN* 6701/37 and landed at Pointe Noire, French Equatorial Africa. Korvettenkapitän Erwin Rostin (Knight's Cross 28.6.42) and crew of 53 were lost on 30.6.42 when U-158 was sunk in the Atlantic 140 miles WNW of Bermuda, in position 32.50N 67.28W by Mariner, pilot Lt Richard E. Schreder of US Navy Bombing Squadron VP-74 based at Bermuda.

*JOHN A. HOLLOWAY* • GRT 1745 • Built 1925 (Canadian)
6.9.42: Torpedoed and sunk by German submarine U-164 (Fechner), in the Caribbean Sea N of Gallinas Punta, Colombia, in position 14.10N 71.30W while sailing independently on a voyage from Mobile to Trinidad via Guantanamo and Key West, with a cargo of 2000 tons of construction material, part of convoy GAT 2. The Master, Capt James Lionel Holmes, and 22 crew landed at Santa Marta, Colombia 12.9.42. 1 US signalman was lost. U-164, commanded by Korvettenkapitän Otto Fechner, was sunk on 6.1.43 in the South Atlantic NE of Camocim, Brazil, in position 01.58S 39.23W by Catalina P-2, pilot Lt William R. Ford of US Navy Bombing Squadron VP-83 based at Natal, Brazil. The U-boat commander and 53 crew were lost. 2 crew were taken prisoner.

## WALLEM & COMPANY – HONG KONG

*ORISKANY* ex-*LA CEIBA* • GRT 1644 • Built 1942
24.2.45: Torpedoed and sunk by German submarine U-480 (Förster), in the Atlantic W of Land's End, in position 50.05N 05.51W while on a voyage from Newport, Mon. to London, with a cargo of coal, part of coastal convoy BTC 78 comprising 9 ships. The Master, Capt David Souter Morrison, Commodore Commander I.N. Macmillan RNR, crew of 21, 7 naval ratings and 4 gunners were lost. Oberleutnant zur See Hans-Joachim Förster (Knight's Cross 20.10.44) and crew of 47 were lost when U-480 was sunk on the same day in the

Atlantic 15 miles WSW of Land's End, in position 49.55N 06.08W by the convoy's escorts, HM frigates *DUCKWORTH* 1085/43 (K.351) (Cdr R.G. Mills) and *ROWLEY* 1085/43 (K.560) (Lt-Cdr F.J.G. Jones) of the 3rd Escort Group.

## WATKINS, WILLIAM LTD – LONDON
## MOWT

*EMPIRE WOLD* (tug) • GRT 269 • Built 1942
10.11.44: Torpedoed and sunk by German submarine U-300 (Hein), in the North Atlantic off Skagi, Iceland, in position 64.08N 22.38W while on a voyage from Loch Ewe to Reykjavik, part of convoy UR 142 comprising 4 ships. The Master, Capt Henry William Draper, and crew of 8 were lost.

## WATTS, WATTS & CO. LTD – LONDON
## Britain SS Co. Ltd

*DEPTFORD* • GRT 4101 • Built 1931
13.12.39: Torpedoed and sunk by German submarine U-38 (Liebe), in the North Sea ¼ mile NNW of Honningsvaag, Norway, in position 62.12N 25.53E while sailing independently on a voyage from Narvik to Middlesbrough, with a cargo of 6000 tons of iron ore. The Master, Capt John William Ferguson, 30 crew and 2 Norwegian pilots were lost. 1 crew was rescued by Norwegian fishing boat *FIRDA* and 3 crew by Norwegian coastal ship *NORDNORGE* and landed at Alesund.

*DARTFORD* • GRT 4093 • Built 1930
12.6.42: Torpedoed and sunk by German submarine U-124 (Mohr), part of the 'Hecht' (Pike) patrol group of six U-boats, in the Atlantic S of Cape Race, in position 49.N 41.33W while on a voyage from the Tyne and Oban 2.6.42 to Sydney CB, in ballast, part of convoy ONS 100 comprising 38 ships. The Master, Capt Samuel Bulmer, 25 crew and 4 gunners were lost. 14 crew and 3 gunners were rescued by rescue ship *GOTHLAND* 1286/32 (Capt James Murray Hadden OBE) and landed at Halifax NS 17.6.42. One of the escorts, FFN corvette *MIMOSA* 925/41 (K.11) (Lt-Cdr J.H. Stubbs), part of the C1 Escort Group, was sunk on 9.6.42 by U-124, in the Atlantic SE of Cape Farewell, in position 52.15N 32.37W.

*WANSTEAD* • GRT 5486 • Built 1928
21.4.43: Torpedoed and damaged by German submarine U-415 (Neide), part of the 'Meise' (Titmouse) patrol group of twenty-eight U-boats, in the Atlantic SE of Cape Farewell, in position 55.46N 45.14W while on a voyage from the Tyne and Oban 8.4.43 to New York, in ballast, part of convoy ONS 3 consisting of 18 ships. Later sunk by HM corvette *POPPY* 925/41 (K.213) (Lt N.K. Boyd DSC). The Master, Capt William B. Johnston, 40 crew and 7 gunners were rescued by HM corvette *POPPY* and HM trawler *NORTHERN GIFT* 655/36 (4.50) (Lt-Cdr A.J. Clemence) and landed at St John's, Newfoundland. 2 crew were lost. U-415, commanded by Oberleutnant zur See Herbert Werner, was lost on 14.7.44 when U-415 struck a mine in the British minefield Jellyfish No. 5 in the Bay of Biscay off Brest, in position 48.22N 04.29W. The U-boat commander and 46 crew were rescued by German craft. 2 crew were lost.

*ASCOT* • GRT 7005 • Built 1942

29.2.44: Torpedoed and sunk by gunfire by Japanese submarine I-37 (Nakagawa), in the Indian Ocean about 800 miles NW of Diego Suarez, in position 05.00S 63.00E while sailing independently on a voyage from Calcutta and Colombo to Diego Suarez and Port Louis, Mauritius, with 9000 tons general cargo including linseed oil, wax, gunnies, pig iron, coconuts and fibre. The survivors were machine-gunned in the water by the Japanese submarine. The Master, Capt James Fawcett Travis, 39 crew and 7 gunners were lost. 4 crew and 3 gunners were rescued by Dutch ship *STRAAT SOENDA* 8184/39 and landed at Aden 3.3.44. I-37 under the command of Lt-Cdr Nobuo Kamimoto was sunk on 12.11.44 in the Pacific 210 miles ENE of Palau Island, part of the Caroline Islands, in position 08.04N 138.03E by US destroyer *NICHOLAS* 2050/42 (DD-449) (Lt-Cdr R.T.S. Keith).

*BLACKHEATH* • GRT 4637 • Built 1936

10.1.45: Torpedoed and damaged by German submarine U-870 (Hechler), in the Atlantic W of Gibraltar, in position 35.49N 06.30W while on government service on a voyage from Greenock and Manchester to Augusta and Ancona, with a cargo of military stores, part of the combined OS 102/KMS 76 comprising 17 ships. She went aground 2 miles S of Cape Spartel, Algeria and became a CTL. The Master, Capt John Norman Garrett, crew of 41 and 9 gunners were rescued by HM frigate *BALLINDERRY* 1370/42 (K.255) (Lt-Cdr E.K. Aikmann) and HM sloop *KILBIRNIE* 795/43 (5.01) (Lt C.T. Letts) ex-USN *BEC 11* and landed at Gibraltar. U-870, commanded by Kapitänleutnant Ernst Hechler (Knight's Cross 21.1.45), was sunk on 30.3.45 by Fortress aircraft of the USAAF at Bremen, in position 53.08N 08.46E.

## MOWT

*EMPIRE MOAT* • GRT 2922 • Built 1941

20.9.41: Torpedoed and sunk by German submarine U-124 (Mohr), in the Atlantic NNE of the Azores, in position 48.07N 22.05W while on a voyage from London and Oban to Gibraltar, in ballast, part of convoy OG 74 comprising 22 ships. The Master, Capt James Fawcett Travis, 28 crew and 3 gunners were rescued by rescue ship *WALMER CASTLE* 906/36, 5 crew were later lost when the *WALMER CASTLE* (Capt Gerald Lewis Clarke) was sunk on 21.9.41 in the Atlantic NE of the Azores, in position 47.16N 22.25W by a Focke-Wulf FW 200 Condor of I/KG 40 Bomb Group based at Bordeaux–Merignac. The Master, Capt J.F. Travis, 23 crew and 3 gunners were rescued after the sinking of the *WALMER CASTLE* by HM corvette *MARIGOLD* 925/40 (K.87) (Lt W.S. Macdonald) and HM sloop *DEPTFORD* 990/35 (L.35) (Lt-Cdr H.R. White) and landed at Gibraltar 28.9.41.

*EMPIRE FUSILIER* ex-*MINCIO* • GRT 5408 • Built 1921

9.2.42: Torpedoed and sunk by German submarine U-85 (Greger), in the Atlantic SE of St John's, Newfoundland, in position 44.45N 47.25W while sailing independently on a voyage from the Tyne to Tampa, in ballast, dispersed from convoy ON 60 comprising 45 ships. The Master, Capt William Reid, 31 crew and 6 gunners were rescued by RCN corvette *BARRIE* 925/40 (K.138) (Chief Skipper G.N. Downey) and landed at Halifax NS. 9 crew were lost. Oberleutnant zur See Eberhard Greger and crew of 44 were lost on 14.4.42 when U-85 was sunk in the Atlantic NE of Cape Hatteras, North Carolina, in position 35.53N 75.13W by US four-stack destroyer *ROPER* 1090/18 (DD-147) (Lt-Cdr Hamilton W. Howe). This was the first U-boat to be sunk by a US warship in the Second World War. The Italian *MINCIO* was taken as a prize on 10.6.40 at Liverpool.

**EMPIRE HARTEBEESTE** ex-*WEST GAMBO* • GRT 5675 • Built 1918
20.9.42: Torpedoed and sunk by German submarine U-596 (Jahn), part of the 'Lohs' patrol group of sixteen U-boats, in the Atlantic SE of Cape Farewell, in position 56.20N 38.10W while on a voyage from New York and Halifax NS 12.9.42 to Hull, with a cargo of 4000 tons of steel, 1000 tons of canned goods, 70 tons of timber and 2000 tons of trucks, part of convoy SC 100 comprising 20 ships. The Master, Capt James Fawcett Travis, 33 crew, 9 gunners and 3 DBS were rescued: the Master and 20 survivors by Norwegian ship *RIO VERDE* 3232/24 and landed at Liverpool 29.9.42, and the Chief Officer and 24 survivors by Norwegian ship *NORHAUK* 6086/19 and landed at Oban 28.9.42.

## WEBSTER, JAMES S. & SONS – KINGSTON, JAMAICA

**ALLISTER** ex-*ALGERIA* ex-*EATON GROVE* ex-*PEREZ* ex-*EASTERN COAST* ex-*POWERFUL* • GRT 1597 • Built 1903
29.5.42: Torpedoed and sunk by German submarine U-504 (Poske), in the Atlantic 54 miles S of Grand Cayman Island, BWI, in position 18.23N 78.50W while sailing independently on a voyage from Kingston, Jamaica to Tampa, with a cargo of 500 tons of bananas. 8 crew landed at Port au Prince, Haiti Republic. 15 crew were lost.

## WEIDNER, HOPKINS & COMPANY – NEWCASTLE UPON TYNE
## MOWT

**EMPIRE ENGINEER** ex-*GIOACCHINO LAURO* ex-*CANADIAN COMMANDER*
GRT 5358 • Built 1921.
4.2.41: Torpedoed and sunk by German submarine U-123 (Moehle), in the Atlantic SE of Cape Farewell, in position 54.00N 34.00W while on a voyage from Sydney CB to Newport, Mon, with a cargo of steel ingots, a straggler from convoy SC 20 comprising 38 ships. The Master, Capt John Whiteley, and crew of 38 were lost. The Italian *GIOACCHINO LAURO* was taken as a prize on 10.6.40 at Hartlepool.

## WEIR, ANDREW & COMPANY – LONDON
**Bank Line**

**CEDARBANK** • GRT 5151 • Built 1924
21.4.40: Torpedoed and sunk by German submarine U-26 (Scheringer), in the North Atlantic NW of Bergen, in position 62.49N 04.10E while on a voyage from Leith to Aalesund, Norway, with a cargo of 400 tons of military stores, ammunition and vehicles. The Master, Capt William James Calderwood, and 29 crew were rescued by HM destroyer *JAVELIN* 1690/38 (F.61) ex-HMS *KASHMIR* (Cdr A.F. Pugsley) landed at Aalesund. 14 crew and 1 gunner were lost. U-26 commanded by Kapitänleutnant Heinz Scheringer was damaged on 1.7.40 in the Atlantic 240 miles W of Ushant, in position 48.03N 11.30W by HM corvette *GLADIOLUS* 925/40 (K.34) (Lt-Cdr Harry M.C. Sanders) and HM sloop *ROCHESTER* 1105/31 (L.50) (Capt G.F. Renwick), and later sunk by Sunderland 'H' P9603, pilot F/Lt W.N. Gibson of No. 10

Squadron RAAF, based at Mount Batten, part of 15 Group. The pilot was awarded the DFC. The U-boat commander and crew of 47 were taken prisoner by HMS *ROCHESTER*.

### *WILLOWBANK* • GRT 5041 • Built 1939

12.6.40: Torpedoed and sunk by German submarine U-46 (Endrass), in the Bay of Biscay about 250 miles WNW of Cape Finisterre, in position 44.16N 13.54W while on a voyage from Durban to Hull via Freetown 31.5.40, with a cargo of 8750 tons of maize, part of convoy SL 34 comprising 30 ships. The Master, Capt Donald Gillies, and crew of 50 were rescued by British ship *SWEDRU* 5379/37.

### *ELMBANK* • GRT 5156 • Built 1925

21.9.40: Torpedoed and damaged by gunfire by German submarines U-99 (Kretschmer) and U-47 (Prien) and later a *coup de grâce* by U-99, in the Atlantic S of Iceland, in position 55.20N 22.30W while on a voyage from Cowichan, British Columbia to Belfast via Panama and Halifax NS, with a cargo of metal and timber, part of convoy HX 72 comprising 47 ships. The Master, Capt Harold Tyler Phillips, and 53 crew were rescued by British ship *PIKEPOOL* 7178/42 and landed at St John's, Newfoundland. 2 crew were lost.

### *TYMERIC* ex-*WAR MAMMOTH* • GRT 5228 • Built 1919

23.11.40: Torpedoed and sunk by German submarine U-123 (Moehle), in the Atlantic 350 miles WNW of Malin Head, in position 57.00N 20.30W while on a voyage from Hull to Buenos Aires, with a cargo of 6150 tons of coal, a straggler from convoy OB 244 comprising 46 ships. The Master, Capt Thomas Fraser, and 4 crew were rescued by HM sloop *SANDWICH* 1043/28 (L.12) (Lt-Cdr R.C. Gervers) and landed at Liverpool. 71 crew were lost.

### *TIELBANK* • GRT 5084 • Built 1937

8.3.41: Torpedoed and sunk by German submarine U-105 (Schewe), in the Atlantic N of the Cape Verde Islands, in position 20.51N 20.32W while on a voyage from Kakinada, EC India and Durban to Oban via Freetown, with a cargo of 743 tons of manganese ingots, 6456 tons of groundnuts and 997 tons of groundnut cake, part of convoy SL 67 comprising 56 ships. The Master, Capt William Broome, 59 crew and 2 gunners were rescued by HM destroyer *FORESTER* 1350/34 (H.74) (Lt-Cdr E.B. Tancock DSC) and landed at Gibraltar 16.3.41. 4 crew were lost.

### *SPRINGBANK* • GRT 5155 • Built 1926 (CAM ship).

27.9.41: Torpedoed and damaged by German submarine U-201 (Schnee) in the Atlantic WSW of Fastnet, in position 49.10N 20.05W, while on a voyage from Gibraltar to the UK, part of convoy HG 73 comprising 25 ships. Later sunk by HM corvette *JASMINE* 925/41 (K.23) (Lt-Cdr C.D.B. Coventry) after becoming a danger to shipping. Lost while employed by the Admiralty as an auxiliary fighter catapult ship. Capt C.H. Godwin DSO and 200 survivors were rescued by HM corvettes *HIBISCUS* 925/40 (K.24) (Lt H. Roach) (landed at Gibraltar) and *PERIWINKLE* 925/40 (K.55) (Lt-Cdr P.G. MacIver) (landed at Milford Haven), part of the 7th Escort Group.

### *THORNLIEBANK* • GRT 5569 • Built 1939

29.11.41: Torpedoed and sunk by German submarine U-43 (Lüth), in the Atlantic N of the Azores, in position 41.50N 29.48E while on government service on a voyage from Barry to the Middle East via Freetown, with general cargo and munitions, part of convoy OS 12 comprising 55 ships. The Master, Capt Sydney Letton, crew of 65 and 9 gunners were lost.

**THURSOBANK** • GRT 5575 • Built 1940
22.3.42: Torpedoed and sunk by German submarine U-373 (Loeser), part of 'Operation Paukenschlag' (Drumbeat), the fourth wave of eleven U-boats in the Atlantic E of Chesapeake Bay, in position 38.05N 68.30W while sailing independently on a voyage from New York to Alexandria via Cape Town with a cargo of 7839 tons of general cargo. The Master, Capt Ralph Brian Ellis, 22 crew and 7 gunners were lost. 26 crew were rescued by Norwegian motor tanker *HAVSTEN* 6161/30 and landed at Halifax NS. U-373, commanded by Oberleutnant zur See Detlef von Lehsten, was sunk on 8.6.44 in the Bay of Biscay 25 miles SW of Ushant, in position 48.27N 05.47W by Liberator 'G', pilot F/O Kenneth Owen Moore (Canadian) of No. 224 Squadron RAF, based at St Eval, part of 19 Group. The pilot was awarded the DSO. The U-boat commander and 43 crew were rescued by a fishing boat and landed in France. 4 crew were lost.

**WEIRBANK** • GRT 5150 • Built 1925
28.7.42: Torpedoed and sunk by German submarine U-66 (Markworth), in the Atlantic about 90 miles SE of Barbados, in position 11.29N 58.51W while sailing independently on a voyage from Alexandria and Durban 27.6.42 to Trinidad and New York, in ballast. The Master, Capt David Alexander Banner Reid, 55 crew and 10 gunners landed at Scarborough, Tobago, BWI 29.7.42. 1 crew was lost.

**TEESBANK** • GRT 5136 • Built 1937
5.12.42: Torpedoed and sunk by German submarine U-128 (Heyse), in the Atlantic N of St Paul Rocks, in position 03.33N 29.35W while sailing independently on a voyage from Port Said and Port Elizabeth 18.11.42 to Demerara, in the ballast. The Master, William George Loraine, was taken prisoner, landed at Lorient 15.1.43 and was taken to Milag Nord. 41 crew were rescued by US tanker *BESSEMER* 4762/19 and landed at Rio de Janeiro and 19 crew by British ship *EAST WALES* 4358/25 landed at Natal, Brazil 23.12.42. 1 crew was lost. Kapitänleutnant Ulrich Heyse was awarded the Knight's Cross (21.1.43). U-128, commanded by Kapitänleutnant Herman Steinert, was damaged on 17.5.43 by Mariner P-5, pilot Lt Harold C. Carey and Mariner P-6, pilot Lt Howland S. Davis of US Navy Bombing Squadron VP–74, based at Aratu, Brazil and was scuttled when US destroyers *MOFFETT* 1850/35 (DD-362) (Cdr J.C. Sowell) and *JOUETT* 1850/38 (DD–396) (Cdr F.L. Tedder) approached in the South Atlantic 200 miles ENE of Bahia, Brazil in position 10.00S 35.35W. The U-boat commander and 46 crew were taken prisoner by USS *MOFFETT* and landed at Recife. 7 crew were lost.

**OAKBANK** • GRT 5154 • Built 1926
27.12.42: Torpedoed and sunk by German submarine U-507 (Schacht), in the South Atlantic 200 miles NNE of Fortaleza, Brazil, in position 00.46S 37.58W while sailing independently on a voyage from Suez and Durban 8.12.42 to Demerara and the UK, in ballast. The Master, Capt John Stuart, 24 crew and 2 gunners were lost. 29 crew and 3 gunners were rescued by Brazilian ship *COMMANDATE RIPPER* 3324/07 and landed at Recife 3.1.43, 1 crew by Argentinian tanker *JUVENAL* 13896/28 and landed at Curacao 8.1.43 and 2 crew on a ship's raft landed at Para 15.1.42. 2 crew were taken prisoner.

**KELVINBANK** ex-*DAGA* ex-*MALIA* • GRT 3872 • Built 1921
9.3.43: Torpedoed and sunk by German submarine U-510 (Neitzel), in the Atlantic NE of Belem, in position 07.24N 52.11W while on a voyage from Alexandria, Aden and Cape Town to Macoris, Cuba via Bahia and Trinidad, in ballast, part of convoy BT 6 comprising 27 ships. The Master, Capt Robert Charles Loraine, 24 crew and 7 gunners were rescued by US liberty ship *GEORGE G. MEADE* 7176/42 and landed at Paramaribo. 27 crew and 1 gunner were lost. Korvettenkapitän Karl Neitzel was awarded the Knight's Cross (27.3.43).

**TINHOW** ex-*HUGHLI* ex-*VALENCIA* • GRT 5232 • Built 1913
11.5.43: Torpedoed and sunk by German submarine U-181 (Lüth), in the Mozambique Channel about 20/25 miles 230° from Limpoo Light, in position 25.25S 33.50E while sailing independently on a voyage from Durban and Beira to Calcutta, with 125 passengers and general cargo, dispersed from convoy DN 37. The Master, Capt Philip Henry Aydon, 24 crew and 50 passengers were lost. 41 crew, 12 gunners and 75 passengers were rescued by Portuguese fishing boats and landed at Lourenco Marques 13.5.43.

**AYMERIC** ex-*WAR NEMESIA* • GRT 5196 • Built 1919
17.5.43: Torpedoed and sunk by submarine U-657 (Göllnitz), part of 'Donau 1' (Danube) patrol group of eleven U-boats, in the Atlantic E of Cape Farewell, in position 59.42N 41.39W while on a voyage from Middlesbrough to New York via Clyde 7.5.43 and Halifax NS, in ballast, part of convoy ONS 7 comprising 40 ships. The Master, Capt Sidney Morris, 18 crew and 6 gunners were rescued by rescue ship *COPELAND* 1526/23 (Capt W.J. Hartley DSC) and HM trawler *NORTHERN WAVE* 655/36 (FY.153) (Lt J.P. Kilbee) and landed at Halifax NS. 25.5.43. 52 crew and 1 gunner were lost. Kapitänleutnant Heinrich Gollnitz and crew of 47 were lost on the same day when U-657 was sunk in the Atlantic 150 miles E of Cape Farewell, in position 58.54N 42.33W by one of the convoy's escorts HM frigate *SWALE* 1370/42 (K.217) (Lt-Cdr J. Jackson). Oberleutnant zur See Karl-Heinz Nagel and crew of 48 were lost on 14.5.43 when U-640 was sunk in the North Atlantic E of Cape Farewell, in position 60.32N 31.05W while shadowing convoy ONS 7 by Catalina 'K', pilot Lt P.A. Bodinet of US Navy VP-84 Patrol Squadron based at Reykjavik.

**INCOMATI** • GRT 7369 • Built 1934
18.7.43: Torpedoed and sunk by gunfire by German submarine U-508 (Staats), in the Atlantic about 200 miles S of Lagos, in position 03.09N 04.15E while sailing independently on a voyage from Takoradi 16.7.43 to Walvis Bay, Durban and the Middle East, with 112 passengers and 7000 tons general cargo including 3600 tons of cocoa, 2600 tons of stores and 2 aircraft. The Master, Capt Stephen Fox, 101 crew, 8 gunners and passengers were rescued by HM destroyer *BOADICEA* 1360/30 (H.65) (Lt-Cdr F.C. Brodrick) and HM sloop *BRIDGEWATER* 1045/28 (L.01) (Cdr N.W.H. Weekes OBE) and landed at Takoradi. 1 crew was lost. Kapitänleutnant Georg Staats (Knight's Cross 14.7.43) and crew of 56 were lost on 12.11.43 when U-508 was sunk in the the Atlantic 130 miles N of Cape Ortegal, in position 46.00N 07.30W by Liberator 'C', pilot Lt Ralph B. Brownell of US Navy Bombing Squadron VB-103 based at Dunkeswell, North Devon. The attacking Liberator was shot down by U-508 and the ten aircrew were lost. The pilot was posthumously awarded the US Navy Cross.

**LARCHBANK** • GRT 5150 • Built 1925

10.9.43: Torpedoed and sunk by Japanese submarine I-27 (Fukumura), in the Indian Ocean W of Cape Comorin, India, in position 07.38N 74.00E while sailing independently on a voyage from Baltimore, Suez and Aden to Colombo and Calcutta, with 7394 tons of general cargo and military stores including 4 tanks, 2 MT boats, 8 amphibious craft and railway iron. The Master, Capt William Arthur McCracken, 36 crew, 6 gunners, 2 DBS and 1 naval petty officer were lost. 16 crew, 4 gunners and 3 DBS landed at Katurunda, Ceylon 28.9.43. The 3rd Officer, 1 cadet, 1 naval petty officer and 4 crew were rescued after 23 days on a raft by Anchor Line ship *TAHAINIA* 7267/42 and landed at Colombo; the 4th Engineer and 2 crew by US ship *PANAMAN* 5283/13 and landed at Fremantle. The *LARCHBANK* sank within 2 minutes.

**CONGELLA** ex-*MINDORO* ex-*SAGAMI* ex-*SECUNDUS* • GRT 4533 • Built 1914

24.10.43: Sunk by gunfire by Japanese submarine I-10 (Tonozuka), in the Indian Ocean NW of Addu Atoll, in position 01.02N 71.14E while sailing independently on a voyage from Calcutta and Colombo to Mombasa and Durban, with a cargo of 8700 tons of general including gunnies, mail, naval stores, tea and wax. The Master, Capt Arthur William Folster, 25 crew and 3 gunners were lost. 33 crew and 4 gunners were rescued by HM whaler *OKAPI* 246/29 ex-AN 5 (Paymaster Lt A.M.H. Baker) and two RAF Catalina flying boats and landed 27.10.43 at Addu Atoll, Maldive Islands. The wireless operator was taken prisoner. I-10 commanded by Lt Sakae Nakajima was sunk on 4.7.44 in the Pacific 210 miles ENE of Guam Island, in position 15.25N 147.48E by US destroyer *DAVID W. TAYLOR* 2050/42 (DD-551) (Cdr W.H. Johnsen) and US destroyer escort *RIDDLE* 1240/43 (DE-185) (Lt-Cdr R.H. Cramer USNR).

## MOWT

**EMPIRE MINIVER** ex-*WEST COBALT* • GRT 6055 • Built 1918

18.10.40: Torpedoed and sunk by German submarine U-99 (Kretschmer), in the Atlantic about 100 miles W by S of Barra Head, in position 56.40N 10.45W while on a voyage from Baltimore to Newport, Mon. via Sydney CB 5.10.40, with a cargo of 4500 tons of pig iron and 6200 tons of steel, part of convoy SC 7 comprising 35 ships. The Master, Capt Robert Smith, and 34 crew were rescued by HM corvette *BLUEBELL* 925/40 (K.80) (Lt-Cdr Robert E. Sherwood) and landed at Greenock 20.10.40. 3 crew were lost.

**EMPIRE HERON** ex-*MOSELLA* • GRT 6023 • Built 1920

16.10.41: Torpedoed and sunk by German submarine U-568 (Preuss), in the Atlantic SE of Cape Farewell, in position 54.55N 27.15W while on a voyage from Freeport, Texas to Manchester via Sydney CB, with a cargo 7673 tons of sulphur, part of convoy SC 48 comprising 50 ships. The Master, Capt James Dick Ross, crew of 33 and 9 gunners were lost. U-568 commanded by Kapitänleutnant Joachim Preuss was sunk on 28.5.42 in the Mediterranean 70 miles NE of Tobruk, in position 32.42N 24.53E by HM destroyers *ERIDGE* 907/40 (L.68) (Lt-Cdr W.F.N. Gregory-Smith), *HERO* 1340/36 (H.99) (Lt-Cdr W.S. Scott) and *HURWORTH* 907/41 (L.28) (Lt-Cdr J.T.B. Birch). The U-boat commander and crew of 46 were taken prisoner by HMS *ERIDGE* and HMS *HURWORTH.*

**ILE DE BATZ** ex-*WEST HOBOMAC* • GRT 5755 • Built 1918

17.3.42: Torpedoed and sunk by gunfire by German submarine U-68 (Merten), in the Atlantic 28 miles SW of Cape Palmas, in position 04.04N 08.04W while sailing independently on a voyage from Rangoon to the UK via Cape Town 4.3.42 and Freetown with 6605 tons of general cargo and rice. The Master, Capt A.J. Watts, 34 crew and 4 gunners landed at Cape Palmas and were brought to Freetown by RCN corvette *WEYBURN* 925/41 (K.173) (Lt Thomas M.H. Golby). 4 crew were lost.

**EMPIRE STEEL** (tanker) • GRT 8138 • Built 1941
24.3.42: Torpedoed and sunk by gunfire by German submarine U-123 (Hardegen), in the Atlantic NE of Bermuda, in position 37.45N 63.17W while sailing independently on a voyage from Baton Rouge 13.3.42 to the UK via Halifax NS, with a cargo of 11000 tons of aviation spirit and kerosene. The Master, Capt William John Gray, 6 crew and 1 gunner were rescued by US tug *EDMUND J. MORAN* 336/40 towing US ship *ROBERT E. LEE* 5184/25 and landed at Norfolk, Virginia. 35 crew and 4 gunners were lost. Kapitänleutnant Reinhard Hardegen was awarded the Knight's Cross (23.1.42) with Oak Leaves (23.4.42).

**EMPIRE ATTENDANT** ex-*DOMALA* • GRT 7524 • Built 1921
15.7.42: Torpedoed and sunk by German submarine U-582 (Schulte), part of the 'Hai' (Shark) patrol group of six U-boats, in the Atlantic S of the Canary Islands, in position 23.48N 21.51W while on a voyage from Liverpool and Durban to Karachi, with a cargo of stores and vehicles, a straggler from convoy OS 33 comprising 41 ships. The Master, Capt Thomas Grundy, crew of 49 and 9 gunners were lost. Kapitänleutnant Werner Schulte and crew of 45 were lost on 5.10.42 when U-582, part of the 'Luchs' (Lynx) patrol group of sixteen U-boats, was sunk in the Atlantic 260 miles S by E of Reykjanes, in position 58.52N 21.42W by Catalina 'I', pilot Lt F.G.F. Swanson of US Navy Bombing Squadron VP-73 based at Reykjavik.

**EMPIRE CITY** • GRT 7295 • Built 1943
6.8.44: Torpedoed and sunk by German submarine U-198 (v. Waldegg), in the Indian Ocean E of Mocimboa, Portuguese East Africa, in position 11.33S 41.25E while on a voyage from Lourenco Marques to Aden and Port Said, with a cargo of 8403 tons of coal, part of convoy DKA 21 comprising 8 ships. The Master, Capt Bernard Henry Jackson, 47 crew and 10 gunners landed at Pekawi, Portuguese East Africa. 2 crew and 10 gunners were lost.

**Inver Tankers Ltd**
**Liffey Transport and Trading Co. Ltd**

**INVERLIFFEY** (tanker) • GRT 9456 • Built 1938
11.9.39: Torpedoed and sunk by gunfire by German submarine U-38 (Liebe), in the Atlantic SW of the Scilly Isles, in position 48.14N 11.48W while sailing independently on a voyage from Trinidad to Coryton, with a cargo of 13000 tons of gasolene. The Master, Capt William Trowsdale, and crew of 48 were rescued by US tanker *R.G. STEWART* 9229/17 and landed at Milford Haven.

**INVERDARGLE** (tanker) • GRT 9456 • Built 1938
16.1.40: Struck a mine, laid on 5.12.39, by German submarine U-28 (Kuhnke) and sank in the Bristol Channel SW of Nash Point, in position 51.16N 03.43W while sailing independently on a voyage from Trinidad to Avonmouth via Halifax NS, with a cargo of 12554 tons of aviation spirit. The Master, Capt Evan Murdock Skelly, and crew of 48 were lost.

*INVERSHANNON* (tanker) • GRT 9154 • Built 1938

21.9.40: Torpedoed and sunk by German submarine U-99 (Kretschmer), in the Atlantic 480 miles W of Bloody Foreland, in position 55.40N 22.04W while on government service on a voyage from Curacao to Scapa Flow, with a cargo of 13241 tons of Admiralty fuel oil, part of convoy HX 72 comprising 47 ships. The Master, Capt William Richardson Forsyth, and 16 crew were rescued by HM sloop *FLAMINGO* 1250/39 (L.18) (Cdr J H Huntley) and landed at Londonderry and 15 crew by HM trawler *FANDANGO* 530/40 (T.107) (Lt G.E. Mabbott) and landed at Belfast 29.9.40. 16 crew were lost.

*INVERSUIR* (tanker) • GRT 9456 • Built 1938

3.6.41: Torpedoed and sunk by gunfire by German submarine U-48 (Schultze), in the Atlantic N of the Azores, in position 48.28N 28.20W while on a voyage from Stanlow 16.5.41 to Aruba, in ballast, dispersed on 1.6.41 in position 52.42N 22.18W from convoy OB 327 comprising 46 ships. The Master, Capt Robert Charles Loraine, and 23 crew were rescued by Norwegian ship *PARA* 3986/21, transferred to HM ocean boarding ship *CORINTHIAN* 3151/38 (F.103) (Cdr E.J.R. Pollitt) and landed at Greenock 21.6.41, 9 crew by HM destroyer *WANDERER* 1100/19 (D.74) (Cdr A.F. St G. Orpen) landed at Holyhead and 12 crew were rescued by an unknown ship and landed at Quebec.

*INVERLEE* (tanker) • GRT 9158 • Built 1938

19.10.41: Torpedoed and sunk by German submarine U-204 (Kell), in the Atlantic 15 miles WSW of Cape Spartel, Morocco while sailing independently on government service on a voyage from Trinidad to Gibraltar, with a cargo of 13880 tons of Admiralty fuel oil. The Master, Capt Thomas Edward Alexander, 20 crew and 1 gunner were lost. 17 crew and 4 gunners were rescued by HM destroyer leader *DUNCAN* 1400/32 (D.99) (Lt-Cdr A.N. Rowell), HM trawlers *LADY HOGARTH* 472/37 (4.89) (Lt S.G. Barnes) and HMS *HAARLEM* 431/38 (FY.306) (Lt L.B. Merrick) and landed at Gibraltar. Kapitänleutnant Walter Kell and crew of 45 were lost on the same day when U-204, part of the 'Breslau' patrol group of six U-boats, was sunk in the Atlantic off Cape Spartel, in position 35.46N 06.02W by HM corvette *MALLOW* 925/40 (K.81) (Lt W.R.B. Noall) and HM sloop *ROCHESTER* 1105/31 (L.50) (Cdr C.B. Allen) of the 37th Escort Group.

*INVERILEN* (tanker) • GRT 9456 • Built 1938

3.2.43: Torpedoed and sunk by German submarine U-456 (Teichert), part of the 'Landsknecht' (Mercenary) patrol of twenty U-boats, in the Atlantic S of Iceland, in position 56.35N 23.30W while on a voyage from New York 22.1.43 to Stanlow, with a cargo of clean petroleum products, part of convoy HX 224 comprising 57 ships. The Master, Capt Joseph Mann, 24 crew and 6 gunners were lost. 14 crew and 2 DBS were rescued by HM corvette *ASPHODEL* 925/41 (K.56) (Lt G.L. Fraser) and landed at Londonderry.

## WEST HARTLEPOOL STEAM NAVIGATION CO. LTD – WEST HARTLEPOOL

*CLIFTONHALL* • GRT 5063 • Built 1938

12.6.42: Torpedoed and sunk by Japanese submarine I-20 (Yamada), in the Mozambique Channel S of Mozambique, in position 16.25S 40.10E while sailing independently on a voyage from Alexandria and Aden to Chile via Cape Town, in ballast. The Master, Capt Frank Hanbury Wainford, and 40 crew landed at Cape Angoche, Portuguese East Africa. 2 crew were lost. Lt Susumu Otsuka and crew were lost on 1.10.43 when I-20 was sunk in the Pacific N of Kolombangara, Solomon Islands, in position 07.40S 157.10E by US destroyer *EATON* 2050/42 (DD-510) (Lt-Cdr E.F. Jackson).

**LINDENHALL** • GRT 5248 • Built 1937
7.11.42: Torpedoed and sunk by German submarine U-508 (Staats), in the Atlantic 40 miles N of Margarita Island, Venezuela, in position 11.34N 63.26W while on a voyage from Rio de Janeiro to the UK via Trinidad 6.11.42 and New York, with a cargo of 8400 tons of iron ore, part of convoy TAG 19 comprising 17 ships. The Master, Capt Frederick Aggebec Kjelgaard, 37 crew and 4 gunners were lost. 5 crew and 1 gunner were rescued by US corvette *SURPRISE* 925/40 (PG.63) ex-HMS *HELIOTROPE* and landed at Havana, Cuba.

## WESTBOURNE SHIPPING CO. LTD – CARDIFF
## MOWT

**DJURDJURA** ex-*PENRITH CASTLE* • GRT 3460 • Built 1922
13.6.41: Torpedoed and sunk by Italian submarine *BRIN* (Loganesi-Cattani), in the Atlantic 428 miles 268° from Slyn Head, Co. Galway, in position 38.53N 23.11W while on a voyage from Pepel to Oban via Freetown, with a cargo of 5000 tons of iron ore, part of convoy SL 76 comprising 60 ships. The Master, Capt Pierre Edward de la Rue Croix de Guerre, and 32 crew were lost. 5 crew were rescued by Portuguese ship *MALANGE* 3155/04.

## WESTERN OIL SHIPPING CO. – LONDON

**KARS** ex-*MINCIO* (tanker) • GRT 8888 • Built 1939
22.2.42: Torpedoed and damaged by German submarine U-96 (Lehmann-Willenbrock), part of 'Operation Paukenschlag' (Drumbeat), the third wave of twelve U-boats, in the Atlantic S of Halifax NS, in position 44.15N 63.25W while on a voyage from Trinidad to Belfast via Halifax NS 14.2.42, with a cargo of 12700 tons of aviation spirit and fuel oil, part of convoy ON 67 comprising 37 ships. The afterpart was towed and beached at Halifax NS. The Master, Capt Arthur Falconer, 45 crew and 4 gunners were lost. 2 crew were rescued by RCN minesweeping sloop *MELVILLE* 590/41 (J.263) (Lt R.T. Ingram) and landed at Halifax NS. Korvettenkapitän Heinrich Lehmann-Willenbrock was awarded the Knight's Cross (26.2.41) with Oak Leaves (31.12.41).

## WESTROLL, JAMES LIMITED – SUNDERLAND
## MOWT

**EMPIRE BELL** ex-*BELGIA* • GRT 2023 • Built 1930
25.9.42: Torpedoed and sunk by German submarine U-442 (Hesse), in the North Atlantic WSW of the Faröe Islands, in position 62.19N 15.27W while on a voyage from the Tyne and Loch Ewe 22.9.42 to Reykjavik, with a cargo of 1832 tons of coal, part of convoy UR 42 comprising 9 ships. The Master, Capt George Charles May, 20 crew and 6 gunners were rescued by Norwegian ship *LYSAKER IV* 1551/24 and landed at Reykjavik. 10 crew were lost.

## WHIMSTER & COMPANY – GLASGOW
### Gart Line Ltd

*GARTAVON* ex-*GELVES* • GRT 1777 • Built 1921
7.9.39: Sunk by gunfire by German submarine U-47 (Prien), in the Atlantic NW of Cape Ortegal, in position 47.04N 11.32W while sailing independently on a voyage from Sete and La Goulette to the Clyde, with a cargo of 1600 tons of iron ore and 500 tons of general cargo including asphalt. The Master, Capt George Smith Hunter, and crew were rescued by Swedish motor tanker *CASTOR* 8914/28 and landed at Horta, Azores 11.9.39.

## WHITWELL, MARK & SON LIMITED – BRISTOL

*SEVERN LEIGH* ex-*QUEEN OLGA* ex-*BEMBRIDGE* ex-*WAR ANCHUSA*
GRT 5242 • Built 1919
23.8.40: Torpedoed and sunk by German submarine U-37 (Oehrn), in the Atlantic S of Iceland, in position 54.31N 25.41W while on a voyage from Hull to St John, New Brunswick, in ballast, part of convoy OA 200 comprising 40 ships. The Master, Capt Robert George Hammett OBE, and 9 crew landed 5.9.40 at Leverburgh, South Uist. 32 crew and 1 gunner were lost. Capt R.G. Hammett was awarded the Lloyd's War Medal for bravery at sea.

## MOWT

*EMPIRE AIRMAN* ex-*BARBANA* ex-*BARBANA G* ex-*TEODO* • GRT 6586 • Built 1915
22.9.40: Torpedoed and damaged by German submarine U-100 (Schepke), in the Atlantic 340 miles W of Bloody Foreland, in position 54.00N 18.00W, taken in tow but sank on 23.9.40 in position 55.11N 15.07W while on a voyage from Wabana, Conception Bay to Cardiff via Halifax NS, with a cargo of iron ore, part of convoy HX 72 comprising 47 ships. The Master, Capt John Brown Raine, and 3 crew were rescued by RCN corvette *LA MALOUINE* 925/40 (K.46) (Lt-Cdr R.W. Keymer) and landed at Greenock. 33 crew were lost. The Italian *BARBANA* was taken as a prize at sea on 10.6.40 and taken to Methil.

*AGNETE MAERSK* ex-*AABENRAA* • GRT 2104 • Built 1921
24.3.41: Torpedoed and sunk by gunfire by Italian submarine *VENIERO* (Petroni), in the Atlantic SW of Fastnet, in position 49.00N 22.55W while sailing independently on a voyage from Ardrossan to St John, New Brunswick, in ballast, dispersed from convoy OG 56 comprising 35 ships. The Master, Capt Rasmus Petter Henry H. Parkholm, and crew of 26 were lost. *VENIERO*, commanded by Lt Elio Zappetta, was sunk on 7.6.42 in the Mediterranean 35 miles SE of Ibiza, Balearic Islands, in position 38.21N 03.21E by Catalina 'M', pilot F/O R.M. Corrie RAAF of No. 202 Squadron RAF, based at Gibraltar. The pilot was awarded the DFC.

*ROSE SCHIAFFINO* ex-*NOTTON* • GRT 3349 • Built 1920
3.11.41: Torpedoed and sunk by German submarine U-374 (v. Fischel), in the North Atlantic 225 miles E of St John's, Newfoundland while sailing independently on a voyage from Wabana, Conception Bay to Cardiff via St John's 31.10.41, with a cargo of iron ore. The Master, Capt Thomas P. Evans, crew of 36 and 4 gunners were lost.

## WILLIAMS, IDAL & COMPANY – CARDIFF
Graig SS Co.

*GRAIGWEN* • GRT 3697 • Built 1926
10.10.40: Torpedoed and damaged by German submarine U-103 (Schütze) and sunk by a *coup de grâce* by U-123 (Moehle), in the Atlantic 37 miles NNW of Rockall, in position 58.11N 13.57W while on a voyage from Montreal to Barry Roads via Sydney CB, with a cargo of 6160 tons of maize, part of convoy SC 6 comprising 38 ships. The Master, Capt Daniel Wright Fowle, 25 crew and 1 gunner were rescued by HM sloop *ENCHANTRESS* 1190/34 (L.56) ex-HMS *BITTERN* (Cdr A.K. Scott-Moncrieff) and landed at Londonderry. 7 crew were lost.

*NEWTON PINE* • GRT 4212 • Built 1925
16.10.42: Torpedoed and sunk by German submarine U-410 (Sturm), part of the 'Wotan' (god of the Vikings) group of ten U-boats, in the Atlantic SE of Cape Farewell, in position 55.00N 30.00W while on a voyage from the UK to New York, in ballast, a straggler from convoy ONS 136 comprising 36 ships. The Master, Capt Evan Owen Thomas, and crew of 39 were lost.

## WILLIAMSON & COMPANY – HONG KONG
Leana SS Co. Ltd

*LEANA* ex-*TAPTI* ex-*ULM* • GRT 4742 • Built 1914
7.7.43: Torpedoed and sunk by gunfire by German submarine U-198 (Hartmann), in the Indian Ocean about 40 miles SE of Zavora Point, Portuguese East Africa, in position 24.55S 35.20E while sailing independently on a voyage from Aden and Mombasa to Lourenco Marques, in ballast, with 1 passenger. The Master, Capt Joseph Crosthwaite, was taken prisoner, landed at Bordeaux 24.9.43 and was taken to Milag Nord. 57 crew, 5 gunners and passenger landed after five days at Inchi-Inchi Lighthouse, near Lourenco Marques, Portuguese East Africa. 2 crew were lost. Kapitänleutnant Werner Hartmann was awarded the Knight's Cross (9.4.40) with Oak Leaves (5.11.44).

## WILTON, T.C. & CO. LTD – NEWCASTLE UPON TYNE
MOWT

*SAINT ENOGAT* ex-*WAR CLARION* • GRT 2360 • Built 1918
19.8.44: Torpedoed and sunk by German submarine U-413 (Sachse), in the English Channel SE of St Catherine's Point, Isle of Wight, in position 50.16N 00.50W while on government service on a voyage from London to Juno beach, Normandy, with a cargo of 1427 tons of government stores, part of coastal convoy ETC 70 comprising 20 ships. The Master, Capt Philip Duggan, 30 crew, 5 gunners and 1 army storekeeper were rescued by Landing Ship Infantry *DUKE OF ARGYLL* 3606/28 and landed at Juno beach. 3 crew and 1 gunner were lost. U-413, commanded by Oberleutnant zur See Dietrich Sachse, was sunk on 20.8.44 in the English Channel 24 miles SSW of Beachy Head, in position 50.21N 00.01W by HM escort destroyer *WENSLEYDALE* 1087/42 (L.86) (Lt-Cdr W.P. Goodfellow) and HM destroyers *FORESTER* 1350/43 (H.74) (Cdr G.W. Gregorie) and *VIDETTE* 1300/18 (F.07) (Lt-Cdr G.S. Woolley). The U-boat commander and 44 crew were lost. 1 officer was taken prisoner.

## WITHERINGTON & EVERETT – NEWCASTLE UPON TYNE
## MOWT

*EMPIRE RIDGE* • GRT 2922 • Built 1941
19.5.41: Torpedoed and sunk by German submarine U-96 (Lehmann-Willlenbrock), in the Atlantic 90 miles W of Bloody Foreland, in position 55.18N 10.49W while on a voyage from Melilla to Workington, with a cargo of 3500 tons of iron ore, part of convoy HG 61 comprising 23 ships. The Master, Capt Ernest William Clark, 27 crew and 3 gunners were lost. 1 crew and 1 gunner were rescued by HM destroyer *VANQUISHER* 1090/17 (D.54) (Lt F.D. Cole), transferred to HM destroyer *LEGION* 1920/39 (F.74) (Cdr R.F. Jessel) and landed at Greenock.

*AVONDALE PARK* • GRT 2878 • Built 1944 (Canadian)
7.5.45: Torpedoed and sunk by German submarine U-2336 (Klusmeyer), in the Firth of Forth, 1 mile E of May Island, in position 56.05N 02.32W while on a voyage from Hull 6.5.45 to Belfast via Methil, with general cargo, part of coastal convoy EN 91 comprising 25 ships. The Master, Capt James Wilson Martin Cushnie, 31 crew and 4 gunners were rescued by the escorts. 2 crew were lost. This was the last British ship to be sunk in the Second World War. U-2336, commanded by Kapitanleutnant Emil Klusmeyer, surrendered to Great Britain. U-2336 sailed on 2.1.46 from Lishally, Loch Foyle under tow by HM destroyer *PYTCHLEY* 907/40 (L.92) (Lt-Cdr D.H. Foulds DSC) and was sunk by gunfire by HM destroyer *OFFA* 1540/41 (G.29) (Lt-Cdr E.M. Thorpe DSO) on the same day at 10.36 hours in the Atlantic SE of Rockall, in position 56.06N 09.00W, part of 'Operation Deadlight', the disposal of 116 U-boats by the Royal Navy.

## YEOWARD BROTHERS – LIVERPOOL
## Yeoward Line

*AQUILA* • GRT 3255 • Built 1917
19.8.41: Torpedoed and sunk by German submarine U-201 (Schnee), in the Atlantic WSW of Fastnet Rock, in position 49.23N 17.56W while on a voyage from Liverpool to Gibraltar and Lisbon, with 91 passengers and 1288 tons of general cargo including mail, part of convoy OG 71 comprising 21 ships. The Master, Capt Arthur Firth, 6 crew, 1 naval staff and 2 passengers were rescued by HM corvette *WALLFLOWER* 925/40 (K.44) (Lt-Cdr I.J. Tyson) and landed at Gibraltar; 6 crew rescued by the *EMPIRE OAK* (tug) 482/41 were later lost when the tug was sunk on 22.8.41 by U-564 (Suhren). Commodore Vice-Admiral Patrick E. Parker DSO RN, 58 crew, 5 gunners, 4 naval staff and 89 passengers were lost.

*AVOCETA* • GRT 3422 • Built 1923
26.9.41: Torpedoed and sunk by German submarine U-203 (Mützelburg), in the Atlantic N of the Azores, in position 47.57N 24.05W while on a voyage from Lisbon to Liverpool, with 88 passengers, 469 tons of general cargo and mail, part of convoy HG 73 comprising 25 ships. The Master, Capt Harold Martin, Commodore Rear-Admiral K.E.L. Creighton MVO RN, 19 crew, 2 gunners, 5 naval staff and 12 passengers were rescued by HM corvette *PERWINKLE* 925/40 (K.55) (Lt-Cdr P.G. MacIver) and landed at Milford Haven. 3 crew were rescued by British ship *CERVANTES* 1810/19, transferred to HM sloop *STARLING* 1350/42 (U.66) (Cdr Frederic John Walker) and landed at Liverpool. 43 crew, 4 gunners and 76 passengers were lost.

# GLOSSARY

## CONVOYS

| | |
|---|---|
| AKD | ex-Aden |
| AT | New York – UK (Military) |
| BC | Beira – Cape Town |
| BT | Sydney NSW – USA (Military) |
| BTC | UK coastal |
| BX | Boston – Halifax, Nova Scotia |
| CB | Cape Town – Beira |
| DN | Durban outwards to dispersal |
| EBC | English Channel |
| EN | Methil – Clyde |
| ET | North African ports – Gibraltar |
| ETC | English Channel |
| FN | Southend – Methil |
| FS | Methil – Southend |
| FXP | English Channel –invasion convoys |
| GAT | Guantanamo – Trinidad |
| GTX | Gibraltar – Tripoli – Alexandria – Port Said |
| GUS | Gibraltar – USA (slow) |
| HC | Calcutta – Colombo |
| HG | Gibraltar – UK |
| HX | Halifax/New York – UK |
| HXF | Halifax/New York – UK (fast) |
| JC | Colombo/Calcutta |
| JT | Rio de Janeiro – Trinidad |
| JW | Loch Ewe – Kola Inlet |
| KJ | Kingston, Jamaica – UK |
| KMF | UK – North Africa to Port Said (fast) |
| KMS | UK – North Africa to Port Said (slow) |
| KRS | UK – North Africa |
| KR | Indian Ocean (military) |
| KX | UK – Gibraltar |
| LMD | Lourenco Marques – Durban |
| MKF | Port Said to North Africa – UK (fast military) |
| MKS | Port Said to North Africa – UK (slow) |
| MWS | Mediterranean West – Alexandria – Malta |
| NA | North America – UK (military) |
| OA | Southend – North America |
| OB | Liverpool – Outward (North America) |
| OC | Australian Coastal convoy |
| OG | UK – Gibraltar |
| ON | Liverpool – North America |
| ONS | UK – North America (slow) |
| OS | UK – Freetown |
| PA | Persian Gulf – Aden |
| PG | Panama – Guantanamo |
| PQ | Iceland – North Russia |
| QP | North Russia – Iceland |
| QS | Quebec – Sydney, Nova Scotia |
| RA | Kola Inlet – Loch Ewe |
| RS | Gibraltar – Freetown |
| RU | Reykjavik – UK |
| SC | Sydney, Nova and New York – UK |
| SG | Sydney, Nova Scotia – Greenland |
| SH | Sydney, CB – Halifax, NS |
| SL | Sierra Leone, Freetown – UK |
| ST | Freetown – Takoradi |
| T | Trinidad to dispersal |
| TA | UK – USA (military) |
| TAG | Trinidad – Guantanamo |
| TAM | English Channel |
| TAW | Trinidad to Aruba – Key West |
| TB | Trinidad – Boston, Mass. |
| TBC | UK Coastal |
| TE | Gibraltar – North African ports |
| TF | Trinidad – Freetown |
| TJ | Trinidad – Rio de Janeiro |
| TM | Trinidad – Gibraltar – Tanker convoy for 'Operation Torch' |
| TS | Takoradi – Freetown |
| TX | Tripoli – Alexandria |
| UC | UK – Caribbean – Tanker convoys |
| UGF | USA – North Africa |
| UGS | USA – Gibraltar (slow) |
| UR | UK – Reykjavik |
| VWP | UK – Coastal |

| | | | |
|---|---|---|---|
| WEC | UK Coastal | MVO | Member of the Royal Victorian Order |
| WP | Bristol Channel – Portsmouth | NWI | Netherland West Indies |
| WS | UK – Middle East and India via Cape of Good Hope (military) | NZ | New Zealand |
| XB | Halifax – Boston, Mass | OBE | Officer of the Order of the British Empire |
| XK | Gibraltar – UK | ORP | Okret Rzeczypospolites Polskiej (Polish Navy) |

**OTHER ABBREVIATIONS USED**

| | | | |
|---|---|---|---|
| | | P/O | Pilot Officer |
| AFC | Air Force Cross | POW | Prisoner-of-War |
| AM | Member of the Order of Australia | RD | Retired |
| BEM | British Empire Medal | RAF | Royal Air Force |
| BWI | British West Indies | RAN | Royal Australian Navy |
| CAM | Catapult Armed Merchantman | RANR | Royal Australian Reserve |
| Capt | Captain (RN and USN) | RANVR | Royal Australian Volunteer Reserve |
| CB | Companion of the Order of the Bath | RCAF | Royal Canadian Airforce |
| CBE | Commander of the Order of the British Empire | RCN | Royal Canadian Navy |
| | | RCNR | Royal Canadian Navy Reserve |
| Cdr | Commander (RN or USN) | RCNVR | Royal Canadian Navy Volunteer Reserve |
| CMG | Companion of the Order of St Michael and St George | REME | Royal Electrical Mechanical Engineers |
| CTL | Constructive Total Loss | | |
| CVO | Commander of the Royal Victorian Order | RHN | Royal Hellenic Navy |
| | | RIN | Royal Indian Navy |
| DBS | Distressed British Seaman | RN | Royal Navy |
| DEMS | Defensive Equipment Merchant Ships | RNR | Royal Navy Reservist |
| | | RNeN | Royal Netherlands Navy |
| DFM | Distinguished Flying Medal | RNoN | Royal Norwegian Navy |
| DSC | Distinguished Service Cross | RNZAF | Royal New Zealand Air Force |
| DSO | Distinguished Service Order | RNZNR | Royal New Zealand Navy Reserve |
| EG | Escort Group | RNZNVR | Royal New Zealand Navy Volunteer Reserve |
| FAA | Fleet Air Arm | | |
| F/Lt | Flight Lieutenant | SAAF | South African Air Force |
| F/O | Flying Officer | SAN | South African Navy |
| F/Sgt | Flight Sergeant | SANVR | South African Navy Volunteer Reserve |
| GRT | Gross Registered Tonnage | | |
| HMCS | His Majesty's Canadian Ship | SO | Senior Officer |
| HMS | His Majesty's Ship | S/Cdr | Squadron Commander (USN) |
| KBE | Knight Commander of the Order of the British Empire | S/Ldr | Squadron Leader |
| | | Sub-Lt | Sub-Lieutenant (RN and Fleet Air Arm) |
| LCI | Land Craft Infantry | | |
| Lt-Cdr | Lieutenant Commander (RN or USN) | USAAF | United States Army Air Force |
| | | USCG | United States Coast Guard |
| MBE | Member of the Order of the British Empire | USN | United States Navy |
| | | USNR | United States Navy Reserve |
| MM | Military Medal | USSR | Union of Soviet Socialist Republics |
| MOS | Ministry of Shipping | VC | Victoria Cross (highest award for bravery) |
| MOWT | Ministry of War Transport | | |
| MTB | Motor Torpedo Boat | W/Cdr | Wing Commander |

# BIBLIOGRAPHY

Adams, Thomas A. & Lees, David J. *Register of Type VII U-boats*, World Ship Society, 1991
*After the Battle* No. 36, 'Operation Deadlight', Battle of Britain Prints International Ltd, 1982
Bagnasco, Erminio. *Submarines of World War II*, Arms & Armour Press, 1977
Baker, Ralph. *Goodnight, Sorry for Sinking You, (City of Cairo)*, Collins, 1984
Beaver, Paul. *The British Aircraft Carrier*, Patrick Stephens, 1984
Bennett G.H. & R. *Survivors: British Merchant Seamen in the Second World War*, Hambledon Press, London. 1998
Blair, Clay. *Hitler's U-boat War, The Hunters, 1939–1942* (Vol 1) and *The Hunted, 1942–1945* (Vol 2 ), Random House, New York, 1998
Bowyer, C. *Men of Coastal Command 1939–1945*, William Kimber
Brown, David. *Warship Losses of World War Two*, Arms and Armour, 1996
Browning, Robert M, Jr. *US Merchant Vessel War Casualties of World War II*, Naval Insitute Press, 1996
Colledge, J.J. *Ships of the Royal Navy* (2 vols) Greenhill, 1987/1989
Costello, John & Hughes, Terry. *The Battle of the Atlantic*, Collins, 1977
Cremer, Peter. *U-333: The Story of a U-boat Ace*, The Bodley Head, 1984
Dittman, F.J. & Colledge, J.J. *British Warships 1914–1919*, Ian Allan, 1972
Dorling, Capt Taprell (Taffrail). *Blue Star Line at War 1939–1945*, Foulsham, 1973
Edwards, Bernard. *Attack & Sink (Convoy SC 42)*, New Guild, 1995
Edwards, Bernard. *Dönitz and the Wolf Packs*, Arms & Armour Press, 1996
Fisher, Robert C. 'Canadian Merchant Ship Losses, 1939–1945', *The Northern Mariner*, Vol. 3, July 1995
Franks, Norman, L.R. *Conflict over the Bay*, William Kimber, 1986
Franks, Norman, L.R. *Search, Find and Kill*, Aston, 1990
Franks, Norman & Zimmerman, Eric. *U-boat versus Aircraft*, Grub Street, 1998
Gasaway, E. Blanchard. *Grey Wolf, Grey Sea – U-124*, A. Barker, 1972
Gill, G. Hermon, *Royal Australian Navy 1942–1945 Vol II* – Australian War Memorial, Canberra, 1968
Gawler, J. *Lloyds Medals 1836–1989*, Hart Publishing, Ontario, n.d.
Hague, Arnold & Ruegg, Bob. *Convoys to Russia 1941–1945*, World Ship Society, 1992
Hague, Arnold. *Convoy Rescue Ships 1940–1945*, World Ship Society, 1998
Halley, James J. *Squadrons of the Royal Air Force & Commonwealth 1918–1988*, Air Britain, 1989
Harrower, John. *Wilson Line*, World Ship Society, 1998
Hashimoto, Mochitsura. *Sunk: The Story of the Japanese Submarine Fleet, 1941–1945*, Cassell, 1954
Haws, Duncan. *Merchant Fleets* – various publications 1982–2001
HMSO. *British Vessels Lost at Sea 1939–1945*, Patrick Stephens, 1983
Hickam, Homer H. Jr. *Torpedo Junction*, Naval Institute Press, 1989
Holman, Gordon. *In Danger's Hour (Clan Line)*, Hodder & Stoughton, 1948
Holme, Richard. *Cairnryan Military Port 1940–1966*, GC Books, 1997
Jane's *Fighting Ships of World War II*, Random House, 1997
Jefford, C.G. *Royal Air Force Squadrons*, Airlife Publishing Ltd, 1988
Jones, Geoffrey. *Autumn of the U-boats*, William Kimber, 1984
Jones, Geoffrey. *Defeat of the Wolf Packs*, William Kimber, 1986
Jones, Geoffrey. *The Month of the Lost U-boats*, William Kimber, 1977
Jones, Geoffrey. *U-boat Aces*, William Kimber, 1988
Kaplan, Philip & Currie, Jack. *Convoy – Merchant Sailors at War 1939–1945*, Aurum Press, 1998
Kaplan, Philip & Currie, Jack. *Wolfpack – U-boats at War 1939–1945*, Aurum Press, 1997

Kelshall, Gaylord T.M. *War in the Caribbean*, Naval Institute Press, 1994

Kemp, Paul. *U-boats Destroyed*, Arms and Armour, 1997

Kerr, George F. *Business in Great Waters, The War History of the P&O 1939–1945*, Faber, 1951

Lenton, H.T. & Colledge, J.J. *Warships of World War II*, Ian Allan, 1964

Lewis, Peter. *Squadron Histories RFC, RNAS & RAF since 1912*. Putman & Co., 1968

*Lloyd's List 1939–1945,* various issues

*Lloyd's Registers 1939–1945*

Lloyd's War Losses, *The Second World War* (Vol 1), Lloyd's of London Press, 1989

Macintyre, Capt Donald. *The Naval War against Hitler*, Batsford, 1971

McKee & Darlington. *The Canadian Naval Chronicle 1939–1945*, Vanwell Publishing, St Catharines, Ontario, 1996

Mallmann Showell, J.P. *U-boats under the Swastika*, Purnell, 1973

Mallmann Showell, J.P. *U-boat Command and the Battle of the Atlantic*, Conway, 1989

Marcus, Alex, *DEMS? What's DEMS?* Boolarong Publications, Australia, 1986

Middlebrook, Martin. *Convoy. The Battle of Convoys SC122 & HX229*, Allen Lane, 1976

Ministry of Defence (Navy). *The U-boat War in the Atlantic 1939–1945*, HMSO, 1989

Mitchell, W.H. and Sawyer, L.A. *The Empire Ships*, 2nd edn, Lloyd's of London Press, 1985

Mitchell, W.H. and Sawyer, L.A. *The Liberty Ships*, David & Charles, 1970

Mitchell, W.H. and Sawyer, L.A. 'The Oceans, the Forts and the Parks', *Journal of Commerce and Shipping Telegraph Ltd*, 1966

Mitchell, W.H. and Sawyer, L.A. *Victory Ships and Tankers*, David & Charles, 1974

Mondey, David. *American Aircraft of World War II*, Chancellor Press, 1996

Mondey, David. *Axis Aircraft of World War II*, Chancellor Press, 1996

Mondey, David. *British Aircraft of World War II*, Chancellor, 1994

Muggenthaler, August Karl, *German Raiders of World War II*, R. Hale, 1978

Musk, George, *Canadian Pacific*, David & Charles, 1981

*The Navy List 1939–1945*

Niestlé, Dr Axel, *German U-boat Losses during World War II*, Greenhill Books, 1998

Padfield, P. *War Beneath the Sea*, John Murray, 1995

Pearce, Frank. *Heroes of the Fourth Service*, Robert Hale, 1996

Peillard, Léonce. *U-Boats to the Rescue: The Laconia Incident*, Jonathan Cape, 1963

Poolman, Kenneth. *Escort Carrier, HMS Vindex at War*, Leo Cooper

Poolman, Kenneth. *Focke-Wulf Condor, Scourge of the Atlantic*, Macdonald and Janes, 1978

Revely, Henry. *The Convoy that Nearly Died (The story of ONS 154)*, William Kimber, 1979

Rohwer, Jürgen. *Axis Submarine Successes 1939–1945*, Patrick Stephens, 1983

Rohwer, Jürgen. *The Critical Convoy Battles of March, 1943*, Ian Allan, 1977

Rohwer, J. & Hummelchen, G. *Chronology of the War at Sea 1939–1945*, Greenhill Books, 1992

Roscoe, Theodore. *United States Destroyer Operations in World War II*, Naval Institute Press, 1953

Roscoe, Theodore. *United States Submarine Operations in World War II*, Naval Institute Press, 1949

Roskill, S.W. *A Merchant Fleet in War 1939–1945 (Alfred Holt & Co.)* Collins, 1962

Roskill, S.W. *The War at Sea 1939–1945*, 3 vols, HMSO, 1954–61

Ruegg, R. & Hague, A. *Convoys to Russia 1941–1945*, World Ship Society, 1992

Savas, Theodore P. *Silent Hunters*, Savas Publishing, 1997

Schoenfeld, Max. *Stalking the U-boat*, Smithsonian Institution Press, 1995

Schofield, B.B. & Martyn, L.F. *The Rescue Ships*, Blackwood, 1968

Sharpe, Peter. *U-boat Fact File*, Midland Publishing, Leicester, 1998

Silverstone, P.H. *US Warships of World War II*, Ian Allan, 1965

Slader, John. *The Fourth Service (Merchantmen at War 1939–1945)*, New Guild, 1995

Slader, John. *The Red Duster at War*, William Kimber, 1988

Stein, Robert C. *U-boats Type VII*, Brockhampton Press, 1998

Tarrant, V.E. *The U-boat Offensive 1914–1945*, Arms & Armour Press 1989

Terraine, John. *Business in Great Waters*, Leo Cooper, 1989

Thomas, David A. *The Atlantic Star 1939–1945*, W.H. Allen, 1990

Thompson, Julian. *The Imperial War Museum Book of the War at Sea*, Sidgwick & Jackson, 1996

Turner, L.C.F., Gordon-Cumming, H.R. and Betzler, J.E. *War in the Southern Oceans*, Oxford University Press, Cape Town, 1961

US Government. *United States Naval Chronology World War II*, US government Printing Office, 1955

US Government. *US Submarine Losses World War II*, US Government Printing Office, 1963

White, John F. *U-boat Tankers 1941–1945*, Airlife Publishing Ltd, 1998

Wiggan, Richard. *Hunt the Altmark*, Robert Hale, 1982

Winton, John. *Ultra at Sea*, Leo Cooper, 1988

Woodman, Richard. *Arctic Convoys*, Murray, 1994

Woodward, David. *The Secret Raiders*. William Kimber, 1955

Wynn, Kenneth. *U-boat Operations of the Second World War* (2 vols) Chatham Publishing, 1997/1998

Young, John M. *Britain's Sea War 1939–1945 (A Diary of Ship Losses 1939–1945)*, Patrick Stephens, 1989

# INDEX OF MERCHANT SHIPS